CLYMER®

YAMAHA

PW50 Y-ZINGER, PW80 Y-ZINGER & BW80 BIG WHEEL • 1981-2002

The world's finest publisher of mechanical how-to manuals

CLYMER®

P.O. Box 12901, Overland Park, Kansas 66282-2901

FIRST EDITION
First Printing July, 1998

SECOND EDITION
First Printing June, 2002
Second Printing December, 2003
Third Printing February, 2007
Fourth Printing September, 2011

Printed in U.S.A.

ISBN-10: 0-89287-828-2

ISBN-13: 978-0-89287-828-4

Library of Congress: 2002106387

MEMBER
MOTORCYCLE INDUSTRY COUNCIL, INC.

TECHNICAL PHOTOGRAPHY: Ron Wright, with assistance by Jordan Engineering. Special thanks to Clawson Motorsports, Fresno, California.

TECHNICAL ILLUSTRATIONS: Steve Amos and Robert Caldwell.

COVER: Mark Clifford Photography, Los Angeles, California.

TOOLS AND EQUIPMENT: K & L Supply Co. at www.klsupply.com.

CLYMER®

Publisher Ron Rogers

EDITORIAL

Editorial Director
James Grooms

Editor
Steven Thomas

Associate Editor
Rick Arens

Authors
Michael Morlan
George Parise
Ed Scott
Ron Wright

Technical Illustrators
Steve Amos
Errol McCarthy
Mitzi McCarthy
Bob Meyer

SALES

Sales Manager–Marine
Jay Lipton

Sales Manager–Powersport/I&T
Matt Tusken

CUSTOMER SERVICE

Customer Service Manager
Terri Cannon

Customer Service Representatives
Dinah Bunnell
Suzanne Johnson
April LeBlond
Sherry Rudkin

PRODUCTION

Director of Production
Dylan Goodwin

Production Manager
Greg Araujo

Senior Production Editors
Darin Watson
Adriane Wineinger

Associate Production Editor
Ashley Bally

Penton

P.O. Box 12901, Overland Park, KS 66282-2901 • 800-262-1954 • 913-967-1719

CLYMER® CLYMER® PROSERIES I&T SHOP SERVICE

More information available at *clymer.com*

CONTENTS

QUICK REFERENCE DATA

MOTORCYCLE INFORMATION

MODEL:______________________________ YEAR:______________

VIN NUMBER:____

ENGINE SERIAL NUMBER:__________________________________

CARBURETOR SERIAL NUMBER OR I.D. MARK:__________________

RECOMMENDED LUBRICANTS AND FUEL

Engine oil	Yamalube 2 or an air cooled 2-stroke engine injection oil
Transmission oil	Yamalube 4 or a comparable 10W-30 SE motor oil
Air filter	Foam air filter oil
Drive chain*	Nontacky O-ring chain lubricant or SAE 30-50 weight engine motor oil
Steering and suspension lubricant	Multipurpose grease
Fuel	Premium unleaded fuel
Control cables	Cable lube**
Drive shaft grease	
PW50	

* Use kerosene to clean O-ring drive chain.

** Do not use drive chain lubricant to lubricate control cables.

OIL TANK CAPACITY

	Liters	U.S. qt.	Imp. qt.
PW50	0.3	0.32	0.26
BW80 and PW80	0.95	1.0	0.84

MAINTENANCE TORQUE SPECIFICATIONS

	N•m	in.-lb.	ft.-lb.
Oil drain bolt			
PW50	14	—	10
BW80 and PW80	20	—	14
Front fork drain bolt			
PW50	—	—	—
BW80 and PW80	20	—	14
Rear brake stay arm nuts at swing arm and brake backing plate			
PW80	16	—	11
Rear axle nut			
PW50	60	—	43
BW80	85	—	61
PW80	60	—	43
Spark plug			
PW50	20	—	14
BW80	20	—	14
PW80	25	—	18

TRANSMISSION OIL CAPACITY

	Millileters	U.S. qt.	Imp. qt.
Oil change			
PW50	300	0.32	0.26
BW80 and PW80	650	0.69	0.57
After engine overhaul			
PW50	350	0.37	0.31
BW80 and PW80	750	0.79	0.66

FUEL TANK CAPACITY

	U.S. gal.	Liters	Imp. gal.
Full			
PW50	0.53	2.0	0.44
BW80	1.06	4.0	0.88
PW80	1.29	4.9	1.08
Reserve			
PW50	*		
BW80	0.11	0.4	0.09
PW80	0.26	1.0	0.22

* Not specified.

TUNE-UP SPECIFICATIONS

Ignition timing	
PW50	16° @ 5,000 rpm
BW80 and PW80	20.6° @ 4,000 rpm
Spark plug	
PW50	NGK BP4HS
BW80	NGK BP7HS
PW80	NGK BP6HS
Spark plug gap	0.6-0.7 mm (0.024-0.028 in.)
Engine idle speed	
PW50 and PW80	Not specified
BW80	1,650-1,750 rpm
Pilot air screw turns out	
PW50	1 3/8
BW80	1 1/4
PW80	1 1/2

DRIVE CHAIN SPECIFICATIONS (BW80 AND PW80)

Type/manufacturer	420M/DAIDO
No. of links	
BW80	89 (plus master link)
PW80	83 (plus master link)
Chain free play	15-20 mm (0.6-0.8 in.)

TIRE INFLATION PRESSURE

	Front kPa (psi)	Rear kPa (psi)
PW50 and PW80	100	15
BW80	29.4	4.3

INTRODUCTION

This detailed, comprehensive manual covers the Yamaha PW50, BW80 and PW80 models. The expert text gives complete information on maintnenance, tune-up, repair and overhaul. Hundreds of photos and drawings guide you through every step. The book includes all you will need to know to keep your Yamaha running right.

A shop manual is a reference. You want to be able to find information fast. As in all Clymer books, this one is designed with you in mind. All chapters are thumb tabbed. Important items are extensively indexed at the rear of the book. All procedures, tables, photos, etc. in this manual are for the reader who may be working on the vehicle for the first time or using this manual for the first time. The *Quick Reference Data* pages at the front of the book summarize the most frequently used specifications.

Keep the book handy in your tool box. It will help you to understand how your vehicle runs, lower repair costs and generally improve your satisfaction with the vehicle.

CHAPTER ONE

GENERAL INFORMATION

This manual covers the Yamaha PW50, BW80 and PW80 models.

Troubleshooting, tune-up, maintenance and repair are not difficult, if you know what tools and equipment to use and what to do. Step-by-step instructions guide you through jobs ranging from simple maintenance to complete engine and suspension overhaul.

This manual can be used by anyone from a first time do-it-yourselfer to a professional mechanic. Detailed drawings and clear photographs give you all the information you need to do the work right.

Some of the procedures in this manual require the use of special tools. The resourceful mechanic can, in many cases, think of acceptable substitutes for special tools—there is always another way. This can be as simple as using a few pieces of threaded rod, washers and nuts to remove or install a bearing or fabricating a tool from scrap material. If you find that a tool can be designed and safely made, but will require some type of machine work, you may want to search out a local community college or high school that has a machine shop curriculum. Some shop teachers welcome this type of outside work for advanced students.

Table 1 lists model coverage with engine serial numbers.

Table 2 lists general vehicle dimensions.

Table 3 lists weight specifications.

Table 4 lists decimal and metric equivalents.

Table 5 lists conversion tables.

Table 6 lists general torque specifications.

Table 7 lists technical abbreviations.

Table 8 lists metric tap drill sizes.

Tables 1-8 are at the end of the chapter.

MANUAL ORGANIZATION

This chapter provides general information and discusses equipment and tools useful both for preventive maintenance and troubleshooting.

Chapter Two provides methods and suggestions for quick and accurate diagnosis and repair of problems. Troubleshooting procedures discuss typical symptoms and logical methods to pinpoint the trouble.

Chapter Three explains all periodic lubrication and routine maintenance necessary to keep your Yamaha operating well. Chapter Three also includes recommended tune-up procedures, eliminating the need to consult other chapters constantly on the various assemblies.

Subsequent chapters describe specific systems such as the engine and transmission, clutch, fuel, exhaust, electrical, oil pump, suspension, drive train, steering, brakes and body panel. Each chapter provides disassembly, repair, and assembly procedures in simple step-by-step form. If a repair is impractical for a home mechanic, it is so indicated. It is usually faster and less expensive to take such repairs to a Yamaha dealership or competent repair shop. Specifications concerning a particular system are included at the end of the appropriate chapter.

NOTES, CAUTIONS AND WARNINGS

The terms NOTE, CAUTION and WARNING have specific meanings in this manual. A NOTE provides additional information to make a step or procedure easier or clearer. Disregarding a NOTE could cause inconvenience, but would not cause damage or personal injury.

A CAUTION emphasizes an area where equipment damage could occur. Disregarding a CAUTION could cause permanent mechanical damage; however, personal injury is unlikely.

A WARNING emphasizes an area where personal injury or even death could result from negligence. Mechanical damage may also occur. WARNINGS *are to be taken seriously*. In some cases, serious injury and death has resulted from disregarding similar warnings.

MESSAGE TO PARENTS

All of the models covered in this manual are designed for beginning riders. And as such, great care and thought must be given to who, when, how and where the motorcycle is serviced. This book is designed to make the job of servicing your child's Yamaha more efficient. It is up to you to decide whether your child is ready to perform the service procedures described in this manual. Of course, this will depend on the child's mental, physical and emotional maturity. If so, provide adult supervision by instructing them on tool, workshop and vehicle safety. Then recheck their work to make sure it was done safely and properly.

Before allowing your child to work on a motorcycle or any type of power driven equipment, note the following precautions:

a. Safety is the first and most important consideration when working in the shop. Thoroughly discuss all of the information listed in the *Safety First* section.
b. Familiarity with tools and service equipment comes through proper instruction and hands-on experience. If this is your child's first experience using tools, discuss proper tool selection, use and safety. Using tools incorrectly may cause personal injury and vehicle damage.
c. Ask your local dealer if he offers any type of basic motorcycle service classes. While these are usually geared to older riders, the information given will provide your child with the fundamentals of motorcycle service and safety.
d. Do not allow a child to work in the shop without adult supervision, depending on their mental, physical and emotional maturity and ability.
e. Before starting work, read all of the procedures carefully. Note where special tools or skills are required. When necessary, refer repairs to a Yamaha dealership or motorcycle service professional.

SAFETY FIRST

Professional mechanics can work for years and never sustain a serious injury. If you observe a few rules of common sense and safety, you can enjoy many safe hours servicing your motorcycle. Ignoring these rules can cause you to hurt yourself or someone working nearby, or cause damage to the motorcycle.

1. *Never* use gasoline or any type of low flash point solvent to clean parts. See *Cleaning Parts* and *Handling Gasoline Safely* in this chapter for additional information on parts cleaning, gasoline use, and safety.

NOTE

Flash point is the lowest temperature at which the vapor of a combustible liquid will ignite momentarily in the air. A solvent with a low flash point will ignite at a lower temperature than one with a high flash point.

2. *Never* smoke or use a torch in the vicinity of flammable liquids, such as gasoline or cleaning solvent, stored in an open container.

3. If welding or brazing is required on the machine, remove the fuel tank, carburetor, and rear shocks to a safe distance, at least 50 feet (15 m) away.

4. Use the proper sized wrenches to avoid damage to fasteners and injury to yourself.

5. When loosening a tight or stuck nut, be guided by what would happen if the tool slips.

6. When replacing a fastener, make sure to use one with the same measurements and strength as the old one. Incorrect or mismatched fasteners can result in damage to the vehicle and possible personal injury. Beware of fastener kits that are filled with cheap and poorly made nuts, bolts, washers and cotter pins. Refer to *Fasteners* in this chapter for additional information.

7. Keep all hand and power tools in good condition. Wipe greasy and oily tools after using them. They are difficult to hold and can cause injury. Replace or repair worn or damaged tools.

8. Keep your work area clean and uncluttered.

9. Wear safety goggles (**Figure 1**) during all operations involving drilling, grinding, the use of a cold chisel, using chemicals, cleaning parts, when using compressed air or *anytime* you feel unsure about the safety of your eyes.

10. Make sure you are wearing the correct type of clothes for the job. Long hair should be tied up or covered by a cap so that it can not accidentally fall out where it could be quickly grabbed by a piece of moving equipment or tool.

1

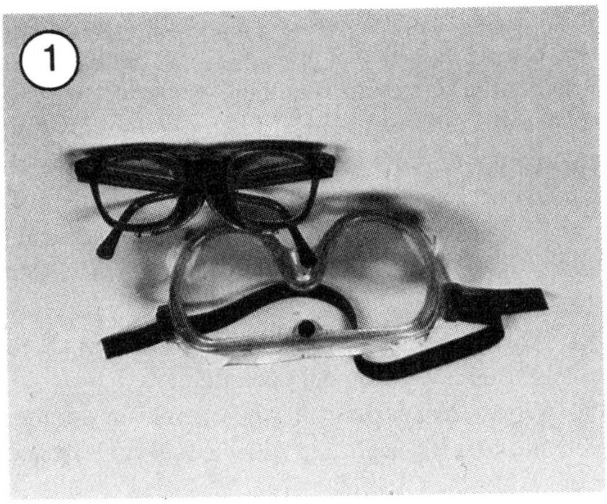

11. Keep an approved fire extinguisher nearby. Be sure it is rated for gasoline (Class B) and electrical (Class C) fires.

12. When drying bearings or other rotating parts with compressed air, never allow the air jet to rotate the bearing or part. The air jet is capable of rotating them at speeds far in excess of those for which they were designed. The bearing or rotating part is very likely to disintegrate and cause serious injury and damage. To prevent bearing damage when using compressed air, hold the inner bearing race by hand.

WARNING

The improper use of compressed air is very dangerous. Using compressed air to dust off your clothes, bike or workbench can cause flying particles to be blown into your eyes or skin. ***Never*** *direct or blow compressed air into your skin or through any body opening (including cuts) as this can cause severe injury or death. Compressed air should be used carefully; never allow children to use or play with compressed air.*

13. Never work on the upper part of the bike while someone is working underneath it.

14. When putting the bike on a stand, make sure the bike is secure before walking away from it.

15. Never carry sharp tools in your pockets.

16. There is always a right and wrong way to use tools. Learn to use them the right way.

17. Do not start and run the motorcycle in an enclosed area. The exhaust gases contain carbon monoxide, a colorless, tasteless, poisonous gas. Carbon monoxide levels build quickly in a small enclosed area and can cause unconsciousness and death in a short time. When it is necessary to start and run the motorcycle during a service procedure, always do so outside, or in a service area equipped with a ventilating system.

CLEANING PARTS

Cleaning parts is one of the more tedious and difficult service jobs performed in the home garage. While there are a number of chemical cleaners and solvents available for home and shop use, most are poisonous and extremely flammable. To prevent chemical overexposure, vapor buildup, fire and serious injury, observe all manufacturer's directions and warnings while noting the following.

1. Read the entire product label before using the chemical. Observe the precautions and warnings on the label. Always know what type of chemical you are using.
2. If the chemical product must be mixed, measure the proper amount according to the directions.
3. When a warning label specifies that the product should only be used with adequate ventilation, care must be taken to prevent chemical vapors from collecting in the shop. Always work in a well-ventilated area. Use a fan or ventilation system in the work area until the vapors are gone. If you are working in a small room or garage, simply opening a door or window may not provide adequate ventilation. Remember, if you can smell the chemical, there is some vapor in the air. The stronger the smell, the stronger the vapor concentration.
4. When a product is listed as combustible, flammable or an extremely flammable liquid, the danger of fire increases as the vapor builds up in the shop.
5. When a product is listed as poisonous, the vapor is poisonous as well as the liquid.
6. To prevent skin exposure, wear protective gloves when cleaning parts. Select a pair of chemical resistant gloves suitable for the type of chemicals you will be working with. Replace the gloves when they become thin, damaged, change color, or show signs of swelling.
7. Wear safety goggles when using chemicals and cleaning parts.
8. Do not use more than one type of cleaning solvent at a time.
9. If a part must be heated to remove a bearing, clean it thoroughly to remove all oil, grease and cleaner residue. Then wash with soapy water and rinse with clear water.
10. Wear a respirator if the instruction label says to do so.
11. Keep chemical products out of reach of children and pets.
12. To prevent sparks, use a nylon bristle brush when cleaning parts.
13. When using a commercial parts washer, read and follow the manufacturer's instructions for selecting the type of solvent to use. Parts washers must be equipped with a fusible link designed to melt and drop the cover in the event of fire.
14. Wash your hands and arms thoroughly after cleaning parts.

HANDLING GASOLINE SAFELY

Gasoline, a volatile flammable liquid, is one of the most dangerous items in the shop. However, because gasoline is used so often, many people forget that it is a dangerous product. Gasoline should be used only as fuel for internal-combustion engines. Never use gasoline to clean parts, tools or to wash your hands with. When working on a motorcycle or any other type of gasoline engine, gasoline will always be present in the fuel tank, fuel line and carburetor. To avoid a disastrous accident when working around gasoline , carefully observe the following cautions:

1. *Never* use gasoline to clean parts. See *Cleaning Parts* in this chapter for additional information on parts cleaning and safety.
2. When working on the fuel system, work outside or in a well-ventilated area.
3. Do not add fuel to the fuel tank or service the fuel system while the motorcycle is in the vicinity of open flames, sparks or where someone is smoking. Gasoline vapors are actually more dangerous than liquid gasoline. Because these vapors are heavier than air, they collect in low areas and are easily ignited.
4. Allow the engine to cool completely before working on any fuel system component.
5. When draining the carburetor, catch the gasoline in a container, then pour it into an approved gas can.
6. Do not store gasoline in any type of glass container. If the glass should break, a serious explosion or fire could occur.
7. Wipe up spilled gasoline immediately with dry rags. Store the rags in a metal container with a lid until they can be properly disposed of, or put them outside in a safe place to dry.
8. Do not pour water onto a gasoline fire. Water spreads the fire and makes it more difficult to put out. Use a class B, BC, or ABC fire extinguisher to smother the flames and put the fire out.
9. Always turn the engine off before refueling. Use a wide mouth funnel to avoid spilling gasoline onto the engine, exhaust pipe or muffler. Do not overfill the fuel tank. Leave an air space at the top of the fuel tank to prevent fuel from spilling out when installing the cap.
10. Always refuel the motorcycle with it parked outside and away from all open flames.
11. When transporting the motorcycle in another vehicle, keep it upright and with the fuel valve turned off.

12. Do not perform a spark test (as described in Chapter Two) if there is any gasoline leaking from the fuel tank, fuel line or carburetor.

SERVICE HINTS

Most of the service procedures covered are straightforward and can be performed by anyone reasonably handy with tools. It is suggested, however, that you consider your own capabilities carefully before attempting any operation involving major disassembly of the engine assembly.

Take your time and do the job right. Do not forget that a newly rebuilt engine must be broken in the same way as a new one. Refer to the *Engine Break-In* procedure listed in Chapter Four or Chapter Five.

1. Front, as used in this manual, refers to the front of the vehicle; the front of any component is the end closest to the front of the vehicle. The left and right-hand sides refer to the position of the parts as viewed by a rider sitting on the seat facing forward. For example, the throttle control is on the right-hand side. These rules are simple, but confusion can cause a major inconvenience during service. See **Figure 2**.
2. Whenever servicing an engine or suspension component, secure the vehicle in a safe manner.
3. Tag all similar internal parts for location and mark all mating parts for position. Record number and thickness of any shims as they are removed. Small parts such as bolts can be identified by placing them in plastic sandwich bags. Seal and label them with masking tape.
4. Tag disconnected wires and connectors with masking tape and a marking pen. Again, do not rely on memory alone.
5. Protect finished surfaces from physical damage or corrosion. Keep gasoline and other chemicals off painted surfaces.
6. Use penetrating oil on frozen or tight bolts, then strike the bolt head a few times with a hammer and punch (use a screwdriver on screws). Avoid the use of heat where possible, as it can warp, melt or affect the temper of parts. Heat also ruins finishes, especially paint and plastics.
7. When a part is a press fit or requires a special tool to remove it, the necessary information or type of tool will be called out in the text. Otherwise, if a part is difficult to remove or install, find out why before proceeding.
8. To prevent small objects and abrasive dust from falling into the engine, cover all openings after exposing them.
9. Read each procedure completely while looking at the actual parts before starting a job. Make sure you thoroughly understand the procedural steps then follow the procedure, step by step.
10. Recommendations are occasionally made to refer service or maintenance to a Yamaha dealership or a specialist in a particular field. In these cases, the work will be done more quickly and economically than if you performed the job yourself.

2

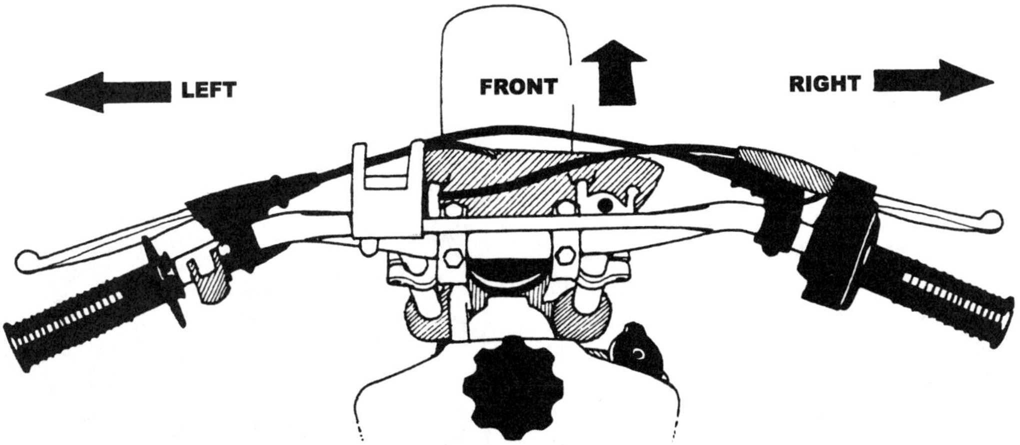

11. In procedural steps, the term *replace* means to discard a defective part and replace it with a new or exchange unit. *Overhaul* means to remove, disassemble, inspect, measure, repair and or replace parts as required.

12. Some operations require the use of a hydraulic press. If you do not own, or know hot to operate a press, it is wiser to have these operations performed at a shop equipped for such work, rather than to try to do the job yourself with makeshift equipment that may damage your machine.

13. Repairs go much faster and easier if the motorcycle is clean before you begin work. There are many special cleaners on the market, like Bel-Ray Degreaser, for washing the engine and related parts. Follow the manufacturer's directions on the container for the best results. Clean all oily or greasy parts with cleaning solvent as you remove them.

WARNING

***Never** use gasoline to clean parts or tools. It presents an extreme fire hazard. Be sure to work in a well-ventilated area when using cleaning solvent. Keep a fire extinguisher, rated for gasoline fires, handy in any case.*

CAUTION

If you use a car wash to clean your motorcycle, do not direct the high pressure water hose at steering bearings, carburetor hoses, suspension components, wheel bearings, muffler outlet, electrical components or the drive chain. The water will flush grease out of the bearings or damage the seals.

14. Much of the labor charge for repairs made at a dealership are for the time involved during the removal, disassembly, assembly, and reinstallation of other parts in order to reach the defective part. It is frequently possible to perform the preliminary operations yourself and then take the defective unit to the dealer for repair at considerable savings.

15. When special tools are required, make arrangements to get them before you start. It is frustrating and time-consuming to get partly into a job and then be unable to complete it.

16. Make diagrams (or take a Polaroid picture) wherever similar-appearing parts are found. For instance, crankcase bolts are often not the same length. You may think you can remember where everything came from, but mistakes are costly. There is also the possibility that you may be sidetracked and not return to work for days or even weeks in which time carefully laid out parts may become disturbed.

17. When assembling parts, be sure all shims and washers are reinstalled exactly as they came out.

18. Whenever a rotating part butts against a stationary part, look for a shim or washer. Use new gaskets if there is any doubt about the condition of the old ones. A thin coat of oil on non-pressure type gaskets may help them seal more effectively.

19. Use cold heavy grease to hold small parts in place if they tend to fall out during assembly. However, keep grease and oil away from electrical and brake components.

SERIAL NUMBERS

Yamaha motorcycles can be identified by serial numbers stamped onto the frame and engine. Always write these numbers down and take them with you when ordering parts. If a question arises about a part number or production change with your motorcycle, these numbers will be required before the part in question can be ordered. These numbers are also useful when trying to identify a motorcycle that may have been repainted or modified in some way.

The vehicle identification number (VIN) is stamped on the right side of the front frame tube (**Figure 3**). Use these numbers to identify and register your Yamaha.

The engine number is stamped on a raised pad on the left crankcase. See **Figure 4** (PW50) or **Figure 5** (BW80 and PW80).

When reading the engine number, the first three digits are the model code number. These digits identify the motorcycles model type and year of manu-

facturer. The remaining digits, separated from the first three by a slash mark, indicate the motorcycle's unit production number. The models numbers for all of the PW50, BW80 and PW80 models covered in this manual are listed in **Table 1**.

WARNING LABELS

A number of warning labels have been attached to the Yamaha motorcycles covered in this manual. These labels contain information that is important to the riders safety. Refer to the Owner's Manual for a description and location of each label. If a label is missing, order a replacement label from a Yamaha dealership.

TORQUE SPECIFICATIONS

The materials used in the manufacturer of your Yamaha can be subjected to uneven torque stresses if the fasteners used to hold the subassemblies are not installed and tightened correctly. Improper bolt tightening can cause cylinder head warpage, crankcase leaks, premature bearing and seal failure and suspension failure. An accurate torque wrench (described in this chapter) must be used with the torque specifications listed at the end of most chapters.

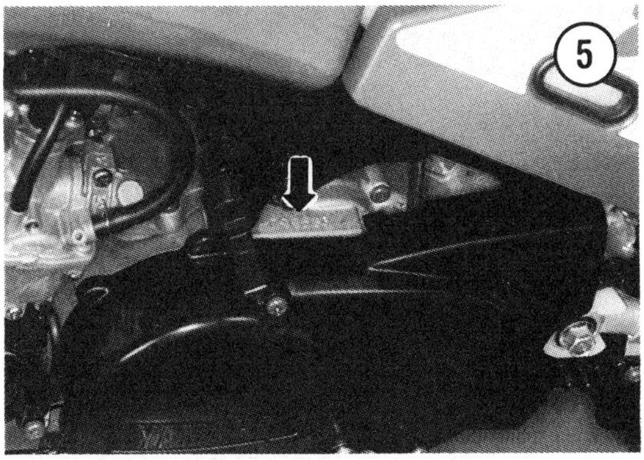

Torque specifications throughout this manual are given in Newton-meters (N•m), foot-pounds (ft.-lb.) and inch-pounds (in.-lb.).

Existing torque wrenches calibrated in meter kilograms can be used by performing a simple conversion. All you have to do is move the decimal point one place to the right; for example, 3.5 mkg = 35 N•m. This conversion is accurate enough for mechanical work even though the exact mathematical conversion is 3.5 mkg = 34.3 N•m.

Refer to **Table 6** for standard torque specifications for various size screws, bolts and nuts that may not be listed in the respective chapters.

FASTENERS

Fasteners (screws, bolts, nuts, studs, pins and clips) are used to secure various pieces of the engine, frame and suspension together. Proper selection and installation of fasteners are important to ensure that the motorcycle operates satisfactorily and can be serviced efficiently. Stripped, broken and missing fasteners cause excessive vibration, oil leaks and other performance and service related problems. For example, a loose or missing engine mount fastener can increase engine vibration that will eventually lead to a cracked frame tube or damaged crankcase.

Threaded Fasteners

Most of the components on your Yamaha are held together by threaded fasteners, such as screws, bolts, nuts, and studs. Most fasteners are tightened by turning clockwise (right-hand threads), although some fasteners may have left-hand threads if rotating parts can cause loosening. When a left-hand thread is used, it is identified in the procedure.

Two dimensions are needed to match threaded fasteners: the number of threads in a given distance and the nominal outside diameter of the threads. Two standards are currently used in the United States to specify the dimensions of threaded fasteners, the U.S. standard system and the metric system (**Figure 6**). Pay particular attention when working with unidentified fasteners; mismatching thread types can damage threads.

NOTE
During reassembly, start all fasteners by hand. This will help you to make sure that the fastener threads are not mismatched or cross-threaded. If a fastener is hard to start or turn, stop and determine the cause before tightening with a wrench.

Metric screws and bolts are classified by length (L, **Figure 7**), diameter (D) and distance between thread crests (T). A typical bolt might be identified by the numbers 8 × 1.25—130, which would indicate that the bolt has a nominal diameter of 8 mm, the distance between threads crests is 1.25 mm and bolt length is 130 mm.

The strength of metric screws and bolts is indicated by numbers located on top of the screw or bolt as shown in **Figure 7**. The higher the number the stronger the screw or bolt. Unnumbered screws and bolts are the weakest.

CAUTION
***Do not** install screws or bolts with a lower strength grade classification than installed originally by the manufacturer. Doing so may cause vehicle failure and possible injury.*

Critical torque specifications are listed in a table at the end of the appropriate chapter. If not, use the torque specifications listed in **Table 6**. The Yamaha torque specifications listed in the manual are for clean, dry threads (unless specified differently in text).

Screws and bolts are manufactured with a variety of head shapes to fit specific design requirements. Your Yamaha is equipped with the common hex, Phillips and Allen head types.

The most common nut used is the hex nut (**Figure 8**). The hex nut is often used with a lockwasher. Self-locking nuts have a nylon insert that prevents loosening; no lockwasher is required. Wing nuts, designed for fast removal by hand, are used for convenience in non-critical locations. Nuts are sized using the same system as screws and bolts. On hex-type nuts, the distance between two opposing flats indicates the proper wrench size to use.

Self-locking screws, bolts and nuts may use a locking mechanism that uses an interference fit between mating threads. Manufacturers achieve interference in various ways: by distorting threads,

6

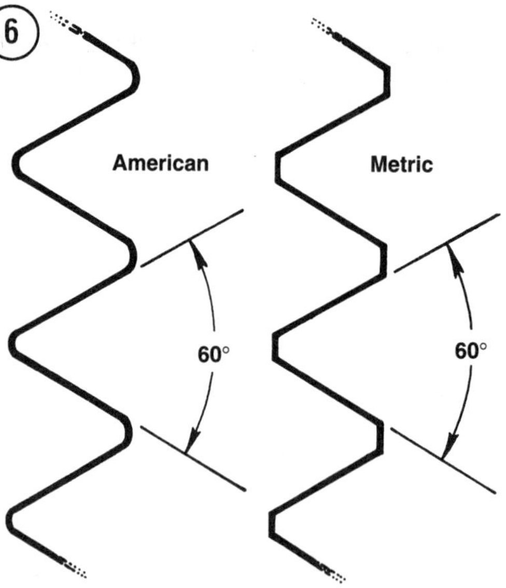

7

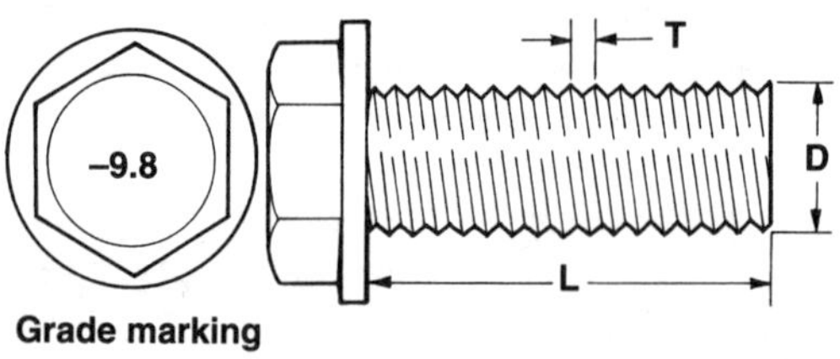

8

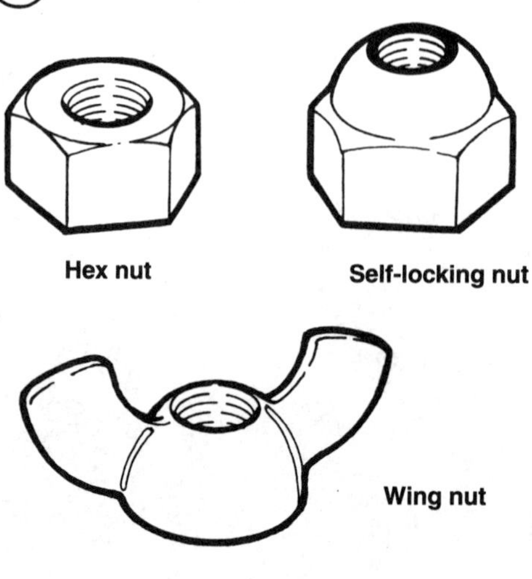

coating threads with dry adhesive or nylon, distorting the top of an all-metal nut, using a nylon insert in the center or at the top of a nut, etc. Self-locking fasteners offer greater holding strength and better vibration resistance than standard fasteners. For greatest safety, install new self-locking fasteners during reassembly.

Washers

There are 2 basic types of washers used on your Yamaha: flat washers and lockwashers. Flat washers are simple discs with a hole to fit a screw or bolt. Lockwashers are designed to prevent a fastener from working loose. **Figure 9** shows several types of washers. Washers can be used in the following functions:

a. As spacers.

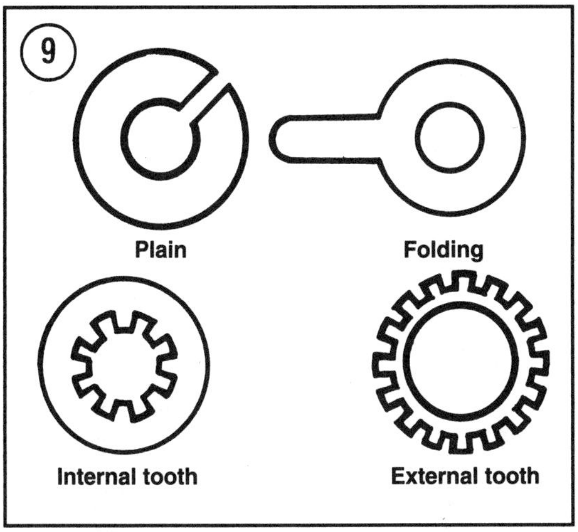

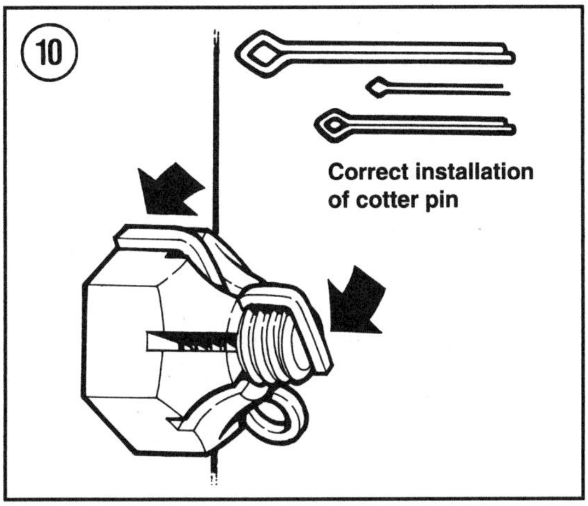

b. To prevent galling or damage of the equipment by the fastener.
c. To help distribute fastener load when tightening the fastener.
d. As fluid seals (copper or laminated washers).

Cotter Pins

Cotter pins (**Figure 10**) secure fasteners in special locations. The threaded stud, bolt or axle must have a hole in it. Its nut or nut lock piece has castellations around its upper edge into which the cotter pin fits to keep it from loosening.

Before installing a cotter pin, tighten the nut to the recommended torque specification. If the castellations in the nut do not align with the hole in the bolt or axle, tighten the nut until the slot and hole align. Do not loosen the nut to make alignment. Insert a *new* cotter pin through the nut and hole, then tap the head lightly to seat it. Bend one arm over the flat on the nut and the other against the top of the axle or bolt (**Figure 10**).

Do not reuse cotter pins.

Circlips

Circlips (snap rings) can be internal or external design (**Figure 11**). Circlips retain items on shafts (external type) or within tubes (internal type). In some applications, circlips of varying thickness' control the end play of assembled parts. These are often called selective circlips. You must replace circlips during reassembly and installation, as removal weakens and deforms them. Two other types of clips used on your Yamaha are the plain snap ring and E-clip (**Figure 11**).

Two basic styles of circlips are available: machined and stamped circlips. Machined circlips (**Figure 12**) can be installed in either direction (shaft or housing) because both faces are machined, thus creating two sharp edges. Stamped circlips (**Figure 13**) are manufactured with one sharp edge and one rounded edge. When installing stamped circlips in a thrust situation, the sharp edge must face away from the part producing the thrust. When installing circlips, observe the following:

a. Remove and install circlips with circlip pliers. See *Circlip Pliers* in this chapter.
b. Compress or expand circlips only enough to install them.

c. After installing a circlip, make sure it seats in its groove completely.

Transmission circlips become worn with use and increase side play. For this reason, always use new circlips whenever a transmission is reassembled.

E-Clips

E-clips (**Figure 11**) are used when it is impractical or impossible to use a circlip. There are many different shapes and types of E-clips available.

Remove E-clips with a flat blade screwdriver—pry between the shaft and E-clip. To install an E-clip, center it over its shaft groove, then tap or push it into place. Replace E-clips when they are easy to install.

LUBRICANTS

Periodic lubrication helps ensure long life for any type of equipment. The *type* of lubricant used is just as important as the lubrication service itself, although in an emergency the wrong type of lubricant is better than none. The following paragraphs describe the types of lubricants used most often when servicing motorcycles. Be sure to follow the manufacturer's recommendations for lubricant types.

Generally, all liquid lubricants are called oil. They may be mineral-based (including petroleum bases), natural-based (vegetable and animal bases), synthetic-based or emulsions (mixtures). Grease is an oil to which a thickening base has been added so that the end product is semi-solid. Grease is often classified by the type of thickener added; lithium soap is commonly used.

Engine Oil

The Yamaha engines covered in this manual are equipped with an oil pump. Premixing of the fuel is not required unless the oil pump is removed from the engine. Yamaha recommends the use of the following 2-stroke engine oils:

a. Yamalube 2-cycle oil injection oil.
b. Any air-cooled 2-stroke engine oil.

Transmission Oil

Yamaha recommends using one of the following 4-cycle engine oils that meet these oil classifications: API Service SE or SF or equivalent:

a. Yamalube 4.
b. SAE 10W-30 motor oil.

Another type of oil to consider is a two-stroke motorcycle transmission oil. This type of oil has the same lubricating qualities as an API SE or SF oil but also has additional shear additives that prevent oil break down and foaming from transmission operation. For example, the Bel-Ray Gear Saver SAE 80W transmission oil replaces SAE 30, SAE 10W-30 and SAE 10W-40 motor oils.

Grease

Grease is graded by the National Lubricating Grease Institute (NLGI). Grease is graded by number according to the consistency of the grease; these range from No. 000 to No. 6, with No. 6 being the most solid. A typical multipurpose grease is NLGI

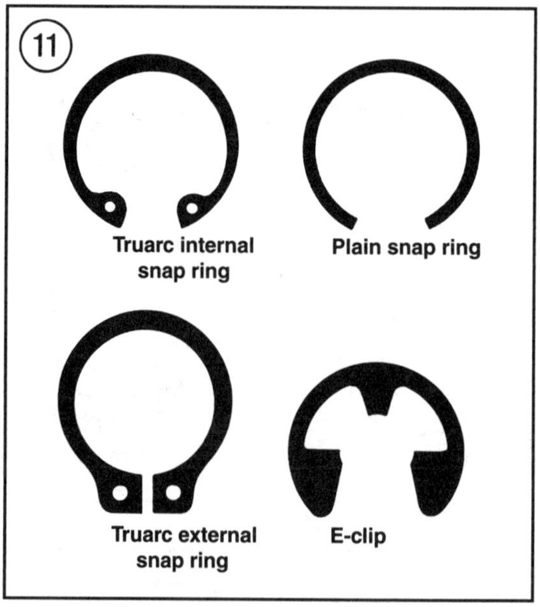

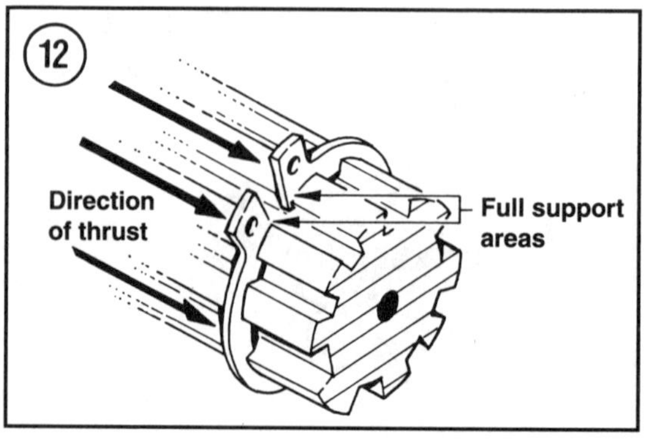

No. 2. For specific applications, equipment manufacturers may require grease with an additive such as molybdenum disulfide (MOS2).

Antiseize Lubricant

An antiseize lubricant may be specified in some assembly applications. The antiseize lubricant prevents the formation of corrosion that may lock parts together.

SEALANT, CEMENTS AND CLEANERS

Sealants and Adhesives

Many mating surfaces of an engine require a gasket or seal between them to prevent fluids and gases from passing through the joint. At times, the gasket or seal is installed as is. However, some times a sealer is applied to enhance the sealing capability of the gasket or seal. Note, however, that a sealing compound may be added to the gasket or seal during manufacturing and adding a sealant may cause premature failure of the gasket or seal.

NOTE
If a new gasket leaks, check the 2 mating component surfaces for warpage, old gasket residue or cracks. Also check to see if the new gasket was properly installed and if the assembly was tightened correctly.

RTV Sealants

One of the most common sealants is RTV (room temperature vulcanizing) sealant. This sealant hardens (cures) at room temperature over a period of several hours, which allows sufficient time to reposition parts if necessary without damaging the gaskets.

13

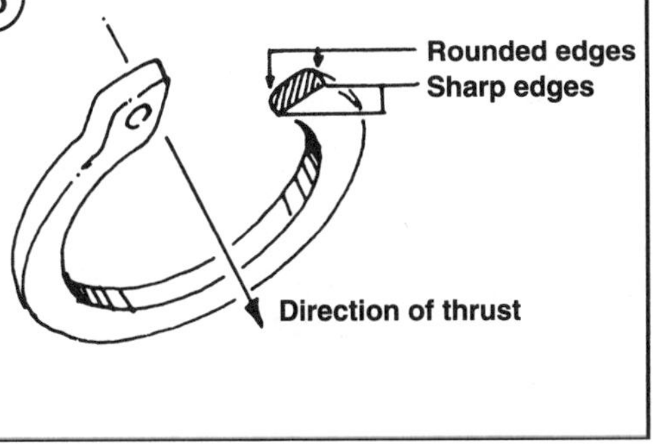

RTV sealant is available for many different applications. For example, while many RTV compounds offer excellent chemical resistance in bonding and sealing applications where oil and water is prevalent, most RTV compounds offer poor resistance to gasoline. Always follow the manufacturer's recommendations when purchasing and using a particular compound.

Cements and Adhesives

A variety of cements and adhesives are available, their use dependent on the type of materials to be sealed, and to some extent, the personal preference of the mechanic. Automotive parts stores offer cements and adhesives in a wide selection. Some points to consider when selecting cements or adhesives: the type of material being sealed (metal, rubber or plastic.), the type of fluid contacting the seal (gasoline, oil or water) and whether the seal is permanent or must be broken periodically, in which case a pliable sealant might be desirable. Unless you are experienced in the selection of cements and adhesives, follow the recommendation if the text specifies a particular sealant.

Cleaners and Solvents

Cleaners and solvents are helpful in removing oil, grease and other residue when maintaining and overhauling your motorcycle. Before purchasing cleaners and solvents, consider how they will be used and disposed of, particularly if they are not water soluble. Local ordinances may require special procedures for the disposal of certain cleaners and solvents.

WARNING
Some cleaners and solvents are harmful and may be flammable. Follow any safety precautions noted on the container or in the manufacturer's literature. Use petroleum-resistant gloves to protect hands and arms from the harmful effect of cleaners and solvents.

Figure 14 shows a variety of cleaners and solvents. Cleaners designed for ignition/electrical contact cleaning are excellent for removing light oil from a part without leaving a residue. Cleaners designed to remove heavy oil and grease residues, called degreasers, contain a solvent that usually must soak awhile to be most effective. Some degreasers will wash off with water. Ease the removal of stubborn gaskets with a gasket remover compound.

One of the more powerful cleaning solutions is carburetor cleaner. It is designed to dissolve the varnish that may build up in carburetor jets and orifices. A good carburetor cleaner is usually expensive and requires special disposal. Carefully read directions before purchase; do not immerse nonmetallic parts in a carburetor cleaner.

Gasket Remover

Stubborn gaskets can present a problem during engine service because they can take a long time and are difficult to remove. Consequently, there is the added problem of secondary damage occurring to the gasket mating surfaces from the incorrect use of gasket scraping tools. To remove stubborn gaskets, use a spray gasket remover. Spray gasket remover can be purchased through any automotive parts store. Follow the manufacturer's directions for use.

THREADLOCKING COMPOUND

A threadlocking compound is a fluid applied to fastener threads. After tightening the fastener, the fluid dries to a solid filler between the mating threads, thereby locking the threads in position. They are also used on threaded parts to help seal against leaks.

Before applying a threadlocking compound, clean the contacting threads with an aerosol electrical contact cleaner. Use only as much threadlocking compound as necessary. Excess fluid can work it way into adjoining parts.

Threadlocking compound is available in different strengths, so follow the manufacturer's instructions when using their particular compound. Two manufacturers of threadlocking compound are ThreeBond of America and the Loctite Corporation. The following threadlocking compounds are recommended for many threadlock requirements described in this manual:

a. ThreeBond 1342: low strength, frequent repair for small screws and bolts.
b. ThreeBond 1360: medium strength, high temperature.
c. ThreeBond 1333B: medium strength, bearing and stud lock.
d. ThreeBond 1303: high strength, frequent repair.
e. Loctite 242 (blue): low strength, frequent repair.
f. Loctite 271 (red): high strength, frequent repair.

There are other quality threadlock brands on the market.

EXPENDABLE SUPPLIES

Certain expendable supplies are required during maintenance and repair work. These include grease, oil, gasket cement, wiping rags and cleaning solvent. Ask your dealer for the special locking compounds, silicone lubricants and other products which make vehicle maintenance simpler and easier. Cleaning solvent or kerosene is available at some service stations, paint or hardware stores.

WARNING
Having a stack of clean shop rags on hand is important when performing engine and suspension service work. However, to prevent the possibility of from spontaneous combustion from a pile of solvent soaked rags, store them in a sealed metal container until they can be washed or discarded properly.

NOTE
To prevent solvent and other chemicals from being absorbed into your skin,

14

wear a pair of petroleum-resistant rubber gloves when cleaning parts. These can be bought through industrial supply houses or well-equipped hardware stores.

BASIC HAND TOOLS

Many of the procedures in this manual can be carried out with simple hand tools and test equipment familiar to the average home mechanic. Keep your tools clean and in a tool box. Keep them organized with the related tools stored together. After using a tool, wipe off dirt and grease with a clean cloth and return the tool to its correct place.

Top quality tools are essential; they are also more economical in the long run. If you are now starting to build your tool collection, stay away from the "advertised specials" featured at some parts houses, discount stores and chain drug stores. These are usually a poor grade tool that can be sold cheaply and that is exactly what they are—*cheap*. They are usually made of inferior material, and are thick, heavy and clumsy. Their rough finish makes them difficult to clean and they usually don't last very long. If it is ever your misfortune to use such tools, you will probably find out that the wrenches do not fit the heads of bolts and nuts correctly and can round-off and damage the fastener heads.

15

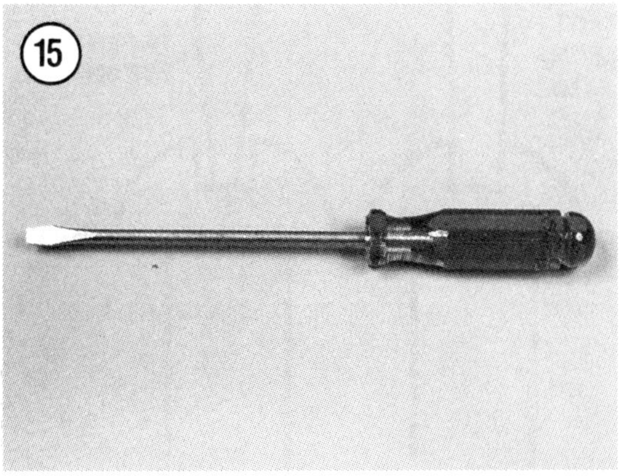

16

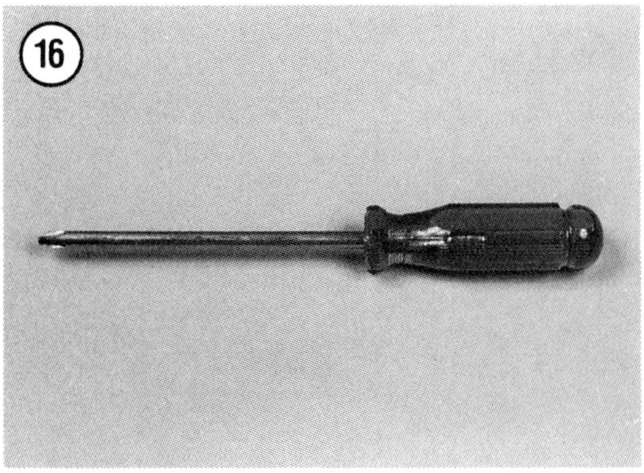

Quality tools are made of alloy steel and are heat treated for greater strength. They are lighter and better balanced than cheap ones. Their surface is smooth, making them a pleasure to work with and easy to clean. The initial cost of good quality tools may be more but they are cheaper in the long run. Do not try to buy everything in all sizes in the beginning; do it a little at a time until you have the necessary tools.

Screwdrivers

The screwdriver is a very basic tool, but if used improperly it will do more damage than good. The slot on a screw has a definite dimension and shape. A screwdriver must be selected to conform with that shape. Use a small screwdriver for small screws and a large one for large screws or the screw head will be damaged.

Two basic types of screwdriver are required: common (flat-blade) screwdrivers (**Figure 15**) and Phillips screwdrivers (**Figure 16**).

Screwdrivers are available in sets which often include an assortment of common and Phillips blades. If you buy them individually, buy at least the following:

a. Common screwdriver—5/16 × 6 in. blade.
b. Common screwdriver—3/8 × 12 in. blade.
c. Phillips screwdriver—size 2 tip, 6 in. blade.
d. Phillips screwdriver—size 3 tip, 6 and 10 in. blade.

Use screwdrivers only for driving screws. Never use a screwdriver for prying or chiseling metal. Do not try to remove a Phillips or Allen head screw with a common screwdriver (unless the screw has a combination head that will accept either type); you can damage the head so that even the proper tool will be unable to remove it.

Keep screwdrivers in the proper condition and they will last longer and perform better. Always keep the tip of a common screwdriver in good condition. **Figure 17** shows how to grind the tip to the proper shape if it becomes damaged. Note the symmetrical sides of the tip.

Pliers

Pliers come in a wide range of types and sizes. Pliers are useful for cutting, bending and crimping. Do not use them to cut hardened objects or to turn bolts or nuts. **Figure 18** shows several pliers useful in motorcycle repair.

Each type of pliers has a specialized function. Slip-joint pliers are general purpose pliers and are used mainly for holding things and for bending.

Needlenose pliers are used to hold or bend small objects. Groove-joint pliers can be adjusted to hold various sizes of objects; the jaws remain parallel to grip around objects such as pipe or tubing. There are many more types of pliers. The ones described here are most suitable for motorcycle service.

Locking Pliers

Locking pliers (**Figure 19**) are used to hold objects very tightly like a vise. Because their sharp jaws can permanently scar the objects they hold, select and use them carefully. Locking pliers are available in many types for more specific tasks.

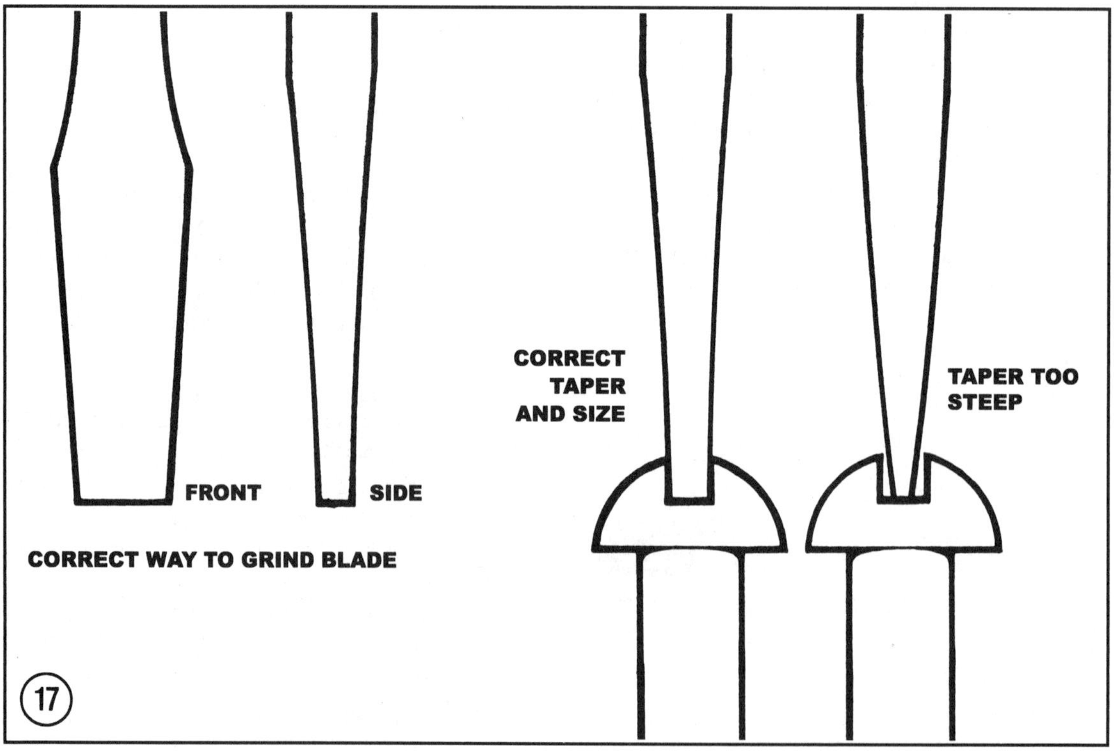

17

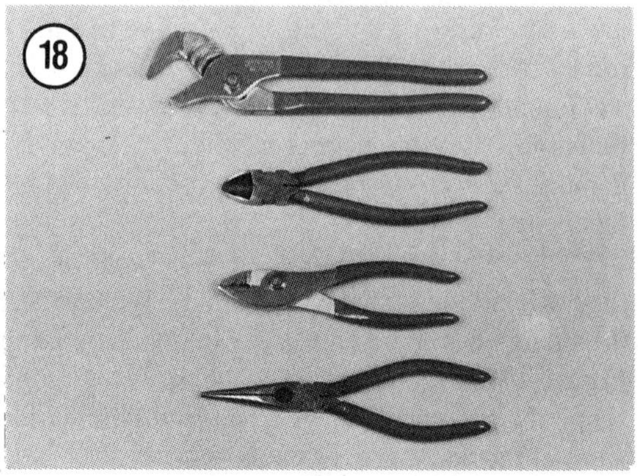
18

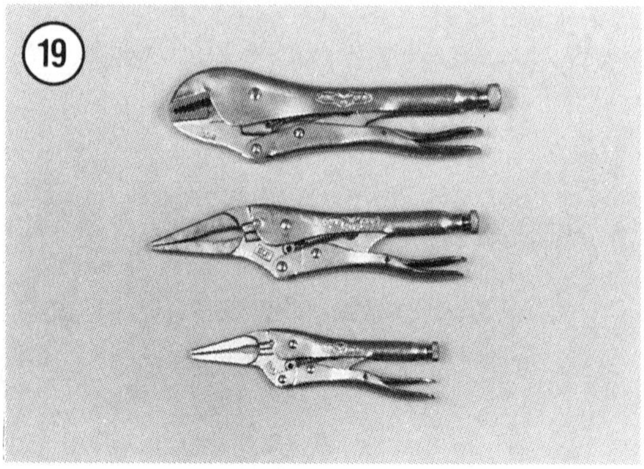
19

Circlip Pliers

Circlip pliers (**Figure 20**) are special in that they are only used to remove circlips from shafts or within engine or suspension housings. When purchasing circlip pliers, there are two kinds to distinguish from. External pliers (spreading) are used to remove circlips that fit on the outside of a shaft. Internal pliers (squeezing) are used to remove circlips which fit inside a gear or housing bore.

20

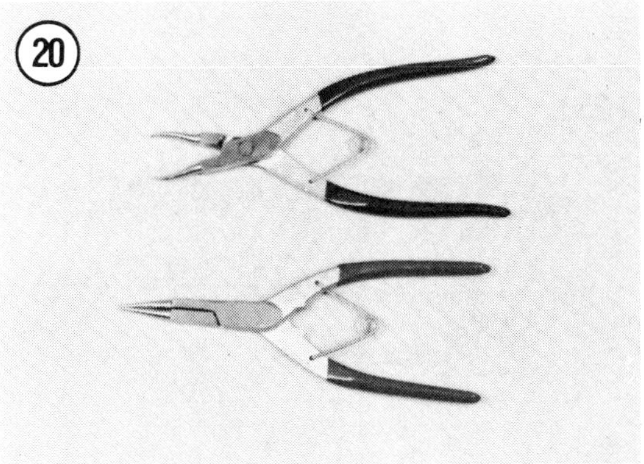

21

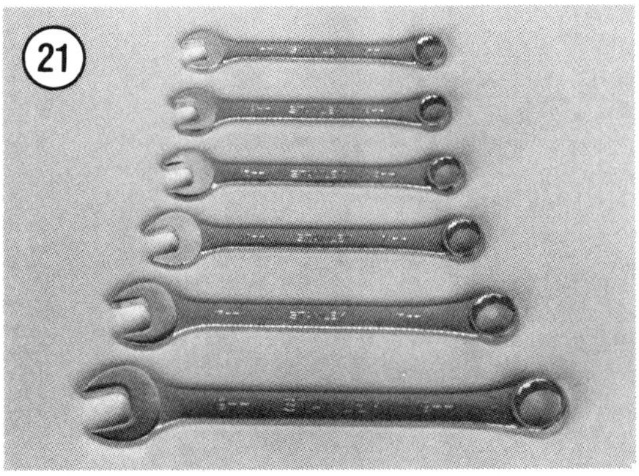

22

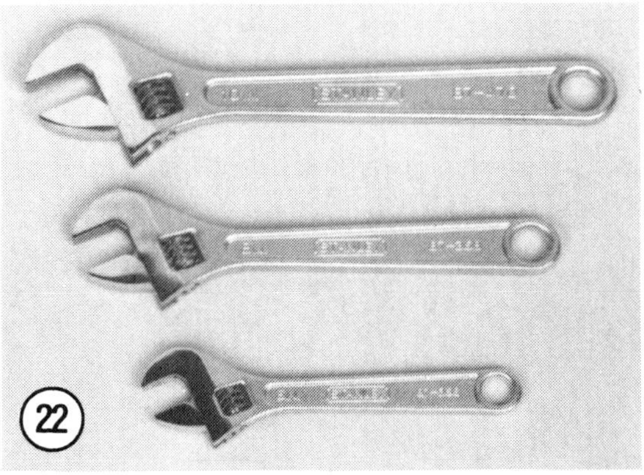

WARNING

Because circlips can slip and fly off when removing and installing them, and broken tips can fly off, always wear safety glasses when using circlip pliers.

Box, Open-end and Combination Wrenches

Box-end, open-end and combination wrenches are available in sets or separately in a variety of sizes. On open and box end wrenches, the number stamped near the end refers to the distance between 2 parallel flats on the hex head bolt or nut. On combination wrenches, the number is stamped near the center.

Box-end wrenches require clear overhead access to the fastener but can work well in situations where the fastener head is close to another part. They grip on all six edges of a fastener for a very secure grip. They are available in either 6-point or 12-point. The 6-point gives superior holding power and durability but requires a greater swinging radius. The 12-point works better in situations with limited swinging radius.

Open-end wrenches are speedy and work best in areas with limited overhead access. Their wide flat jaws make them unstable for situations where the bolt or nut is sunken in a well or close to the edge of a casting. These wrenches grip only two flats of a fastener so if either the fastener head or the wrench jaws are worn, the wrench may slip off.

Combination wrenches (**Figure 21**) have open-end on one side and box-end on the other with both ends being the same size. These wrenches are favored by professionals because of their versatility.

Adjustable Wrenches

An adjustable wrench can be adjusted to fit nearly any nut or bolt head which has clear access around its entire perimeter. Adjustable wrenches (**Figure 22**) are best used as a backup wrench to keep a large nut or bolt from turning while the other end is being loosened or tightened with a proper wrench.

Adjustable wrenches have only two gripping surfaces which make them more subject to slipping off the fastener and damaging the part and possibly injuring your hand. The fact that one jaw is adjustable only aggravates this shortcoming.

These wrenches are directional; the solid jaw must be the one transmitting the force. If you use the adjustable jaw to transmit the force, it will loosen and possibly slip off.

Adjustable wrenches come in all sizes. A wrench in the 10 to 12 in. range is recommended as an all-purpose wrench.

Socket Wrenches

This type is undoubtedly the fastest, safest and most convenient to use. Sockets which attach to a ratchet handle (**Figure 23**) are available with 6-point or 12-point openings and 1/4, 3/8 and 1/2 in. drives. The drive size indicates the size of the square hole which mates with the ratchet handle (**Figure 24**).

When purchasing and using sockets, note the following:

a. When working on your Yamaha, use metric sockets. Individual sockets can be identified by the bolt-head sizes stamped on the side of the socket.
b. While you will be using metric sockets, the drive hole in the bottom of all sockets is always measured in inches: 1/4, 3/8 and 1/2 inch drive (larger drive sizes are available for industrial use).
c. Sockets are available with either 6- or 12-points. Point size refers to the number of points between the grooves cut inside the socket walls.
d. The 6-point socket provides greater holding power and durability than a 12-point socket.
e. Some sockets are also available with 4- and 8-points. These sizes are useful for turning square shafts.

Allen Wrenches

Allen wrenches are available in sets or separately in a variety of sizes. These sets come in SAE and metric size, so be sure to buy a metric set (**Figure 25**). Allen bolts are sometimes called socket bolts.

Impact Driver

The hand impact driver may have been designed with the motorcycle rider in mind. This tool makes removal of fasteners easy and eliminates damage to bolts and screw slots. Impact drivers and interchangeable bits (**Figure 26**) are available at most large hardware, motorcycle or auto parts stores. While sockets can also be used with a hand impact driver, they must be designed for impact use. Use only impact sockets with impact drivers and air tools. Do not use regular hand sockets as they may shatter during use.

Hammers

The correct hammer (**Figure 27**) is necessary for certain repairs. Use only a hammer with a face (or head) of rubber or plastic or the soft-faced type that is filled with steel or lead shot. These are sometimes

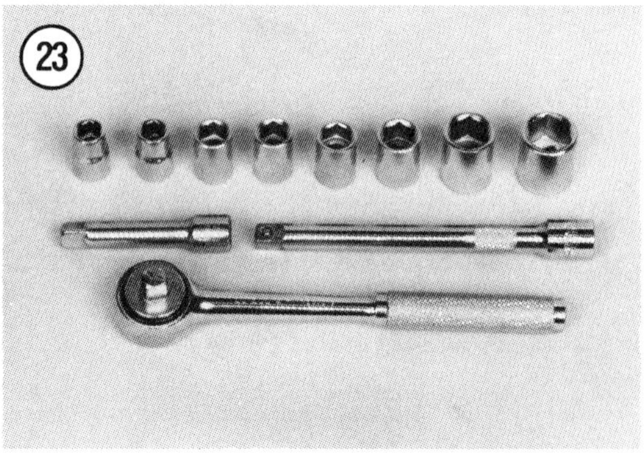

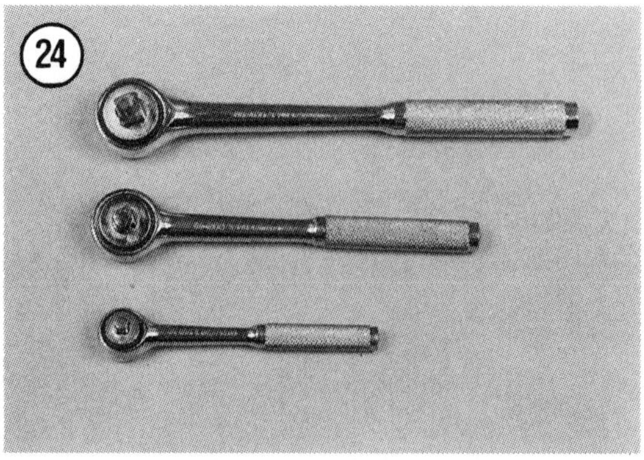

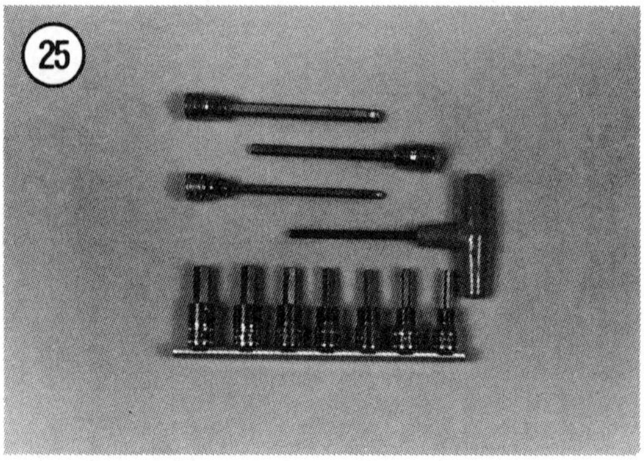

necessary in engine teardowns. *Never* use a metal-faced hammer on engine or suspension parts, as severe damage will result in most cases. Ball-peen or machinist's hammers are required when striking another tool, such as a punch or impact driver. When it is necessary to strike hard against a steel part without damaging it, a brass or lead hammer should be used.

When using a hammer, note the following:

a. *Always* wear safety glasses when using a hammer.
b. Inspect the hammer for a damaged or broken handle. Repair or replace the hammer as required. Do *not* use a hammer with a cracked handle.
c. The head of the hammer should always strike the object squarely. Do not use the side of the hammer or handle to strike an object.
d. Always wipe oil or grease off of the hammer *before* using it.
e. Always use the correct hammer for the job.

26

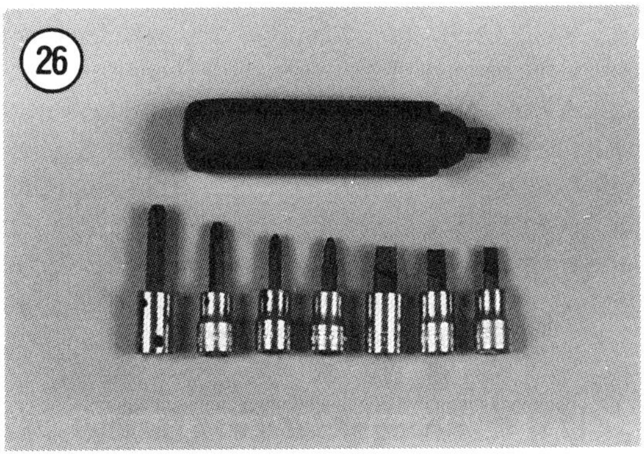

27

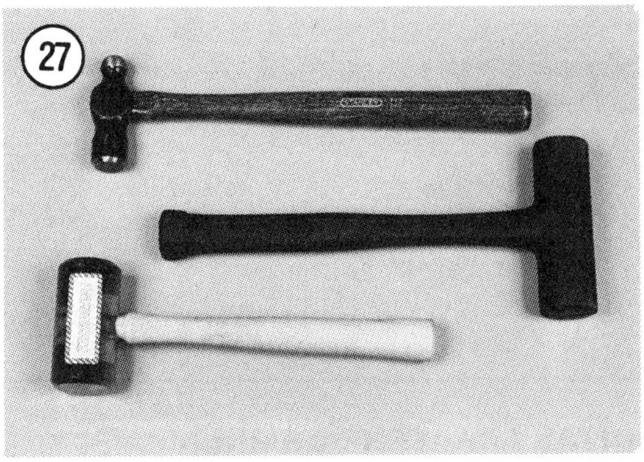

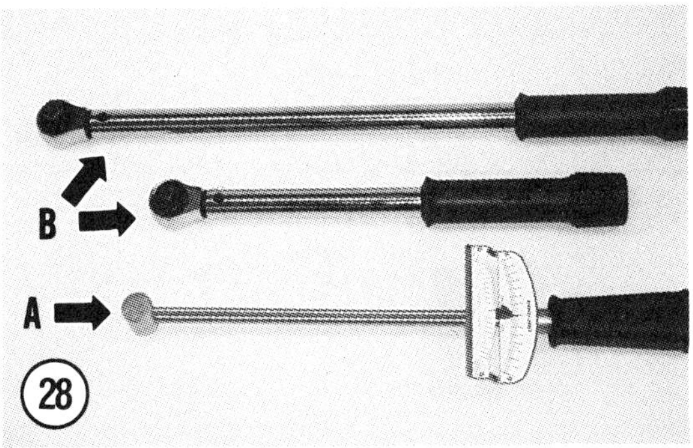

28

Torque Wrench

A torque wrench is used with a socket, torque adapter or similar extension to measure how tightly a nut, bolt or other fastener is installed. They come in a wide price range and with either 1/4, 3/8 or 1/2 in. square drive. The drive size indicates the size of the square drive which mates with the socket, torque adapter or extension. Popular types are the deflecting beam (A, **Figure 28**), the dial indicator and the audible click (B, **Figure 28**) torque wrenches. As with any series of tools, there are advantages and disadvantages with each type of torque wrench. When choosing a torque wrench, consider its torque range, accuracy rating and price. The torque specifications listed at the end of most chapters in this manual will give you an idea on the range of torque wrench needed to service your Yamaha.

Because the torque wrench is a precision tool, don't throw it in with other tools and expect it to hold its accuracy. Always store a torque wrench in its carrying case or in a padded tool box drawer. All torque wrenches require periodic recalibration. To find out more about this, read the information that came with the torque wrench or write to the manufacturer.

Torque Wrench Adapters

Torque adapters and extensions allow you to extend or reduce the reach of your torque wrench. For example, the torque adapter wrench shown in **Figure 29** can be used to extend the length of the torque wrench to tighten fasteners that cannot be reached with a torque wrench and socket. When a torque adapter lengthens or shortens the torque wrench (**Figure 29**), the torque reading on the torque wrench will not be the same amount of torque that is applied to the fastener. It is then necessary to recalibrate the torque specification to compensate for the effect of the added or reduced torque adapter length. When a torque adapter is used and it does not change the length of the torque wrench (explained below), recalibration is not necessary.

When it is necessary to recalculate a torque reading when using a torque adapter, you must know the lever length of the torque wrench, the length of the adapter from the center of square drive to the center of the nut or bolt, and the actual amount of torque desired at the nut or bolt (**Figure 30**). The formula can be expressed as:

$$TW = \frac{TA \times L}{L + A}$$

TW = This is the torque setting or dial reading to set on the torque wrench when tightening the fastener.

TA = Actual torque setting. This is the torque specification listed in the service manual and will be the actual amount of torque applied to the fastener.

A = This is the length of the adapter from the centerline of the square drive (at the torque wrench) to the centerline of the nut or bolt. If the torque adapter extends straight from the end of the torque wrench (**Figure 31**), the center line of the torque adapter and torque wrench are the same.

However, when the center lines of the torque adapter and torque wrench do not line up, the distance must be measured as shown in **Figure 31**. Also note in **Figure 31** that when the torque adapter is set at a right-angle to the torque wrench, no calculation is needed (the lever length of the torque wrench did not change).

L = This is the lever length of your torque wrench. This specification is usually listed in the instruction manual that came with your torque wrench, or you can determine its length by measuring the distance from the center of the square drive on the torque wrench to the center of the torque wrench handle (**Figure 30**).

Example:

What should the torque wrench preset reading or dial reading be when :

TA = 20 ft.-lb.

A = 3 in.

L = 14 in.

$$TW = \frac{20 \times 14}{14 + 3} = \frac{280}{17} = 16.5 \text{ ft.-lb.}$$

In this example, the recalculated torque value of 16.5 ft.-lb. would be the amount of torque to set on the torque wrench. When using a dial or beam-type torque wrench, apply torque until the pointer aligns with the 16.5 ft.-lb. dial reading. When using a click type torque wrench, the micrometer dial would be pre-set to 16.5 ft.-lb. In all cases, even though the torque wrench dial or pre-set reading was 16.5 ft.-lb., the fastener would actually be tightened to 20 ft.-lb.

29

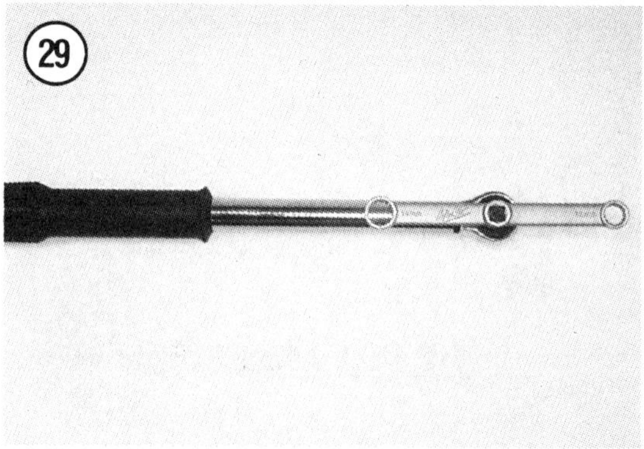

30

TORQUE WRENCH AND HORIZONTAL ADAPTER FORMULA

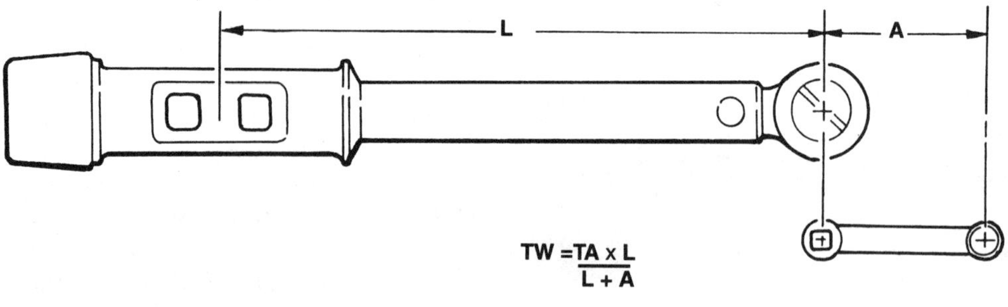

PRECISION MEASURING TOOLS

Measurement is an important part of motorcycle service. When performing many of the service procedures in this manual, you will be required to make a number of measurements. These include basic checks such as engine compression and spark plug gap. As you become more involved with engine work, measurements will be required to determine the size and condition of the piston and cylinder bore, crankshaft runout and so on. When making these measurements, the degree of accuracy will dictate which tool is required. Precision measuring tools are expensive. If this is your first experience at engine or suspension service, it may be more worthwhile to have the checks made at a Yamaha dealership or machine shop. However, as your skills and enthusiasm for doing your own service work increase, you may want to begin purchasing some of these specialized tools. The following is a descrip-

(31)

HOW TO MEASURE TORQUE WRENCH EFFECTIVE LENGTH

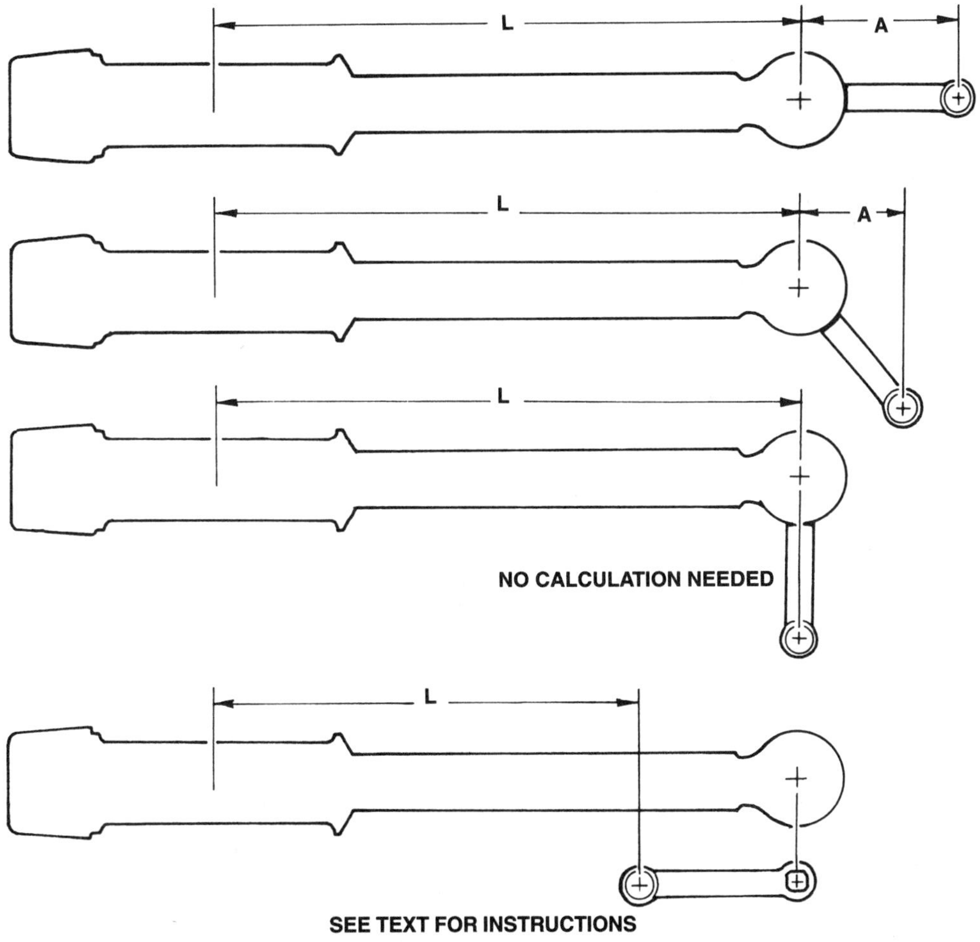

tion of the measuring tools required to perform the service procedures described in this manual.

Feeler Gauge

Feeler gauges come in assorted sets and types. The feeler gauge is made of either a piece of a flat or round hardened steel of a specified thickness. Wire gauges (**Figure 32**) are used to measure spark plug gap. Flat gauges (**Figure 33**) are used for most other measurements.

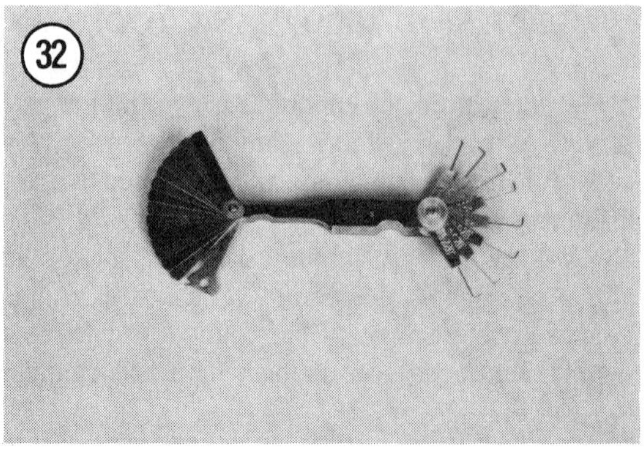

Vernier Caliper

This tool (**Figure 34**) is used to take inside, outside and depth measurements. Although this tool is not as precise as a micrometer, it allows reasonably accurate measurements, typically to within 0.025 mm (0.001 in.). Common uses of a vernier caliper are measuring the length of clutch springs, the thickness of clutch plates, shims and thrust washers, brake pad thickness or the depth of a bearing bore. The jaws of the caliper must be clean and free of burrs at all times in order to obtain an accurate measurement. There are several types of vernier calipers available. The standard vernier caliper (**Figure 34**) has a highly accurate graduated scale on the handle in which the measurements must be calculated. The dial indicator caliper (**Figure 35**) is equipped with a small dial and needle that indicates the reading, and the digital electronic type has an LCD display that shows the measurement on the small display screen. Some vernier calipers must be calibrated (zeroed) prior to making a measurement to ensure an accurate measurement. Refer to the manufacturer's instructions for this procedure.

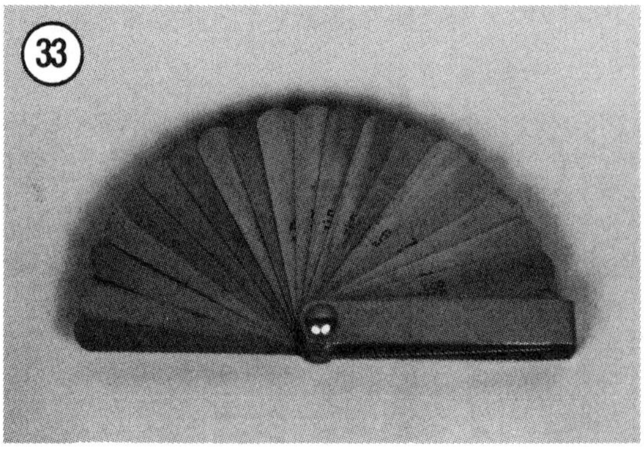

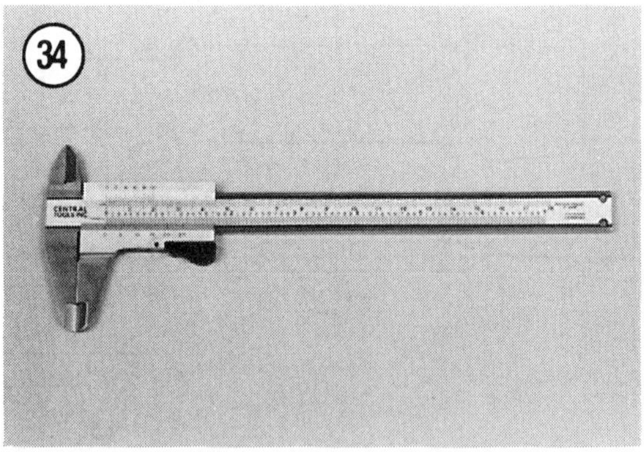

Outside Micrometer

An outside micrometer is a precision tool used to measure parts accurately using decimal divisions of the inch or meter (**Figure 36**). While there are many types and styles of micrometers, this section describes how to use the outside micrometer. The outside micrometer is the most common type of micrometer used when servicing motorcycles. It is used to accurately measure the outside diameter, length and thickness of parts. These parts include the piston, piston pin, crankshaft, piston rings and shims. The outside micrometer is also used to meas-

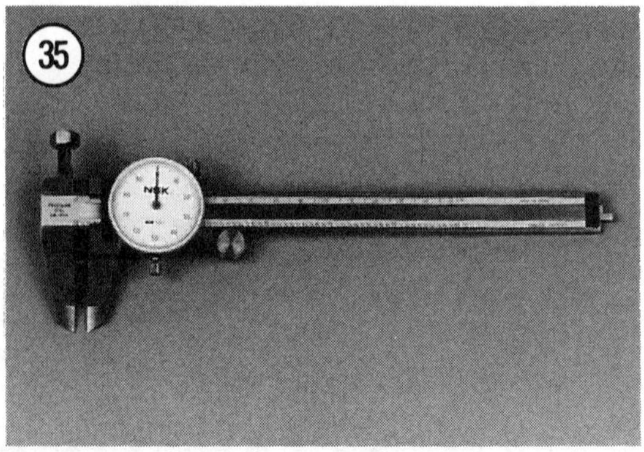

ure the dimension taken by a small hole gauge or a telescoping gauge described later in this section. After the small hole gauge or telescoping gauge has been carefully expanded to a limit within the bore of the component being measured, carefully remove the gauge and measure the distance across its arms with the outside micrometer. Other types of micrometers include the depth micrometer and screw thread micrometer. **Figure 37** illustrates the various parts of an outside micrometer with its part names and markings identified.

Micrometer Range

A micrometer's size indicates the minimum and maximum size of a part that it can measure. The most common sizes are: 0-1 in. (0-25 mm), 1-2 in. (25-50 mm), 2-3 in. (50-75 mm) and 3-4 in.(75-100 mm). These micrometers use fixed anvils.

Some micrometers use the same frame with interchangeable anvils of different lengths. This allows you to install the correct length anvil for a particular job. For example, a 0-4 in. interchangeable micrometer is equipped with four different length anvils. While purchasing one or two micrometers to cover a range from 0-4 or 0-6 in. is less expensive, its overall frame size makes it less convenient to use.

How to Read a Micrometer

When reading a micrometer, numbers are taken from different scales, then added together. The following sections describe how to read the standard inch micrometer, the vernier inch micrometer, the standard metric micrometer and the metric vernier micrometer.

Standard inch micrometer

The standard inch type micrometer is accurate up to one-thousandth of an inch (0.001 in.). The heart of the micrometer is its spindle screw with 40 threads per inch. Every turn of the thimble will move the spindle 1/40 of an inch or 0.025 in.

Before you learn how to read a micrometer, study the markings and part names in **Figure 37**. Then take your micrometer and turn the thimble until its zero mark aligns with the zero mark on the sleeve line. Now turn the thimble counterclockwise and align the next thimble mark with the sleeve line. The micrometer now reads 0.001 in. (one one-thousandth) of an inch. Thus each thimble mark is equal to 0.001 in. Every fifth thimble mark is numbered to help with reading: 0, 5, 10, 15 and 20.

Reset the micrometer so that the thimble and sleeve line zero marks line up. Then turn the thimble counterclockwise one complete revolution and align the thimble zero mark with the first line on the sleeve line. The micrometer now reads 0.025 in. (twenty-five thousandths) of an inch. Thus each sleeve line represents 0.025 in.

Now turn the thimble counterclockwise while counting the sleeve line marks. Every fourth mark on the sleeve line is marked with a number ranging from 1 through 9. The last digit on the sleeve line is usually a zero (0) mark. The zero mark indicates that you have reached the end of the micrometer's measuring range. Each sleeve number represents 0.100 in.

(36)

DECIMAL PLACE VALUES*

0.1	Indicates 1/10 (one tenth of an inch or millimeter)
0.01	Indicates 1/100 (one one-hundredth of an inch or millimeter)
0.001	Indicates 1/1,000 (one one-thousandth of an inch or millimeter)

* This chart represents the values of figures placed to the right of the decimal point. Use it when reading decimals from one-tenth to one one-thousandth of an inch or millimeter. It is not a conversion chart (for example: 0.001 in. is not equal to 0.001 mm).

For example, the number 1 represents 0.100 in. and the number 9 represents 0.900 in.

When reading a standard inch micrometer, take the 3 measurements described and add them together. The first 2 readings are taken from the sleeve. The last reading is taken from the thimble. The sum of the 3 readings provide the measurement in thousandths of an inch (0.001 in.).

To read a standard inch micrometer, perform the following steps while referring to the example in **Figure 38**.

1. Read the sleeve line to find the largest number visible—each sleeve number mark equals 0.100 in.
2. Count the number of sleeve marks visible between the numbered sleeve mark and the thimble edge—each sleeve mark equals 0.025 in. If there is no visible sleeve marks, continue with Step 3.
3. Read the thimble mark that lines up with the sleeveline—each thimble mark equals 0.001 in.

NOTE

If a thimble mark does not align exactly with the sleeve line but falls between 2 lines, estimate the decimal amount between the lines. For a more accurate reading, you must use a vernier inch micrometer.

4. Adding the micrometer readings in Steps 1, 2 and 3 gives the actual measurement.

Vernier inch micrometer

A vernier inch micrometer can accurately measure in ten-thousandths of an inch (0.0001 in.) increments. While it has the same markings as a standard micrometer, a vernier scale scribed on the sleeve (**Figure 39**) makes it unique. The vernier scale consists of eleven equally spaced lines marked 1-9 with

(37)

STANDARD INCH MICROMETER

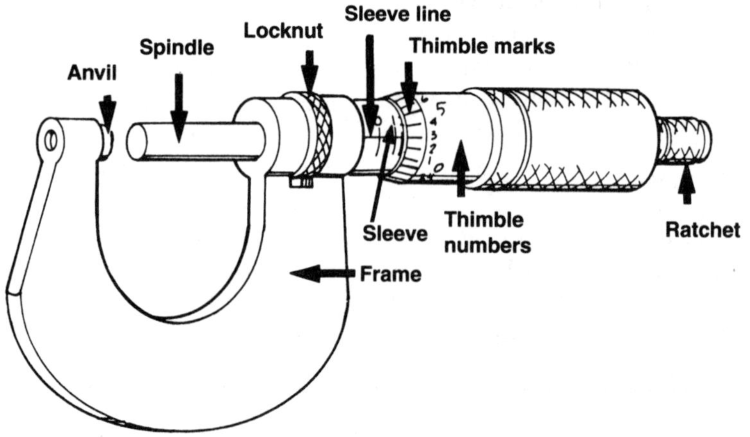

(38)

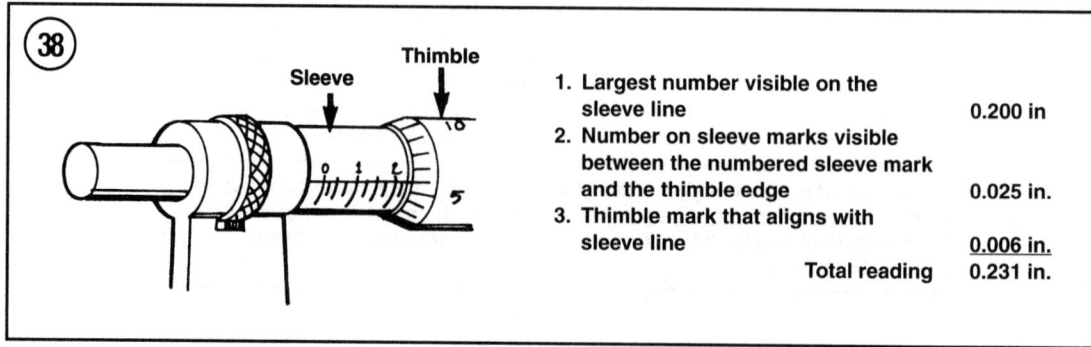

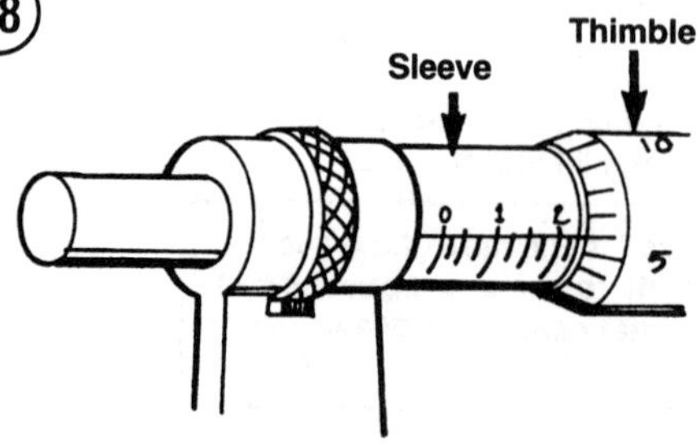

1. Largest number visible on the sleeve line		0.200 in
2. Number on sleeve marks visible between the numbered sleeve mark and the thimble edge		0.025 in.
3. Thimble mark that aligns with sleeve line		0.006 in.
	Total reading	0.231 in.

a 0 on each end. These lines run parallel on the top of the sleeve where each line is equal to 0.0001 in. Thus the vernier scale divides a thousandth of an inch (0.001 in.) into ten-thousandths of an inch (0.0001 in.).

To read a vernier inch micrometer, perform the following steps while referring to the example in **Figure 40**.

1. Read the micrometer in the same way as the standard inch micrometer. This is your initial reading.
2. If a thimble mark aligns exactly with the sleeve line, reading the vernier scale is not necessary. If a thimble mark does not align exactly with the sleeve line, read the vernier scale in Step 3.
3. Read the vernier scale to find which vernier mark align with one thimble mark. The number of that

VERNIER INCH MICROMETER

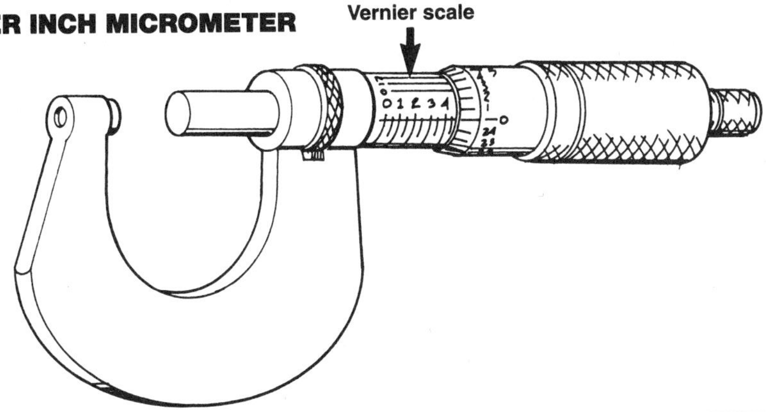

39

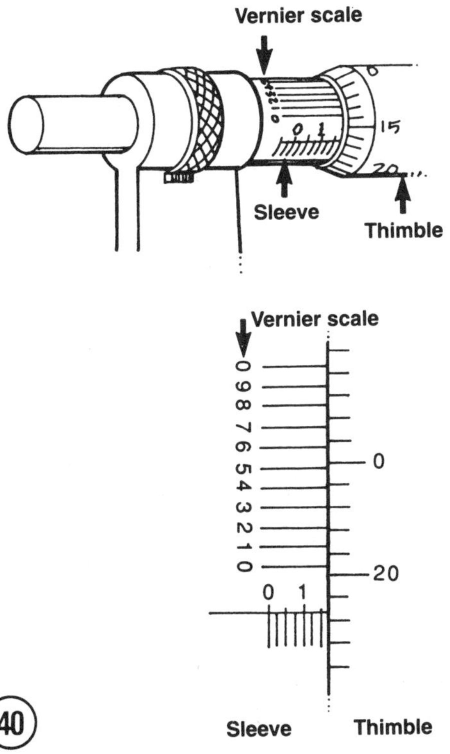

1. Largest number visible on sleeve line — 0.100 in.
2. Number of sleeve marks visible between the numbered sleeve mark and the thimble edge — 0.050 in.
3. Thimble is between 0.018 and 0.019 in. on the sleeve line — 0.018 in.
4. Vernier line coinciding with thimble line — 0.0003 in.

Total reading — 0.1683 in.

40

vernier mark is the number of ten-thousandths of an inch to add to the initial reading taken in Step 1.

Metric micrometer

The metric micrometer is very similar to the standard inch type. The differences are the graduations on the thimble and sleeve as shown in **Figure 41**.

The standard metric micrometer is accurate of measuring to a one one-hundredth of a millimeter (0.01 mm). On the metric micrometer, the spindle screw is ground with a thread pitch of one-half millimeter (0.5 mm). Thus every turn of the thimble will move the spindle 0.5 mm.

The sleeve line is graduated in millimeters and half millimeters. The marks on the upper side of the sleeve line are equal to 1.00 mm. Every fifth mark above the sleeve line is marked with a number. The actual numbers will depend on the size of the micrometer. For example, on a 0-25 mm micrometer, the sleeve marks are numbered 0, 5, 10, 15, 20 and 25. On a 25-50 mm micrometer, the sleeve marks are numbered 25, 30, 35, 40, 45 and 50. This numbering sequence continues with larger micrometers (50-75

41

STANDARD METRIC MICROMETER

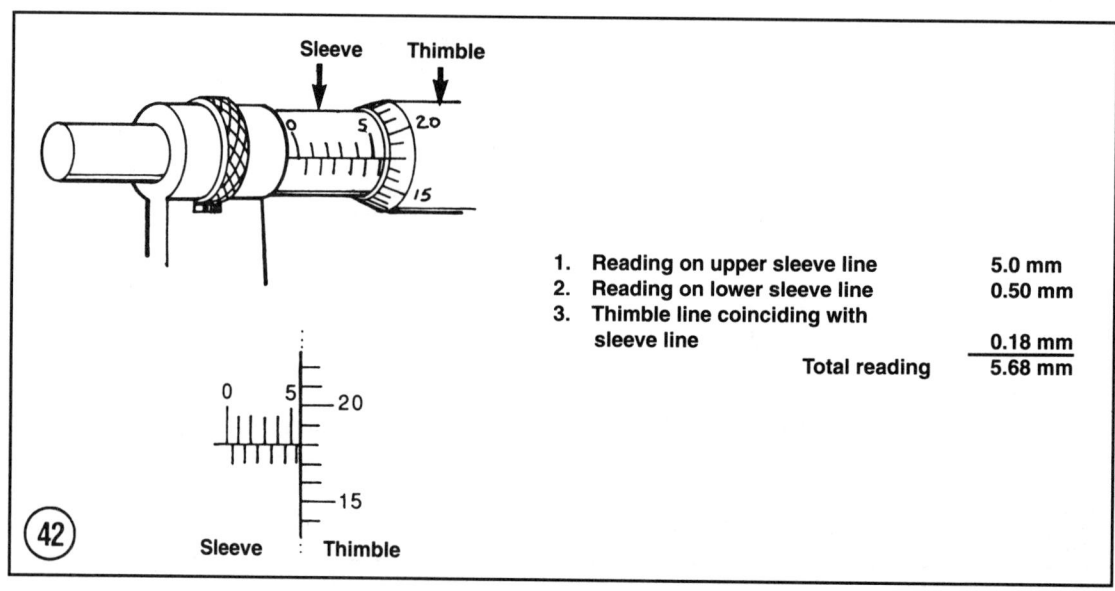

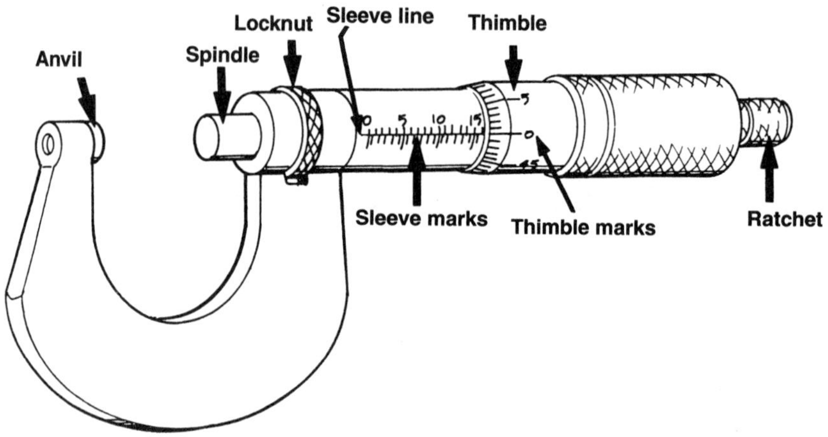

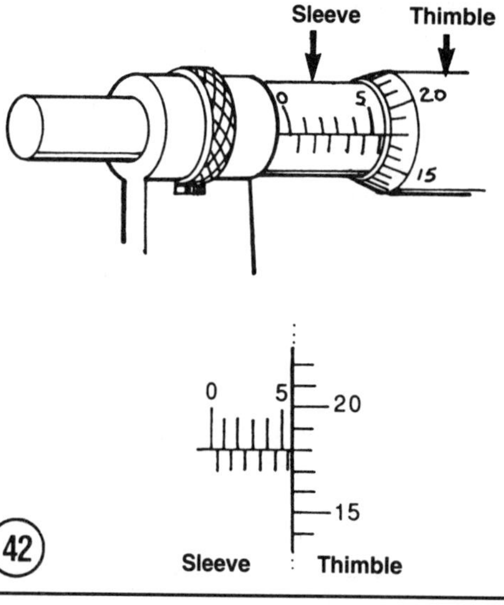

1. Reading on upper sleeve line — 5.0 mm
2. Reading on lower sleeve line — 0.50 mm
3. Thimble line coinciding with sleeve line — 0.18 mm

Total reading — 5.68 mm

42

and 75-100). Each mark on the lower side of the sleeve line is equal to 0.50 mm.

The thimble scale is divided into fifty graduations where one graduation is equal to 0.01 mm. Every fifth thimble graduation is numbered 0-45 to help with reading. The thimble edge is used to indicate which sleeve markings to read.

To read a metric micrometer, add the number of millimeters and half-millimeters on the sleeve line to the number of one one-hundredth millimeters on the thimble. To do so, perform the following steps while referring to the example in **Figure 42**.

1. Take the first reading by counting the number of marks visible on the upper sleeve line. Record the reading.
2. Look below the sleeve line to see if a lower mark is visible directly past the upper line mark. If so, add 0.50 to the first reading.
3. Now read the thimble mark that aligns with the sleeve line. Record this reading.

NOTE
If a thimble mark does not align exactly with the sleeve line but falls between 2 lines, estimate the decimal amount between the lines. For a more accurate reading, you must use a metric vernier micrometer.

4. Adding the micrometer readings in Steps 1, 2 and 3 gives the actual measurement.

Metric vernier micrometers

A metric vernier micrometer is accurate to 2 thousandths of a millimeter (0.002 mm). While it has the same markings as a standard metric micrometer, a vernier scale scribed on the sleeve (**Figure 43**) makes it unique. The vernier scale consists of five equally spaced lines marked 0, 2, 4, 6 and 8. These lines run parallel on the top of the sleeve where each line is equal to 0.002 mm.

To read a metric vernier micrometer, perform the following steps while referring to the example in **Figure 44**:

1. Read the micrometer in the same way as on the metric standard micrometer. This is the initial reading.
2. If a thimble mark aligns exactly with the sleeve line, reading the vernier scale is not necessary. If a thimble mark does not align exactly with the sleeve line, read the vernier scale in Step 3.
3. Read the vernier scale to find which vernier mark lines up with one thimble mark. The number of that vernier mark is the number of thousandths of a millimeter to add to the initial reading taken in Step 1.

Micrometer Accuracy Check

Before using a micrometer, check its accuracy as follows:

(43) **VERNIER METRIC MICROMETER**

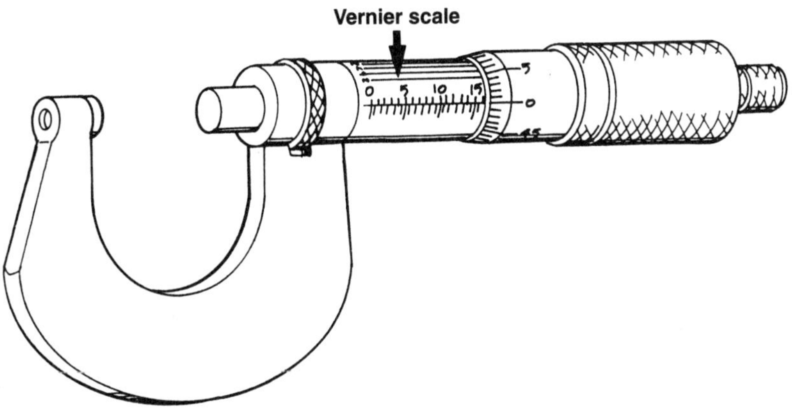

1. Make sure the anvil and spindle faces (**Figure 37** or **Figure 41**) are clean and dry.

2. To check a 0-1 in. or 0-25 mm micrometer, perform the following:

   a. Turn the thimble until the spindle contacts the anvil. If the micrometer has a ratchet stop, use it to ensure that the proper amount of pressure is applied against the contact surfaces.

   b. Read the micrometer. If the adjustment is correct, the 0 mark on the thimble will align exactly with the 0 mark on the sleeve line. If the 0 marks do not align, the micrometer is out of adjustment.

   c. To adjust the micrometer, follow its manufacturer's instructions given with the micrometer.

3. To check the accuracy of micrometers above the 1 in. or 25 mm size, perform the following:

   a. Manufacturers usually supply a standard gauge with these micrometers. A standard is a steel block, disc or rod that is ground to an exact size to check the accuracy of the micrometer. For example, a 1-2 in. micrometer is equipped with a 1 inch standard gauge. A 25-50 mm micrometer is equipped with a 25 mm standard gauge.

   b. Place the standard gauge between the micrometer's spindle and anvil and measure its outside diameter or length. Read the micrometer. If the adjustment is correct, the 0 mark on the thimble will align exactly with the 0 mark on the sleeve line. If the 0 marks do not align, the micrometer is out of adjustment.

   c. To adjust the micrometer, follow its manufacturer's instructions given with the micrometer.

Proper Care of the Micrometer

The micrometer is a precision instrument and must be used correctly and with great care. When handling a micrometer, note the following:

1. Store a micrometer in its box or in a protected place where dust, oil, and other debris cannot come in contact with it. Do not store micrometers in a drawer with other tools or hang them on a tool board.

2. When storing a 0-1 in. (0-25 mm) micrometer, turn the thimble so the spindle and anvil faces do not contact each other. If they do, rust may form on the

44

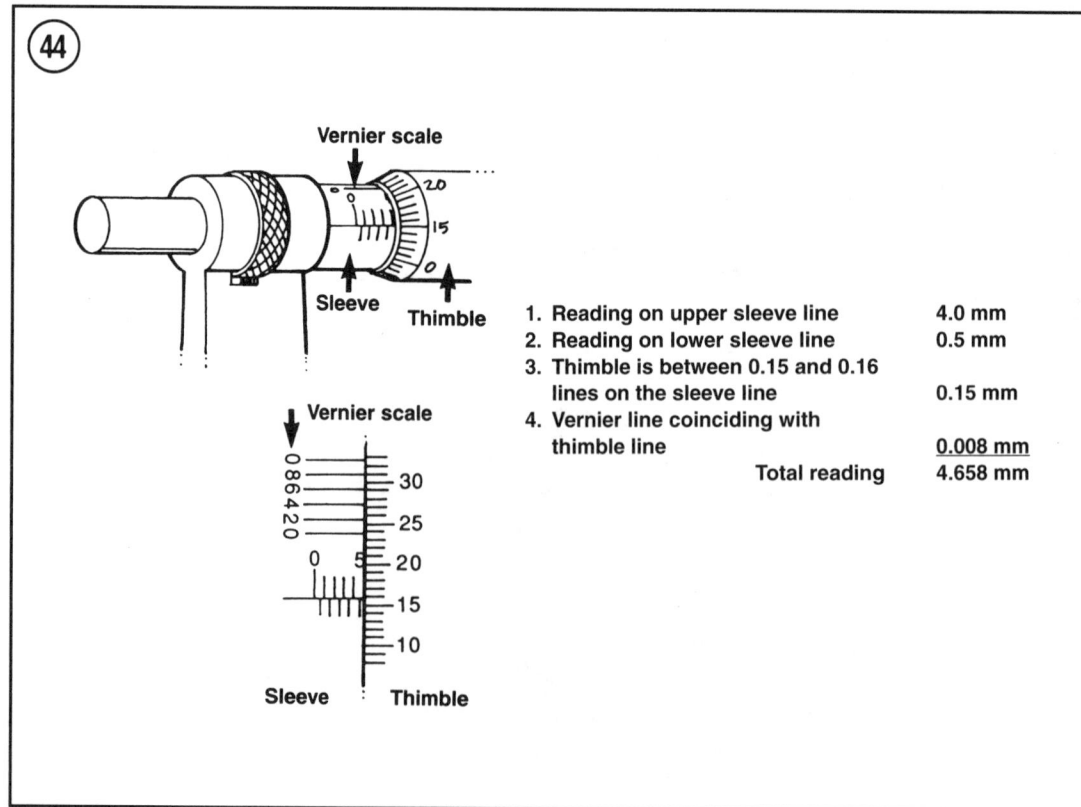

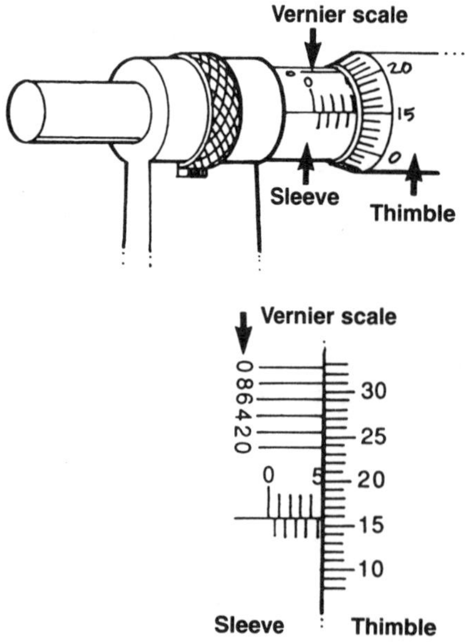

1. Reading on upper sleeve line		4.0 mm
2. Reading on lower sleeve line		0.5 mm
3. Thimble is between 0.15 and 0.16 lines on the sleeve line		0.15 mm
4. Vernier line coinciding with thimble line		0.008 mm
	Total reading	4.658 mm

45

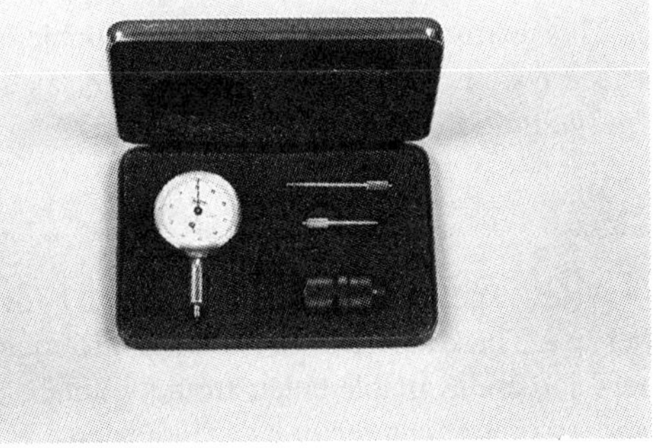

46

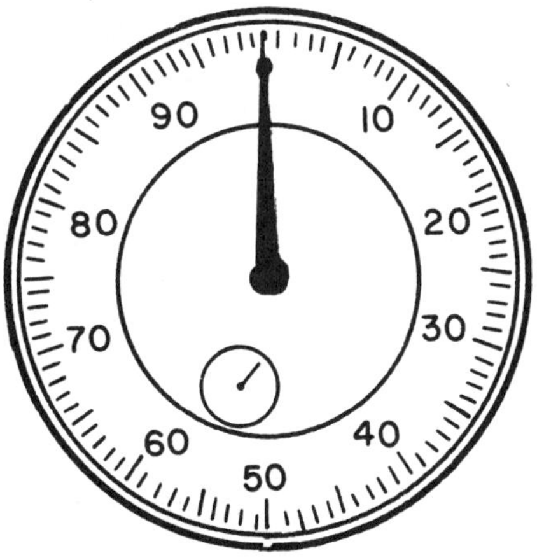

47

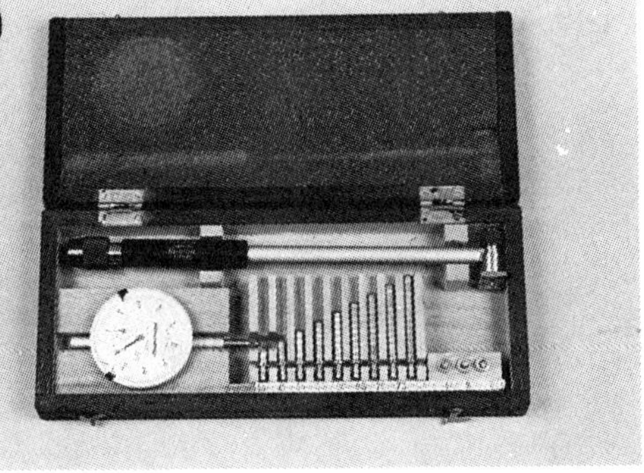

contact ends or the spindle can be damaged from temperature changes.

3. Do not clean a micrometer with compressed air. Dirt forced into the tool can cause premature wear.

4. Occasionally lubricate the micrometer with a light weight oil to prevent rust and corrosion.

5. Before using a micrometer, check its accuracy. Refer to *Micrometer Accuracy Check* in this section.

Dial Indicator

Dial indicators (**Figure 45**) are precision tools used to check dimensional variations on machined parts such as transmission shafts and axles and to check crankshaft and axle shaft end play. Dial indicators are available with various dial types; for motorcycle repair, select an indicator with a continuous dial face (**Figure 46**).

Cylinder Bore Gauge

The cylinder bore gauge is a very specialized precision tool. The gauge set shown in **Figure 47** is comprised of a dial indicator, handle and a number of length adapters to adapt the gauge to different bore sizes. The bore gauge can be used to make cylinder bore measurements such as bore size, taper and out-of-round. In some cases, an outside micrometer must be used to calibrate the bore gauge to a specific bore size.

Select the correct length adapter for the size of the bore to be measured. Calibrate the bore gauge according to its manufacturer's instructions, insert the bore gauge into the cylinder, carefully move it around in the bore to make sure it is centered and that the gauge foot is sitting correctly on the bore surface. This is necessary to obtain a correct reading. Refer to the manufacturer's instructions for reading the actual measurement obtained.

V-Blocks

V-blocks (**Figure 48**) are precision ground blocks used to hold a round object when checking its runout or condition. V-blocks can be used when checking the runout of such items as the transmission shafts and axles.

TEST EQUIPMENT

Spark Tester

A quick way to check the ignition system is to connect a spark tester to the end of the spark plug wire and operate the engine's kickstarter. A visible spark should jump the gap on the tester. A variety of spark testers is available from engine and aftermarket manufacturers. This tool is shown in Chapter Two.

Compression Gauge

An engine with low compression cannot be properly tuned and will not develop full power. A compression gauge (**Figure 49**) measures engine compression. The one shown has a flexible stem with an extension that can allow you to hold it while kicking the engine over. Open the throttle all the way when checking engine compression. See Chapter Three.

Crankcase Pressure Tester

A pressure tester checks for air leaks in a 2-stroke engine. This test should be made when troubleshooting a 2-stroke engine, after installing the reed valve assembly or after reassembling the engine's top end. Air leaks through the engine seals and/or gaskets can cause engine seizure, carburetor problems and power loss. This test is fully described in Chapter Two.

Strobe Timing Light (BW80 and PW80)

Use this instrument to check ignition timing. By flashing a light at the precise instant the spark plug fires, the position of the timing mark can be seen. The flashing light makes a moving mark appear to stand still opposite a stationary mark.

Suitable lights range from inexpensive neon bulb types to powerful xenon strobe lights. A light with an inductive pickup is recommended to eliminate any possible damage to ignition wiring. Use according to manufacturer's instructions. This procedure is described in Chapter Three.

Multimeter or VOM

This instrument (**Figure 50**) is invaluable for electrical system troubleshooting. See *Electrical Troubleshooting* in Chapter Two for its use.

SPECIAL TOOLS

A few special tools will be required for major service. These are described in the appropriate chapters and are available either from a Yamaha dealership or other manufacturers as indicated.

MECHANIC'S TIPS

Removing Frozen Nuts and Screws

When a fastener rusts and cannot be removed, several methods may be used to loosen it. First, apply penetrating oil such as Liquid Wrench or WD-40 (available at hardware or auto supply stores). Apply it liberally and let it penetrate for 10-15 minutes. Rap the fastener several times with

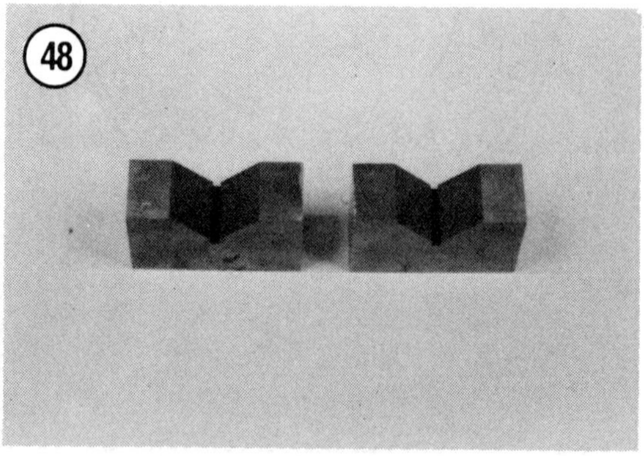

48

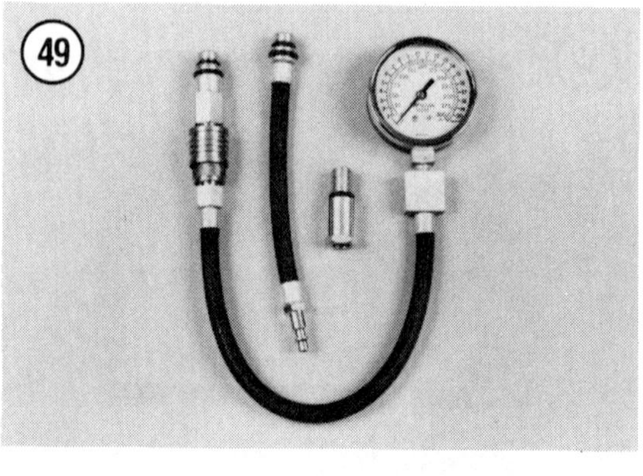

49

a small hammer; do not hit it hard enough to cause damage. Reapply the penetrating oil if necessary.

For frozen screws, apply penetrating oil as described, then insert a screwdriver in the slot and rap the top of the screwdriver with a hammer. This loosens the rust so the screw can be removed in the normal way. If the screw head is too chewed up to use this method, try to grip the fastener head with locking pliers and twist the screw out.

Avoid applying heat unless specifically instructed, as it may melt, warp or remove the temper from parts.

Removing Broken Screws or Bolts

When the head breaks off a screw or bolt, several methods are available for removing the remaining portion.

If a large portion of the remainder projects out, try gripping it with locking pliers. If the projecting portion is too small, file it to fit a wrench or cut a slot in it to fit a screwdriver. See **Figure 51**.

If the head breaks off flush, use a screw extractor. To do this, centerpunch the exact center of the remaining portion of the screw or bolt. Drill a small hole in the screw and tap the extractor into the hole. Back the screw out with a wrench on the extractor. See **Figure 52**.

50

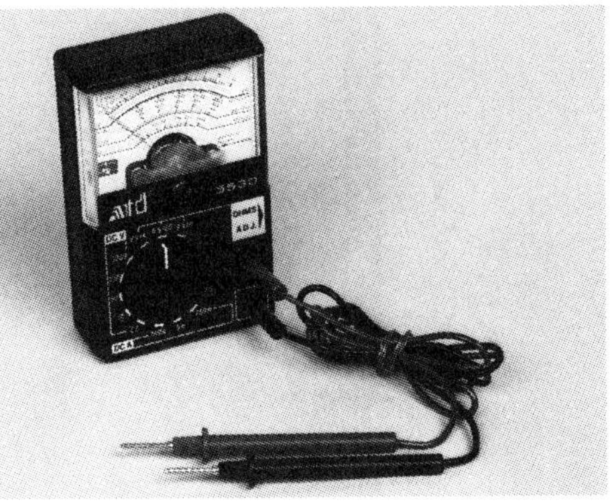

51

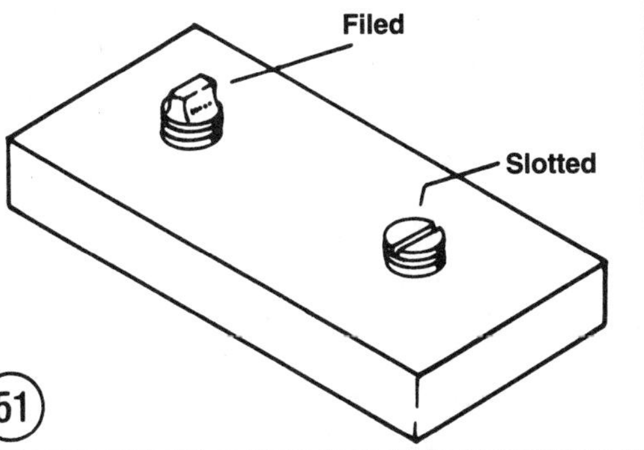

Remedying Stripped Threads

Occasionally, threads are stripped through carelessness or impact damage. Often the threads can be cleaned up by running a tap (for internal threads on nuts) or die (for external threads on bolts) through the threads. See **Figure 53**. To clean or repair spark plug threads, use a spark plug tap.

If an internal thread is damaged, it may be necessary to install a thread insert. These are available for individual thread sizes and in large sets. Follow the manufacturer's instructions when installing their insert.

If it is necessary to drill and tap a hole, refer to **Table 8** for metric tap drill sizes.

Replacing Studs

1. Measure the height of the installed stud so that the new stud can be installed correctly.

2A. If some threads of a stud are damaged, but some remain, you may be able to removed the stud as follows. If there are no usable threads, remove the stud as described in Step 2B.

   a. Thread two nuts onto the damaged stud (**Figure 54**), then tighten the nuts against each other so that they are locked.
   b. Turn the bottom nut (**Figure 55**) and unscrew the stud.

2B. If the threads on the stud are damaged, remove the stud with a stud remover or, if possible, with a pair of locking pliers.

3. Clean the threads with solvent or contact cleaner and allow to dry thoroughly.

4. Clean the threaded hole with contact cleaner or solvent and a wire brush. Try to remove as much of the threadsealer residue from the hole as possible.

5. Install 2 nuts on the top half of the new stud as in Step 2A. Make sure they are locked securely.

6. Apply a high-strength threadlocking compound to the bottom threads on the new stud.

7. Turn the top nut and thread the new stud in. Install the stud to its correct height position (Step 1) or tighten it to its correct torque specification (see appropriate chapter).

8. Remove the nuts and repeat for each stud as required.

BALL BEARING REPLACEMENT

Ball bearings (**Figure 56**) are used throughout the engine and chassis to reduce power loss, heat and noise resulting from friction. Because ball bearings are precision-made parts, they must be maintained by proper lubrication and maintenance. If a bearing is damaged, replace it immediately. However, when installing a new bearing, use caution to prevent damage to the new bearing. While bearing replacement is covered in the individual chapters, the following should be used as a guideline.

NOTE
Unless otherwise specified, install bearings with their manufacturer's mark or number facing outward.

Purchasing New Bearings

Replacement bearings can be purchased through a Yamaha dealership or from a local bearing supply house. When you purchase a bearing through your dealer, a part number recorded off the dealer's microfiche card or computer will be used to order and identify the bearing. When using a local bearing supply house, the code number listed on the side of the bearing will be used to identify the bearing. When replacing a bearing, do not discard the old

52

REMOVING BROKEN SCREWS AND BOLTS

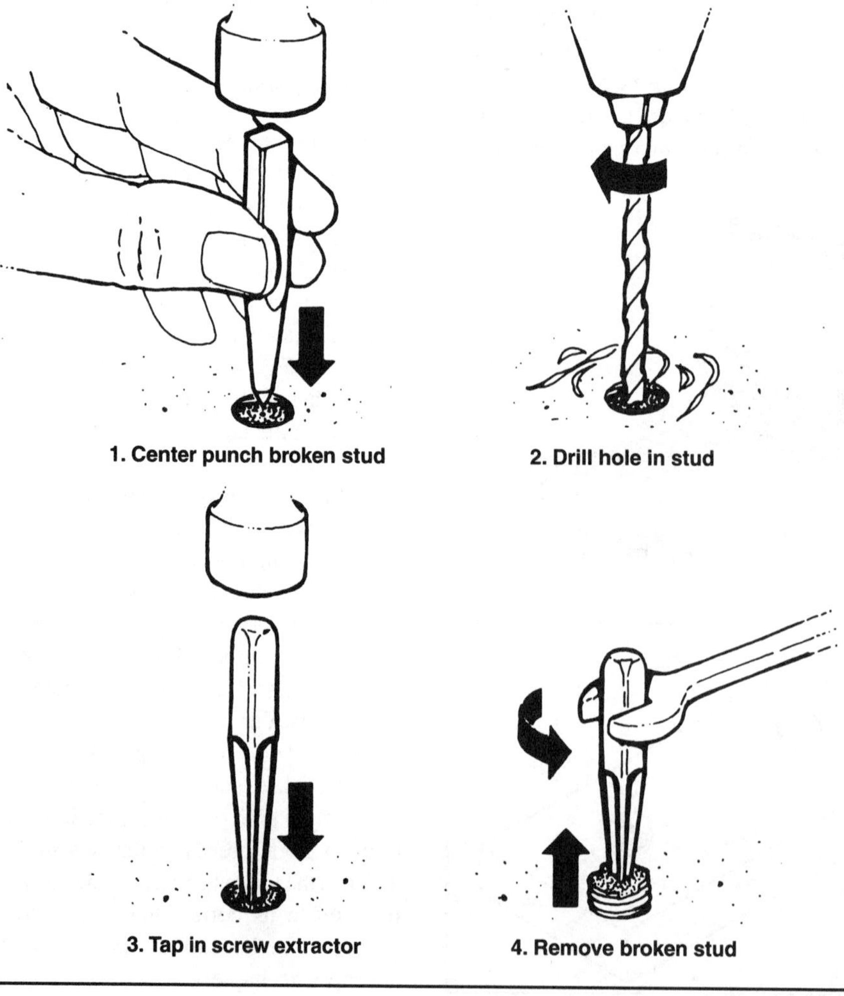
1. Center punch broken stud
2. Drill hole in stud
3. Tap in screw extractor
4. Remove broken stud

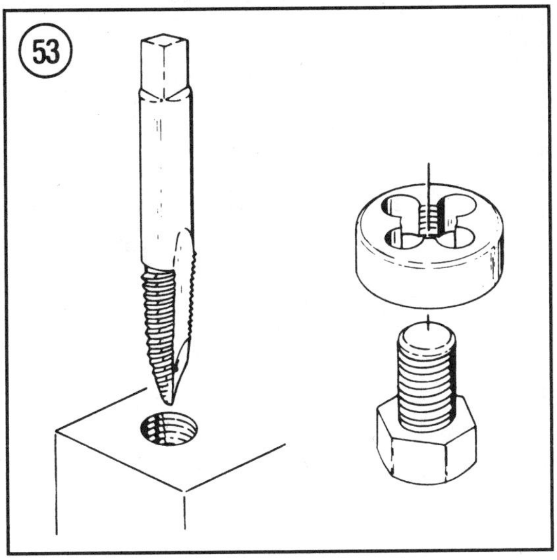
53

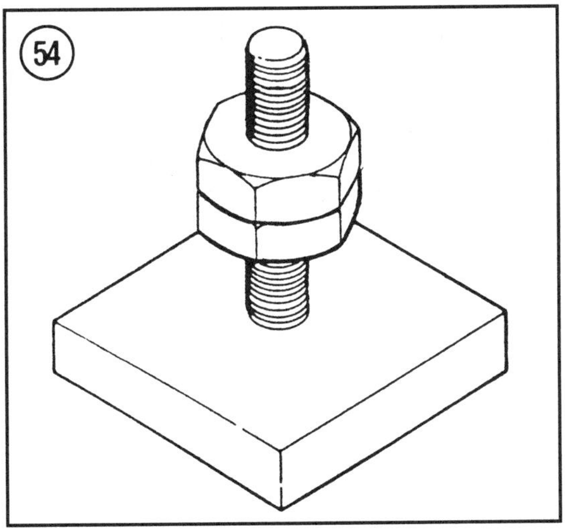
54

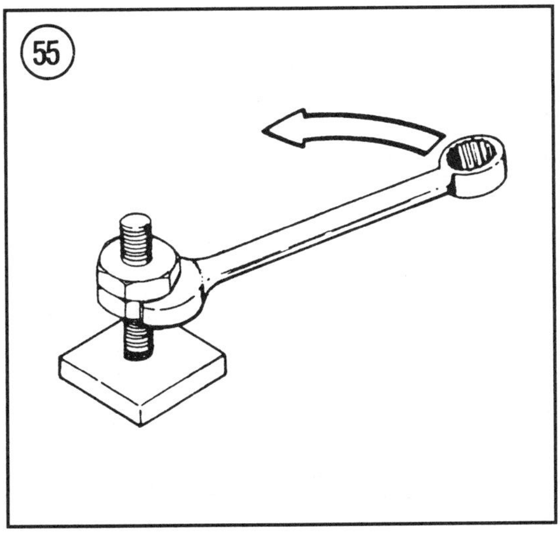
55

bearing until you are sure that the new bearing is an identical match.

Ball bearings are available in many types and series, for example, light, medium, heavy and max. They are also available where they are open on both sides, use one shield or two shields or use one or two seals. Principal bearing dimensions are width, outside diameter and inside diameter.

Bearing Removal

While bearings are normally removed only if damaged, there may be times when it is necessary to remove a bearing that is in good condition. However, improper bearing removal may damage the bearing and its housing or shaft. Note the following when removing bearings.

1. When using a puller to remove a bearing from a shaft, take care that the shaft is not damaged. Always place a piece of metal (**Figure 57**) between the end of the shaft and the puller screw. In addition, place the puller arms next to the bearing's inner bearing.

56

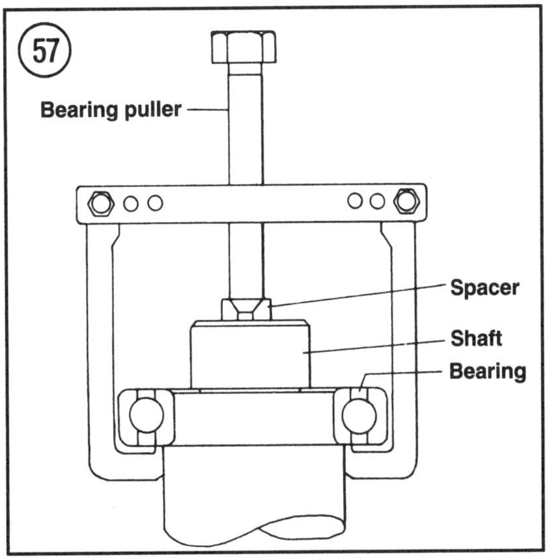

2. When using a hammer to drive a shaft off of a bearing, do not strike the shaft with the hammer. Doing so can crack or spread the end of the shaft, permanently damaging it. Instead, use a brass or aluminum driver between the hammer and shaft, while supporting both bearing races with wooden blocks as shown in **Figure 58**.

3. The ideal method of bearing removal is with a hydraulic press. However, certain procedures must be followed or damage may occur to the bearing, bearing bore or shaft. Note the following when using a press:

a. Always support the inner and outer bearing races with a suitable size wood or aluminum spacer (**Figure 59**). If only the outer race is supported, the balls and/or the inner race will be damaged.

b. Make sure the press ram (**Figure 59**) aligns with the center of the shaft. If the ram is not centered, it may damage the bearing and/or shaft.

c. The moment the shaft is free of the bearing, it will drop to the floor. Secure or hold the shaft to prevent it from falling.

58

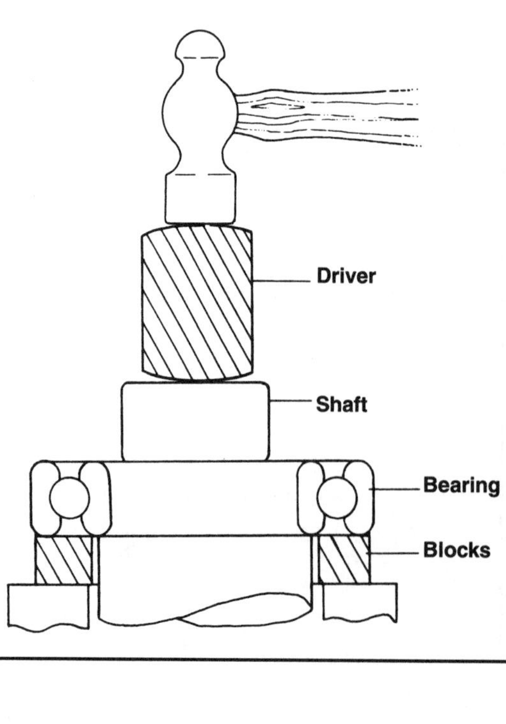

59

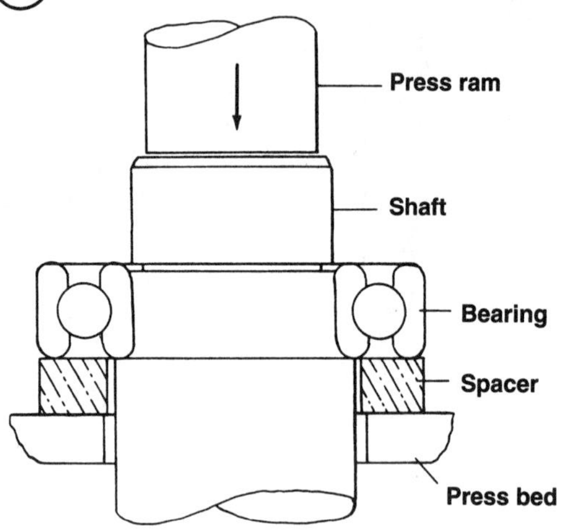

60

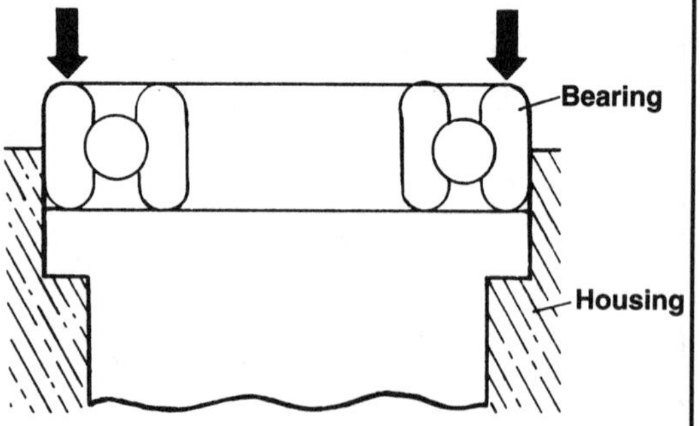

61

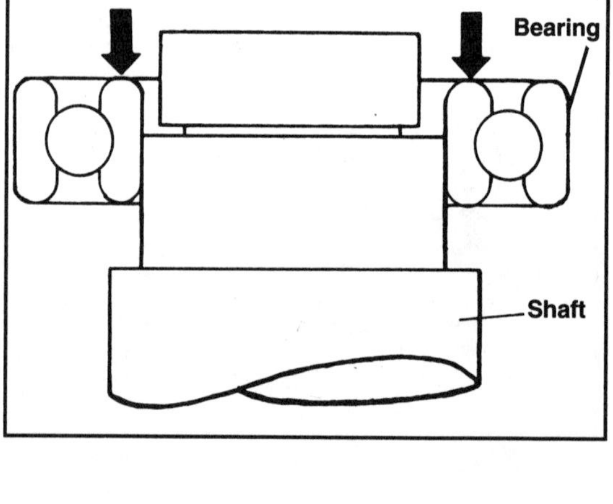

Bearing Installation

Refer to the following when installing bearings.

1. When installing a bearing in a housing, apply pressure to the *outer* bearing race (**Figure 60**). When installing a bearing on a shaft, apply pressure to the *inner* bearing race (**Figure 61**).
2. When installing a bearing as described in Step 1, some type of driver is required. Never strike the bearing directly with a hammer or the bearing will be damaged. When installing a bearing, a bearing driver or a socket with an outside diameter that matches the bearing race is required. **Figure 62** shows the correct way to use a bearing driver and hammer when installing a bearing over a shaft.
3. Step 1 describes how to install a bearing in a housing and over a shaft. However, when installing a bearing over a shaft and into a housing at the same time, a snug fit is required for both outer and inner bearing races. In this situation, a spacer must be installed underneath the driver tool to apply pressure evenly across *both* races (**Figure 63**). If the outer race is not supported as shown in **Figure 63**, the balls will push against the outer bearing race and damage it.

62

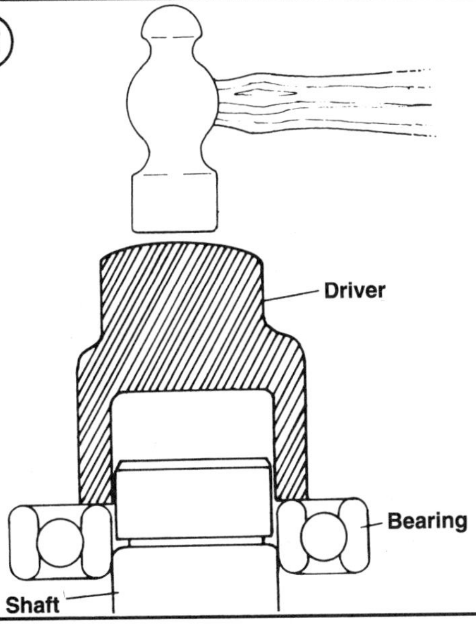

63

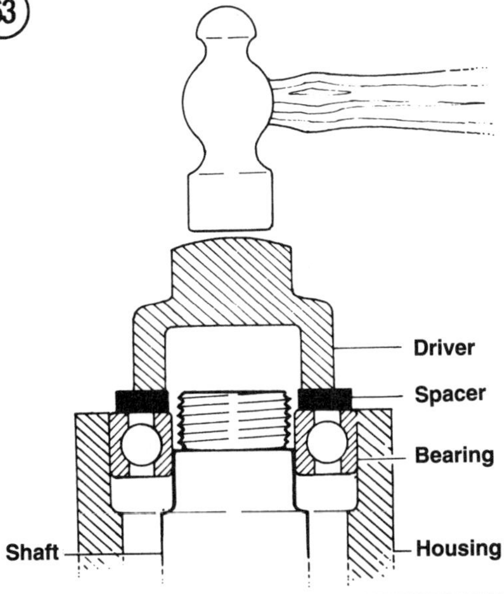

Shrink Fit

1. *Installing a bearing over a shaft*: If a tight fit is required, the bearing inside diameter will be smaller than the shaft. In this case, driving the bearing on the shaft using normal methods may cause bearing damage. Instead, heat the bearing before installation. Note the following:
   a. Secure the shaft so that it is ready for bearing installation.
   b. Clean the bearing surface on the shaft of all residue. Remove burrs with a file or sandpaper.
   c. Fill a suitable pot or beaker with clean mineral oil. Place a thermometer (rated higher than 120° C [248° F]) in the oil. Support the thermometer so that it does not rest on the bottom or side of the pot.
   d. Secure the bearing with a piece of heavy wire bent to hold it in the pot. Hang the bearing in the pot so that it does not touch the bottom or sides of the pot.
   e. Turn the heat on and monitor the thermometer. When the oil temperature rises to approximately 120° C (248° F), remove the bearing from the pot and quickly install it. If necessary, place a socket on the inner bearing race (**Figure 61**) and tap the bearing into place. As the bearing chills, it will begin to tighten on the shaft. To prevent the bearing from locking onto the shaft at the wrong spot, work quickly when installing it. Make sure the bearing is installed all the way.
2. *Installing a bearing in a housing*: Bearings are generally installed in a housing with a slight inter-

ference fit. Driving the bearing into the housing using normal methods may damage the housing or cause bearing damage. Instead, the housing should be heated before the bearing is installed. Note the following.

CAUTION
Before heating the housing in this procedure to remove the bearings, wash the housing thoroughly with detergent and water. Rinse and rewash the housing as required to remove all traces of oil and other chemical deposits.

a. Heat the housing to a temperature of about 100° C (212° F) in a shop oven or on a hot plate. An easy way to see if it is at the proper temperature is to drop tiny drops of water on the housing; if they sizzle and evaporate immediately, the temperature is correct. Heat only one housing at a time.

CAUTION
Do not heat the housing with a torch (propane or acetylene)—never bring open flames into contact with the bearing or housing. The direct heat will destroy the case hardening of the bearing and will likely warp the housing.

b. Remove the housing from the oven or hot plate. Hold onto the housing with a kitchen pot holder, heavy gloves, or heavy shop cloths—*it is hot.*

NOTE
A suitable size socket and extension work well for removing and installing bearings.

c. Hold the housing with the bearing side down and tap the bearing out. Repeat for all bearings in the housing.
d. Before heating the housing, place the new bearings in a freezer, if possible. Chilling them will slightly reduce their overall diameter while the hot housing assembly is larger due to heat expansion. This will make installation much easier.

NOTE
Always install bearings with their manufacturer's mark or number facing outward unless the text directs otherwise.

e. While the housing is still hot, install the new bearing(s) into the housing. Install the bearings by hand, if possible. If necessary, lightly tap the bearing(s) into the housing with a socket placed on the outer bearing race. *Do not* install new bearings by driving on the inner bearing race. Install the bearing(s) until it seats completely.

SEALS

Seals (**Figure 64**) are used to prevent leakage of oil, grease or combustion gasses from between a housing and a shaft. The seal has a rubber or neoprene lip that rests against the shaft to form a seal. Depending on the application, the seal may have one or more lips, as well as a garter spring behind the lip to increase pressure on the seal lips. Improper procedures to remove a seal can damage the housing or shaft. Improper installation can damage the seal. Note the following:

a. Prying is generally the easiest and most effective method of removing a seal from a housing. However, always place a rag underneath the pry tool to prevent damage to the housing.
b. Pack grease in the seal lips before installing the seal. If the procedure does not specify a certain type of grease, use a waterproof grease.

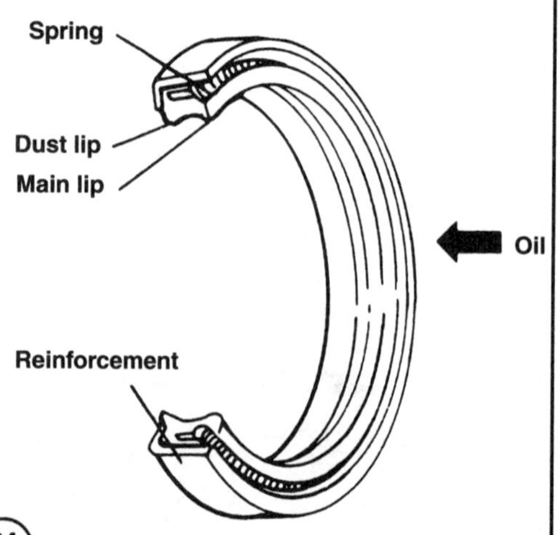

64

c. Install seals with their manufacturer's marks facing out, unless the text directs otherwise.
d. A socket of the correct size can often be used as a seal driver. Select a socket that fits the seal's outer diameter properly and clears any protruding shafts.
e. Some seals can be installed by pressing them into place with your fingers. When doing so, make sure the seal is positioned squarely in its bore.
f. Make sure the seal is driven squarely into the housing. Never install a seal by hitting directly against the top of the seal with a hammer.

Table 1 ENGINE AND FRAME SERIAL NUMBERS

Year and model	Engine and frame serial number*
PW50H (1981)	4x4-000101-on
PW50J (1982)	4x4-200101-on
PW50K (1983)	4x4-260101-on
PW50N (1985)	36E-000101-on
PW50S (1986)	36E-020101-on
PW50T (1987)	36E-040101-on
PW50A (1990)	3PT-000101-on
PW50B (1991)	3PT-027101-on
PW50D (1992)	3PT-051101-on
PW50E (1993)	3PT-070101-on
PW50F (1994)	3PT-099101-on
PW50G (1995)	3PT-138101-on
PW50H1 (1996)	3PT-167101-on
PW50J1 (1997)	**
PW50K1 (1998)	**
PW50L (1999)	**
PW50M1 (2000)	**
PW50N1 (2001)	**
PW50P (2002)	**

(continued)

Table 1 ENGINE AND FRAME SERIAL NUMBERS (continued)

Year and model	Engine and frame serial number*
BW80S (1986)	1RY-000101-on
BW80T (1987)	1RY-020101-on
BW80U (1988)	1RY-056101-on
BW80A (1990)	3TW-000101-on
PW80K (1983)	21W-000101-on
PW80N (1985)	21W-000101-on
PW80B (1991)	3RV-000101-on
PW80D (1992)	3RV-010101-on
PW80E (1993)	3RV-020101-on
PW80F (1994)	3RV-032101-on
PW80G (1995)	3RV-044101-on
PW80H (1996)	3RV-061101-on
PW80J (1997)	**
PW80K1 (1998)	**
PW80L (1999)	**
PW80M1 (2000)	**
PW80N1 (2001)	**
PW80P (2002)	**

* End numbers not listed.
** Not specified for this model year.

Table 2 GENERAL DIMENSIONS

	mm	in.
Overall length		
PW50	1,245	49.0
BW80	1,575	62.0
PW80	1,540	60.6
Overall width		
PW50	575	22.6
BW80 and PW80	640	25.2
Overall height		
PW80	715	28.1
BW80	875	34.4
PW80	880	34.6
Seat height		
PW50	485	19.1
BW80	630	24.8
PW80	635	25.0
Minimum ground clearance		
PW50	105	4.1
BW80	180	7.1
PW80	185	7.3

Table 3 WEIGHT SPECIFICATIONS

	kg	lb.
Vehicle weight with full oil and full tanks		
PW50	39	86
BW80	110	243
PW80	61	134

Table 4 DECIMAL AND METRIC EQUIVALENTS

Fractions	Decimal in.	Metric mm	Fractions	Decimal in.	Metric mm
1/64	0.015625	0.39688	33/64	0.515625	13.09687
1/32	0.03125	0.79375	17/32	0.53125	13.49375
3/64	0.046875	1.19062	35/64	0.546875	13.89062
1/16	0.0625	1.58750	9/16	0.5625	14.28750
5/64	0.078125	1.98437	37/64	0.578125	14.68437
3/32	0.09375	2.38125	19/32	0.59375	15.08125
7/64	0.109375	2.77812	39/64	0.609375	15.47812
1/8	0.125	3.1750	5/8	0.625	15.87500
9/64	0.140625	3.57187	41/64	0.640625	16.27187
5/32	0.15625	3.96875	21/32	0.65625	16.66875
11/64	0.171875	4.36562	43/64	0.671875	17.06562
3/16	0.1875	4.76250	11/16	0.6875	17.46250
13/64	0.203125	5.15937	45/64	0.703125	17.85937
7/32	0.21875	5.55625	23/32	0.71875	18.25625
15/64	0.234375	5.95312	47/64	0.734375	18.65312
1/4	0.250	6.35000	3/4	0.750	19.05000
17/64	0.265625	6.74687	49/64	0.765625	19.44687
9/32	0.28125	7.14375	25/32	0.78125	19.84375
19/64	0.296875	7.54062	51/64	0.796875	20.24062
5/16	0.3125	7.93750	13/16	0.8125	20.63750
21/64	0.328125	8.33437	53/64	0.828125	21.03437
11/32	0.34375	8.73125	27/32	0.84375	21.43125
23/64	0.359375	9.12812	55/64	0.859375	22.82812
3/8	0.375	9.52500	7/8	0.875	22.22500
25/64	0.390625	9.92187	57/64	0.890625	22.62187
13/32	0.40625	10.31875	29/32	0.90625	23.01875
27/64	0.421875	10.71562	59/64	0.921875	23.41562
7/16	0.4375	11.11250	15/16	0.9375	23.81250
29/64	0.453125	11.50937	61/64	0.953125	24.20937
15/32	0.46875	11.90625	31/32	0.96875	24.60625
31/64	0.484375	12.30312	63/64	0.984375	25.00312
1/2	0.500	12.70000	1	1.00	25.40000

Table 5 CONVERSION TABLES

Multiply	By	To get equivalent of
Length		
Inches	25.4	Millimeter
Inches	2.54	Centimeter
Miles	1.609	Kilometer
Feet	0.3048	Meter
Millimeter	0.03937	Inches
Centimeter	0.3937	Inches
Kilometer	0.6214	Mile
Meter	3.281	Feet
Fluid volume		
U.S. quarts	0.9463	Liters
U.S. gallons	3.785	Liters
U.S. ounces	29.573529	Milliliters
Imperial gallons	4.54609	Liters
Imperial quarts	1.1365	Liters
Liters	0.2641721	U.S. gallons
Liters	1.0566882	U.S. quarts
Liters	0.8799	Imperial quarts

(continued)

Table 5 CONVERSION TABLES (continued)

Multiply	By	To get equivalent of
Fluid volume (cont.)		
Liters	33.814023	U.S. ounces
Liters	0.22	Imperial gallons
Milliliters	0.033814	U.S. ounces
Milliliters	1.0	Cubic centimeters
Milliliters	0.001	Liters
Torque		
Foot-pounds	1.3558	Newton-meters
Foot-pounds	0.138255	Meters-kilograms
Inch-pounds	0.11299	Newton-meters
Newton-meters	0.7375622	Foot-pounds
Newton-meters	8.8507	Inch-pounds
Meters-kilograms	7.2330139	Foot-pounds
Volume		
Cubic inches	16.387064	Cubic centimeters
Cubic centimeters	0.0610237	Cubic inches
Temperature		
Fahrenheit	$(F - 32) \times 0.556$	Centigrade
Centigrade	$(C \times 1.8) + 32$	Fahrenheit
Weight		
Ounces	28.3495	Grams
Pounds	0.4535924	Kilograms
Grams	0.035274	Ounces
Kilograms	2.2046224	Pounds
Pressure		
Pounds per square inch	0.070307	Kilograms per square centimeter
Kilograms per square centimeter	14.223343	Pounds per square inch
Kilopascals	0.1450	Pounds per square inch
Pounds per square inch	6.895	Kilopascals
Speed		
Miles per hour	1.609344	Kilometers per hour
Kilometers per hour	0.6213712	Miles per hour

Table 6 GENERAL TORQUE SPECIFICATIONS

Fastener size or type	N•m	in.-lb.	ft.-lb.
5 mm screw	4	35	—
5 mm bolt and nut	5	44	—
6 mm screw	9	80	—
6 mm bolt and nut	10	88	—
6 mm flange bolt (8 mm head, small flange)	9	80	—
6 mm flange bolt (10 mm head) and nut	12	106	—
8 mm bolt and nut	22	—	16
8 mm flange bolt and nut	27	—	20
10 mm bolt and nut	35	—	25
10 mm flange bolt and nut	40	—	29
12 mm bolt and nut	55	—	40

Table 7 TECHNICAL ABBREVIATIONS

ABDC	After bottom dead center
ATDC	After top dead center
BBDC	Before bottom dead center
BDC	Bottom dead center
BTDC	Before top dead center
C	Celsius (Centigrade)
cc	Cubic centimeters
CDI	Capacitor discharge ignition
cu. in.	Cubic inches
F	Fahrenheit
ft.-lb.	Foot-pounds
gal.	Gallons
H/A	High altitude
hp	Horsepower
in.	Inches
kg	Kilogram
kg/cm^2	Kilograms per square centimeter
kgm	Kilogram meters
km	Kilometer
L	Liter
m	Meter
MAG	Magneto
ml	Milliliter
mm	Millimeter
N•m	Newton-meters
oz.	Ounce
psi	Pounds per square inch
PTO	Power take off
pt.	Pint
qt.	Quart
rpm	Revolutions per minute

Table 8 METRIC TAP DRILL SIZES

Metric (mm)	Drill size	Decimal equivalent	Nearest fraction
3 × 0.50	No. 39	0.0995	3/32
3 × 0.60	3/32	0.0937	3/32
4 × 0.70	No. 30	0.1285	1/8
4 × 0.75	1/8	0.125	1/8
5 × 0.80	No. 19	0.166	11/64
5 × 0.90	No. 20	0.161	5/32
6 × 1.00	No. 9	0.196	13/64
7 × 1.00	16/64	0.234	15/64
8 × 1.00	J	0.277	9/32
8 × 1.25	17/64	0.265	17/64
9 × 1.00	5/16	0.3125	5/16
9 × 1.25	5/16	0.3125	5/16
10 × 1.25	11/32	0.3437	11/32
10 × 1.50	R	0.339	11/32
11 × 1.50	3/8	0.375	3/8
12 × 1.50	13/32	0.406	13/32
12 × 1.75	13/32	0.406	13/32

CHAPTER TWO

TROUBLESHOOTING

Diagnosing mechanical or electrical problems is relatively simple if you use orderly procedures and keep a few basic principles in mind. The first step in any troubleshooting procedure is to define the symptoms as closely as possible and then localize the problem. Subsequent steps involve testing and analyzing those areas which could cause the symptoms. A haphazard approach may eventually solve the problem, but it can be very costly in terms of wasted time and unnecessary parts replacement.

Proper lubrication, maintenance and periodic tune-ups as described in Chapter Three will reduce the necessity for troubleshooting. Even with the best of care, however, all motorcycles are prone to problems which will require troubleshooting.

Never assume anything. Check all switches and other starting procedures. If the engine won't start, is the spark plug cap on tight? Is the engine flooded with fuel?

If the engine suddenly quits, what sound did it make? Consider this and check the easiest, most accessible problem first. If the engine sounded like it ran out of fuel, check to see if there is fuel in the tank. If there is fuel in the tank, is it reaching the carburetor? If not, check the fuel system, starting with the fuel tank vent hose and finishing at the carburetor. Check all of the parts within the system to locate the problem.

If nothing obvious turns up in a quick check, look a little further. Learning to recognize and describe symptoms will make repairs easier for you or a mechanic at the dealership. If you do take your motorcycle to the dealership, describe the problem accurately and fully.

Gather as many symptoms as possible to aid in diagnosis. Note whether the engine lost power gradually or all at once, what color smoke (if any) came from the exhaust and so on.

After defining the symptoms, problem areas can be tested and analyzed. Guessing at the cause of a problem may provide the solution, but it usually leads to frustration, wasted time and a series of expensive, unnecessary parts replacements.

You do not need expensive equipment or complicated test gear to determine whether you should attempt repairs at home. A few simple checks could save a large repair bill and lost time while your motorcycle sits in a dealership service department. On the other hand, be realistic and attempt repairs that are within your abilities and shop experience. Service departments tend to charge heavily for putting together an engine that someone else has disassembled or damaged. Some won't even take on such a job, so use common sense and don't get in over your head.

OPERATING REQUIREMENTS

An engine needs 3 basics to run properly: correct fuel/air mixture, sufficient compression and a spark at the right time (**Figure 1**). If one basic requirement is missing, the engine will not run. Two-stroke engine operating principles are described in this chapter.

If the motorcycle has been sitting for any length of time and refuses to start, check and clean the spark plug. If the plug is not fouled, inspect the fuel delivery system. This includes the fuel tank, fuel shutoff valve, in-line fuel filter (if used) and fuel line. Gasoline deposits may have gummed up the carburetor's fuel inlet needle, jets and small air passages. Gasoline loses its potency after standing for long periods. Condensation may also contaminate it with water. Drain the old gas and try starting with a fresh mixture.

1

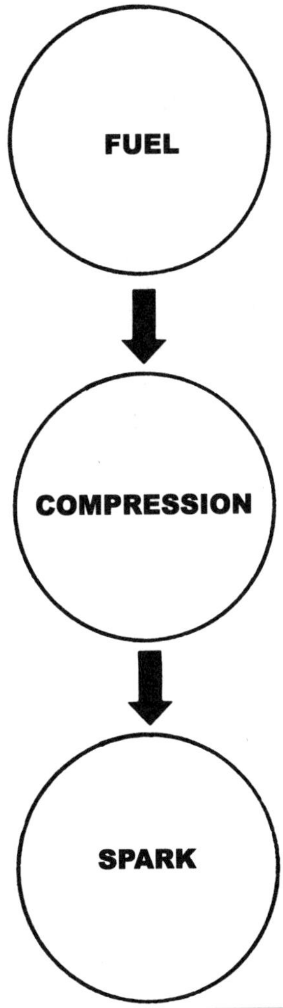

ENGINE OPERATING PRINCIPLES

Figure 2 explains how a 2-stroke engine operates. Understanding the principles and knowing what must happen for the engine to run will help you troubleshoot problems if the engine does not start or run properly.

STARTING THE ENGINE

If your engine refuses to start, frustration can cause you to forget basic starting principles and procedures. The following outline will guide you through the basic starting procedures for the engines covered in this manual. In all cases, make sure that there is an adequate supply of fresh fuel in the tank and that the engine oil tank is full of oil.

Engine Starting Procedures

A rich air/fuel mixture is required when starting a cold engine. To accomplish this, a separate choke circuit is installed inside the carburetor. The choke circuit is controlled by a hand-operated choke lever; see **Figure 3** (PW50) or **Figure 4** (BW80 and PW80). A cable connects the choke lever to the choke circuit. To *open* the choke circuit for starting a cold engine, pull the choke lever up. To *close* the choke circuit after the engine has warmed up or when starting a warm or hot engine, push the choke lever down.

Pre-operation checks

Before starting the engine, make the following checks. If an adjustment or further inspection is required, refer to the appropriate section in Chapter Three.

1. *Air filter*—Check that it is clean and oiled.
2. *Brakes*—Check the operation and adjustment of the front and rear brakes.

2

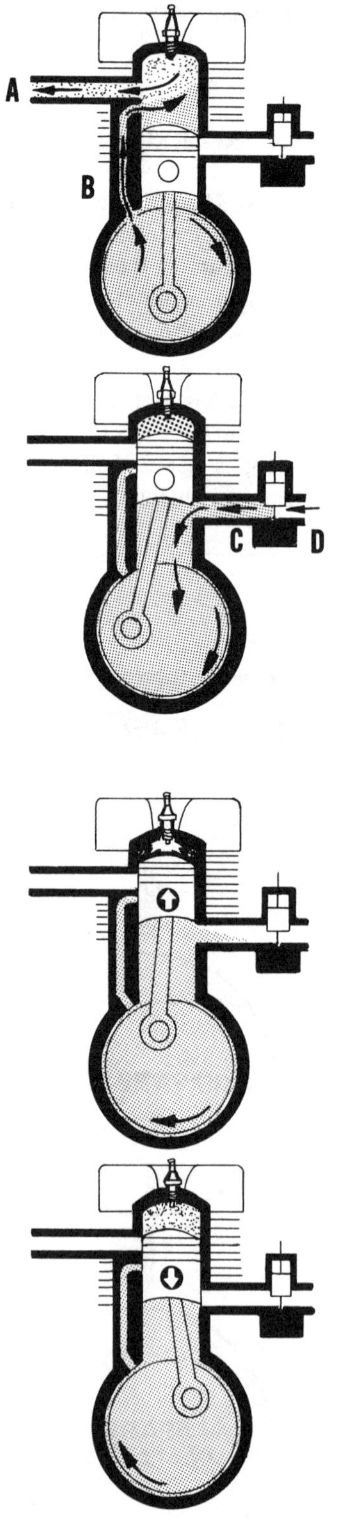

2-STROKE OPERATING PRINCIPLES

The crankshaft in this discussion is rotating in a clockwise direction.

As the piston travels downward, it uncovers the exhaust port (A) allowing the exhaust gases, which are under pressure, to leave the cylinder.

A fresh fuel/air charge, which has been compressed slightly, travels from the crankcase into the cylinder through the transfer port (B). Since this charge enters under pressure, it also helps to push out the exhaust gases.

While the crankshaft continues to rotate, the piston moves upward, covering the transfer port (B) and exhaust port (A). The piston is now compressing the new fuel/air mixture and creating a low pressure area in the crankcase at the same time. As the piston continues to travel, it uncovers the intake port (C). A fresh air/fuel charge, from the carburetor (D), is drawn into the crankcase through the intake port, because of the low pressure within it.

Now, as the piston almost reaches the top of its travel, the spark plug fires, thus igniting the compressed fuel/air mixture. The piston continues to top dead center (TDC) and is pushed downward by the expanding gases.

As the piston travels down, the exhaust gases leave the cylinder and the complete cycle starts all over again.

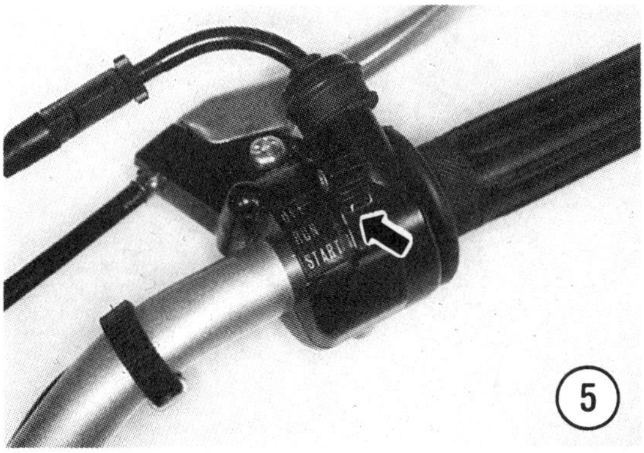

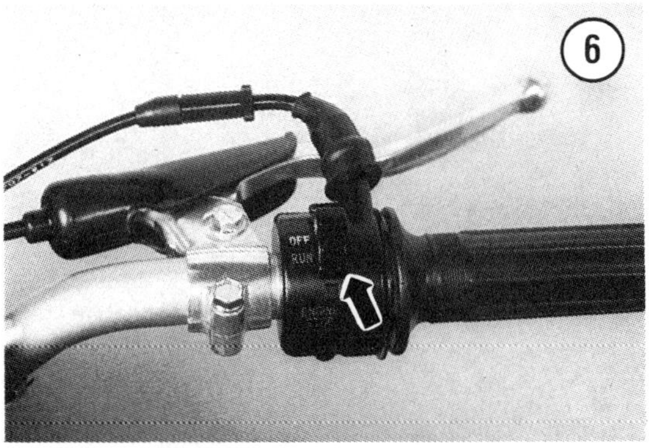

3. *Hose fittings and fasteners*—Check for leaks and tightness.

4. *Throttle*—Check the operation and adjustment of the throttle cable assembly.

5. *Transmission*—Change oil when necessary. Repair any leaks.

6. *Spark plug*—Check color and condition. Make sure the spark plug cap is on tight.

7. *Wheels and tires*—Check axle nut tightness, tire condition and air pressure.

8. *Drive chain (BW80 and PW80)*—Check chain tension and alignment. Lubricate drive chain.

Starting a cold engine

WARNING

Before starting the engine in freezing weather, check that the throttle cable assembly (including the oil pump cable) moves freely. Operating the motorcycle with a sluggish or tight throttle cable can cause you to lose control.

1. On PW50 models, support the bike on its centerstand.

2. Perform the steps listed under *Pre-Operation Checks* in this section.

WARNING

If any pre-operation check is not working properly, adjust or repair it before starting and riding the motorcycle.

2. Turn the fuel valve to its ON position.

3A. On PW50 models, move the ignition control switch to its START position (**Figure 5**).

3B. On BW80 and PW80 models, move the engine stop switch to its RUN position (**Figure 6**).

4. Move the choke lever up (**Figure 3** or **Figure 4**) to open the choke circuit.

5. With the throttle completely *closed*, crank the engine.

6. When the engine starts, allow the engine to idle until it will idle cleanly with the throttle lever moved down (closing the choke circuit). Warm the engine for 1-2 minutes.

7. On PW50 models, perform the following:
   a. Move the motorcycle off its centerstand.
   b. With the throttle grip closed, move the ignition control switch to its RUN position (**Figure 5**).

Starting a warm or hot engine

1. Perform Steps 1-4 under *Starting a Cold Engine* in this section.
2. With the throttle completely *closed*, crank the engine.
3. When the engine starts, idle the engine until the throttle responds cleanly with the throttle lever moved down (closing the choke circuit). Warm the engine for 1-2 minutes.
4. On PW50 models, perform the following:
   a. Move the motorcycle off its centerstand.
   b. With the throttle grip closed, move the ignition control switch to its RUN position (**Figure 5**).

Starting a flooded engine

If the engine is hard to start and there is a strong gasoline smell, the engine is probably flooded. If so, close the choke (**Figure 3** or **Figure 4**). On PW50 models, move the ignition control switch to its START position (**Figure 5**). On BW80 and PW80 models, move the engine stop switch to its RUN position (**Figure 6**). On PW50 models, make sure the bike is resting on its centerstand. On BW80 and PW80 models, the transmission must be in NEUTRAL. Then open the throttle all the way and kick the engine over until it starts. Depending on how badly the engine is flooded, it will generally start after a few hard kicks. If the engine is flooded badly, you may have to remove the spark plug and dry its insulator, or install a new plug before the engine will run. When a flooded engine first starts to run, it will initially cough and run slowly as it burns the excess fuel. Then as this excess fuel is burned, the engine will accelerate quickly. Release the throttle grip at this point and work it slowly to make sure the engine is running cleanly. Because a flooded engine smokes badly when it first starts to run, always start it outside and in a well-ventilated area with its muffler pointing away from all objects. Do not start a flooded engine in a garage or other closed area.

NOTE
On PW50 models, if the speed limiter is being used to control engine speed, remove it so the throttle can be opened all the way. Then, after the engine starts and runs cleanly, reinstall the speed limiter screw and set at its original adjustment position.

NOTE
If the engine still refuses to start, check the carburetor overflow hose attached to the fitting at the bottom of the float bowl. If fuel is running out of the hose, the inlet valve is stuck open, allowing the carburetor to overfill. Service the carburetor as described in Chapter Seven.

STARTING DIFFICULTIES

If the engine is difficult to start, or will not start at all, check for obvious problems even before getting out your tools. Go down the following list step by step. Perform each step while remembering the 3 engine operating requirements described under *Operating Requirements* in this chapter.

1. Is the choke in the right position? Lift the choke lever for a cold engine and push it down for a warm or hot engine. See **Figure 3** or **Figure 4**.
2. Is there fuel in the tank? Fill the tank if necessary. Check for a clogged fuel tank vent tube (**Figure 7**). Remove the tube from the filler cap, wipe off one

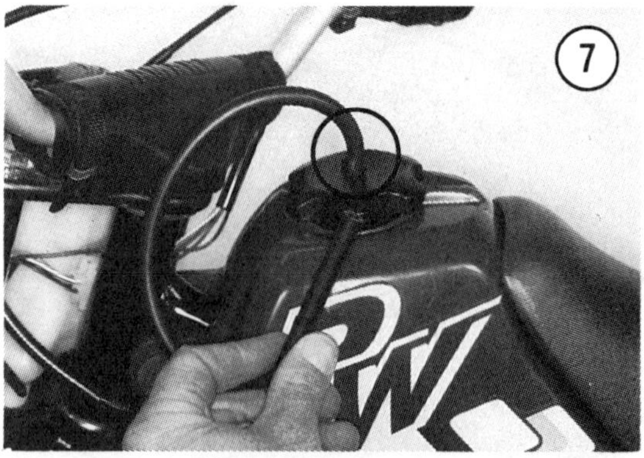

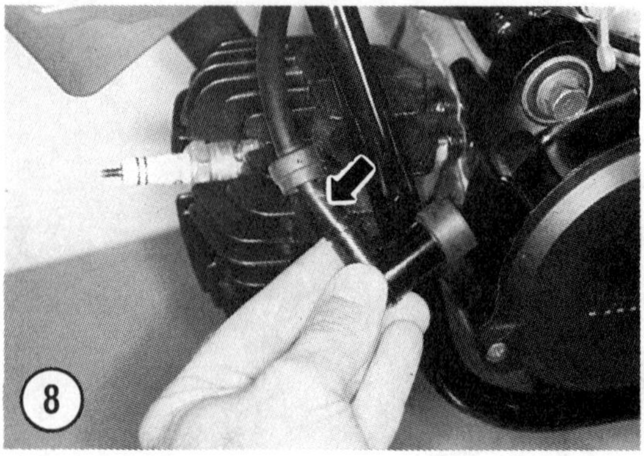

end and blow through it. Remove the filler cap and check its air vent passage for any obstructions.

WARNING
Do not use an open flame to check in the fuel tank. A serious explosion is certain to result.

3. Pull off the fuel line at the carburetor and insert the end of the hose into an empty plastic container. Turn the fuel valve on and check fuel flow through the hose. If the hose is plugged, remove the hose and fuel filter (if equipped), then turn the fuel valve on again. If fuel flows, the hose or filter is clogged; clean the fuel hose or replace the clogged fuel filter. If there is no fuel flow through the valve, the valve is blocked by foreign matter, or the fuel cap vent may be plugged. Service the fuel valve as described in Chapter Seven.
4. If you suspect that the cylinder is flooded, remove the spark plug. If the spark plug is wet, the engine is flooded. A strong gasoline smell around the engine and exhaust pipe also indicates engine flooding. To start a flooded engine, refer to *Starting A Flooded Engine* in this chapter.
5. Check the carburetor overflow hose on the bottom of the float bowl. If fuel is running out of the hose, the float is stuck open. Turn the fuel valve off and tap the float bowl a few times to help break any sediment loose and allow the fuel valve to close. Check again by turning the fuel valve back on. If fuel continues to run out of the overflow hose, remove and service the carburetor as described in Chapter Seven. Check the carburetor vent hoses to make sure they are clear. Check the end of the hoses for contamination.

NOTE
If fuel is reaching the carburetor, the fuel system could still be the problem. The pilot jet could be clogged or the air filter could be severely restricted. If the choke lever must be opened to start a warm or hot engine, suspect a plugged pilot jet. Opening the choke lever richens the air/fuel mixture and helps to compensate for the fuel that is not passing through the plugged pilot system.

6A. On PW50 models, make sure the ignition control switch (**Figure 5**) is in the START position.
6B. On BW80 and PW80 models, make sure the engine stop switch (**Figure 6**) is in the RUN position.

NOTE
If necessary, test the switches as described under **Switches** *in Chapter Eight.*

7. Is the spark plug cap screwed tightly into the ignition coil secondary wire and making good contact (**Figure 8**)? Hold the secondary wire and turn the cap to check its tightness. If the cap is loose, unscrew it all the way and check its mating terminal (A, **Figure 9**) for corrosion or damage. Then check the secondary wire to make sure you can see the individual wire leads inside the wire (B, **Figure 9**). On models where the spark plug cap has been removed and installed a number of times, these wires can weaken from being turned so often and break off. To test the spark plug cap, refer to *Ignition Coil Testing* in Chapter Eight.
8. Perform a spark test as described under *Engine Fails to Start (Spark Test)* in this chapter. If there is a strong spark, perform Step 9. If there is no spark, or if the spark is very weak, test the ignition system as described in this chapter.

NOTE
If the fuel and ignition systems are working properly, the mechanical system should be checked next. Unless the engine is locked up, mechanical problems affecting the top end generally occur over a period of time. Isolate the mechanical problem to one of these areas: top end, bottom end, clutch or transmission. The top and bottom end (as they relate to engine compression) are covered in Step 9. Clutch and transmission problems are covered in this chapter.

9. Check cylinder compression as follows:
   a. On PW50 models, move the ignition control switch to its OFF position (**Figure 5**).
   b. On BW80 and PW80 models, move the engine stop switch to its OFF position (**Figure 6**).
   c. Turn the fuel valve off.
   d. Remove and ground the spark plug shell against the cylinder head (**Figure 10**).
   e. Put your finger tightly over the spark plug hole.
   f. Operate the kickstarter. When the piston comes up on the compression stroke, pressure in the cylinder should force your finger from the spark plug hole. If your finger pops off, the cylinder probably has sufficient compression to start the engine.

NOTE
*You may still have a compression problem even though it seems good with the previous test. Check engine compression with a compression gauge as described under **Engine Compression Check** in Chapter Three.*

NOTE
*If the cylinder compression is sufficient, the engine may be suffering from a loss of crankcase pressure. During 2-stroke operation, the air/fuel mixture is compressed twice, first in the crankcase and then in the combustion chamber. Crankcase pressure forces the air/fuel mixture to flow from the crankcase chamber through the transfer ports and into the combustion chamber. Before continuing, perform the **2-Stroke Crankcase Pressure Test** as described in this chapter to help isolate any problems in this area.*

ENGINE STARTING PROBLEMS

An engine that refuses to start or is difficult to start is very frustrating. Usually, the problem is minor and can be found with a simple and logical troubleshooting approach. The following items show a beginning point from which to isolate engine starting problems.

Engine Fails to Start (Spark Test)

Perform the following spark test to determine if the ignition system is producing adequate spark to start the engine.

CAUTION
Before removing the spark plug in Step 1, clean all dirt and debris away from the plug base. Dirt that falls into the cylinder will cause rapid engine wear.

1. Disconnect the plug wire and remove the spark plug.

NOTE
*A spark tester (**Figure 11**) is a useful tool for checking the ignition system. This tool is inserted in the spark plug cap and its base is ground against the cylinder head. Because the tool's air gap is adjustable, it allows you to see and hear the spark while testing the intensity of the spark. A number of different spark testers are available through motorcycle and automotive parts stores. The spark tester shown in **Figure 11** is manufactured by Motion Pro.*

2. If using an adjustable spark tester, set its air gap to 6 mm (0.24 in.).

3. Insert the spark plug (or spark tester) into the plug cap and touch its base against the cylinder head to ground it (**Figure 10**). Position the plug so you can see the electrodes.

10

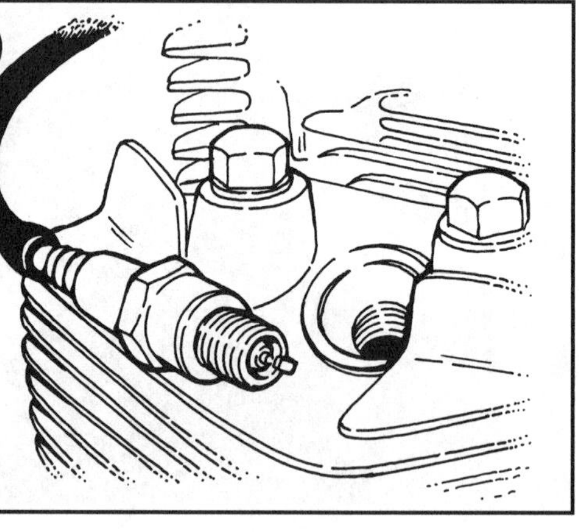

CAUTION
Mount the spark plug or spark tester away from the plug hole in the cylinder head so the spark from the plug or tester cannot ignite the gasoline vapor in the cylinder.

4. Crank the engine over with the kickstarter. A fat blue spark should be evident across the spark plug electrodes or spark tester terminals.

WARNING
Do not hold or touch the spark plug (or spark checker), wire or connector when making a spark check. A serious electrical shock may result.

5. If the spark is good, check for one or more of the following possible malfunctions:
   a. Obstructed fuel line or fuel filter (if used).
   b. Low compression or engine damage.
   c. Flooded engine.
6. If the spark is weak (white or yellow in color) or if there is no spark, check for one or more of the following conditions:
   a. Fouled or wet spark plug. If you get a spark across a spark tester but not across the original spark plug, the plug is fouled. Repeat the spark test with a new plug.
   b. Loose or damaged spark plug cap connection. Hold the secondary wire and turn the spark plug cap (**Figure 8**) to tighten it. The install the spark plug into the cap and repeat the spark test.
   c. Loose or damaged high tension wiring connections (at coil and plug cap). See **Figure 9**.
   d. Faulty ignition coil or faulty ignition coil ground wire connection.

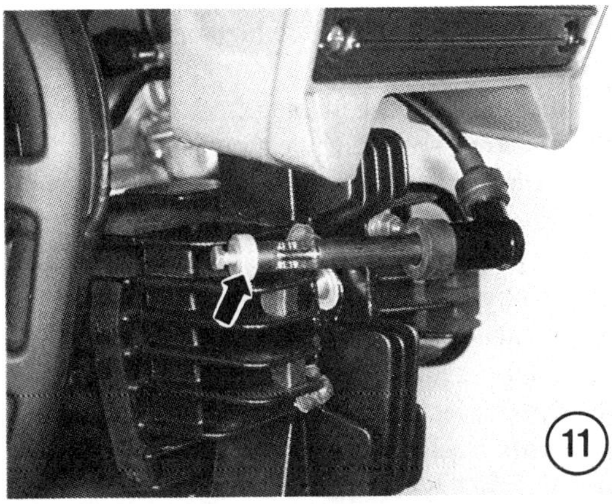
11

   e. Faulty CDI unit or stator coil(s).
   f. Sheared flywheel key.
   g. Loose flywheel nut.
   h. Loose electrical connections.
   i. Dirty electrical connections.

NOTE
If the engine backfires when you attempt to start it, the ignition timing may be incorrect. A loose flywheel, sheared flywheel key, loose stator plate mounting screws or a defective ignition component will change the ignition timing.

Engine is Difficult to Start

If the motorcycle has spark, compression and fuel, but it is difficult to start, check for one or more of the following possible malfunctions:

1. Incorrect air/fuel mixture:
   a. Clogged air filter element.
   b. Incorrect carburetor adjustment.
   c. Clogged pilot jet.
   d. Clogged air passage.
2. Flooded engine:
   a. Incorrect starting procedure.
   b. Incorrect fuel level (too high).
   c. Worn carburetor float valve and seat assembly.
   d. Float valve stuck open.
   e. Damaged float.
3. No fuel flow:
   a. Clogged fuel line.
   b. Clogged fuel filter (if used).
   c. Clogged fuel valve.
   d. Clogged or restricted fuel valve.
   e. Clogged fuel tank cap vent hose (**Figure 7**).
   f. Fuel valve turned off.
   g. No fuel.
4. Weak spark:
   a. Fouled or wet spark plug.
   b. Loose or damaged spark plug cap connection.
   c. Loose or damaged secondary lead connection at spark plug cap or coil.
   d. Faulty ignition coil.
   e. Faulty CDI unit.
   f. Faulty stator plate coils.
   g. Sheared flywheel key.
   h. Loose flywheel nut.
   i. Loose electrical connections.
   j. Dirty electrical connections.
5. Low engine compression:

a. Loose spark plug or missing spark plug gasket.
b. Stuck piston ring.
c. Excessive piston ring wear.
d. Excessively worn piston and/or cylinder.
e. Loose cylinder head fasteners.
f. Cylinder head incorrectly installed and/or torqued down.
g. Warped cylinder head.
h. Blown head gasket.
i. Blown base gasket.
j. Damaged reed valve assembly.

6. Excessively worn, cracked or broken reed valves.

Engine Will Not Turn Over

If a mechanical problem prevents the engine from being kicked or turned over, check for one or more of the following possible conditions:

NOTE
After referring to the following list, refer to ***Drive Train Noise*** *in this chapter for additional information.*

a. Defective kickstarter and/or gear.
b. Broken kick shaft return spring.
c. Damaged kickstarter ratchet gear.
d. Seized piston.
e. Broken piston skirt.
f. Seized crankshaft bearings.
g. Seized connecting rod small end bearing.
h. Seized connecting rod big end bearing.
i. Broken connecting rod.
j. Seized primary drive gear/clutch assembly.

ENGINE PERFORMANCE

This section describes conditions where the engine is running but at a reduced performance level. Use the information described here as a starting point from which to isolate the problem.

Engine Will Not Idle or the Throttle Sticks Open

a. Damaged throttle cable assembly (check all 3 cables).
b. Damaged throttle lever.
c. Incorrect throttle cable routing.
d. Dirt is trapped between the carburetor throttle valve and bore.
e. Excessively worn carburetor throttle valve and/or bore.

Engine Will Not Idle

Poor idle speed performance is usually traced to a carburetor problem. If the engine will not idle as described in Chapter Three, check the following:

a. Stuck or damaged choke lever assembly.
b. Incorrect carburetor adjustment.
c. Loose or clogged pilot jet.

NOTE
If the engine starts with the choke on but cuts out when the choke is closed, or will idle only if the choke is on, check for a plugged pilot jet.

d. Obstructed fuel line or fuel shutoff valve.
e. Fouled or improperly gapped spark plug.
f. Leaking head gasket.
g. Loose carburetor hose clamps.

Poor Low Speed Performance

Check for one or more of the following possible malfunctions:

1. Incorrect air/fuel mixture:
   a. Clogged air filter element.
   b. Incorrect carburetor adjustment.
   c. Clogged pilot jet.
   d. Clogged air passage.
   e. Loose or cracked air box boot.
   f. Loose carburetor hose clamps.
   g. Clogged fuel tank cap vent hose (**Figure 7**).
   h. Carburetor choke stuck open.
   i. Incorrect fuel level (too high or too low).
2. Weak spark:
   a. Fouled or wet spark plug.
   b. Incorrect spark plug heat range.
   c. Loose or damaged spark plug cap connection.
   d. Loose or damaged secondary coil wire at coil or plug cap.
   e. Faulty ignition coil.
   f. Faulty CDI unit.
   g. Faulty stator coils.
   h. Loose electrical connections.
   i. Dirty electrical connections.
   j. Incorrect ignition timing.

3. Low engine compression:
   a. Loose spark plug or missing spark plug gasket.
   b. Stuck piston ring.
   c. Excessive piston ring wear.
   d. Excessively worn piston and/or cylinder.
   e. Loose cylinder head fasteners.
   f. Cylinder head incorrectly installed and/or torqued down.
   g. Warped cylinder head.
   h. Damaged cylinder head gasket.
   i. Blown base gasket.
   j. Loose cylinder base nuts.
4. Excessively worn, cracked or broken reed valves.
5. Dragging brakes. Refer to *Brakes* in this chapter for additional information.

Poor High-Speed Performance

Check for one or more of the following possible malfunctions:

1. Incorrect air/fuel mixture:
   a. Clogged air filter element.
   b. Clogged carburetor air vent tubes.
   c. Incorrect jet needle clip position.
   d. Incorrect main jet.
   e. Clogged main jet.
   f. Worn jet needle and/or needle jet.
   g. Clogged air jet or air passage.
   h. Loose or cracked air box boot.
   i. Loose carburetor hose clamps.
   j. Clogged fuel tank cap vent hose (**Figure 7**).
   k. Worn float valve and seat.
   l. Incorrect fuel level (too high or too low).
   m. Clogged fuel line.
   n. Clogged fuel filter.
   o. Clogged fuel valve.
   p. Fuel tank contaminated with water.
2. If the engine speed drops off or cuts out abruptly:
   a. Clogged air filter element.
   b. Restricted silencer.
   c. Clogged exhaust system.
   d. Clutch slippage.
   e. Clogged main jet.
   f. Incorrect fuel level (too high or too low).
   g. Choke valve partially stuck.
   h. Throttle valve does not open all the way.
   i. Dragging brakes.
   j. Engine overheating.
   k. Fuel tank contaminated with water.
3. Low engine compression:
   a. Loose spark plug or missing spark plug gasket.
   b. Stuck piston ring.
   c. Excessive piston ring wear.
   d. Excessively worn piston and/or cylinder.
   e. Loose cylinder head fasteners.
   f. Cylinder head incorrectly installed and/or torqued down.
   g. Warped cylinder head.
   h. Damaged cylinder head gasket.
   i. Blown base gasket.
   j. Cracked or broken reed valves.

Engine Overheating

Check for one or more of the following possible malfunctions:

1. Clogged, broken or missing cylinder head and cylinder cooling fins.
2. Overrunning the engine in sand.
3. Oil injection pump system:
   a. Air in oil hose or delivery line(s).
   b. Empty oil tank.
   c. Oil injection pump or drive gear failure.
4. Other causes of engine overheating are:
   a. Excessive carbon buildup in the combustion chamber.
   b. Incorrect air/fuel mixture.
   c. Clutch slippage.
   d. Brake drag.
   e. Transmission oil level too high.

Black Exhaust and Engine Runs Roughly

a. Clogged air filter element.
b. *Carburetor adjustment incorrect*—Mixture too rich.
c. Carburetor floats damaged or incorrectly adjusted.
d. Choke not operating correctly.
e. Water or other contaminants in fuel.
f. Excessive piston-to-cylinder clearance.

Engine Loses Power

a. Incorrect carburetor adjustment.
b. Engine overheating.
c. Ignition timing incorrect due to improper timing or defective ignition component(s).

d. Incorrectly gapped spark plug.
e. Cracked or broken reed valve.
f. Plugged cylinder exhaust port.
g. Obstructed muffler.
h. Brake drag.

Engine Lacks Acceleration

a. Incorrect carburetor adjustment.
b. Clogged fuel line.
c. Ignition timing incorrect due to improper timing or faulty ignition component(s).
d. Cracked or broken reed valve.
e. Plugged cylinder exhaust port.
f. Obstructed muffler.
g. Dragging brake.

ENGINE

Engine problems are generally symptoms of something wrong in another system, such as ignition, fuel or starting.

Preignition

Preignition is the premature burning of fuel and is caused by hot spots in the combustion chamber. The fuel ignites before it is supposed to. Glowing deposits in the combustion chamber, inadequate cooling or an overheated spark plug can all cause preignition. This is first noticed as a power loss but will eventually result in damage to the internal parts of the engine because of higher combustion chamber temperatures.

Detonation

Commonly called spark knock or fuel knock, detonation is the violent explosion of fuel in the combustion chamber instead of a controlled burn that occurs during normal combustion. Severe damage can result. Use of low octane gasoline is a common cause of detonation.

Even when using a high octane gasoline, detonation can still occur. Other causes are over-advanced ignition timing, lean fuel mixture at or near full throttle, inadequate engine cooling, or the excessive accumulation of deposits in the combustion chamber (cylinder head and piston crown).

Power Loss

Several factors can cause a lack of power and speed. Look for a clogged air filter or a fouled or damaged spark plug. A piston or cylinder that is galled, incorrect piston clearance or worn or stuck piston rings may be responsible. Look for loose bolts, defective gaskets or leaking machined mating surfaces on the cylinder head, cylinder or crankcase. Also check for damaged crankshaft seals; refer to *Two-Stroke Crankcase Pressure Test* in this chapter.

Piston Seizure

This is caused by incorrect bore clearance, piston rings with an improper end gap, compression leak, incorrect engine oil, damaged oil pump, spark plug of the wrong heat range or incorrect ignition timing. Overheating from any cause may result in piston seizure.

Piston Slap

Piston slap is an audible slapping or rattling noise resulting from excessive piston-to-cylinder clearance. If allowed to continue, piston slap will eventually cause the piston skirt to shatter.

To prevent piston slap from occurring, measure the cylinder bore and piston diameter on a regular schedule. If you hear piston slap, disassemble the top end and measure the cylinder bore and piston diameter and check for excessive piston to cylinder clearance. Replace parts that exceed wear limits or show damage.

ENGINE NOISES

1. *Knocking or pinging during acceleration*—Caused by using a low octane or poor quality gasoline. Pinging can also be caused by a spark plug of the wrong heat range and incorrect carburetor jetting. Refer to *Correct Spark Plug Heat Range* in Chapter Three. Check also for excessive carbon buildup in the combustion chamber or a faulty CDI unit.
2. *Slapping or rattling noises at low speed or during acceleration*—May be caused by piston slap, i.e., excessive piston-cylinder wall clearance. Check also for a bent connecting rod or worn piston pin and/or piston pin holes in the piston.

3. *Knocking or rapping while decelerating*—Usually caused by excessive rod bearing clearance.

4. *Persistent knocking and vibration or other noise*—Usually caused by worn main bearings. If the main bearings are okay, consider the following:

   a. Loose engine mounts.
   b. Cracked frame.
   c. Leaking cylinder head gasket.
   d. Exhaust pipe leakage at cylinder head.
   e. Stuck piston ring.
   f. Broken piston ring.
   g. Partial engine seizure.
   h. Excessive small end connecting rod bearing clearance.
   i. Excessive big end connecting rod bearing clearance.
   j. Excessive crankshaft runout.
   k. Work or damaged primary drive gear.

5. *Rapid on-off squeal*—Compression leak around cylinder head gasket or spark plug.

2-STROKE CRANKCASE PRESSURE TEST

Owners of 2-stroke motorcycles are sometimes plagued by hard starting and generally poor running, for which there seems to be no cause. Carburetion and ignition may be good, and compression tests may show that all is well in the engine's upper end.

What a compression test does not show is a lack of primary compression. The crankcase in a 2-stroke engine must be alternately under pressure and vacuum. After the piston closes the intake port, further downward movement of the piston causes the entrapped mixture to be pressurized so that it can rush quickly into the cylinder when the scavenging ports are opened. Upward piston movement creates a slight vacuum in the crankcase, enabling the air/fuel mixture to be drawn in from the carburetor.

NOTE
*The operational sequence of a 2-stroke engine is illustrated under **Engine Operating Principles** in this chapter.*

If the crankcase seals or engine gaskets leak, the crankcase cannot hold pressure or vacuum and proper engine operation becomes impossible. Any other source of leakage such as a defective cylinder base gasket or porous or cracked crankcase castings will result in the same condition (**Figure 12**).

It is possible, however, to test for and isolate primary compression leakage. The test is simple but will require the use of a pressure tester like the one shown in **Figure 13**. To perform a crankcase pressure test, all engine openings are first sealed off. Then a small amount of air pressure is pumped into the engine. If the engine does not hold air, a leak is

(12) **2-STROKE CRANKCASE PRESSURE TESTING**

Excessive exhaust smoke, oil-fouled spark plug or transmission and clutch oil loss	Check: •Leaking right side crankshaft seal •Leaking crankcase mating seal •Porous cylinder head casting
White spark plug reading, pinging or preignition, power surging, piston seizure or holed piston	Check: •Leaking spark plug seal •Leaking left side crankshaft seal •Leaking intake manifold •Leaking crankcase mating seal •Porous cylinder head casting
Difficult starting, white spark plug reading or low compression	Check: •Leaking spark plug seal •Leaking head gasket •Porous cylinder head casting

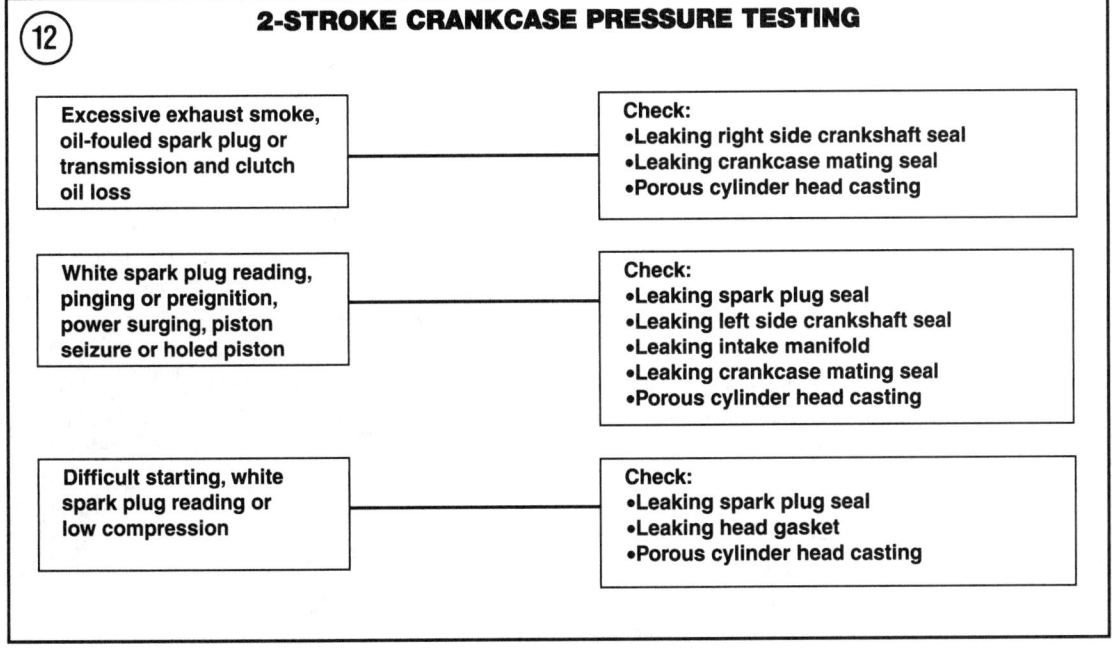

indicated. Then it is only necessary to locate and repair the leak.

The following procedure describes how to perform a crankcase pressure test.

1. Remove the exhaust pipe (Chapter Four or Chapter Five).
2. Remove the carburetor (Chapter Seven).

NOTE
Do not remove the intake manifold from the crankcase. The manifold should remain on the engine during this test as it may be leaking.

3. Remove the flywheel and stator plate (Chapter Eight) to access the left side oil seal.
4. Turn the crankshaft so that the piston is at bottom dead center (BDC).
5. To block the exhaust port, perform the following:
   a. Cut an aluminum plate and a thick piece of rubber (an old inner tube will do) large enough to block the exhaust port.
   b. Align the aluminum plate and rubber gasket with each other, then drill 2 holes through them the same distance apart as the threaded holes in the front of the cylinder (exhaust port side).
   c. Mount the rubber gasket and aluminum plate onto the cylinder and secure it with 2 bolts as shown in **Figure 14**.
6. To block the intake manifold, perform the following:
   a. If your pressure tester applies pressure to the engine through a spark plug adapter, remove the spark plug and install the adapter into the spark plug hole. Then block the intake manifold with a piece of hose or rubber plug.
   b. If tester applies pressure to the engine through the intake manifold, leave the spark plug in place. Then mount the tester and its adapter onto the intake manifold (A, **Figure 15**).

CAUTION
In the following steps, do not apply more than 6-8 psi or the crankcase seals can pop out of the crankcase.

7. Squeeze the pressure gauge lever or bulb until the gauge (B, **Figure 15**) indicates 5-6 psi (34-41 kPa).
8. Read the pressure gauge. A pressure drop of less than 1 psi (6.9 kPa) in several minutes indicates a properly sealed engine. A good rule of thumb is that an engine should hold 6 psi (41 kPa) for 5-6 minutes. Any immediate pressure loss or a pressure loss of 1 psi (6.9 kPa) or more in 1 minute indicates serious sealing problems. Before condemning the engine, first make sure that there are no leaks in the test equipment or sealing plugs. Check the equipment sealing points by spraying them with soapy water (**Figure 16**). When all of the test equipment and its hose fittings are air tight, go over the entire engine carefully. If the pressure gauge shows a loss of pressure, check all of the engine sealing points (**Figure 16**). Where there is a leak, bubbles will form as air leaks out of the engine and mixes with the soapy water. Some possible leakage points are listed below:
   a. Left side crankshaft seal.
   b. Right side crankshaft seal.
   c. Spark plug.
   d. Cylinder head joint.
   e. Intake manifold.

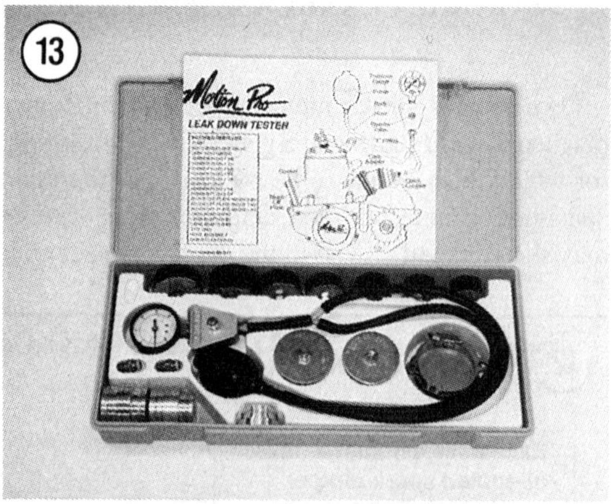

13

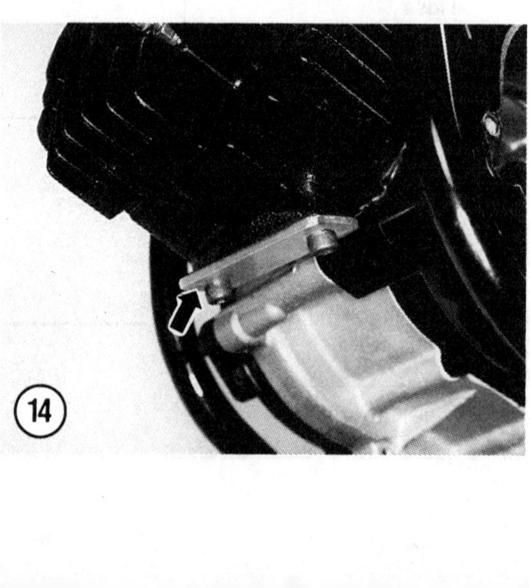
14

f. Cylinder base joint.
g. Crankcase joint.
h. Porous crankcase, cylinder or cylinder head casting.

9. When a leak is detected, repair it or replace the damaged part. Repeat the test after replacing or repairing damaged parts and after reassembling the engine.
10. Remove the test equipment and reverse Steps 1-3 to complete engine assembly.

FUEL SYSTEM

Many riders automatically assume that the carburetor is at fault if the engine runs poorly. While fuel system problems do occur, carburetor adjustment is seldom the answer. In many cases, adjusting the carburetor only compounds the problem by making the engine run worse.

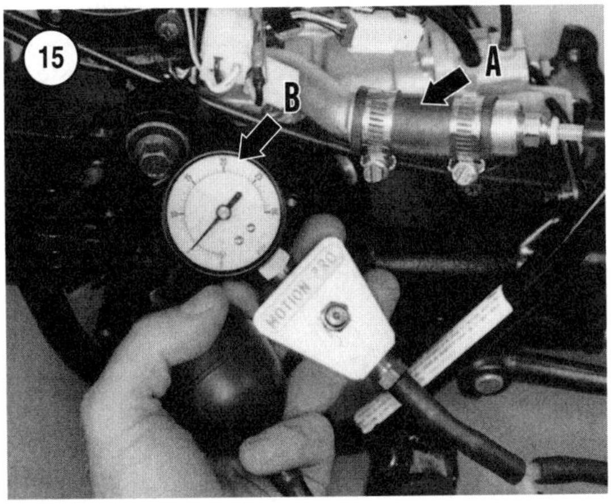

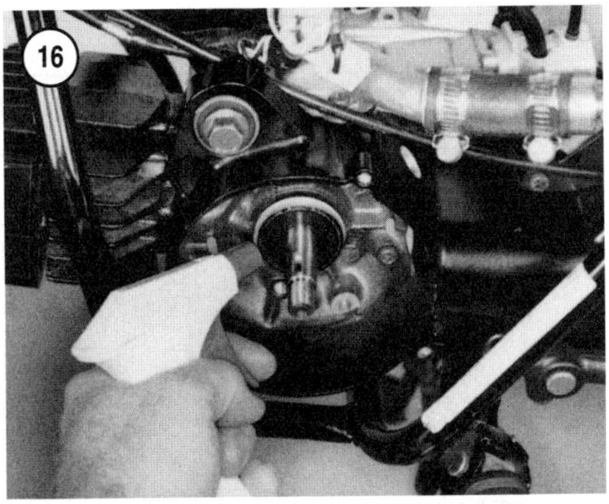

When troubleshooting the fuel system, start at the fuel tank and work through the system, reserving the carburetor as the final point. Most fuel system problems result from an empty fuel tank, a plugged fuel filter or fuel valve, or sour fuel. Fuel system troubleshooting is covered thoroughly under *Starting Difficulties*, *Engine Starting Troubles* and *Engine Performance* in this chapter.

A malfunctioning carburetor choke can also cause engine starting and operating problems. Check the choke by opening and closing the choke lever (**Figure 3** or **Figure 4**). The choke lever must open and close without binding either position. If necessary, remove the choke (Chapter Seven) and inspect its plunger and spring for severe wear or damage.

ELECTRICAL TROUBLESHOOTING

Electrical troubleshooting can by very time-consuming and frustrating without proper knowledge and a suitable plan. Refer to the wiring diagrams at the end of this book to help you determine how the circuits should work. Use them to trace the current paths from the power source through the circuit components to ground.

As with all troubleshooting procedures, analyze typical troubleshooting symptoms in a systematic procedure. Never assume anything and do not overlook the obvious like an electrical connector that has separated. Test the simplest and most obvious cause first and try to make tests at easily accessible points on the bike.

Preliminary Checks and Precautions

a. Disconnect each electrical connector in the suspect circuit and check that there are no bent terminals on either side of the electrical connector (**Figure 17**). A bent terminal will not attach to its mate.
b. Make sure that the terminals (**Figure 18**) are pushed all the way into the plastic connector. To check, carefully push them in with a narrow blade screwdriver.
c. Check all electrical wires where they enter the connector. Make sure the wires are not damaged where they attach to the terminal.

d. Make sure all electrical terminals within the connector are clean and free of corrosion. Clean, if necessary, and pack the connectors with a dielectric grease
e. After all is checked out, push the connectors together and make sure they are fully engaged and locked together (**Figure 19**).
f. Never pull on the electrical wires when disconnecting an electrical connector–pull only on the connector plastic housing.

IGNITION SYSTEM

All models are equipped with a capacitor discharge igntion (CDI) system. This solid state system uses no contact breaker point or other moving parts. Because of the solid state design, problems with the capacitor discharge system are relatively few. However, if an ignition malfunction occurs, it generally causes the ignition system to have a weak spark or no spart at all. It is relatively easy to troubleshoot an ignition system with weak or no spark. It is difficult, however, to troubleshoot an intermittent ignition malfunction that occurs only if the engine is hot or under load.

Ignition System Troubleshooting

If there is no spark or if the spark is intermittent, perform the following steps in order.

NOTE
If the problem is intermittent, perform the tests with the engine cold, then hot.

1. Remove the seat (Chapter Fifteen).
2. Remove the fuel tank (Chapter Eight).
3. Perform the spark test as described under *Engine Fails to Start (Spark Test)* in this chapter. If there is no spark, continue with Step 4.
4. Unscrew the spark plug cap from the ignition coil secondary wire (**Figure 9**) and hold the end of the wire 6 mm (0.24 in.) from the cylinder head and away from the spark plug hole as shown in **Figure 20**. Have an assistant operate the kickstarter. A fat blue spark should be evident passing from the end of the wire to the cylinder head. Note the following:
   a. If there is no spark, perform Step 5.
   b. If there is a spark, the plug cap is probably faulty. Test the spark plug resistance as described under *Ignition Coil Testing* in Chapter Eight. Replace the spark plug cap and retest.
5. Test the ignition control switch (PW50) or the engine stop switch (BW80 and PW80) as described under *Switch Testing* in Chapter Eight. Note the following:
   a. If the switch is good, perform Step 6.
   b. If the switch fails to pass the test as described in Chapter Eight, the switch is faulty and must be replaced. Replace the switch and retest the ignition system.
6. Test the ignition coil secondary and primary resistance as described under *Ignition Coil Testing* in Chapter Eight. Note the following:
   a. If the ignition coil is good, perform Step 7.
   b. If the ignition coil fails to pass the test described in Chapter Eight, replace the ignition coil and retest the ignition system.
7. Test the stator plate coils as described under *Stator Coil Testing and Replacement* in Chapter Eight. Note the following:
   a. If both coils are good, perform Step 8.
   b. If one or both coils are defective, replace the damaged coil(s) and retest the ignition system.
8. If you have not been able to locate the damaged component, check the ignition system wiring har-

17

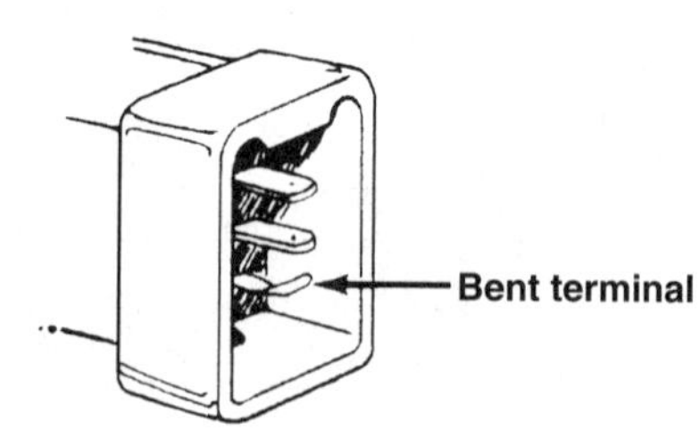

18

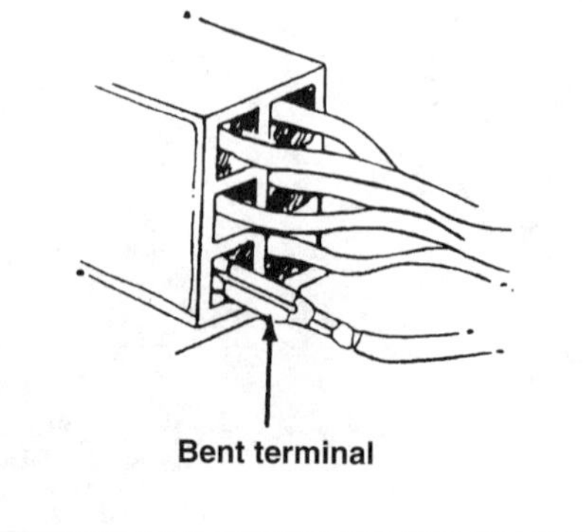

ness and connectors. Check for damaged wires or loose, dirty or damaged connectors. If the wiring and connectors are in acceptable condition, the CDI unit is faulty and must be replaced. See *CDI Unit* in Chapter Eight.

NOTE
At this point, you must decide whether or not to replace the CDI unit. If your test results are accurate, the CDI unit is faulty and must be replaced. If you missed something during this procedure, replacing the CDI unit may not fix the problem. Ignition problems are more often caused by an open or short circuit or by a poor connection or damaged wire. Because most dealerships do not accept returns on electrical parts, make sure the CDI unit is the problem before purchasing a new one. If you are unsure, take the motorcycle to a Yamaha dealership and have them troubleshoot the ignition system for you.

9. Install all parts previously removed.

19

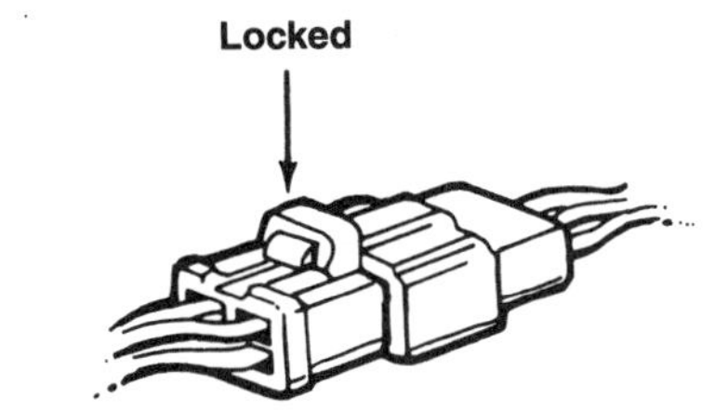

20

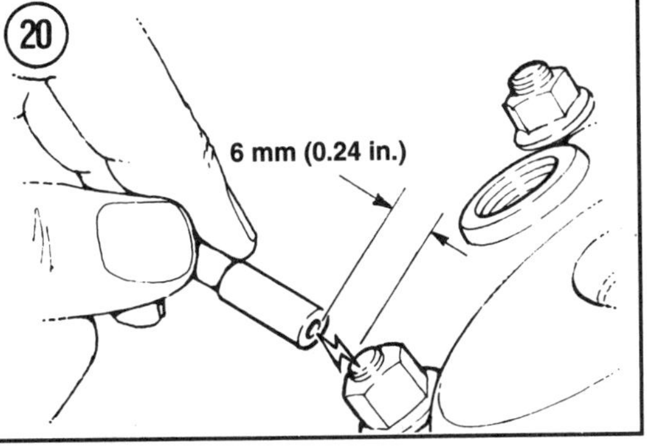

CLUTCH AND GEARSHIFT LINKAGE

A centrifugal clutch is used on the models covered in this manual. The clutch will engage and disengage at an engine rpm or speed just above idle. The main clutch problems are listed below. Because there is no external clutch adjustment on these models, further inspection will require that the clutch be removed from the engine.

This section also lists shifting problems that can be caused by a faulty external shift mechanism assembly used on BW80 and PW80 models. Because the PW50 uses a direct drive transmission, suspect a faulty clutch when experiencing off-idle clutch and transmission engagement problems. Problems directly related to the transmission for all models are listed under *Transmission* in this chapter.

Motorcycle Creeps With the Engine Idling (PW50)

a. Warped clutch shoe assembly.
b. Partially seized or damaged clutch housing.
c. Severely worn or damaged clutch springs.
d. Faulty clutch weight shafts.
e. Incorrect transmission oil weight.

Motorcycle Creeps With the Engine Idling (BW80 and PW80)

a. Incorrect clutch adjustment (internal).
b. Warped clutch plates.
c. Faulty clutch weight assembly.
d. Incorrect transmission oil weight.

Clutch Slips During Acceleration (BW50)

a. Worn or damaged clutch shoe lining(s).
b. Weak clutch springs.
c. Worn or damaged clutch housing.
d. Worn or damaged clutch weight shaft(s).
e. Transmission oil contaminated with a graphite or molybdenum additive.

Clutch Slips During Acceleration (BW80 and PW80)

a. Worn clutch discs.
b. Weak clutch springs.

c. Worn or damaged clutch boss.
d. Worn or damaged clutch housing ball ramps.
e. Transmission oil contaminated with a graphite or molybdenum additive.

Hard to Shift (BW80 and PW80)

a. Incorrect clutch adjustment (internal).
b. Loose stopper lever bolt.
c. Faulty stopper lever assembly.
d. Faulty shift shaft assembly.

Shift Shaft Will Not Return (BW80 and PW80)

a. Bent shift shaft assembly.
b. Damaged shift shaft selector arm.
c. Incorrectly installed or damaged shift shaft return spring.

TRANSMISSION

This section lists problems and possible causes related to the transmission. The PW50 uses a direct drive transmission while the BW80 and PW80 models use a 3-speed constant mesh transmission.

Excessive Noise

a. Worn or damaged transmission bearing(s).
b. Damaged gear(s).

No Transmission Engagement (PW50)

a. Faulty clutch.
b. Damaged mainshaft and driven pinion gears.
c. Damaged drive shaft assembly.
d. Damaged ring gear assembly.

Hard to Shift (BW80 and PW80)

a. Incorrect clutch operation.
b. Bent shift fork.
c. Bent shift fork shaft.
d. Worn or damaged countershaft and first gear engagement balls and slots.
e. Damaged shift drum grooves.
f. Damaged shift drum pins.
g. Faulty shift shaft.

Transmission Jumps Out of Gear (BW80 and PW80)

a. Damaged stopper lever assembly.
b. Damaged shift drum pin(s).
c. Bent shift fork.
d. Bent shift fork shaft.
e. Worn or damaged gear dogs or slots.
f. Worn or damaged countershaft and first gear engagement balls and slots.

KICKSTARTER

Refer to the following troubleshooting information for a list of common kickstarter symptoms and possible causes.

Kickstarter Lever or Shaft Slips

a. Severely worn or damaged kickstarter shaft.
b. Severely worn or damaged kick gear.
c. Weak or damaged kick clip spring.
d. Kick clip coming out of kick gear groove.
e. Deteriorated transmission oil.

Kickstarter Does Not Return

a. Damaged kickstarter return spring.
b. Kickstarter return spring is disengaged from one or both ends.
c. Kick clip coming out of kick gear groove.
d. Incorrectly assembled kickstarter assembly.

Kickstarter is Hard to Kick Over

1. *Kickstarter axle*—Check the following:
   a. Seized kickstarter gear.
   b. Incorrect kick clip (too tight).
2. *Engine*—Check the following:
   a. Seized piston and cylinder.
   b. Broken piston.
   c. Damaged crankcase assembly.
   d. Seized or broken crankshaft.
   e. Seized crankshaft main bearings.
3. *Transmission oil*—Check the following:

a. Low viscosity gear oil.
b. Deteriorated gear oil.

DRIVE TRAIN NOISE (PW50)

The final drive assembly consists of the drive shaft and housing, final drive housing and ring gear assembly. If there is an abnormal noise coming from the drive train, remove and inspect these components as described in Chapter Twelve. Because the final drive assembly is lubricated with grease instead of oil, long intervals between cleaning and regreasing the ring gear assembly can increase drive train noise and wear. Also check the rear wheel engagement points at the final drive assembly for damage.

DRIVE TRAIN NOISE (BW80 AND PW80)

This section deals with noises that are restricted to the drive train assembly—drive chain, clutch and transmission. While some drive train noises have little meaning, abnormal noises are a good indicator of a developing problem. The problem is recognizing the difference between a normal and abnormal noise. A new noise, no matter how minor, must be investigated.

1. *Drive chain noise*—Normal drive chain noise can be considered a low-pitched, continuous whining sound. The noise will vary, depending on the speed of the motorcycle and the terrain you are riding on, as well as proper lubrication, wear (both chain and sprocket) and alignment. When checking abnormal drive chain noise, consider the following:
   a. *Inadequate lubrication*—A dry chain will give off a loud whining sound. Clean and lubricate the drive chain at regular intervals; see Chapter Three.
   b. *Incorrect chain adjustment*—Check and adjust the drive chain as described in Chapter Three.
   c. *Worn chain*—Check chain wear at regular intervals, and replace it when it's overall length exceeds the wear limit specified in Chapter Three.
   d. *Worn or damaged sprockets*—Worn or damaged sprockets accelerate chain wear. Inspect the sprockets carefully as described in Chapter Three.
   e. *Worn, damaged or missing drive chain slider*—The chain slider is in constant contact with the chain. Check it often for loose, damaged or missing parts. A damaged chain slider will increase chain slack and can cause rapid wear against the frame or swing arm.
2. *Clutch noise*— Investigate any noise that develops in the clutch. First, drain the transmission oil (Chapter Three), checking for bits of metal or clutch plate material. If the oil looks and smells okay, remove the clutch (Chapter Six) and inspect it for damage.
3. *Transmission noise*—The transmission will exhibit more normal noises than the clutch, but like the clutch, a new noise in the transmission should be investigated. Drain the transmission oil (Chapter Three) into a clean container. Wipe a small amount of oil on a finger and rub the finger and thumb together. Check for the presence of metallic particles. Inspect the oil in the drain pan for metal deposits.

NOTE
If metallic particles are found in Step 2 or Step 3, remove and inspect the clutch, then, if necessary, disassemble the engine and inspect the transmission.

OIL INJECTION PUMP

All models covered in this manual are lubricated by an oil injection pump. On this system, the pump feeds oil directly into the carburetor where it is mixed with the fuel.

The oil pump is driven off the primary drive gear and meters oil to the engine with respect to engine speed. When a problem is experienced with the oil injection system, do not attempt to disassemble and repair the oil pump. The oil pump is a sealed unit; there are no replacement parts or overhaul gaskets available. Furthermore, the pump itself is seldom the problem as it is highly reliable and requires no maintenance, other than cable adjustment.

If a problem is experienced with the engine oil system, note the following:

1. The oil pump must be bled if one of the following conditions is met:
   a. The oil tank is empty.
   b. If any of the oil injection hoses are disconnected.
   c. The machine was dropped on its side.

2. Always make sure the engine oil tank is full of oil. If necessary, fill the tank with the correct type of 2-stroke injection oil as described in Chapter Three.
3. If there is little or no oil reaching the engine and the oil tank is full, check the oil line between the oil tank and oil pump. If the line seems okay, disconnect the line at the oil pump. With the line disconnected, oil should flow freely from the line. If there is no oil flow from the line, check for a plugged or damaged line.
4. If oil flows from the oil line, check the oil delivery line connected between the oil pump and carburetor.
5. Repair any loose or damaged hose. Bleed the oil pump (Chapter Nine) if a hose was loose or disconnected.

HANDLING

Poor handling can cause you to lose control of the motorcycle. When experiencing handling problems, check the following items:

1. *Handlebars*—Check the following:
   a. Loose or damaged handlebar clamps.
   b. Incorrect handlebar clamp installation.
   c. Bent or cracked handlebar.
2. *Tires*—Check the following:
   a. Incorrect tire pressure.
   b. Worn or damaged tires.
3. *Wheels*—Check the following:
   a. Loose or damaged hub bearings.
   b. Loose or bent wheel axle.
   c. Damaged wheel.
   d. Loose axle nut.
   e. Excessive wheel run out.
4. *Steering*—Check the following:
   a. Incorrect steering adjustment.
   b. Dry or damaged steering shaft bearings.
   c. Bent steering shaft or frame neck.
   d. Loose steering, fork tube and front wheel fasteners.
5. *Swing arm on BW80 and PW80 models*—Check the following:
   a. Damaged swing arm.
   b. Severely worn or damaged swing arm bushings.
   c. Improperly tightened swing arm pivot shaft.
   d. Bent or seized pivot shaft.
6. *Shock absorbers*—Check the following:
   a. Damaged damper rod.
   b. Leaking damper housing.
   c. Sagged shock springs.
   d. Loose or damaged shock mount bolts.
7. *Frame*—Check the following:
   a. Damaged frame.
   b. Cracked or broken engine mount brackets.

BRAKES

The front and rear drum brakes are critical to riding performance and safety. Inspect the brakes frequently and repair or replace damaged parts immediately. Adjust the front and rear brakes as described in Chapter Three.

Brake Squeal

a. Glazed or contaminated brake linings.
b. Glazed or contaminated brake drum.
c. Worn brake linings.
d. Worn brake drum.
e. Loose or damaged brake component.
f. Damaged brake backing plate.

Poor Brake Performance

a. Glazed brake linings.
b. Glazed brake drum.
c. Worn brake linings or drum.
d. Incorrect brake adjustment.
e. Worn or damaged brake cable.
f. Worn or damaged brake return springs.
g. Incorrect brake arm and brake cam engagement angle.
h. Damaged brake arm and brake cam splines.
i. Incorrectly installed brake shoes.

Brakes Grab or Drag

a. Incorrect brake adjustment.
b. Worn or damaged brake return springs.
c. Brake drum out-of-round.
d. Warped or damaged brake shoe.
e. Cracked brake drum.
f. Damaged wheel hub.
g. Loose or severely worn wheel bearings.

Incorrect Brake Lever or Pedal Operation

a. Incorrect brake adjustment.

b. Bent brake lever or damage lever perch.
c. Bent or damaged brake pedal or pivot shaft.
d. Worn or damaged brake lever mounting bolt.
e. Damaged brake cable or brake rod (BW80 and PW80).
f. Missing or damaged brake cable or brake rod spring.
g. Dry, rusted or kinked brake cable.
h. Worn or damaged brake return springs.
i. Brake drum contamination.
j. Incorrect brake arm and brake cam engagement angle.
k. Stripped brake arm and brake cam splines.

CHAPTER THREE

LUBRICATION, MAINTENANCE AND TUNE-UP

Your Yamaha requires periodic maintenance to operate efficiently without breaking down. This chapter covers all of the required periodic service procedures that do not require major disassembly. Regular, careful maintenance is the best guarantee for a trouble-free, long lasting motorcycle. All motorcycles designed for off-road use require proper lubrication, maintenance and tune-up to maintain a high level of performance and extend engine, suspension and chassis life. Procedures at the end of this chapter also describe steps on how to store your Yamaha for long periods of nonuse.

You can do your own lubrication, maintenance and tune-up if you follow the correct procedures and use common sense. Always remember that damage can result from improper tuning and adjustment. In addition, where special tools or testers are called for during a particular maintenance or adjustment procedure, the tool should be used or you should refer service to a qualified Yamaha dealership or repair shop.

Tables 1-10 are at the end of this chapter.

SERVICE INTERVALS

The intervals shown in **Tables 1-3** are recommended by Yamaha for the routine service of your motorcycle. Strict adherence to these recommendations will ensure long service from your motorcycle. However, if the motorcycle is run in an area of high humidity the lubrication and services must be done more frequently to prevent possible rust damage. This is also true when riding through water (especially salt water) and sand or if the motorcycle is used in competition.

TUNE-UP

The number of definitions of the term tune-up is probably equal to the number of people defining it. For the purpose of this book, a tune-up is a general adjustment and maintenance to ensure peak engine and suspension performance.

Tune-up procedures are usually listed in some logical order. For example, some procedures should be done with the engine cold and others with the engine hot. For example, check the cylinder head nuts when the engine is cold and adjust the carburetor and drain the transmission oil when the engine is hot. Also, because the engine needs to run as well as possible when adjusting the carburetor, service the air filter and spark plug first. If you adjust the carburetor, then find that the air filter needs service, you may have to readjust the carburetor.

After completing a tune-up, write down the date, the motorcycle operating time interval, and the type of service performed at the back of this book or in a suitable notebook. This information will provide an accurate record on the type of service performed. This record can also be used to schedule future service procedures at the correct time.

To perform a tune-up on your Yamaha, service the following engine and chassis items as described in this chapter:

Engine Tune-Up Procedure

a. Tighten cylinder head nuts (Chapter Four or Chapter Five).
b. Clean muffler (Chapter Four or Chapter Five).
c. Check exhaust pipe fasteners for tightness (Chapter Four or Chapter Five).
d. Clean and oil air filter.
e. Check and service spark plug.
f. Check compression.
g. Adjust carburetor.
h. Check throttle operation and cables.
i. Check oil pump cable adjustment.
j. Start engine and allow to warm to normal operating temperature.
k. Adjust carburetor.
l. Change transmission oil.
m. Check all exposed engine nuts and bolts for tightness.

Chassis Tune-Up Procedure

a. Clean and lubricate drive chain (BW80 and PW80).
b. Check drive chain tension and alignment (BW80 and PW80).
c. Check brake operation and cable adjustment.
d. Check wheel rims and tires.
e. Change front fork oil (BW80 and PW80).
f. Check operation of front and rear suspension.
g. Check all exposed steering and suspension nuts and bolts for tightness.

Test Ride

The test ride is an important part of the tune-up or service procedure because it is here where you will find out whether the motorcycle is ready to ride or if it needs more work. When test riding a motorcycle, always start slowly and ride in a safe place away from all other vehicles and people. Concentrate on the areas that were worked on and how they can effect other systems. If the brakes were worked on, never apply full brake pressure at high speed (emergencies excepted). It is safer to check the brakes at slower speeds and with moderate pressure. Do not continue to ride the motorcycle if the engine, brakes or any suspension or steering component is not working correctly.

ENGINE OIL

All the engines described in this manual are equipped with a gear driven oil injection system where oil is injected into the carburetor. The amount of oil injected into the engine is determined by throttle position and engine rpm where the throttle and oil pump cables are connected together. When the throttle is turned to open the carburetor, the oil pump cable simultaneously operates the oil pump. This system automatically maintains the optimum fuel/oil ratio according to engine speed. The oil mixes with the incoming fuel charge and circulates through the crankcase and enters the combustion chamber where it is burned with the fuel. The 2-stroke engine components (piston, rings, cylinder, connecting rod, crankshaft, and main bearings) are lubricated by the oil as it passes through the crankcase and cylinder.

Refer to Chapter Nine for oil pump service procedures.

Engine Oil Level Check and Adjustment

Check the oil level in the tank before starting the engine. Continue to check the oil throughout the day.

1. Park the motorcycle on a level surface and check the oil level in the tank. See **Figure 1** (PW50) or **Figure 2** (BW80 and PW80). On BW80 and PW80 models, the oil level must be above the L mark on the oil tank. If it is necessary to add oil, continue with Step 2.

CAUTION

If the oil tank is empty the oil pump must be bled before restarting the engine; otherwise, air drawn into the system can interrupt the flow of oil to the engine. Depending on how long the engine is run, this condition can cause severe engine damage. Fill the oil tank as described in this chapter, then bleed the oil pump as described in Chapter Nine.

2A. On PW50 models, the oil tank is mounted on the steering stem and behind the number plate. To add oil, perform the following:

a. Wipe off the area around the oil tank cap so that no dirt can fall into the tank.
b. Remove the oil fill cap (**Figure 3**) from the oil tank.
c. Add the recommended type of *2-stroke engine oil* listed in **Table 4**. **Table 5** lists oil tank capacity.
d. Install and tighten the oil fill cap (**Figure 3**).

2B. On BW80 and PW80 models, the oil tank is mounted underneath the seat. To add oil, perform the following:

a. Remove the seat (Chapter Fifteen).
b. Remove the oil fill cap (**Figure 4**).
c. Add the recommended type of *2-stroke engine oil* listed in **Table 4**. **Table 5** lists oil tank capacity.
d. Push the oil fill cap (**Figure 4**) firmly into the tank.
e. Install the seat (Chapter Fifteen).

TRANSMISSION OIL

The transmission oil lubricates components that operate behind the clutch cover and within the transmission portion of the crankcase. The transmission oil does not lubricate the 2-stroke engine components (piston, rings, cylinder, connecting rod, crankshaft, and main bearings).

Yamaha suggests the use of a high-quality 10W-30 motor oil with an API rating of SE. The API rating is stamped or printed on top of the can or label on plastic bottles (**Figure 5**).

Another type of oil to consider is a gear oil designed exclusively for use in 2-stroke transmissions. This type of oil has the same lubricating qualities as an API SE motor oil but are formulated with different load carrying agents and extreme pressure additives that prevent oil break down and foaming caused by clutch and transmission operation. For example, the Bel-Ray Gear Saver SAE 80W transmission oil shown in **Figure 6** is a light bodied oil that corresponds to motor oil grades SAE 30, SAE 10W-30 and SAE 10W-40. There are a number of 2-stroke transmission oils available for use in the transmission. However, do not confuse this type of gear oil with a hypoid gear oil used in motorcycle and ATV shaft drive units. Before using a gear oil, pay atten-

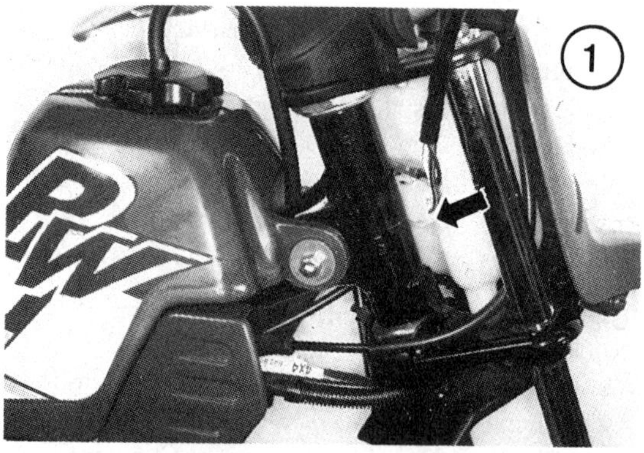

1

2

3

4

tion to its service designation, making sure it is specified for use in motorcycle transmissions only.

Try to use the same brand of oil at each oil change. Yamaha cautions against the use of oil additives as it may cause clutch slippage.

Oil Level Check (PW50)

On the PW50 engine, there is no means of checking the transmission oil level. The oil fill cap (**Figure 7**) is not equipped with a dipstick and there is no sight window or oil check bolt on the clutch cover. The best way to maintain the oil level on the PW50 models is to change the oil regularly and to repair any oil leaks. Because the clutch and transmission assembly does not consume oil, the oil level should remain constant as long as there is no oil leakage. Possible oil leak points are:

a. Clutch cover.

b. Kickstarter shaft seal.

c. Engine oil drain bolt and gasket.

d. Right side crankshaft seal.

If the right side crankshaft seal becomes worn or damaged, it will allow the engine to draw in oil from the clutch and transmission side of the engine. Depending on the condition of the seal and how the long the bike is ridden under these conditions, an appreciable amount of transmission oil can be used. If the engine starts to run rich at all engine speeds and the oil pump is properly adjusted, perform the 2-stroke crankcase pressure test described in Chapter Two. This test will check the engine for air and oil leakage and will help to pinpoint the leak's location.

Oil Level Check (BW80 and PW80)

Check the transmission oil level with the dipstick mounted on the bottom of the clutch oil fill cap.

1. Start the engine and let it idle approximately 2-3 minutes. Then turn the engine off and allow the oil to settle for a few minutes before checking the oil level.

2. Support the bike so it is resting straight up. Do not rest it on its sidestand when checking the transmission oil level as you will get an incorrect reading.

3. Remove the dipstick (**Figure 8**) and wipe it off, then reinstall the dipstick so that it rests on the clutch cover threads. Do *not* screw the cap in.

4. Remove the dipstick and read the oil level. The oil level should be between the upper and lower oil level marks on the dipstick (**Figure 9**). If necessary, add oil through the oil fill hole to bring the level up to the upper dipstick mark. Top off the oil with the correct type of *transmission oil* listed in **Table 4**. Do not overfill.

Oil Change

Regular oil changes will contribute to increased crankcase bearing, transmission and clutch component service life. The factory recommended oil change interval is listed in **Tables 1-3**. Change the oil more often if racing or if operating under harsh or dusty conditions.

To change the engine oil and filter you need:

a. Drain pan.
b. Funnel.
c. 12 mm wrench or socket.
d. Transmission oil (see **Table 4** and **Table 7**).

NOTE
*Never dispose of motor oil in the trash, on the ground, or down a storm drain. Many service stations accept used motor oil and waste haulers provide curbside used motor oil collection. Do not combine other fluids with motor oil to be recycled. To locate a recycler, contact the American Petroleum Institute (API) at **www.recycleoil.org**.*

1. Start the engine and warm it up to normal operating temperature, then turn the engine off.

NOTE
Warming the engine allows the oil to heat; thus it flows freely and carries contamination and sludge out with it.

2. Park the PW50 on its centerstand. On BW80 and PW80 models, support the bike so it is resting upright.
3. Place a clean drain pan underneath the engine and remove the oil drain bolt and gasket. See **Figure 10** (PW50) or **Figure 11** (BW80 and PW80).
4. Remove the oil fill cap (**Figure 8**) to help speed the flow of oil.
5. Allow the oil to drain completely.
6. Clean and inspect the oil drain bolt and gasket. Replace the drain bolt if its hex corners are starting to round off or if the threads are damaged. Replace the gasket if it is warped, grooved or if oil was leaking from around the drain bolt.
7. After all the oil has drained, inspect the oil drain bolt hole threads in the crankcase for damage. Wipe off this area with a clean rag before installing the drain bolt.
8. Install the oil drain bolt and gasket and tighten as specified in **Table 6**.
9. Insert a funnel into the oil fill hole and fill the transmission with the correct type (**Table 4**) and quantity (**Table 7**) transmission oil.

NOTE
*The oil capacity reading cast into the top of the clutch cover beside the oil fill cap (**Figure** 7, typical) is the amount of oil that should be added during a routine oil change. If the engine was disassembled, use the **after engine overhaul** capacity listed in **Table** 7.*

10. Install the oil fill cap and its O-ring and tighten securely. See **Figure 7** (PW50) or **Figure 8** (BW80 and PW80).
11. Start the engine and allow it to idle.
12. Check the oil drain bolt for leaks.
13. On BW80 and PW80 models, turn the engine off and after waiting 2-3 minutes for the oil to settle, check the engine oil level (**Figure 9**). Add more oil if necessary to bring the oil level up to the upper mark on the dipstick.

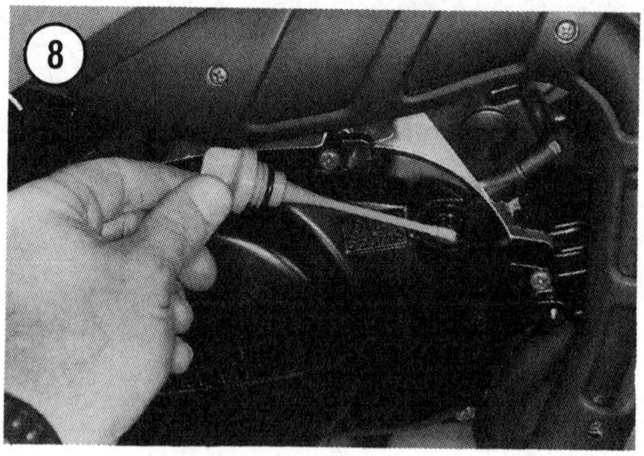

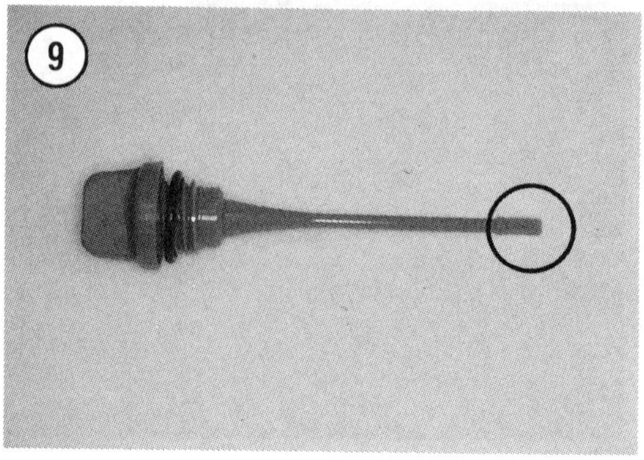

WARNING
Prolonged contact with used oil may cause skin cancer. It is advisable to thoroughly wash your hands with soap and water as soon as possible after handling or coming in contact with any type of engine or transmission oil.

AIR FILTER

The job of an air filter is to trap dift, grit, sand and other arbrasive particles before they enter the engine. And even though the air filter is one of the cheapest parts on your Yamaha, it is often neglected at the expense of engine performance and wear. Never run the engine without a property oiled and installed air filter element. Likewise, running the engine with a dry or damaged air filter element will allow unfiltered air to enter the engine. A well-oiled but dirty or clogged air filter will reduce the amount of air that enters the engine and cause a rich air/fuel mixture, resulting in poor engine starting, spark plug fouling and reduced performance. Frequent air filter inspection and cleaning service is a critical part of minimizing engine wear and maintaining engine performance.

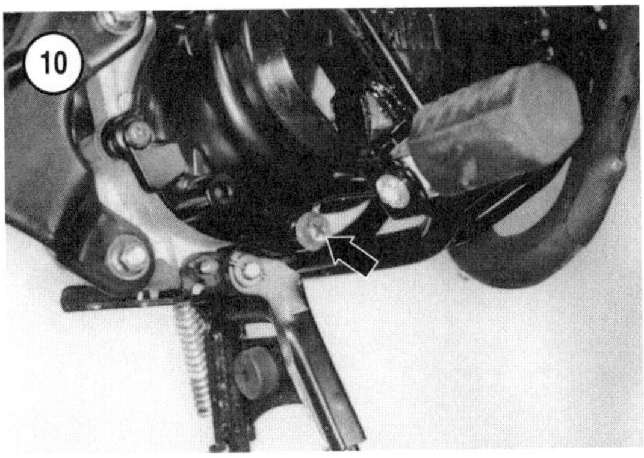

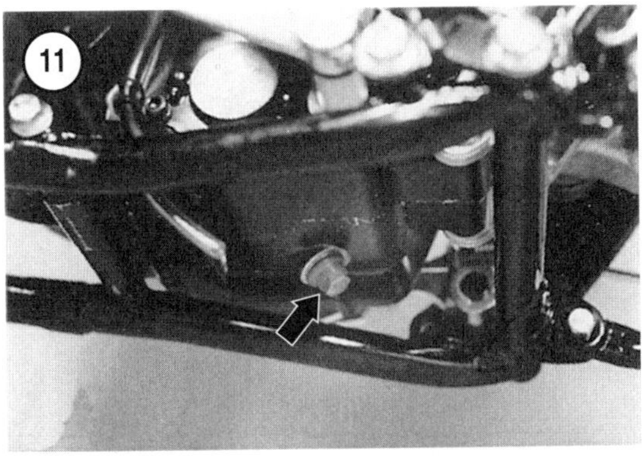

Tables 1-3 list intervals for cleaning the air filter. Clean the air filter more often if racing, riding in sand or in wet and muddy conditions.

3

Air Filter Removal/Installation (PW50)

Refer to **Figure 12** for this procedure.

1. Remove the seat (Chapter Fifteen).
2. Remove the air box screw (A, **Figure 13**). Then spread the hose clamp (B, **Figure 13**) and remove the air box (C, **Figure 13**) assembly.
3. Remove the screw and washer (A, **Figure 14**) and remove the rear cover (B, **Figure 14**).
4. Remove the air filter element (**Figure 15**) from its housing.
5. Clean and dry the element housing (A, **Figure 16**) and rear cover.
6. If the connecting hose was removed, install it by aligning the notch in the hose with the fixed tab on the air box housing (**Figure 17**).
7. Inspect, clean and reoil the air filter element (B, **Figure 16**) as described in this section.

NOTE
Continue with Step 8 only after reoiling the air filter element.

8. Install the air filter element onto the housing as shown in **Figure 15**. Make sure the element seats evenly around the housing. Then install the rear cover (B, **Figure 14**) and secure it with its mounting screw and washer (A, **Figure 14**).
9. Spread the air box clamp (B, **Figure 13**) and slide the air box hose over the carburetor. Then install and tighten the air box mounting screw (A, **Figure 13**).

NOTE
To prevent air leaks and dirty air from entering the engine, make sure all connections between the carburetor, air boot and air box are sealed properly.

10. Install the seat (Chapter Fifteen).

(12)

AIR FILTER (PW50)

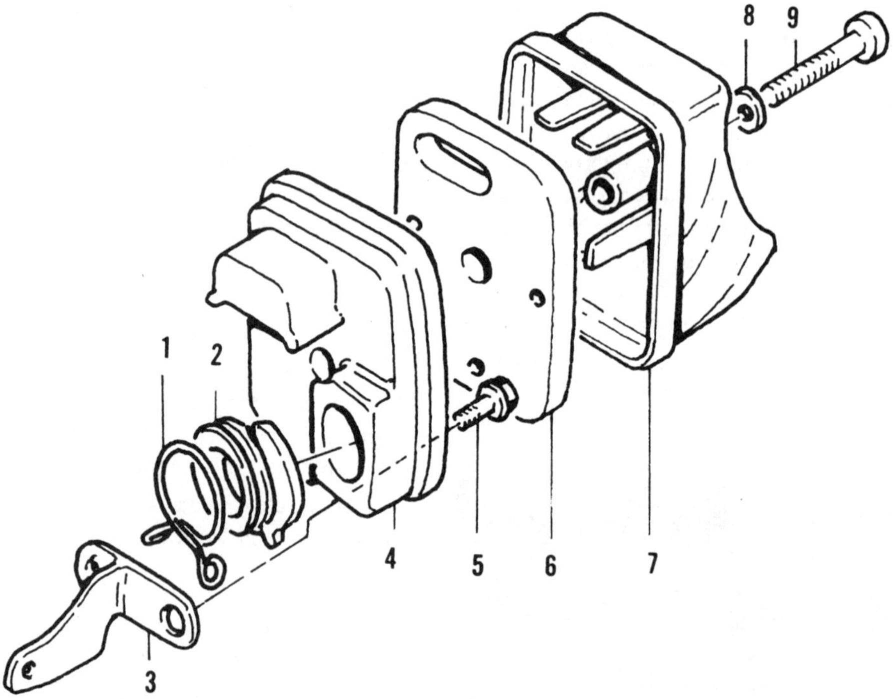

1. Clamp
2. Hose
3. Bracket
4. Air box
5. Bolt
6. Filter element
7. Cover
8. Washer
9. Bolt

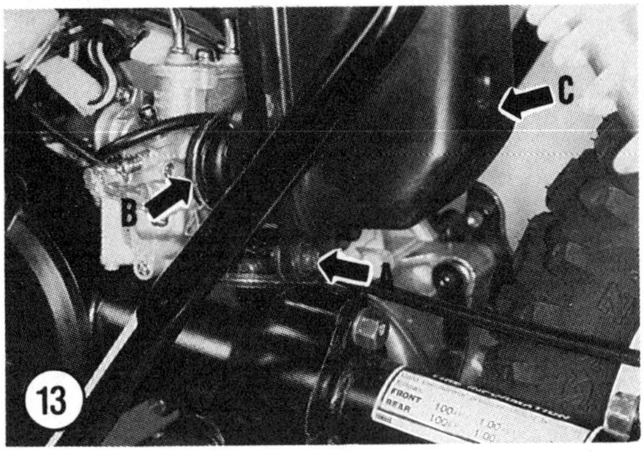

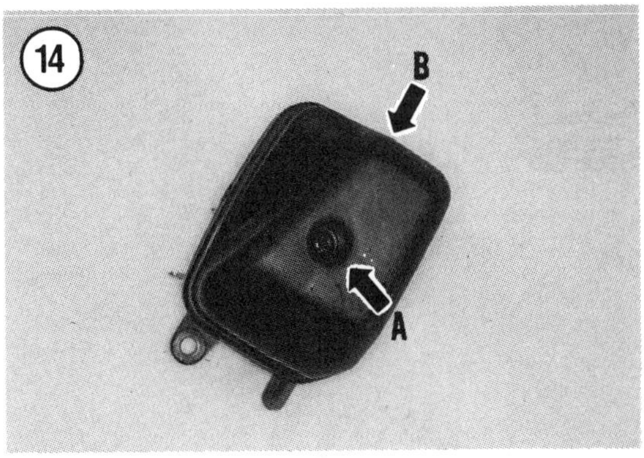

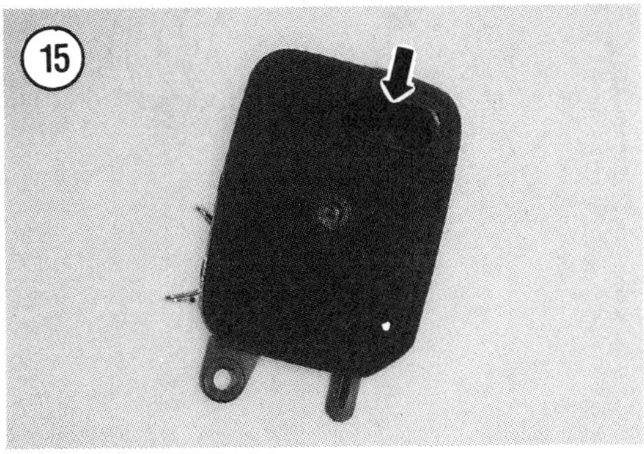

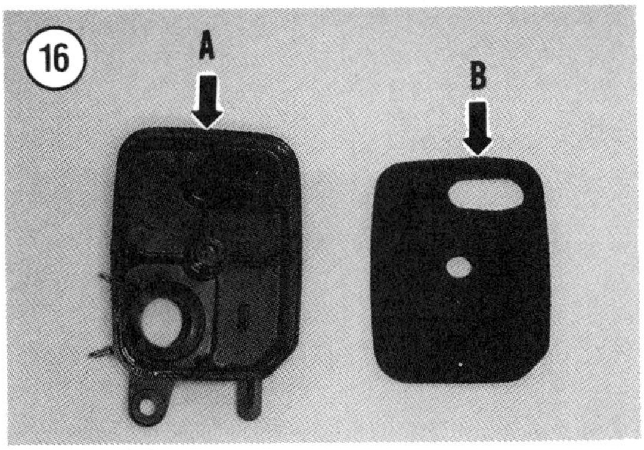

Air Filter Removal/Installation (BW80 and PW80)

Refer to **Figure 18** for this procedure.

1. Support the bike on its side stand.

2. Remove the screws (**Figure 19**) securing the air box cover, holder and element to the air box and remove them as an assembly. See **Figure 20**.

3. Remove air filter element (A, **Figure 21**) from the holder.

4. Clean and dry the cover, holder (A, **Figure 22**) and housing (**Figure 23**).

5. Inspect, clean and reoil the air filter element (B, **Figure 22**) as described in this section.

NOTE
Continue with Step 6 only after reoiling the air filter element.

6. Install the air filter element onto its holder by aligning the element tab (B, **Figure 21**) with the matching tab on the holder. At the same time, install the element holes over the 2 projecting arms on the holder.

7. Apply a thick wheel bearing grease all the way around the outer edge of the filter element (B, **Figure 21**) where the element seats against the inside (sealing surface) of the air box housing.

8. Install the air box cover, holder and element assembly (**Figure 20**) and secure it with the mounting screws (**Figure 19**). The 2 lower screws (3, **Figure 18**) are longer than the 2 upper screws. Tighten the screws securely.

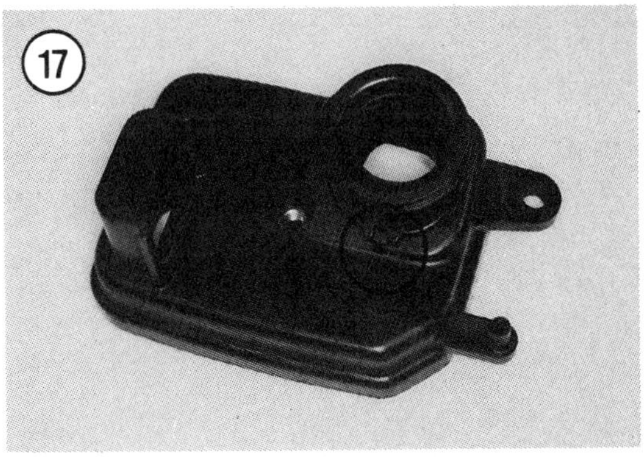

(18)

AIR FILTER (BW80 AND PW80)

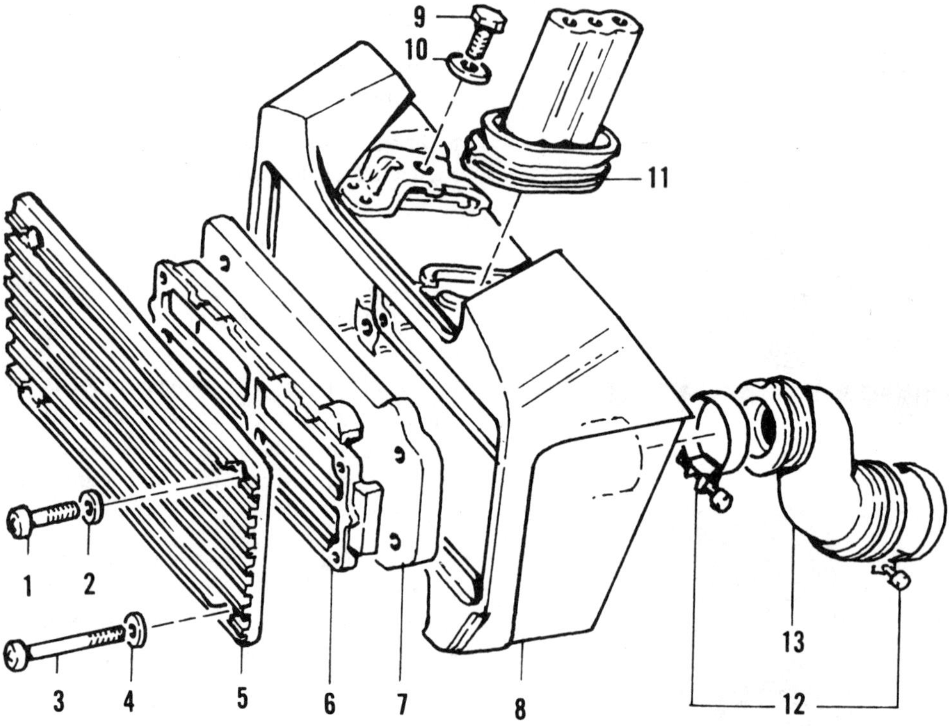

1. Screw
2. Washer
3. Screw
4. Washer
5. Cover
6. Holder
7. Filter element
8. Air box
9. Bolt
10. Washer
11. Air intake
12. Clamps
13. Boot

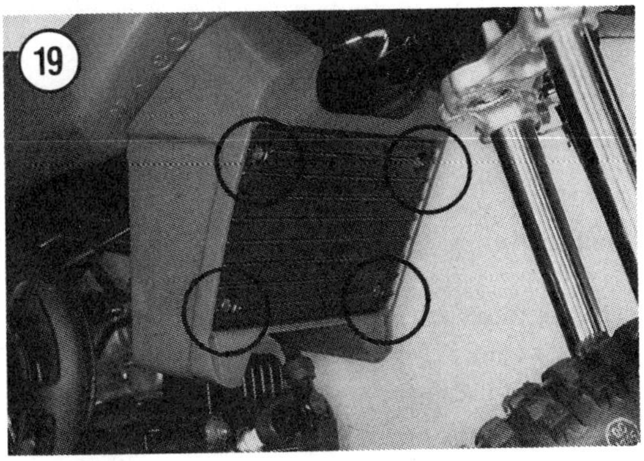

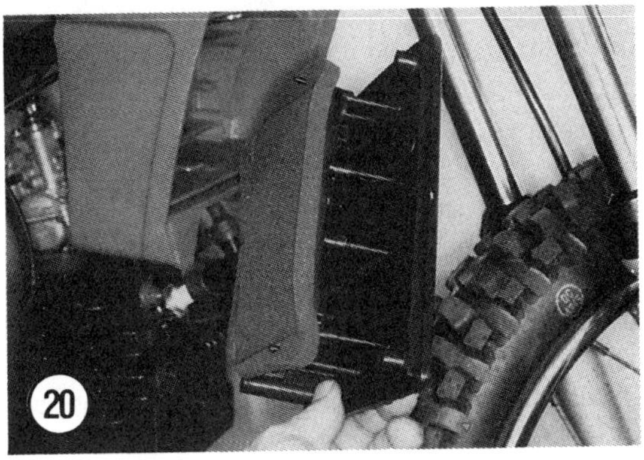

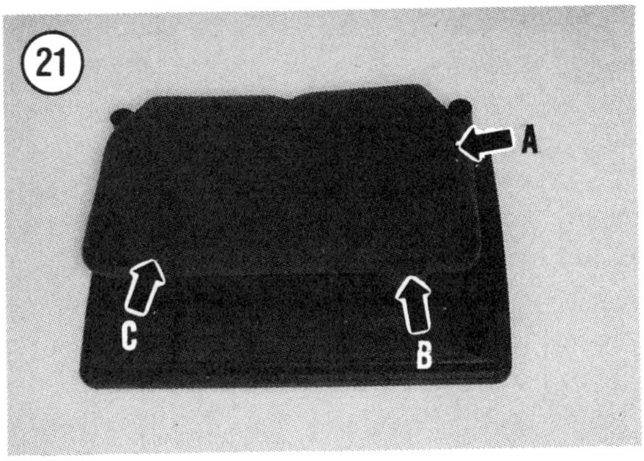

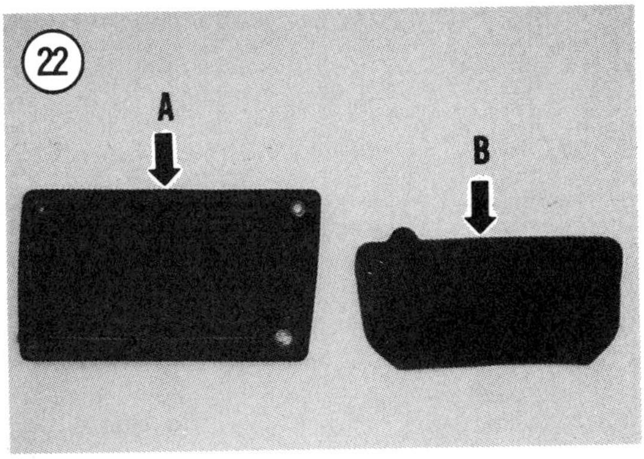

Air Filter Element Cleaning, Inspection and Reoiling

1. Before cleaning the air filter element (B, **Figure 16** or B, **Figure 22**), check it for brittleness, separation or other damage. Replace the filter if damaged or if its condition is questionable. If the air filter is in good condition, continue with Step 2.

WARNING
Do not clean the air filter element with gasoline or any other low-flash point solvent.

CAUTION
When cleaning the air filter in the following steps, do not wring or twist the element. This will damage the filter and allow unfiltered air to enter the engine.

2. Soak the air filter into a container filled with kerosene or an air filter cleaner. Gently squeeze the filter to dislodge and remove the oil and dirt from the filter pores. Swish the filter around in the cleaner while repeating this step a few times, then remove the air filter and set aside to air-dry.
3. Fill a clean pan with warm soapy water.
4. Submerge the filter into the cleaning solution and gently work the cleaner into the filter pores. Soak and squeeze (gently) the filter to clean it.
5. Rinse the filter under warm water while gently squeezing it.
6. Repeat Steps 4 and 5 two or three times or until there are no signs of dirt being rinsed from the filter.
7. After cleaning the element, inspect it again. Replace the air filter if it is torn or broken in any area. Do not run the engine with a damaged element as it may allow dirt to enter the engine.
8. Set the filter aside and allow to air-dry.

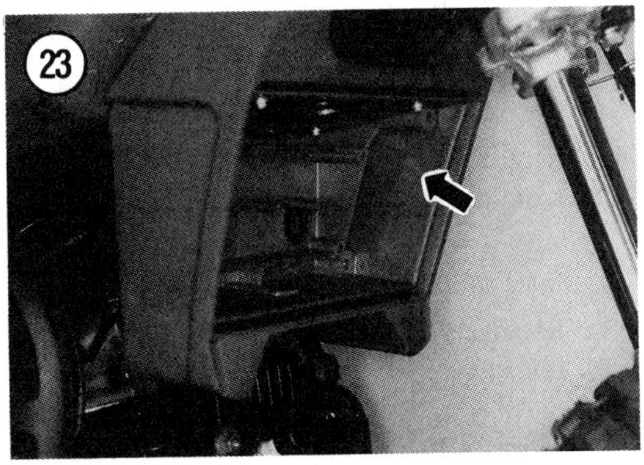

3

CAUTION
A damp filter will not trap fine dust. Make sure the filter is dry before oiling it.

9. Correctly oiling an air filter element is a messy job. Wear a pair of disposable rubber gloves when performing this procedure. Oil the filter as follows:
   a. Place the air filter into a gallon size storage bag.
   b. Pour an air filter oil onto the filter to soak it completely.

NOTE
Engine oil is too thin to be used on air filters. When engine oil is applied to an air filter, some of the oil drains down the filter and collects in the bottom of the air box and carburetor boot. When the engine is running, this excess oil and some of the other oil in the filter pores is drawn into the engine, thus richening the air/fuel mixture and causing the engine to sputter and run roughly. The engine will eventually smooth out after the excess oil is consumed, but because there is less oil on the filter, dirt is more likely to pass through the air filter and into the engine. Air filter oils are specially formulated for use in polyurethane foam air filters. A low viscosity solvent in the filter oil helps the oil to be applied easily to the filter pores. This solvent evaporates after application and leaves behind a tacky, viscous fluid that stays in the filter pores while allowing maximum air flow through filter.

   c. Gently squeeze and release the filter to soak filter oil into the filter's pores. Repeat until all of the filter's pores are saturated with the oil.
   d. Remove the filter from the bag and check the pores for uneven oiling. This is indicated by light or dark areas on the filter. If necessary, soak the filter and squeeze it again.
   e. When the filter oiling is even, squeeze the filter a final time.
   f. Remove the air filter from the bag and inspect it for any excessive oil or uneven oiling. Remove any excessive oil from the filter with a paper towel.

SPARK PLUG

Table 8 lists the standard heat range spark plug for the models covered in this manual.

Correct Spark Plug Heat Range

Spark plugs are available in various heat ranges, hotter or colder (**Figure 24**) than the plug originally installed at the factory.

Select a spark plug of the heat range designed for the loads and conditions under which your Yamaha will be operating under. Use of incorrect heat ranges can cause the plug to foul, engine overheating and piston damage.

In general, use a hot plug for low speeds and low temperatures. Use a cold plug for high speeds, high engine loads and high temperatures. The plug must operate hot enough to burn off unwanted deposits, but not so hot that it causes engine overheating and preignition. A spark plug of the correct heat range will show a light tan color on the portion of the insulator within the cylinder after the plug has been in service.

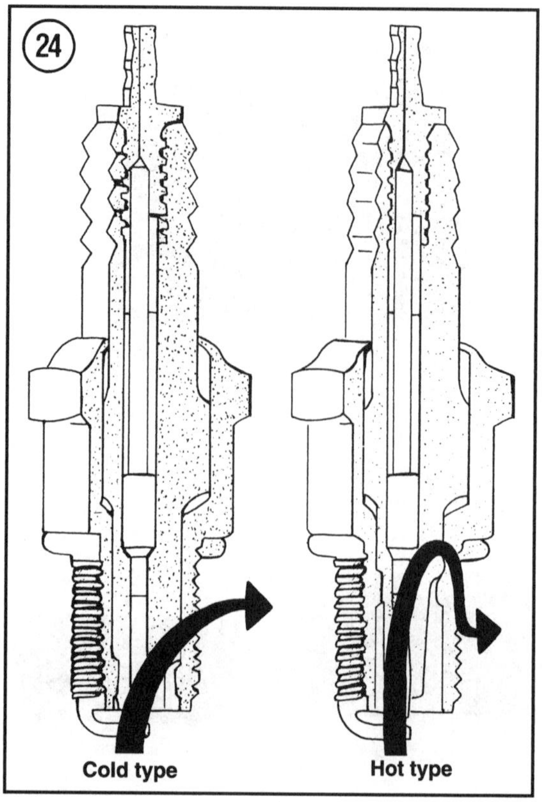

25

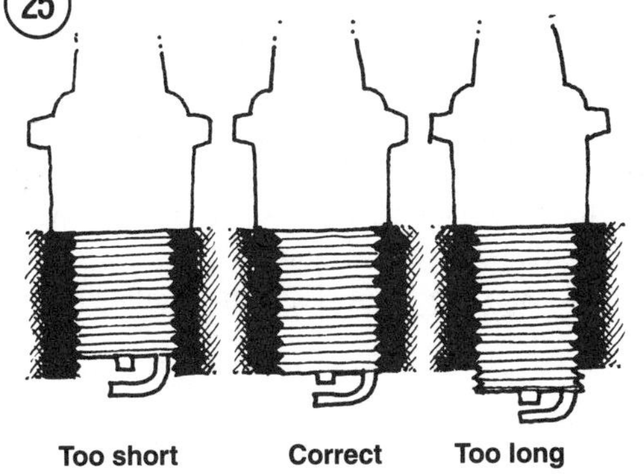

26

27

28

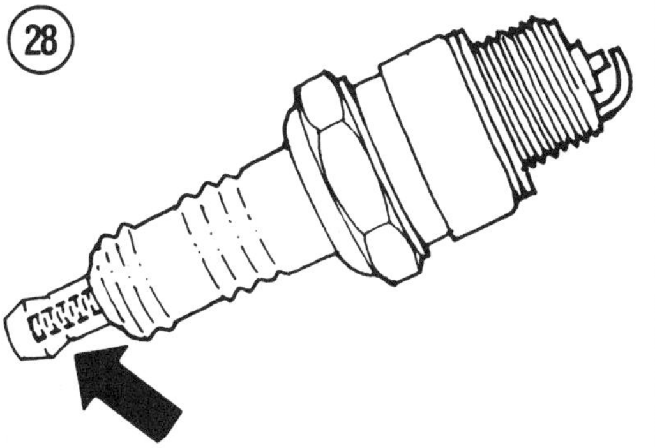

The reach (length) of a plug is also important. A too short plug will cause excessive carbon buildup, hard starting and plug fouling (**Figure 25**).

Spark Plug Removal

1. Grasp the spark plug lead as near the plug as possible and pull it off the plug (**Figure 26**). If it is stuck to the plug, twist it slightly to break it loose.
2. Blow any dirt and other debris away from the spark plug and spark plug hole in the cylinder.

CAUTION
Dirt that falls through the spark plug hole will increase piston, ring and cylinder wear.

3. Remove the spark plug with a 14 mm spark plug wrench.

NOTE
If the plug is difficult to remove, apply penetrating oil, like WD-40 or Liquid Wrench, around the base of the plug and let it soak in about 10-20 minutes.

4. Inspect the plug (**Figure 27**) carefully. Look for a broken center porcelain, excessively eroded electrode, and excessive carbon or oil fouling.

Gapping and Installing the Plug

Gap the new spark plug to ensure a reliable, consistent spark. Use a spark plug gapping tool and a wire feeler gauge as described in this procedure.
1. When using the stock spark plugs caps, the small terminal adapter (**Figure 28**) is not required.
2. Refer to the spark plug gap listed in **Table 8**. Then insert a wire feeler gauge between the center and side electrode (**Figure 29**). If the gap is correct, you will feel a slight drag as you pull the wire through. If there is no drag, or the gauge will not pass through, bend the side electrode with a gapping tool (**Figure 30**) to set the proper gap.

NOTE
Do not use a flat feeder gauge to check the spark plug gap on a used spark plug or too large of a gap will result.

3. Apply an antiseize lubricant to the plug threads before installing the spark plug.

3

4. Screw the spark plug in by hand until it seats. Very little effort should be required. If force is necessary, the plug may be cross-threaded. Unscrew it and try again.

5. Tighten the spark plug to the torque specification in **Table 6** or use a spark plug wrench and tighten the plug an additional 1/4 to 1/2 turn after the gasket has made contact with the head. If you are installing an old, regapped plug and reusing the old gasket, only tighten an additional 1/4 turn.

NOTE
Do not overtighten. This may squash the gasket and cause a compression leak.

6. Install the spark plug cap (**Figure 26**) onto the spark plug. Make sure it is on tight.

CAUTION
Make sure the spark plug wire is pulled away from the exhaust pipe.

Reading Spark Plugs

Careful examination of the spark plug can determine valuable engine and spark plug information. This information is only valid after performing the following steps.

1. Ride the motorcycle at full throttle in a suitable area.

NOTE
You must ride the motorcycle long enough to obtain an accurate reading or color on the spark plug. If the original plug was fouled, use a new plug.

2. Push the engine stop switch to OFF before closing the throttle and coasting to a stop.
3. Remove the spark plug and examine it. Compare it to **Figure 31** and note the following:

Normal condition

If the plug has a light tan- or gray-colored deposit and no abnormal gap wear or erosion, good engine, carburetion and ignition condition are indicated. The plug in use is of the proper heat range and may be serviced and returned to use.

Carbon fouled

Soft, dry, sooty deposits covering the entire firing end of the plug are evidence of incomplete combustion. Even though the firing end of the plug is dry, the plug's insulation decreases. An electrical path is formed that lowers the voltage from the ignition system. Engine misfiring is a sign of carbon fouling.

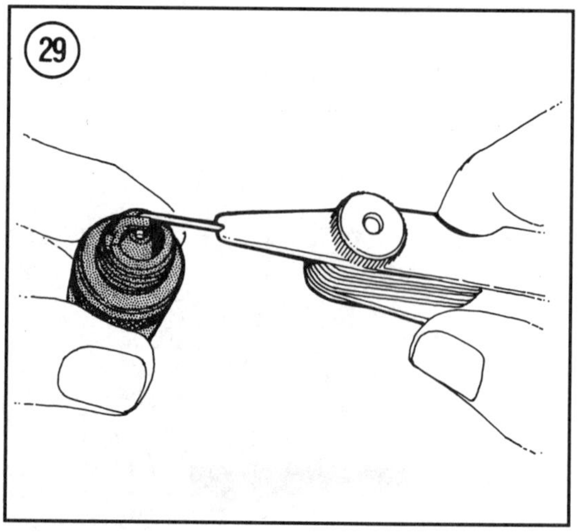

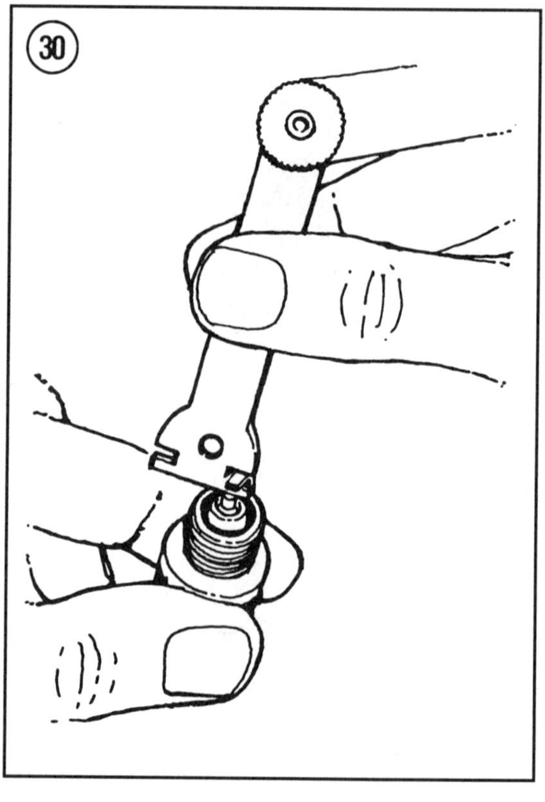

(31)

SPARK PLUG CONDITIONS

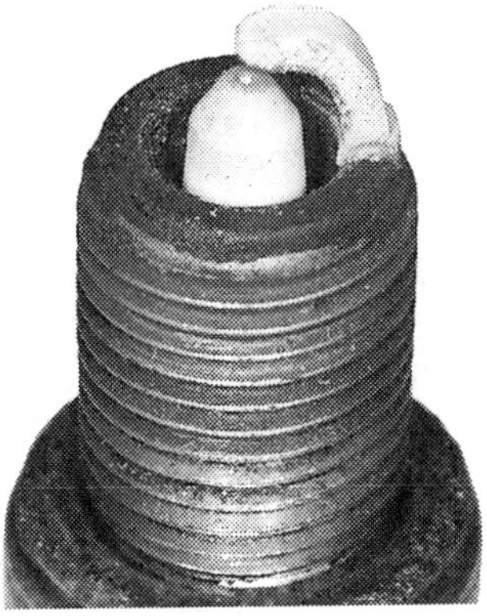

Normal

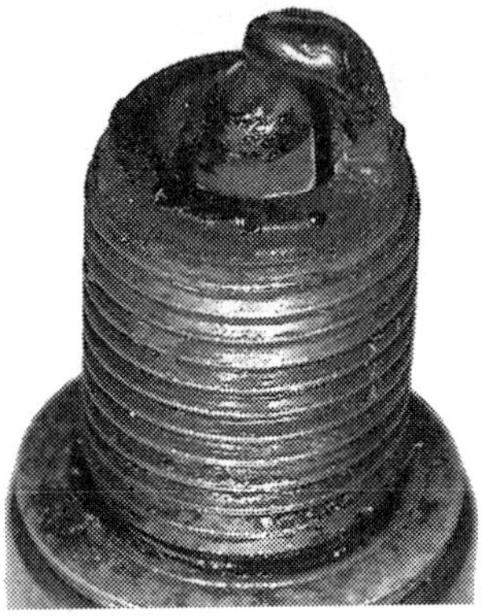

Gap bridged

Carbon fouled

Overheated

Oil fouled

Sustained preignition

Carbon fouling can be caused by one or more of the following:

a. Too rich fuel mixture.
b. Spark plug heat range too cold.
c. Clogged air filter.
d. Over-retarded ignition timing.
e. Ignition component failure
f. Low engine compression.
g. Prolonged idling.

Oil fouled

The tip of an oil fouled plug has a black insulator tip, a damp oil film over the firing end and a carbon layer over the entire nose. The electrodes will not be worn. Common causes for this condition are:

a. Incorrect carburetor jetting.
b. Low idle speed or prolonged idling.
c. Ignition component failure.
d. Spark plug heat range too cold.
e. Engine still being broken in.

An oil fouled spark plug may be cleaned in an emergency, but it is better to replace it. It is important to correct the cause of fouling before you return the engine to service.

Gap bridging

A plug with this condition exhibits gaps shorted out by combustion deposits between the electodes. The engine can still run with a bridged spark plug, but it will miss badly. If you encounter this condition, check for an improper oil type or excessive carbon in the combustion chamber. Be sure to find and correct the cause of this condition.

Overheating

Badly worn electrodes and premature gap wear are signs of overheating, along with a gray or white "blistered" porcelain insulator surface. The most common cause for this condition is using a spark plug of the wrong heat range (too hot). If you have not changed to a hotter spark plug and the plug is overheated, consider the following causes:

a. Lean fuel mixture.
b. Ignition timing too advanced.
c. Incorrect oil pump flow.
d. Engine air leak.
e. Improper spark plug installation (overtightening).
f. No spark plug gasket.

Worn out

Corrosive gases formed by combustion and high voltage sparks have eroded the electrodes. A spark plug in this condition requires more voltage to fire under hard acceleration. Replace with a new spark plug.

Preignition

If the electrodes are melted, preignition is almost certainly the cause. Check for carburetor mounting or intake manifold leaks and advanced ignition timing. It is also possible that a plug of the wrong heat range (too hot) is being used. Find the cause of the preignition before returning the engine into service.

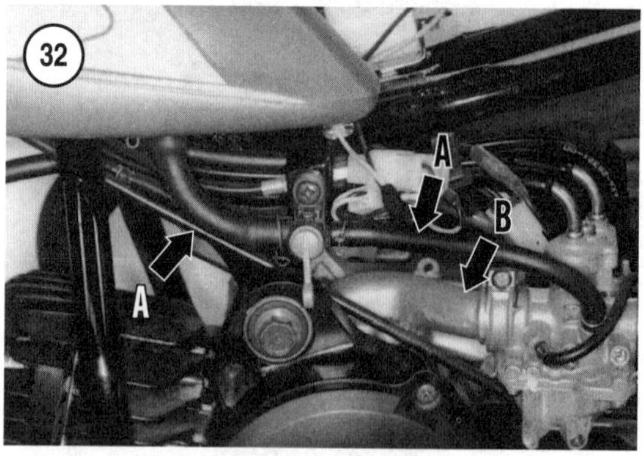

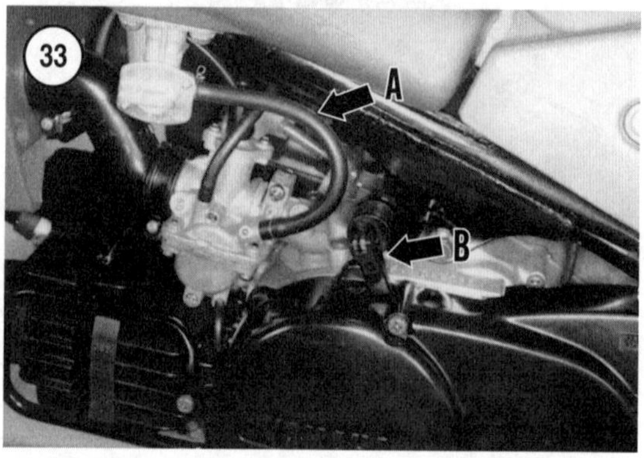

CARBURETOR

This section describes service to the fuel hose, shutoff valve, intake manifold and carburetor.

Fuel Hose and Shutoff Valve Inspection

Inspect the fuel hose for any leaks, a damaged hose or missing or weak hose clamps. Replace the fuel hose and hose clamps if damaged. See A, **Figure 32** (PW50) or A, **Figure 33** (BW80 and PW80).

Inspect the fuel shutoff valve for any leaks or damage. O-rings installed in the valve can go bad and cause the valve to leak fuel. If there is insufficient fuel flow from the ON or RES fuel lever positions, the screen mounted at the top of each pickup tube may be partially clogged. To service the fuel valve, refer to *Fuel Tank* in Chapter Eight.

WARNING

A leaking fuel hose may cause the engine to catch on fire. Do not start the engine with a leaking or damaged fuel hose or fuel shutoff valve.

34

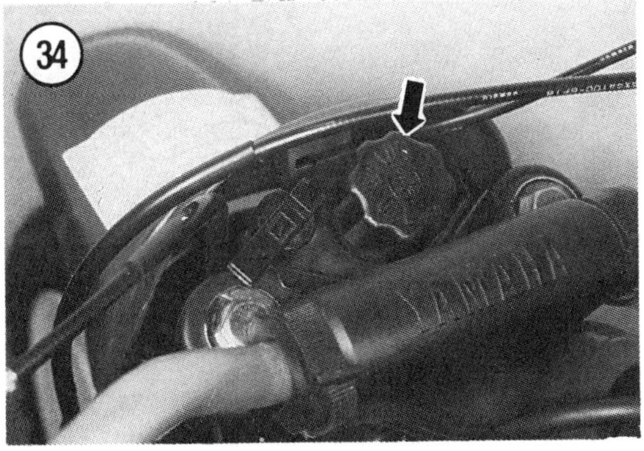

35

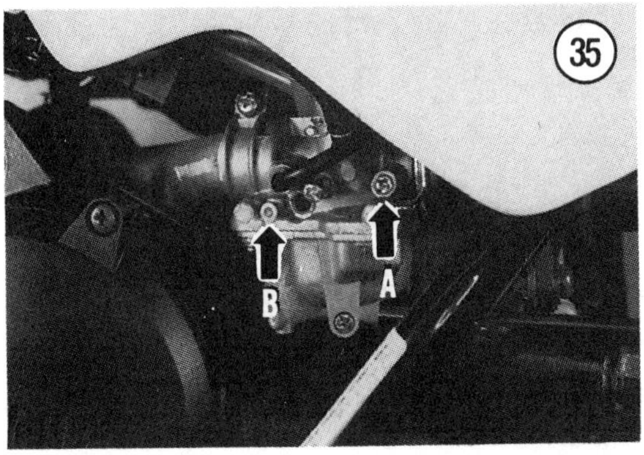

Intake Manifold Inspection

The intake manifold mounts to the top of the cylinder and connects the reed valve and carburetor to the engine; see B, **Figure 32**, typical. A loose or damaged intake manifold will allow air to leak into the engine and cause a lean air/fuel mixture. To accurately check for a loose or damaged intake manifold, perform the *2-Stroke Crankcase Pressure Test* in Chapter Two.

Inspect the intake manifold for loose mounting screws and a loose or damaged carburetor hose clamp.

Carburetor Choke

Check the choke by lifting up and pushing down the choke lever. See **Figure 34** (PW50) or B, **Figure 33** (BW80 and PW80). The choke lever, cable and valve should move smoothly and lock in both positions. To check the choke, perform the following:

1. Start the engine and allow it to warm to normal operating temperature.
2. When the engine has warmed completely, lift the choke lever to open the choke circuit inside the carburetor. When doing so the engine should stall. If the engine does not stall, the choke may not be working correctly.

NOTE

Lifting the choke lever opens the choke circuit. Pushing the choke lever down closes the choke circuit.

3. If necessary, refer to Chapter Seven to service the choke or choke cable.

Carburetor Idle Speed and Mixture Adjustment

Proper idle speed is a balance between a low enough idle to give adequate compression braking and a high enough idle to prevent engine stalling. The idle air/fuel mixture affects transition from idle to 1/8 throttle openings.

Turning the pilot air screw in enriches the fuel mixture and turning it out leans the mixture. See A, **Figure 35** (PW50) or A, **Figure 36** (BW80 and PW80).

1. Make sure that the throttle cable free play is correct. Check and adjust the throttle cable as described in this chapter.

2. Turn the pilot air screw in until it seats lightly, then back it out the number of turns indicated in **Table 8**. See A, **Figure 35** (PW50) or A, **Figure 36** (BW80 and PW80).

CAUTION
Never turn the pilot air screw in tightly against its seat as you will damage the screw or the soft aluminum seat in the carburetor.

3. Connect a portable tachometer to the engine following its manufacturer's instructions.

NOTE
If a tachometer is not available, set the idle speed fast enough so the engine idles smoothly without stalling, but, not so fast that the automatic (centrifugal) clutch engages.

4. Start the engine and warm it to normal operating temperature.
5. Remove the seat.
6. Turn the throttle stop screw to set the engine idle speed to the speed listed in **Table 8**. See B, **Figure 35** (PW50) or B, **Figure 36** (BW80 and PW80).
7. Now turn the pilot air screw clockwise or counterclockwise to obtain the highest idle speed as possible. See A, **Figure 35** (PW50) or A, **Figure 36** (BW80 and PW80).

NOTE
Do not open the pilot air screw more than 3 turns or it may vibrate out. If you cannot get the engine to idle properly, first make sure the air filter is clean. If air filter is good and other engine systems are operating correctly, the pilot jet size may be incorrect. Refer to Chapter Seven for information on jetting the carburetor.

8. Finally, turn the throttle stop screw to set the engine idle speed within the rpm range listed in **Table 8**. See B, **Figure 35** (PW50) or B, **Figure 36** (BW80 and PW80).
9. Open and then close the throttle a few times, making sure the idle speed returns to the range listed in **Table 8**.
10. Turn the engine off and remove the tachometer.
11. Install the seat.
12. Test ride the motorcycle. Throttle response from idle must be rapid and without hesitation. If there is any hesitation, readjust the carburetor.

WARNING
With the engine idling, move the handlebar from side to side. If idle speed increases during this movement, the throttle cable needs adjusting or it may be incorrectly routed through the frame. Correct this problem immediately. Do not ride the motorcycle in this unsafe condition.

EXHAUST SYSTEM

To maintain engine performance, inspect and service the exhaust system at regular intervals.

Inspection

Refer to Chapter Four (PW50) or Chapter Five (BW80 and PW80) for service and repair procedures called out in this section.

1. Inspect the exhaust pipe for cracks or dents which could alter performance. See **Figure 37** (PW50) or **Figure 38** (BW80 and PW80).
2. Check all of the exhaust pipe fasteners and mounting points for loose or damaged parts.
3. Check the exhaust pipe where it is bolted against the exhaust port on the front of the cylinder (**Figure 39**). Make sure the 2 nuts or bolts are tight and that there are no exhaust leaks. If the exhaust pipe is leaking at this point, remove the exhaust pipe and replace the gasket installed between the pipe and cylinder.
4. Decarbonize the exhaust pipe and spark arrestor when servicing the engine's top end.

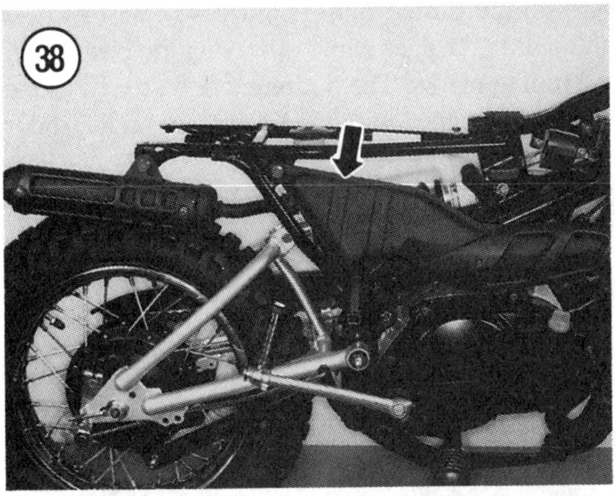
38

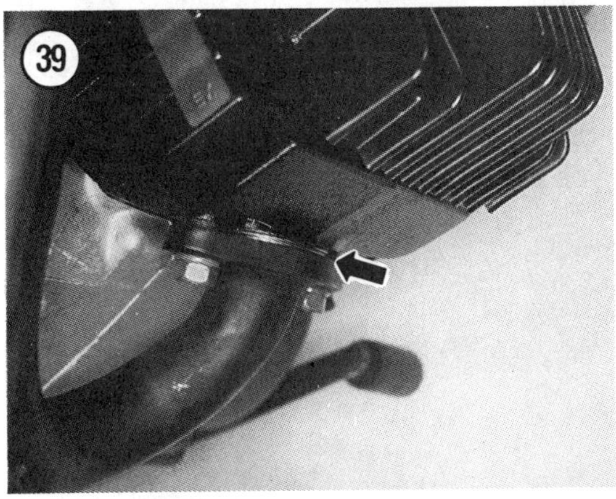
39

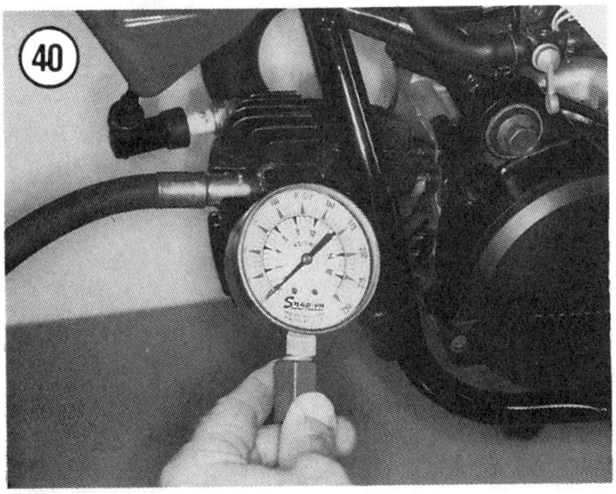
40

OIL PUMP AND ENGINE OIL LINES

The oil pump supplies oil to the engine. To prevent any engine lubrication problems, periodically inspect the engine oil lines and the pump assembly for loose, missing or damaged parts. Refer to Chapter Nine for all oil pump and oil line inspection and service procedures.

CAUTION
*If the oil tank is empty, or a new oil tank was installed, fill it as described under **Engine Oil** in this chapter, then bleed the oil pump before starting the engine; otherwise, air trapped in the delivery line will prevent oil from reaching the engine. This will cause engine damage at start-up. Refer to Chapter Nine to bleed the oil pump.*

ENGINE COMPRESSION CHECK

A cylinder cranking compression check is one of the quickest ways to check the internal condition of the engine: rings, piston, cylinder and head gasket. It's a good idea to check compression at each tune-up, write it down, and compare it with the reading you get at the next tune-up. This will help you identify any developing problems.

1. Clean the area around the spark plug, then remove it from the cylinder head.
2. Thread or insert the tip of a compression gauge into the cylinder head spark plug hole (**Figure 40**). Make sure the gauge is seated properly.
3. Move the engine stop switch to its OFF position.
4. Hold the throttle wide open and kick the engine over until the gauge needle gives its highest reading.

Yamaha does not list a compression reading for the engines covered in this manual. If the compression reading is low, the engine top end should be disassembled and the parts measured to find the worn parts. See Chapter Four or Chapter Five for engine top end service.

5. If the reading is excessively high, there may be a buildup of carbon deposits in the combustion chamber or on the piston crown.

NOTE
If the compression is low, the engine cannot be tuned to maximum performance. The worn parts must be replaced or the engine rebuilt.

6. Push the release button on the compression gauge, then remove it from the cylinder. Reinstall the spark plug cap and connect its spark plug cap.

IGNITION TIMING

Adjustment (PW50)

The ignition timing is not adjustable since the stator plate (**Figure 41**) position is fixed to the crankcase (the mounting screw holes are not slotted for adjustment) and the flywheel is not equipped with timing marks. If you feel there is a problem with the ignition system, make sure all electrical connections are clean and properly connected. If you cannot find a problem here, troubleshoot the ignition system as described in Chapter Two.

Adjustment (BW80 and PW80)

On these models, the stator plate position is fixed to the crankcase (the mounting screw holes are not slotted for adjustment). However, the flywheel is equipped with timing marks that allow the ignition timing to be checked with a timing light.

You need a timing light, 6-volt battery and portable tachometer for this procedure. Check and set the ignition timing as follows:

NOTE
Follow the operating instructions listed by the timing light and tachometer manufacturers. In particular, make sure the timing light and tachometer cords are routed away from the flywheel.

1. Support the bike on its sidestand.
2. Remove the shift pedal and the left side cover (**Figure 42**).
3. Connect a portable tachometer and timing light to the engine following their manufacturer's instructions.
4. Start the engine and warm it to normal operating temperature.
5. After the engine has warmed to operating temperature, open and hold the throttle so the engine is running at 4,000 rpm.
6. Aim the timing light (**Figure 43**) the flywheel and pull the trigger while observing the position of the timing marks. The timing mark on the flywheel should be aligned with the fixed mark on the stator

41

42

43

plate (**Figure 44**). Turn the engine off and note the following:

a. If the timing marks are aligned (**Figure 44**), the ignition timing is correct.

b. If the timing marks are not aligned, first check that the stator plate mounting screws and the flywheel mounting nut are tight. Then check that all of the electrical connectors are clean and properly connected. If you cannot find a problem here, troubleshoot the ignition system as described in Chapter Two. A faulty component in the ignition system is probably causing the incorrect ignition timing reading.

7. Disconnect the timing light and tachometer leads.

8. Install the left side cover and the shift pedal (**Figure 42**).

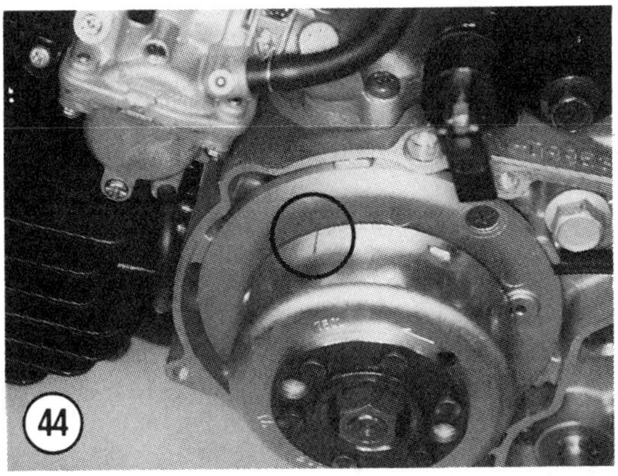

44

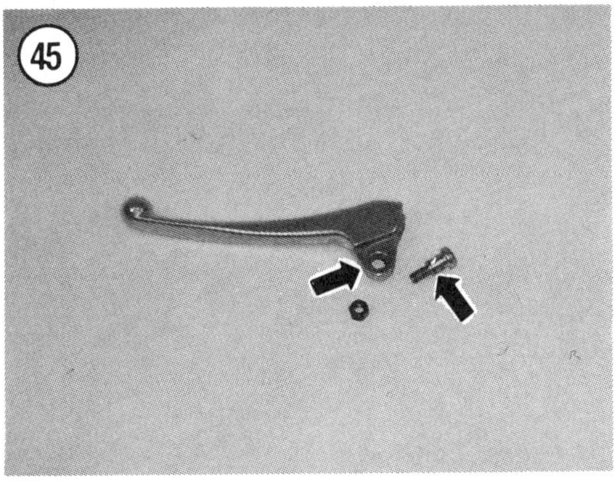

45

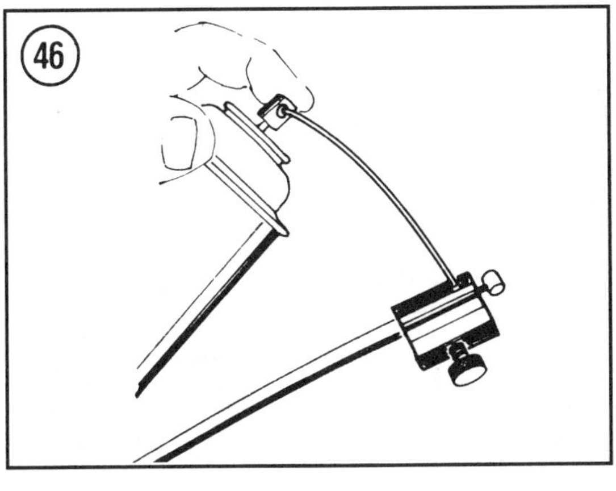

46

CONTROL CABLE LUBRICATION

This section describes complete lubrication procedures for the control cables and control lever assemblies.

Brake Lever Pivot Bolt Lubrication

Periodically, remove the brake lever pivot bolt(s) (**Figure 45**) at the handlebar and lubricate the bolts with 10W-30 motor oil. Replace the bolts if their shoulders become grooved or excessively worn. At the same time inspect the pivot hole in the levers and replace the levers if the holes have grooves or show severe wear. Reinstall the pivot bolts and nuts and tighten securely. Make sure the lever pivots smoothly and that there is no binding or roughness.

Control Cable Lubrication

Clean and lubricate the throttle and brake cables at the intervals indicated in **Tables 1-3**. In addition, check the cables for kinks and signs of wear, damage or fraying that could cause a cable to stick or break during use. Cables are expendable items and won't last forever under the best of conditions.

Lubricate the stock or aftermarket steel lined control cables with a cable lubricator (**Figure 46**) and a can of cable lube or a multipurpose lubricant Do *not* use a chain lube to lubricate control cables unless it is also specified as a control cable lubricant. If the stock cables were replaced with Teflon type control cables, follow the manufacturer's instructions regarding cleaning and servicing these cables.

1. Disconnect the front and rear (PW50) brake cable(s) as described the appropriate brake cable replacement procedure in Chapter Fourteen.

2. Disconnect the choke, throttle and oil pump cables as described in Chapter Seven. Then separate

each cable from the connector housing and lubricate the cables separately. See **Figure 47**, typical.

CAUTION
*Do not lubricate the choke cable or the throttle cable with the lower cable ends (**Figure 48**) attached to the carburetor assembly. Oil and dirt that is flushed from the end of the cable will enter the top of the carburetor. This could cause severe wear to the carburetor bore, choke and throttle valves. The contamination may also cause the throttle valve to stick open while the motorcycle is being ridden.*

3. Wipe off the cable ends and inspect them (**Figure 47**, typical) for any fraying, bending or other damage. Replace damaged cables as described in Chapter Seven (choke, oil pump and throttle) or Chapter Fourteen (brake).

4. Attach a cable lubricator to the end of the cable following the manufacturer's instructions (**Figure 46**).

5. Insert the lubricant can nozzle into the lubricator, press the button on the can and hold down until the lubricant begins to flow out of the other end of the cable. If you cannot get the cable lube to flow through the cable at one end, remove the lubricator and try at the opposite cable end.

NOTE
Place a shop cloth at the end of the cable to catch the oil as it runs out.

6. Disconnect the lubricator.

7. Lightly grease the cable ends, except the throttle cable end (**Figure 48**) before reconnecting them.

8. Reverse Steps 1 and 2 to reconnect the control cables.

9. Adjust all of the control cables as described in this chapter.

10. Check that each cable operates correctly and does not bind or move roughly.

WARNING
Do not ride the motorcycle until all of the control cables are properly adjusted.

THROTTLE AND OIL PUMP CABLE ADJUSTMENT (PW50)

Cable wear will affect the operation of the throttle, oil pump and carburetor. Normal amounts of cable wear can be controlled by the free play adjustments described in this section. If you cannot adjust a cable within its adjustment limits, the cable is excessively worn or damaged and requires replacement. Also, do not adjust cables that show visible damage or suffer from rust damage.

Free play is the distance the throttle moves before the throttle valve and oil pump pulley move.

Throttle Cable Adjustment

The throttle cable is a subassembly consisting of 3 separate cables and a connector housing. The upper cable is connected between the throttle housing and connector housing. The 2 lower cables are connected between the connector housing and then separately to the carburetor and oil pump.

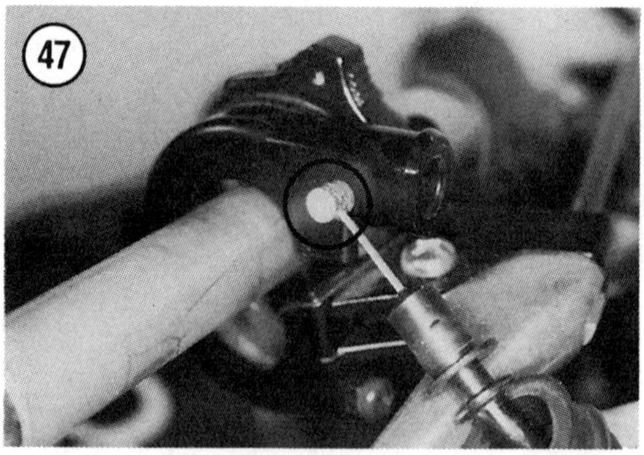

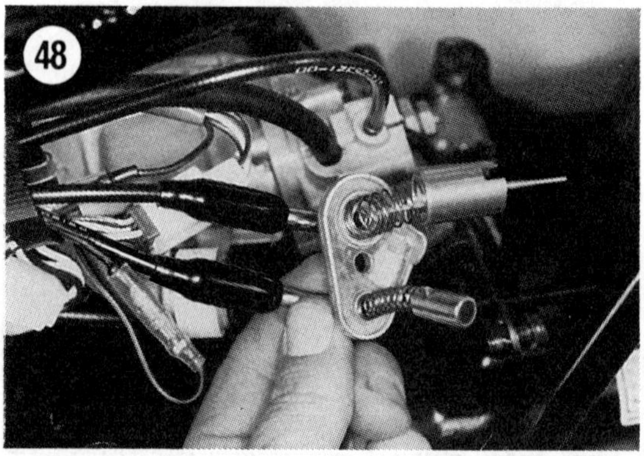

Some throttle cable play is necessary to prevent changes in the idle speed when you turn the handlebar.

Yamaha specifies a separate free play measurement for the upper and lower throttle cables. Adjust the lower throttle cable first, and then the upper throttle cable as described in the following procedure.

1. Set the engine idle speed as described under *Idle Speed Adjustment* in this chapter.

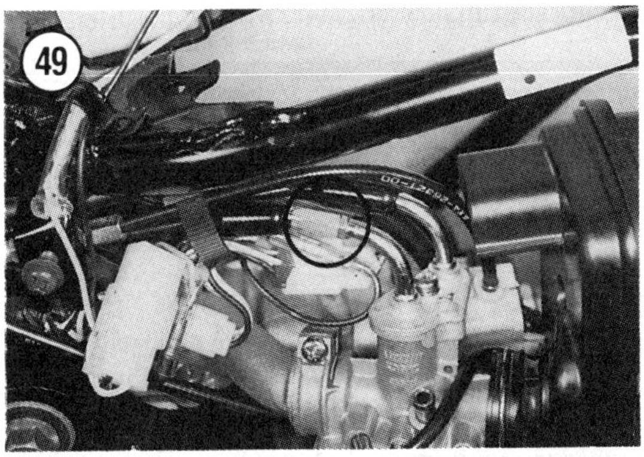

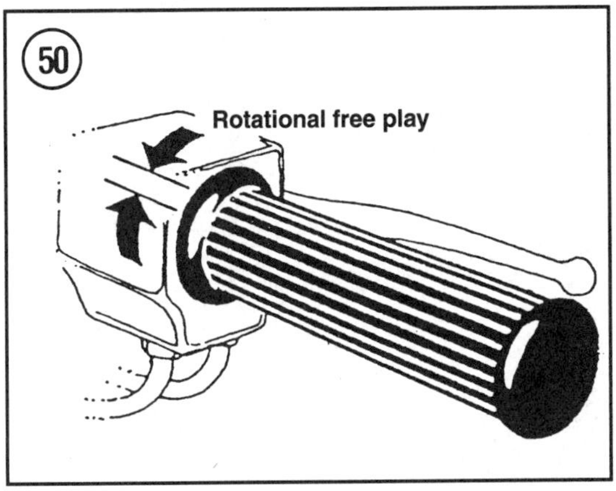

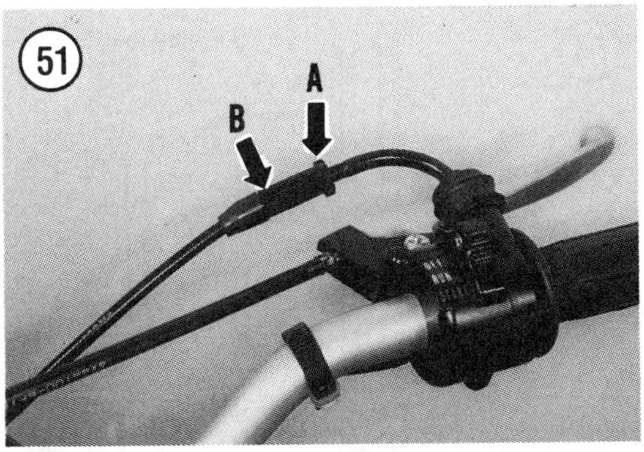

2. Before checking the cable adjustment, check each throttle cable to make sure each cable end is connected and routed properly.

NOTE

Steps 3-5 describe adjustment of the lower throttle cable (attached between the connector housing and carburetor).

3. At the top of the carburetor, slide the rubber boot up the throttle cable and completely off the throttle cable adjuster (**Figure 49**).

4. Tug on the cable while measuring its movement at the adjuster. The cable should have 1.0 mm (0.04 in.) of free play. If necessary, loosen the adjuster locknut and turn the adjuster (**Figure 49**) until the free play measurement is correct. Then tighten the locknut and recheck the free play.

5. Slide the rubber boot down the throttle cable and over the adjuster.

NOTE

Steps 6 and 7 describe adjustment of the upper throttle cable (attached between the throttle and connector housing).

6. Turn the throttle and measure the free play at the throttle grip flange (**Figure 50**). The upper cable should have 1.5-3.5 mm (0.06-0.14 in.) of free play at the throttle grip flange. If the free play measurement is incorrect, continue with Step 7.

7. At the throttle housing, loosen the throttle cable adjuster locknut (A, **Figure 51**) and turn the adjuster (B, **Figure 51**) in or out to achieve the proper amount of cable free play. Tighten the locknut and recheck the free play.

8. Open and release the throttle, making sure it moves smoothly with no binding or roughness.

9. Check the oil pump cable adjustment as described in this chapter.

10. Start the engine and allow it to idle in NEUTRAL. Turn the handlebar from side to side. If the idle increases, the throttle cable is routed incorrectly or there is not enough cable free play.

WARNING

Do not ride the motorcycle with a sticking throttle cable or throttle.

Oil Pump Cable Adjustment

The oil pump cable is part of the throttle cable assembly. It is connected between the throttle cable connector housing and oil pump.

1. First check the throttle cable adjustment as described in this section. Adjust the cable, if necessary, then adjust the oil pump cable.
2. Remove the oil pump cover screws and cover (**Figure 52**).
3. Check the oil pump pulley alignment marks. The 2 raised marks on the pulley (A, **Figure 53**) should be aligned with the Phillips screw (B, **Figure 53**) mounted onto the adjusting plate. See **Figure 54**. Note the following:
   a. If the adjustment is incorrect, continue with Step 4.
   b. If the adjustment is correct, go to Step 7.
4. Remove the fuel tank (Chapter Seven).
5. Locate the oil pump cable adjuster mounted on the left side of the engine. Loosen the oil pump cable adjuster locknut (A, **Figure 55**) and turn the cable adjuster (B, **Figure 55**) in or out to align the raised marks on the pulley with the Phillips screw (B, **Figure 53**). Then tighten the locknut and recheck the adjustment.
6. Install the fuel tank (Chapter Seven).
7. Install the oil pump cover and tighten its mounting screw.

THROTTLE AND OIL PUMP CABLE ADJUSTMENT (BW80 AND PW80)

Cable wear will adversely affect the operation of the throttle, oil pump and carburetor. Normal cable wear can be controlled by the free play adjustments described in this section. If you cannot adjust a cable within its adjustment limits, the cable is severely worn or damaged and requires replacement. Also, do not adjust cables that show visible damage.

Free play is the distance the throttle moves before the throttle valve and oil pump pulley move.

Throttle Cable Adjustment

The throttle cable is a subassembly consisting of 3 separate cables and a connector housing. The upper cable is connected between the throttle housing and connector housing. The 2 lower cables are connected between the connector housing and then separately to the carburetor and oil pump.

Some throttle cable play is necessary to prevent changes in the idle speed when you turn the handlebars.

1. Set the engine idle speed as described under *Idle Speed Adjustment* in this chapter.
2. Before checking the throttle cable adjustment, check each throttle cable to make sure each cable end is connected and routed properly.
3. Turn the throttle and measure the free play at the throttle grip flange (**Figure 50**). The throttle cable

52

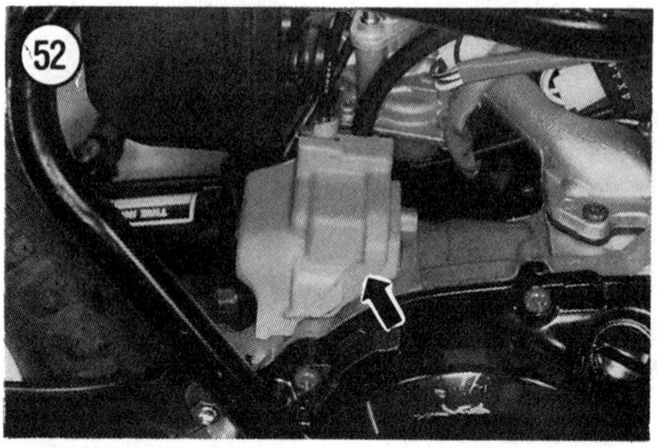

53

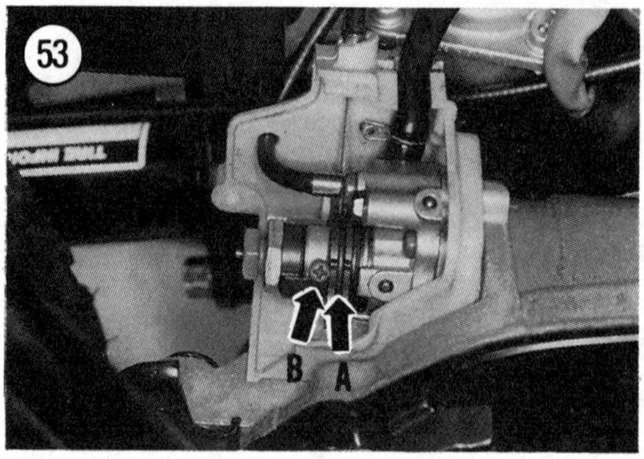

54

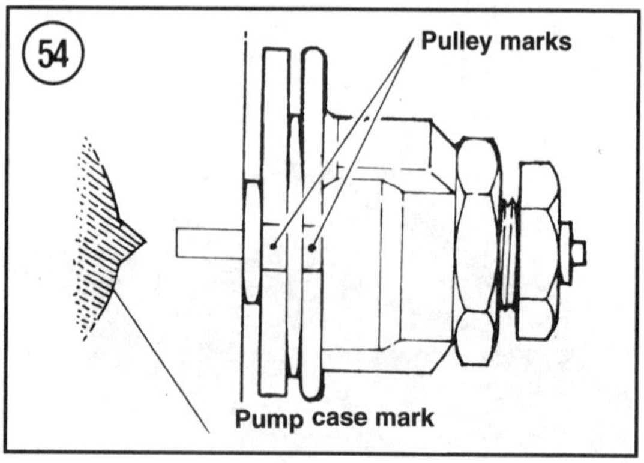

should have 5 mm (0.2 in.) of free play at the throttle grip flange. If the free play measurement is incorrect, continue with Step 4.

4. At the throttle housing, loosen the throttle cable adjuster locknut (A, **Figure 51**) and turn the adjuster (B, **Figure 51**) in or out to achieve the proper amount of cable free play. Tighten the locknut and recheck the free play.

5. Open and release the throttle, making sure it moves smoothly with no binding or roughness.

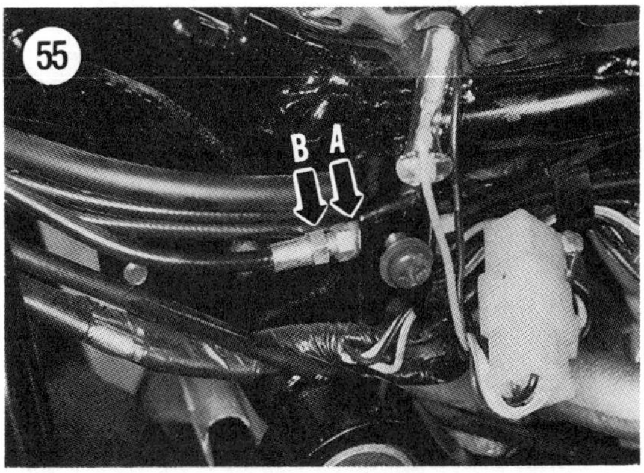

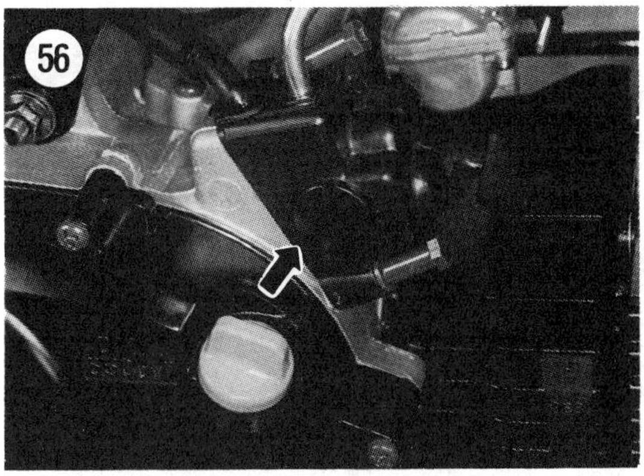

6. Check the oil pump cable adjustment as described in this chapter.

7. Start the engine and allow it to idle in NEUTRAL. Turn the handlebar from side-to-side. If the idle increases, the throttle cable is routed incorrectly or there is not enough cable free play.

WARNING
Do not ride the motorcycle with a sticking throttle cable or throttle.

Oil Pump Cable Adjustment

The oil pump cable is part of the throttle cable assembly. It is connected between the throttle cable connector housing and oil pump.

1. Check the throttle cable adjustment as described in this section. Adjust the cable, if necessary.

2. Remove the grommet (**Figure 56**) from the oil pump cover hole.

WARNING
When performing the following steps, do not start and run the motorcycle in a closed area. The exhaust gases contain carbon monoxide, a colorless, tasteless, poisonous gas. Carbon monoxide levels build quickly in a small enclosed area and can cause unconsciousness and death in a short time.

3. Start the engine and allow to idle. Then turn the throttle until all cable slack is removed from the throttle cable and the engine speed starts to increase. Hold the throttle at this position and check the oil pump pulley alignment marks. The 2 raised marks on the pulley (A, **Figure 57**) should be aligned with the raised mark on the oil pump case (B, **Figure 57**). Note the following:

  a. If the adjustment is incorrect, perform Step 4.
  b. If the adjustment is correct, go to Step 6.

4. Locate the oil pump cable adjuster. Loosen the oil pump cable adjuster locknut (A, **Figure 58**) and turn the cable adjuster (B, **Figure 58**) in or out to align the raised marks on the pulley (A, **Figure 57**) with the raised mark on the oil pump case (B, **Figure 57**). Then tighten the locknut and recheck the adjustment as described in Step 3.

5. Turn the engine off.

6. Install the grommet (**Figure 56**) into the oil pump cover hole.

SPEED LIMITER ADJUSTMENT (PW50)

The throttle housing is equipped with a speed limiter (**Figure 59**) that can be used to limit the range of throttle opening. The speed limiter is designed primarily to limit engine speed for beginning riders. It can also be used to control engine speed when breaking in a new or rebuilt engine.

NOTE
While the speed limiter adjustment described here is not a functional part of engine maintenance, it is included here to complement the information found in the Yamaha PW50 Owner's Service Manual. When the speed limter is used to control the speed of the motorcycle for a young rider, always refer to the information listed in the Yamaha PW50 Owner's Service Manual.

The speed limiter adjustment is set by varying the length of the speed limiter screw mounted in the throttle housing. Turning the screw in (clockwise) decreases engine speed. Turning the screw out (counterclockwise) or removing the screw altogether increases engines speed. If the screw is removed from the throttle housing, plug the exposed hole opening with the rubber plug originally equipped with the motorcycle.

BRAKE LUBRICATION, INSPECTION AND CABLE ADJUSTMENT

This section describes lubrication, inspection and adjustment procedures for the front and rear brake assemblies.

Refer to Chapter Fourteen for complete brake lining and drum inspection and repair procedures.

Brake Lever Lubrication

Refer to *Control Cable Lubrication* in this chapter.

Rear Brake Pedal Pivot Shaft Lubrication (BW80 and PW80)

At the intervals specified in **Table 2** or **Table 3**, remove the rear brake pedal assembly and then lubricate the brake pedal pivot shaft with a waterproof grease. Refer to *Rear Brake Pedal and Rod (BW80 and PW80)* in Chapter Fourteen.

Brake Camshaft and Pivot Pin Lubrication

Lubricate the front and rear brake camshafts and pivot pins as indicated in **Tables 1-3**.

1. Remove the brake shoes from the backing plate as described in Chapter Fourteen.
2. Wipe away old grease from the camshaft and pivot pins. Also clean the pivot hole and the contact area of each shoe. Do no get any grease on the brake linings.
3. Apply a light film of high-temperature grease to the camshaft and pivot pin contact surfaces. See **Figure 60**, typical.
4. On PW50 models, wipe away old grease from the backing place oil seal lip and repack with the same high-temperature grease used in Step 3.
5. Reassemble the brake shoes as described in Chapter Fourteen.

Brake Lining and Drum Inspection

Because the brake drums are not equipped with wear indicators, the wheels must be removed to inspect the brake linings and drums. Refer to Chapter Fourteen.

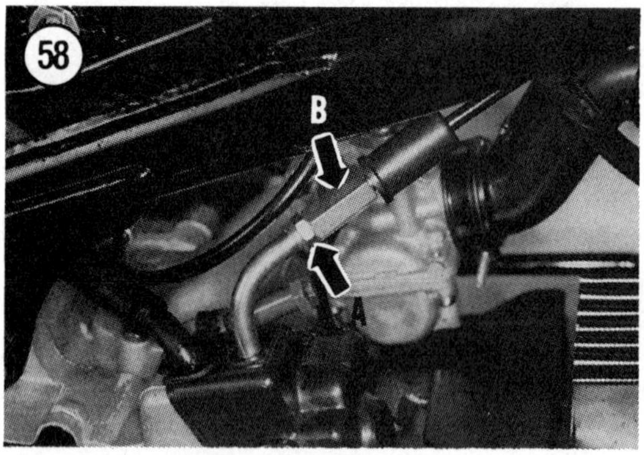

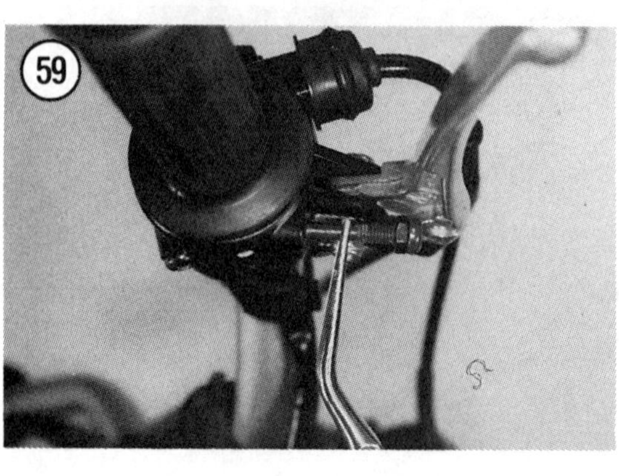

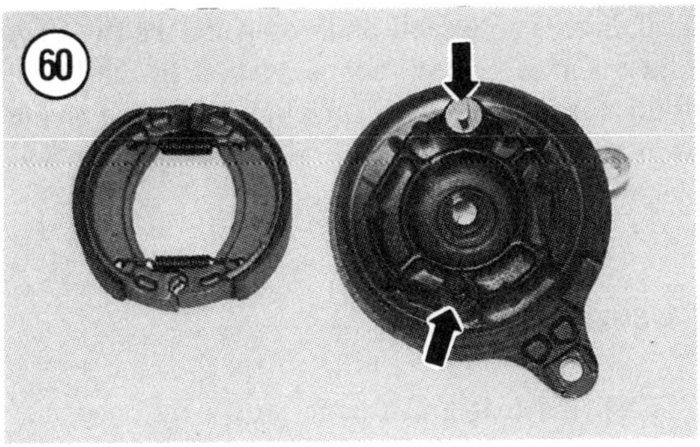

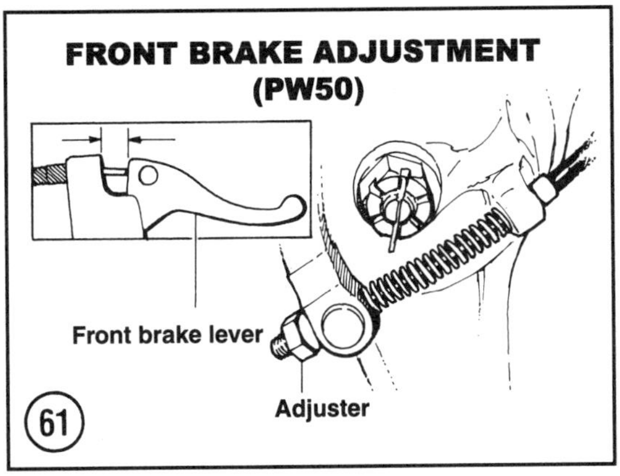

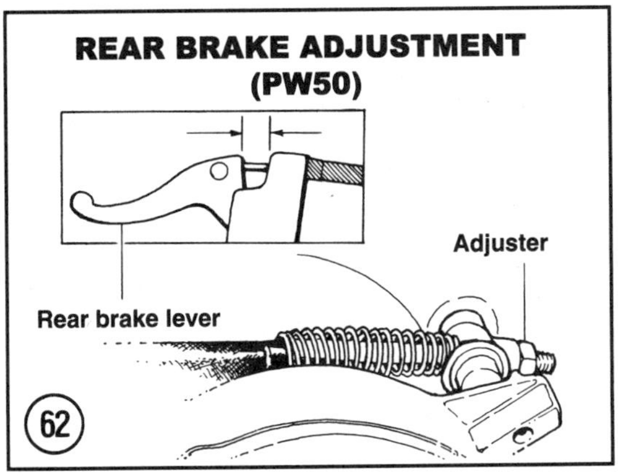

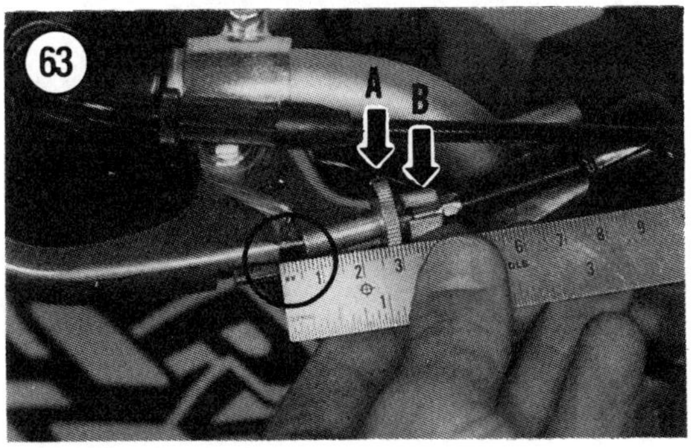

Brake Cable Adjustment

As the brake linings wear, they are positioned farther away from the brake drum lining surface, thus increasing the brake lever or pedal free play. As the free play increases, the brake lever or pedal must travel farther before the brake takes effect. Brake adjustment compensates for brake lining wear by setting the free play to the manufacturer's standard setting. Free play is the distance the brake lever or pedal moves before the brakes take hold. Always check brake adjustment at the intervals listed in **Tables 1-3** or whenever the brake lever or pedal travel has increased. If the brakes cannot be adjusted as described in this section, the brake linings may be severely worn. Brake cable free play is necessary to prevent brake drag and to compensate for brake lining wear. The brakes must not be adjusted so closely that the brake linings contact the brake drum with the lever or pedal (BW80 and PW80) relaxed.

WARNING

Do not attempt to compensate for excessively worn brake linings by overadjusting the brake or repositioning the brake arm on the brake cam. An incorrect brake arm angle (usually in excess of 90°) can allow the cam to go overcenter (turn horizontal) and lock up the wheel, causing the rider to lose control.

PW50

The front brake lever is mounted on the left side of the handlebar. The rear brake lever is mounted on the right side of the handlebar.

1. Pull the front brake lever until resistance is felt and hold in this position. Then measure the distance between the brake lever perch and brake lever as shown in **Figure 61**. The correct free play measurement is 3-5 mm (0.12-0.20 in.). If the free play measurement is incorrect, turn the brake adjuster (**Figure 62**) in or out until the correct adjustment is obtained.
2. Pull the rear brake lever until resistance is felt and hold in this position. Then measure the distance between the brake lever perch and brake lever as shown in **Figure 62**. The correct free play measurement is 3-5 mm (0.12-0.20 in.). If the free play measurement is incorrect, turn the brake adjuster (**Figure 63**) in or out until the correct adjustment is obtained.

3. Support the bike so the wheel to be checked is off the ground. Spin the wheel by hand and check for brake drag. Also operate the brake lever several times to make sure it returns to the at-rest position immediately after release.
4. If there is noticeable brake drag and the free play adjustment is correct, contamination in the brake drum area may be causing the linings to drag on the drum. Remove the wheel for further inspection and cleaning.

BW80 and PW80 front brake

The front brake is equipped with two adjustments. Minor adjustments should be made at the brake lever and major adjustments should be made at the brake adjuster at the brake panel.

1. Slide back the rubber protective boot at the hand lever.
2. Pull the front brake lever until resistance is felt and hold in this position. Then measure the distance between the brake lever perch and brake lever as shown in **Figure 63**. The correct free play measurement is 5-8 mm (0.2-0.30 in.) on BW80 models and 5 mm (0.2 in.) on PW80 models. If the free play measurement is incorrect, continue with Step 3.
3. Loosen the locknut (A, **Figure 63**) and turn the adjuster (B, **Figure 63**) to achieve the correct amount of free play. Tighten the locknut and recheck the adjustment.
4. Because of normal brake wear, the upper end adjustment will eventually be used up. It is then necessary to loosen the locknut and screw the adjuster all the way toward the hand grip. Tighten the locknut.
5. At the brake panel, loosen the locknut (A, **Figure 64**) and turn the adjuster (B, **Figure 64**) until the brake lever adjuster (B, **Figure 63**) can be used once again for minor adjustments. Tighten the locknut (A, **Figure 64**).
6. At the hand lever, loosen the locknut (A, **Figure 63**) and turn the adjuster (B, **Figure 63**) to achieve the correct amount of free play (Step 2). Tighten the locknut.
7. Slide the rubber protective boot back into place.
8. Support the bike so that the front wheel is off the ground. Spin the wheel by hand and check for brake drag. Also operate the brake lever several times to make sure it returns to the at-rest position immediately after release.
9. If there is noticeable brake drag and the free play adjustment is correct, contamination in the brake drum area may be causing the linings to drag on the drum. Remove the wheel for further inspection and cleaning, refer to Chapter Eleven.

BW80 and PW80 rear brake

1. Push the rear brake pedal down by hand and measure the distance from its at-rest position to the point where resistance is felt (**Figure 65**). This distance is rear brake pedal free play. The correct free play distance is 20-30 mm (0.8-1.2 in.).
2. To adjust, turn the rear brake adjuster (A, **Figure 66**) in or out until the free play distance is correct.
3. Support the bike so that the rear wheel is off the ground. Spin the wheel by hand and check for brake drag. Also operate the brake pedal several times to make sure it returns to the at-rest position immediately after release.
4. If there is noticeable brake drag and the free play adjustment is correct, contamination in the brake drum area may be causing the linings to drag on the

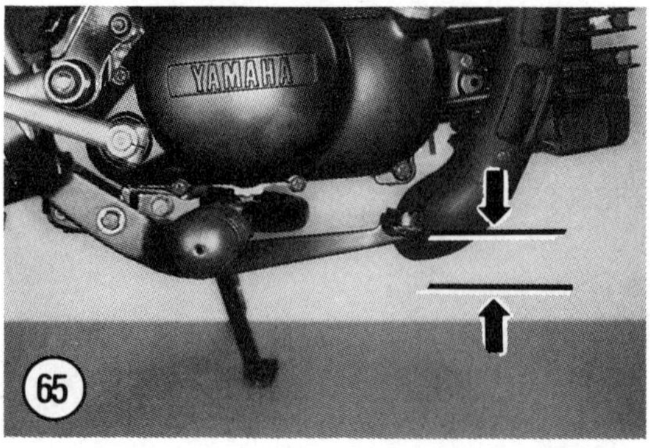

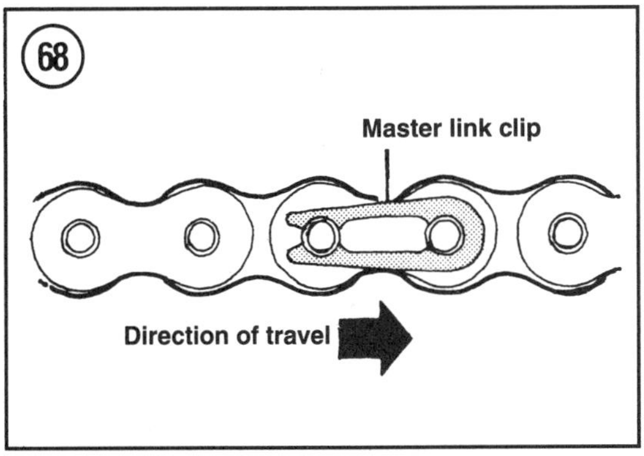

drum. Remove the wheel for further inspection and cleaning, refer to Chapter Twelve.

Brake Stay Arm (PW80)

When servicing the PW80 brakes in this section, check the brake stay arm (B, **Figure 66**) for loose or missing fasteners. Tighten the rear brake stay arm mounting nuts as specified in **Table 6**. Secure each nut with a new cotter pin and bend the ends over completely.

FINAL GEAR LUBRICATION (PW50)

At the intervals specified in **Table 1**, remove and disassemble the final gear assembly (**Figure 67**). Clean the assembly of all old grease and then repack with new grease. Refer to *Final Drive* in Chapter Twelve for service and lubrication procedures.

DRIVE CHAIN (BW80 AND PW80)

Service the drive chain at the intervals listed in **Table 2** or **Table 3** or earlier after riding the motorcycle in muddy or sandy conditions.

Drive Chain Master Link Inspection

It is a good idea to check the master link before riding the motorcycle and after cleaning or adjusting the drive chain. Check that the master link is properly installed and secured to the drive chain. The spring clip must be installed so its closed end (**Figure 68**) faces in the direction of chain travel.

Chain Slider Inspection

The chain slider (**Figure 69**) protects the swing arm from chain contact and damage. Inspect the chain slider frequently and replace it when severely worn or damaged. To replace the chain slider (**Figure 69**), remove the swing arm as described in Chapter Thirteen.

Drive Chain Lubrication

Lubricate the drive chain every 1/2 to 1 hour of riding time. If the chain is caked with mud, clean both sides of the drive chain using a wire brush before lubricating it. If the contamination is severe, or if the links are kinked or tight, remove and clean the drive chain as described in this section.

1. Ride the motorcycle for 5 minutes to pre-heat the chain. Then turn the engine off.
2. Support the motorcycle with the rear wheel off the ground.
3. Shift the transmission into NEUTRAL.
4. Turn the rear wheel and lubricate the chain with a commercial type chain lubricant. Spray the lubricant between the side plates and on the center rollers. Do not overlubricate as this will cause dirt to collect on the chain and sprockets.
5. Wipe off all excess chain lubricant from the rear hub, rim and tire.

Drive Chain Cleaning

1. Support the bike with the rear wheel off the ground.
2. Shift the transmission into NEUTRAL.
3. Remove the upper chain guard.

70

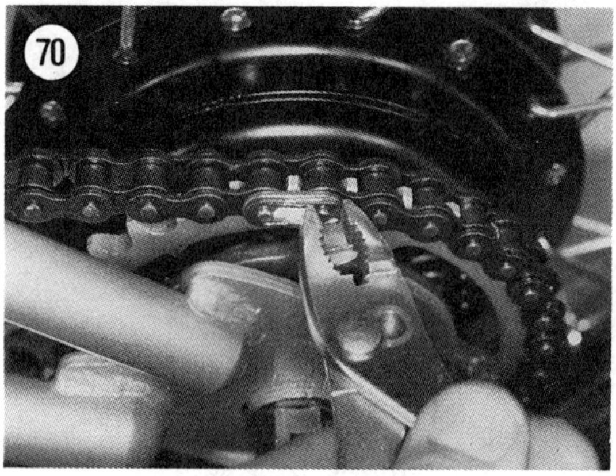

71

MASTER LINK

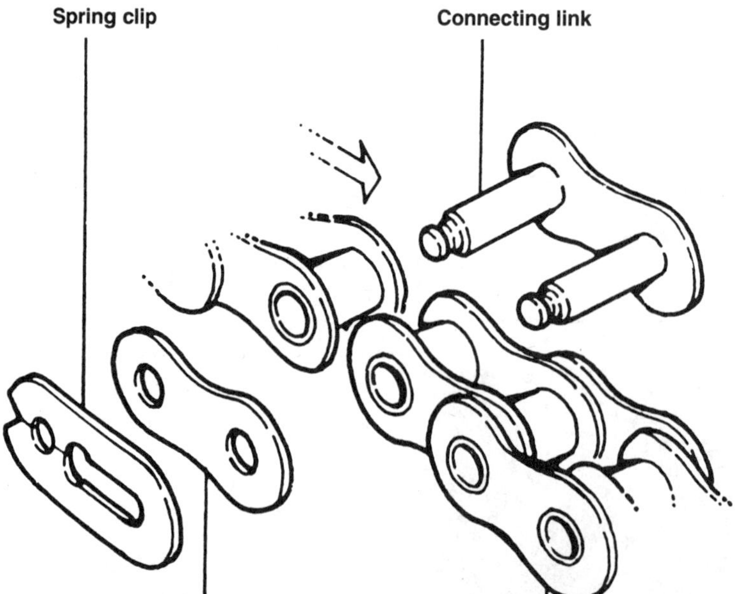

4. Remove the drive chain as follows:
   a. Turn the rear wheel until the master link is accessible.
   b. Remove the master link spring clip with a pair of pliers (**Figure 70**). Then remove the side plate and connecting link (**Figure 71**) and separate the drive chain.
   c. Remove the drive chain.

5. Clean the drive chain in a pan partially filled with kerosene. Remove any caked on dirt and oil using a stiff brush.

6. Examine the chain while you clean it in Step 5. Look for damaged rollers and pins, kinked chain links and rust damage. If the chain does not show any type of visible damage, soak it for about a half hour. Tight or kinked links may free up after a thorough cleaning. However, if some of the chain links are still kinked or tight, or if there is visible chain damage, the chain should be replaced.

7. After cleaning the chain, hang it up to allow to the chain to dry. Place a container underneath the chain to catch any fluid and contamination that runs off.

72

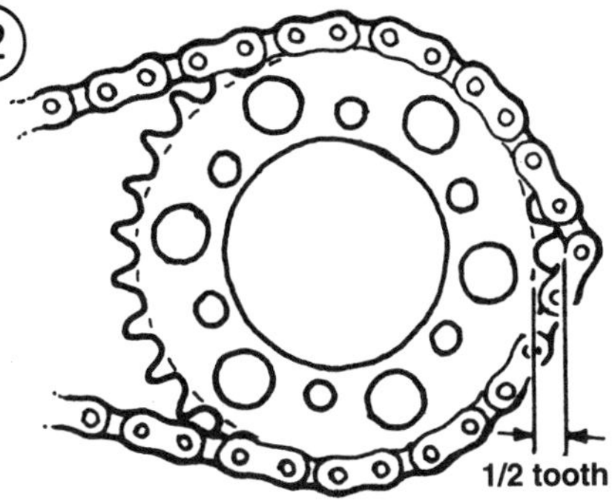

73

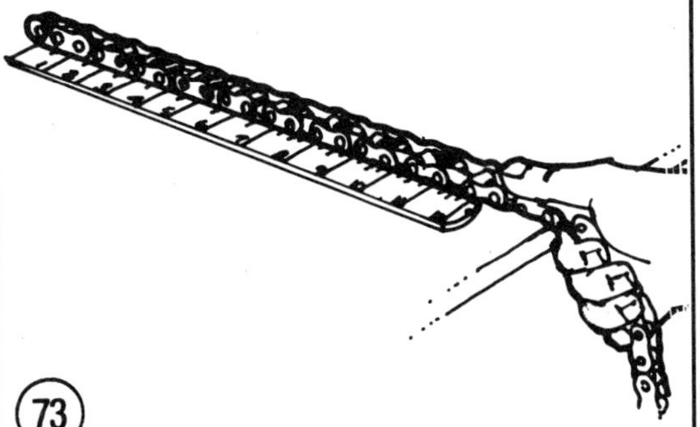

8. To check the chain for excessive wear, measure it as described under *Drive Chain/Sprocket Wear and Inspection Check* in this section.

9. Lubricate the drive chain with a commercial type chain lubricant.

10. Before installing the drive chain, remove any caked on dirt and oil from the sides of both sprockets with a paint scraper.

11. Reinstall the chain on the motorcycle. Use a new master link spring clip (**Figure 71**) and install it so that the closed end of the clip is facing the direction of chain travel (**Figure 68**).

WARNING

Always check the master link spring clip after the bike has been rolled backward, such as unloading from a truck or trailer. The master link clip may have snagged on the chain guard and become disengaged. Obviously, losing a chain while riding can cause a serious spill not to mention the chain damage which may occur.

12. Check and adjust the drive chain tension and alignment as described in this chapter.

Drive Chain/Sprocket Wear and Inspection Check

The drive chain should be checked frequently and replaced when excessively worn or damaged.

A quick check will give you an indication of when to actually measure chain wear. At the rear sprocket, pull one of the links away from the sprocket (**Figure 72**). If the link pulls away more than 1/2 the height of a sprocket tooth, the chain is excessively worn.

To accurately measure chain wear, perform the following:

1. Support the motorcycle with the rear wheel off the ground.
2. Loosen the rear axle nut.
3. Loosen the chain adjuster locknuts.
4. Tighten the chain adjusters to move the rear axle rearward until the drive chain is tight (no slack).

NOTE

*If you are making this check with the chain off of the motorcycle, lay the chain on your workbench and stretch it tightly (**Figure 73**). Hook one end of the chain*

3

on a nail or screw to anchor it in place when measuring its length in Step 5.

5. Lay a scale along the top chain run, and measure the length of any 21 pins in the chain. Measure from the inside of the first pin to the inside of the twenty-first pin as shown in **Figure 74**. Turn the wheel and repeat the measurement with a different set of links along the drive chain. If the measurement is greater than 262 mm (10-5/16 in.), the drive chain is excessively worn and should be replaced.
6. Check the inner plate chain faces. They should be lightly polished on both sides. If they show uneven wear on one side, the sprockets are not aligned. Severe wear requires chain and sprocket replacement.
7. Inspect the drive and driven sprockets (**Figure 75**) for:
   a. Undercutting or sharp teeth.
   b. Broken teeth.
8. If wear is evident, replace the chain and both sprockets as a set, or the new chain will soon wear out. Replace the drive chain and sprockets as described in Chapter Thirteen.
9. Adjust the drive chain as described in this chapter.

Drive Chain Adjustment

The drive chain must have adequate play so the chain is not too tight when the swing arm is horizontal. Conversely, too much play can allow the chain to jump off the sprockets, possibly causing the rear wheel to lock up. A thrown chain can also catch and bind between the drive sprocket and crankcase, cracking the crankcase.

(74) **DRIVE CHAIN WEAR**

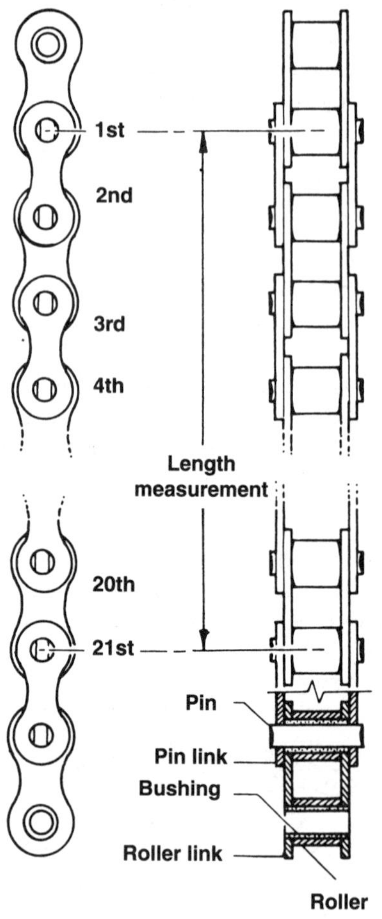

(75)

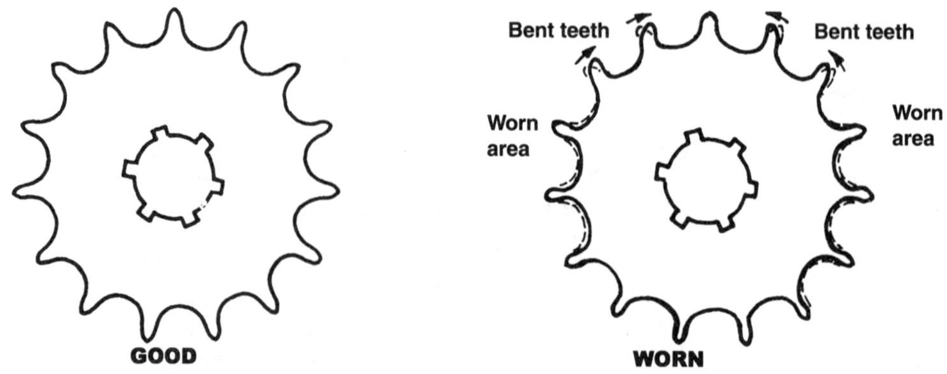

Check the drive chain free play and alignment before each ride, and throughout the riding day as required. Drive chain free play is listed in **Table 9**.

1. Remove the upper and lower chain guards (**Figure 76**).
2. Because the chain wears unevenly, its tightness will vary. This condition is normal. However, to avoid overtightening the chain when adjusting it, this tight spot must be found and the chain tension measured and adjusted at this point. If the chain is tightened at a looser spot, the chain will become too tight and may break or jump off the sprockets under riding conditions. Before adjusting the chain, perform the following:
   a. Support the bike on a stand with the rear wheel off the ground.
   b. Slowly turn the rear wheel and check the chain for binding and tight spots by moving the links up and down by hand. Each link must move freely against its connecting links. If a group of chain links or the entire chain is tight, remove and clean the drive chain as described in this section. Do not attempt to adjust and align a kinked drive chain.
   c. Slowly turn the rear wheel and check the chain tightness at several spots in the middle of the upper chain run (**Figure 77**). Find the tightest part on the chain and adjust it at this point.

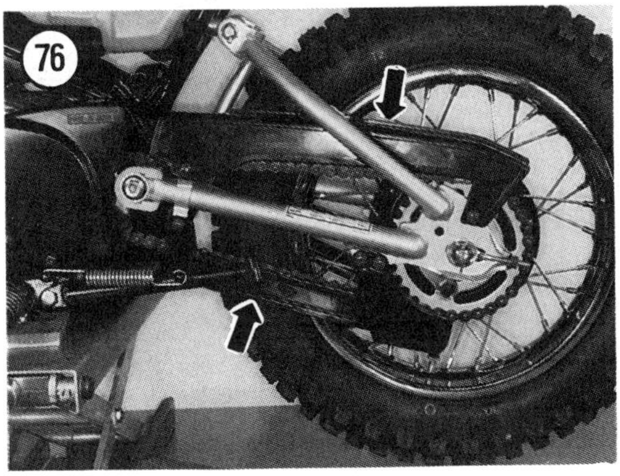

3. Remove the bike from its stand and support it so that it is standing upright with both wheels on the ground and without a rider.
4. Move the chain up and down on its upper chain run and midway between both sprockets. Measure the chain movement with a ruler (**Figure 77**) and compare with the free play specification in **Table 9**. If the chain free play is incorrect, adjust it as follows.

NOTE

When adjusting the drive chain, you must also maintain rear axle alignment. A misaligned rear axle can cause poor handling and pulling to one side or the other, as well as increased chain and sprocket wear. All models have wheel alignment marks on the rear swing arm and chain adjusters.

5. Remove the cotter pin and loosen the rear axle nut (**Figure 78**). Discard the cotter pin.
6. Loosen the chain adjuster locknuts (A, **Figure 79**) and turn the adjuster bolts (B, **Figure 79**) so that the index mark on each adjuster aligns with the same mark (or point between each mark) on each side of the swing arm.
7. When chain free play is correct, check wheel alignment by sighting along the chain from the rear sprocket. It should leave the sprocket in a straight line (A, **Figure 80**). If it is cocked to one side or the

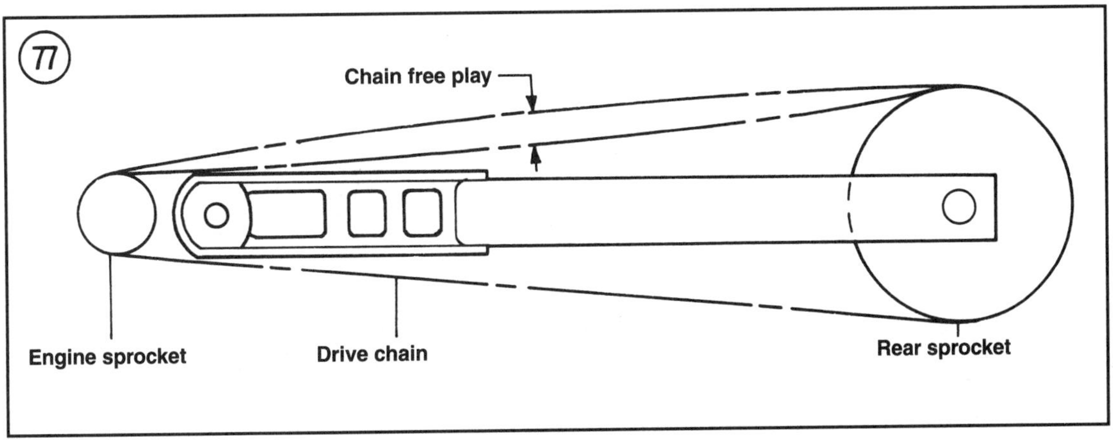

other, adjust wheel alignment by turning one adjuster or the other. Then check the chain free play.

8. Tighten the chain adjuster locknuts (A, **Figure 79**) tightly.

9. Tighten the rear axle nut as specified in **Table 6**. Then install a new cotter pin through the axle nut and rear axle and bend the ends over to lock it in place (**Figure 81**). If the nut slot and axle hole do not align, tighten the axle to align them.

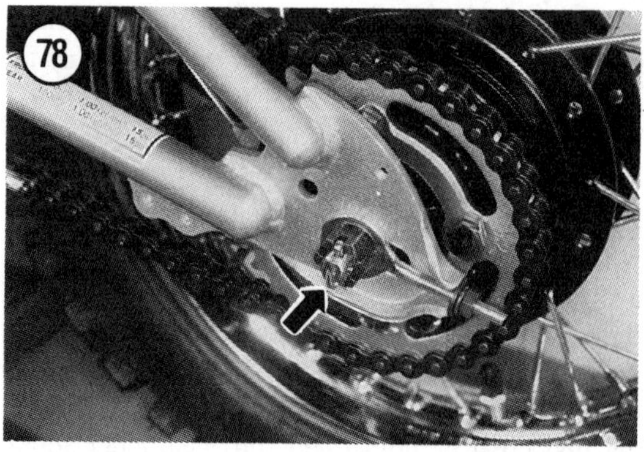

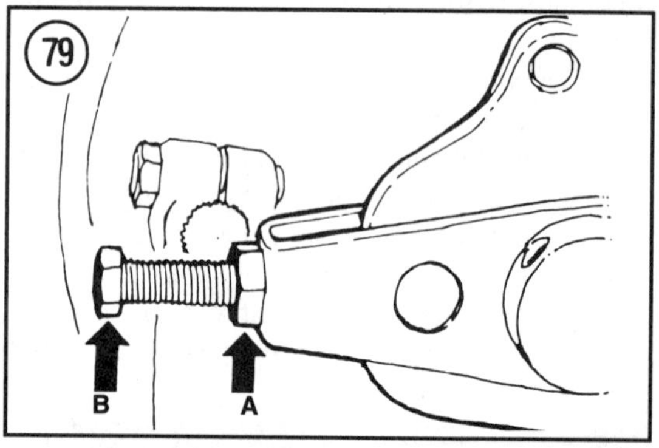

TIRES, WHEELS AND BEARINGS

Tire Pressure

Check and set the tire pressure to maintain good traction and handling and to prevent rim damage. Keep an accurate tire gauge (**Figure 82**) in your tool box. **Table 10** lists the standard tire pressure for the front and rear wheels.

Tire Inspection

The tires take a lot of punishment due to the variety of terrain they are subjected to. Inspect them weekly for excessive wear, cuts, abrasions, etc. To check for internal sidewall damage, remove the tire from the rim as described in Chapter Eleven. Run your hand around the inside tire casing, checking for tears or sharp objects imbedded in the casing.

While checking the tires on PW50 and PW80 models, check the position of the valve stem. If a valve stem is turned sideways (**Figure 83**), the tire and tube have slipped on the rim. The valve stem will eventually pull out of the tube, causing a flat. The BW80 is equipped with tubeless tires.

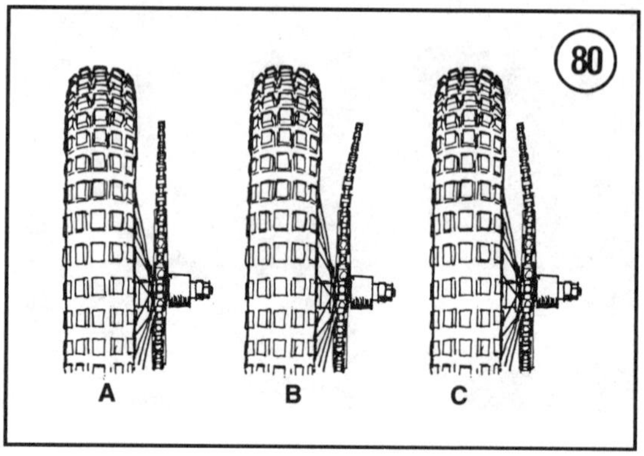

Wheel Spoke Tension (PW80)

Check each spoke for tightness with a spoke wrench (**Figure 84**). If the spokes are loose, tighten them as described in Chapter Eleven.

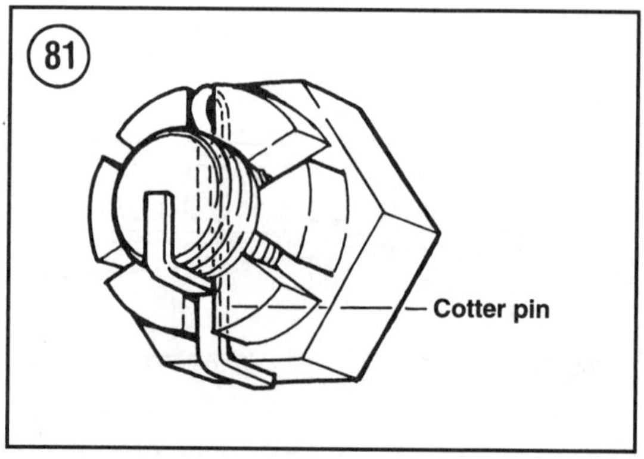

Rim Inspection and Runout

Inspect the rims for cracks, warpage or dents. Replace damaged rims.

Wheel rim runout is the amount of wobble a wheel shows as it rotates. You can check runout with the

82

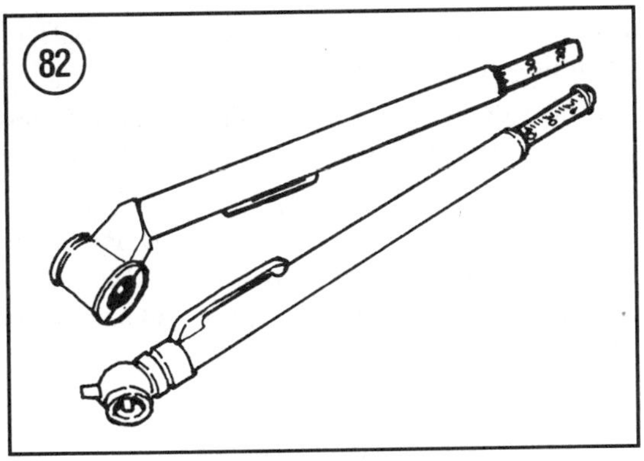

83

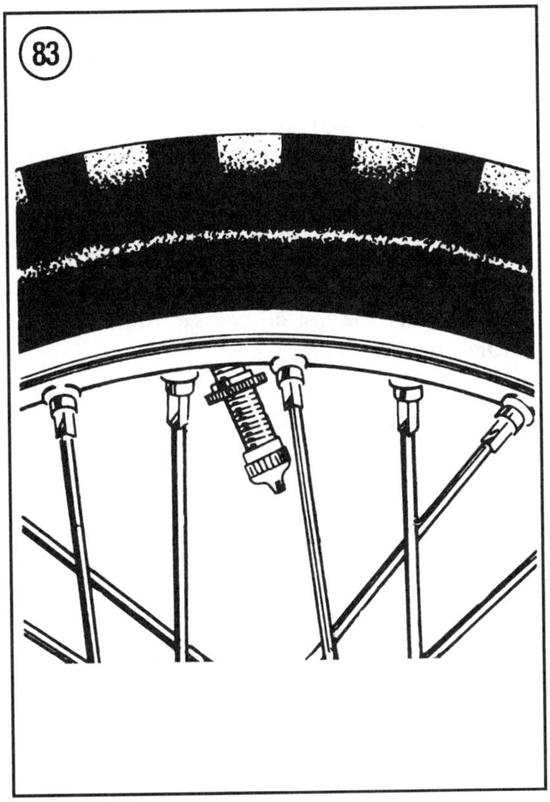

84

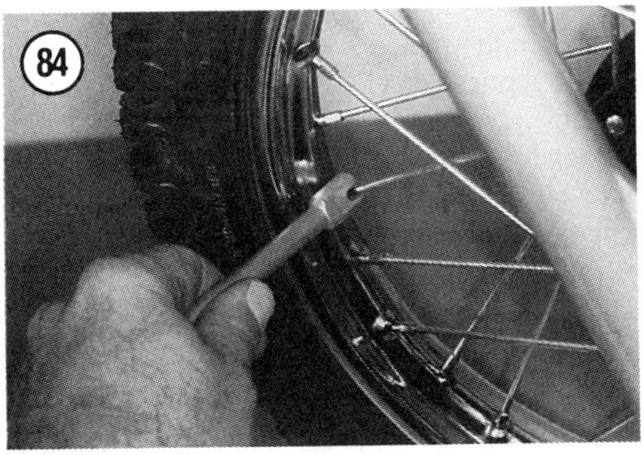

wheels on the bike by simply supporting the wheel off the ground and turning the wheel slowly while you hold a pointer solidly against a fork leg or the swing arm. To check the rims more accurately, refer to Chapter Ten or Chapter Eleven.

Wheel Bearings Inspection and Lu ication

At the service intervals listed in **Tables 1-3**, remove the wheels and inspect the wheel bearings. Clean and repack the open bearings. Refer to Chapters Ten through Fourteen for complete inspection and service procedures.

STEERING

Steering Bearing Lubrication

At the intervals specified in **Tables 1-3**, repack the steering bearings with grease. See Chapter Ten or Chapter Eleven for complete inspection, lubrication and adjustment procedures.

FRONT FORK OIL CHANGE (BW80 AND PW80)

The BW80 and PW80 models are not equipped with drain screws. It is necessary to remove the fork assembly and partially disassemble the fork to replace the fork oil. Refer to *Fork Oil Change* under *Front Forks* in Chapter Eleven.

REAR SUSPENSION

Perform the following rear suspension inspection and lubrication procedures at the intervals listed in **Tables 1-3**.

Rear Suspension Check

Check the rear suspension for loose or missing fasteners. Tighten all fasteners to the torque specification specified in Chapter Twelve or Chapter Thirteen.

Rear Swing Arm Pivot Shaft Lubrication (BW80 and PW80)

Remove the swing arm and lubricate the pivot shaft and rear swing arm bushings with grease. Refer to Chapter Thirteen for complete service procedures.

SIDESTAND (BW80 AND PW80)

At the intervals specified in **Table 2** or **Table 3**, lubricate the sidestand pivot bolt with a waterproof grease.

FRAME

When inspecting the suspension components, inspect the frame and all of its welded joints for cracks, bent parts or other damage. Refer all frame repair to a qualified welding and metal fabrication shop.

NUTS, BOLTS AND OTHER FASTENERS

Constant vibration can loosen many of the fasteners on the motorcycle. Check the tightness of all fasteners, especially those on:

a. Engine mounting hardware.
b. Engine crankcase covers.
c. Handlebar.
d. Gearshift lever.
e. Brake pedal and lever.
f. Exhaust system.
g. Steering and suspension components.

STORAGE

Several months of inactivity can cause serious problems and a general deterioration of the motorcycle's condition. This is especially true in areas of weather extremes. During the winter months or during long periods of nonuse, it is advisable to prepare your Yamaha for storage.

Selecting a Storage Area

Most riders store their motorcycles in their home garage. If you do not have a garage, facilities suitable for long-term storage are readily available for rent or lease in most areas. In selecting a building, consider the following points.

1. The storage area must be dry. Heating is not necessary, but the building should be well insulated to minimize extreme temperature variations.
2. Buildings with large window areas should be avoided, or such windows should be masked (also a good security measure) if direct sunlight can fall on the motorcycle.

Preparing Motorcycle for Storage

Careful preparation will minimize deterioration and make it easier to restore the motorcycle to service later. Use the following procedure.

1. Wash the motorcycle completely. Make certain to remove dirt in all the hard to reach parts like the cooling fins on the head and cylinder. Completely dry all parts of the bike to remove moisture.
2. Run the engine for about 20-30 minutes to warm up the transmission oil. Drain the oil, regardless of the time since the last oil change. Refill with the normal quantity and type of oil.
3. Drain all gasoline from the fuel tank, interconnecting hose, and the carburetor.
4. Clean and lubricate the drive chain and control cables; refer to specific procedures in this chapter.
5. Remove the spark plug and add about one teaspoon of engine oil into the cylinder. Reinstall the spark plug and turn the engine over to distribute the oil to the cylinder wall and piston.
6. Tape or tie a plastic bag over the end of the silencer to prevent the entry of moisture.
7. Check the tire pressure, inflate to the correct pressure and move the motorcycle to the storage area. Place it securely on a stand with both wheels off the ground.
8. Cover the motorcycle with a tarp, blanket or heavy plastic drop cloth. Place this cover over the bike mainly as a dust cover—do not wrap it tightly, especially any plastic material, as it may trap moisture causing condensation. Leave room for air to circulate around the motorcycle.

Inspection During Storage

Try to inspect the motorcycle weekly while in storage. Any deterioration should be corrected as soon as possible. For example, if corrosion is observed, cover them with a light coat of grease or silicone spray.

Turn the engine over a couple of times. Do not start it.

Restoring Motorcycle to Service

A motorcycle that has been properly prepared and stored in a suitable area requires only light maintenance to restore to service.

1. Check and clean the motorcycle of any spider webs (especially black widow spiders) and wasp nests that may have taken up residence during the motorcycle's storage.
2. Before removing the motorcycle from the storage area, reinflate the tires to the correct pressures. Air loss during storage may have nearly flattened the tires.
3. When the motorcycle is brought to the work area, refill the fuel with fresh gasoline.
4. Check the engine oil tank (described in this chapter) and bleed the oil pump (Chapter Nine).
5. Install a fresh spark plug and start the engine.
6. Check the operation of the engine stop switch. Oxidation of the switch contacts during storage may make it inoperative.
7. Clean and test ride the motorcycle.

3

Table 1 MAINTENANCE AND LUBRICATION SCHEDULE (PW50)*

Initial 1 month; thereafter every 3 months
Inspect spark plug
Check carburetor adjsutment
Check oil pump adjustment and operation
Check front and rear brake operation and adjustment
Check tire pressure and wheel runout
Check suspension system operation
Check fuel system; flush fuel tank when required
Check all fittings and fasteners
Initial 1 month; thereafter every 6 months
Change transmission oil
Initial 3 months; thereafter every 6 months
Inspect and lubricate control cables
Lubricate brake lever and brake camshaft
Clean and lubricate air filter
Check all carburetor hoses and fittings
Initial 6 months; thereafter every 6 months
Clean and lubricate throttle grip and housing
Initial 6 months; thereafter every year
Clean carburetor
Initial 6 months; thereafter every 2 years
Inspect and repack wheel bearings
Every year
Inspect and repack wheel bearings
Every 2 years
Clean and grease middle and final gear assembly

* This maintenance schedule must be considered a guide to general maintenance and lubrication intervals. Harder than normal use (racing) and exposure to mud, water and high humidity will require more frequent attention to most maintenance items.

Table 2 MAINTENANCE AND LUBRICATION SCHEDULE (BW80)*

Every month
Check drive chain adjustment and wear
Clean and lubricate drive chain
Initial 1 month; thereafter every 6 months
Check spark plug
Check carburetor adjustment
Check oil pump adjustment and operation
Check all fasteners and fittings
Check sidestand operation
Initial 1 month; thereafter every 12 months
Check steering adjustment
Initial 1 month; thereafter every 2 months
Change transmission oil
Every 6 months
Clean and oil air filter
Check fuel system for leaks
Check front and rear brake operation and adjustment
Check wheels for damage and runout
Check wheel bearings
Check front forks for oil leaks and damage
Check rear shock absorbers for oil leaks and damage
Every 12 months
Check fuel tank filter and flush fuel tank
Clean and lubricate rear swing arm
Every 2 years
Clean and lubricate steering bearings
* This maintenance schedule must be considered a guide to general maintenance and lubrication intervals. Harder than normal use (racing) and exposure to mud, water and high humidity will require more frequent attention to most maintenance items.

Table 3 MAINTENANCE AND LUBRICATION SCHEDULE (PW80)*

Every 1/2 hour to hour
Lubricate drive chain
Every 20 hours
Clean and lubricate air filter
Initial 10 hours; thereafter every 20 hours
Inspect spark plug
Check wheels and spokes
Check all fittings and fasteners
Check drive chain tension and alignment
Check oil injection system adjustment and operation
Initial 10 hours; thereafter every 40 hours
Check fuel filter and flush fuel tank
Initial 20 and then 40 hours; thereafter every 40 hours
Check front and rear brakes
Check clutch internal adjustment
Initial 20, 40 and 80 hours; thereafter every 80 hours
Check ignition timing
Check carburetor adjustment
Check engine compression
Initial 20 hours, thereafter every 80 hours
Decarbonize engine
Initial 20 and then 40 hours; thereafter every 80 hours
Change transmission oil
Lubricate control cables
Initial 40 hours; thereafter every 80 hours
Lubricate rear brake pedal shaft
Lubricate sidestand pivot shaft

(continued)

Table 3 MAINTENANCE AND LUBRICATION SCHEDULE (PW80)* (continued)

Initial 80 hours; thereafter every 40 hours
  Inspect and lubricate wheel bearings
Initiial 80 hours; thereafter every160 hours
  Inspect and lubricate steering bearings
Every 80 hours
  Change fork oil

* This maintenance schedule must be considered a guide to general maintenance and lubrication intervals. Harder than normal use (racing) and exposure to mud, water and high humidity will require more frequent attention to most maintenance items.

Table 4 RECOMMENDED LUBRICANTS AND FUEL

Engine oil	Yamalube 2 or air cooled 2-stroke engine injection oil
Transmission oil	Yamalube 4 or comparable 10W-30 SE motor oil
Air filter	Foam air filter oil
Drive chain*	Chain lubricant or SAE 30-50 engine motor oil
Steering and suspension lubricant	Multipurpose grease
Fuel	Premium unleaded fuel
Drive shaft grease	Cable lube**
PW50	

* Use kerosene to clean O-ring drive chain.
** Do not use drive chain lubricant to lubricate control cables.

Table 5 OIL TANK CAPACITY

	Liters	U.S. qt.	Imp.qt.
PW50	0.3	0.32	0.26
BW80 and PW80	0.95	1.0	0.84

Table 6 MAINTENANCE TORQUE SPECIFICATIONS

	N•m	in.-lb.	ft.-lb.
Oil drain bolt			
PW50	14	—	10
BW80 and PW80	20	—	14
Rear brake stay arm nuts at swing arm and brake backing plate			
PW80	16	—	11
Rear axle nut			
PW50	60	—	44
BW80	85	—	62
PW80	60	—	44
Spark plug			
PW50	20	—	14
BW80	20	—	14
PW80	25	—	18

Table 7 TRANSMISSION OIL CAPACITY

	Milliliters	U.S. qt.	Imp. qt.
Oil change			
PW50	300	0.32	0.26
BW80 and PW80	650	0.69	0.57
After engine overhaul			
PW50	350	0.37	0.31
BW50 and PW80	750	0.79	0.66

Table 8 TUNE-UP SPECIFICATIONS

Ignition timing	
PW50	16° @ 4500 rpm
BW80 and PW80	20.6° @ 4000 rpm
Spark plug	
PW50	NGK BP4HS
BW80	NGK BP7HS
PW80	NGK BP6HS
Spark plug gap	0.6-0.7 mm (0.024-0.028 in.)
Engine idle speed	
PW50 and PW80	Not specified
BW80	1650-1750 rpm
Initial pilot air screw setting (turns out)	
PW50	1 3/8
BW80	1 1/4
PW80	1 1/2

Table 9 DRIVE CHAIN FREE PLAY MEASUREMENT

	mm	in.
BW80 and PW80	15-20	0.6-0.8

Table 10 TIRE INFLATION PRESSURE

	Front kPa (psi)	Rear kPa (psi)
PW50 and PW80	100 (15)	(15) 100
BW80	29.4 (4.3)	4.3 (29.4)

CHAPTER FOUR

ENGINE (PW50)

This chapter covers information on servicing the following engine components:

a. Exhaust pipe.
b. Cylinder head.
c. Cylinder.
d. Reed valve.
e. Piston and rings.
f. Clutch.
g. Primary drive gear.
h. Kickstarter.
i. Oil pump drive gear.
j. Kick pinion gear.
k. Transmission.
l. Crankcases.
m. Crankshaft.

Service to the flywheel and stator plate assembly is described in Chapter Eight.

With the exception of servicing the engine top end (cylinder head, cylinder and piston) and the flywheel and stator plate assembly (Chapter Eight), the engine must be removed from the frame to service the engine components.

Before starting any work, read the information listed under *Service Hints* in Chapter One. You will do a better job with this information fresh in your mind.

Make certain that you have all of the necessary special tools. All of the fasteners used on your Yamaha are metric; make sure to use metric wrenches and sockets.

One of the more important aspects of engine overhaul is preparation. Throwing all of the parts in one or two boxes will make it difficult to rebuild the engine. Use boxes (**Figure 1**) and small plastic bags during disassembly and label the parts as required.

The text often refers to the left and right sides of the engine. The terms left and right side refer to the engine as it is mounted in the frame—the flywheel is on the left side; the clutch is on the right side.

Engine specifications are listed in **Tables 1-6** at the end of the chapter.

ENGINE IDENTIFICATION

The engine is a single cylinder, air-cooled 2-stroke engine. This engine is very simple in design in that it only uses three moving parts: the piston assembly, connecting rod and crankshaft. See **Table 1** for general engine specifications.

The engine consists of an upper and lower end. To prevent confusion, the following lists identify these engine subassemblies as they are called out in this manual:

a. *Engine top end*—Cylinder head, cylinder, piston, rings, needle bearing and piston pin. This needle bearing and pin assembly is often referred to as the upper end bearing.
b. *Engine lower end*—Crankshaft assembly, main bearings and oil seals. The crankshaft assembly consists of the left and right side crank wheels, connecting rod, washers, pin and needle bearing. This needle bearing and pin assembly is often referred to as the lower end bearing.

2

EXHAUST SYSTEM (PW50)

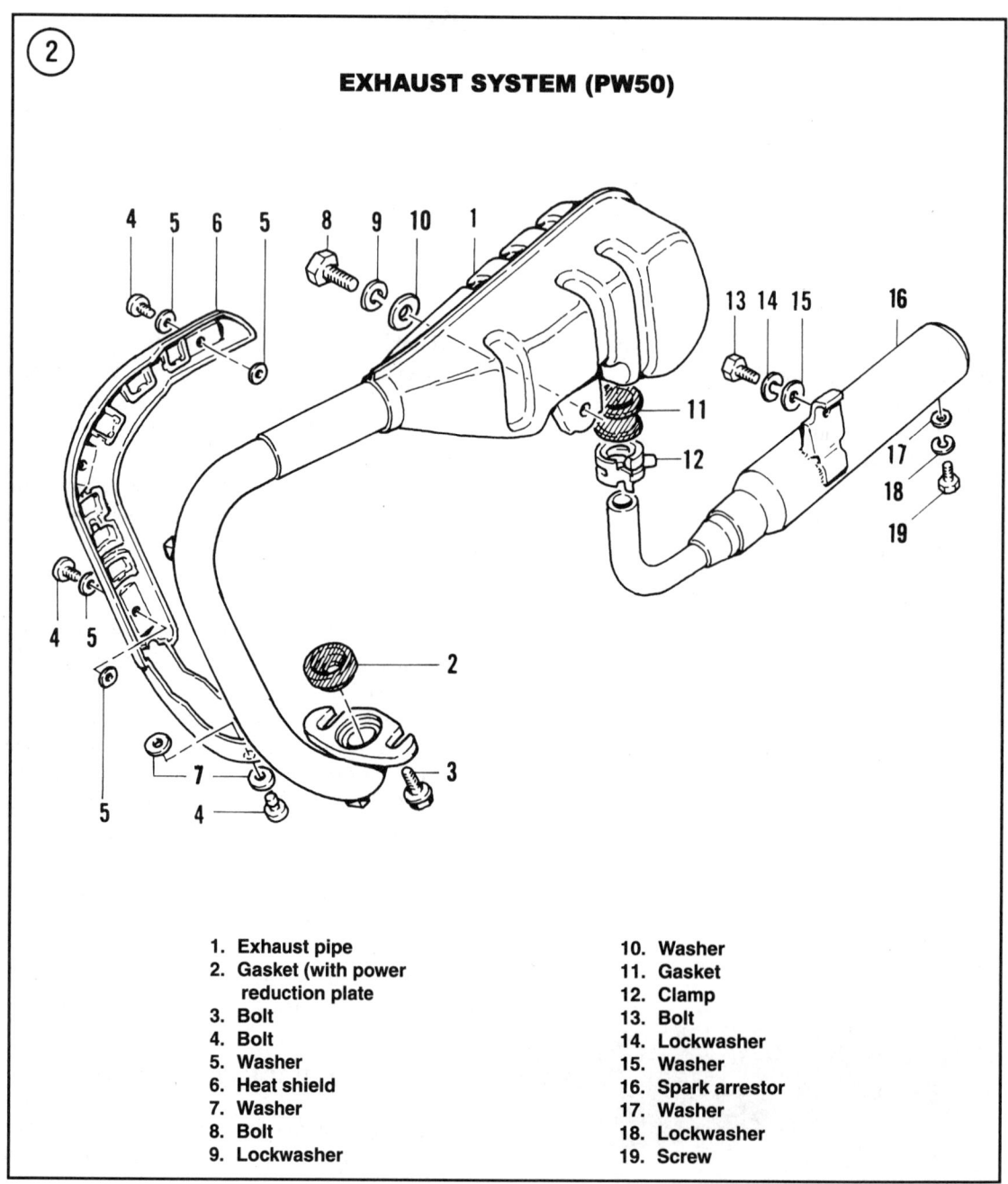

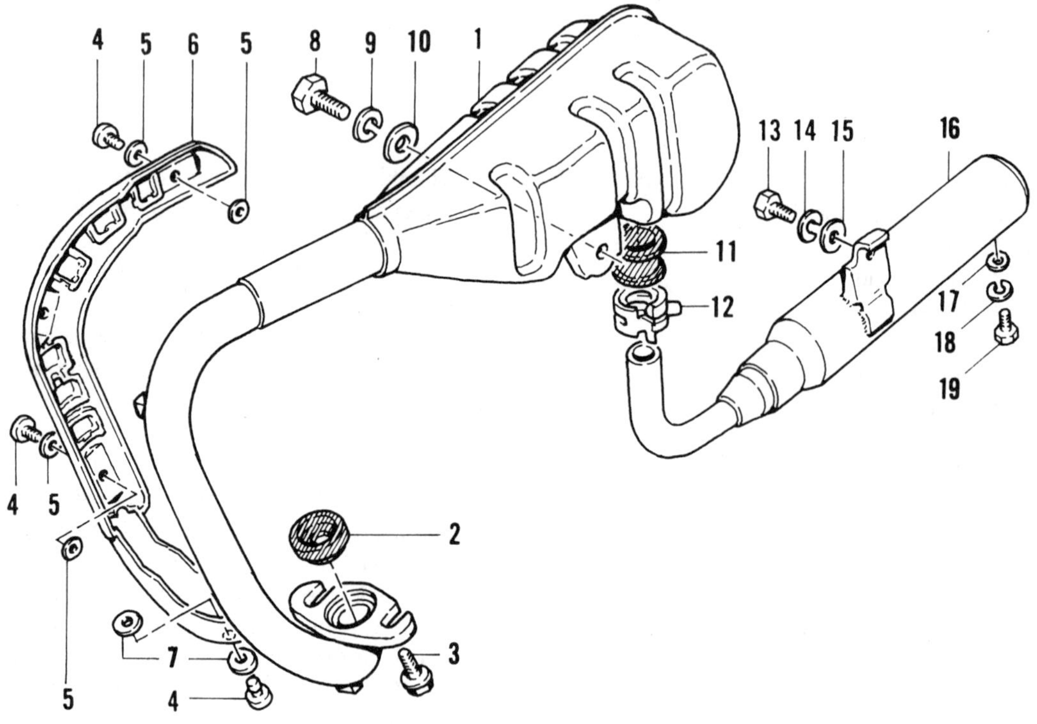

1. Exhaust pipe
2. Gasket (with power reduction plate
3. Bolt
4. Bolt
5. Washer
6. Heat shield
7. Washer
8. Bolt
9. Lockwasher
10. Washer
11. Gasket
12. Clamp
13. Bolt
14. Lockwasher
15. Washer
16. Spark arrestor
17. Washer
18. Lockwasher
19. Screw

The crankcase combines the engine top and lower end assemblies as well as the clutch, kickstarter and transmission assembly. Where the engine top and lower end assemblies operate, the crankcase must be airtight.

The engine top and bottom end assemblies are lubricated by the Autolube oil injection pump. The clutch and transmission assemblies are lubricated by the transmission oil added through the oil fill hole on the right crankcase cover.

ENGINE LUBRICATION

The PW50 2-stroke engine is lubricated by the Yamaha Autolube oil injection system. Oil is injected into the carburetor where it mixes with the air/fuel mixture before entering the engine. The oil is burned with the fuel and expelled through the exhaust. The engine top and bottom end components are lubricated by this oil, which clings to the various parts as it passes through the crankcase and cylinder. This oil is not reused and the amount of oil in the oil tank will diminish as the oil is being used during engine operation.

Check the oil level in the oil tank daily and whenever refueling the vehicle. Refer to Chapter Three for oil tank refilling. Refer to Chapter Nine for Autolube pump service.

CLEANLINESS

Repairs go much faster and easier if your engine is clean before you begin work. When servicing the engine top end with the engine installed in the frame, dirt trapped underneath the fuel tank and upper frame tube can fall into the cylinder or crankcase opening; remove the fuel tank and wrap the frame tube with a large, clean cloth.

EXHAUST SYSTEM

The exhaust system (**Figure 2**) includes the exhaust pipe/muffler, heat shield, power reduction plate (if used), and a Yamaha-Krizman type spark arrester.

The exhaust pipe is not a tuned exhaust system, but instead, a combination exhaust pipe and muffler assembly. Fiberglass is packed around the inside of the exhaust pipe to help reduce noise. This fiberglass packing is not replaceable.

The spark arrestor helps eliminate the danger of fire when the motorcycle is ridden off-road. As the exhaust gas travels through the exhaust pipe, solid pieces of carbon, knocked loose from the engine and exhaust pipe, are carried with it. Because some of these carbon particles are red-hot, they must be trapped inside the exhaust system. If not, a grass or forest fire could result. The Krizman type spark arrestor uses swirl vanes or blades that force the exhaust gases to swirl as they pass through the spark arrester. During this swirling action, centrifugal force throws the carbon particles to the outside of the spark arrestor where they are caught in a special trap. When you remove a spark arrestor and shake it, you can hear the carbon particles moving around in the trap. Because the spark arrestor gradually fills with carbon, it must be cleaned regularly. If not, the carbon particles will build to a point where some will be forced to pass through the spark arrester. Never run the motorcycle with a damaged or improperly installed spark arrester, or with the spark arrestor removed from the exhaust system.

Periodically check the exhaust pipe and spark arrestor for loose or missing fasteners. Loose mounting bolts will allow the pipe and spark arrestor to rattle and vibrate. This increases engine noise and will eventually cause damage to the exhaust pipe and its mounting brackets. An exhaust leak between the exhaust pipe and cylinder will leave a messy residue of oil, rob the engine of power, and can cause engine damage.

Exhaust pipe decarbonization and spark arrestor cleaning intervals are listed in Chapter Three (**Table 1**). Clean the exhaust pipe assembly at these intervals to ensure good performance.

Power Reduction Plate

Because the PW50 is designed for young riders, it is critical to limit the speed of the motorcycle to match the rider's skill and experience. The PW50 is equipped with two safety devices: a power reduction plate (governor) and a speed limiter on the throttle housing. The speed limiter is discussed in Chapter Three.

The power reduction plate (**Figure 3**) is located between the exhaust port and exhaust pipe. Consisting of a round plate with a small hole, it effectively blocks off most of the exhaust port opening to reduce the power output of the engine. The power reduction plate is mounted to the exhaust pipe gasket and can be separated from the gasket at a suitable time determined by the rider's parent or guardian. See the PW50 owner's service manual for more information on both safety devices.

Removal

WARNING
A hot exhaust pipe and spark arrestor can cause serious burns. Do not touch or service the exhaust pipe assembly until it cools off.

1. Support the bike on its centerstand.
2. Remove the bolt, lockwasher and flat washer (A, **Figure 4**) securing the spark arrestor to the rear arm. Then pull the spark arrestor down to disconnect it from the exhaust pipe (B, **Figure 4**) and remove it from the bike. See **Figure 5**.
3. Loosen the rear exhaust pipe mounting bolt (**Figure 6**).
4. Remove the 2 exhaust pipe mounting bolts at the cylinder (**Figure 7**).
5. Remove the rear exhaust pipe mounting bolt (**Figure 6**), then slide the exhaust pipe forward and remove it from between the frame and engine.
6. Remove the exhaust pipe gasket (**Figure 8**) from the exhaust pipe or exhaust port. If the gasket is stuck, remove it with a thin-bladed screwdriver.

Inspection

1. Service the spark arrestor as described under *Spark Arrestor Cleaning* in this section.
2. Check the exhaust pipe (**Figure 9**) for cracks, leaks or a damaged mounting bracket. Make sure the welded bracket at the front of the pipe is tight. Refer exhaust pipe repair to a welding repair shop.
3. Rap the exhaust pipe with a plastic or rubber hammer to break loose some of the carbon stuck to the inside pipe walls. Be careful not to dent or damage the exhaust pipe.
4. Clean oil and carbon built up in the front of the exhaust pipe with a scraper.
5. Check that the heat shield (**Figure 10**) is in place and that all of its mounting screws are tight. Tighten the screws to the torque specification in **Table 6**.
6. Inspect the exhaust pipe-to-spark arrestor gasket (**Figure 11**) and replace if worn or damaged.

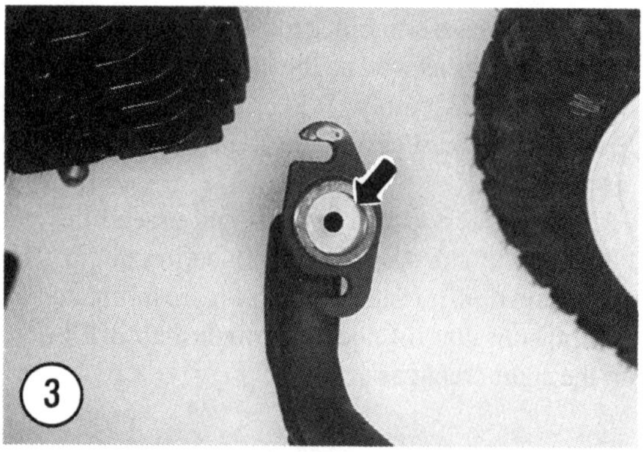
3

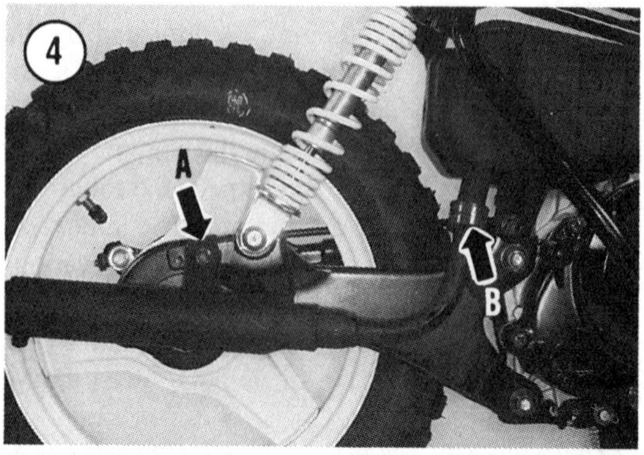

4

5

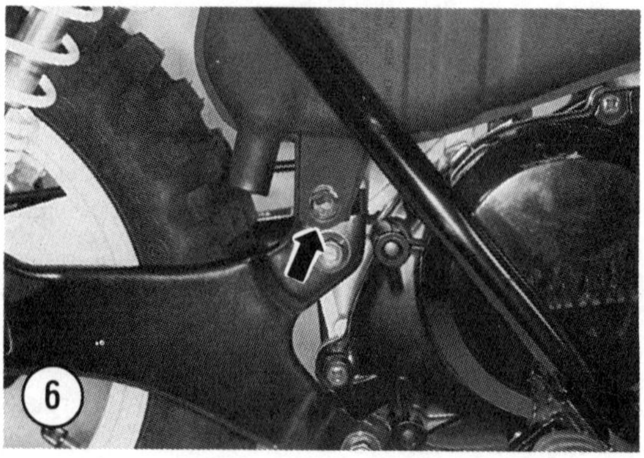
6

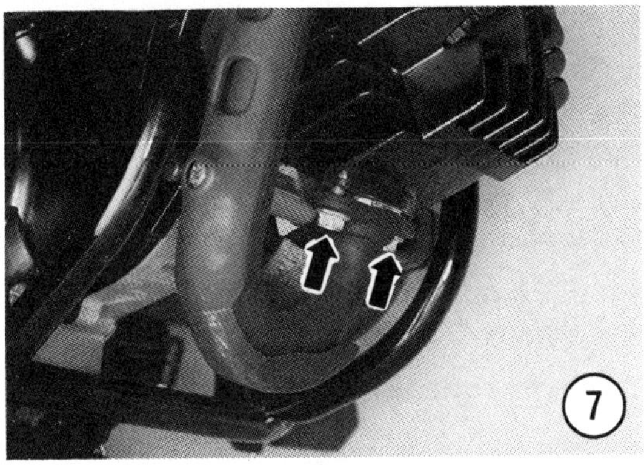

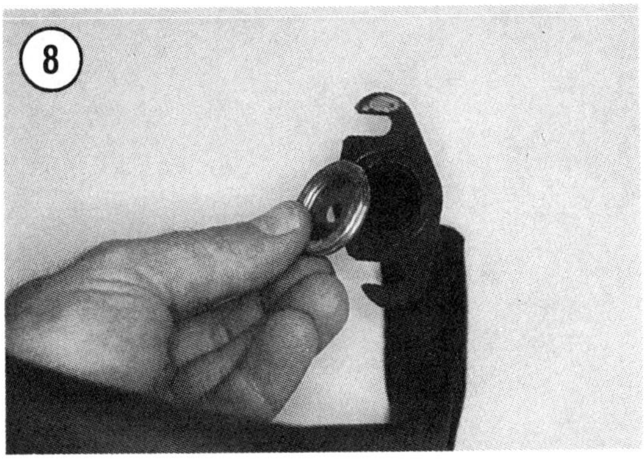

7. Replace the exhaust pipe gasket (**Figure 8**) if leaking or damaged.

NOTE
A power reduction plate is installed on OEM replacement exhaust pipe gaskets.

Spark Arrestor Cleaning

Refer to **Figure 12** for this procedure.

NOTE
It may be easier to remove the spark arrestor baffle with the spark arrestor mounted on the bike.

WARNING
A hot exhaust pipe and spark arrestor can cause a serious burn. Do not touch or service the exhaust pipe assembly until it cools off.

1. Support the bike on its centerstand.
2. Rap the spark arrestor with a plastic or rubber hammer to loosen some of the carbon deposits in the

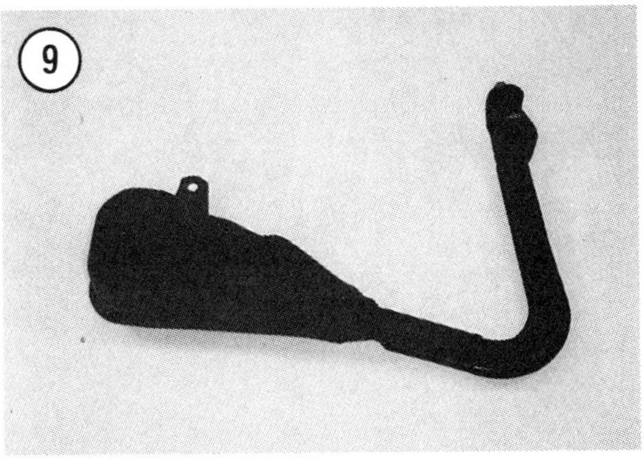

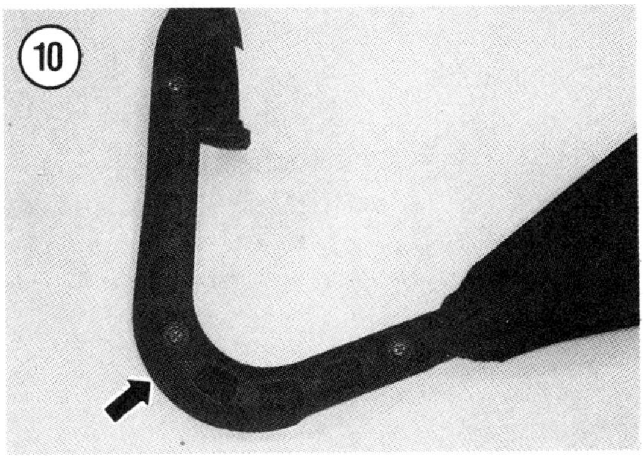

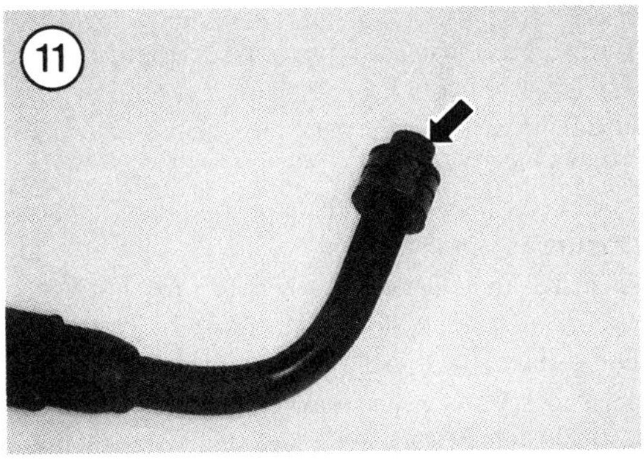

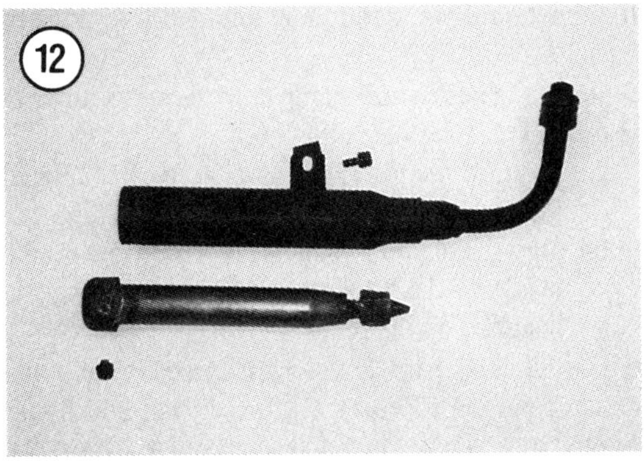

spark arrestor and its housing walls. Be careful not to dent or damage the silencer housing.

3. Remove the screw and washers (A, **Figure 13**), then twist and pull the baffle (B, **Figure 13**) out of its housing. If the baffle is stuck or rusted in place, remove it as described in Step 4.
4. Perform these steps to remove a stuck baffle:
   a. Assemble a slide hammer using a weight (or large socket), long bolt and flange nut as shown in **Figure 14**.
   b. Hook the flange nut against the inside of the baffle opening, then operate the slide hammer and pull the baffle out of its housing (**Figure 15**).
5. Remove the spark arrestor housing from the bike.
6. Initially clean the baffle and housing (**Figure 12**) with a scraper and stiff wire brush. Then clean the baffle and housing in solvent and dry thoroughly.
7. Inspect the baffle (**Figure 12**) for cracks or other damage.
8. Install the baffle into its housing, aligning the 2 mounting holes. Then install and tighten the screw and washers.

Installation

1. Install a new exhaust pipe gasket (**Figure 8**) into the exhaust pipe. If using the power reduction plate, install the gasket so the plate sets against the exhaust pipe and not the cylinder.
2. Loosely install the 2 exhaust pipe mounting bolts (**Figure 16**) into the cylinder.
3. Install the exhaust pipe between the frame and engine, then seat its bracket slots past the 2 mounting bolts. Make sure that the exhaust pipe gasket did not get knocked out of position.
4. Hold the exhaust pipe and hand-tighten the 2 mounting bolts (**Figure 7**), then install and hand-tighten the rear mounting bolt and washers (**Figure 6**).
5. Slide the gasket and clamp onto the spark arrestor (**Figure 11**). Note the following:
   a. Position the lower edge of the gasket against the raised knob on the spark arrestor tube.
   b. Turn the clamp so that its arms face toward the inside of the bike when the spark arrestor is installed on the bike.
6. Install the spark arrestor (**Figure 5**) onto the exhaust pipe (B, **Figure 4**), then install and hand-tighten its mounting bolt and washers (A, **Figure 4**).
7. Tighten the exhaust pipe fasteners in the following order:
   a. Tighten the front exhaust pipe mounting bolts (**Figure 7**) as specified in **Table 6**.
   b. Tighten the rear exhaust pipe mounting bolt (**Figure 6**) securely.
   c. Tighten the spark arrestor mounting bolt (A, **Figure 4**) as specified in **Table 6**.
8. Start the engine and check for exhaust leaks.

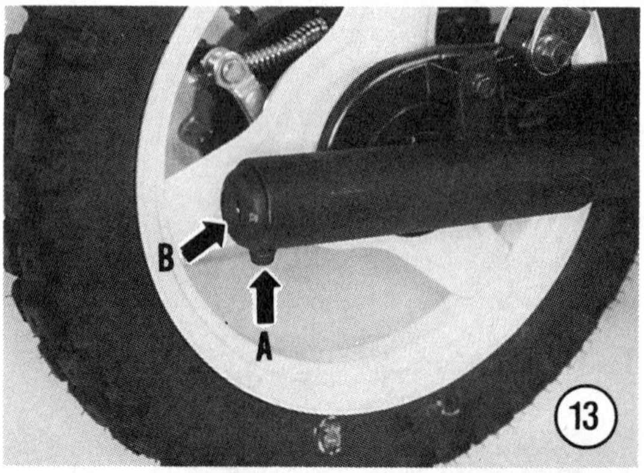

ENGINE

This section describes 2 procedures to remove and install the engine. Follow the procedure that best describes the type of service that will be performed to the motorcycle. Note the following:

a. Procedure I: This procedure separates the engine from the final drive unit,then removes it from the frame. Follow this procedure if transmission service or engine disassembly is required.
b. Procedure II: This procedure removes the engine from the frame without disconnecting the final drive unit from the engine. The engine can then be worked on while it is supported by its centerstand, drive shaft and rear wheel assembly. Follow this procedure if servicing the clutch, kickstarter or primary drive gear assembly (parts mounted behind the right crankcase cover).

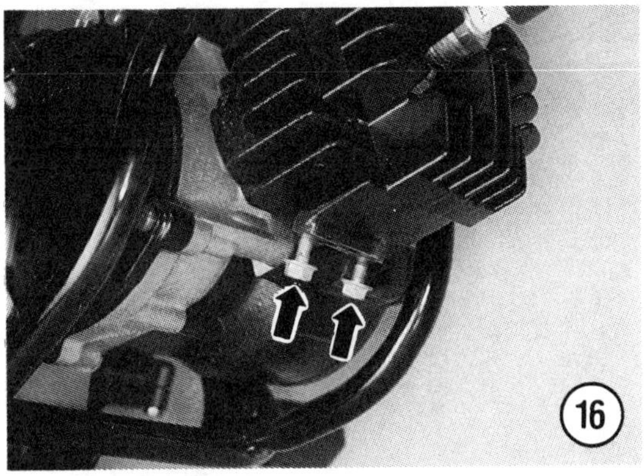

16

17

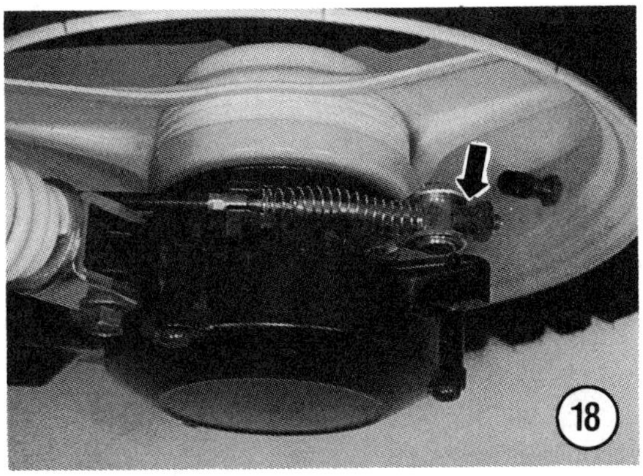

18

Engine Removal (Procedure I)

1. Support the bike on its centerstand.
2. If the clutch or engine is going to be disassembled, drain the transmission oil (Chapter Three).
3. Remove the seat (Chapter Fifteen).
4. Remove the fuel tank (Chapter Seven).
5. Remove the carburetor (Chapter Seven).
6. Remove the exhaust system as described in this chapter.

7A. Remove the flywheel and stator plate, if necessary, as described in Chapter Eight.

7B. If the flywheel and stator plate are not going to be removed, disconnect the stator plate electrical connectors (**Figure 17**) from the left side of the engine.

8. Disconnect the spark plug wire at the spark plug.
9. Support the bike with a stand placed in front of the centerstand, then raise the centerstand. Tie the front of the bike down so that it cannot pivot backwards.

NOTE
Steps 10-16 describe removal of the rear wheel and drive shaft assembly.

10. Disconnect the rear brake cable (**Figure 18**) from the rear hub.
11. Remove the 2 rear arm nuts and washers (**Figure 19**).
12. Remove the screw (A, **Figure 20**), washer and plate (B, **Figure 20**) from the engine.
13. Remove the 2 rear arm mounting bolts (**Figure 21**) from the crankcase.
14. Remove the upper bolt and washer (**Figure 22**) from each shock absorber. Do not pull the shock absorbers off of their frame mounts at this time.

15. Remove the 3 drive shaft bolts and washers (**Figure 23**) at the engine.

NOTE
Reroute the rear brake cable so that it will not grab onto the rear arm assembly in the following steps.

16. Slide both shock absorbers off of their upper frame mount (A, **Figure 24**), then pull the rear wheel and drive shaft assembly back and remove it from the frame. At the same time, the drive shaft will disconnect from the engine. See **Figure 25**.

17. Remove the centerstand assembly (**Figure 26**) as follows:

WARNING
*A high-tension spring (**Figure 27**) is used on the centerstand assembly. To prevent eye injury from a flying spring or tool, wear safety glasses when removing and installing the spring.*

a. Hook a spring removal tool onto the spring, then disconnect it from the centerstand.
b. Remove the hitch pin and flat washer (**Figure 28**) from the pivot shaft.
c. Push the pivot shaft out and remove the centerstand.

18. Remove the oil pump by performing the following steps:

a. Remove the screw cover from the rear of the oil pump.

NOTE
Unless you are going to service the oil pump, it is not necessary to disconnect the hoses or cable from the pump.

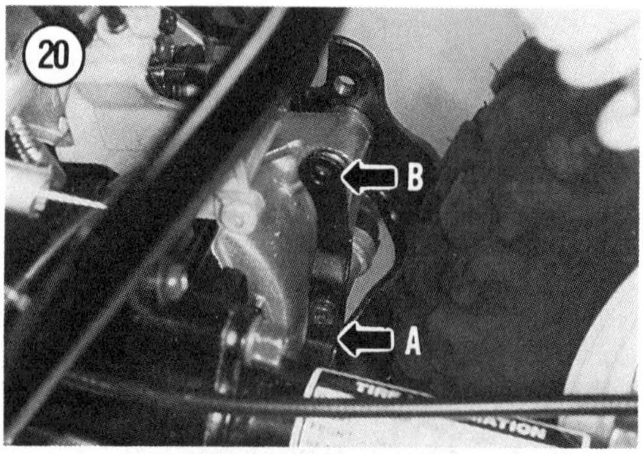

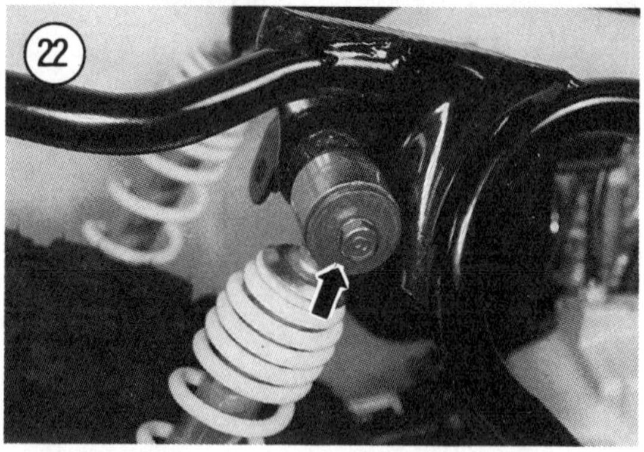

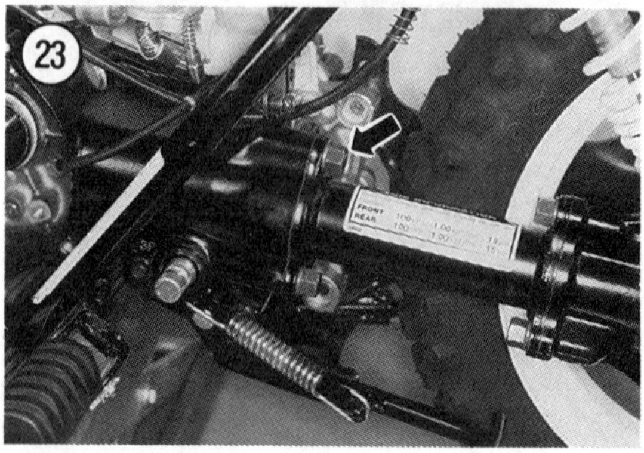

b. Remove the 2 Phillips screws (**Figure 29**) securing the oil pump to the engine.

c. Remove the oil pump from the engine together with its cover (**Figure 30**). Tie the oil pump against the frame.

19. Check the engine to make sure there are no hoses or cables attached to it.

20. If the flywheel was removed, either reinstall the flywheel cover or thread the flywheel nut (A, **Figure 31**) onto the end of the crankshaft to protect the crankshaft threads from damage.

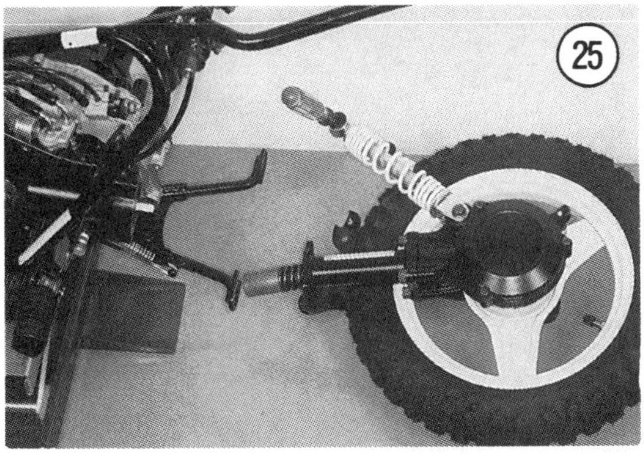

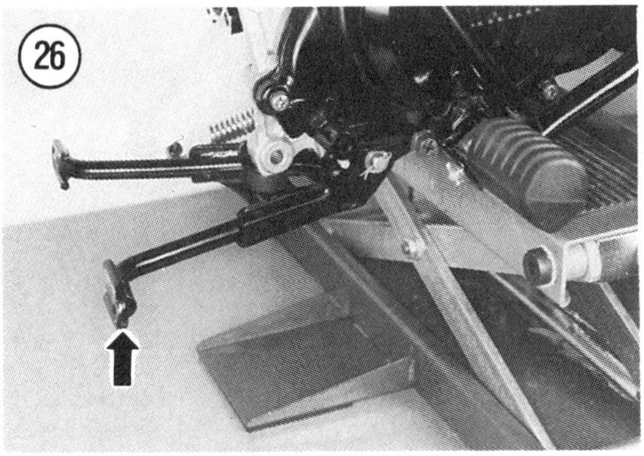

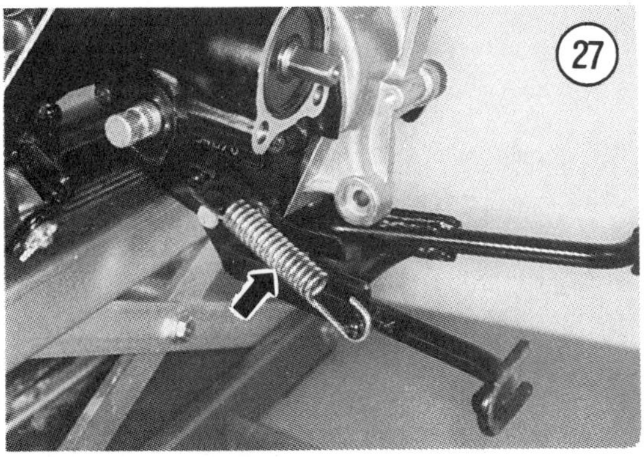

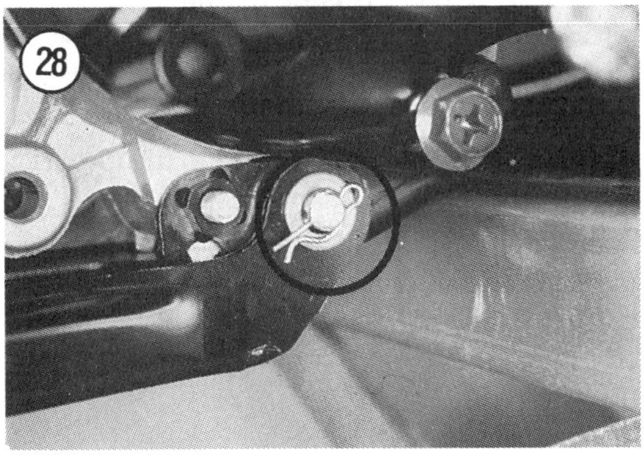

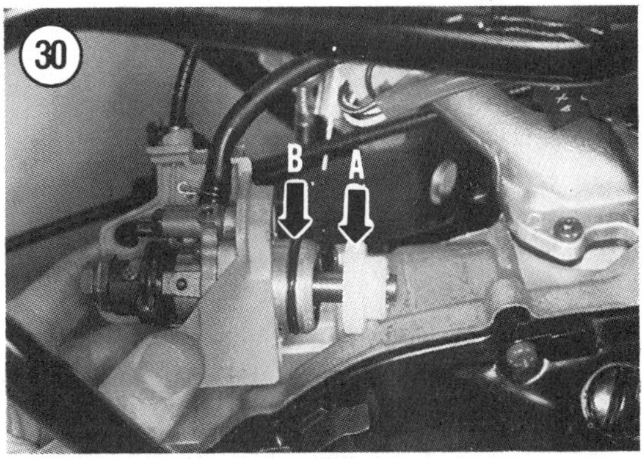

21. Remove the pivot shaft nut (**Figure 32**) from the right side of the engine.

22. Remove the pivot shaft (B, **Figure 31**), then remove the engine through the rear of the frame. See **Figure 33**.

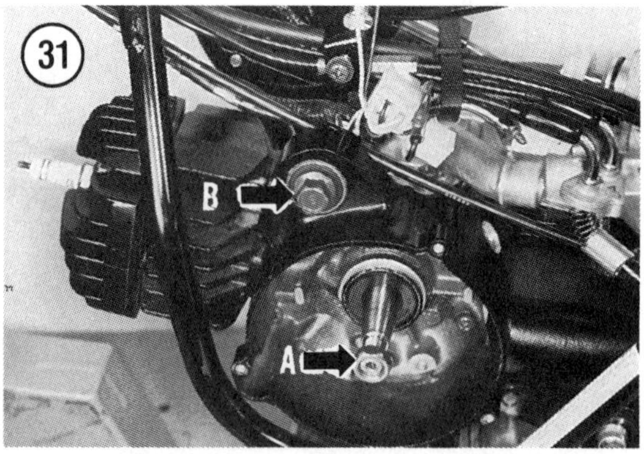

31

32

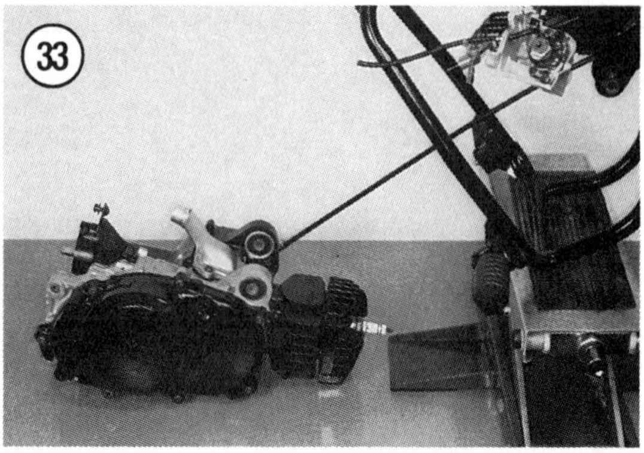
33

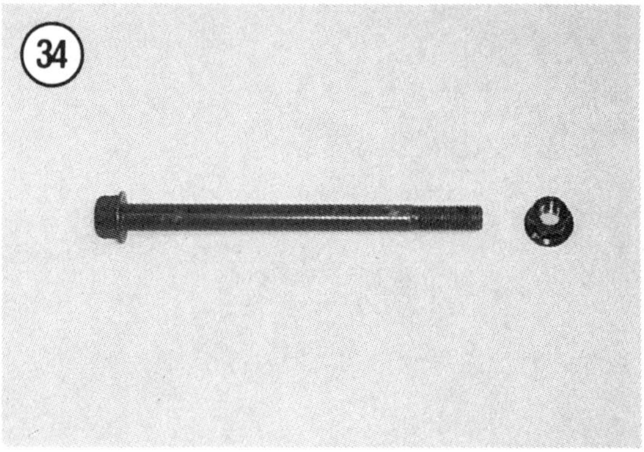
34

Inspection (Procedure I)

1. Clean and inspect the pivot shaft and nut (**Figure 34**). Replace if bent or damaged.

2. Inspect the frame (**Figure 35**) for any cracks or other damage. Check the pivot shaft area on the frame for cracks or severe wear. Refer repair to a welding shop familiar with motorcycle frame repair.

3. Clean all of the disconnected electrical connectors with a spray type electrical contact cleaner.

4. Replace all damaged fasteners before installing the engine in the frame. Fasteners with rounded-off heads or damaged threads cannot be tightened properly.

Engine Installation (Procedure I)

1. Position the engine in the frame, then install the pivot shaft (B, **Figure 31**) from the left side of the engine. Install the pivot shaft nut (**Figure 32**) and tighten hand-tight.

2. Route the rear brake cable as follows:
   a. Route over the top of the pivot shaft.
   b. Route underneath and toward the outside of the air box bracket.
   c. Route underneath the intake manifold (**Figure 36**).

3. Install the oil pump as follows:

NOTE
If the oil pump was removed completely from the motorcycle, install it as described in Chapter Nine.

   a. Lubricate the O-ring (B, **Figure 30**) with engine oil.
   b. Install the oil pump (**Figure 30**) into the crankcase—engage the oil pump driven gear (A, **Figure 30**) with the oil pump drive gear mounted on the mainshaft. See A, **Figure 37**.

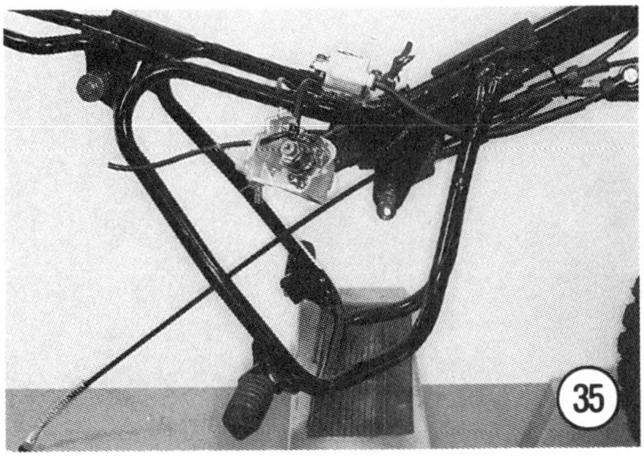

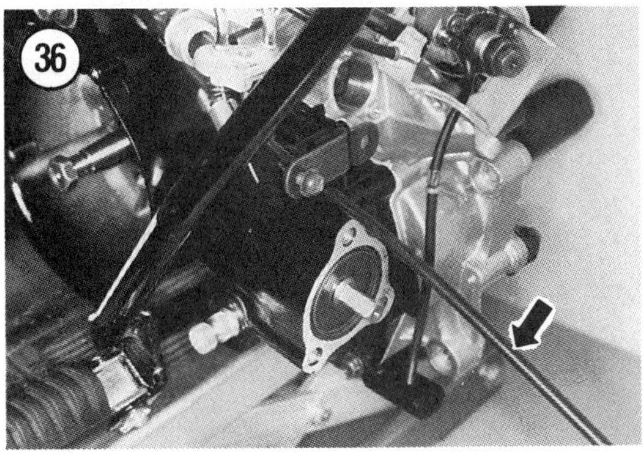

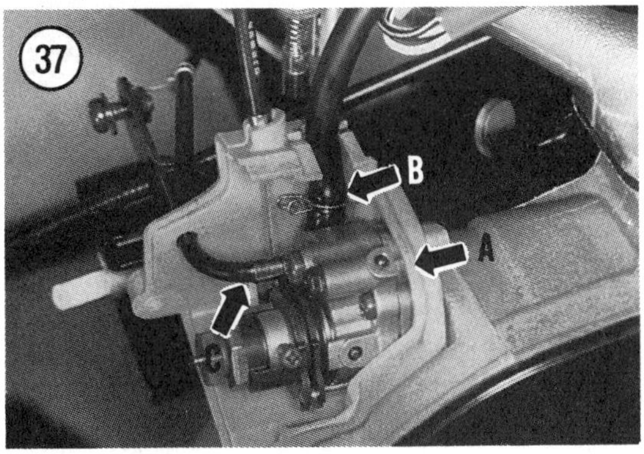

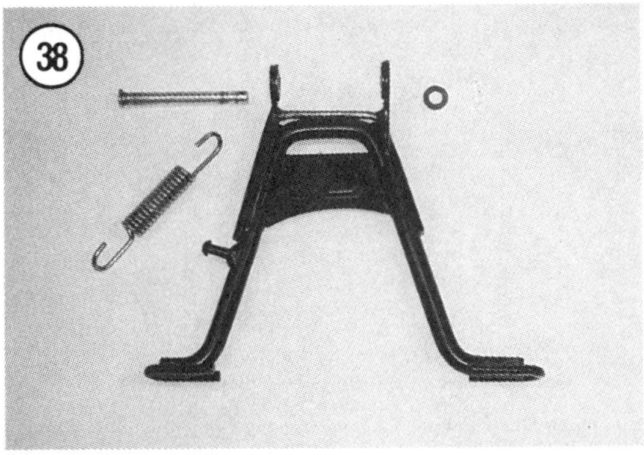

NOTE
You can see the oil pump drive gear through the large crankcase oil pump mounting hole.

c. Install and tighten the 2 oil pump mounting screws (**Figure 29**) as specified in **Table 6**.

d. Check that the oil delivery hose (from the oil tank [B, **Figure 37**]) and the oil discharge hose (C, **Figure 37**) are clamped to the correct oil pump hose nozzles.

4. Install the centerstand assembly (**Figure 38**) as follows:

a. Make sure the rubber damper is mounted on top of the centerstand.

b. Position the centerstand (A, **Figure 39**) on its mounting bracket, then install its pivot shaft (B, **Figure 39**) from the left side.

c. Install the flat washer onto the pivot shaft and secure it with its hitch pin (**Figure 28**).

CAUTION
*A high tension spring (**Figure 27**) is used on the centerstand assembly. To prevent eye injury from a flying spring or tool, wear safety glasses when installing the spring.*

d. Install the spring between the pin on the centerstand bracket and the pin on the centerstand (**Figure 27**).

e. Operate the centerstand to make sure the spring operates with sufficient spring tension to prevent the centerstand from dropping down while the motorcycle is being ridden. If the spring is weak, replace it.

WARNING
A weak or damaged spring will not keep the centerstand positioned up against the engine. If the centerstand falls as the motorcycle is being ridden, it could cause the rider to lose control.

NOTE
*Steps 5-13 describe installation of the drive shaft, rear arm, and rear wheel assembly (***Figure 40***).*

5. If removed, install the drive shaft into its housing—the long shoulder on the drive shaft (**Figure 41**) must face toward the engine. Install the square hole in the end of the drive shaft over the drive pinion shaft.

6. Lift the rear wheel assembly up, then slide the upper right side shock mount onto the upper frame mount as shown in **Figure 42**. Secure the shock with its flat washer and bolt.

7. Turn the rear wheel while watching the drive shaft; the drive shaft must turn at the same time. If not, engage the drive shaft with the drive pinion shaft.

8. Pivot the rear wheel assembly toward the left side, then install the drive shaft (A, **Figure 43**) over the driven pinion shaft while seating the drive shaft housing against the engine. If necessary, turn the rear wheel to align the parts.

9. Install the 3 mounting bolts (**Figure 44**), lockwashers and flat washers. Tighten each bolt hand-tight at this time.

10. Install the left side shock absorber over its frame mount, then install its washer and bolt. Tighten the bolt hand-tight.

11. Install the 2 rear arm mounting bolts (**Figure 45**) through the crankcase and rear arm (**Figure 46**),

41

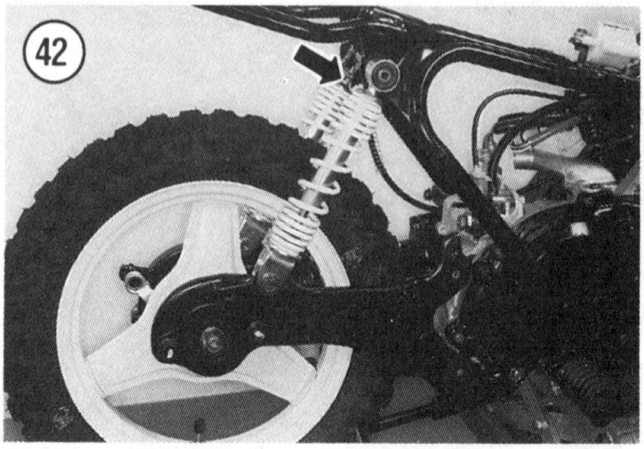
42

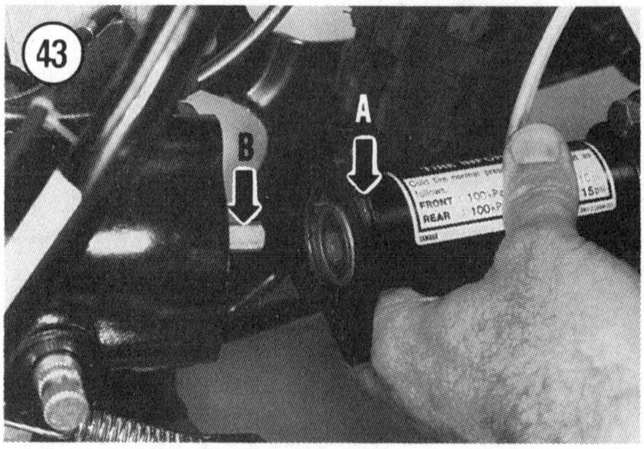

43

40

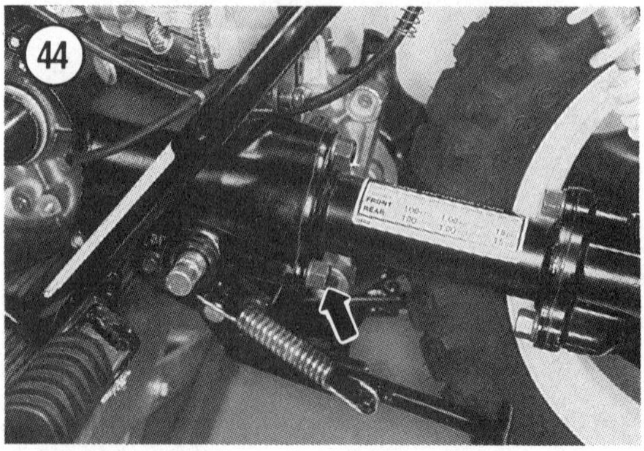
44

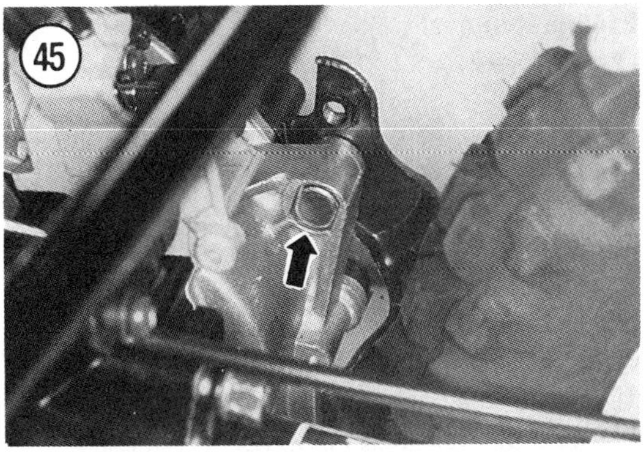

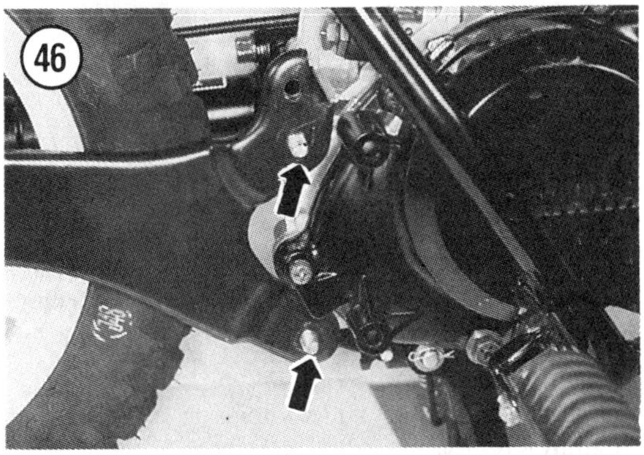

then install the washers and nuts. Tighten the nuts hand-tight.

12. Install the plate (A, **Figure 47**), washers and screw (B, **Figure 47**) at the back of the crankcase, then tighten the screw securely.

13. Tighten the following nuts and bolts as specified in **Table 6**.

a. Engine pivot shaft nut (**Figure 32**).

b. Drive shaft housing bolts (**Figure 44**).

NOTE
*A torque adapter (**Figure 48**) is required to tighten the drive shaft housing bolts accurately.*

c. Rear arm nuts (**Figure 49**).

d. Left and right side upper shock absorber mounting bolts.

14. Remove the workstand from underneath the bike, then support it with its centerstand.

15. Reconnect the rear brake cable at the rear hub as follows:

a. Slide the rear brake cable through the cable guide hole (A, **Figure 50**) on the rear hub.

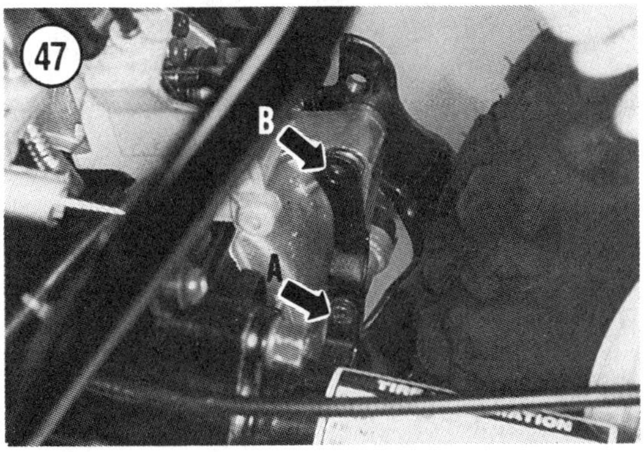

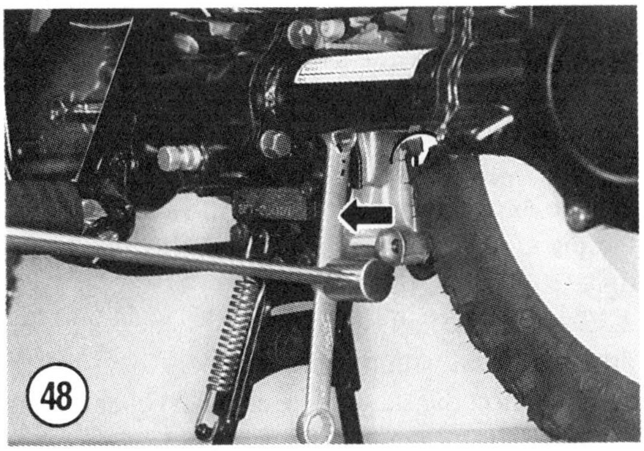

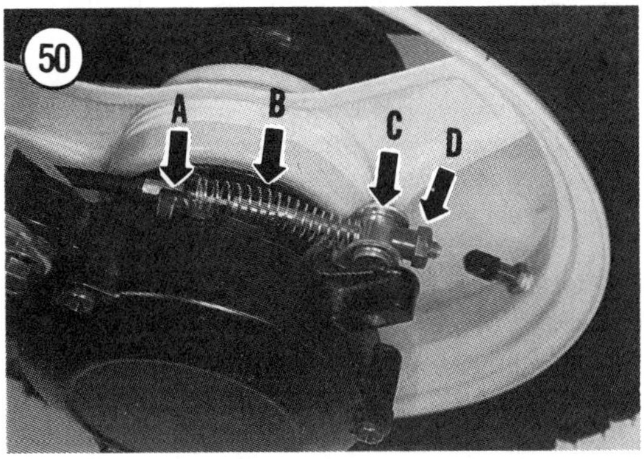

b. Install the return spring over the end of the cable and seat it against the hub's cable guide (B, **Figure 50**).
c. Install the pivot pin (C, **Figure 50**) in the brake arm, then apply the rear brake (to pull the cable forward) and slide the brake cable through the pivot pin.
d. Screw the adjust nut (concave side facing in) onto the brake cable (D, **Figure 50**).
e. Adjust the rear brake as described in Chapter Three.

CAUTION
Overtightening the rear brake adjustment can cause brake drag.

16. Reconnect the spark plug cap at the spark plug.
17. If removed, install the stator plate and flywheel as described in Chapter Eight.
18. Reconnect the stator plate electrical connectors at the left side of the engine.
19. If necessary, refill the crankcase with the correct type and quantity of transmission oil as described in Chapter Three.
20. Install the carburetor as described in Chapter Seven.
21. Install the fuel tank as described in Chapter Seven.

WARNING
When bleeding the oil pump in Step 22, do not start and run the motorcycle in an enclosed area. The exhaust gases contain carbon monoxide, a colorless, tasteless, poisonous gas. Carbon monoxide levels build quickly in a small enclosed area and can cause unconsciousness and death in a short time.

22. Start the engine and bleed the oil pump as described in Chapter Nine.

WARNING
The engine will be hot after bleeding the oil pump. Do not install the exhaust system until after the engine cools.

23. Install the exhaust system as described in this chapter.
24. Install the seat.
25. Restart engine and check the exhaust system for leaks.

Engine Removal (Procedure 2)

This procedure allows the engine to be separated from the frame while it is still attached to the rear drive shaft, rear wheel and center stand assembly. These items support the engine while allowing easy access to the clutch, primary drive, kickstarter, and transmission assemblies mounted behind the clutch cover.

1. Support the bike on its centerstand.
2. Drain the transmission oil (Chapter Three).
3. Remove the exhaust system as described in this chapter.
4. Remove the rear arm (Chapter Twelve).
5. Disconnect the rear brake cable (**Figure 50**) from the brake lever at the rear wheel.
6. Remove the air box and carburetor (Chapter Seven).
7. Remove the oil pump (Chapter Nine).
8. Disconnect the stator plate electrical connectors from the main wiring harness mounted on the left side of the engine.
9. Remove the left side shock absorber lower mounting bolt at the drive shaft unit.
10. Remove the pivot shaft nut (**Figure 32**) from the right side of the engine.
11. Remove the pivot shaft (B, **Figure 31**) from the left side of the engine, then roll the frame and front wheel assembly away from the engine. See **Figure 51**.

Inspection (Procedure 2)

Perform the steps under *Inspection (Procedure 1)* in this section.

Engine Installation (Procedure 2)

1. Roll the frame and front wheel assembly over the engine (**Figure 51**), then install the pivot shaft (B, **Figure 31**) from the left side of the engine. Install the pivot shaft nut (**Figure 32**) and tighten hand-tight.
2. Connect the left side shock absorber onto the drive shaft unit with its mounting bolt.
3. Reconnect the stator plate electrical connectors.
4. Install the oil pump (Chapter Nine).

5. Install the carburetor and air box (Chapter Seven).
6. Install the rear arm as described in Chapter Twelve. Tighten its rear mounting nuts (**Figure 49**) at the engine hand-tight. Do not tighten the other fasteners at this time.
7. Tighten the following nuts and bolts as specified in **Table 6**:
   a. Engine pivot shaft nut (**Figure 32**).
   b. Rear arm nuts (**Figure 49**).
   c. Left shock absorber lower mounting bolt.
8. Reconnect the rear brake cable at the rear hub as follows:
   a. Slide the rear brake cable through the cable guide hole (A, **Figure 50**) on the rear hub.
   b. Install the return spring over the end of the cable and seat it against the hub's cable guide (B, **Figure 50**).
   c. Install the pivot pin (C, **Figure 50**) in the brake arm, then apply the rear brake (to pull the cable forward) and slide the brake cable through the pivot pin.
   d. Screw the adjust nut (concave side facing in) onto the brake cable (D, **Figure 50**).
   e. Adjust the rear brake as described in Chapter Three.

CAUTION
Overtightening the rear brake adjustment can cause brake drag.

9. Refill the crankcase with the correct type and quantity of transmission oil as described in Chapter Three.

WARNING
When bleeding the oil pump in Step 10, do not start and run the motorcycle in an enclosed area. The exhaust gases contain carbon monoxide, a colorless, tasteless, poisonous gas. Carbon monoxide levels build quickly in a small enclosed area and can cause unconsciousness and death in a short time.

10. Start the engine and bleed the oil pump as described in Chapter Nine.

4

51

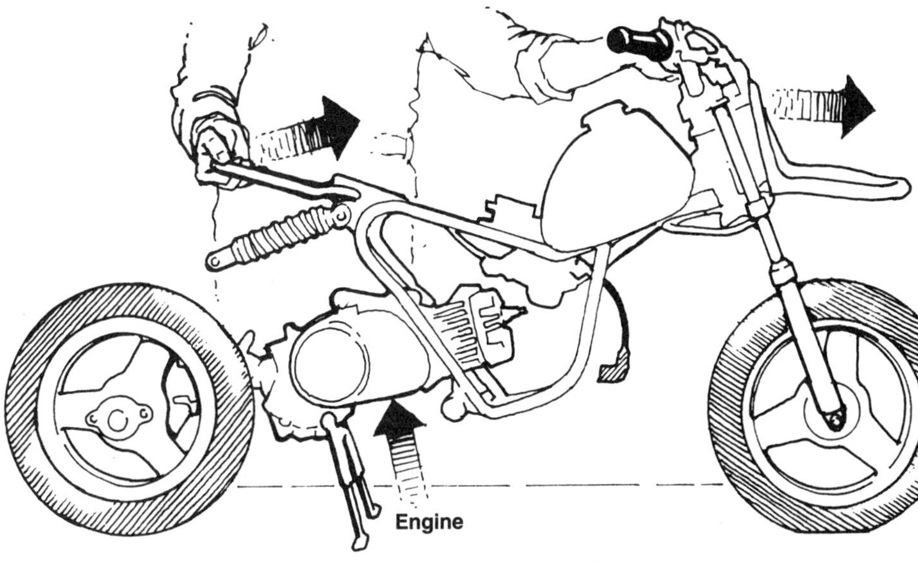

WARNING
The engine will be hot after bleeding the oil pump. Do not install the exhaust system until after the engine cools down.

11. Install the exhaust system as described in this chapter.
12. Restart engine and check the exhaust system for leaks.

CYLINDER HEAD

The cylinder head (**Figure 52**) can be removed with the engine mounted in the frame.

Before working on the top end, clean all dirt and grease from the outside of the engine and the frame area surrounding the cylinder head.

Removal

CAUTION
To avoid possible warping of the cylinder head, wait until the engine has cooled before removing the cylinder head.

1. Remove the seat (Chapter Fifteen) and fuel tank (Chapter Seven).
2. Perform the *Two-Stroke Leak Down Test* described in Chapter Two to check for any cylinder head or other engine leaks.
3. Disconnect the spark plug wire at the plug, then loosen the spark plug.
4. Loosen the cylinder head nuts 1/4 turn at a time in a crisscross pattern. Then remove the nuts.
5. Remove the cylinder head (**Figure 53**).
6. Remove and discard the cylinder head gasket (**Figure 54**).
7. Lay a clean rag over the cylinder to prevent dirt from falling into the cylinder.
8. Inspect the cylinder head as described in this chapter.

52

ENGINE TOP END

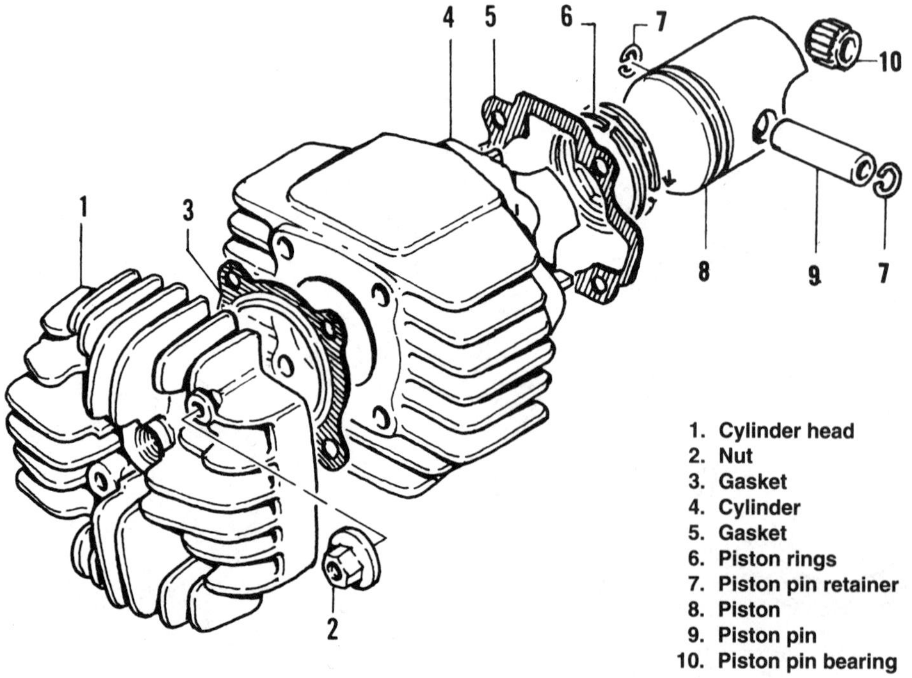

1. Cylinder head
2. Nut
3. Gasket
4. Cylinder
5. Gasket
6. Piston rings
7. Piston pin retainer
8. Piston
9. Piston pin
10. Piston pin bearing

53

54

55

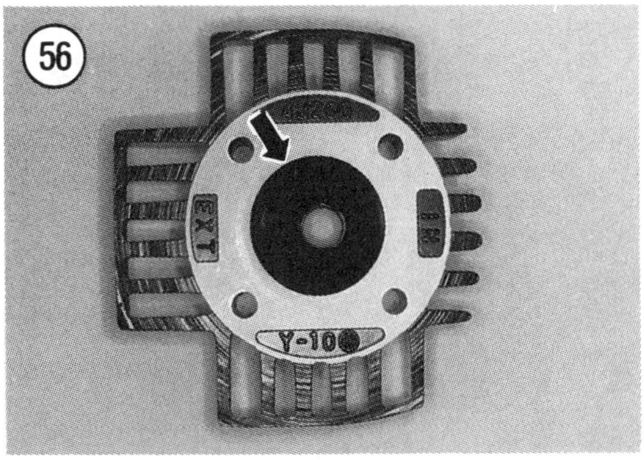

56

Inspection

1. Check the cylinder head for cracked or missing cooling fins (A, **Figure 55**). Refer repair to your dealership or a welding shop.

CAUTION

Damaged or missing cylinder head cooling fins can cause the engine to run hot. Repair or replace the cylinder head before running the engine.

CAUTION

Do not gouge the gasket or combustion chamber surfaces when cleaning the cylinder head in Step 2. Burrs created from improper cleaning may cause compression loss, preignition, or heat erosion.

2. Wipe away any soft deposits on the cylinder head combustion chamber (**Figure 56**). Remove hard deposits with a wire brush mounted in a drill or drill press, or with a soft metal scraper.
3. Remove the spark plug and check the cylinder head threads (B, **Figure 55**) for carbon buildup or thread damage. Use a spark plug tap to clean or repair slightly damaged threads. If thread damage is severe, install new threads with a thread repair kit.
4. Measure the cylinder head flatness with a straightedge and feeler gauge (**Figure 57**). If the cylinder head warpage exceeds the service limit in **Table 2**, resurface the head as follows:
   a. Tape a piece of 400-600 grit wet emery sandpaper onto a piece of thick plate glass or surface plate (**Figure 58**).
   b. Slowly resurface the head by moving it in figure-eight patterns on the emery sandpaper.

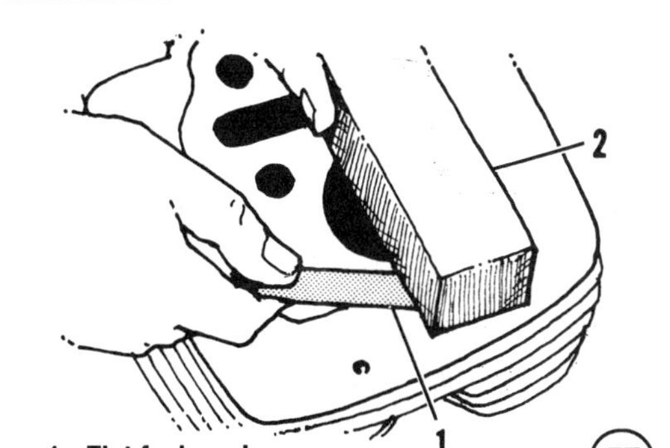

1. **Flat feeler edge**
2. **Straightedge**

57

c. Rotate the head several times to avoid removing too much material from one side. Check the progress often with the straightedge and feeler gauge.
d. If the cylinder head warpage still exceeds the service limit, take the cylinder head to your dealership for further inspection and repair, or replace the cylinder head.

5. Clean and inspect the cylinder head nuts. Replace nuts with damaged threads or rounded off hex corners.
6. Check for loose or damaged cylinder head studs. Replace or tighten studs as described in Chapter One.
7. Wash the cylinder head in hot soapy water and rinse with clean, cold water.

Installation

1. Clean and inspect the cylinder head as described under *Inspection* in this chapter.
2. Wipe the cylinder gasket surface with solvent and allow to air dry.
3. Install a new cylinder head gasket (**Figure 54**) over the cylinder studs.
4. Install the cylinder head as follows:
   a. The cylinder head is directional and can be installed backwards. Refer to the EXT and IN marks in the bottom of the cylinder head to identify cylinder head alignment.
   b. Install the cylinder head with its EXT mark (**Figure 59**) facing toward the front or exhaust side of the engine.

CAUTION
*The cylinder head is designed with more cooling fin area on the exhaust side of the engine (**Figure 59**). If the cylinder head is installed backward, cylinder head warpage and engine overheating may result.*

5. Install the cylinder head nuts and tighten finger-tight. Then tighten the nuts in a crisscross pattern and in two steps as follows:
   a. First tighten the cylinder head nuts to half of their torque specified in **Table 6**.
   b. Then tighten the cylinder head nuts to the final torque specified in **Table 6**.
   c. Go over each nut a final time to make sure none have been missed.

6. Install the spark plug and tighten as specified in **Table 6**. Reconnect the spark plug lead.
7. Install the fuel tank (Chapter Seven) and seat (Chapter Fifteen).
8. Perform the *2-Stroke Crankcase Pressure Test* in Chapter Two to check for engine leaks.
9. If a new major component of the upper or lower end was installed (piston, rings, connecting rod, etc.), perform the engine break-in procedure described in this chapter.

CYLINDER

The cylinder can be serviced with the engine mounted in the frame.

Refer to **Figure 52** when servicing the cylinder .

Removal

1. Remove the exhaust pipe as described in this chapter.
2. Remove the cylinder head as described in this chapter.

58

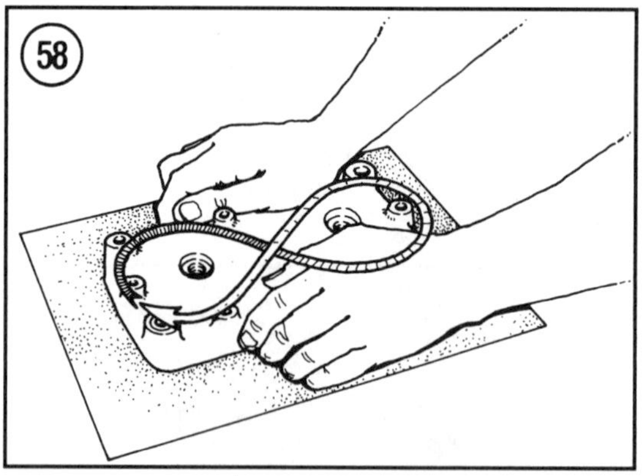

59

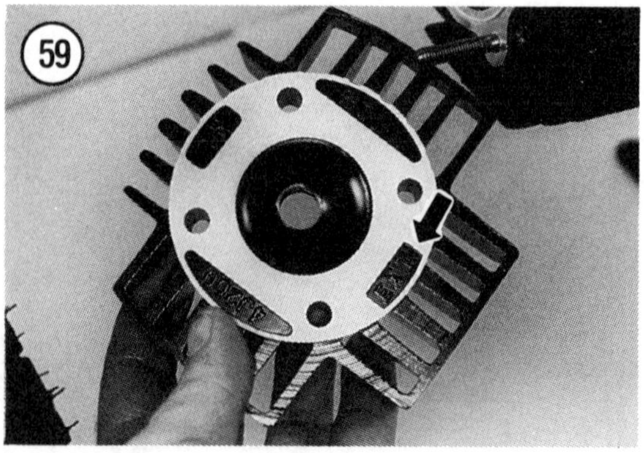

3. Tap the cylinder (**Figure 60**) to break its seal, then slide it off the piston and crankcase studs. If the cylinder is stuck to the crankcase or piston, do not pry it off as marks left between the mating surfaces could cause an air leak. Use a plastic or rubber hammer and carefully tap the cylinder loose.

NOTE
A seized piston or rusted and corroded cylinder bore will make it difficult to remove the cylinder. If the cylinder lifts off the crankcase, but is stuck to the piston, soak the piston crown and cylinder bore with a penetrating liquid. If the seizure or corrosion is severe, you may have to break the piston to separate it from the cylinder bore.

60

61

62

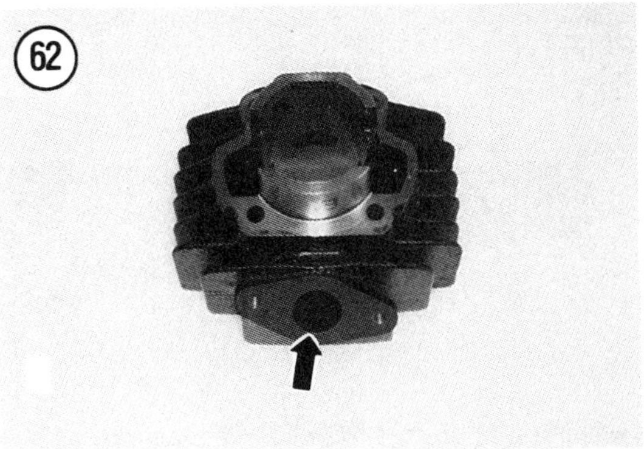

4. Slide a piece of hose (A, **Figure 61**) over both lower studs to protect the piston and rings from damage. Then stuff clean rags around the connecting rod to keep dirt and loose parts from entering the crankcase.

5. Remove and discard the cylinder base gasket.

6. Carefully scrape the crankcase to remove any base gasket residue. Be careful not to gouge the gasket surfaces.

Inspection

The original cylinder block uses a cast-iron liner. It can be bored to accept oversize pistons. Yamaha offers 2 oversize pistons.

A bore gauge and a 50-75 mm (2-3 in.) micrometer or an inside micrometer will be required to measure the cylinder bore accurately. If you do not have these tools, have the measurements performed by a dealership or qualified machine shop.

1. Remove all gasket and carbon residue from both cylinder gasket surfaces. Be careful not to gouge or damage the surfaces.

2. Remove hard carbon deposits from the exhaust port (**Figure 62**) with a drill mounted wire wheel or scraper. Be careful not to damage the cylinder bore or change the exhaust port chamfer.

NOTE
A good way to protect the cylinder bore when cleaning the exhaust port is to block off the exhaust port with an old piston or with a piece of plastic or cardboard.

3. Measure the cylinder bore with a bore gauge (**Figure 63**) or an inside micrometer at the 4 depth positions (A, B, C and D) shown in **Figure 64**. Except for the bottom measurement, measure both in line with the piston pin and at 90° to the pin. Note the following:

   a. Use the largest bore measurement to determine cylinder wear.
   b. Record measurements for cylinder wear, taper and out-of-round.

4

c. If the cylinder bore, taper or out-of-round measurement exceed the wear limits in **Table 2**, the cylinder bore must be rebored to the next oversize and fitted with a new piston.

4. To determine piston-to-cylinder clearance, refer to *Piston/Cylinder Clearance* in this chapter.

5. When installing new piston rings, hone the cylinder with a ball hone (**Figure 65**) to deglaze the cylinder and help the new rings to seat. If necessary, refer this service to a dealership or motorcycle repair shop.

6. After the cylinder has been bored or honed, the edges of the ports must be chamfered to prevent the rings from snagging a port. This service is usually performed by the machinist or technician after the cylinder machining operation. If you are doing the work yourself, use a fine cut file to chamfer the port as shown in **Figure 66**.

7. Before installing the cylinder, wash the bore in hot soapy water and rinse with clear water. Then check the bore cleanliness by running a white cloth over the bore surface. Repeat this wash process until the white cloth comes out clean—no smudge or dark marks.

8. Dry the cylinder with compressed air, then lubricate the bore with 2-stroke oil to prevent the liner from rusting.

Cylinder Installation

Make sure all engine parts are clean before starting assembly.

1. Clean the cylinder bore as described in this section.

2. Install a new base gasket (**Figure 67**).

3. If removed, install the piston as described in this chapter.

4. Lubricate the piston skirt, piston ring and cylinder bore with 2-stroke injection oil.

5. Check that the piston pin clips are seated in the piston grooves completely.

6. Center the piston ring end gaps around the piston ring locating pins as shown in B, **Figure 61**.

7. Compress the rings with your fingers and start the bottom edge of the cylinder over the piston (**Figure 68**). Then hold the piston and slide the cylinder down until it covers the rings. Continue to slide the cylinder down over the crankcase mounting studs, and seat it against the base gasket.

63

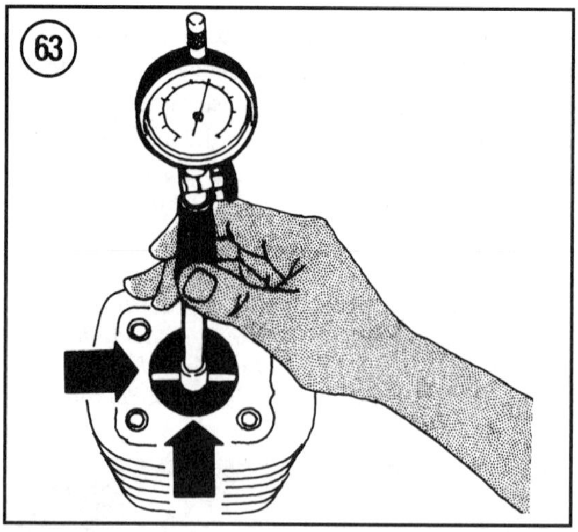

64

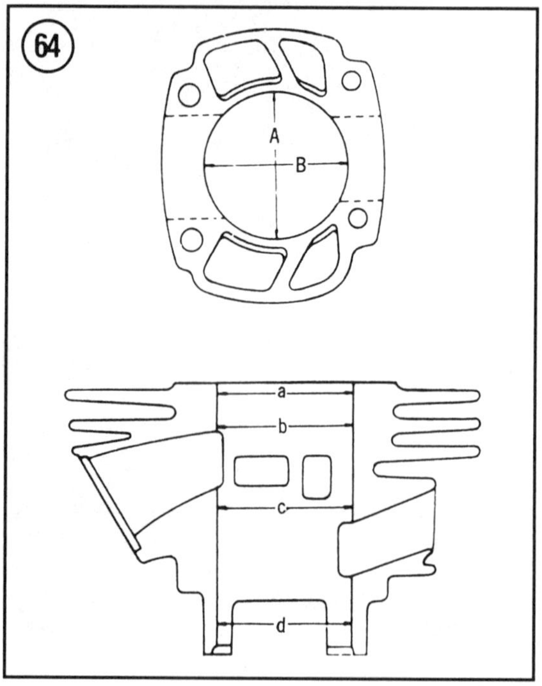

65

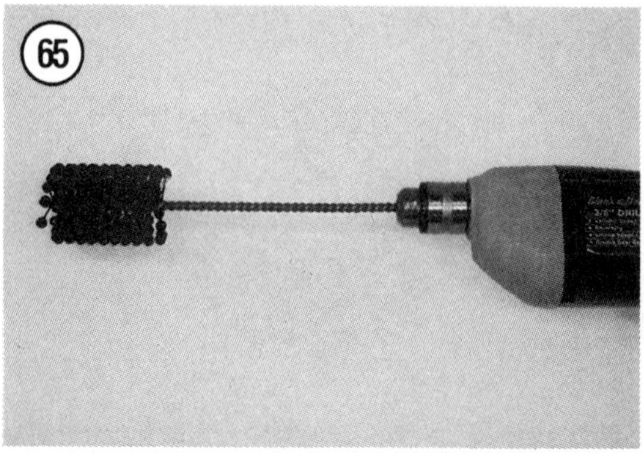

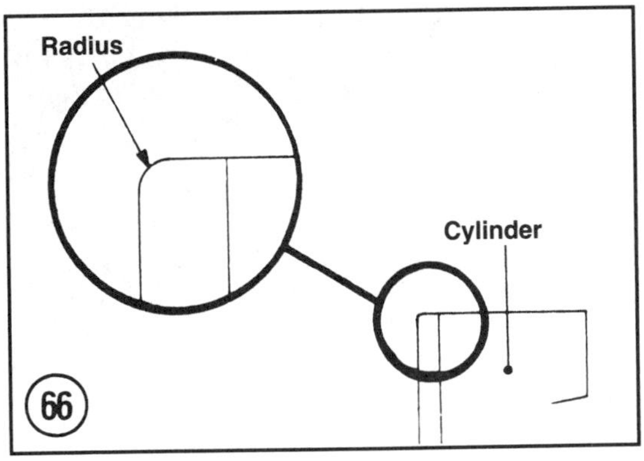

66

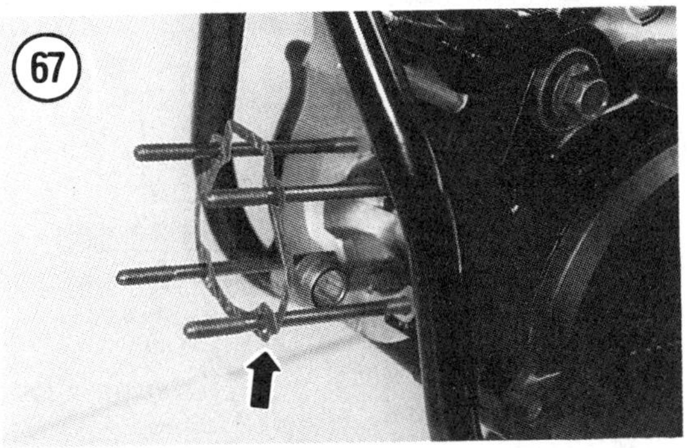

67

68

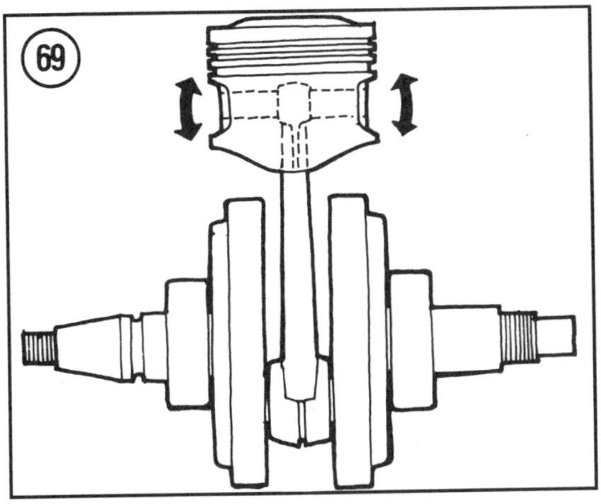

69

8. Hold the cylinder in place with one hand and operate the kickstarter lever with your other hand. If the piston catches or stops in the cylinder, one or both piston rings were not aligned properly. The piston must move up and down the cylinder bore smoothly.

NOTE
If the ring is not correctly aligned with the locating pins, remove the cylinder and check for damage. Reposition the piston rings correctly.

9. Install the head gasket and cylinder head as described in this chapter.
10. Perform the *Two-Stroke Crankcase Pressure Test* in Chapter Two to ensure that the engine is air tight.
11. Install the exhaust system as described in this chapter.
12. Follow the *Engine Break-In* procedure in this chapter if the cylinder was rebored or honed or a new piston or piston rings were installed.

PISTON, PISTON PIN AND PISTON RINGS

The piston is made of an aluminum alloy. The piston pin is a precision fit and is held in place by a clip at each end. A caged needle bearing is used on the small end of the connecting rod.

Piston and Piston Ring Removal

1. Remove the cylinder as described in this chapter.
2. Before removing the piston, hold the connecting rod tightly and rock the piston as shown in **Figure 69**. Any rocking motion (do not confuse with the normal side-to-side sliding motion) indicates wear of the piston pin, needle bearing, piston pin bore, or more likely a combination of all three. If there is any play, pay particular attention to the inspection of these items.
3. Wrap a clean shop cloth under the piston so that the clips cannot fall into the crankcase.

WARNING
Piston pin clips can slip and fly off forcefully during removal. Wear safety glasses to prevent eye injury.

4. Remove one or both piston pin clips with a pair of needlenose pliers (**Figure 70**). Hold your thumb

4

over one edge of the clip when removing it to help prevent it from springing out.

5. Hold the piston securely, then push the piston pin (**Figure 71**) out of the piston with a wooden dowel or socket extension.

CAUTION

The piston pin is a floating type and should slide out with only slight hand pressure. If the engine ran hot or seized, piston distortion may lock the piston pin in place, making it difficult to remove. If the piston pin is tight, do not drive it out of the piston. Doing so may damage the piston, needle bearing and connecting rod. To remove a stuck piston pin, use the tool and procedure described in Step 6.

6. If the piston pin is tight, remove it with a piston pin removal tool, or fabricate the tool shown in **Figure 72**. Assemble the tool onto the piston and pull the piston pin out of the piston. Install a pad between the piston and piece of pipe to prevent the tool from damaging the piston.

7. Lift the piston off the connecting rod.

8. Remove the needle bearing (**Figure 73**).

NOTE

*While the top (A, **Figure 74**) and bottom (B, **Figure 74**) piston rings have the same sectional dimensions (**Table 3**), their outer coating materials are different. If the piston rings are going to be reused, identify them for reassembly.*

9. Remove the upper piston ring by spreading the ring ends with your thumbs just enough to slide the ring up over the piston (**Figure 75**).

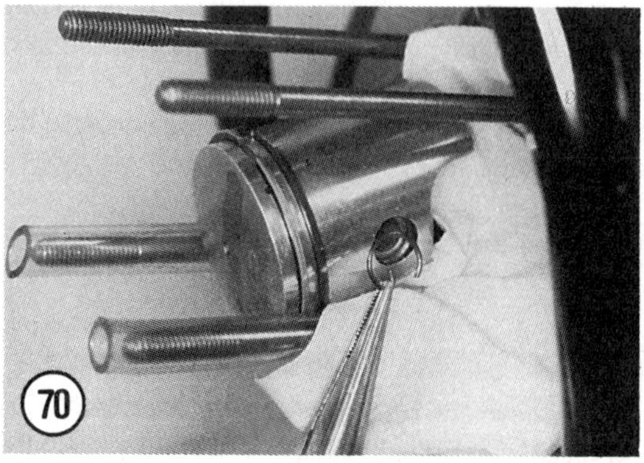
70

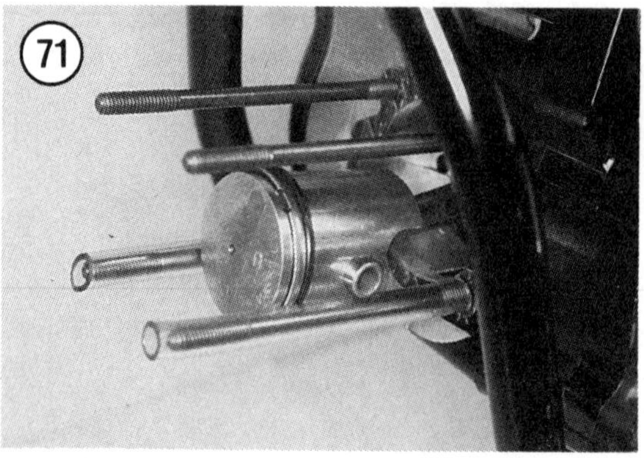
71

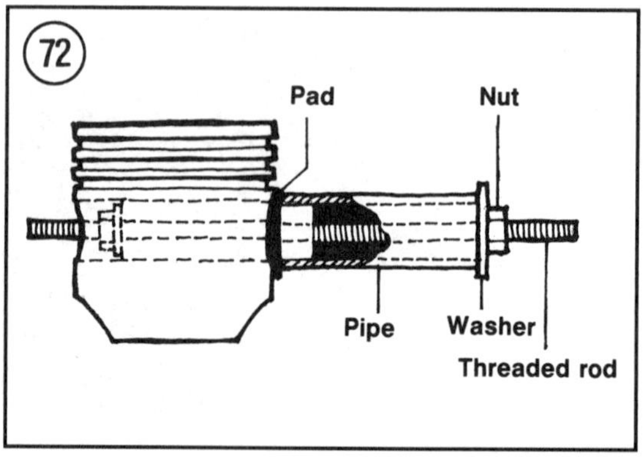

72

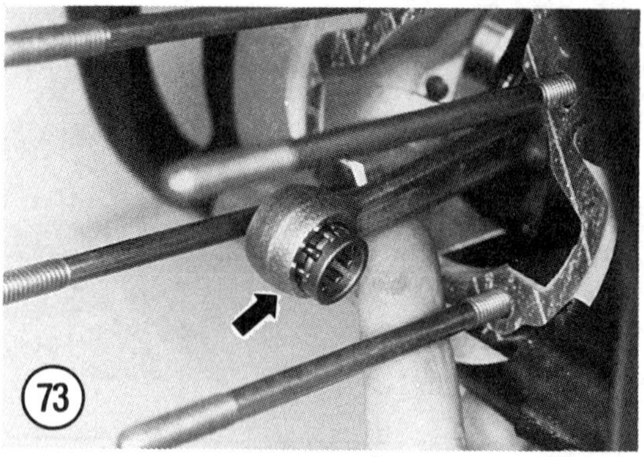
73

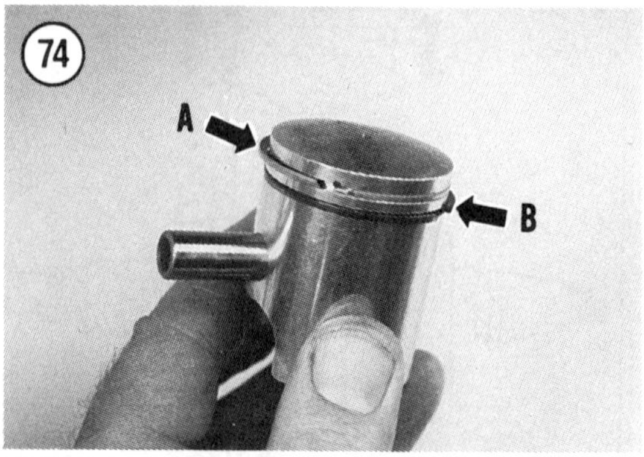

74

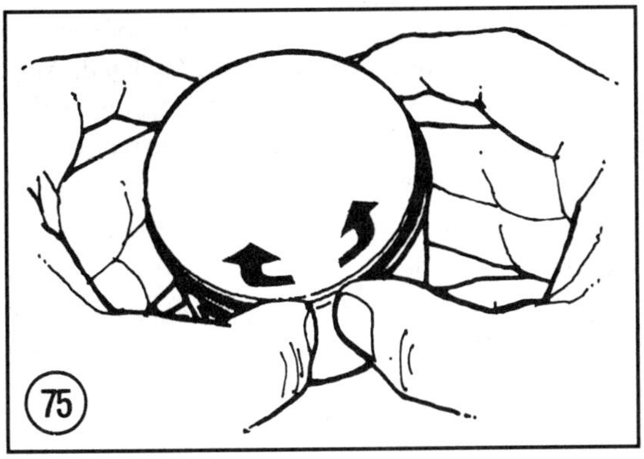

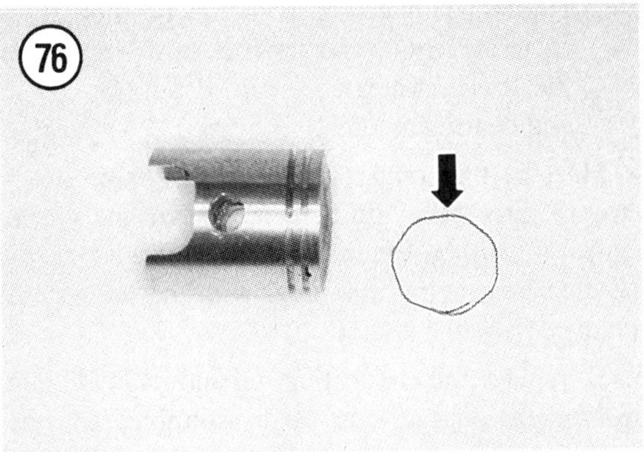

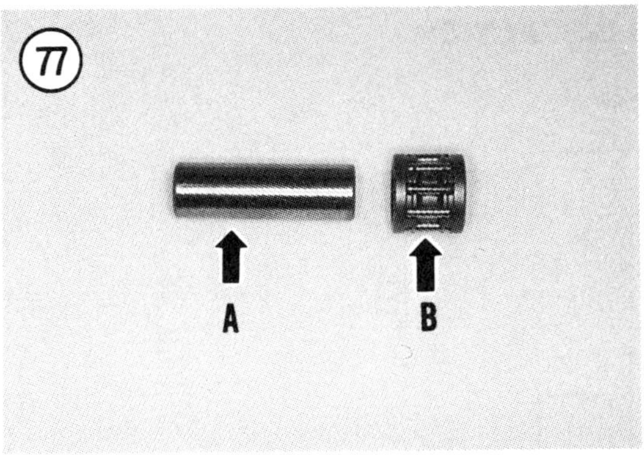

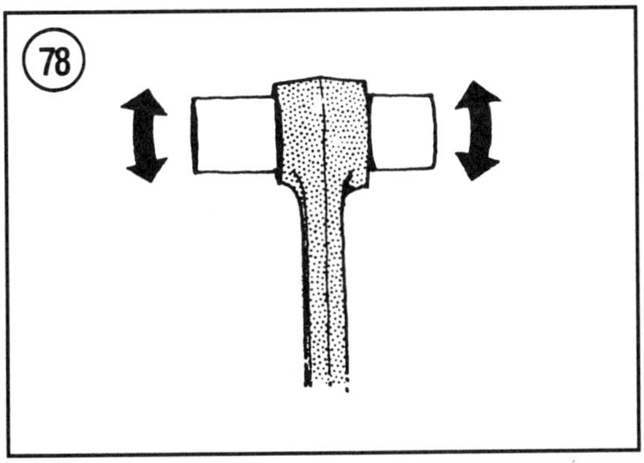

10. Repeat Step 9 to remove the bottom piston ring. Then carefully remove the expander spacer (**Figure 76**) from the bottom ring groove.

Piston Pin and Needle Bearing Inspection

Yamaha does not list operating clearances for the piston pin and piston. This procedure describes basic visual and free play checks that can be made to these parts. Since the piston pin-to-piston clearance is small, refer inspection to a dealership if there is any questionable play.

1. Clean and dry the piston pin and needle bearing.
2. Check the piston pin (A, **Figure 77**) for excessive wear, scoring and cracks along its outer diameter. Replace the piston pin if necessary.
3. Inspect the needle bearing (B, **Figure 77**) for:
   a. Needle wear, flat spots or damage.
   b. A damaged bearing cage.
4. Lubricate the needle bearing and piston pin and install them into the connecting rod (**Figure 78**). Try to move the piston pin back and forth as shown in **Figure 78**. There must be no noticeable play in either direction. If there is free play, repeat the check with a new bearing and pin. If there is still free play, replace the connecting rod.
5. Install the piston pin partway into one side of the piston as shown in **Figure 79**. Try to move the piston pin in each of the 4 positions shown in **Figure 79**. Repeat for the other side of the piston. There must be no noticeable play in either direction. If there is free play, repeat the check with a new piston pin. If there is free play with the new piston pin, the piston is worn and must be replaced.

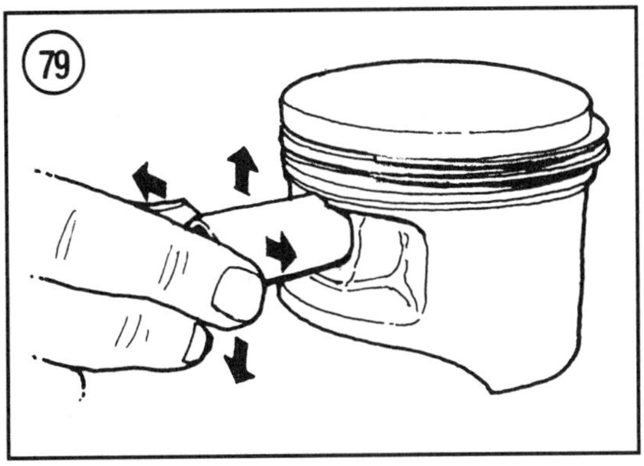

Connecting Rod Inspection

The following checks can be made with the crankshaft installed in the engine and the engine installed in the frame. When checking the connecting rod, compare the actual measurements to the specifications in **Table 4**. Replace the connecting rod if any measurement is out of specification as described in this section.

1. Visually inspect the connecting rod small and large ends for galling, cracks or other damage.

2. Measure connecting rod small end free play (**Figure 80**) as follows:
   a. Turn the crankshaft so the connecting rod is at top dead center (TDC).
   b. Mount a dial indicator so that its plunger contacts the connecting rod small end (**Figure 81**).
   c. Slide the connecting rod over so that it seats against the crankshaft's lower thrust washer that is on the same side the dial indicator is installed on. Hold the connecting rod in this position.
   d. While holding the lower part of the connecting rod, try to move the upper end by hand. Any movement is small end free play. Compare the actual reading to the small end free play clearance in **Table 4**.

3. Check connecting rod big end radial clearance (**Figure 80**) as follows:
   a. Turn the crankshaft so that the connecting rod is at TDC.
   b. Move the connecting rod over so that it seats against one of the crankshaft's lower thrust washers.
   c. Hold the connecting rod in this position, then try to move it up and down as shown in **Figure 80**. If radial clearance can be felt, the lower end bearing assembly is worn.

4. Measure the connecting rod big end side clearance (**Figure 80**) with a feeler gauge and check against the dimension in **Table 4**. **Figure 82** shows the clearance being measured with the crankshaft removed from the engine.

5. To replace the connecting rod and its lower end bearing, the engine must be disassembled and the

80 CONNECTING ROD INSPECTION

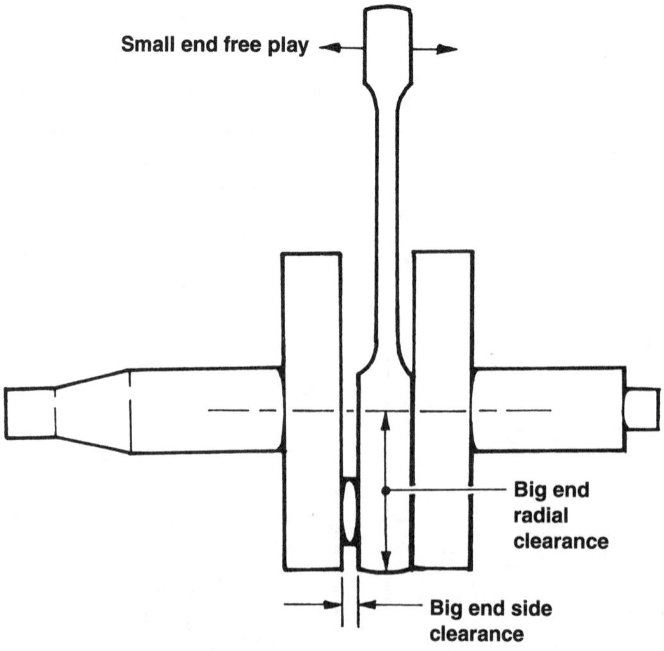

crankshaft overhauled. Crankcase disassembly is described later in this chapter.

Piston and Ring Inspection

When measuring the piston and ring components in this section, compare the actual measurements to the new and service limit specifications in **Table 2**. Replace parts that are out of specification or show damage as described in this section.

1. Check the piston for hairline cracks at the transfer cutaways (A, **Figure 83**) and along the piston skirt (B, **Figure 83**).
2. Check the piston skirt for brown varnish deposits. More than a slight amount is evidence of worn or sticking rings.
3. Check the intake side of the piston skirt for abrasive scratches which indicates that dirt is passing through the air filter.
4. Check the piston skirt for galling and abrasion which may have resulted from piston seizure. If light

81

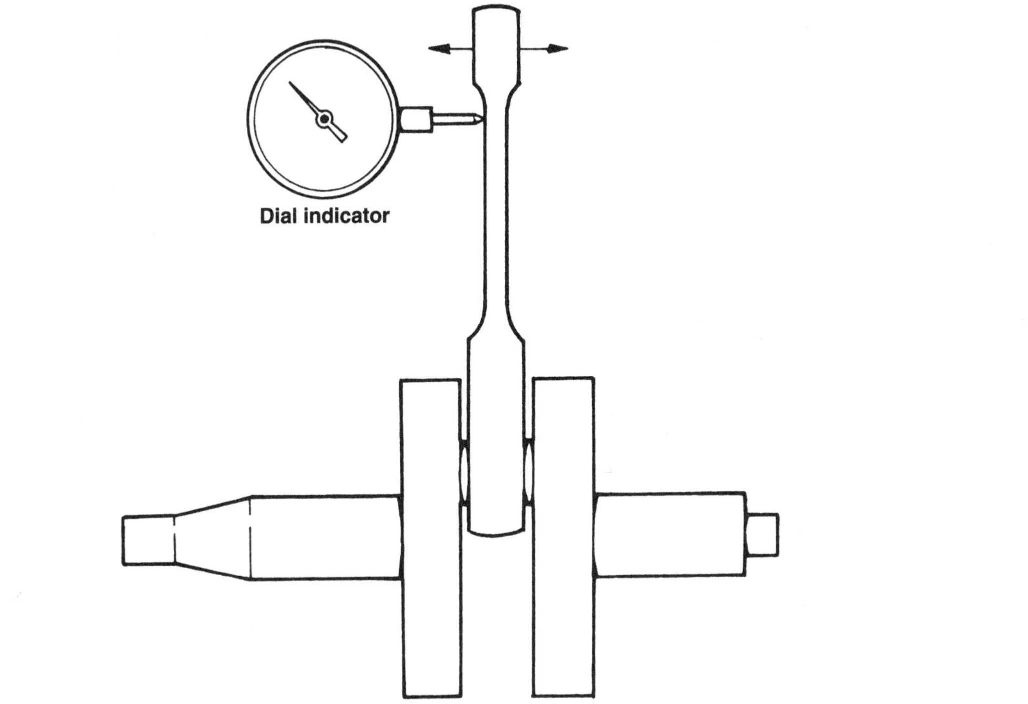

82

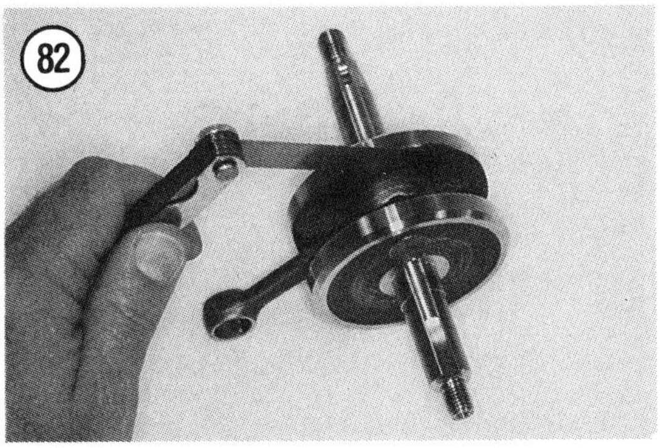

83

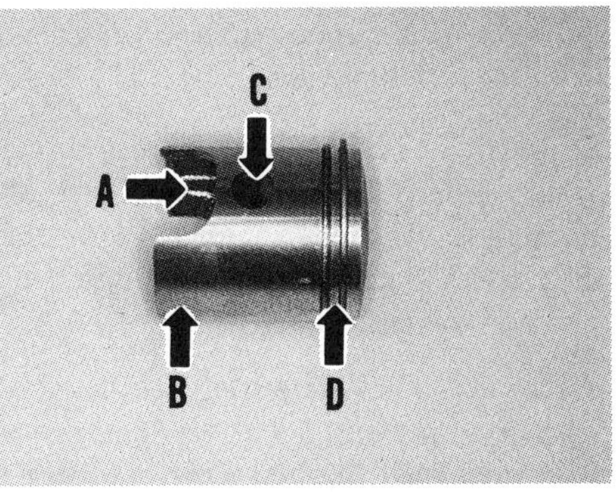

galling is present, lightly smooth these areas with No. 400 sandpaper or with fine emery cloth and oil. However, if the galling is severe or if the piston is deeply scored or cracked, replace the piston.

NOTE
If there is evidence of piston seizure, there is probably some aluminum deposits or other damage on the cylinder liner.

5. Check for a loose or damaged ring locating pin (**Figure 84**). Each pin must be tight with no outer cracks or other damage. Replace the piston if either pin is loose or damaged.

CAUTION
*If a piston ring locating pin falls out, the piston ring can rotate in its groove. This will allow the ring's end gap to catch in a port and cause the type of damage shown in **Figure 85**.*

6. Check the piston pin clip grooves (C, **Figure 83**) for severe wear or damage.
7. Check the condition and color of the piston crown (**Figure 86**). Remove normal carbon buildup with a wire wheel mounted in a drill. If there is any erosion of metal on the piston crown, the engine is operating with a lean air/fuel mixture, a too hot spark plug or incorrect ignition timing. This condition should be corrected immediately after a new piston has been installed and the engine reassembled.

CAUTION
Do not use a wire brush to clean the piston skirt or gouge the piston when cleaning it.

CAUTION
*Because the stock piston uses Keystone rings (**Figure 87**), do not clean the piston ring grooves with a plain or square type piston ring. Doing so will damage the piston ring land.*

8. Remove carbon buildup from the ring groove with a broken Keystone ring (**Figure 88**). Work carefully to avoid removing any piston material from the grooves. If the carbon buildup is severe, soak the piston in solvent.

NOTE
Any deposits left in the grooves will contribute to ring sticking and may result in loss of power and possible piston seizure.

9. Inspect the ring grooves (D, **Figure 83**) for burrs, nicks, or broken and cracked lands. Replace the piston if either ring groove is severely worn or damaged.
10. Roll the ring around its groove (**Figure 89**) and check for tight spots in the groove. If any tight spots are found, check the piston carefully for warpage, cracks or other damage. Repair minor damage with a fine-cut file only after determining that the piston

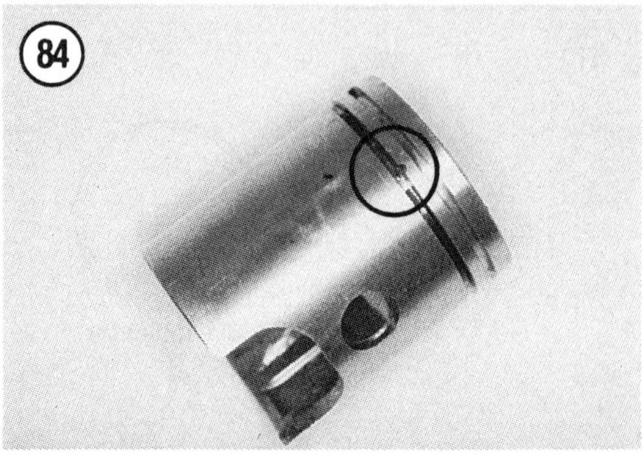

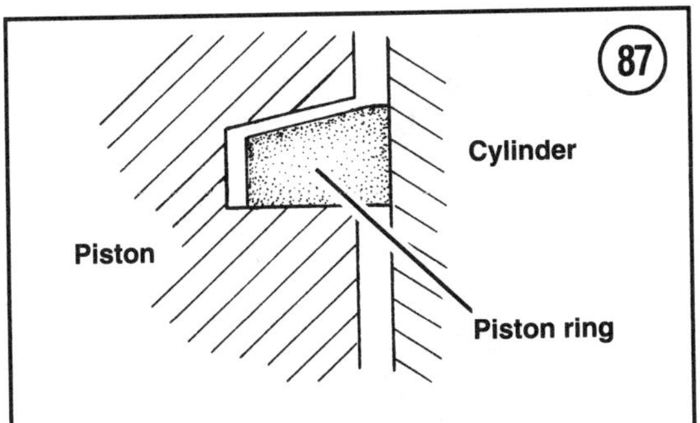

87

Keystone piston and piston ring

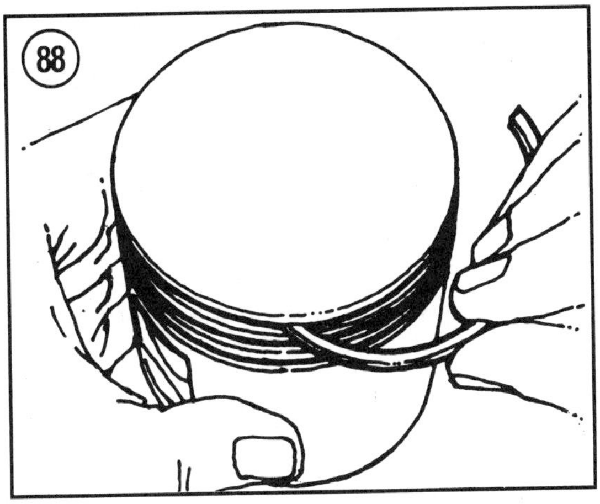

88

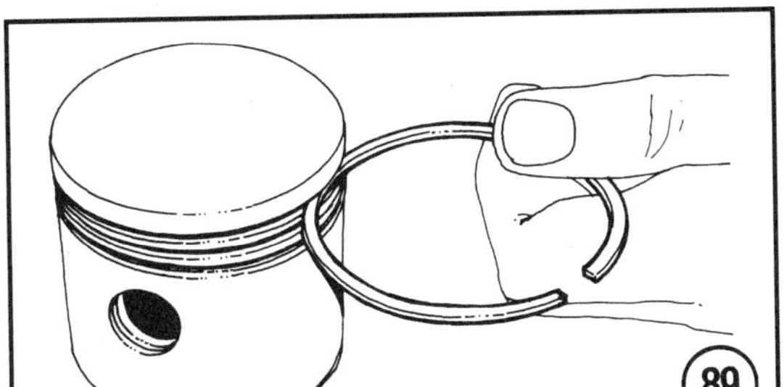

89

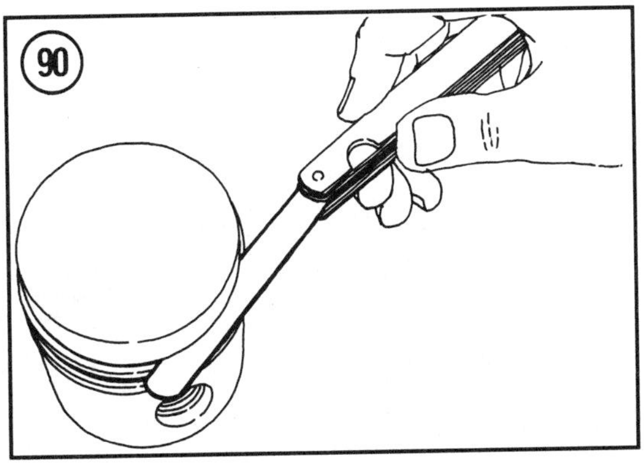

90

is not permanently damaged. Replace the piston if there is any doubt as to its condition.

11. Install each ring in its groove and measure the piston ring-to-groove side clearance (**Figure 90**) with a feeler gauge. If the clearance is out of specification, the next step would be to recheck the clearance with a new piston ring. However, this is not always a practical step for the home mechanic. Instead, measure the side clearance of each groove using the bottom ring. Because this ring normally receives less wear than the upper ring, you may be able to better approximate whether the wear is caused by the ring or piston (or both).

12. Measure the piston ring end gap as follows. Place a ring into the bottom of the cylinder and push it in down approximately 20 mm (0.79 in.). Position the ring so that it is parallel with the bottom edge of the cylinder. Then measure the ring gap with a flat feeler gauge (**Figure 91**). Replace the rings as a set if the end gap of any ring is out of specification.

13. Measure the piston outside diameter as described under *Piston/Cylinder Clearance* in this chapter.

Piston/Cylinder Clearance

Yamaha does not list service limit specifications for their standard and oversize piston sizes. They only list new piston sizes (**Table 2**). To determine piston wear, first measure the cylinder bore wear. If it is within specification, measure the piston outside diameter and then subtract this dimension from the bore inside diameter to determine the piston-to-cylinder clearance. If the piston clearance is good, the piston diameter is good. If the piston clearance is out of specification (and the bore wear is good), the

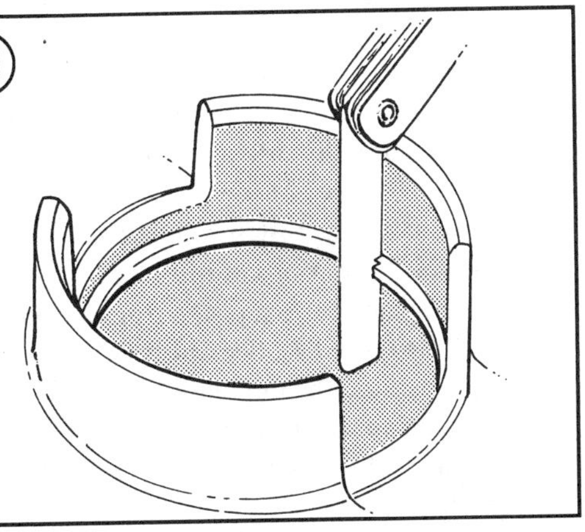

91

4

piston is worn and must be replaced. If the piston clearance is just out of specification, and the cylinder bore wear is minimal, it may be possible to install a new piston to help take up some of the excessive piston-to-cylinder clearance. If the piston-to-cylinder clearance is excessive, and the bore wear is just within specification, it may be better to rebore the cylinder to the next oversize.

1. Measure the cylinder bore with a bore gauge (**Figure 92**) or an inside micrometer at the 3 depth positions (A, B, C and D) shown in **Figure 93**. Except for the bottom measurement, measure both in line with the piston pin and at 90° to the pin. Note the following:
   a. Use the largest bore measurement to determine cylinder wear.
   b. Record measurements for cylinder wear, taper and out-of-round.
   c. If the cylinder bore, taper or out-of-round measurement exceeds the wear limit in **Table 2**, the cylinder bore must be rebored to the next oversize and fitted with a new piston.
2. Measure the piston diameter at a point 5 mm (0.2 in.) from the bottom edge of the piston skirt and at a 90° angle to the piston pin as shown in **Figure 94**.
3. Subtract the piston skirt diameter from the maximum cylinder bore diameter to determine the piston-to-cylinder clearance. Compare this measurement with the service limit in **Table 2**. If out of specification, replace with the same size piston or rebore the cylinder and fit an oversize piston.

Piston Ring Installation

1. Check the piston ring end gap before assembling the piston and rings; refer to *Piston Inspection* in this chapter. The end gap measurement must be within specification (**Table 2**). If the end gap is too narrow after boring the cylinder, remeasure the cylinder bore to make sure it is within specification. If it is, enlarge the gap by carefully filing the ring ends with a fine-cut file (**Figure 95**).
2. Clean and dry the piston and rings.
3. Install the piston rings as follows:
   a. The top and bottom piston rings are Keystone rings (**Figure 87**). See **Table 3** for piston ring dimensions. The top ring (A, **Figure 74**) has a chrome outer surface. The bottom ring (B, **Figure 74**) does not have the chrome outer surface.

92

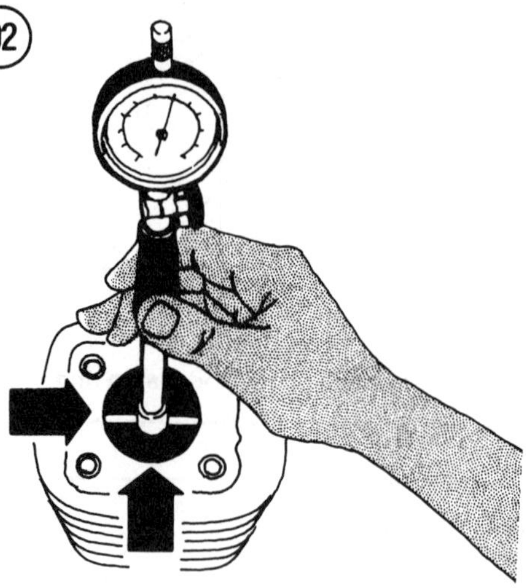

93

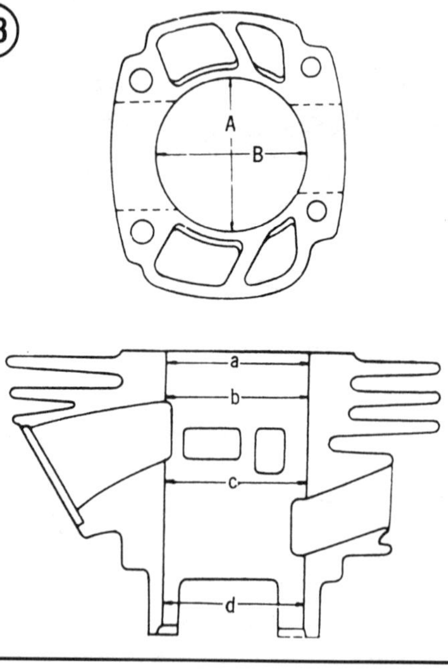

94

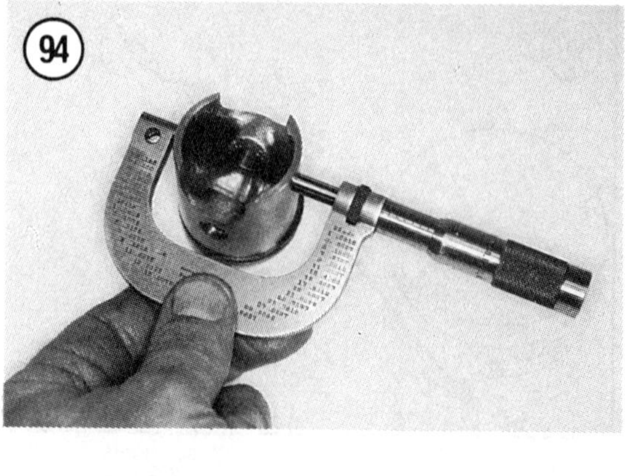

95

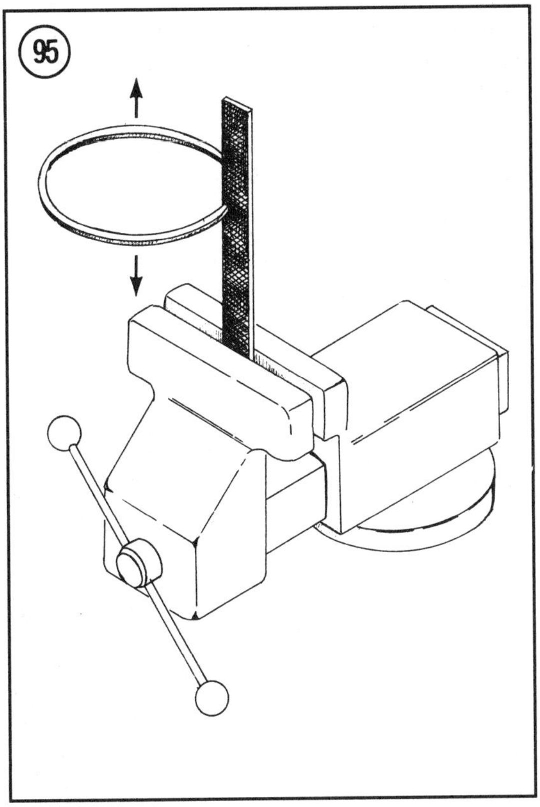

96

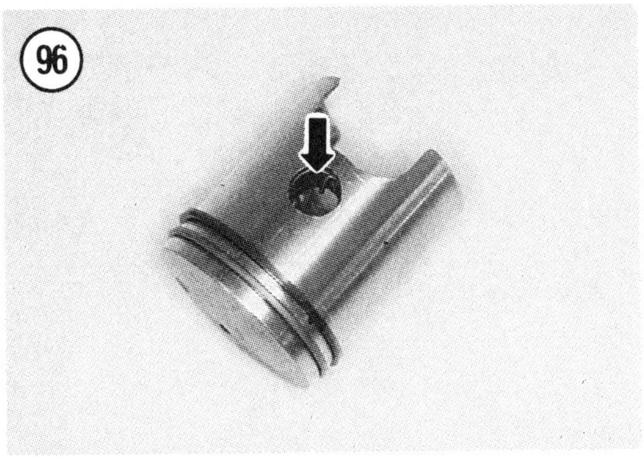

97

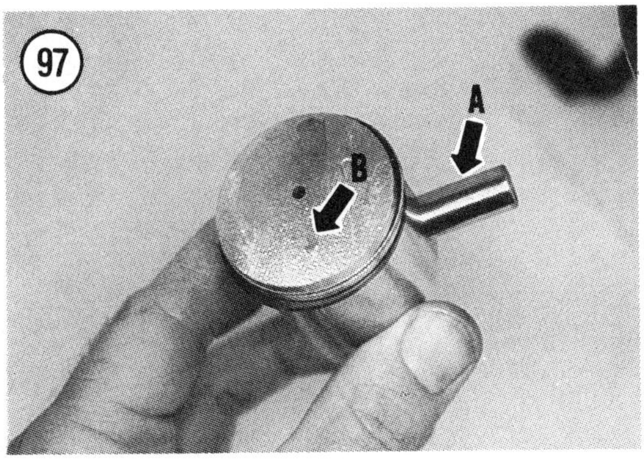

b. Install the expander spacer (**Figure 76**) into the bottom ring groove. Center the spacer's end gap around the piston ring locating pin (**Figure 84**).

c. Install used piston rings in their original mounting position. Refer to your identification marks made during removal.

d. Install both piston rings with their manufacturer's marks facing up.

e. Install the bottom piston ring (B, **Figure 74**) by carefully spreading its ends your thumbs and slipping it over the top of the piston (**Figure 75**). Center the ring end gap around the pin in the ring groove (**Figure 84**).

f. Repeat to install the top piston ring.

4. Make sure each ring floats smoothly in its ring groove.

Piston Installation

Make sure all engine parts are clean before starting assembly. Use a 2-stroke engine when oil is called for in the following steps.

1. Lightly oil the needle bearing and install it in the connecting rod (**Figure 73**).

CAUTION
Do not install used piston pin clips.

WARNING
Piston pin clips can slip and fly off during installation. Wear safety glasses to prevent eye injury.

2. Install the first *new* piston pin clip (**Figure 96**) into one of the piston clip groove's. Make sure the clip seats in the groove completely. Turn the clip so that its bent arm is at the 12 or 6 o'clock position.

3. Oil the piston pin and install it partway into the piston (A, **Figure 97**).

4. Place the piston over the connecting rod with its arrow mark (B, **Figure 97**) facing toward the exhaust side of the engine. Line up the piston pin with the bearing, then push the pin (**Figure 98**) into the piston.

NOTE
If the arrow mark is not visible on the piston crown, install the piston with its ring locating pins facing toward the intake side of the engine.

CAUTION

If the piston pin will not slide in the piston smoothly, use the home-made tool described during ***Piston Removal*** *to install the piston pin.*

5. Wrap a clean shop cloth under the piston so that the clip cannot fall into the crankcase.

WARNING

Piston pin clips can slip and fly off during installation. Wear safety glasses to prevent eye injury.

6. Install the second *new* piston pin clip (**Figure 99**) into the clip groove in the piston. Make sure the clip is seated in the groove (**Figure 100**) completely. Turn the clip so that its bent arm is at the 12 or 6 o'clock position.
7. Make sure both rings are seated in their grooves with their end gaps centered around their ring locating pins.

REED VALVE ASSEMBLY

The reed valve assembly can be serviced with the engine mounted in the frame. This procedure shows reed valve service with the engine removed for clarity.

Refer to **Figure 101** when servicing the reed valve in this section.

NOTE

If your model is equipped with an aftermarket reed valve, refer to the manufacturer's instructions on removal, installation and inspection procedures.

Removal/Installation

1. If the engine is mounted in the frame, remove the air box and carburetor (Chapter Seven).
2. Remove the intake manifold mounting screws and remove the manifold (**Figure 102**).
3. Remove the reed block and both gaskets (**Figure 103**).
4. Inspect the reed valve assembly as described in this chapter.
5. Remove all gasket residue from the intake manifold, reed block and crankcase mating surfaces.
6. Install a new lower gasket (A, **Figure 104**) onto the crankcase (**Figure 105**), then install the reed block (**Figure 103**).
7. Install a new upper gasket (B, **Figure 104**) onto the reed block (**Figure 103**).
8. Install the intake manifold (**Figure 102**) and its mounting screws. Tighten the screws in a crisscross pattern as specified in **Table 6**.
9. If necessary, install the carburetor and air box (Chapter Seven).

98

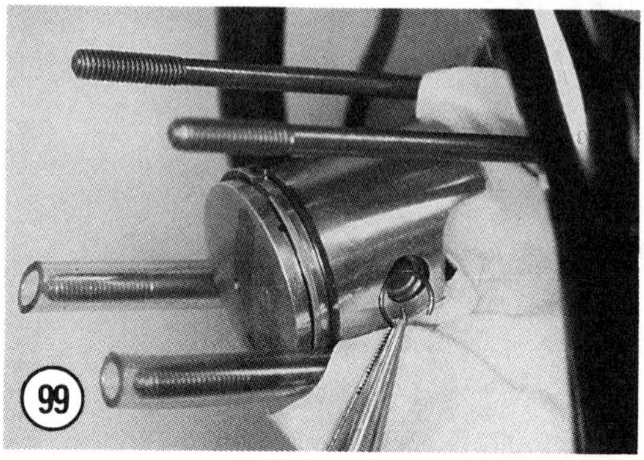

99

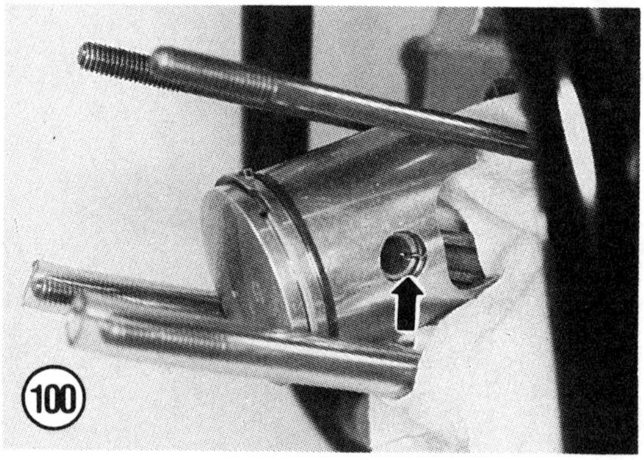

100

101

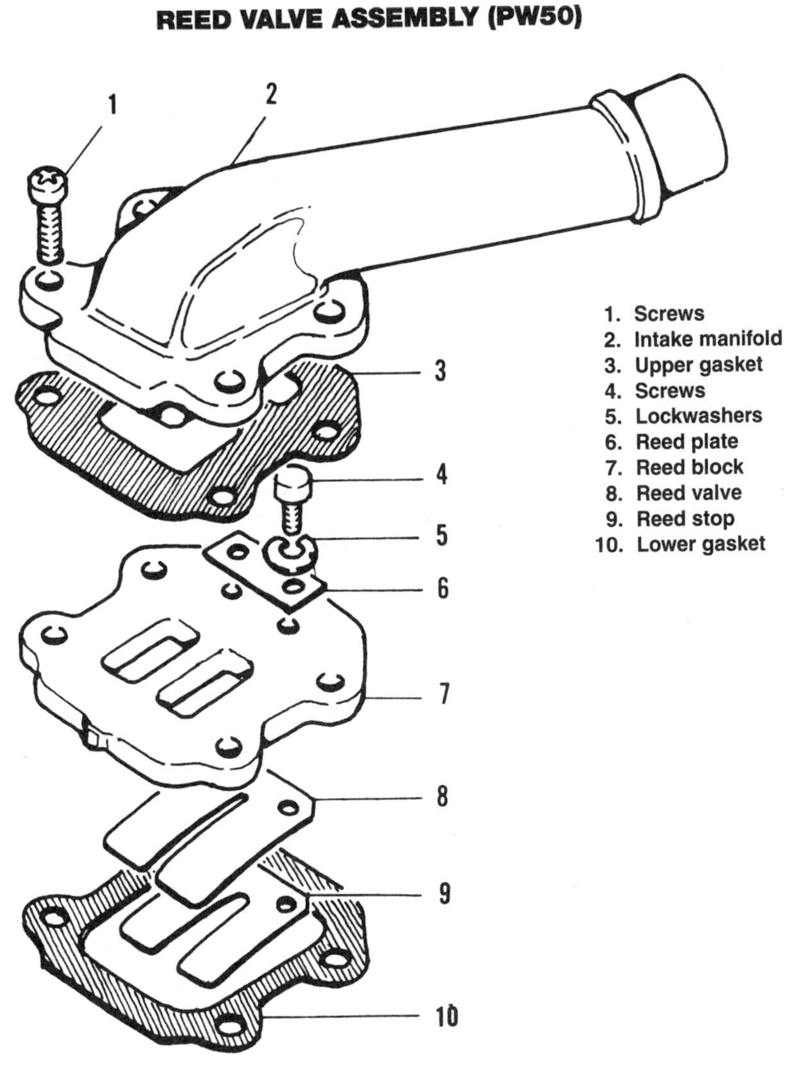
REED VALVE ASSEMBLY (PW50)
1
2
3
4
5
6
7
8
9
10
1. Screws
2. Intake manifold
3. Upper gasket
4. Screws
5. Lockwashers
6. Reed plate
7. Reed block
8. Reed valve
9. Reed stop
10. Lower gasket

102

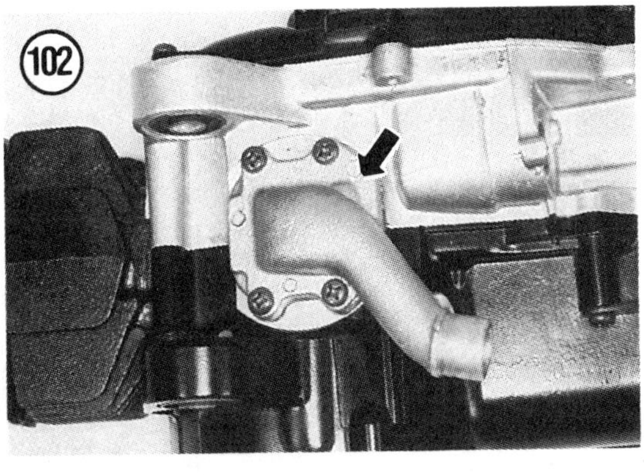

103

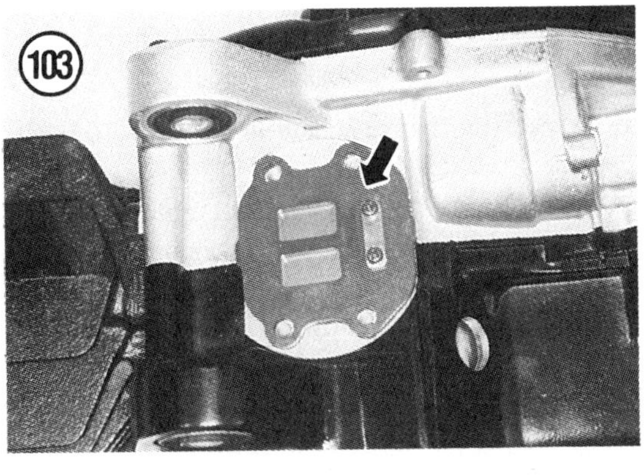

Inspection

When measuring the reed valve components, compare the actual measurements to the specifications in **Table 2**. Replace parts that are out of specification or show damage as described in this section.

1. Carefully examine the reed block (A, **Figure 106**) for excessive wear, distortion or damage.

2. Check the reed valve (B, **Figure 106**) for cracks or other damage. A damaged reed valve will cause hard engine starting and reduce engine performance.

3. Check the reed stop (C, **Figure 106**) for cracks or other damage.

4. Use a flat feeler gauge and measure the clearance between the reed valve and the reed block sealing surface (**Figure 107**). Replace the reed valve if its bend clearance exceeds the service limit.

CAUTION
Many riders turn reed valves over when out of tolerance; however, bear in mind an out of tolerance condition is caused by metal fatigue. Metal fatigue may cause the reed valve to break and enter the engine, resulting in serious and expensive damage. Fiber reed valves are available and do not cause engine damage when they break.

5. Measure the reed stop height distance as shown in **Figure 108**. If the reed valve stop height measures 0.4 mm (0.016 in.) more or less than the specification in **Table 2**, either remove the reed stop and bend it back into specification, or replace it. Do *not* try to bend the reed stop while it is mounted on the reed block.

CAUTION
After bending the reed stop, check it carefully for cracks or other damage before reinstalling it back into the engine.

6. Inspect the intake manifold (**Figure 109**) and replace if cracked or damaged.

7. Measure the intake manifold flatness with a straightedge and feeler gauge. If the intake manifold warpage exceeds the service limit in **Table 2**, resurface the manifold as follows:

   a. Tape a piece of 400-600 grit wet emery sandpaper onto a piece of thick plate glass or surface plate.
   b. Slowly resurface the intake manifold by moving it in figure-eight patterns on the emery sandpaper.
   c. Rotate the manifold several times to avoid removing too much material from one side. Check progress often with the straightedge and feeler gauge.
   d. If the warpage cannot be corrected by this method, replace the intake manifold.

Reed Valve/Reed Stop Replacement

1. Remove the screws (A, **Figure 110**) securing the reed stop, reed valve and reed plate (B, **Figure 110**) to the reed block.

2. Clean and dry all parts. Remove all thread sealer residue from the mounting screws and the threaded holes in the reed stop.

3. Check the reed valve and replace if worn or damaged.

4. Replace the screws if the threads or screw head is damaged.

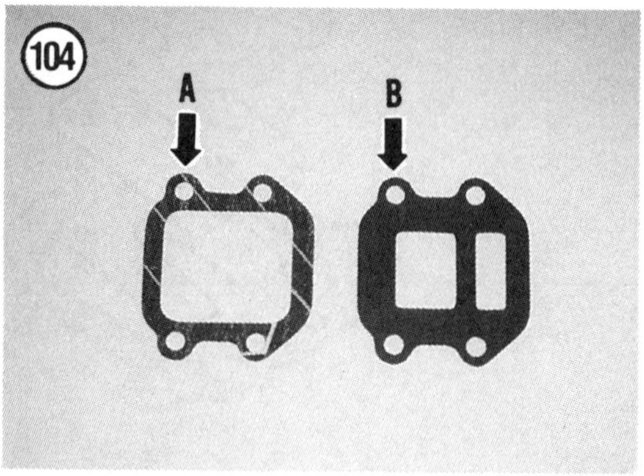

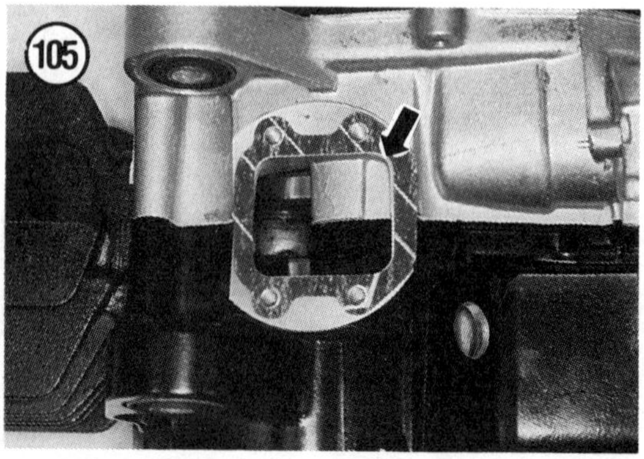

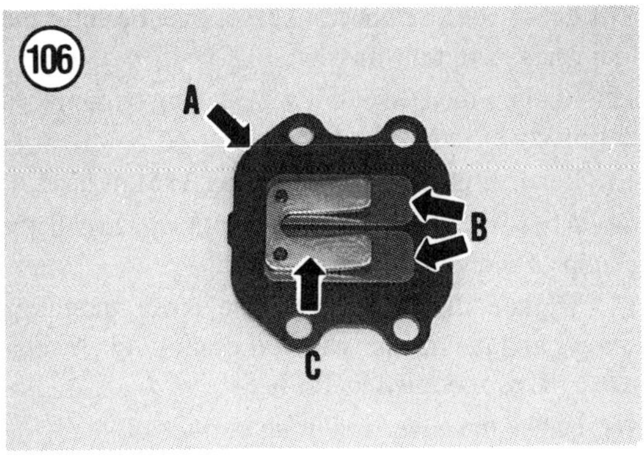

106

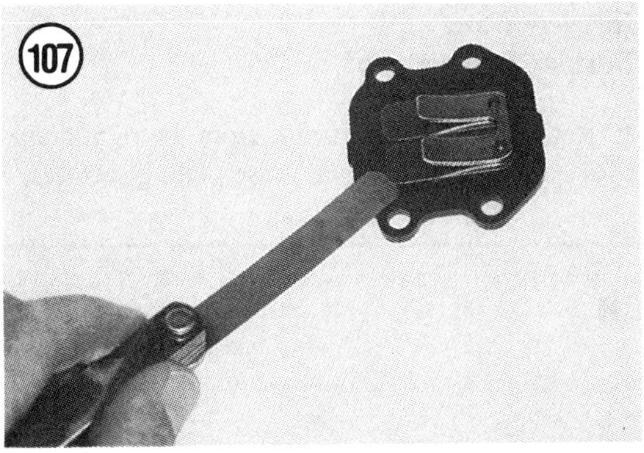
107

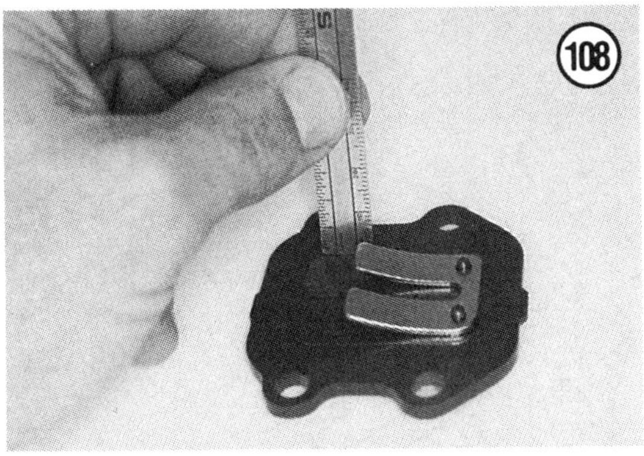
108

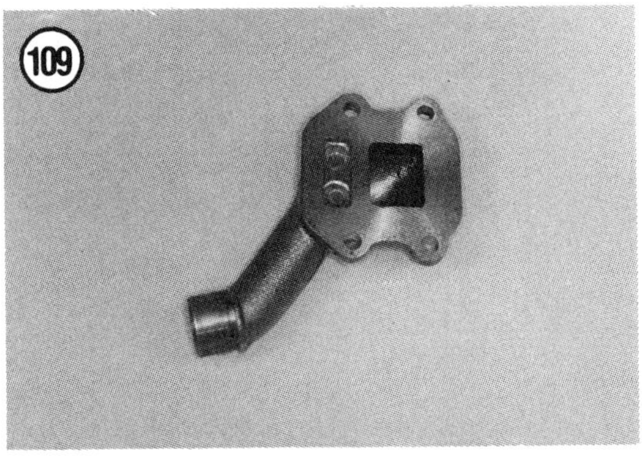
109

5. Reassemble the reed cage as follows:
   a. The reed pedal is not perfectly flat, but instead, one side will bow out slightly. Install the reed plate so that the bowed section faces out.
   b. Apply ThreeBond TB1342 or an equivalent threadlocking compound to the mounting screws prior to installation. Assemble the reed valve, reed stop and reed plate (**Figure 101**) and secure with the mounting screws and lockwashers. Tighten the screws securely.

CLUTCH

A centrifugal automatic clutch (**Figure 111**) is used on the PW50. This section describes service to the right crankcase cover and clutch assembly. The engine must be removed from the frame to service the right crankcase cover and clutch.

Right Crankcase Cover Removal/Installation

Refer to **Figure 112** for this procedure.

1. Support the bike on its centerstand.
2. Drain the transmission oil (Chapter Three).

3A. If the engine crankcases are also going to be disassembled, remove the engine from the frame as described under *Engine Removal (Procedure 1)* in this chapter.

3B. If only clutch, primary drive or kickstarter service is required, remove the engine from the frame as described under *Engine Removal (Procedure 2)* in this chapter.

4. Remove the screw and clamp (A, **Figure 13**), second screw (B) and protector cover (C) from the right crankcase cover.

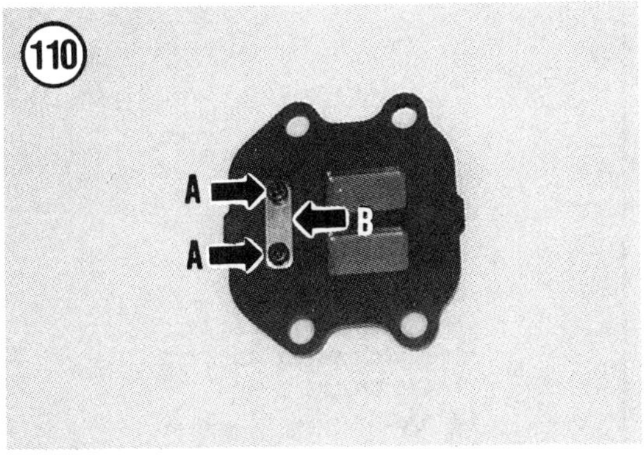

110

5. Remove the transmission oil drain plug and washer (A, **Figure 114**) and the remaining cover screws, then remove the right crankcase cover (B, **Figure 114**).

6. Remove the gasket (A, **Figure 115**).

7. Remove the 2 dowel pins (B, **Figure 115**).

8. If no additional engine disassembly is required, make a stop plate (use a flat piece of aluminum or steel) and bolt it onto the crankcase so that one ends seats against the kickstarter assembly as shown in **Figure 116**. The stop plate will prevent the kickstarter from accidentally moving outward and disengaging from the engine.

9. Perform the inspection procedures to clean the cover and inspect the cover bushing.

10. Reverse these steps to install the right crankcase cover, plus the following.

11. Lubricate the right crankcase cover bushing and mainshaft with transmission oil.

12. Replace the gasket if it was leaking or damaged during cover removal.

13. Remove the stop plate (**Figure 116**), if used.

14. After installing the protector cover, install the clamp as shown in **Figure 117**.

15. Tighten the right crankcase cover mounting screws and the transmission oil drain plug (A, **Figure 114**) as specified in **Table 6**.

16. Check the cover and drain bolt for oil leaks.

Inspection and Bushing Replacement

1. Remove all gasket residue from the right crankcase cover and engine crankcase mating surfaces.

(111) **CLUTCH**

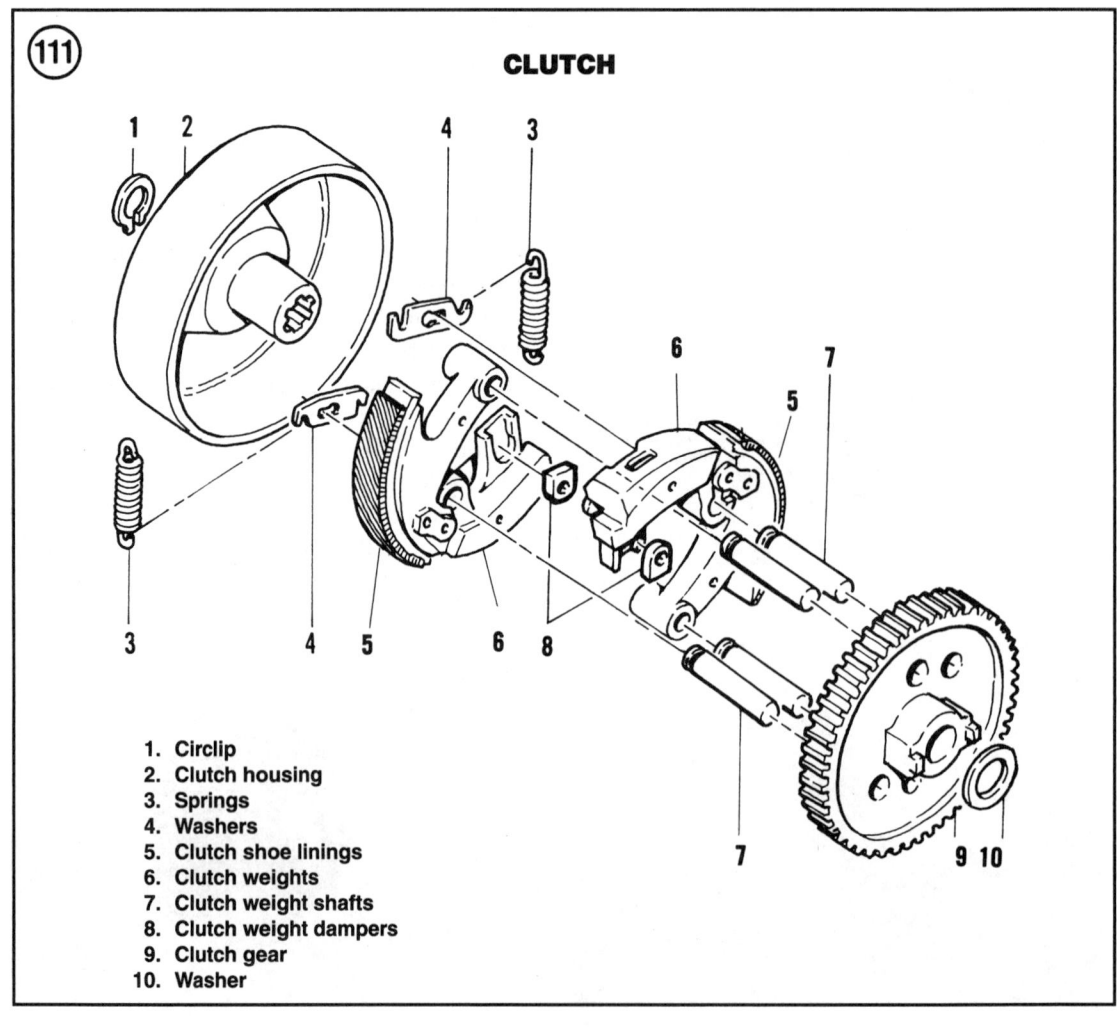

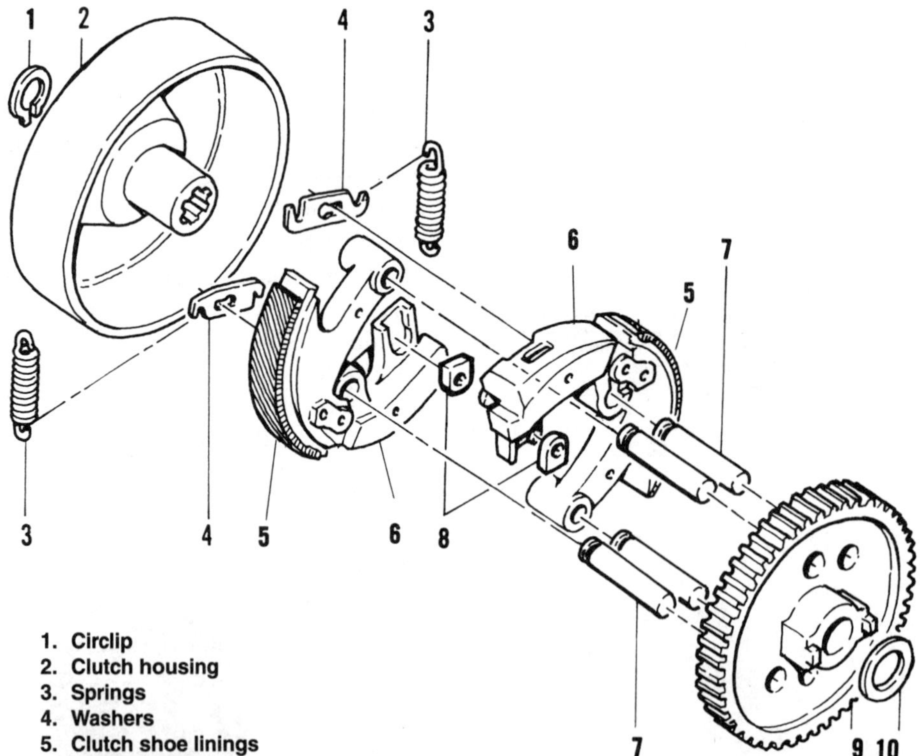

1. Circlip
2. Clutch housing
3. Springs
4. Washers
5. Clutch shoe linings
6. Clutch weights
7. Clutch weight shafts
8. Clutch weight dampers
9. Clutch gear
10. Washer

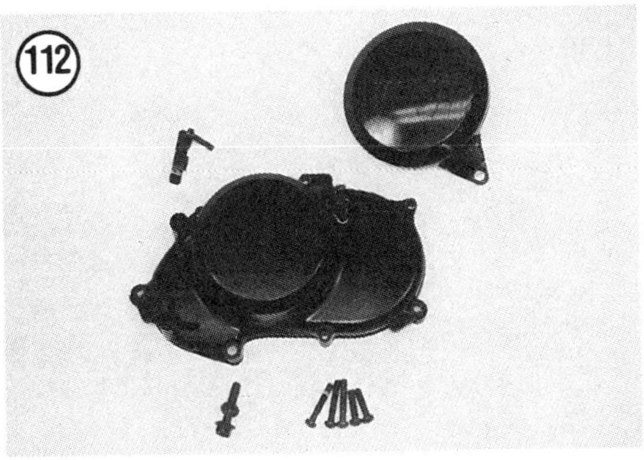
112

2. Clean and dry both covers and all fasteners.

3. Inspect the cover for any cracks or other damage. Repair small leaks or cracks with a suitable epoxy.

4. Inspect the right crankcase cover bushing (**Figure 118**) for wear, looseness or other damage. If necessary, replace the bushing as follows:

NOTE
If the bushing is excessively worn or damaged, check the end of the mainshaft for damage.

113

114

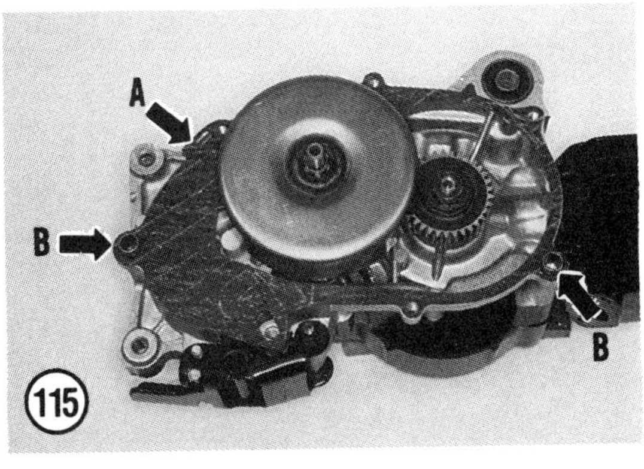

115

116

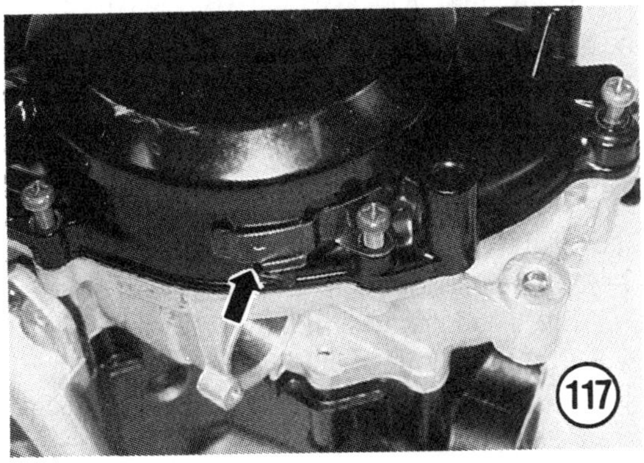
117

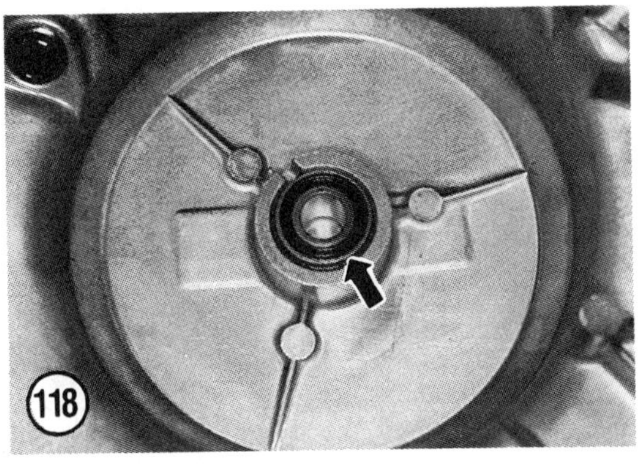
118

a. Support the cover and remove the bushing with a blind bearing remover. If the bushing is a loose fit in the cover, examine the mounting bore in the cover for cracks or severe wear. Replace the cover if there is any damage. The bushing must be a tight fit in the cover.
b. Clean the mounting bore.
c. Press the new bushing into the cover mounting bore.

Clutch Removal

Refer to **Figure 111** for this procedure.

1. Remove the right crankcase cover as described in this section.
2. Remove the circlip (A, **Figure 119**) from the groove in the mainshaft.
3. Slide off the clutch housing (B, **Figure 119**).

NOTE
If the primary drive gear is going to be removed, loosen its locknut (A, ***Figure 120****) before removing the clutch in Step 4. Refer to* ***Primary Drive Gear*** *in this chapter.*

4. Remove the clutch assembly (B, **Figure 120**).
5. Remove the flat washer (**Figure 121**).

Clutch Disassembly

1. Remove the clutch springs (A, **Figure 122**) as shown in **Figure 123**.
2. Remove the 2 washers (B, **Figure 122**).
3. Slide the clutch weight halves off of the clutch weight shafts as shown in **Figure 124**.
4. Pull the 2 clutch weight halves apart and remove the 2 clutch weight dampers (**Figure 125**).

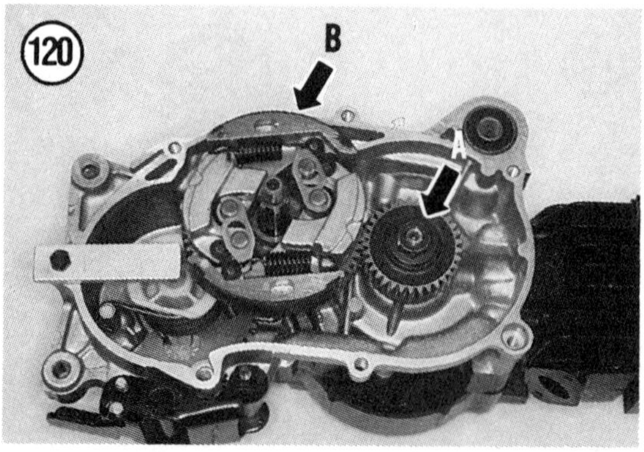

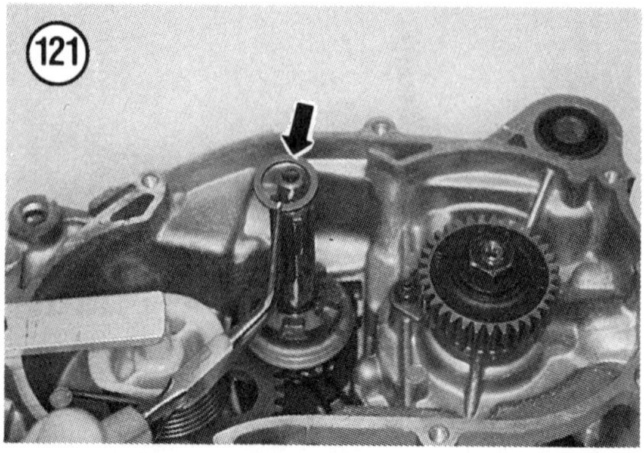

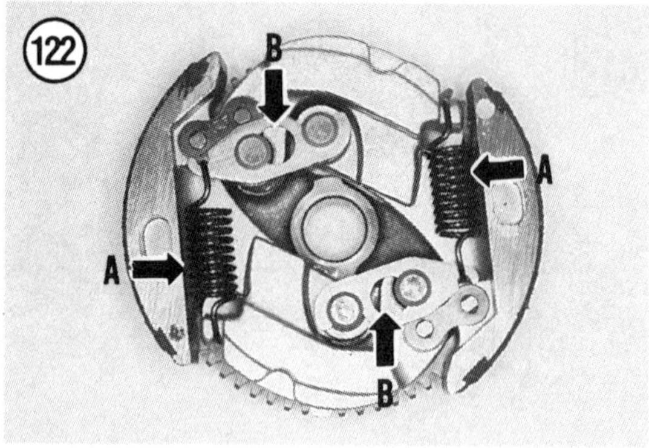

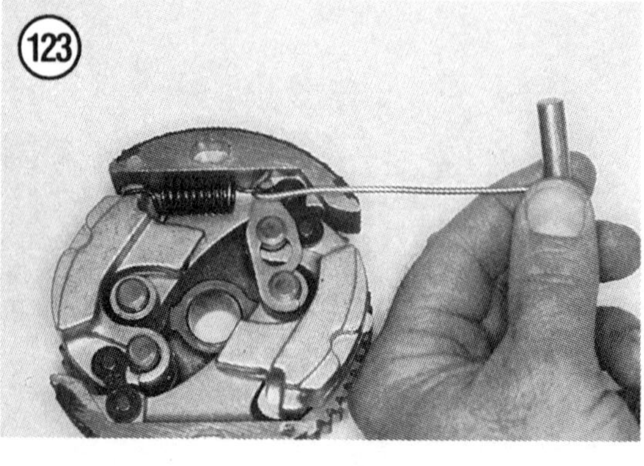

124

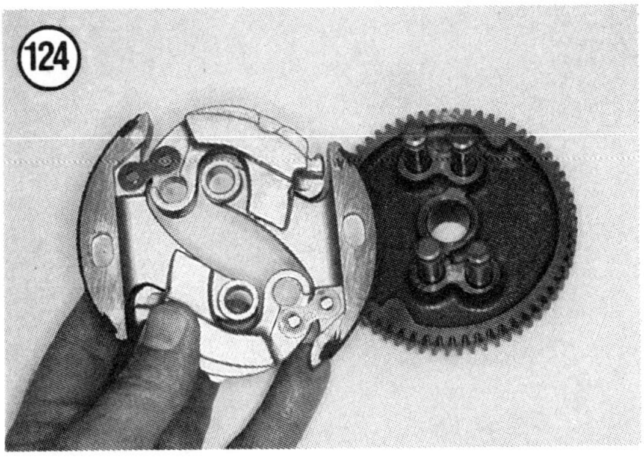

125

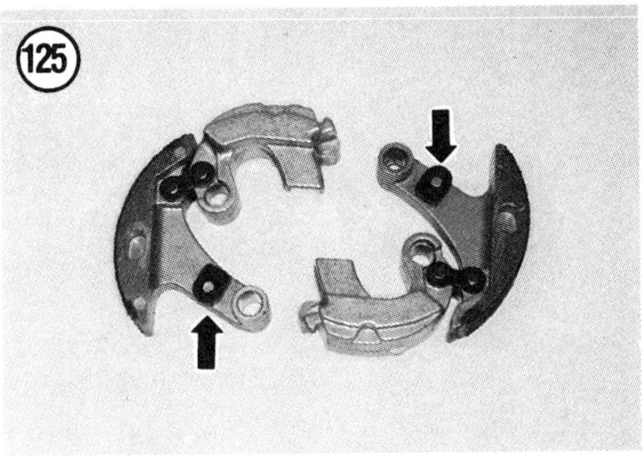

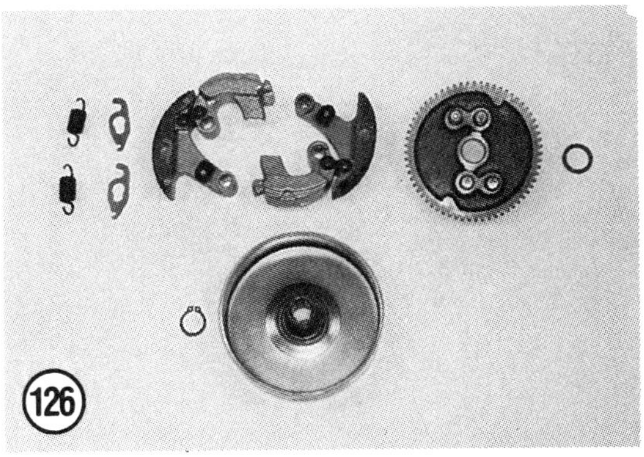

126

Clutch

Cleaning and Inspection

When measuring the clutch components, compare the actual measurements to the specifications in **Table 5**. Replace the part if its measurement is out of specification or shows damage as described in this section.

1. Clean and dry all parts (**Figure 126**).
2. Inspect the clutch housing inside wall (A, **Figure 127**) for steps, cracks or other damage. Then inspect the splines and bore (B, **Figure 127**) for damage.
3. Inspect the outer circlip and inner washer (**Figure 126**) for severe wear or damage.

NOTE

*The clutch shoe linings (5, **Figure 111**) are bonded onto the clutch weights (6, **Figure 111**).*

4. Inspect the clutch shoe linings (A, **Figure 128**) for signs of damage, overheating or a burnt smell. Replace the clutch weights if the lining surface is damaged.
5. Measure the thickness of each clutch shoe lining as shown in **Figure 129**. Replace both clutch weights if the thickness of either clutch shoe lining is out of specification.
6. Inspect the link (B, **Figure 128**) connecting the 2 clutch weight halves.
7. Inspect the clutch springs (A, **Figure 130**) for fatigue, stretched coils or other damage.
8. Measure the clutch shoe spring free length with calipers as shown in **Figure 131**. Replace both springs as a set if the free length of one spring is out of specification.
9. Inspect the washers (B, **Figure 130**) and replace if bent or damaged.

127

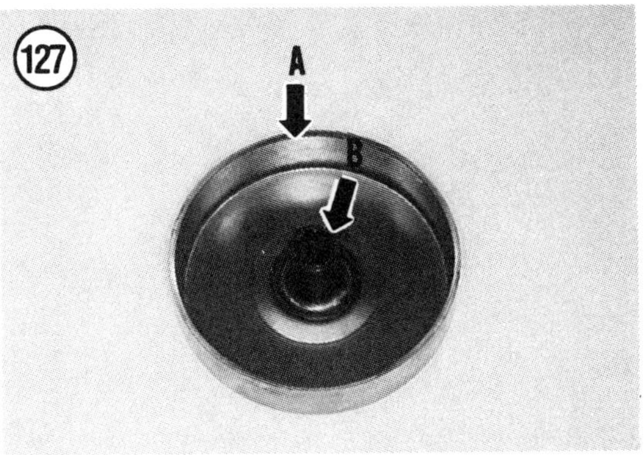

128

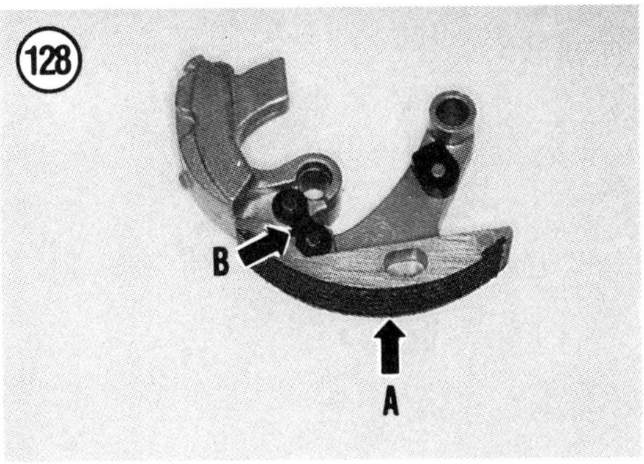

4

10. Inspect the clutch weight dampers (**Figure 132**) and replace if worn or damaged.

11. Inspect the clutch gear (**Figure 133**) for:
   a. Missing, broken or chipped gear teeth.
   b. Worn, damaged or rounded-off gear lugs.
   c. Cracked or worn shaft bore.

12. Inspect the clutch weight shafts (**Figure 134**) for wear or damage. If necessary, replace the shafts as follows:
   a. Measure the shafts installed height with a caliper (**Figure 135**). Record the height dimension.
   b. Press the old shafts out of the clutch gear.
   c. Press in the new shafts to the height dimension recorded in substep a.

Clutch Assembly

1. Install a clutch damper (**Figure 125**) on each clutch weight pin.
2. Join the clutch weight halves as follows:
   a. Align the notch in the end of each clutch weight with its mating clutch weight damper (**Figure 136**).

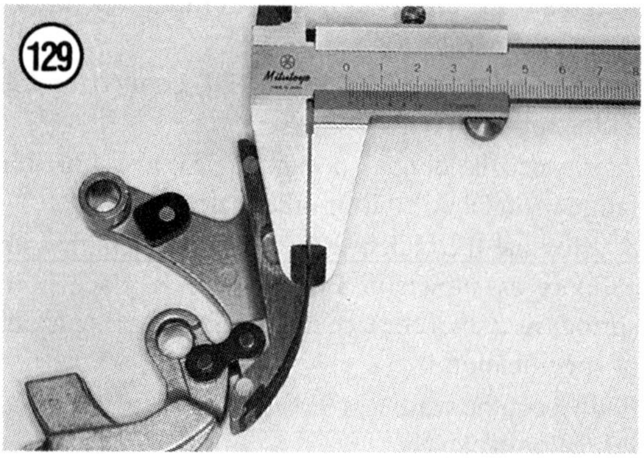

129

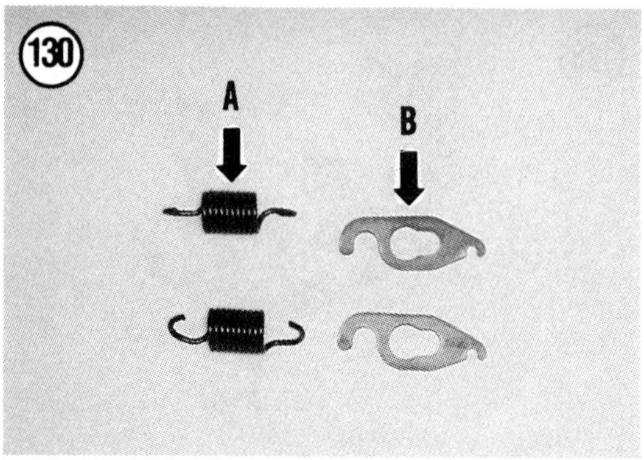

130

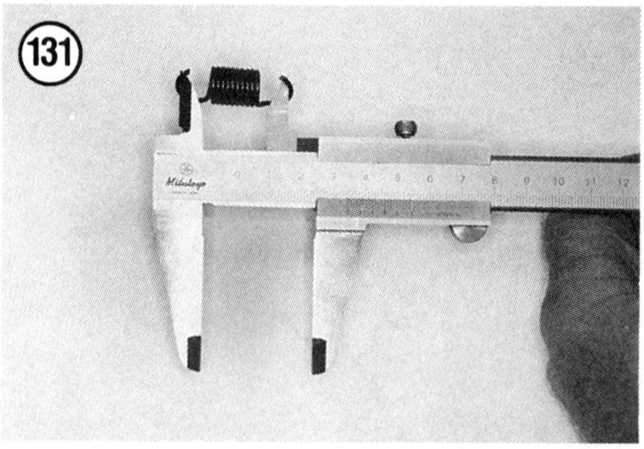

131

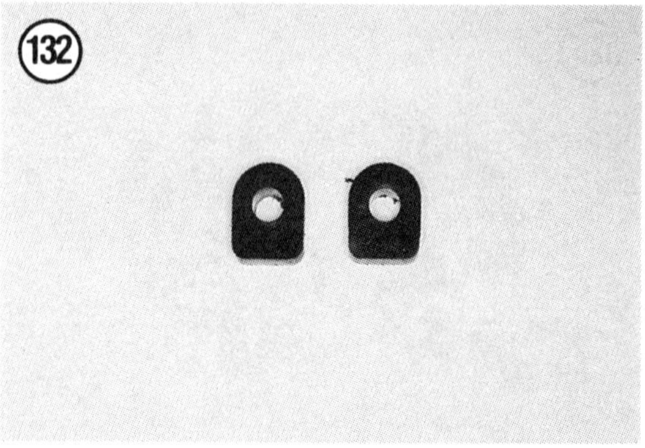

132

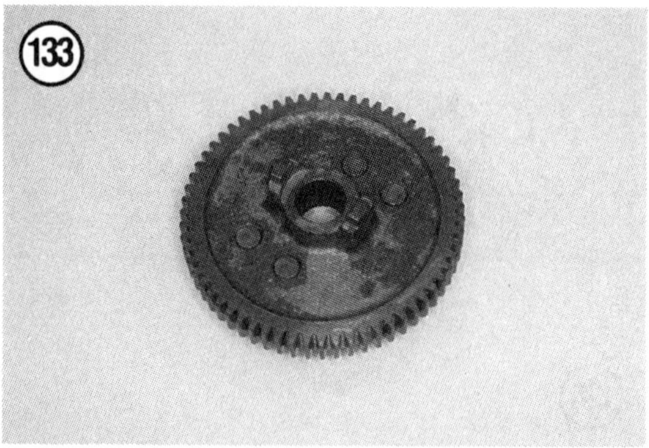

133

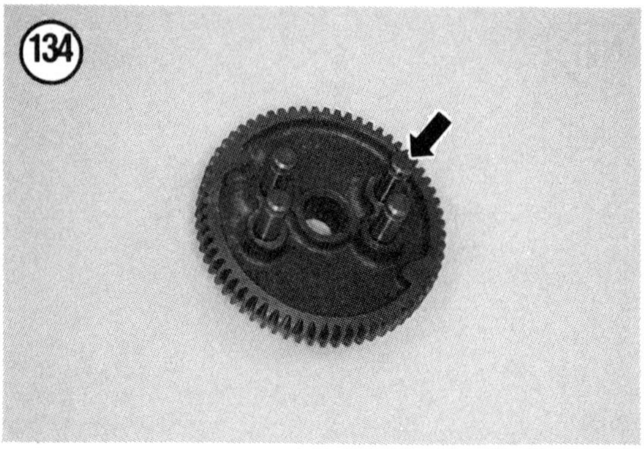

134

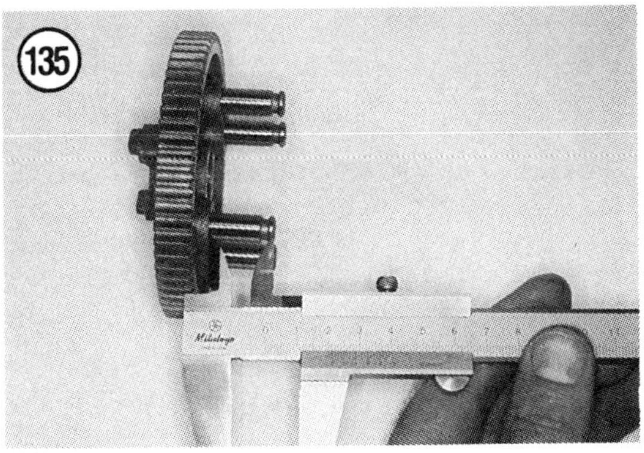

135

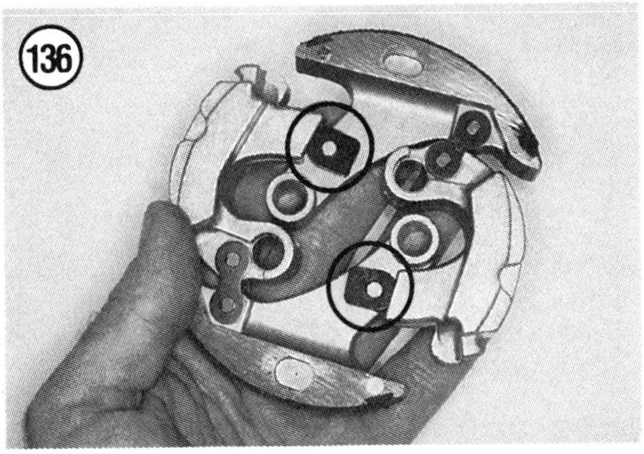

136

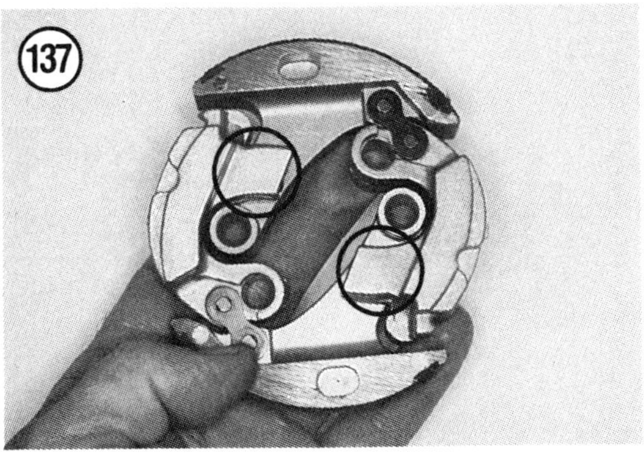

137

138

b. Turn each clutch weight damper so its curved end faces into its clutch weight (**Figure 136**).

c. Then push the clutch weight over its damper (**Figure 137**). The 2 clutch weight halves should now be joined together.

3. Install the clutch weight halves (**Figure 124**) over the clutch weight shafts as shown in **Figure 138**.

NOTE

*The 2 washers and 2 springs (**Figure 130**) are identical (same part numbers).*

4. Install the first washer over the clutch weight shaft shown in **Figure 139**. Then pull and turn the washer to lock it against the opposite clutch weight shaft groove as shown in **Figure 140**.

5. Hook the spring between the clutch weight and washer hook as shown in **Figure 141**. Hook the spring ends with a tool like shown in **Figure 123**.

6. Repeat Steps 4 and 5 to install the other washer and spring. See **Figure 142**.

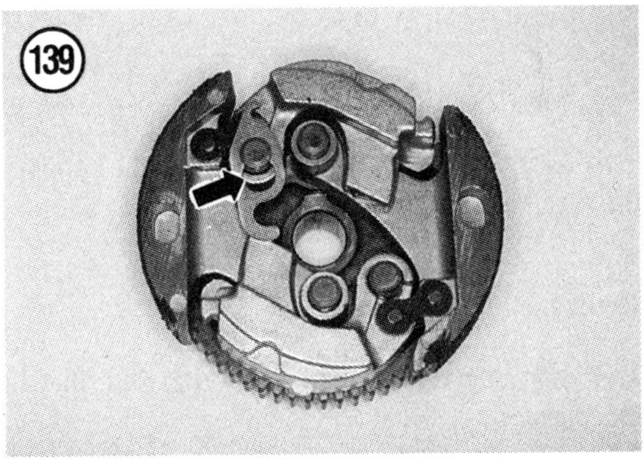

139

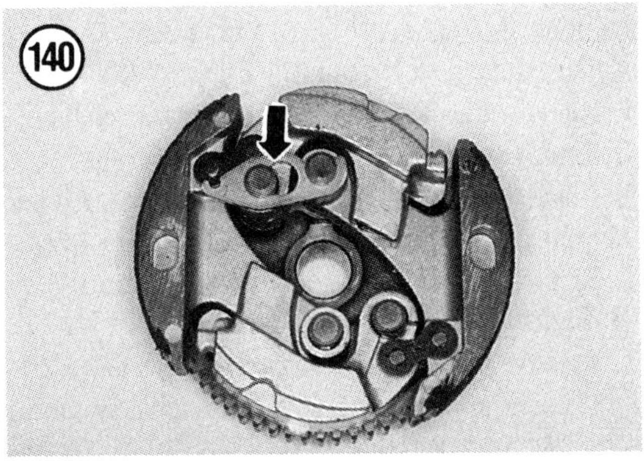

140

Clutch Installation

Refer to **Figure 143** for this procedure.

1. Lubricate the mainshaft, clutch gear bore and clutch housing inside wall and spline bore with transmission oil.
2. Install the flat washer—machined side facing out—over the mainshaft. See **Figure 144**.
3. Install the clutch (**Figure 145**) by meshing the 2 dogs on the back of the clutch gear with 2 notches in the oil pump drive gear.
4. Lubricate the clutch shoe linings with transmission oil.
5. Install the clutch housing (A, **Figure 146**).
6. Install the circlip—flat side facing out—into the groove in the end of the mainshaft (B, **Figure 146**). Make sure the circlip seats in the groove completely.

NOTE

If the circlip groove is not visible above the clutch housing, the clutch gear dogs are not meshed with the oil pump drive gear notches.

7. Install the right crankcase cover as described in this section.

PRIMARY DRIVE GEAR

Refer to **Figure 147** when servicing the primary drive gear assembly.

Removal

1. Remove the right crankcase cover as described in this chapter.
2. Lock the primary drive gear to the clutch gear by stuffing a thick folded rag (several layers thick) at the point shown in A, **Figure 148**. Then loosen the primary drive gear locknut (B, **Figure 148**).
3. Remove the clutch as described in this chapter.
4. Remove the locknut (B, **Figure 148**).
5. Remove the spring washer (A, **Figure 149**) and the primary drive gear assembly (B, **Figure 149**).
6. Remove the key (A, **Figure 150**) and thrust plate (B, **Figure 150**).
7. Remove the collar (A, **Figure 151**).
8. If necessary, remove the seal retainer mounting screw and retainer (B, **Figure 151**).

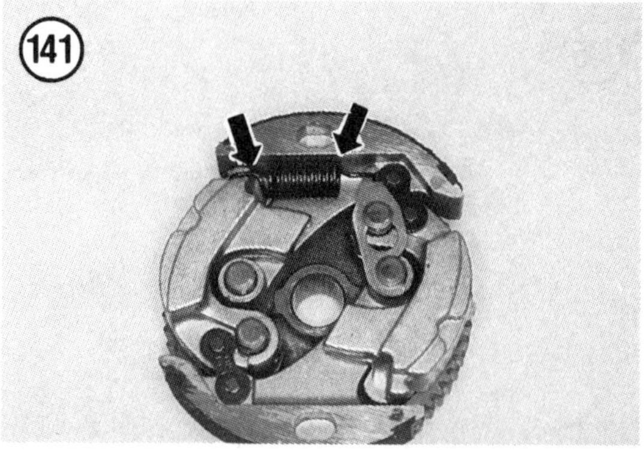
141

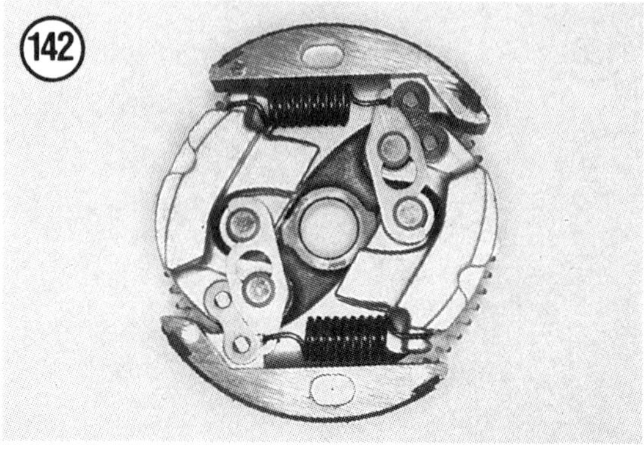
142

143

144

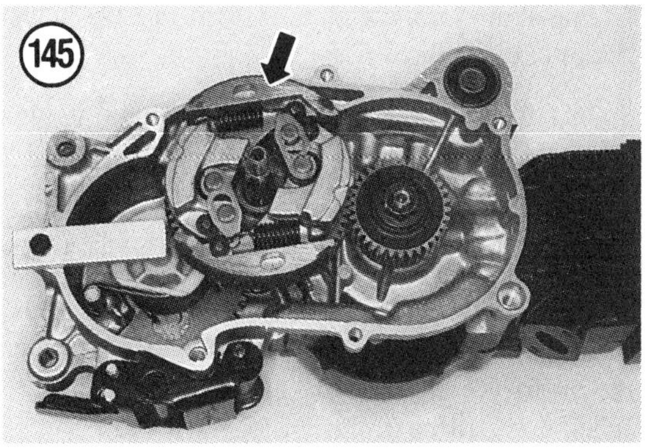

4

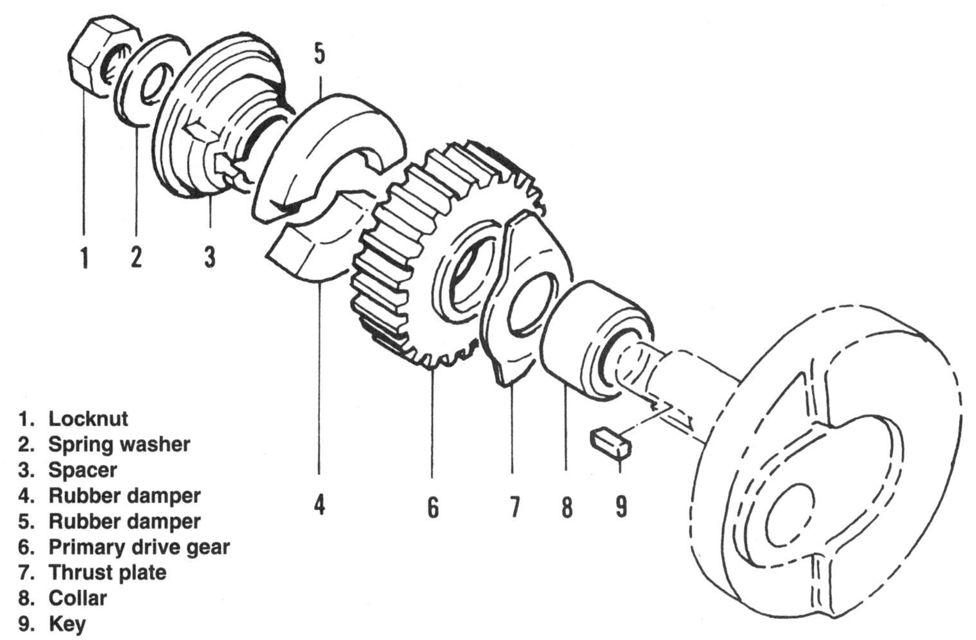

1. Locknut
2. Spring washer
3. Spacer
4. Rubber damper
5. Rubber damper
6. Primary drive gear
7. Thrust plate
8. Collar
9. Key

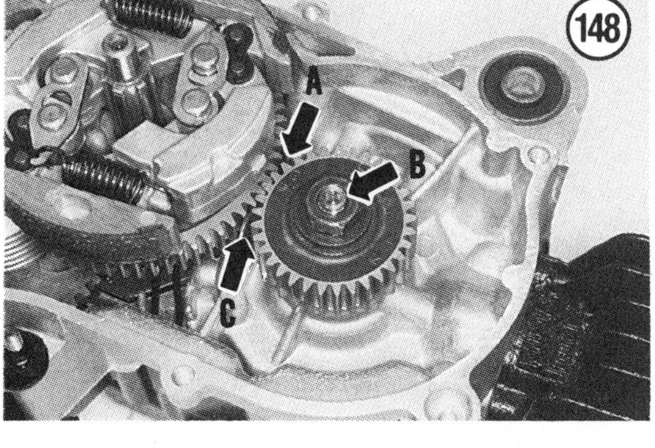

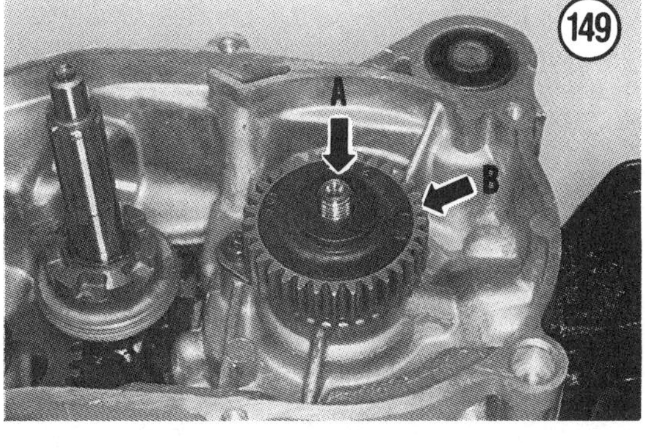

9. To separate the primary drive gear assembly, remove the spacer and the 2 rubber dampers (**Figure 152**).

Inspection

Replace all parts that show damage as described in this section.

1. Clean and dry all parts (**Figure 153**).
2. Inspect the primary drive gear assembly (**Figure 152**) for:
   a. Missing, broken or chipped teeth.
   b. Cracked or scored gear bore.
   c. Damaged keyway.
   d. Damaged spacer.
   e. Worn or damaged rubber dampers.
3. Inspect the thrust plate, key and collar for damage.

Installation

1. If removed, install the seal retainer (B, **Figure 151**) and its mounting screw. Use a medium strength threadlock on the retainer screw and tighten securely.
2. Lubricate the collar with grease, then install it over the crankshaft and into the seal with its chamfered side (**Figure 154**) facing out. See A, **Figure 151**.
3. The thrust plate tabs (**Figure 155**) are bent toward one side. Install the thrust plate (B, **Figure 150**) with its bent tabs facing out (away from engine).
4. Install the key (A, **Figure 150**) into the crankshaft keyway.
5. Assemble the primary drive gear assembly (**Figure 152**) as follows:
   a. Install the 2 rubber dampers into the primary drive gear cavity so that they are separated by the metal boss inside the gear as shown in A, **Figure 156**.
   b. Install the spacer by inserting its raised boss (B, **Figure 156**) in the gap between the 2 rubber dampers (C, **Figure 156**). See **Figure 157**.
6. Install the primary drive gear by aligning the keyway in the spacer with the key in the crankshaft. The spacer side of the primary drive gear should face out as shown in B, **Figure 149**.
7. Install the spring washer (A, **Figure 149**) so that its convex side faces out.
8. Install the locknut (B, **Figure 148**) and tighten finger tight.
9. Install the clutch as described in this chapter.
10. Lock the primary drive gear to the clutch gear by stuffing a thick folded rag (several layers thick) at the point shown in C, **Figure 148**. Then tighten the primary drive gear locknut (B, **Figure 148**) as specified in **Table 6**.

153

154
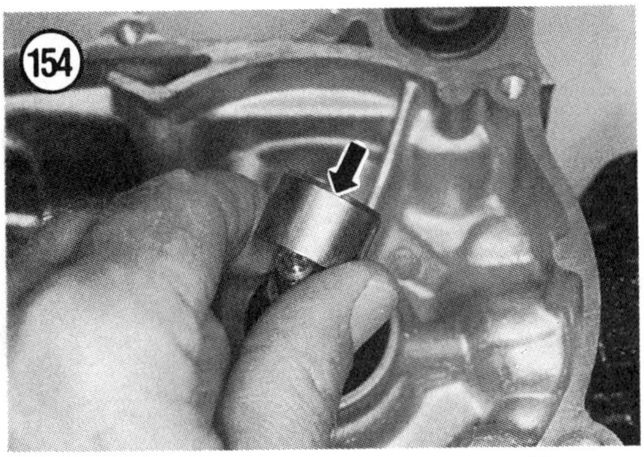

155

156
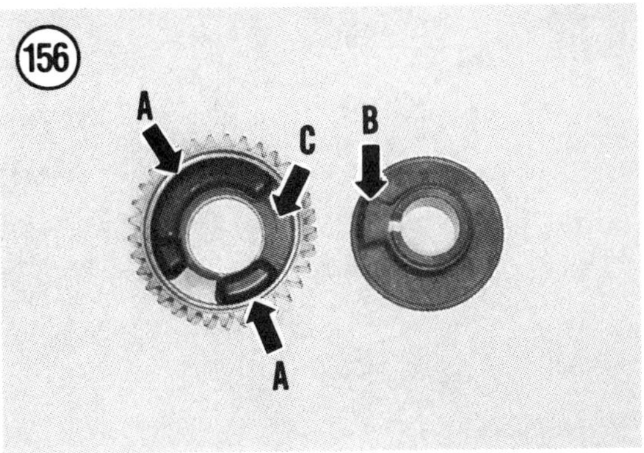

11. Install the right crankcase cover as described in this chapter.

KICKSTARTER, OIL PUMP DRIVE GEAR AND KICK PINION GEAR

Refer to **Figure 158** for this procedure.

Removal

1. Remove the clutch as described in this chapter.
2. Remove the circlip (A, **Figure 159**) and the oil pump drive gear (B, **Figure 159**).
3. Unhook the kick spring (**Figure 160**) and allow the spring to unwind.
4. Remove the kickstarter pedal from the left side of the engine.
5. See **Figure 161**. Remove the spring guide (A), kick spring (B) and kick shaft (C).
6. Remove the kick pinion gear (A, **Figure 162**)and clip (B).

Inspection

Replace all damaged parts as described in this section.

1. Clean and dry all parts (**Figure 163**).
2. Inspect the kick shaft (A, **Figure 164**) for:
   a. Missing, broken or chipped kick shaft gear teeth.
   b. Bent kick shaft.
   c. Stripped kick shaft splines.
3. Inspect the kick spring (B, **Figure 164**) for:
   a. Spread or damaged coils.
   b. Damaged spring ends.
4. Inspect the spring guide (C, **Figure 164**) for:

157

158

KICKSTARTER, OIL PUMP DRIVE GEAR AND KICK PINION GEAR

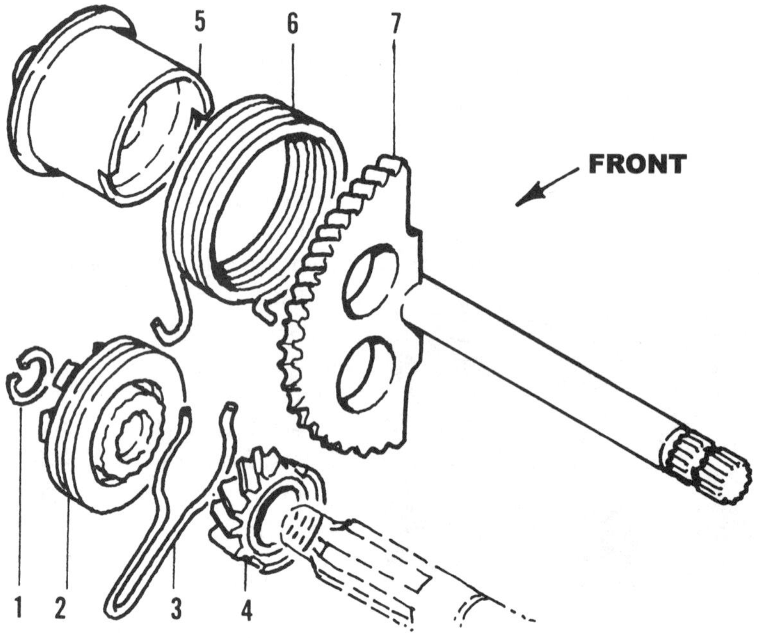

1. Circlip
2. Oil pump drive gear
3. Clip
4. Kick pinion gear
5. Spring guide
6. Kick spring
7. Kick shaft

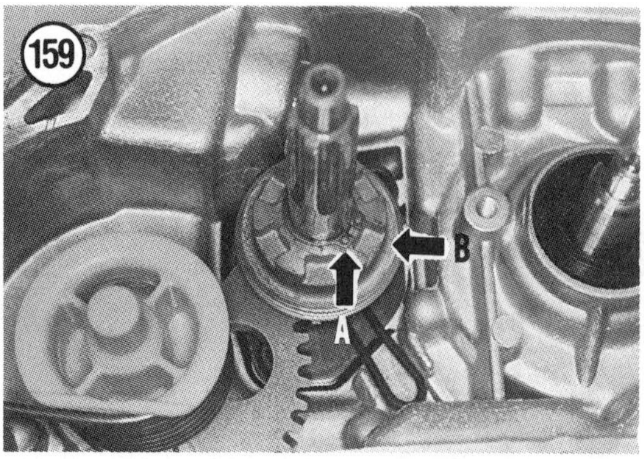

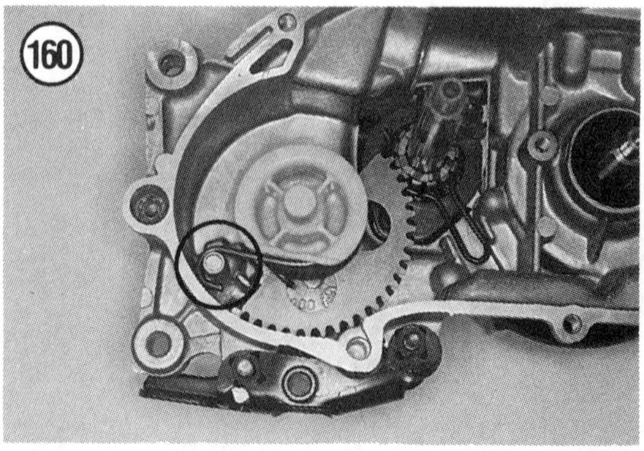

a. Excessively worn or damaged outer surface.

b. Cracked or damaged bore inside diameter.

5. Replace the oil pump drive gear circlip (A, **Figure 165**).

6. Inspect the oil pump drive gear (B, **Figure 165**) for:

a. Worn or damaged clutch engagement tabs (B, **Figure 165**).

b. Damaged oil pump threads (C, **Figure 165**).

NOTE

If the oil pump threads are damaged, inspect the oil pump driven gear teeth for damage.

c. Damaged kick pinion engagement teeth (**Figure 166**).

7. Inspect the kick pinion gear (D, **Figure 165**) for:

a. Worn or damaged oil pump gear engagement tabs.

b. Worn or damaged kick shaft gear teeth.

8. Replace the clip (E, **Figure 165**) if weak or damaged.

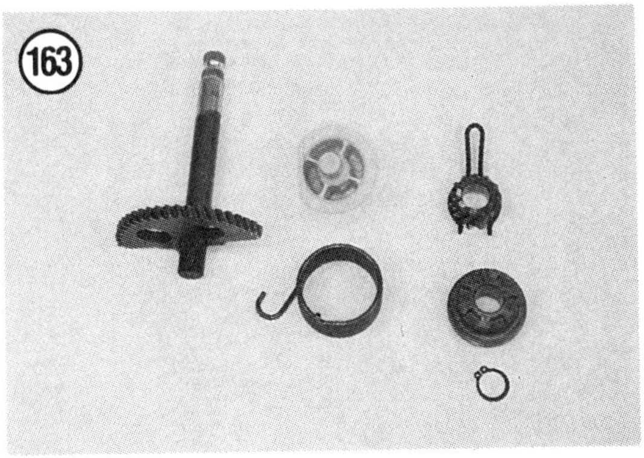

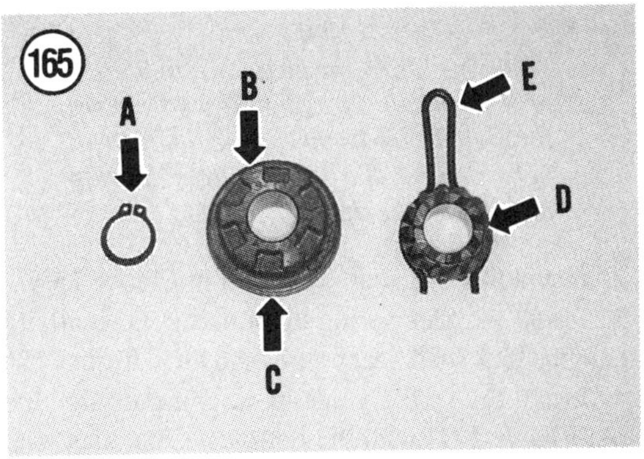

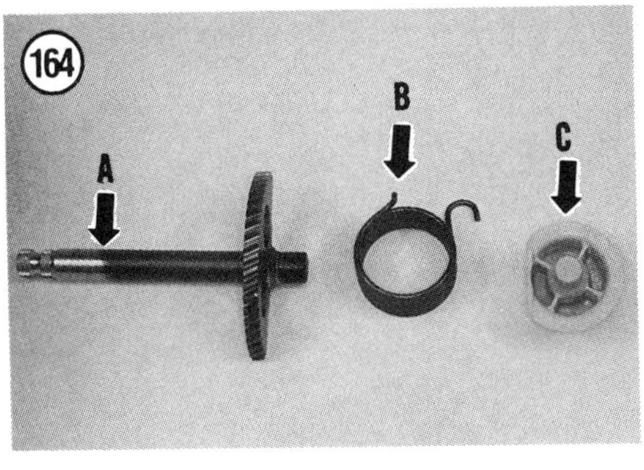

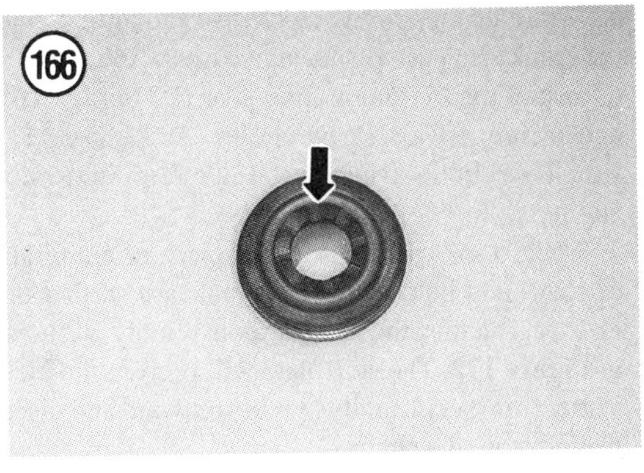

Kick Shaft Seal Replacement

The kick shaft seal (**Figure 167**) can be replaced with the engine cases assembled.

1. Remove the kick shaft as described in this section.
2. Pry the seal out of its mounting bore using a screwdriver as shown in **Figure 168**. Pad the bottom of the screwdriver to prevent crankcase damage.
3. Clean the mounting bore, then check it for cracks or other damage.
4. Pack the lips of the new with grease.
5. Install the new oil by pressing it into its mounting bore with your fingers, or install it with a socket and hammer. Install the seal so that its closed side (**Figure 167**) faces out.
6. Install the kick shaft as described in this section.

Installation

1. Install the kick pinion gear (A, **Figure 162**) and clip. Seat the clip between the 2 crankcase bosses as shown in B, **Figure 162**. Install the pinion gear with the oil pump engagement gear teeth facing up.

NOTE

When installing the kick shaft in Step 2, turn the shaft as its spline end passes through the left crankcase seal. This will help prevent the splines from tearing and damaging the seal.

2. Install the kick shaft as shown in **Figure 169**.
3. Install the kick spring by hooking its small arm onto the kick shaft gear hole as shown in **Figure 170**.
4. Install the spring guide by aligning its shoulder (A, **Figure 171**) with the flat part of the kick shaft gear (B, **Figure 171**). See A, **Figure 161**.
5. Wind the kick spring clockwise and hook it onto the crankcase post as shown in **Figure 160**.
6. Install the oil pump drive gear (B, **Figure 159**) and secure it with a new circlip (A, **Figure 159**). Install the circlip so that its flat side faces in (toward engine).
7. Make a stop plate (use a flat piece of aluminum or steel) and bolt it onto the crankcase so that one end seats against the kickstarter assembly as shown in **Figure 172**. The stop plate will prevent the kickstarter from accidentally moving outward and disengaging from the engine.
8. Install the kickstarter pedal (**Figure 173**) and operate it by hand. Make sure the kick shaft turns and engages the kick pinion gear, then returns under spring pressure.

NOTE

Leave the stop plate mounted onto the engine until just before the right crankcase cover is installed.

9. Install the clutch as described in this chapter.

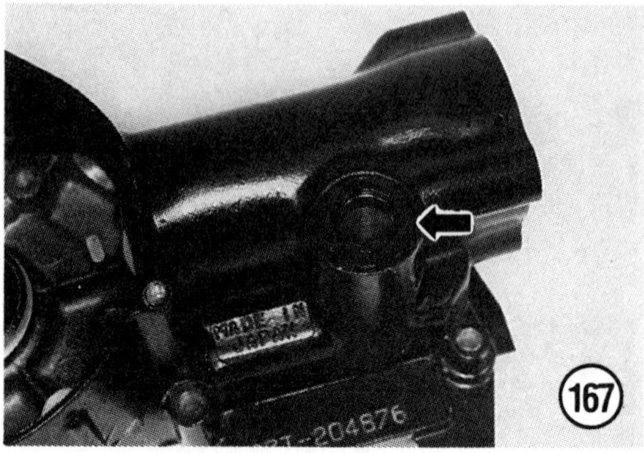

167

168

169

170

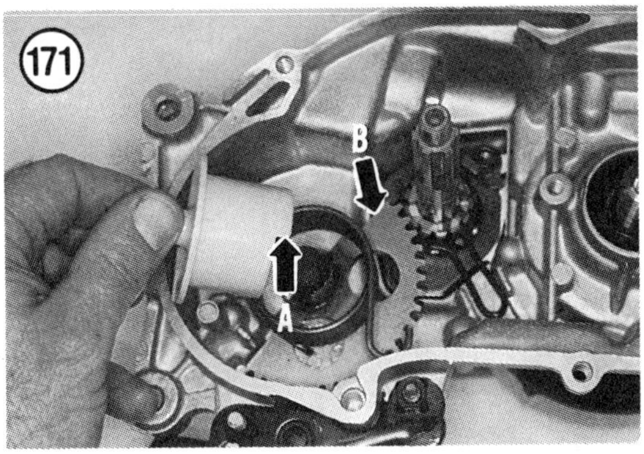

171

172

173

TRANSMISSION

Refer to **Figure 174** when servicing the transmission in this section.

Removal

1. Remove the kickstarter, oil pump drive gear and kick pinion gear as described in this chapter.
2. See **Figure 175**. Remove the 2 Allen bolts (A), stop plate (B) and cover plate (C).
3. Pull the mainshaft (**Figure 176**) out of the crankcase along with the pinion shim (**Figure 177**).
4. Remove the driven pinion shaft seal (**Figure 178**) as follows.
   a. A hand drill, 2 sheet metal screws, a suitable size drill bit, drill stop, and a pair of pliers are required for this procedure. The drill stop mounts onto the drill bit to prevent the drill bit from going in too far and damaging the engine case or hex screw.

   NOTE

   *The driven pinion shaft seal (**Figure 178**) can be difficult to remove, especially on an older machine. Yamaha recommends to insert the end of a pair of needlenose pliers into the seal and pry it out. This method is difficult as the seal has a metal backing, making it difficult to penetrate. The following procedure works well if you follow the steps and use a drill stop on the drill bit. In all cases, when removing the seal, make sure you do not damage the crankcase bore surface.*

   b. Mount a drill stop onto the drill bit and set it to a depth of 3 mm (1/8 in.).

   NOTE

   *Drill stops are available commercially, or you can improvise with a piece of masking or duct tape as shown in **Figure 179**.*

   c. Drill 2 holes, 180° apart (**Figure 180**) through the seal. See **Figure 181**.
   d. Thread the 2 sheet metal screws through the holes in the seal (**Figure 182**). Thread the screws far enough into the oil seal to make complete thread engagement, but not so deep that contact is made with the cover nut.

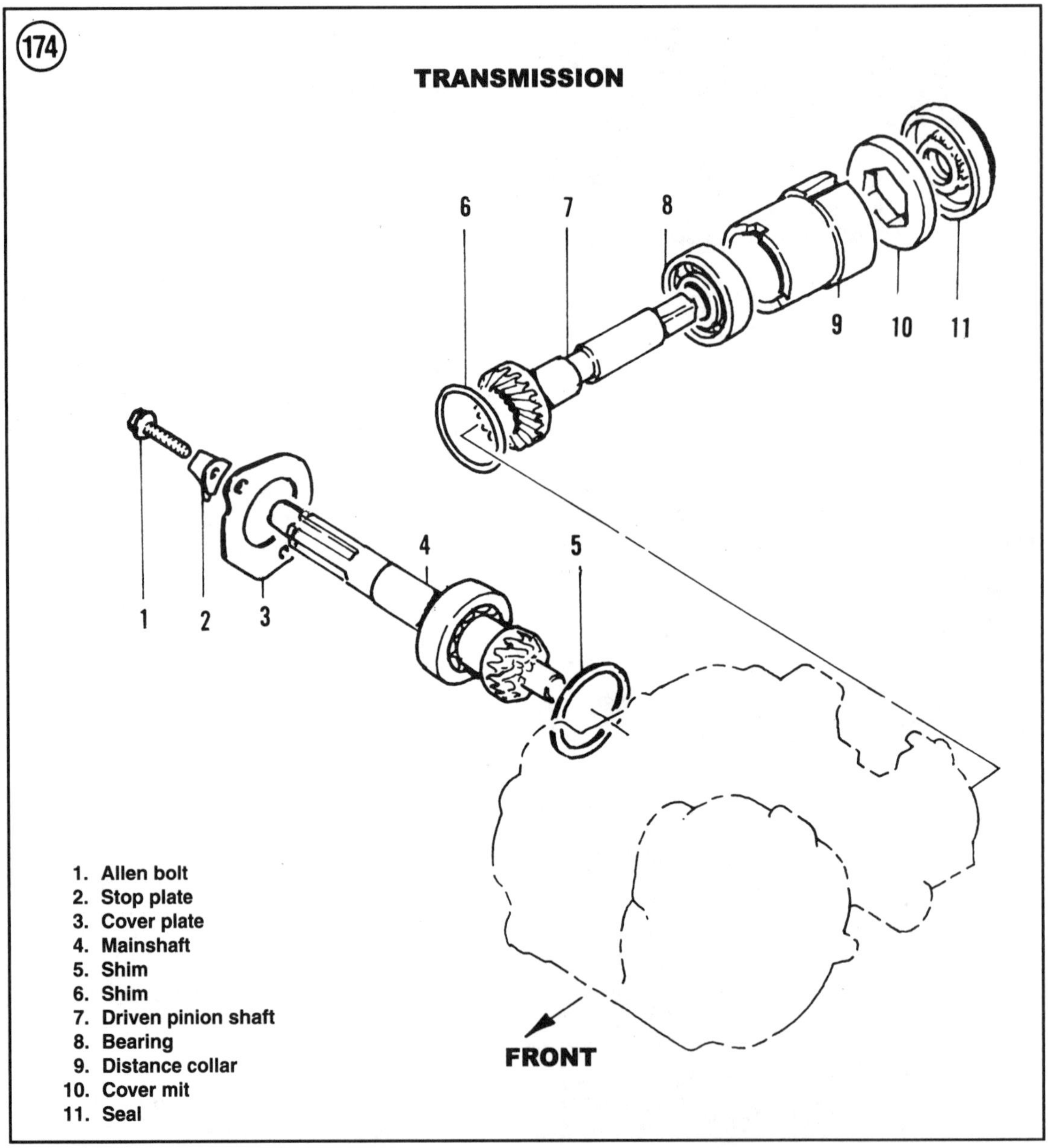
174
TRANSMISSION
6
7
8
9
10
11
1
2
3
4
5
FRONT
1. Allen bolt
2. Stop plate
3. Cover plate
4. Mainshaft
5. Shim
6. Shim
7. Driven pinion shaft
8. Bearing
9. Distance collar
10. Cover mit
11. Seal

175
C
B
A

176

e. Remove the seal by pulling first on one screw and then the other. Repeat this sequence to prevent the seal from binding in its mounting bore. See **Figure 183**.

5. Remove the 25 mm cover nut (**Figure 184**) as follows:

NOTE
*A 25 mm hex wrench (Yamaha part No. YM-01306 or equivalent) with a hollow center is required to remove and install the cover nut (**Figure 184**). We used the outside hex part of a 27/32 in. plumber's faucet socket (available at most large hardware stores) and a 17 mm hex socket inserted into the opposite end of the faucet socket. See **Figure 185**. While the 17 mm hex socket is not required to loosen the nut, it allows a means of using a torque wrench to tighten the nut during reassembly. While it may be nec-*

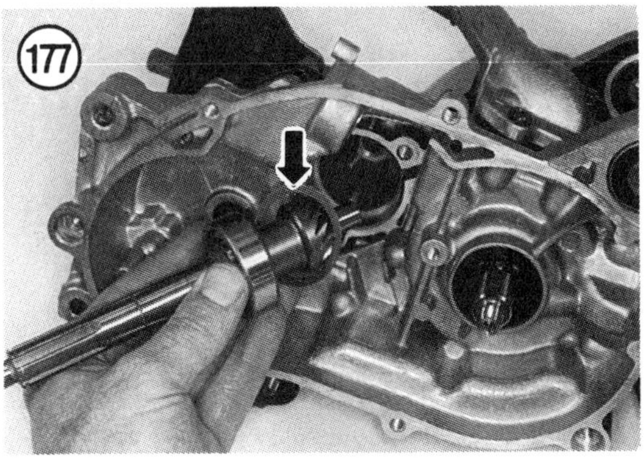
177

178

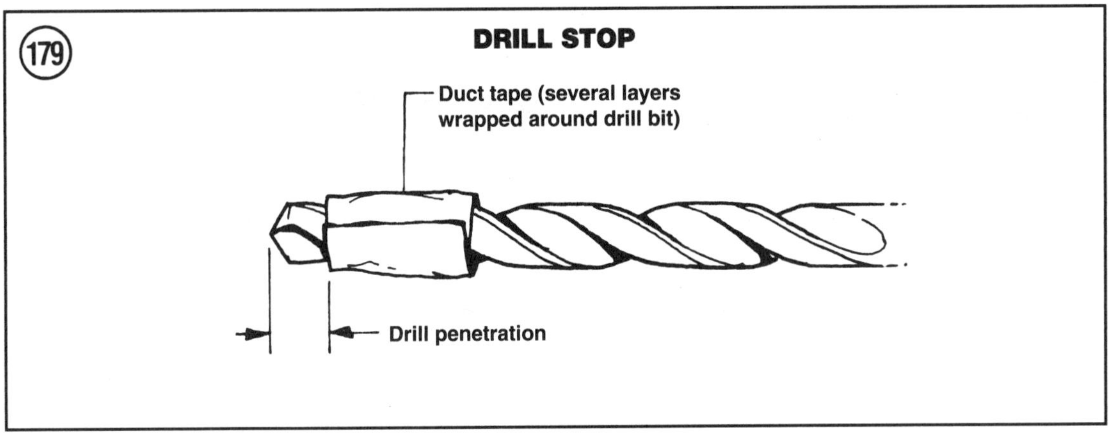

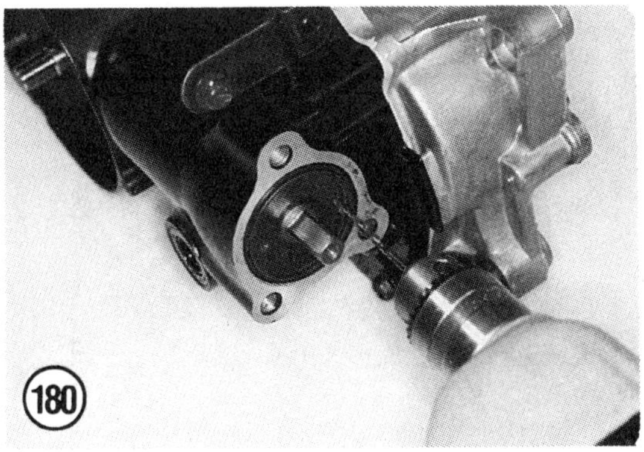
180

181

essary to file the outside of the plumber's faucet to allow it to fit the cover nut, this tool setup works well for removing and tightening the nut.

CAUTION
The cover nut has left-hand threads (turn clockwise to loosen).

a. The cover nut uses left-hand threads. This is indicated by the clockwise arrow cast into the front of the nut (**Figure 184**).
b. Insert the plumber's socket or Yamaha hex wrench into the nut (**Figure 186**), then turn it clockwise to loosen and remove it. See **Figure 187**.

6. Remove the driven pinion shaft (**Figure 188**), distance collar and thrust shim assembly. See **Figure 189**.

Mainshaft Inspection

Replace parts that are out of specification or show damage as described in this section.

1. Clean and dry all parts (**Figure 190**).

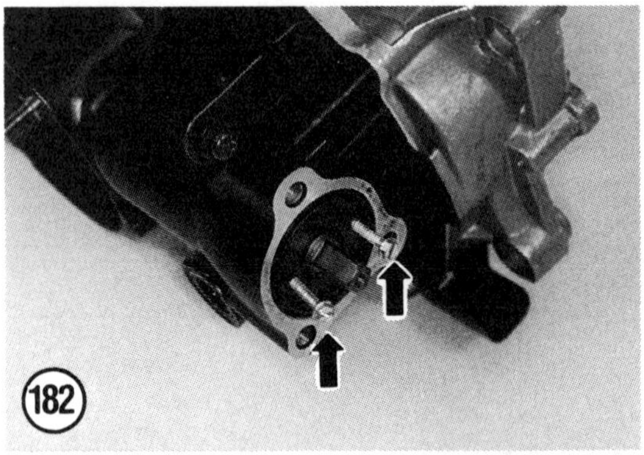
182

183

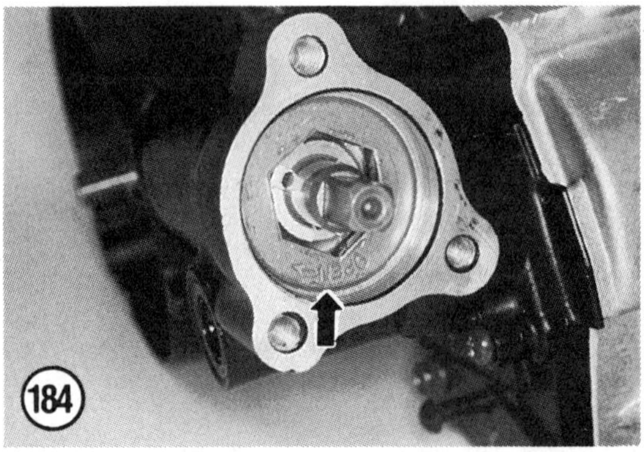
184

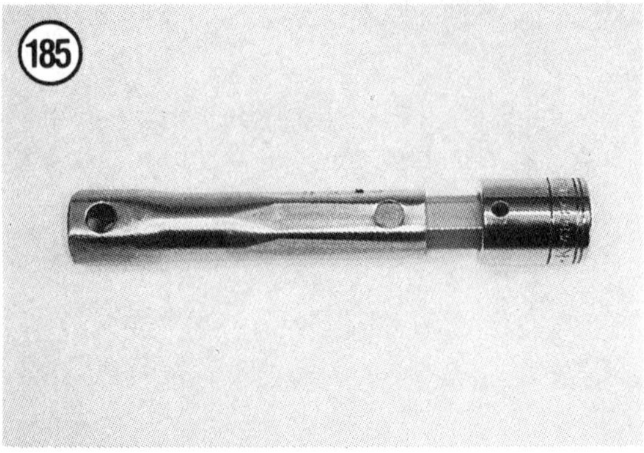
185

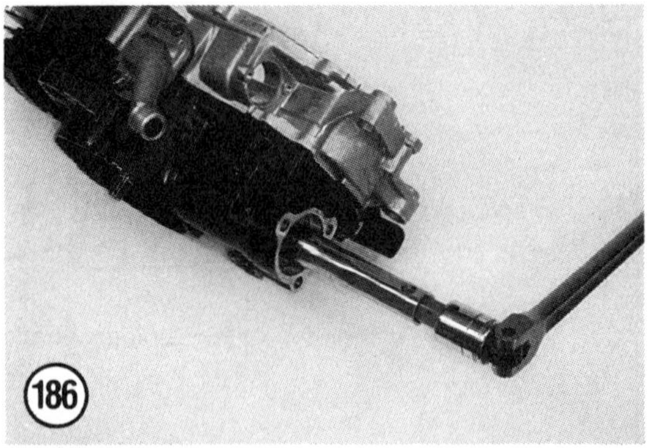
186

187

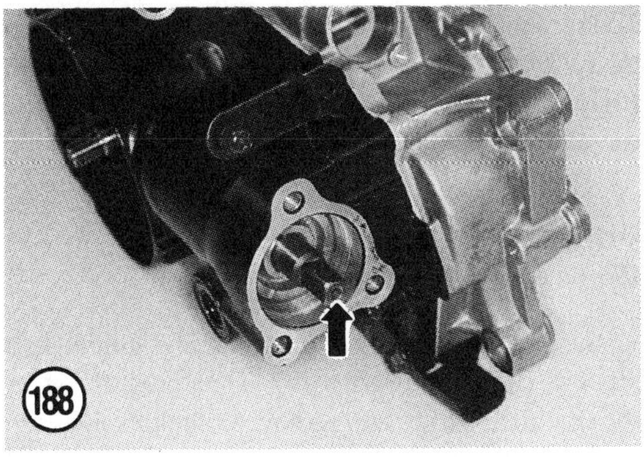

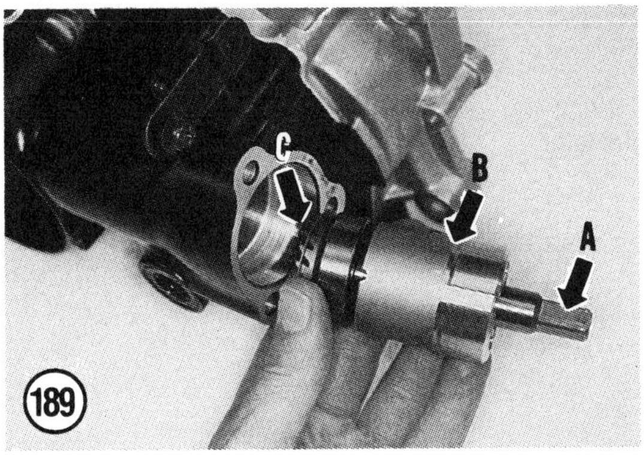

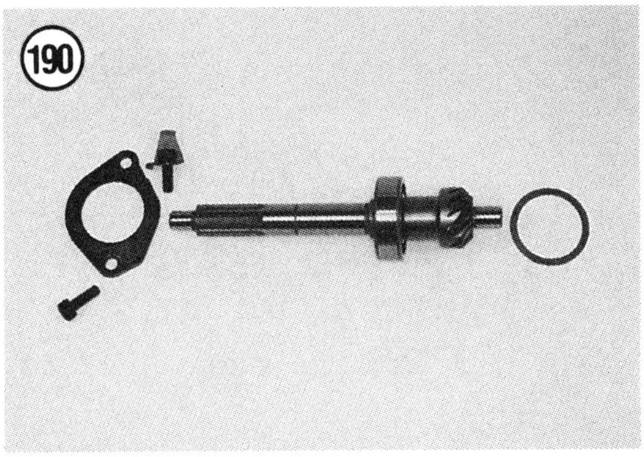

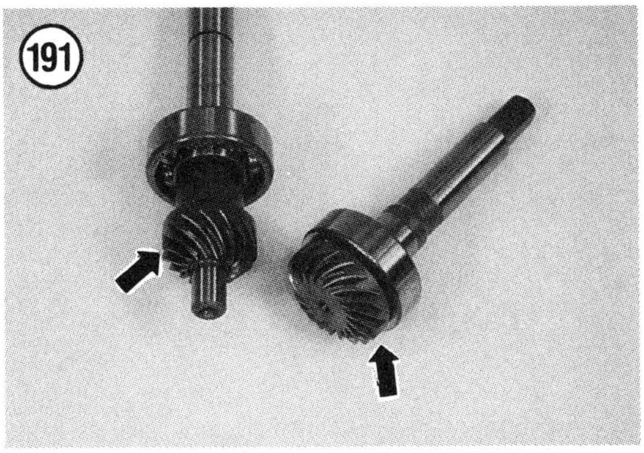

2. Inspect the cover plate and stop plate (**Figure 190**) and replace if damaged.
3. Replace the pinion shim (**Figure 190**) if bent or otherwise damaged.
4. Visually inspect the mainshaft (**Figure 190**) for:
   a. Worn or damaged splines.
   b. Cracked or rounded-off circlip groove.
   c. Worn or damaged bearing surfaces.
   d. Damaged mainshaft gear. If the mainshaft gear is damaged, check the driven pinion shaft gear (**Figure 191**) for damage also.
5. Inspect the mainshaft bearing (**Figure 192**) for visual damage. Then spin the bearing by hand. The bearing must turn smoothly without binding or excessive noise. If the bearing is damaged, replace the mainshaft as an assembly. The mainshaft bearing cannot be replaced separately.
6. Place the mainshaft between centers and measure runout with a dial indicator as shown in **Figure 193**. Replace the mainshaft if the runout exceeds the service limit in **Table 5**.

Driven Pinion Shaft Inspection

Replace parts that are out of specification or show damage as described in this section.
1. Clean and dry all parts (**Figure 194**).
2. Inspect the cover nut (**Figure 194**) and replace it if damaged.
3. Replace the thrust shim (**Figure 194**) if bent or otherwise damaged.
4. Inspect the distance collar (**Figure 195**) for:
   a. Cracks or damaged.
   b. Worn or damaged bearing surfaces.

4

5. Visually inspect the driven pinion shaft (**Figure 194**) for:
   a. Worn or damaged shaft square.
   b. Worn or damaged bearing surfaces.
   c. Damaged driven pinion shaft gear. If the driven pinion is damaged, check the main shaft gear (**Figure 191**) for damage also.

6. Inspect the driven pinion shaft bearing (**Figure 196**) for visual damage. Then spin the bearing by hand. The bearing must turn smoothly without binding or excessive noise. If the bearing is damaged, replace it as described in this section.

7. Place the driven pinion shaft between centers and measure runout with a dial indicator as shown in **Figure 193**. Replace the driven pinion shaft if the runout exceeds the service limit in **Table 5**.

Driven Pinion Shaft Bearing Replacement

1. Support the bearing with a bearing splitter in a press as shown in **Figure 197**. Then press the shaft through the bearing and remove both parts. Discard the bearing.

193

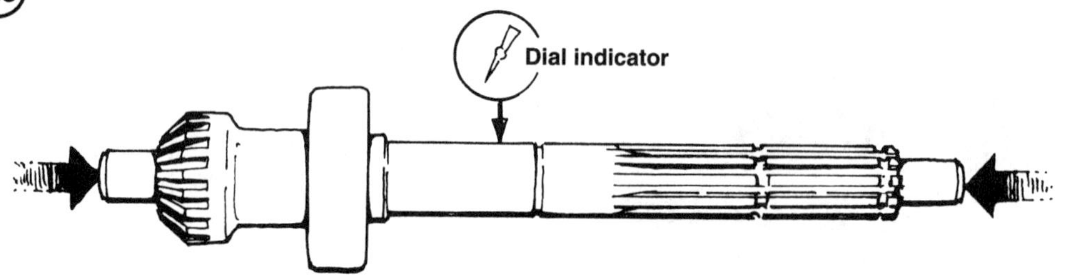

194

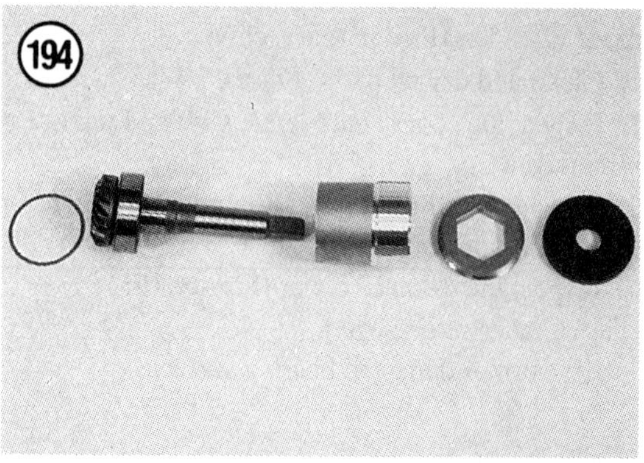

196

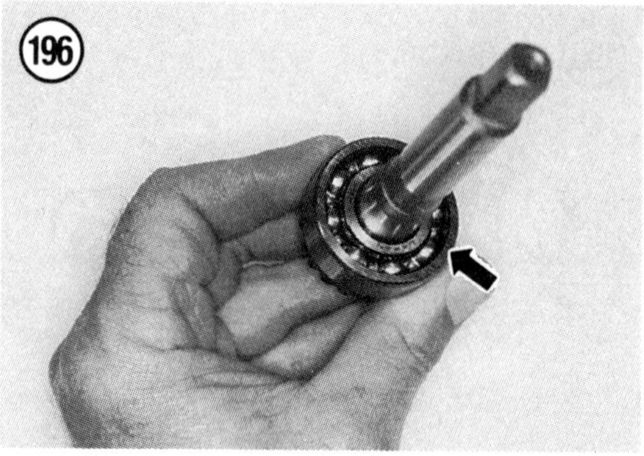

195

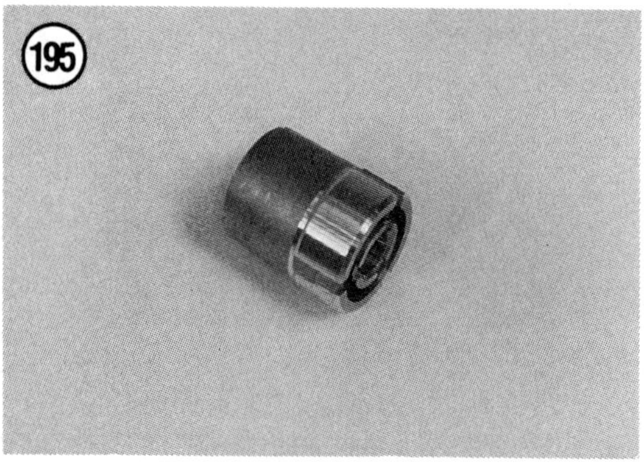

197

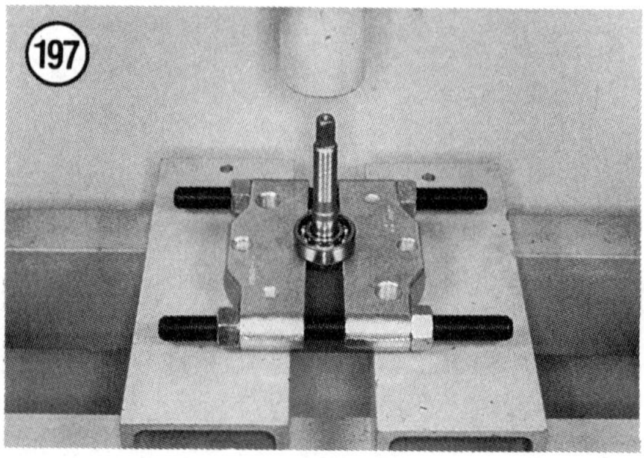

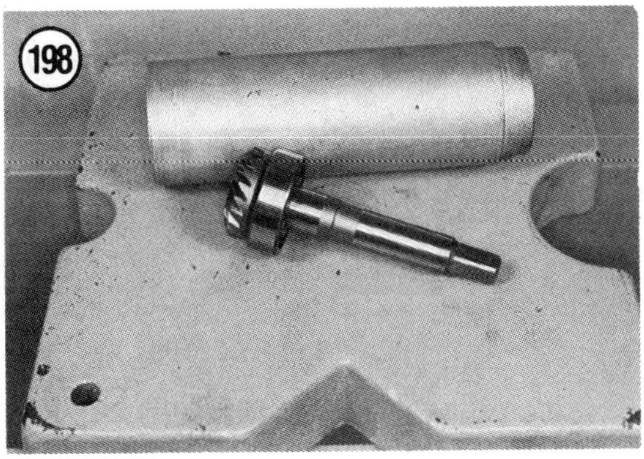
198

2. Clean and inspect the driven pinion shaft.
3. Place the driven pinion shaft in a press so the gear side faces down. Then press the new bearing onto the shaft with a driver placed on the inner bearing race. Install the bearing until it bottoms on the shaft (**Figure 198**).

Installation

Refer to **Figure 199** when installing the transmission assembly.

1. Make sure all transmission parts are clean before starting assembly.

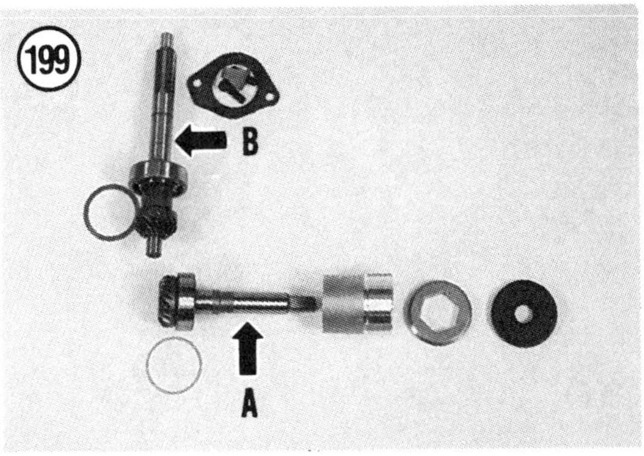

199

NOTE
*Steps 2-6 describe installation of the driven pinion shaft assembly (A, **Figure 199**).*

2. Lubricate the thrust shim, bearing and all bearing surfaces on the distance collar and driven pinion shaft (**Figure 194**) with transmission oil.
3. See **Figure 189**. Install the thrust shim (C) and distance collar (B) onto the driven pinion shaft (A).
4. Install the driven pinion shaft assembly (**Figure 188**) into the crankcase. Make sure the shaft is fully seated in its mounting bore.

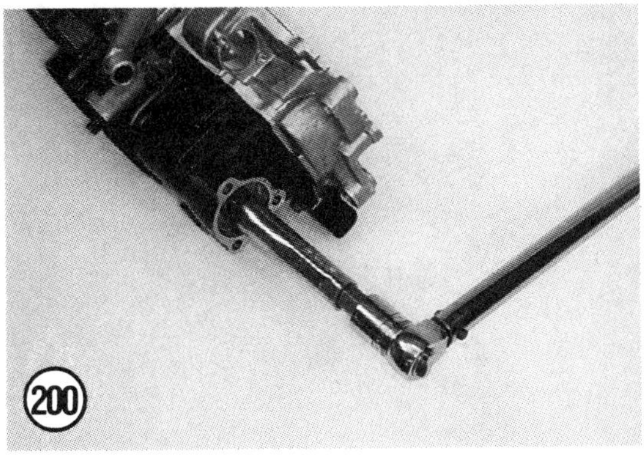
200

CAUTION
*The cover nut (**Figure 187**) has left-hand threads. Turn the nut counter-clockwise to tighten it.*

5. Thread the cover nut (**Figure 184**) into the crankcase by hand). Then, using the same tool as during disassembly, tighten the cover nut (**Figure 200**) as specified in **Table 6**. Turn the middle driven pinion shaft by hand, making sure it turns smoothly.
6. Install the seal as follows:
   a. Pack the seal lip (**Figure 201**) with grease.
   b. Install the seal with its closed side facing out (away from engine).
   c. Install the seal by tapping it into its mounting bore with a bearing driver or socket (**Figure 202**) of the same size. Install the seal until its outer surface is flush with or slightly below the oil seal mounting bore inside surface (**Figure 203**). Make sure the seal is properly installed.

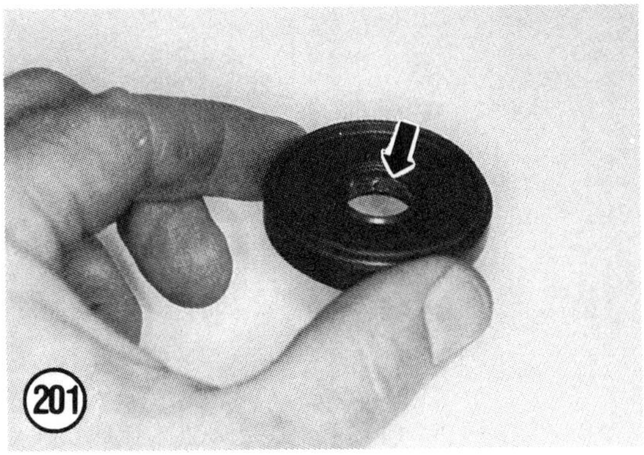
201

NOTE
*Steps 7-10 describe installation of the mainshaft assembly (B, **Figure 199**).*

7. Lubricate the pinion shim, bearing and all mainshaft (**Figure 190**) and crankcase bearing surfaces with transmission oil.
8. Install the pinion shim onto the mainshaft as shown in **Figure 177**.
9. Install the mainshaft into the crankcase and engage its gear with the middle driven pinion shaft gear (**Figure 176**). Turn the mainshaft, making sure that the middle driven pinion shaft turns also.
10. Install the mainshaft cover (A, **Figure 204**) and stop plate (B, **Figure 204**) as follows:
   a. Install the cover plate so its notch is at the top right corner as shown in A, **Figure 205**.
   b. Install the cover plate lower mounting bolt (B, **Figure 205**).
   c. Install the upper mounting bolt through the stop plate, then install the stop plate so its arm faces down and toward the mainshaft as shown in **Figure 206**.
   d. Tighten the mainshaft cover plate mounting bolts as specified in **Table 6**.
11. Turn the mainshaft once again, making sure that the middle driven pinion shaft turns. If there is any binding or roughness, remove the transmission and check the parts.
12. Install the kick pinion gear, oil pump drive gear and kickstarter as described in this chapter.

CRANKCASE AND CRANKSHAFT

The crankcase is made in 2 halves of a precision diecast aluminum alloy.

The crankshaft assembly is made up of 2 full-circle flywheels pressed together on a hollow crankpin. The connecting rod big end bearing on the crankpin is a needle bearing assembly. The crankshaft assembly is supported by 2 ball bearings in the crankcase.

Special Tools

To disassemble and reassemble the crankcase assembly you will need the following special tools or their equivalents. These tools allow easy disassembly and reassembly of the engine without prying or hammer use.

   a. Yamaha crankcase separating tool (part No. YU-01135) or equivalent; see **Figure 207**. This tool threads into the crankcase and is used to separate the crankcase halves and to press the crankshaft out of the crankcase.

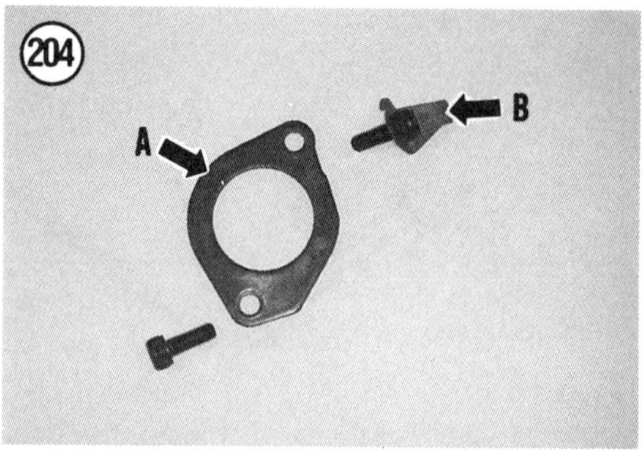

206

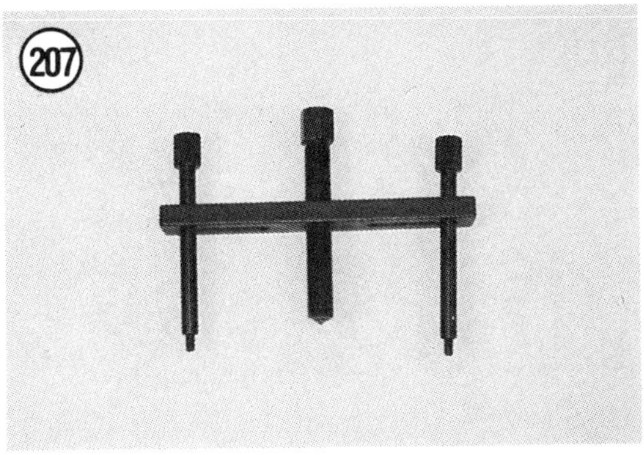

207

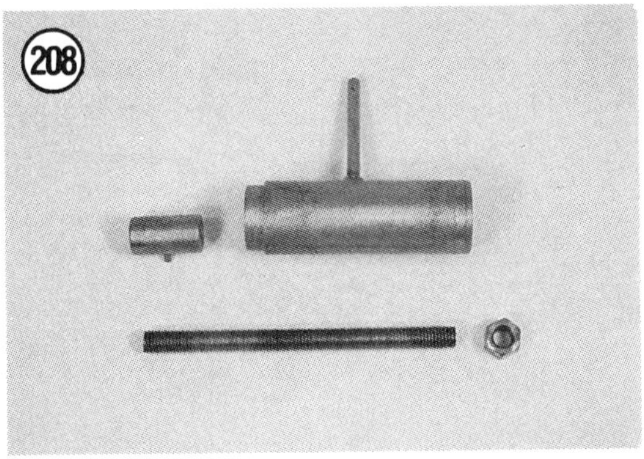

208

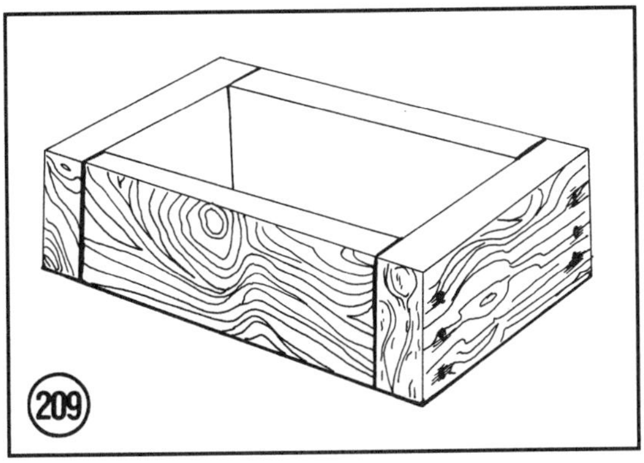

209

b. Yamaha crankshaft installing tool (part No. YU-90500) and adapter (part No. YU-90063); see **Figure 208**.
c. When handling the engine cases, 2 wooden blocks or a fixture made of wood (**Figure 209**) will assist in engine disassembly and reassembly and will help to prevent damage to the crankshaft and transmission shafts.

Crankcase Disassembly

This procedure describes disassembly of the crankcase halves and removal of the crankshaft.

1. Remove the flywheel and stator plate (Chapter Eight).
2. Remove the Woodruff key (**Figure 210**) from the crankshaft keyway.

NOTE

The Woodruff key must be removed before removing the crankshaft from the engine; otherwise, it will hang up on the left main bearing during crankshaft removal and cause crankshaft and bearing damage.

3. Remove the following engine assemblies as described in this chapter.
   a. Cylinder head, cylinder and piston.
   b. Remove the engine from the frame.
   c. Intake manifold and reed valve assembly.
   d. Right crankcase cover.
   e. Clutch and primary drive gear system.
   f. Kickstarter, oil pump drive gear and kick pinion gear.
   g. Transmission assembly.

210

4. Place the engine assembly on wooden blocks with the left side facing up (**Figure 211**).
5. Place a plastic hose over each cylinder stud (**Figure 212**) to protect them during the following steps.
6. Remove the center stand mounting bracket (A, **Figure 211**).
7. Remove the air filter mounting bracket (B, **Figure 211**).
8. Loosen the remaining crankcase screws one-quarter turn at a time and in a crisscross pattern.
9. Before removing the crankcase mounting screws, draw an outline of the crankcase on a piece of cardboard (**Figure 213**) and punch holes along the outline for the placement of each mounting screw.
10. Remove the left crankcase mounting screws and place them in the corresponding holes in the cardboard (**Figure 213**).

NOTE
When separating the crankcase halves in Step 12, the crankshaft will remain in the left case half.

11. Turn the engine over so the right side faces up (**Figure 214**). Then tap and remove the right crankcase half (**Figure 215**). As the case halves separate, make sure they come apart evenly at the front and back. If not, make sure all of the crankcase screws are removed.

CAUTION
The right case half should come off fairly easily as the right main bearing and right crank half are a slip fit. Never pry between the case halves or you may cause permanent damage to the mating surfaces resulting in an air and/or oil leak.

211

212

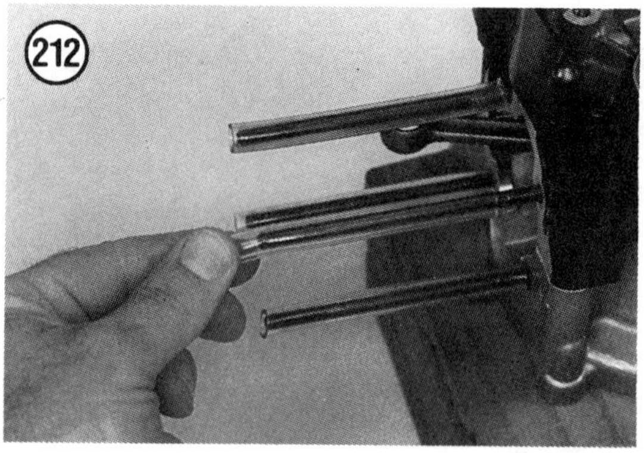

213

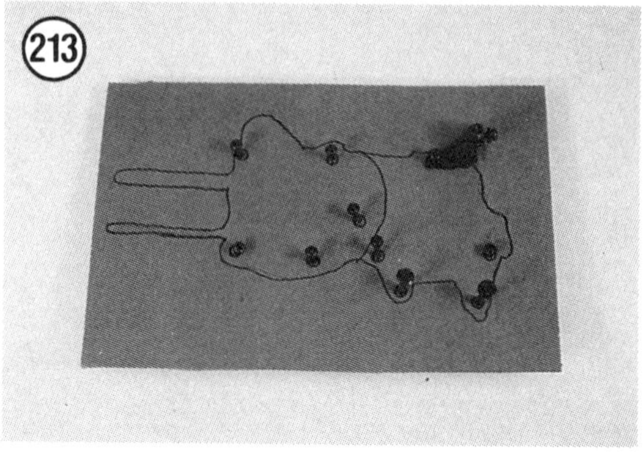

214

215

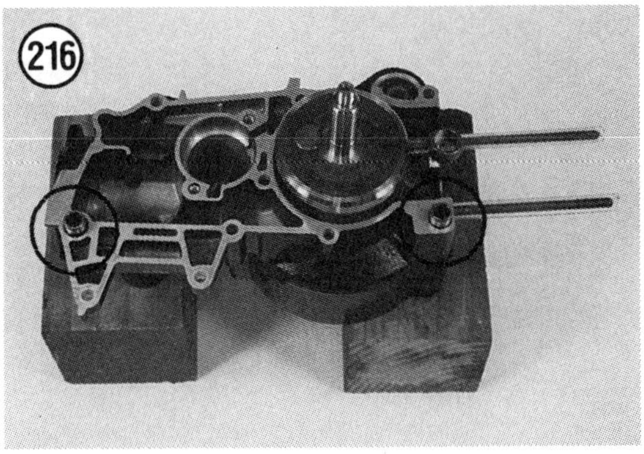
216

12. Remove the 2 dowel pins (**Figure 216**).

NOTE
*Steps 13-17 describe crankshaft (**Figure 216**) removal. If the special tool is not available, have the crankshaft removed at a dealership. Do not drive on the end of the crankshaft to remove it. This will severely damage the crankshaft threads.*

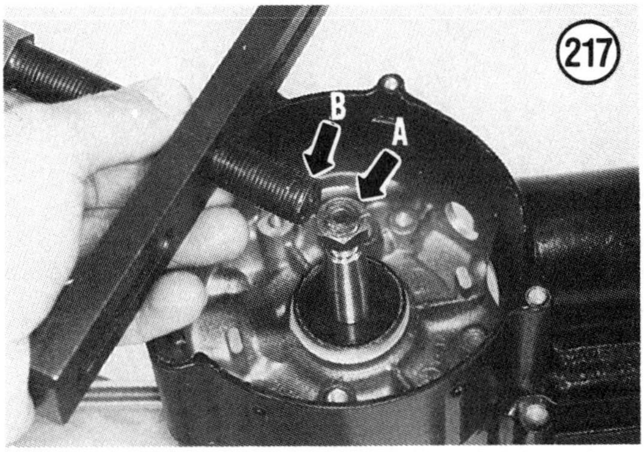

217

13. Install the flywheel nut (A, **Figure 217**) onto the end of the crankshaft.

14. Apply some grease onto the end of the crankshaft and the crankcase separating tool's pressure bolt (B, **Figure 217**).

15. Mount the crankcase separating tool onto the crankcase and over the crankshaft as shown in **Figure 218**.

16. Run the tool's pressure bolt against the end of the crankshaft. Then check to make sure the tool's body is parallel with the crankcase (**Figure 218**). If not, readjust the tool's mounting bolts.

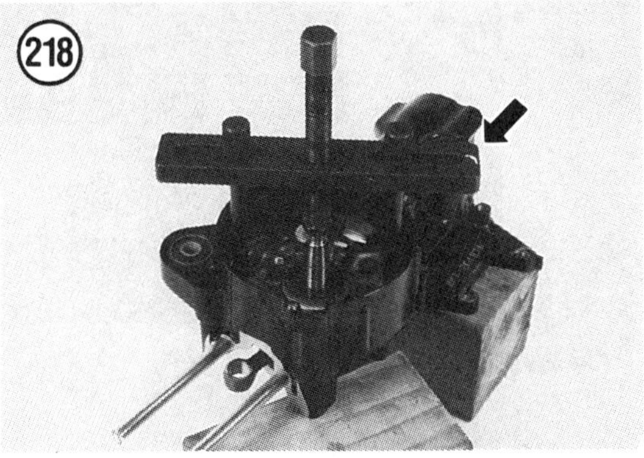
218

17. Hold the crankshaft with one hand and then turn the tool's pressure bolt *clockwise* until the crankshaft begins to move out of its bearing. You may hear a loud pop when the crankshaft starts to move. This is normal, but stop and investigate all the way around the crankshaft and bearing. If everything is normal, continue until the crankshaft is free. Then remove the flywheel nut (**Figure 219**) and slide the crankshaft out of its bearing. See **Figure 220**.

18. Clean and inspect the crankcase halves, bearings and crankshaft as described in this chapter.

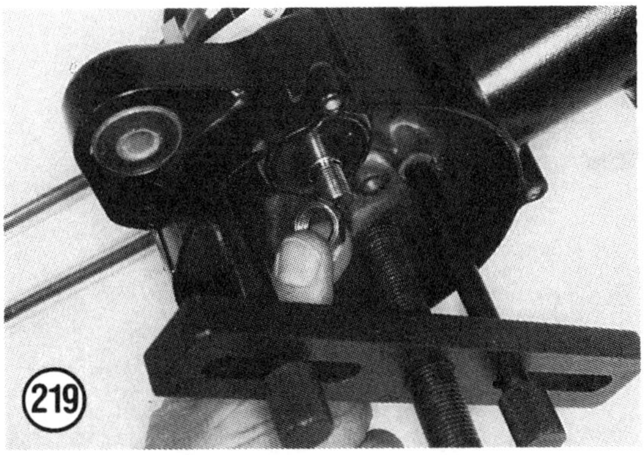
219

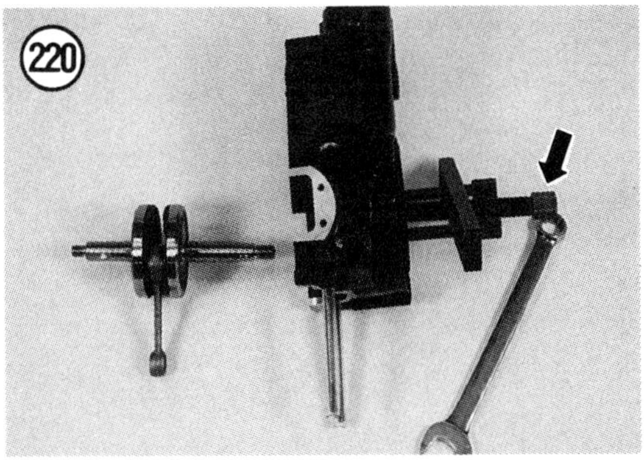
220

Crankcase Cleaning and Inspection

1. Remove the crankcase seals as described under *Seal Replacement* in this chapter.
2. Remove all gasket and sealer residue from both crankcase mating surfaces.
3. Clean both crankcase halves (**Figure 221**).
4. Dry the case halves and bearings with compressed air. When doing so, hold the inner bearing races to prevent them from turning. When the bearings are dry, lubricate them with oil.
5. Check the crankcase halves (**Figure 221**) for cracks or fractures in the stiffening webs, around the bearing bosses, and at threaded holes.
6. Inspect machined surfaces for burrs, cracks or other damage. Repair minor damage with a fine-cut file or oilstone. A severely damaged mating surface may require welding and machining.

NOTE

If cracks or fractures are found, have them repaired at a reputable shop experienced in this type of welding and repair.

7. Check the cylinder studs (**Figure 222**) and threaded holes for stripping, cross-threading or deposit buildup. Clean threaded holes with compressed air. If necessary, repair threads with a tap or die. Replace damaged studs as described under *Stud Replacement* in Chapter One.
8. Check the pivot shaft bushings (**Figure 223**) for severe wear, age deterioration or other damage. Replace both bushings as set. Replace the bushing with a press.
9. Check the main bearings (**Figure 224** and **Figure 225**) for pitting, galling, and wear. Rotate the bearings by hand and feel for roughness and excessive

222

223

224

221

225

226

227

play. They should turn smoothly and evenly and there should be no apparent radial play. If any bearing is in questionable condition, replace it as described in this section.

Crankcase Seal Replacement

Seals are identified as follows:

a. Left main bearing seal (**Figure 226**).

b. Kick shaft seal (**Figure 227**).

c. Right main bearing seal (**Figure 228**).

1. Before removing the seals, inspect them for damage or any unusual type of wear.

2A. Because of the deep case recess, remove the left main bearing seal with a hooked tool as shown in **Figure 229**.

2B. Remove the kick shaft and right main bearing seals with a screwdriver, taking care not to damage the case bore. Pad the pry area under the screwdriver to avoid damaging the crankcase. See **Figure 230** and **Figure 231**.

3. Inspect and service the main bearings before installing the new oil seals. Refer to *Crankshaft Bearing Replacement* in this section.

228

230

229

231

4. Compare the new and old seals before installation.
5. Pack grease between the oil seal lips (**Figure 232**).
6. Using your hands, press the new oil seals into their mounting bores (**Figure 233**). If necessary, use a suitable socket or bearing driver to install the oil seals. Install the oil seals with their manufacturer's marks facing out (away from crankcase). Press in each oil seal until its outer surface is flush with or slightly below the oil seal bore inside surface.

Main Bearing Replacement

This section describes replacement of the left (**Figure 224**) and right (**Figure 225**) main bearings.

1. All bearings are marked on one side with its respective size code and usually with some type of manufacturer code or name. Before removing the bearings, note and record the direction in which the manufacturer's marks face for proper assembly. Bearings are usually installed with these marks facing out (the marks are visible from the side the bearing is installed from).
2. If a bearing came off with the crankshaft, remove it with a bearing puller.

NOTE
*Two methods of replacing the crankcase bearings are described below. Before you begin, read the **Ball Bearing Replacement** section in Chapter One.*

3A. To replace the bearings using heat, perform the following steps:

a. Before heating the case half, select all of the appropriate bearing drivers for the bearings being removed.
b. Before heating the case half, place the new bearings in a freezer. Chilling them will slightly reduce their overall diameter while the hot crankcase is slightly larger due to heat expansion. This will make installation much easier.

CAUTION
Before heating the crankcases to remove the bearings, wash the cases thoroughly with detergent and water. Rinse and rewash the cases as required to remove all traces of oil and other chemical deposits.

c. The bearings are installed with a slight interference fit. Heat the crankcase halves to a temperature of about 212° F (100° C) in a shop oven or on a hot plate. Heat only one case at a time.

CAUTION
Do not heat the case halves with a torch (propane or acetylene)—never bring a flame into contact with the bearing or case. The direct heat can warp the case half.

232

233

234

d. Wearing a pair of welding gloves, remove the case from the shop oven or hot plate—*it is hot*.

e. Support the crankcase on wooden blocks and drive the bearing out from its opposite side.

NOTE

Install new bearings so that their manufacturer's name and size code faces in the same direction recorded before disassembly. If you did not record this information, install the bearings so that their marks are visible from the side the bearing is installed from.

f. While the crankcase is still hot, install the new bearing into the crankcase. Install the bearing into its bore and drop it into place. If necessary, lightly tap the bearing into the case with a socket placed on the outer bearing race. *Do not* install the new bearing by driving on the inner bearing race. Install the bearing until it seats completely.

3B. To replace bearings with a press:

a. Support the crankcase on 2 wooden blocks and center the bearing under the press ram. See **Figure 234** or **Figure 235**.

b. Press the bearing out of the crankcase.

c. Support the crankcase on 2 wooden blocks and center the bearing and bearing bore under the press ram.

d. Place a bearing driver on the outer bearing race (**Figure 236** or **Figure 237**) and press the bearing into the crankcase until it bottoms out. See **Figure 224** or **Figure 225**.

4. Install the oil seals as described under *Crankcase Oil Seal Replacement* in this chapter.

235

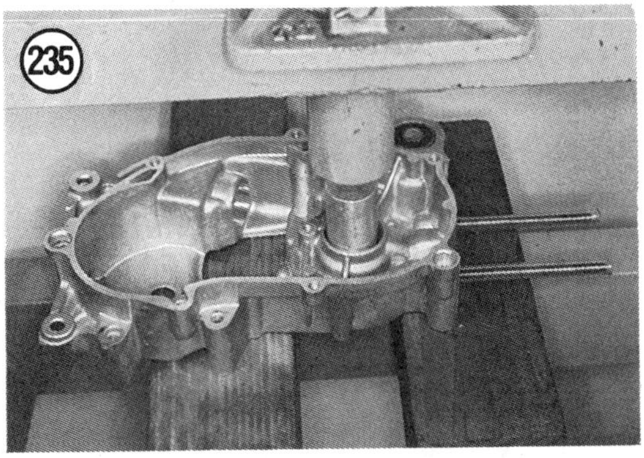

236

237

Crankshaft Inspection

When measuring the crankshaft in this section, compare the actual measurements to the new and service limit specifications in **Table 4**. Replace the connecting rod assembly if it is out of specification or shows damage as described in this section. To replace the connecting rod assembly, a 20-30 ton press and adapters, V-blocks or crankshaft truing stand, and dial indicator are required. If necessary, refer crankshaft overhaul to a dealer or service shop. You can save considerable expense by disassembling the engine and just taking the crankshaft in for repair at a dealership or machine shop familiar with this type of work.

When rebuilding a crankshaft, always install a new connecting rod, pin, bearing and both thrust washers (**Figure 238**).

1. Clean and dry the crankshaft. Then lubricate the bottom end bearing and crankshaft journals with 2-stroke engine oil.

2. Check the crankshaft journals (A, **Figure 239**) for scratches, heat discoloration or other defects.

3. Check the crankshaft seal for grooving, pitting or scratches.

238

CRANKSHAFT

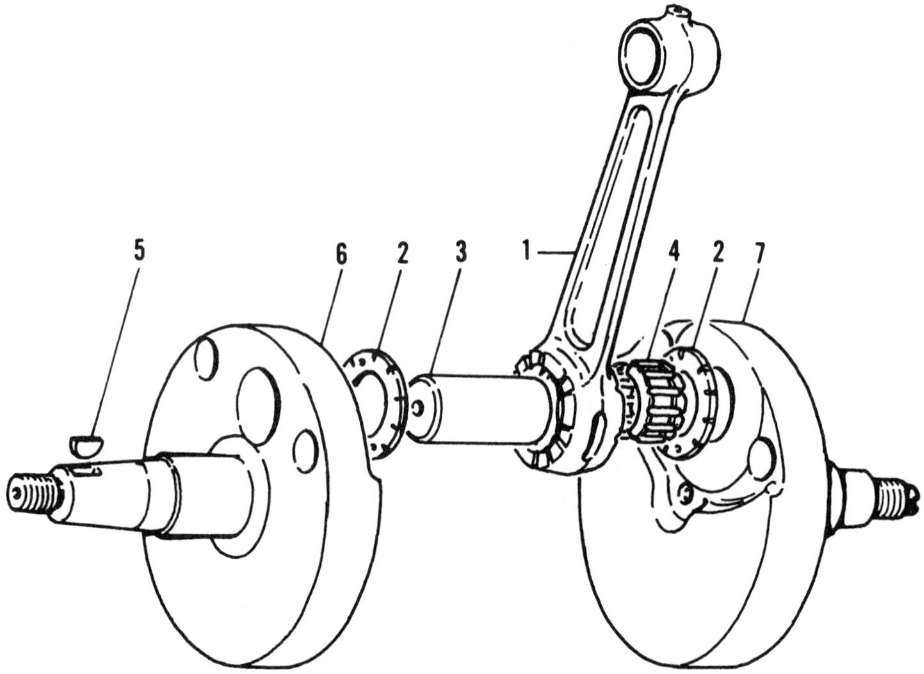

1. Connecting rod
2. Thrust washer
3. Crankpin
4. Needle bearing
5. Woodruff key
6. Left-hand crank half
7. Right-hand crank half

239

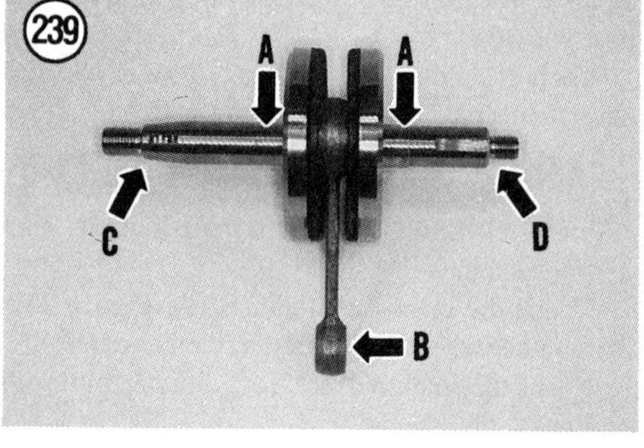

240

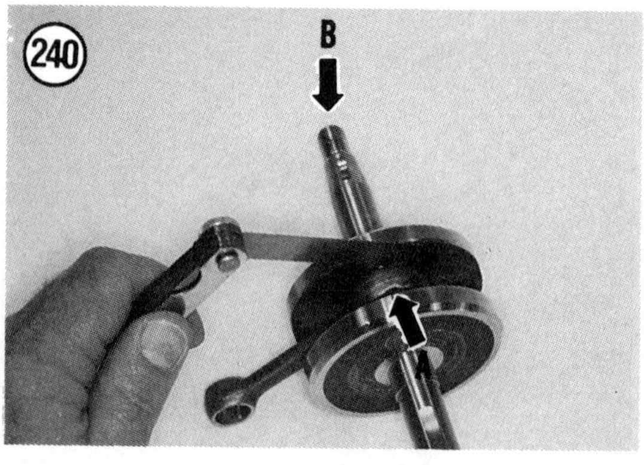

4. Check the crankshaft bearing surfaces for chatter marks and excessive or uneven wear. Clean minor damage with a 320 grit carborundum cloth.

5. Check the left crank half flywheel taper, threads and keyway (C, **Figure 239**) for damage.

6. Check the right crank half keyway and threads (D, **Figure 239**) for damage.

7. Check the connecting rod big end (A, **Figure 240**) for signs of heat or damage. Check the needles and cage for visible damage.

8. Check the connecting rod small end (B, **Figure 239**) for signs of heat or damage. To determine wear at the rod's small end, perform the *Piston Pin and Needle Bearing Inspection* procedure in this chapter.

9. Measure the connecting rod side clearance between the connecting rod and thrust washer with a feeler gauge (A, **Figure 240**). Replace the connecting rod assembly if the clearance is out of specification.

10. Measure connecting rod small end free play (**Figure 241**) as follows:

   a. Mount the crankshaft on a set of V-blocks.
   b. Turn the crankshaft so that the connecting rod is at top dead center (TDC).
   c. Mount a dial indicator so that its plunger contacts the connecting rod small end (**Figure 242**).
   d. Slide the connecting rod over so that it seats against the lower thrust washer that is on the same side the dial indicator is installed on. Hold the connecting rod in this position.
   e. While holding the lower part of the connecting rod, try to move the upper end by hand. Any movement is small end free play.
   f. Replace the connecting rod if the clearance is out of specification.

11. Measure connecting rod big end radial clearance (**Figure 241**) as follows:

   a. Turn the crankshaft so that the connecting rod is at TDC.
   b. Move the connecting rod over so that it seats against one of the lower thrust washers.
   c. Mount a dial indicator with its plunger contacting the connecting rod big end.
   d. Hold the connecting rod in this position, then try to move it up and down as shown in **Figure 241**. Any movement is big end radial clearance.

4

241

CONNECTING ROD INSPECTION

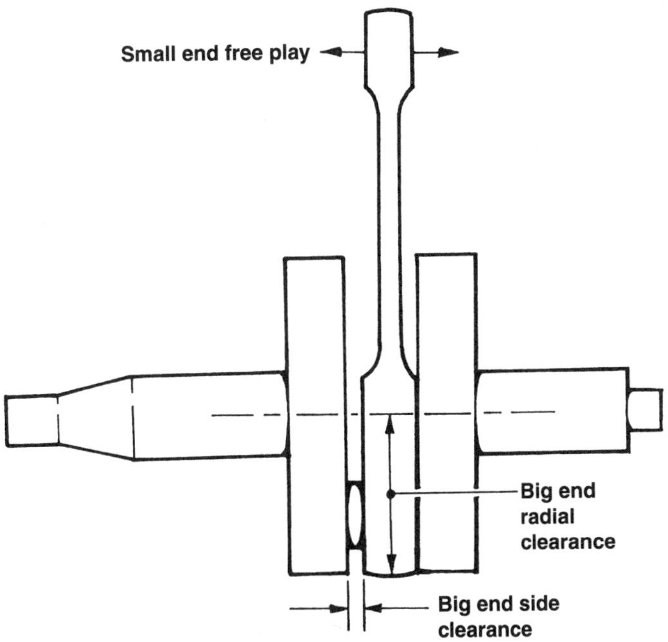

e. Replace the connecting rod if the clearance is out of specification.

12. Measure the crank wheel width every 90° at its machined edge with a micrometer (**Figure 243**) or vernier caliper. Retrue the crankshaft if out of specification.

13. Measure crankshaft runout with a dial indicator and V-blocks as shown in **Figure 244**. Retrue the crankshaft if out of specification.

Crankshaft Installation

The crankshaft is installed in the left case half (**Figure 245**) using the Yamaha crankcase tools described under *Special Tools* in this chapter. The tools are identified as follows:

a. Threaded adapter (A, **Figure 246**).
b. Installing pot (B, **Figure 246**).
c. Threaded rod and nut (C, **Figure 246**).

CAUTION
If you do not have access to these or similar crankshaft tools, take the crankshaft and case half to a dealership for installation. Do not drive the crankshaft into the crankcase with a hammer.

1. Clean the crankshaft before installation. Lubricate the big end bearing (A, **Figure 240**) with 2-stroke injection oil.

2. Install the left crankcase seal as described under *Seal Replacement* in this chapter.

3. Lubricate the left crankshaft main bearing with 2-stroke engine oil.

4. Remove the Woodruff key from the crankshaft keyway.

5. Carefully install the crankshaft's left end (side with taper) into the left side main bearing. Push it in until it stops (**Figure 247**).

6. Thread the Yamaha threaded adapter (part No. YU-90063) onto the crankshaft until it bottoms out, then back out 1/2 turn. See A, **Figure 248**.

7. Thread the threaded rod (B, **Figure 248**) all the way into the adapter.

8. Install the installing pot (A, **Figure 249**) over the threaded rod and engage its slot with the pin in the adapter to lock them together. Then install the nut

242

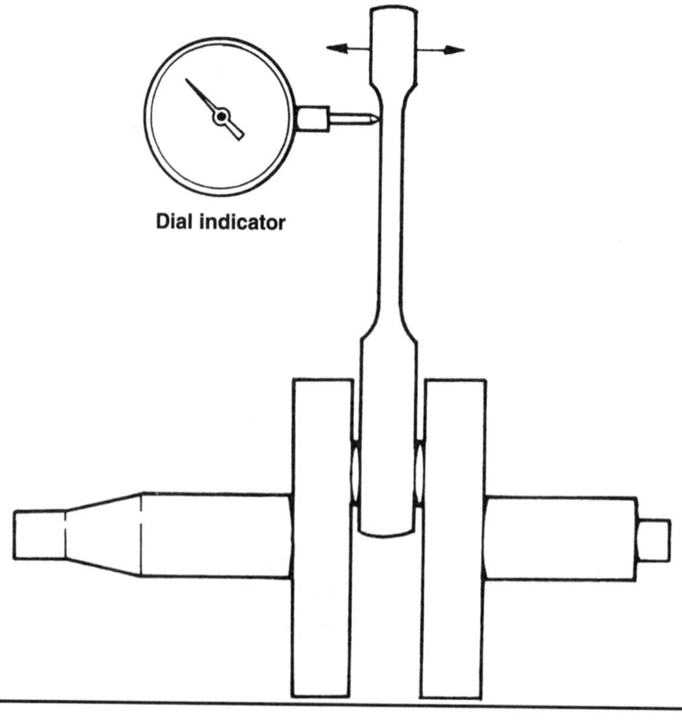

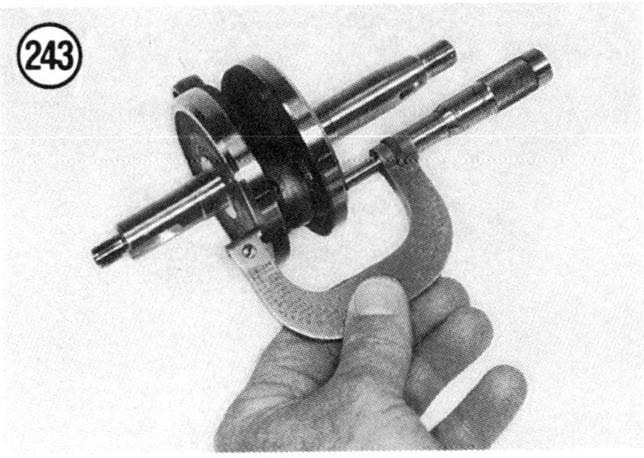

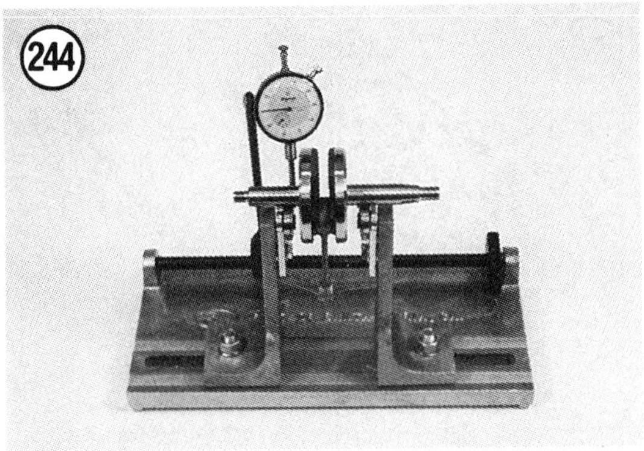

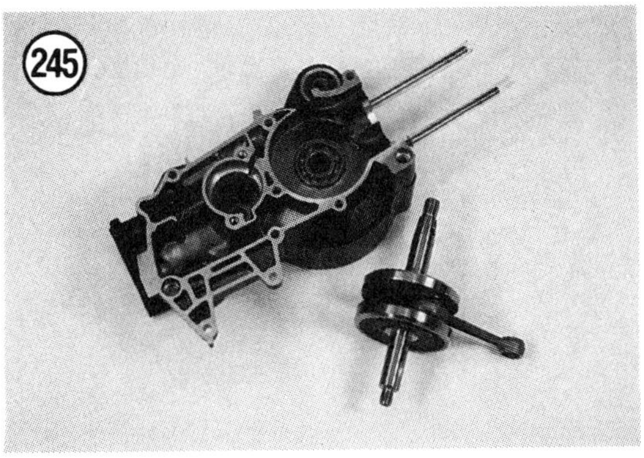

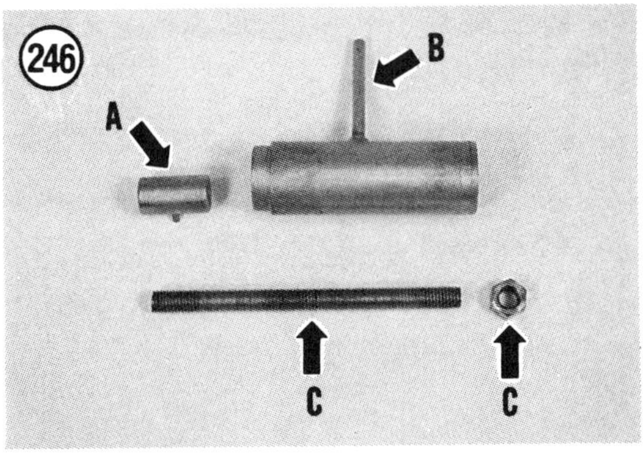

(B, **Figure 249**) and thread it against the installing pot.

CAUTION

*Hold the connecting rod (**Figure 250**) at TDC or BDC when pressing the crankshaft into its main bearing; otherwise the rod may contact the side on the crankcase, causing rod and crankcase damage.*

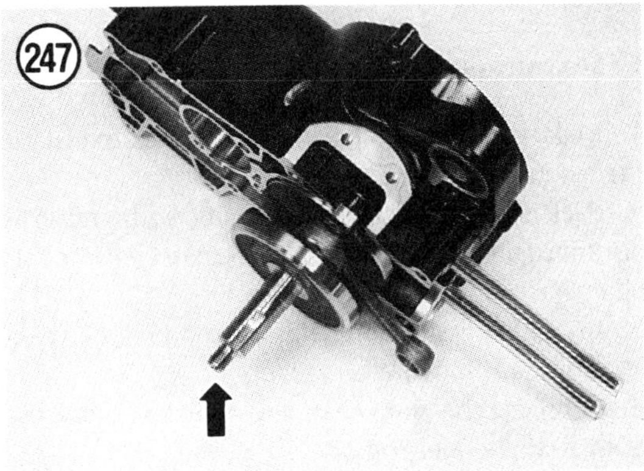

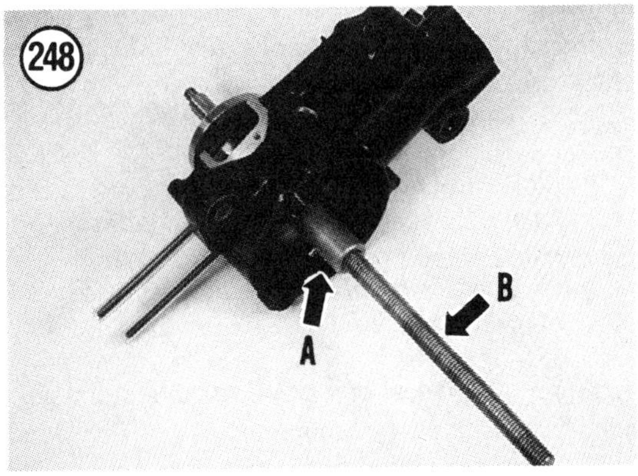

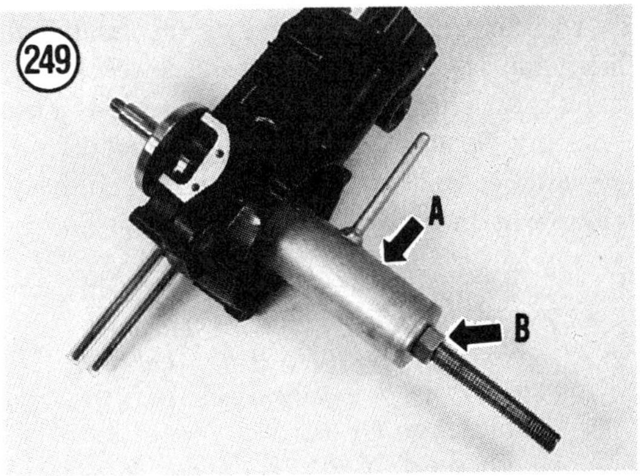

9. Hold the installing pot rod, then turn the nut (**Figure 251**) to pull the crankshaft into its main bearing. Continue until you feel crankshaft shoulder bottom out against the bearing.

10. Remove the tools from the end of the crankshaft, then place the crankcase assembly on wooden blocks (**Figure 252**).

11. Correctly position the connecting rod in the crankcase opening, then spin the crankshaft by hand, making sure it turns smoothly with no roughness or binding.

250

Crankcase Assembly

1. Make sure all engine parts are clean before starting assembly.
2. Pack all of the crankcase seal lips with grease as described under *Crankcase Seal Replacement* in this chapter.
3. Install the crankshaft as described under *Crankshaft Installation* in this chapter.
4. Lubricate the crankshaft and right main bearing with 2-stroke injection oil.
5. Support the left crankcase assembly on wooden blocks.
6. Install the 2 dowel pins (**Figure 252**) into the crankcase holes.

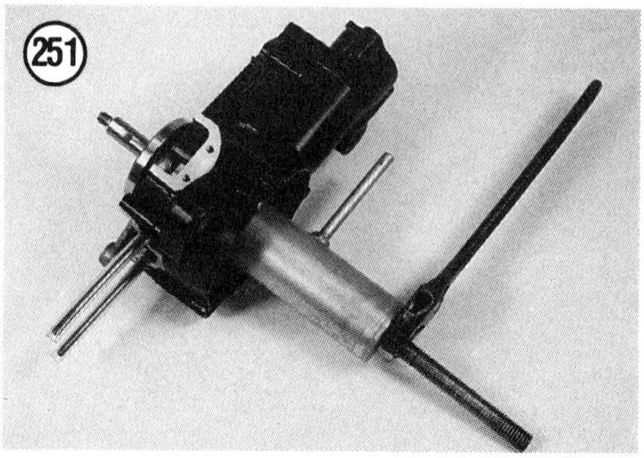
251

NOTE

Make sure both crankcase mating surfaces are clean and free of all old gasket sealer residue or oil. If necessary, clean with an electrical contact cleaner and allow to air dry.

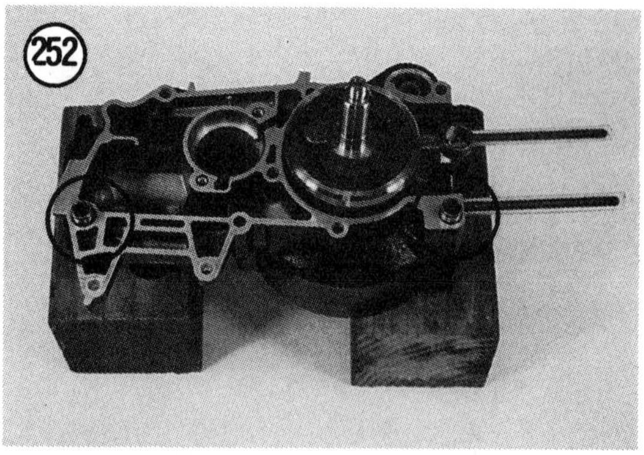
252

7. Apply a light coat of a *nonhardening* liquid gasket sealer, such as Yamabond No. 4 or ThreeBond 1104, onto the right side crankcase gasket surface (**Figure 253**).
8. Align the right crankcase with the crankshaft, then install it over the crankshaft and dowel pins and seat it against the left case half (**Figure 254**). Then check that the gasket surfaces are flush all the way around the case halves. Turn the crankshaft by hand. It must turn smoothly with no roughness or binding.

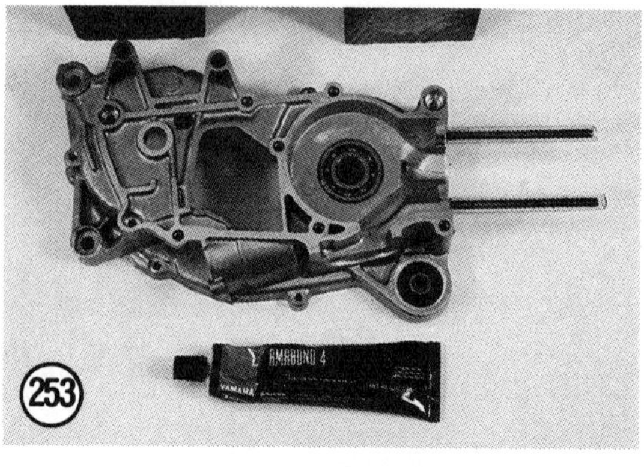
253

CAUTION

The crankcase halves should fit together without excessive force. If the crankcase halves do not fit together completely, do not pull them together with the crankcase screws. If the crankshaft turns

254

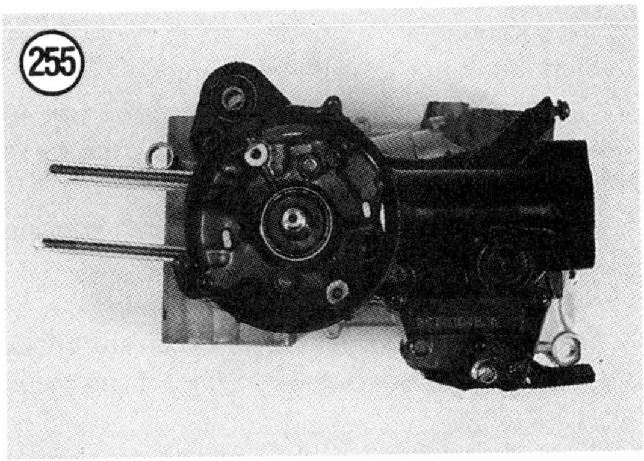

255

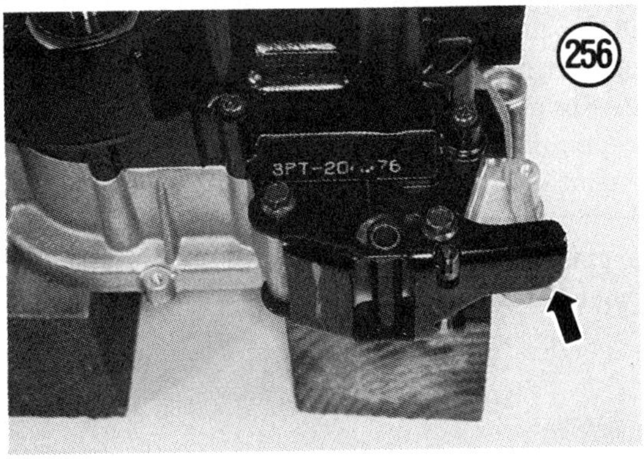

256

257

*roughly or is binding, it may be off center in the cases; tap one end of the crank lightly with a soft-faced mallet and check that it turns freely. If the crankshaft is properly centered in the right case main bearing, it may not be installed properly in the left case main bearing (it did not bottom against the bearing). If the crankshaft was rebuilt, measure the crankshaft wheel width with a micrometer (**Figure 243**) and compare to the specification in **Table 4**. If the wheels are spaced too far apart, they can interfere with crankcase assembly. If necessary, separate the crankcase halves and investigate the cause of the interference. Do not risk damage by trying to force the cases together.*

9. Turn the engine over so that the left side faces up (**Figure 255**).
10. Install the center stand mounting bracket (**Figure 256**).
11. Install the air filter mounting bracket (**Figure 257**).
12. Install all of the crankcase mounting screws finger-tight.

NOTE

If the crankcase mounting screws were not identified during disassembly, check that each one sticks up the same amount before you screw them all in. If not, there is a short screw in a long hole, and vice versa.

13. Tighten the crankcase mounting screws in 2 stages and in a crisscross pattern as specified in **Table 6**.
14. Rotate the crankshaft and check for binding; the crankshaft must turn freely.
15. Install the following engine assemblies as described in this chapter.
    a. Transmission assembly.
    b. Kickstarter, oil pump drive gear and kick pinion gear.
    c. Clutch and primary drive gear system.
    d. Right crankcase cover.
    e. Intake manifold and reed valve assembly.
    f. Install the engine in the frame.
    g. Cylinder head, cylinder and piston.
16. Install the Woodruff key into the crankshaft keyway.

17. Install the stator plate and flywheel (Chapter Eight).

18. After filling the transmission with gear oil and bleeding the oil pump, start the engine and check for leaks. Check the throttle and clutch operation and adjust if necessary.

ENGINE BREAK-IN

Engine performance and durability will depend on a sensible and accurate engine break-in procedure. If the rings were replaced, a new piston installed, the cylinder rebored, the crankshaft rebuilt or replaced, or new engine bearings installed, the engine must be broken in just as if it were new. If a proper engine break-in procedure is not followed, accelerated engine wear and overheating will result, reducing engine life.

Before starting the break-in procedure, note the following:

a. Make sure the engine oil tank is full (Chapter Three) and the oil pump bled of all air (Chapter Nine).
b. Make sure the air filter is clean, oiled, and properly installed.
c. Make sure the correct heat range spark is installed in the engine.
d. Perform the break-in procedure on flat ground. To prevent engine overheating, avoid riding in sand, mud or up hills.
e. Do not run the engine with the throttle in the same position for more than a few seconds.
f. Short bursts of full throttle operation (no more than 2-3 seconds at a time) are acceptable. However, rest the engine after each full throttle operation by cruising at a low engine speed for a few minutes. This will allow the engine to rid itself of any excessive heat buildup.
h. Check the spark plug frequently during the break-in procedure. The electrode should be dry and clean and the color of the insulation should be light to medium tan. Refer to Chapter Three for further information on spark plug reading.
i. Keep accurate time records of the break-in procedure.

1. Start the engine and allow to warm up.
2. Operate the engine at lower speeds for 8 to 10 minutes. Turn the engine off and check the spark plug.
3. Allow the engine to cool down before restarting it.
4. Restart the engine and allow to warm up.
5. Repeat Step 2 for 5 minutes. Periodically check full throttle response. Turn the engine off and check the spark plug.
6. Allow the engine to cool down before restarting it. During this time, check the motorcycle for loose or missing fasteners. Check the front and rear brake adjustments.
7. Restart the engine and allow to warm up. Run the engine through its full operating range, then turn the engine off and recheck the spark plug condition.
8. If the spark plug reading is okay, restart the engine and ride for 10-15 minutes. At this point, the engine break-in is complete.

Table 1 GENERAL ENGINE SERVICE SPECIFICATIONS (PW50)

Type	Air-cooled 2 stroke, reed valve induction
Cylinder arrangement	Single cylinder, forward inclined
Displacement	49 cc
Bore × stroke	40 × 39.2 mm (1.575 × 1.543 in.)
Compression ratio	6.0:1
Starting system	Kickstarter
Lubrication system	Autolube oil injection pump
Clutch	Wet, centrifugal automatic
Transmission	
Primary reduction system	Gear
Primary reduction ratio	63/33 (1.909)
Secondary reduction system	Shaft drive
Secondary reduction ratio	19/15 × 54/11 (6.218)

Table 2 ENGINE TOP END SERVICE SPECIFICATIONS

	New mm (in.)	Service limit mm (in.)
Cylinder head warpage limit	—	0.03 (0.0012)
Cylinder		
Bore size	39.993-40.012 (1.5745-1.5753)	—
Taper limit	—	0.05 (0.0020)
Out-of-round limit	—	0.01 (0.0004)
Piston		
Diameter	39.952-39.972 (1.5729-1.5737)	—
Piston measuring point	5 (0.2)	—
Piston clearance	0.034-0.047 (0.0013-0.0019)	0.07 (0.0030)
Piston offset (exhaust side)	0.2 (0.008)	—
Piston rings (top and second rings)		
End gap	0.15 (0.006)	0.35 (0.014)
Side clearance	0.020 (0.0008)	0.060 (0.0024)
Intake manifold warp limit	—	0.1 (0.004)
Reed valve		
Thickness	0.2 (0.0008)	—
Reed stop height	4.6-5.0 (90.181-0.197)	—
Reed valve bend clearance limit	—	0.2 (0.008)

Table 3 PISTON RING SECTIONAL DIMENSIONS

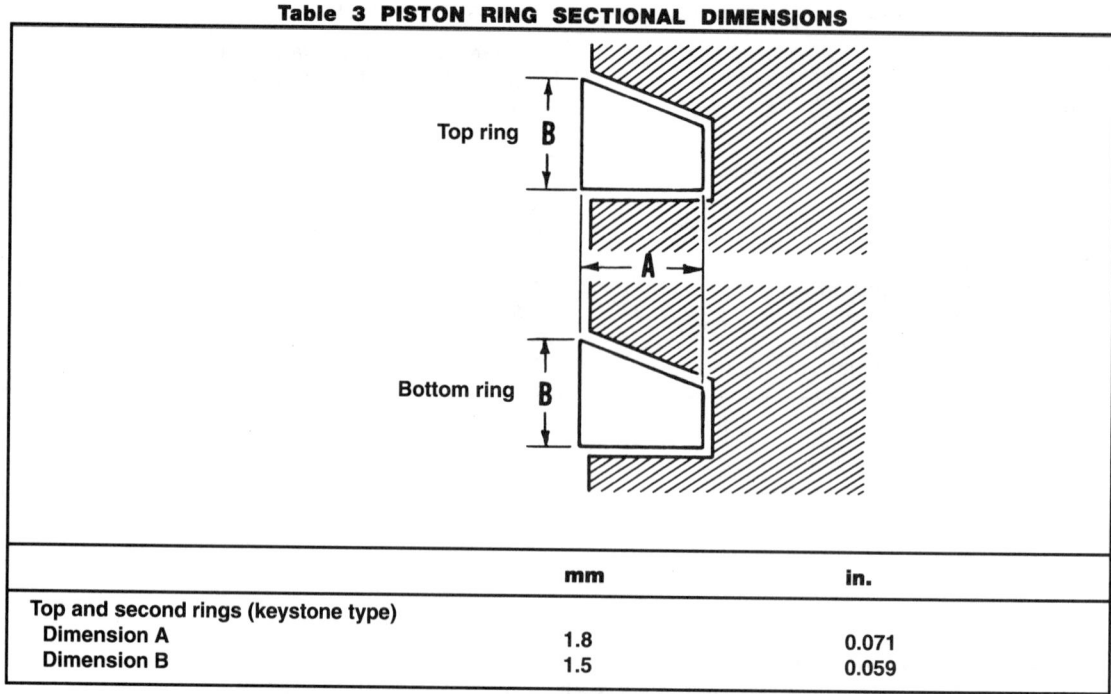

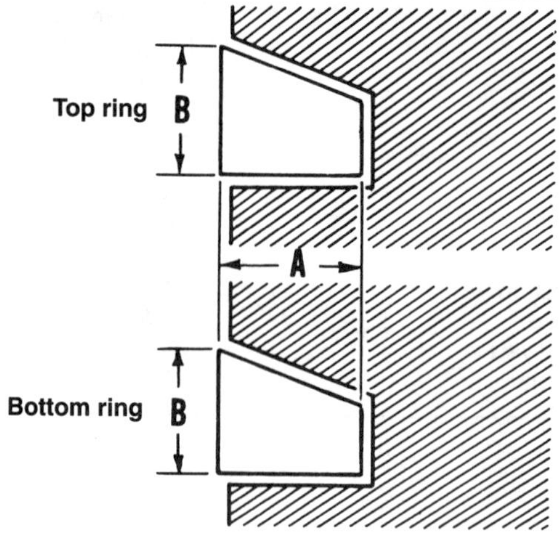

	mm	in.
Top and second rings (keystone type)		
Dimension A	1.8	0.071
Dimension B	1.5	0.059

Table 4 CRANKSHAFT SERVICE SPECIFICATIONS

	New mm (in.)	Service limit mm (in.)
Crankshaft wheel width	37.90-37.95 (1.492-1.494)	—
Runout limit	—	0.05 (0.0020)
Connecting rod big end side clearance	0.35-0.55 (0.014-0.022)	—
Connecting small end free play	0.4-0.8 (0.016-0.031)	—

Table 5 CLUTCH AND TRANSMISSION SERVICE SPECIFICATIONS

	New mm (in.)	Service limit mm (in.)
Clutch shoe lining thickness	1.0 (0.40)	0.7 (0.028)
Clutch shoe spring free length	34.5 (1.36)	35.5 (1.40)
Transmission shafts runout limit	—	0.25 (0.010)

Table 6 ENGINE TIGHTENING TORQUES

	N•m	in.-lb.	ft.-lb.
Air filter housing mounting screw	9	80	—
Crankcase mounting screws	9	80	—
Cylinder head nuts	10	88	—
Drive shaft housing mounting bolts			
at engine	26	—	19
Engine pivot shaft nut	48	—	35
Exhaust pipe assembly			
Front exhaust pipe mounting bolts			
at cylinder	9	80	—
Exhaust pipe heat shield	9	80	—
Spark arrestor mounting bolt	18	—	13
Flywheel mounting nut	43	—	31
Intake manifold mounting screws	9	80	—
Kickstarter pinch bolt	10	88	—
Left crankcase cover mounting screws	4	35	—
Mainshaft cover plate mounting bolts	12	106	—
Middle driven pinion shaft hex screw	60	—	43
Oil drain bolt	14	—	10
Oil pump cover	4	35	—
Oil pump mounting screws	4	35	—
Primary drive gear locknut	30	—	22
Rear arm mounting nuts at engine	29	—	21
Rear shock absorber mounting bolts			
Upper	11	—	8
Lower	23	—	17
Right crankcase cover mounting screws	9	80	—
Spark plug	20	—	14
Stator plate mounting screws	9	80	—

CHAPTER FIVE

ENGINE (BW80 AND PW80)

This chapter covers information on servicing the following engine components:

a. Exhaust pipe.
b. Cylinder head.
c. Cylinder.
d. Reed valve.
e. Piston and rings.
f. Clutch.
g. Primary drive gear.
h. Kickstarter.
i. Oil pump drive gear.
j. Kick pinion gear.
k. Transmission.
l. Crankcases.
m. Crankshaft.

Service to the flywheel and stator plate assembly is described in Chapter Eight.

Before starting any work, read the information listed under *Service Hints* in Chapter One. You will do a better job with this information fresh in your mind.

Make certain that you have all of the necessary special tools. All of the fasteners used on your Yamaha are metric; make sure to use metric wrenches and sockets.

One of the more important aspects of engine overhaul is preparation. Throwing all of the parts in one or two boxes will make it difficult to rebuild the engine. Use boxes (**Figure 1**) and small plastic bags during disassembly and label the parts as required.

The text often refers to the left and right sides of the engine. The terms left and right side refer to the engine as it is mounted in the frame—the flywheel is on the left side; the clutch is on the right side.

Engine specifications are listed in **Tables 1-6** at the end of the chapter.

ENGINE IDENTIFICATION

The engine is a single cylinder, air-cooled 2-stroke engine. This engine is very simple in design in that it only uses three moving parts: piston assembly,

1

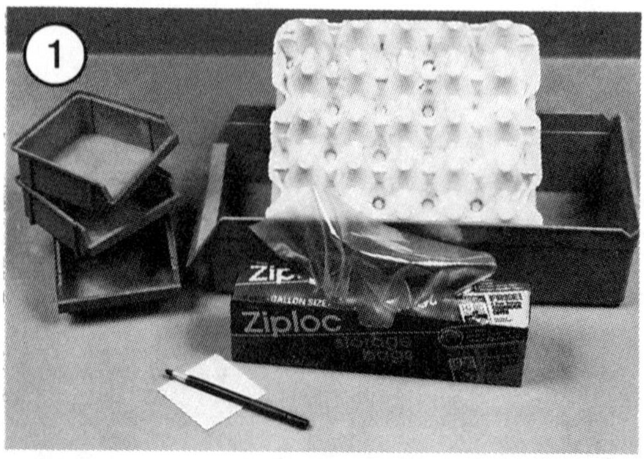

connecting rod and crankshaft. See **Table 1** for general engine specifications.

The engine consists of an upper and lower end. To prevent confusion, the following lists identifies these engine subassemblies as they are called out in this manual:

a. *Engine top end*—Cylinder head, cylinder, piston, rings, needle bearing and piston pin. This needle bearing and pin assembly is often referred to as the upper end bearing.
b. *Engine lower end*—Crankshaft assembly, main bearings and oil seals. The crankshaft assembly consists of the left and right side crank wheels, connecting rod, washers, pin and needle bearing. This needle bearing and pin assembly is often referred to as the lower end bearing.

The crankcase combines the engine top and lower end assemblies as well as the clutch, kickstarter and transmission assembly. Where the engine top and lower end assemblies operate, the crankcase must be airtight.

A major difference to distinguish between the different engine assemblies is that of lubrication. The engine top and bottom end assemblies are lubricated by the Autolube oil injection pump. The clutch and transmission assemblies are lubricated by the transmission oil added through the oil fill hole on the right crankcase cover.

ENGINE LUBRICATION

The 2-stroke engine is lubricated by the Yamaha Autolube oil injection system. Oil is injected into the carburetor where it mixes with the air/fuel mixture before entering the engine. The oil is burned with the fuel and expelled through the exhaust. The engine top and bottom end components are lubricated by this oil, which clings to the various parts as it passes through the crankcase and cylinder. This oil is not reused and the amount of oil in the oil tank will diminish as the oil is being used.

Check the oil level in the oil tank daily and whenever refueling the vehicle. Refer to Chapter Three for oil tank refilling. Refer to Chapter Nine for oil pump service.

CLEANLINESS

Repairs go much faster and easier if your engine is clean before you begin work. When servicing the engine top end with the engine installed in the frame, dirt trapped underneath the fuel tank and upper frame tube can fall into the cylinder or crankcase opening, remove the fuel tank and wrap the frame tube with a large, clean cloth.

EXHAUST SYSTEM

The exhaust system (**Figure 2**) includes the exhaust pipe/muffler, heat shield, power reduction plate (if used), and a Yamaha-Krizman type spark arrester.

The exhaust pipe is not a tuned exhaust system, but instead, a combination exhaust pipe and muffler assembly. Fiberglass is packed around the inside of the exhaust pipe to help reduce noise. This fiberglass packing is not replaceable.

The spark arrestor helps eliminate the danger of fire when the motorcycle is ridden off-road. As the exhaust gas travels through the exhaust pipe, solid pieces of carbon, knocked loose from the engine and exhaust pipe, are carried with it. Because some of these carbon particles are red-hot, they must be trapped inside the exhaust system. If not, and the carbon passes through the spark arrester, a grass or forest fire could result. The Krizman type spark arrestor uses swirl vanes or blades that force the exhaust gases to swirl as they pass through the spark arrester. During this swirling action, centrifugal force throws the carbon particles to the outside of the spark arrestor where they are caught in a special trap. When you remove a spark arrestor and shake it, you can hear the carbon particles moving around in the trap. Because the spark arrestor trap gradually fills with carbon, it must be cleaned regularly. If not, the carbon particles will build to a point where some will be forced to pass through the spark arrester. Never run the motorcycle with a damaged or improperly installed spark arrester, or with the spark arrestor removed from the exhaust system.

Periodically check the exhaust pipe and spark arrestor for loose or missing fasteners. Loose mounting bolts will allow the pipe and spark arrestor to rattle and vibrate. This increases engine noise and will eventually cause damage to the exhaust pipe and its mounting brackets. An exhaust leak between the

(2)

EXHAUST SYSTEM (BW80 AND PW80)

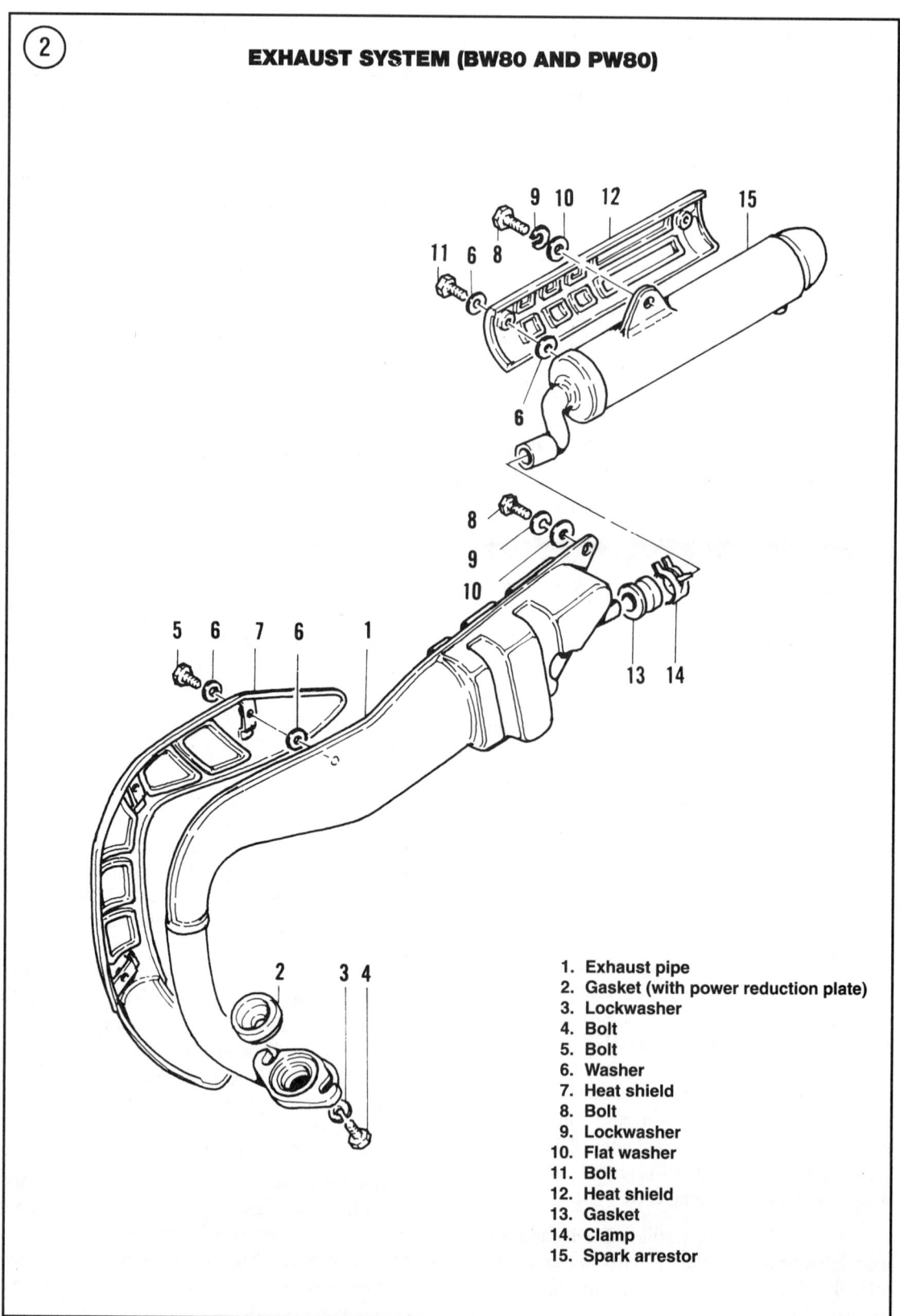

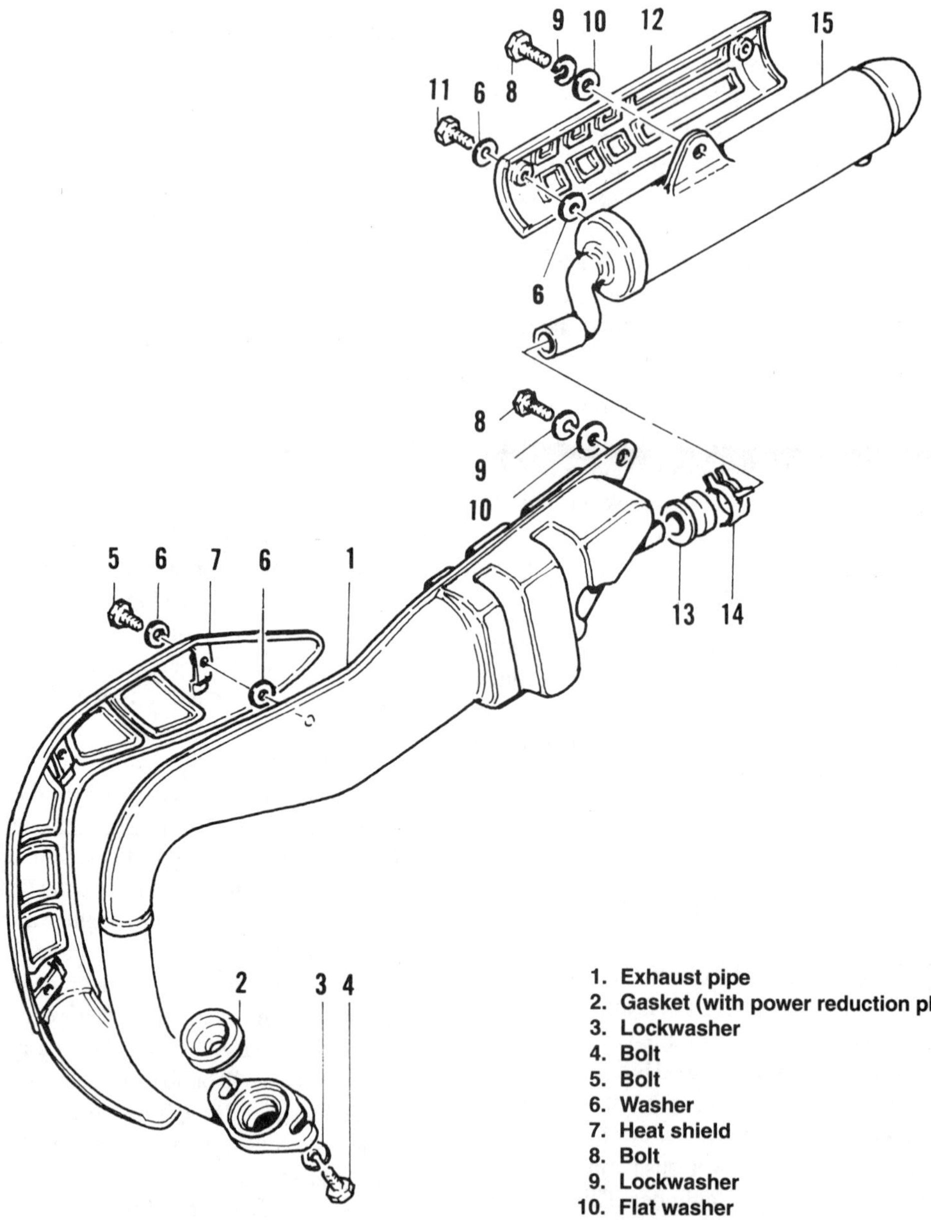

1. Exhaust pipe
2. Gasket (with power reduction plate)
3. Lockwasher
4. Bolt
5. Bolt
6. Washer
7. Heat shield
8. Bolt
9. Lockwasher
10. Flat washer
11. Bolt
12. Heat shield
13. Gasket
14. Clamp
15. Spark arrestor

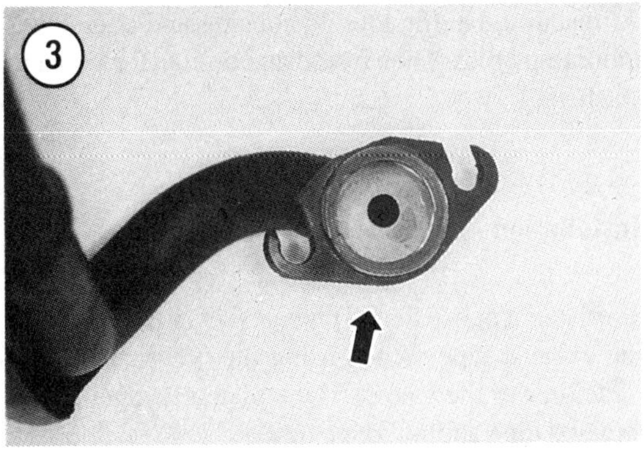

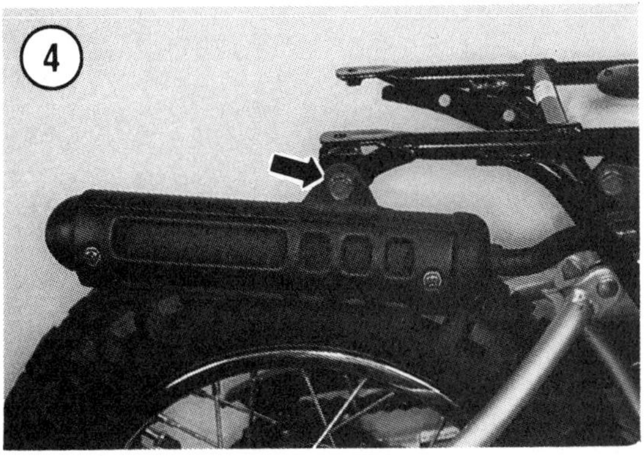

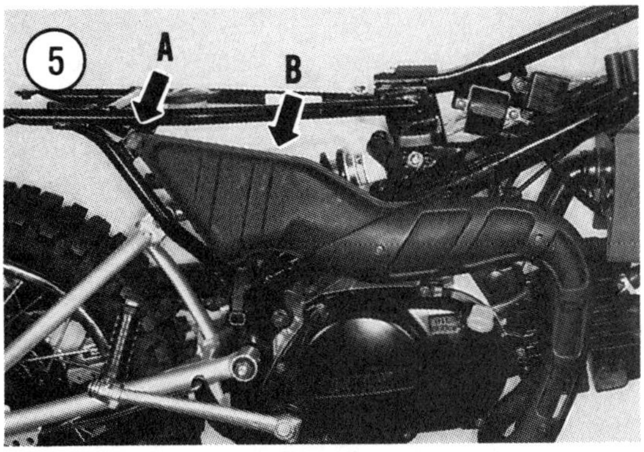

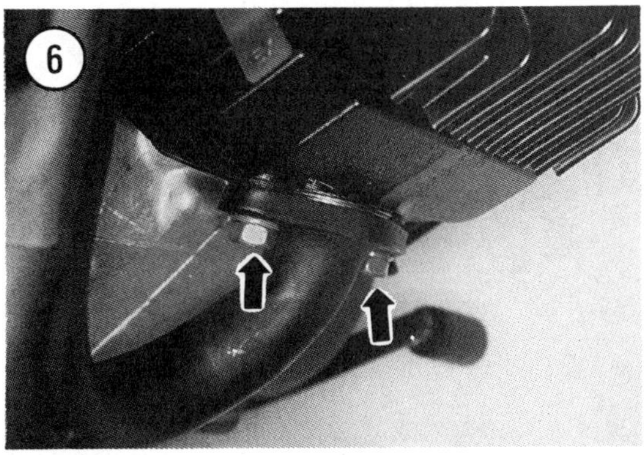

exhaust pipe and cylinder will leave a messy residue of oil, decrease power, and can cause engine damage.

Exhaust pipe decarbonization and spark arrestor cleaning intervals are listed in Chapter Three (**Table 2** and **3**). Clean the exhaust pipe assembly at these intervals to ensure good performance.

Power Reduction Plate

Because the BW80 and PW80 models are designed for young riders, it is critical to limit the speed of the motorcycle to correspond to the rider's skill and experience. Both the BW80 and the PW80 are originally equipped with a power reduction plate (governor).

The power reduction plate (**Figure 3**) is installed between the exhaust port and exhaust pipe. Consisting of a round plate with a small hole, it effectively blocks off most of the exhaust port opening to reduce the power output of the engine. The power reduction plate is mounted onto the exhaust pipe gasket and can be separated from the gasket at a suitable time determined by the rider's parent or guardian. See the BW80 or PW80 owner's service manual for more information on both safety devices.

Removal

WARNING
A hot exhaust pipe and spark arrestor can cause serious burns. Do not touch or service the exhaust pipe assembly until it cools off.

1. Support the bike on its sidestand.
2. Remove nut (BW80) or the bolt, lockwasher and flat washer (PW80) securing the spark arrestor (**Figure 4**) to its frame bracket and remove it from the exhaust pipe.
3. Loosen the rear exhaust pipe mounting bolt (A, **Figure 5**).
4. Remove the 2 exhaust pipe mounting bolts at the cylinder (**Figure 6**).
5. Remove the rear exhaust pipe mounting bolt, then slide the exhaust pipe (B, **Figure 5**) forward and remove it from the engine.
6. Remove the exhaust pipe gasket (**Figure 3**) from the exhaust pipe or exhaust port.

Inspection

1. Service the spark arrestor as described under *Spark Arrestor Cleaning* in this section.
2. Check the exhaust pipe for cracks, leaks or a damaged mounting bracket. Check also that the welded bracket at the front of the pipe is not cracked. Refer exhaust pipe repair to a welding repair shop.
3. Rap the exhaust pipe with a plastic or rubber hammer to break loose some of the carbon stuck to the inside pipe walls. Be careful not to dent or damage the exhaust pipe.
4. Clean oil and carbon buildup in the front of the exhaust pipe with a scraper.
5. Make sure the heat shield is in place and that all of its mounting screws are tight.
6. Replace the exhaust pipe-to-spark arrestor gasket (**Figure 2**) if leaking or damaged.
7. Replace the exhaust pipe gasket (**Figure 3**) if leaking or damaged.

NOTE
A power reduction plate is installed on all OEM replacement exhaust pipe gaskets.

Spark Arrestor Cleaning

NOTE
It may be easier to remove the spark arrestor baffle with the spark arrestor mounted on the bike.

WARNING
A hot exhaust pipe and spark arrestor can cause serious burns. Do not touch or service the exhaust pipe assembly until it cools off.

1. Support the bike on its sidestand.
2. Rap the spark arrestor with a plastic or rubber hammer to loosen some of the carbon deposits stuck to the spark arrestor and its housing walls. Be careful not to dent or damage the silencer housing.
3. Remove the bolt and washers (**Figure 7**), then twist and pull the baffle (**Figure 8**) out of its housing.
4. Remove the spark arrestor housing from the bike.
5. Initially clean the baffle (**Figure 9**) and housing with a scraper and stiff wire brush. Then clean the baffle and housing in solvent and dry thoroughly.
6. Inspect the baffle (**Figure 9**) for cracks or other damage.
7. Install the baffle into its housing and align the 2 mounting holes. Then install and tighten the bolt and washers.

Installation

1. Install a new exhaust pipe gasket (**Figure 3**) into the exhaust pipe. When using the power reduction plate, install the gasket so the plate sets against the exhaust pipe and not the cylinder.

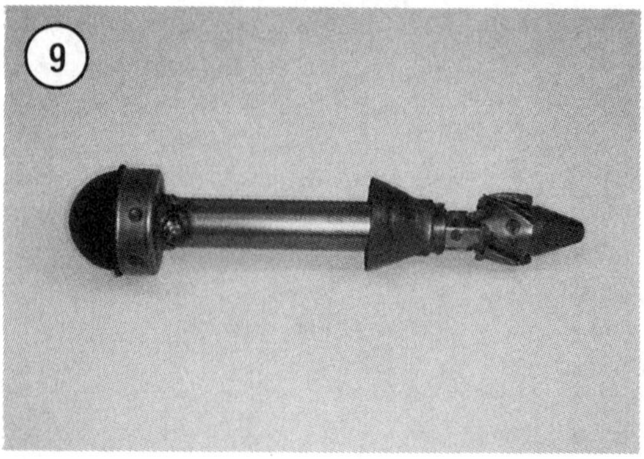

NOTE
In Step 2, tighten the mounting bolts finger-tight only. Final tightening will take place after the complete exhaust system is mounted on the bike.

2. Install the exhaust pipe (B, **Figure 5**) and secure it with its 2 front mounting bolts and washers (**Figure 6**) and rear mounting bolt (A, **Figure 5**). Make sure that the exhaust pipe gasket did not fall out of position.

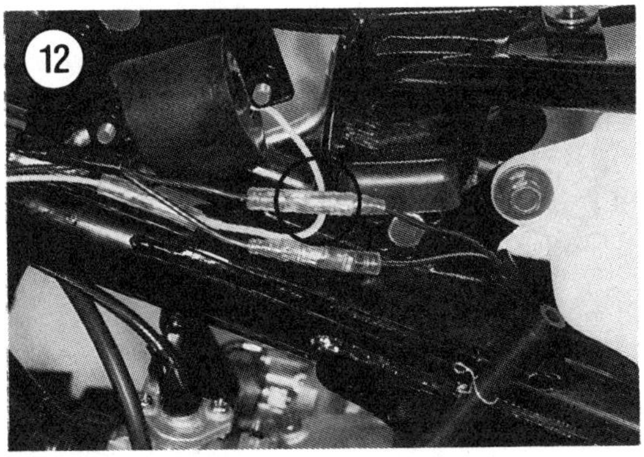

3. Slide the gasket and clamp onto the spark arrestor (**Figure 2**).
4. Install the spark arrestor (**Figure 4**) onto the exhaust pipe, then install and hand-tighten its nut (BW80) or mounting bolt and washers (PW80).
5. Tighten the exhaust pipe fasteners in the following order:
   a. Tighten the front exhaust pipe mounting bolts (**Figure 6**) as specified in **Table 6**.
   b. Tighten the rear exhaust pipe mounting bolt (A, **Figure 5**) as specified in **Table 6**.
   c. Tighten the spark arrestor nut or mounting bolt securely.
6. Start the engine and check for exhaust leaks.

ENGINE

Removal/Installation

1. Support the bike on its sidestand.
2. If the clutch or engine is going to be disassembled, drain the transmission oil (Chapter Three).
3. Remove the seat (Chapter Fifteen).
4. Remove the fuel tank (Chapter Seven).
5. Remove the air box and carburetor (Chapter Seven).
6. Remove the exhaust system as described in this chapter.
7. Remove the shift pedal (A, **Figure 10**) and the left side cover (B, **Figure 10**).
8. Remove the circlip (A, **Figure 11**) and drive sprocket (B, **Figure 11**).

9A. Remove the flywheel and stator plate, if necessary, as described in Chapter Eight.

9B. If the flywheel and stator plate are going to be left on the engine, disconnect the stator plate electrical connectors (**Figure 12**) from the left side of the engine.

10. Disconnect the spark plug wire at the spark plug.

11A. Remove the oil pump as described in Chapter Nine.

11B. If the oil pump is going to be left on the engine, perform the following:
   a. Remove the oil pump cover mounting bolts and lift the cover (**Figure 13**) partway off the oil pump.
   b. Disconnect the oil pump cable from the oil pump (**Figure 14**), then remove the cover.

c. Disconnect the oil feed hose (**Figure 15**) at the oil pump. Plug the hose opening.
d. Cover the oil feed hose nozzle on the oil pump to prevent dirt from falling into the pump.

12. If complete engine disassembly is required, remove the following components while the engine is mounted in the frame:
a. Engine top end (cylinder head, cylinder and piston).
b. Clutch (Chapter Six).
c. Primary drive gear.
d. External shift mechanism.
e. Kickstarter.

13. Check the engine to make sure there are no hoses or cables attached to it.
14. Loosen the 3 engine mount bolts and nuts (**Figure 16**). Remove the nuts and washers from the top and rear mounting bolts.
15. Remove the lower engine mount bolt and washers (**Figure 17**).
16. Remove the top and rear mounting bolts, then remove the engine (**Figure 18**) from the frame. If the engine is completely assembled, remove it from the right side.
17. Do not loosen the rubber dampers (**Figure 19**) mounted in the engine.
18. Perform the *Inspection* procedure.
19. To install the engine in the frame, reverse these removal steps, while noting the following.
20. Tighten the engine mount bolts as specified in **Table 6**.
21. Install the drive sprocket with its stamped number side facing out.
22. If necessary, refill the crankcase as described in Chapter Three.
23. Bleed the oil pump as described in Chapter Nine.

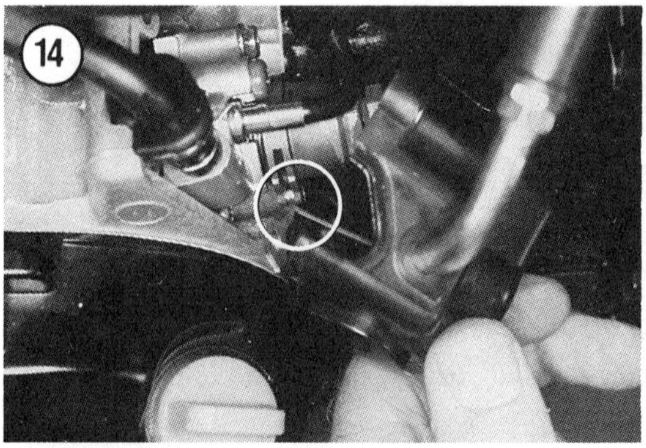

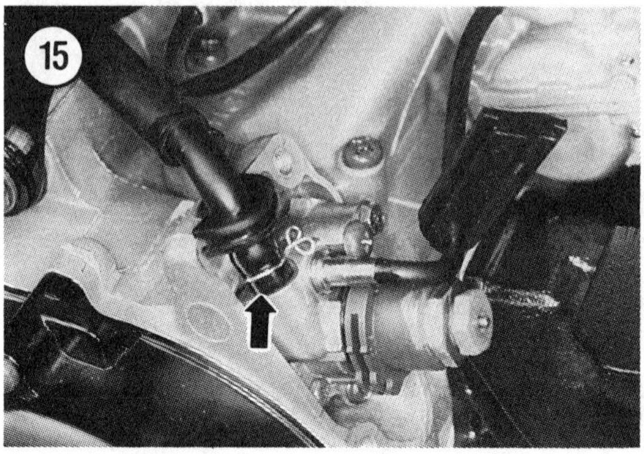

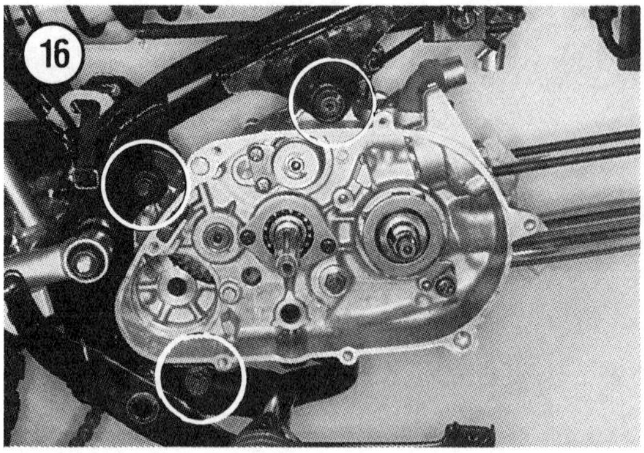

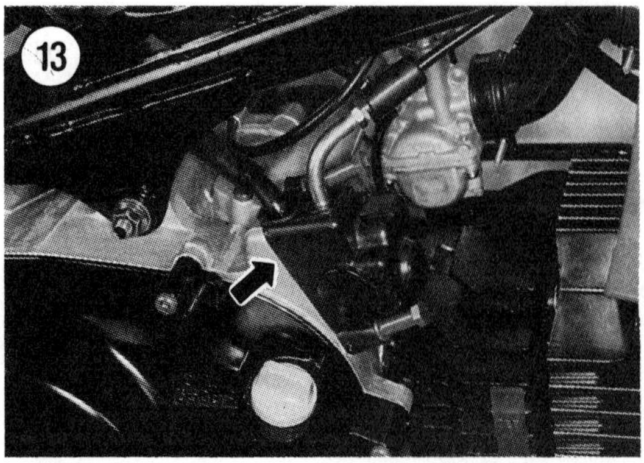

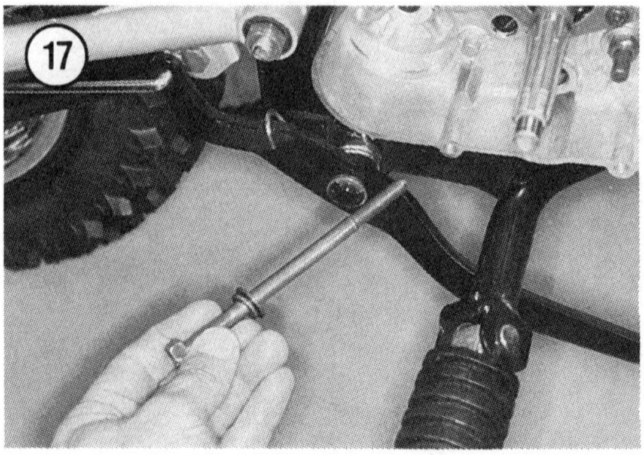

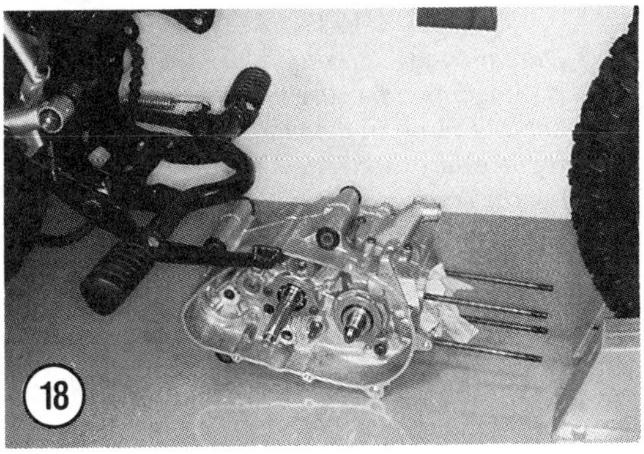

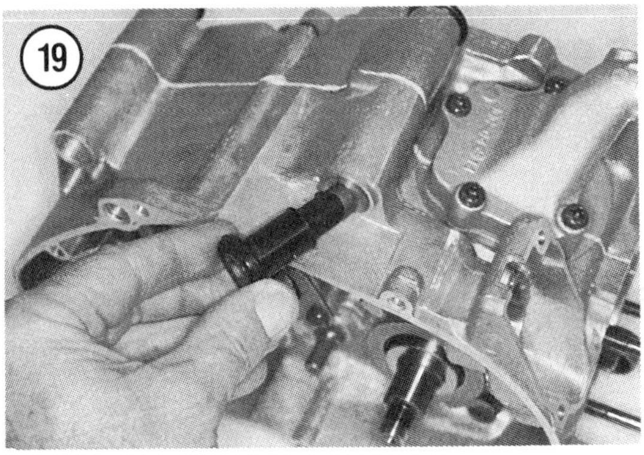

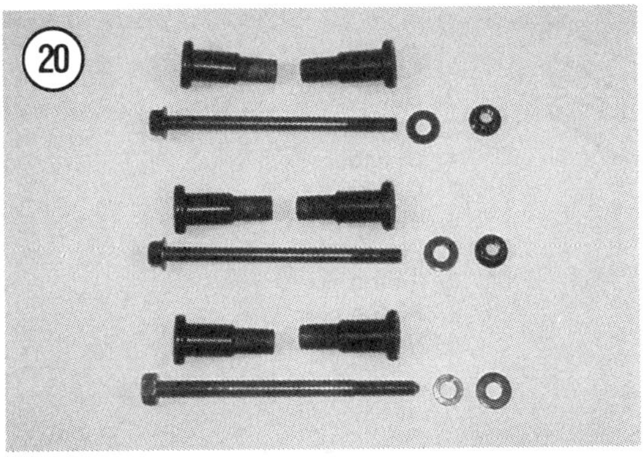

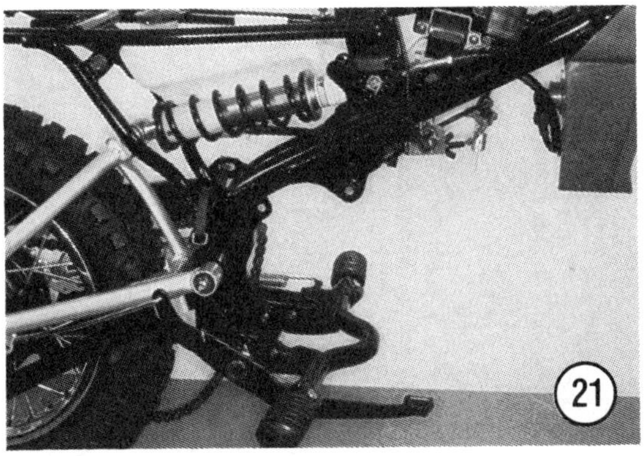

24. Tighten the oil pump cover (**Figure 13**) mounting bolts as specified in **Table 6**.
25. Tighten the left crankcase cover (**Figure 10**) mounting screws as specified in **Table 6**.
26. Tighten the shift pedal pinch bolt (**Figure 10**) as specified in **Table 6**.
27. Start the engine and check for leaks.

Inspection

Replace all damaged or worn parts as described in this section. Fasteners with rounded-off heads or damaged threads cannot be tightened properly.

1. Clean and inspect the engine mount bolts and rubber dampers (**Figure 20**).
2. Inspect the frame (**Figure 21**) for any cracks or other damage. Check the engine mount areas on the frame for cracks or severe wear. Refer repair to a welding shop familiar with motorcycle frame repair.
3. Clean all of the disconnected electrical connectors with a spray type electrical contact cleaner.

CYLINDER HEAD

The cylinder head (**Figure 22**) can be removed with the engine mounted in the frame.

Before working on the top end, clean all dirt and grease from the outside of the engine and the frame area surrounding the cylinder head.

Removal

CAUTION

To avoid possible warping of the cylinder head, wait until the engine has cooled down before removing the cylinder head.

1. Remove the seat (Chapter Fifteen) and fuel tank (Chapter Seven).
2. Perform the *Crankcase Pressure Test* described in Chapter Two to check for any cylinder head or other engine leaks.
3. Disconnect the spark plug wire from the plug, then loosen the spark plug.
4. Loosen the cylinder head nuts 1/4 turn at a time and in the crisscross pattern. Then remove the nuts.
5. Remove the cylinder head (**Figure 23**).
6. Remove and discard the cylinder head gasket (**Figure 24**).

7. Lay a clean rag over the cylinder to prevent dirt from falling into the cylinder.

8. Inspect the cylinder head as described in this chapter.

Inspection

1. Check the cylinder head for cracked or missing cooling fins (A, **Figure 25**). Refer repair to your dealer or a welding shop.

CAUTION

Damaged or missing cylinder head cooling fins can cause the engine to run hot and result in detonation. Repair or replace the cylinder head before operating the engine.

CAUTION

Do not gouge the gasket or combustion chamber surfaces when cleaning the cylinder head in Step 2. Burrs created from improper cleaning may cause com-

22

ENGINE TOP END

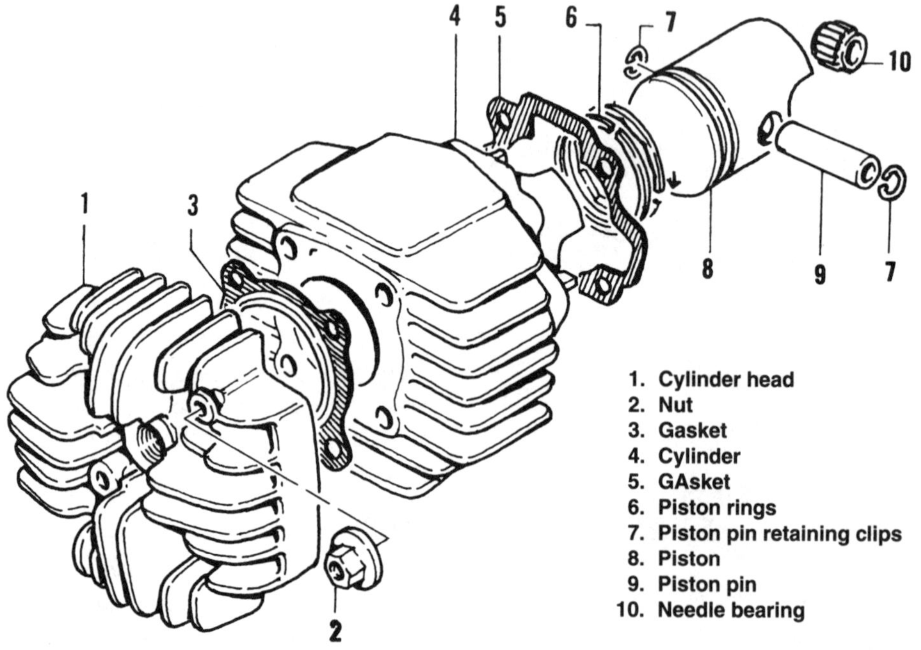

23

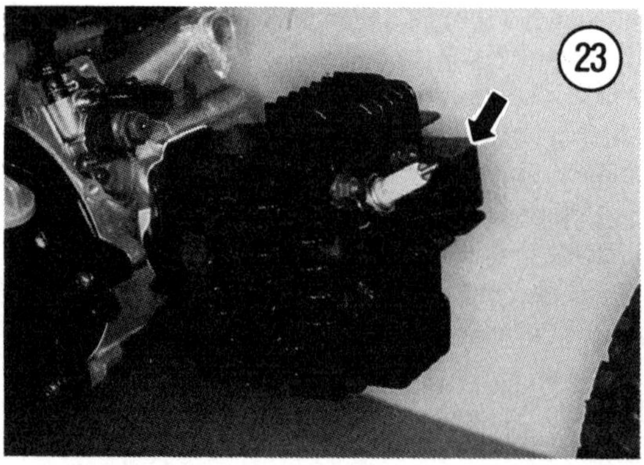

24

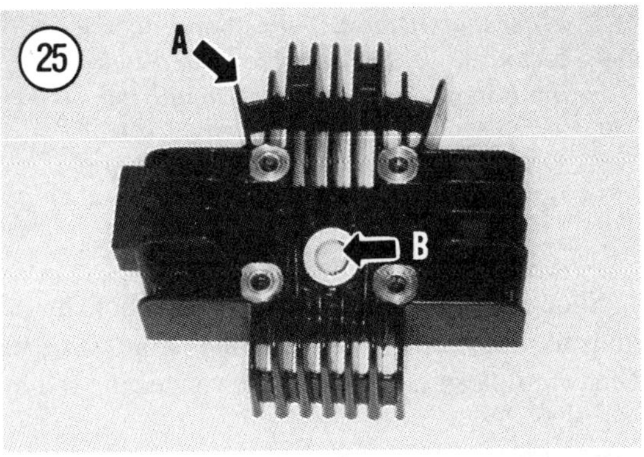

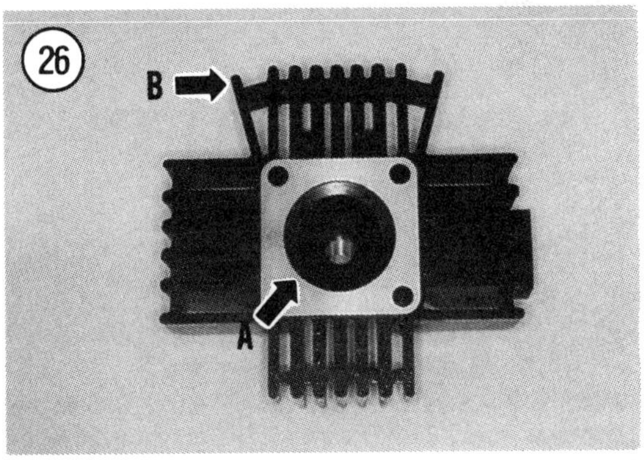

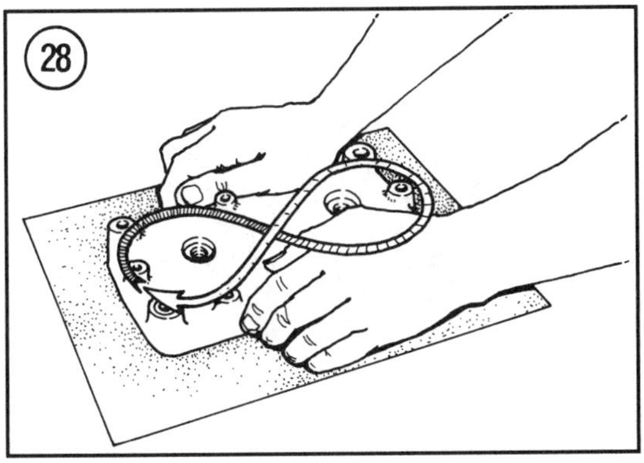

pression loss, preignition or heat erosion.

2. Wipe away any soft deposits from the cylinder head combustion chamber (A, **Figure 26**). Remove hard deposits with a wire brush mounted in a drill or drill press, or with a soft metal scraper.

3. Remove the spark plug and check the cylinder head threads (B, **Figure 25**) for carbon buildup or thread damage. Use a spark plug tap to clean or repair slightly damaged threads. If thread damage is severe, install new threads with a thread repair kit.

4. Measure the cylinder head flatness with a straightedge and feeler gauge (**Figure 27**). If the cylinder head warpage exceeds the service limit in **Table 2**, resurface the head as follows:

   a. Tape a piece of 400-600 grit wet emery sandpaper onto a piece of thick plate glass or surface plate (**Figure 28**).
   b. Slowly resurface the head by moving it in figure-eight patterns on the sandpaper.
   c. Rotate the head several times to avoid removing too much material from one side. Check the progress often with the straightedge and feeler gauge.
   d. If the cylinder head warpage still exceeds the service limit, take the cylinder head to your dealer for further inspection and repair, or replace the cylinder head.

5. Clean and inspect the cylinder head nuts. Replace nuts with damaged threads or rounded off hex corners.

6. Check for loose or damaged cylinder head studs (**Figure 24**). Replace or tighten studs as described in Chapter One.

7. Wash the cylinder head in hot soapy water and rinse with clean, cold water.

Installation

1. Clean and inspect the cylinder head as described under *Inspection* in this chapter.

2. Wipe the cylinder gasket surface with solvent and allow to air dry.

3. Install a new cylinder head gasket (**Figure 24**) over the cylinder studs.

4. Install the cylinder head with its larger fin area (B, **Figure 26**) facing toward the exhaust port side of the engine. See **Figure 23**.

CAUTION

*The cylinder head is designed with more cooling fin area on the exhaust side of the engine (B, **Figure 26**). If the cylinder head is installed backward, cylinder head warpage and engine overheating may result.*

5. Install the cylinder head nuts and tighten finger-tight. Then tighten the nuts in a crisscross pattern and in two steps as follows:
   a. First tighten the cylinder head nuts to half of their torque specified in **Table 6**.
   b. Then tighten the cylinder head nuts to the final torque specified in **Table 6**.
   c. Go over each nut a final time to make sure none have been missed.
6. Install the spark plug and tighten as specified in **Table 6**. Reconnect the spark plug lead.
7. Install the fuel tank (Chapter Seven) and seat (Chapter Fifteen).
8. Perform the *Crankcase Pressure Test* in Chapter Two to check for engine leaks.
9. If a new major component of the upper or lower end was installed (piston, rings, connecting rod, etc.), perform the engine break-in procedure described in this chapter.

CYLINDER

The cylinder can be serviced with the engine mounted in the frame.

Refer to **Figure 22** when servicing the cylinder head in this section.

Removal

1. Remove the exhaust pipe as described in this chapter.
2. Remove the cylinder head as described in this chapter.
3. Tap the cylinder (**Figure 29**) and then slide it off the piston and crankcase studs. If the cylinder is stuck to the crankcase or piston, do not pry it off as marks left between the mating surfaces could cause an air leak. Use a plastic or rubber hammer and carefully tap the cylinder loose.

NOTE

A seized piston or rusted and corroded cylinder bore will make it difficult to remove the cylinder. If the cylinder lifts off the crankcase, but is stuck to the piston, soak the piston crown and cylinder bore with a penetrating liquid. If the seizure or corrosion is severe, you may have to break the piston to separate it from the cylinder bore.

4. Slide a piece of hose (**Figure 30**) over both lower studs to protect the piston and rings from damage. Then stuff clean rags around the connecting rod to

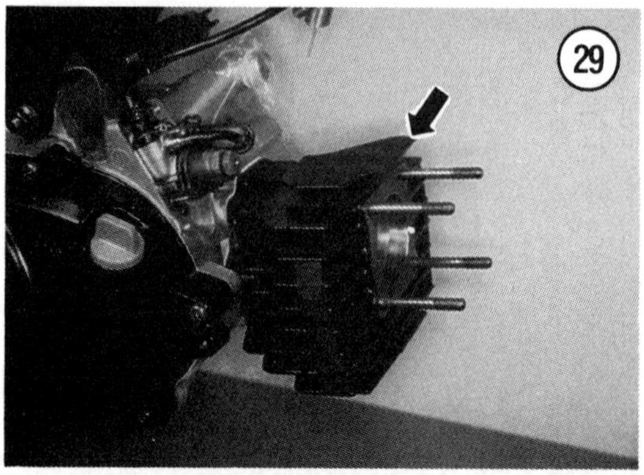
29

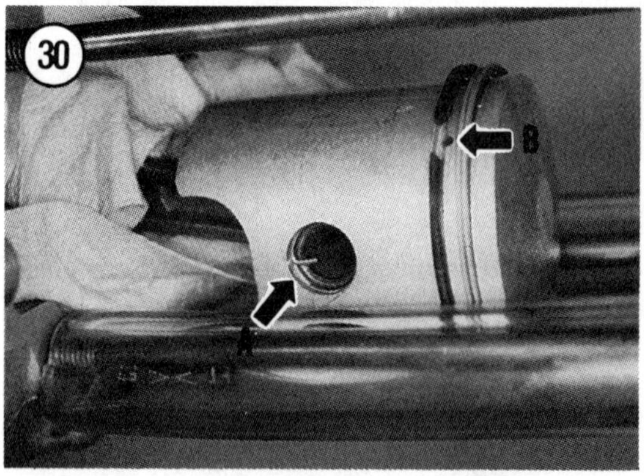

30

31

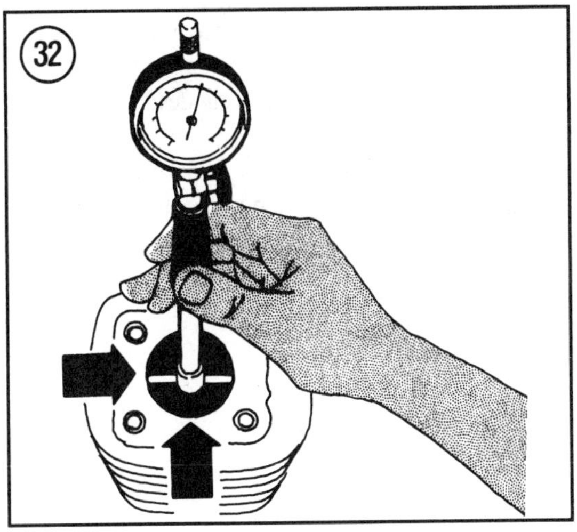

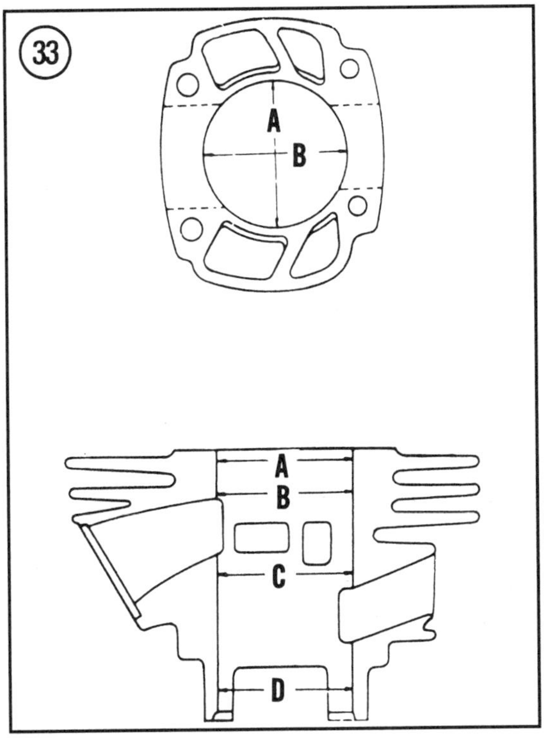

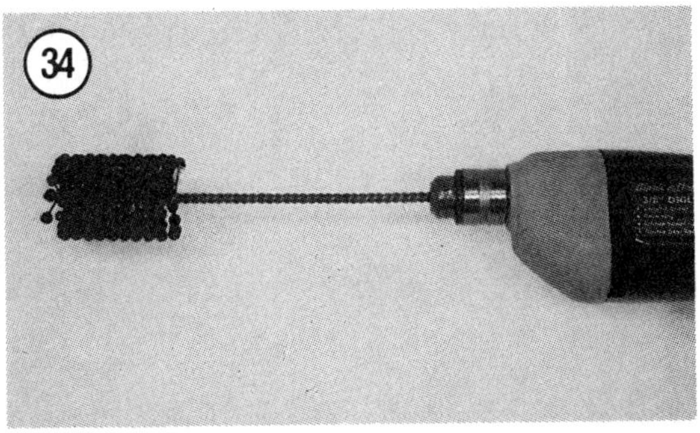

keep dirt and loose parts from entering the crankcase.

5. Remove and discard the cylinder base gasket.

6. Carefully scrape the crankcase to remove any base gasket residue. Be careful not to gouge the gasket surfaces.

Inspection

The original cylinder block uses a cast-iron liner. It can be bored to accept oversize pistons. Yamaha offers 2 oversize pistons.

A bore gauge and a 50-75 mm (2-3 in.) micrometer or an inside micrometer will be required to measure the cylinder bore accurately. If you do not have these tools, have the measurements performed by a dealership or qualified machine shop.

1. Remove all gasket and carbon residue from both cylinder gasket surfaces. Be careful not to gouge or damage the surfaces.

2. Remove hard carbon deposits from the exhaust port (**Figure 31**) with a drill mounted wire wheel or scraper. Be careful not to damage the cylinder bore or change the exhaust port chamfer.

NOTE

A good way to protect the cylinder bore when cleaning the exhaust port is to block off the exhaust port with an old piston or with a piece of plastic or cardboard.

3. Measure the cylinder bore with a bore gauge (**Figure 32**) or an inside micrometer at the 4 depth positions (A, B, C and D) shown in **Figure 33**. Except for the bottom measurement, measure both in line with the piston pin and at 90° to the pin. Note the following:

   a. Use the largest bore measurement to determine cylinder wear.
   b. Record measurements for cylinder wear, taper and out-of-round.
   c. If the cylinder bore, taper or out-of-round measurements exceed the wear limits in **Table 2**, the cylinder bore must be rebored to the next oversize and fitted with a new piston.

4. To determine piston-to-cylinder clearance, refer to *Piston/Cylinder Clearance* in this chapter.

5. When installing new piston rings, hone the cylinder with a ball hone (**Figure 34**) to deglaze the cylinder and help the new rings to seat. If necessary,

refer this service to a dealer or motorcycle repair shop.

6. After the cylinder has been bored or honed, the edges of the ports must be chamfered to prevent the rings from snagging a port. This service is usually performed by the machinist or technician after the cylinder machining operation. If you are doing the work yourself, use a fine cut file to chamfer the port as shown in **Figure 35**.

7. Before installing the cylinder, wash the bore in hot soapy water and rinse with clear water. Then check the bore cleanliness by running a white cloth over the bore surface. Repeat this step until the white cloth comes out clean—no smudge or dark marks.

8. Dry the cylinder with compressed air, then lubricate the bore with 2-stroke oil to prevent the liner from rusting.

Cylinder Installation

Make sure all engine parts are clean before starting assembly.

1. Clean the cylinder bore as described in this section.
2. Install a new base gasket (**Figure 36**).
3. If removed, install the piston as described in this chapter.
4. Lubricate the piston skirt, piston ring and cylinder bore with 2-stroke injection oil.
5. Make sure the piston pin clips (A, **Figure 30**) are seated in the piston grooves completely.
6. Center the piston ring end gaps around the piston ring locating pins as shown in B, **Figure 30**.
7. Compress the rings with your fingers and start the bottom edge of the cylinder over the piston (**Figure 37**). Then hold the piston and slide the cylinder down until it covers the rings. Continue to slide the cylinder down over the crankcase mounting studs, and seat it against the base gasket. See **Figure 29**.
8. Hold the cylinder in place with one hand and operate the kickstarter lever with your other hand. If the piston catches or stops in the cylinder, one or both piston rings are not aligned properly. The piston must move up and down the cylinder bore smoothly.

NOTE

If the rings are not aligned, remove the cylinder and check for damage. Reposition the piston rings correctly.

9. Install the head gasket and cylinder head as described in this chapter.
10. Perform the *Crankcase Pressure Test* in Chapter Two to ensure that the engine is air tight.
11. Install the exhaust system as described in this chapter.
12. Follow the *Engine Break-In* procedure in this chapter if the cylinder was rebored or honed or a new piston or piston rings were installed.

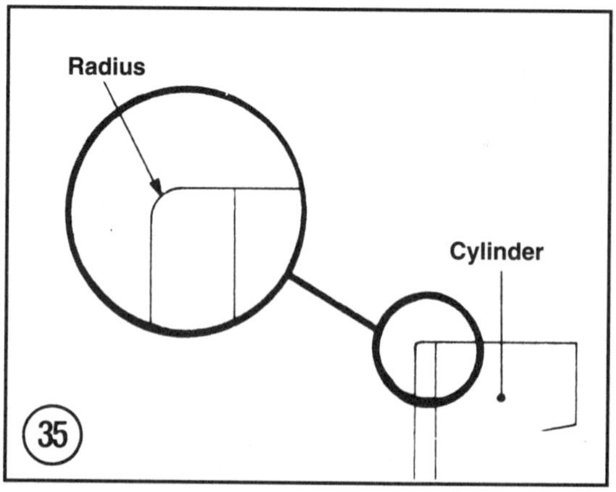

35

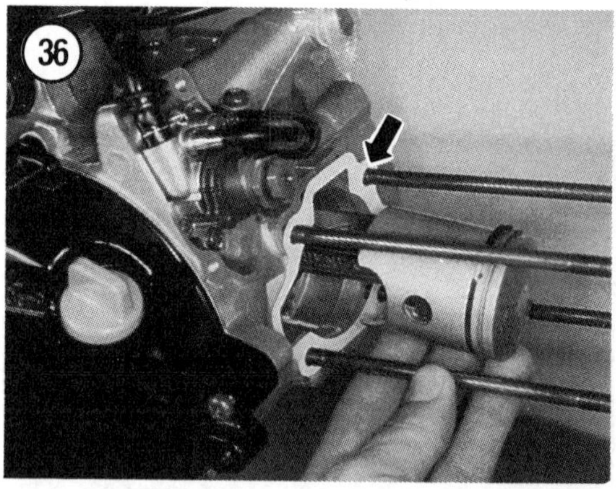

36

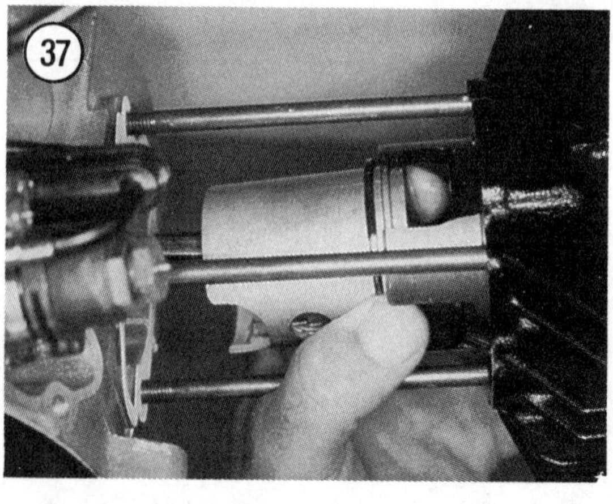

37

PISTON, PISTON PIN, AND PISTON RING

The piston is made of an aluminum alloy. The piston pin is a precision fit and is held in place by a clip at each end. A caged needle bearing is used on the small end of the connecting rod.

See **Figure 22** for this procedure.

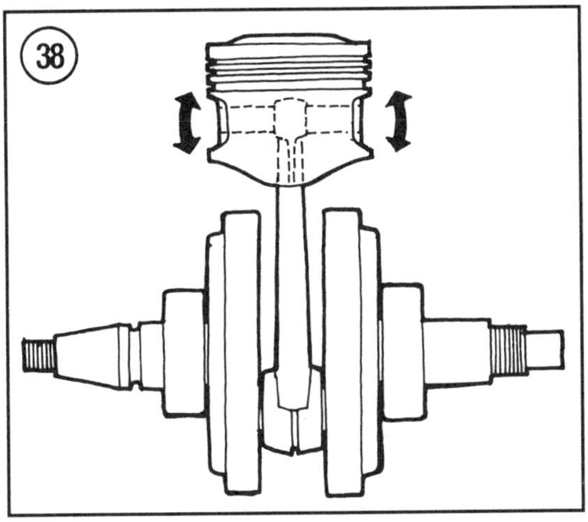

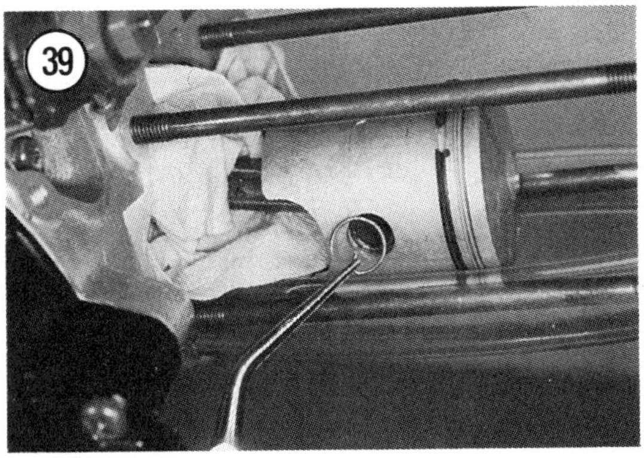

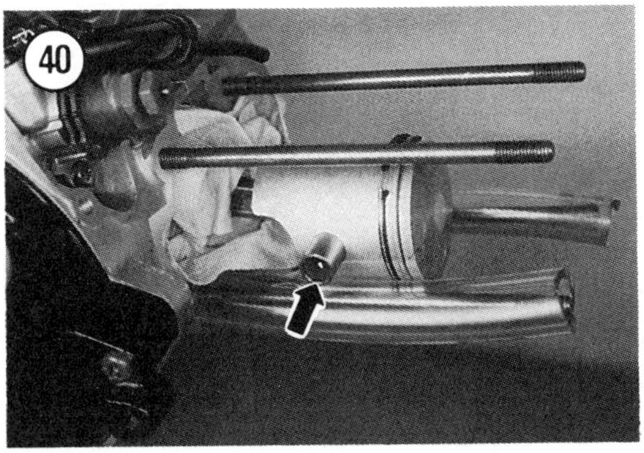

Piston and Piston Ring Removal

1. Remove the cylinder as described in this chapter.
2. Before removing the piston, hold the connecting rod tightly and rock the piston as shown in **Figure 38**. Any rocking motion (do not confuse with the normal side-to-side sliding motion) indicates wear of the piston pin, needle bearing, piston pin bore, or more likely a combination of all three. If there is any play, pay particular attention to the inspection of these items.
3. Wrap a clean shop cloth under the piston so that the clips cannot fall into the crankcase.

WARNING
Piston pin clips can slip and fly off forcefully during removal. Wear safety glasses to prevent eye injury.

4. Remove one or both piston pin clips with a pair of needlenose pliers (**Figure 39**). Hold your thumb over one edge of the clip when removing it to help prevent it from springing out.
5. Hold the piston securely, then push the piston pin (**Figure 40**) out of the piston with a wooden dowel or socket extension.

CAUTION
The piston pin is a floating type and should slide from the piston/connecting ring with only slight hand pressure. If the engine ran hot or seized, piston distortion may lock the piston pin in place, making it difficult to remove. If the piston pin is tight, do not drive it out of the piston. Doing so may damage the piston, needle bearing and connecting rod. To remove a stuck piston pin, use the tool and procedure described in Step 6.

6. If the piston pin is tight, remove it with a piston pin removal tool, or fabricate the tool shown in **Figure 41**. Assemble the tool onto the piston and pull the piston pin out of the piston. Install a pad between the piston and piece of pipe to prevent the tool from damaging the piston.
7. Lift the piston off the connecting rod.
8. Remove the needle bearing (**Figure 42**).

NOTE
*While the top (A, **Figure 43**) and bottom (B, **Figure 43**) piston rings have the same sectional dimensions (**Table 3**),*

their outer coating materials are different. If the piston rings are going to be reused, identify them for correct reassembly.

9. Remove the upper piston ring by spreading the ring ends with your thumbs just enough to slide the ring up over the piston (**Figure 44**).
10. Repeat Step 9 to remove the bottom piston ring.

Piston Pin and Needle Bearing Inspection

Yamaha does not list operating clearances for the piston pin and piston. This procedure describes basic visual and free play checks that can be made to these parts. Since piston pin-to-piston clearances are small, refer inspection to a dealership if there is any questionable play.

1. Clean and dry the piston pin and needle bearing.
2. Check the piston pin (A, **Figure 45**) for severe wear, scoring and cracks along the outer diameter. Replace the piston pin if necessary.
3. Inspect the needle bearing (B, **Figure 45**) for:
   a. Needle wear, flat spots or damage.
   b. A damaged bearing cage.
4. Lubricate the needle bearing and piston pin and install them into the connecting rod (**Figure 46**). Try to move the piston pin back and forth as shown in **Figure 46**. There must be no noticeable play in either direction. If there is free play, repeat the check with a new bearing and pin. If there is still free play, replace the connecting rod.
5. Install the piston pin partway into one side of the piston as shown in **Figure 47**. Try to move the piston pin in each of the four directions shown in **Figure 47**. Repeat for the other side of the piston. There must be no noticeable play in either direction. If there is free play, repeat the check with a new piston pin. If there is free play with the new piston pin, the piston is worn and must be replaced.

Connecting Rod Inspection

The following checks can be made with the crankshaft installed in the engine and the engine installed in the frame. When checking the connecting rod in this section, compare the actual measurements to the specifications in **Table 4**. Replace the connecting

41

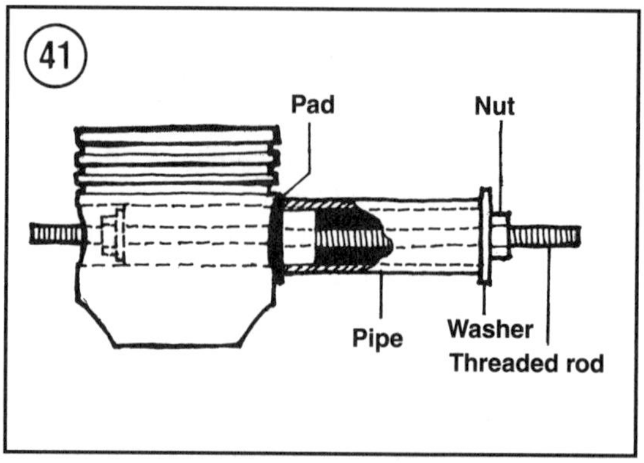

42

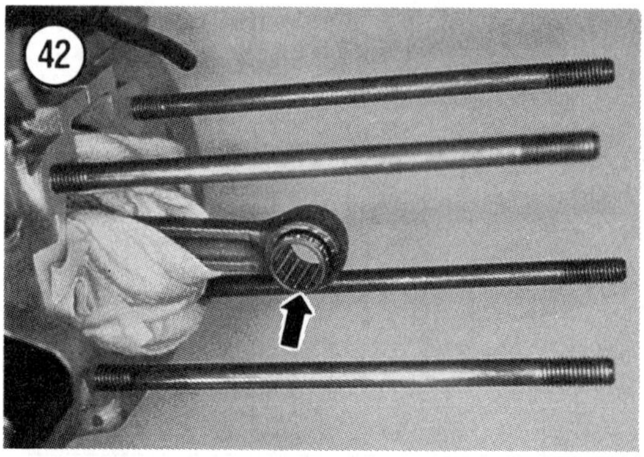

43

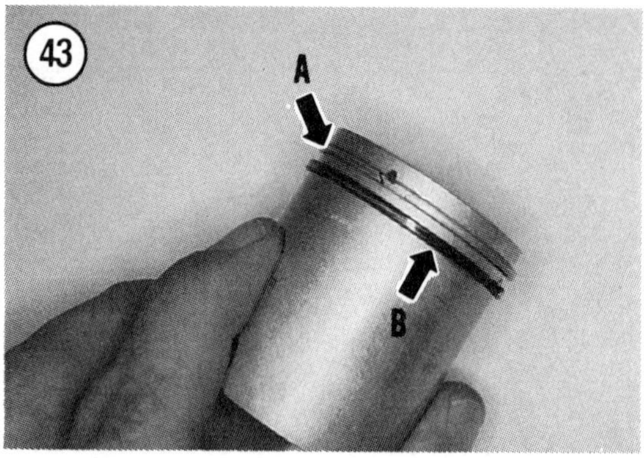

44

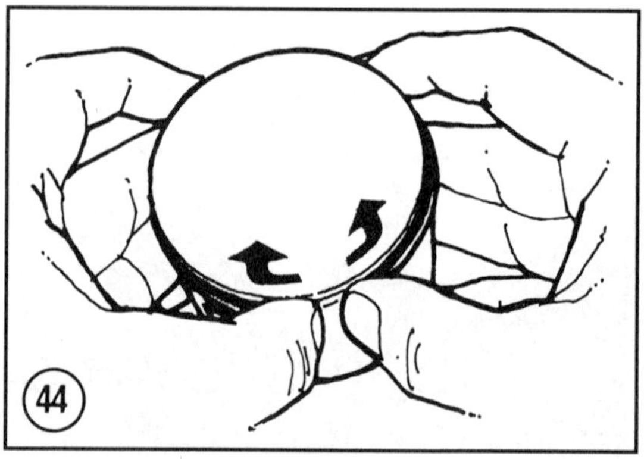

rod if damaged or any measurement is out of specification.

1. Visually inspect the connecting rod small and large ends for galling, cracks or other damage.

2. Measure connecting rod small end free play (**Figure 48**) as follows:

   a. Turn the crankshaft so that the connecting rod is at top dead center (TDC).

   b. Mount a dial indicator so that its plunger contacts the connecting rod small end (**Figure 49**).

45

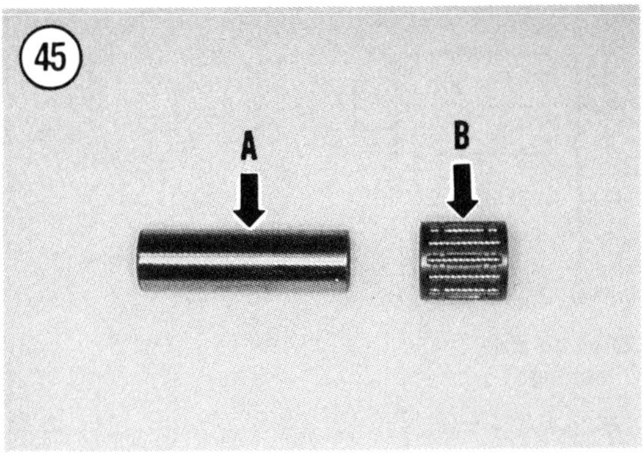

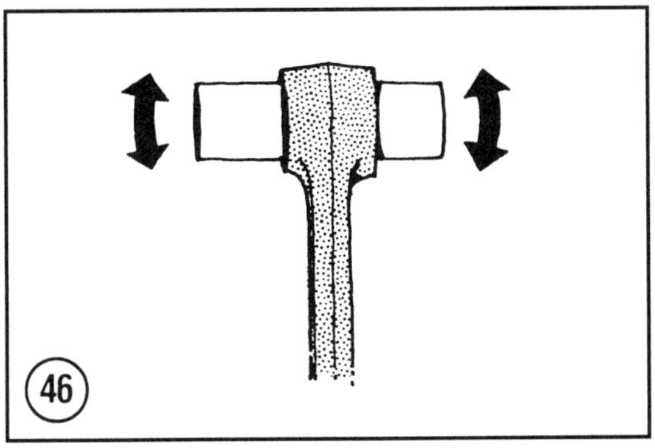

46

47

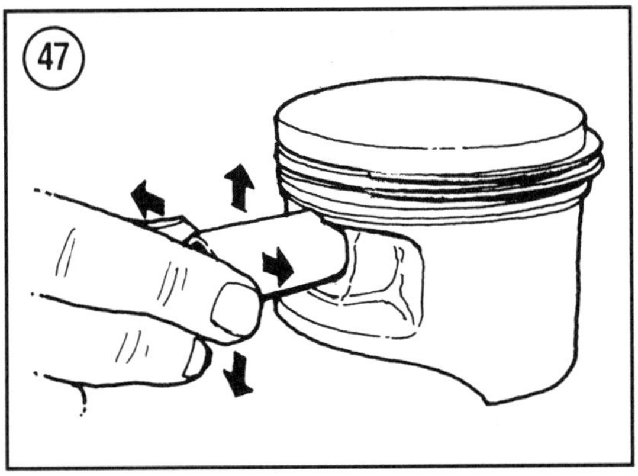

   c. Slide the connecting rod over so that it seats against the crankshaft's lower thrust washer that is on the same side the dial indicator is installed on. Hold the connecting rod in this position.

   d. While holding the lower part of the connecting rod, try to move the upper end by hand. Any movement is small end free play. Compare the actual reading to the small end free play clearance in **Table 4**.

3. Check connecting rod big end radial clearance (**Figure 48**) as follows:

   a. Turn the crankshaft so that the connecting rod is at TDC.

   b. Move the connecting rod over so that it seats against one of the cankshaft's lower thrust washers.

   c. Hold the connecting rod in this position, then try to move it up and down as shown in **Figure 48**. If radial clearance can be felt, the lower end bearing assembly is worn.

4. Measure the connecting rod big end side clearance (**Figure 48**) with a feeler gauge and check against the specification in **Table 4**. **Figure 50** shows the clearance being measured with the crankshaft removed from the engine.

5. To replace the connecting rod and its lower end bearing, the engine must be disassembled and the crankshaft rebuilt. Crankcase disassembly is described later in this chapter.

Piston and Ring Inspection

When measuring the piston and ring components in this section, compare the actual measurements to the new and service limit specifications in **Table 2**. Replace parts that are out of specification or show damage as described in this section.

1. Check the piston for hairline cracks at the transfer cutaways (A, **Figure 51**) and along the piston skirt (B, **Figure 51**).

2. Check the piston skirt for brown varnish deposits. More than a slight amount is evidence of worn or sticking rings.

3. Check the intake side of the piston skirt for abrasive scratches which indicates that dirt is passing through the air filter.

4. Check the piston skirt for galling and abrasion which may have resulted from piston seizure. If light galling is present, lightly smooth the area with No.

(48)

CONNECTING ROD INSPECTION

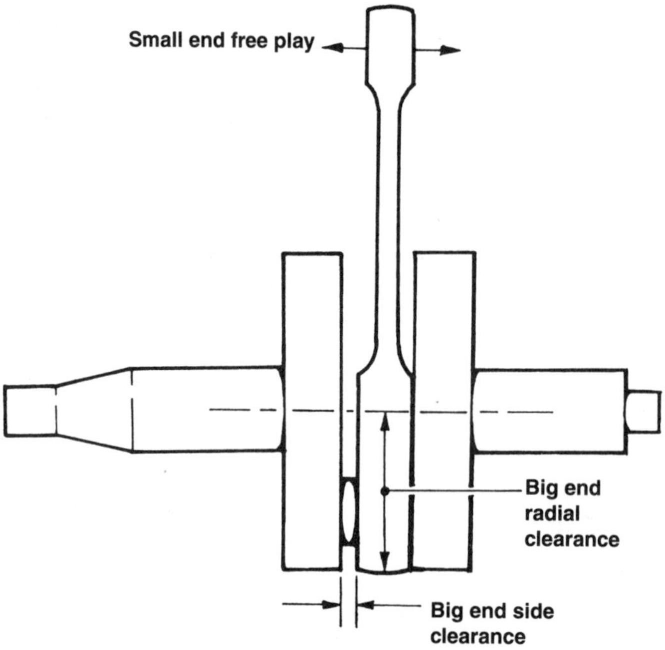

(49)

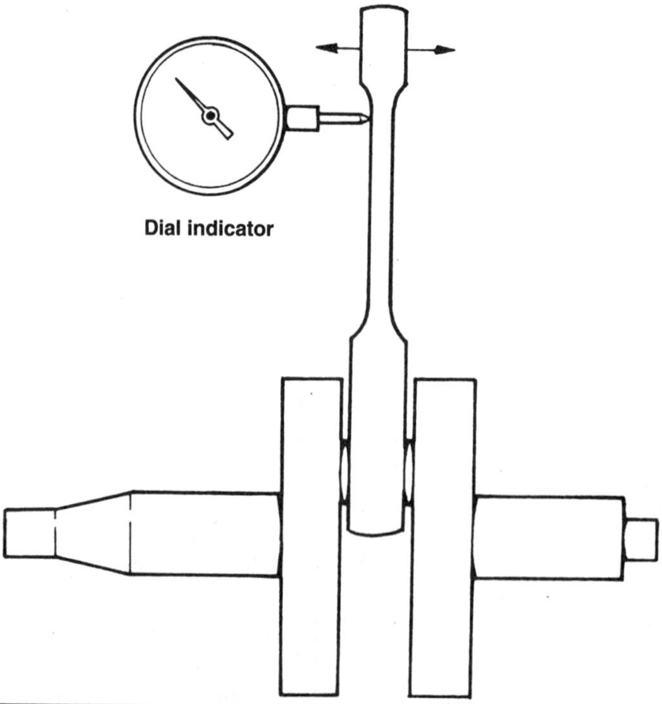

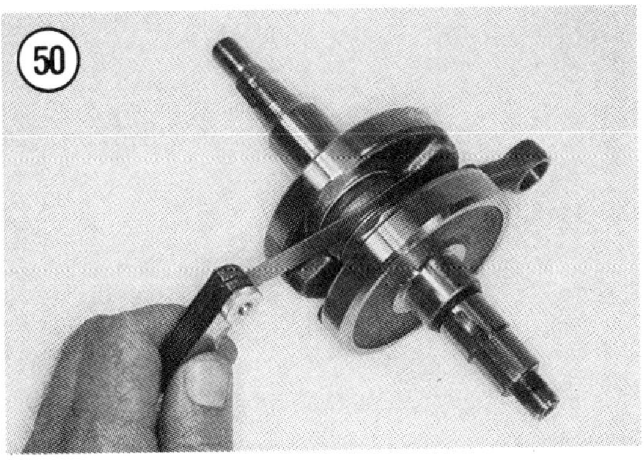

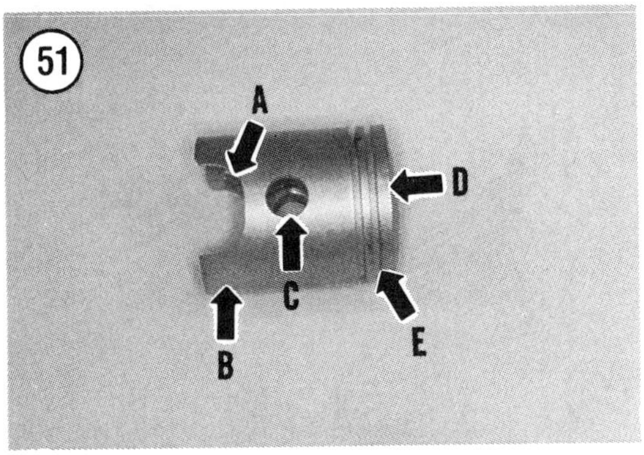

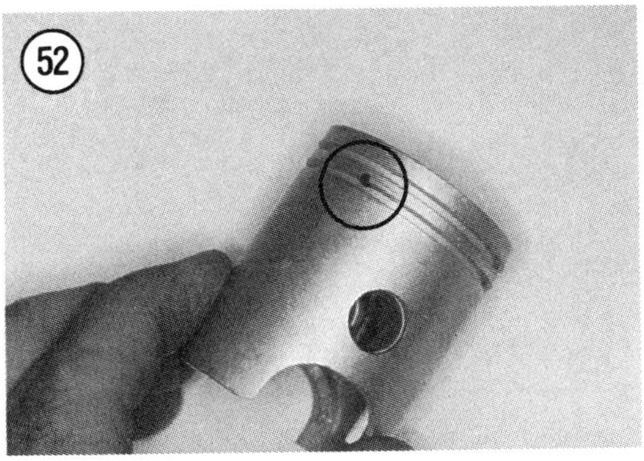

400 sandpaper or with fine emery cloth and oil. However, if the galling is severe or if the piston is deeply scored or cracked, replace the piston.

NOTE

If there is evidence of piston seizure, there is probably some aluminum deposits or other damage on the cylinder liner.

5. Check for loose or damaged ring locating pins (**Figure 52**). Each pin must be tight with no outer cracks or other damage. Replace the piston if either pin is loose or damaged.

CAUTION

*If a piston ring locating pin falls out, the piston ring can rotate in its groove. This will allow the ring's end gap to catch in a port and cause the type of damage shown in **Figure 53**.*

6. Check the piston pin clip grooves (C, **Figure 51**) for wear or damage.
7. Check the condition and color of the piston crown (D, **Figure 51**). Remove normal carbon buildup with a wire wheel mounted in a drill. If there is any erosion of metal on the piston crown, the engine is operating with a lean air/fuel mixture, a too hot spark plug or incorrect ignition timing. This condition should be corrected immediately after a new piston has been installed and the engine reassembled.

CAUTION

Do not use a wire brush to clean the piston skirt or gouge the piston when cleaning it.

CAUTION

*Because the stock piston uses Keystone rings (**Figure 54**), do not clean the piston ring grooves with a plain or square type piston ring. Doing so will damage the piston ring land.*

8. Remove carbon buildup from the ring groove with a broken Keystone ring (**Figure 55**). Work carefully to avoid removing any piston material from the grooves. If the carbon buildup is severe, soak the piston in solvent before trying to remove it.

NOTE

Any deposits left in the grooves will contribute to ring sticking and may re-

sult in loss of power and possible piston seizure.

9. Inspect the ring grooves (E, **Figure 51**) for burrs, nicks, or broken and cracked lands. Replace the piston if either ring groove is severely worn or damaged.
10. Roll the ring around its groove (**Figure 56**) and check for tight spots in the groove. If any tight spots are found, check the piston carefully for warpage, cracks or other damage. Repair minor damage with a fine-cut file only after determining that the piston is not permanently damaged. Replace the piston if there is any doubt as to its condition.
11. Install each ring in its groove and measure the piston ring-to-groove side clearance (**Figure 57**) with a feeler gauge. If the clearance is out of specification, the next step would be to recheck the clearance with a new piston ring. However, this is not always a practical step for the home mechanic. Instead, measure the side clearance of each groove using the bottom ring. Because this ring normally receives less wear than the upper ring, you may be able to better approximate whether the wear is caused by the ring or piston (or both).
12. Measure the piston ring end gap as follows. Place a ring into the bottom of the cylinder and push it in down approximately 20 mm (0.79 in.). Position the ring so that it is parallel with the bottom edge of the cylinder. Then measure the ring gap with a flat feeler gauge (**Figure 58**). Replace the rings as a set if the end gap of any ring is out of specification.
13. Measure the piston outside diameter as described under *Piston/Cylinder Clearance* in this chapter.

Piston/Cylinder Clearance

Yamaha does not list service limit specifications for their standard and oversize piston sizes. They only list new piston sizes (**Table 2**). To determine piston wear, first measure the cylinder bore wear. If it is within specification, measure the piston outside diameter and then subtract this dimension from the bore inside diameter to determine the piston-to-cylinder clearance. If the piston clearance is good, the piston diameter is good. If the piston clearance is out of specification (and the bore wear is good), the piston is worn and should be replaced. If the piston clearance is just out of specification, and the cylinder bore wear is minimal, it may be possible to install a

54

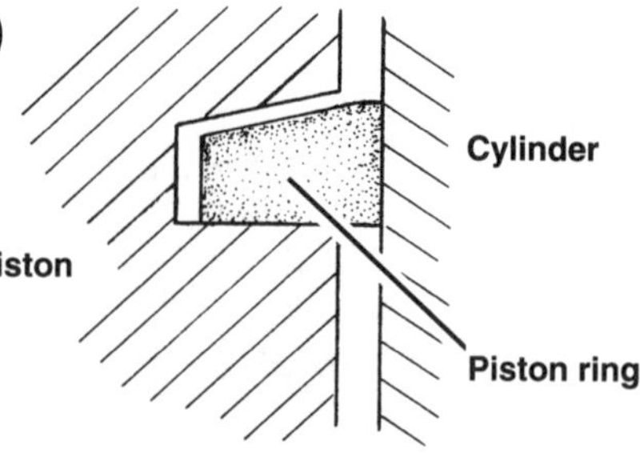

Keystone piston and piston ring

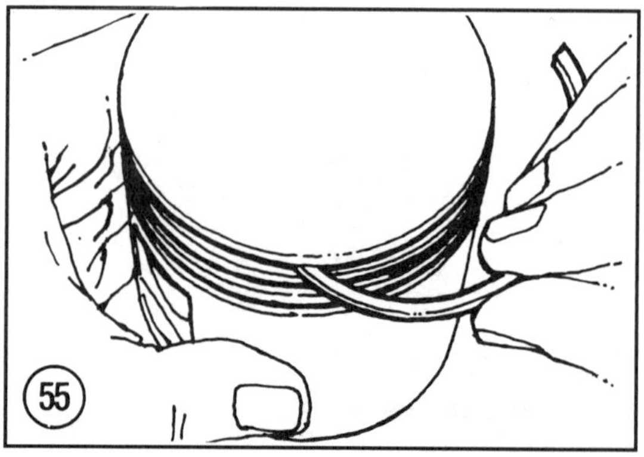

55

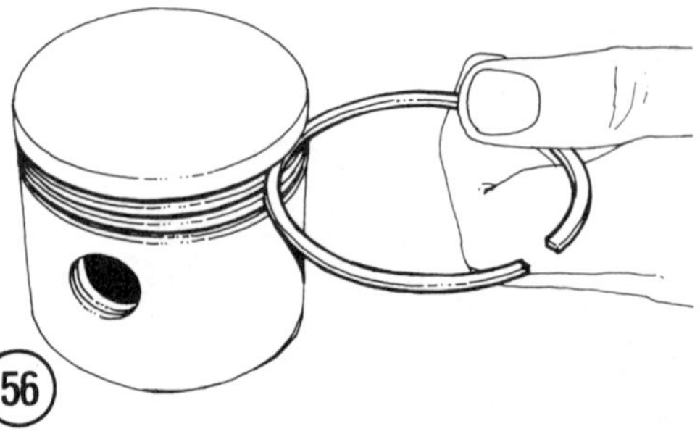

56

57

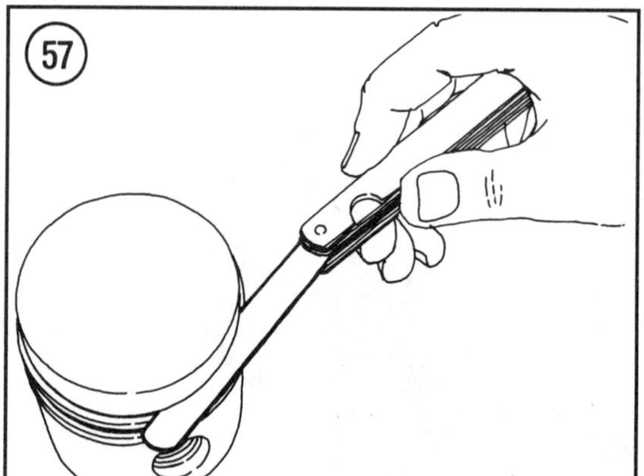

58

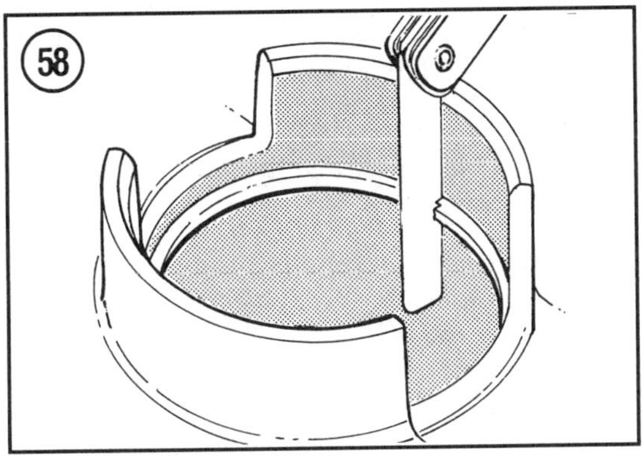

59

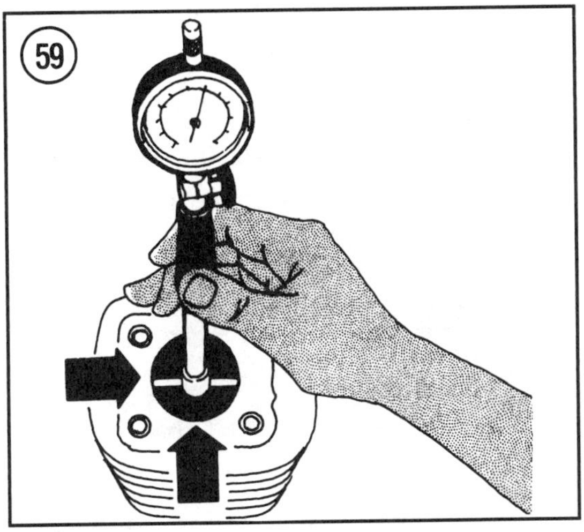

60

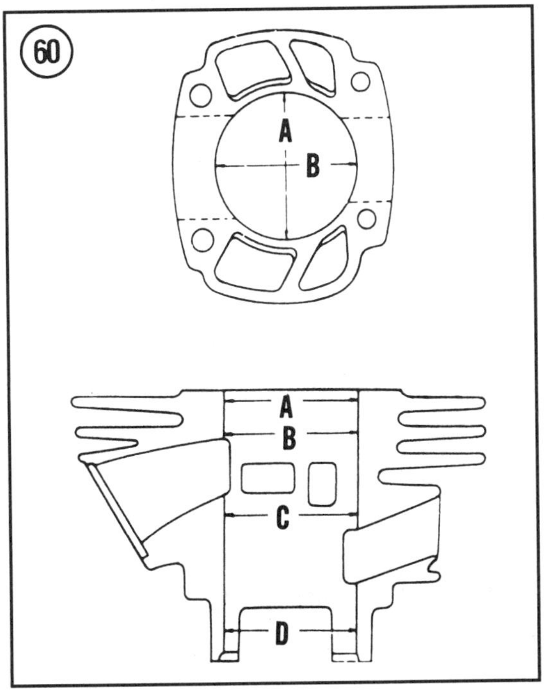

new piston to help take up some of the excessive piston-to-cylinder clearance. If the piston-to-cylinder clearance is excessive, and the bore wear is just within specification, it may be better to rebore the cylinder to the next oversize.

1. Measure the cylinder bore with a bore gauge (**Figure 59**) or an inside micrometer at the 3 depth positions (A, B, C and D) shown in **Figure 60**. Except for the bottom measurement, measure both in line with the piston pin and at 90° to the pin. Note the following:
   a. Use the largest bore measurement to determine cylinder wear.
   b. Record measurements for cylinder wear, taper and out-of-round.
   c. If the cylinder bore, taper or out-of-round measurement exceeds the wear limit in **Table 2**, the cylinder bore must be rebored to the next oversize and fitted with a new piston.

2. Measure the piston diameter at a point 5 mm (0.2 in.) from the bottom edge of the piston skirt and at a 90° angle to the piston pin as shown in **Figure 61**.

3. Subtract the piston skirt diameter from the maximum cylinder bore diameter to determine the piston-to-cylinder clearance. Compare this measurement with the service limit in **Table 2**. If out of specification, replace with the same size piston or rebore the cylinder and fit an oversize piston.

Piston Ring Installation

1. Check the piston ring end gap before assembling the piston and rings; refer to *Piston Inspection* in this chapter. The end gap measurement must be within specification (**Table 2**). If the end gap is too narrow after boring the cylinder, remeasure the cylinder bore

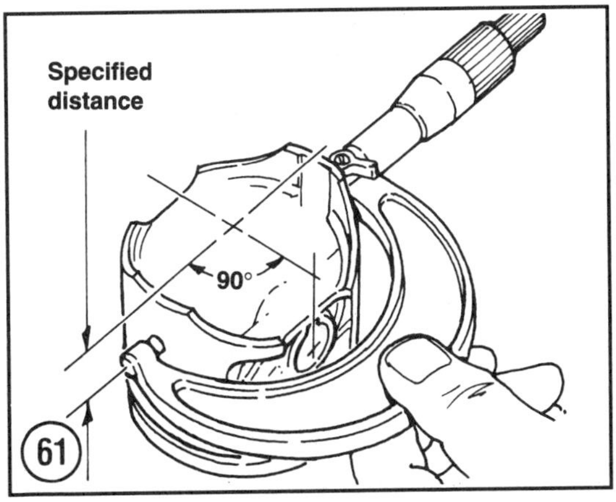

61

to make sure it is within specification. If it is, enlarge the gap by carefully filing the ring ends with a fine-cut file (**Figure 62**).

2. Clean and dry the piston and rings.
3. Install the piston rings as follows:
   a. The top and bottom piston rings are Keystone rings (**Figure 54**). See **Table 3** for piston ring dimensions. The top ring (A, **Figure 63**) has a chrome outer surface. The bottom ring (B, **Figure 63**) has a black surface color.
   b. Install used piston rings in their original mounting position. Refer to your identification marks made during removal.
   c. Install both piston rings with their manufacturer's marks facing up.
   d. Install the bottom piston ring (B, **Figure 63**) by carefully spreading its ends your thumbs and slipping it over the top of the piston (**Figure 44**). Center the ring end gap around the pin in the ring groove (**Figure 63**).
   e. Repeat to install the top piston ring.
4. Make sure each ring floats smoothly in its ring groove.

Piston Installation

Make sure all engine parts are clean before starting assembly. Use a 2-stroke engine when oil is called for in the following steps.

62

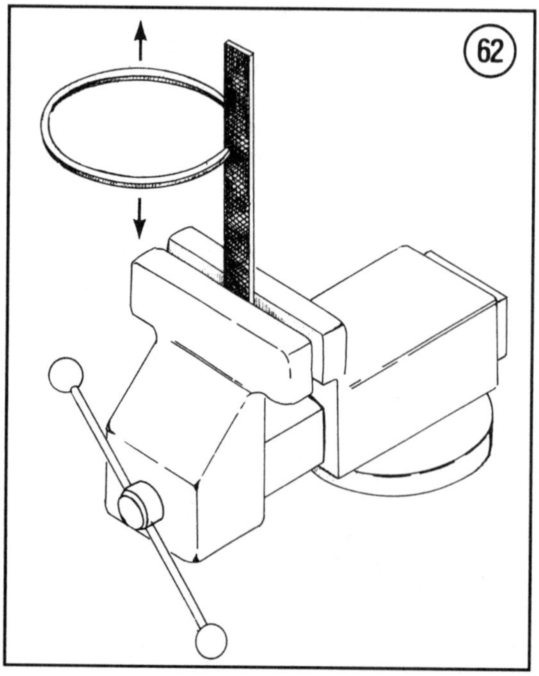

1. Lightly oil the needle bearing and install it in the connecting rod (**Figure 42**).

CAUTION
Do not install used piston pin clips.

WARNING
Piston pin clips can slip and fly off during installation. Wear safety glasses to prevent eye injury.

2. Install the first *new* piston pin clip (**Figure 64**) into one of the piston clip grooves. Make sure the clip seats in the groove completely. Turn the clip so that its bent arm is at the 12 or 6 o'clock position.

63

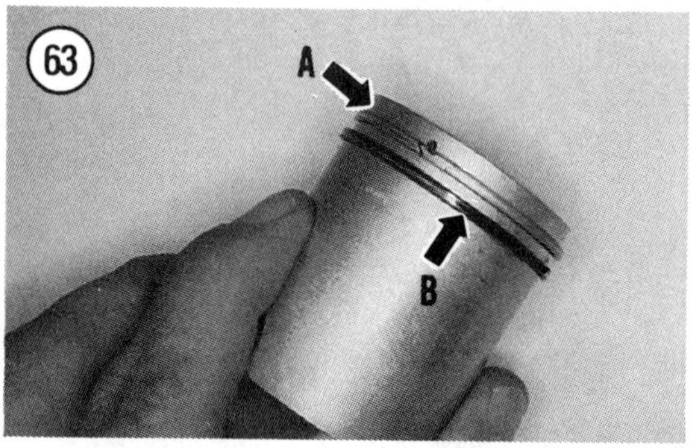

64

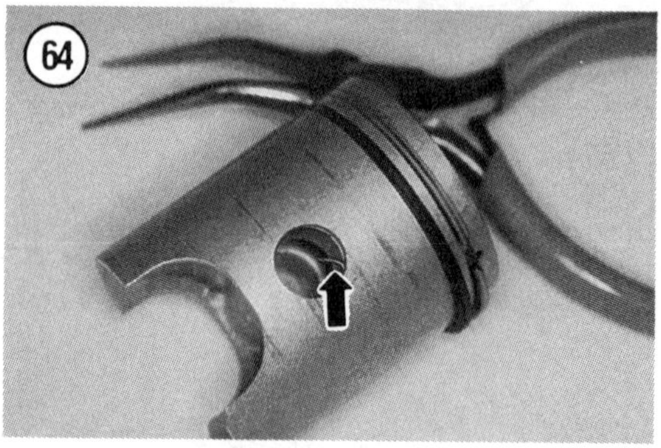

65

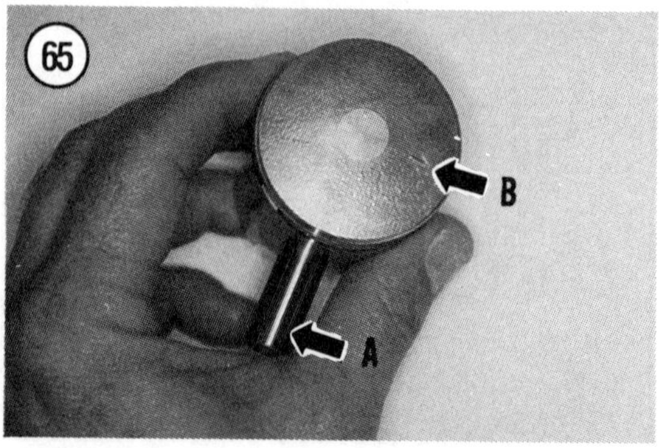

3. Oil the piston pin (A, **Figure 65**) and install it partway into the piston.
4. Place the piston over the connecting rod with its arrow mark (B, **Figure 65**) facing toward the exhaust side of the engine. Align the piston pin with the bearing, then push the pin (**Figure 66**) into the piston.

NOTE
If the arrow mark is not visible on the piston crown, install the piston with its ring locating pins facing toward the intake side of the engine.

66
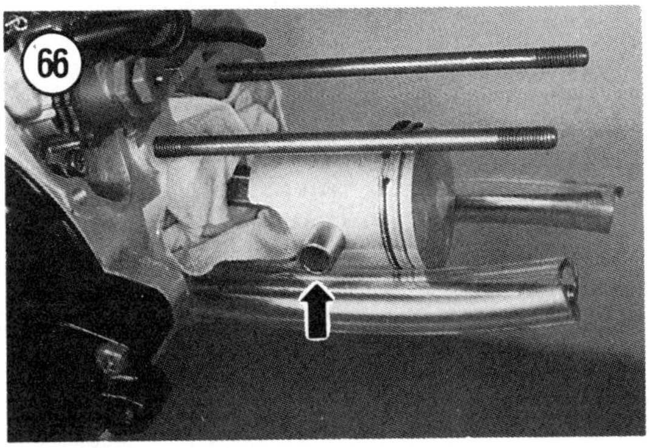

67
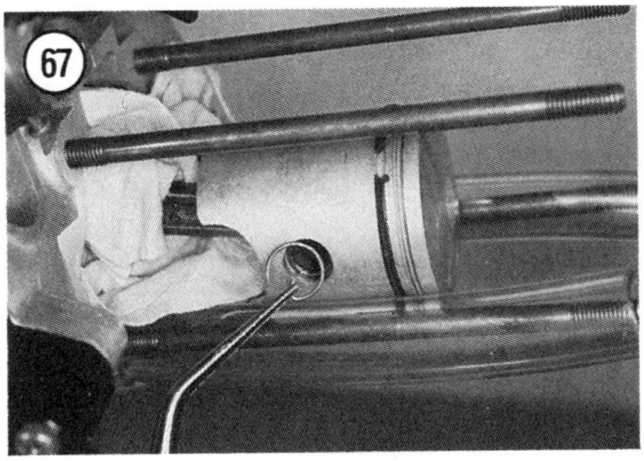

68

CAUTION
If the piston pin is not a slip fit in the piston, install it with the tool described under ***Piston Removal*** *in this chapter.*

5. Wrap a clean shop cloth under the piston so that the clip cannot fall into the crankcase.

WARNING
Piston pin clips can slip and fly off during installation. Wear safety glasses to prevent eye injury.

6. Install the second *new* piston pin clip (**Figure 67**) into the clip groove in the piston. Make sure the clip is seated in the groove (**Figure 68**) completely. Turn the clip so that its bent arm is at the 12 or 6 o'clock position.
7. Make sure both rings are seated in their grooves with their end gaps centered around their ring locating pins.

REED VALVE ASSEMBLY

The reed valve assembly can be serviced with the engine mounted in the frame. This procedure shows reed valve service with the engine removed for clarity.

Refer to **Figure 69** when servicing the reed valve in this section.

NOTE
If your model is equipped with an aftermarket reed valve, refer to its manufacturer's instructions on removal, installation and inspection procedures.

Removal/Installation

1. If the engine is mounted in the frame, remove the air box and carburetor (Chapter Seven).
2. Remove the intake manifold mounting screws and remove the manifold (**Figure 70**).
3. Remove the reed block and both gaskets. See **Figure 71**.
4. Inspect the reed valve assembly as described in this chapter.
5. Remove all gasket residue from the intake manifold, reed block and crankcase mating surfaces.
6. Install a new lower gasket (**Figure 72**) onto the crankcase, then install the reed block (A, **Figure 73**).
7. Install a new upper gasket (B, **Figure 73**) onto the reed block.

5

(69)

REED VALVE ASSEMBLY (BW80 AND PW80)

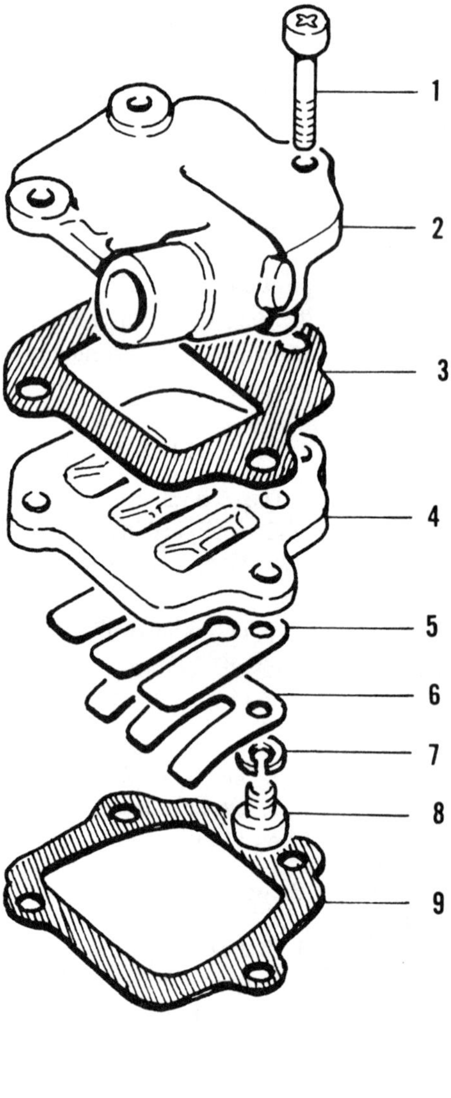

1. Screws
2. Intake manifold
3. Upper gasket
4. Reed block
5. Reed valve
6. Reed stop
7. Lockwashers
8. Screws
9. Lower gasket

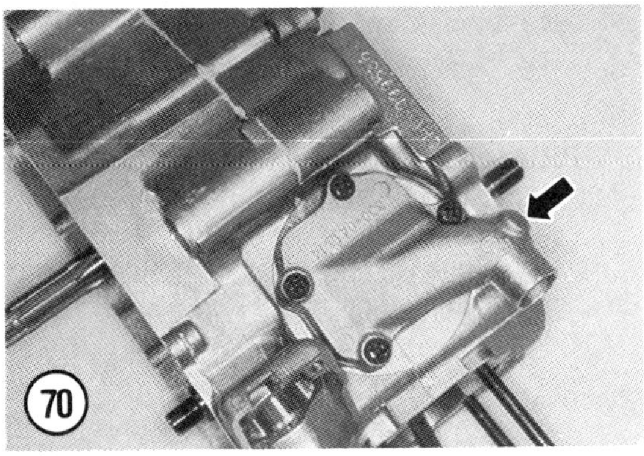

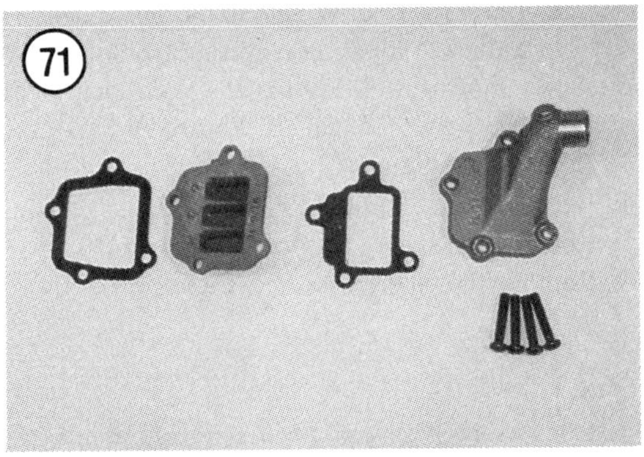

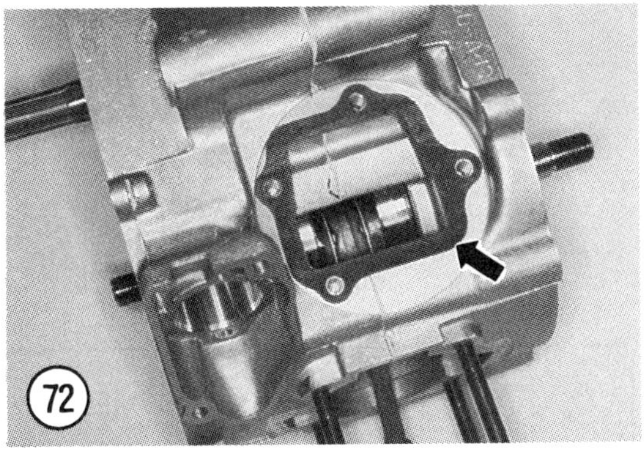

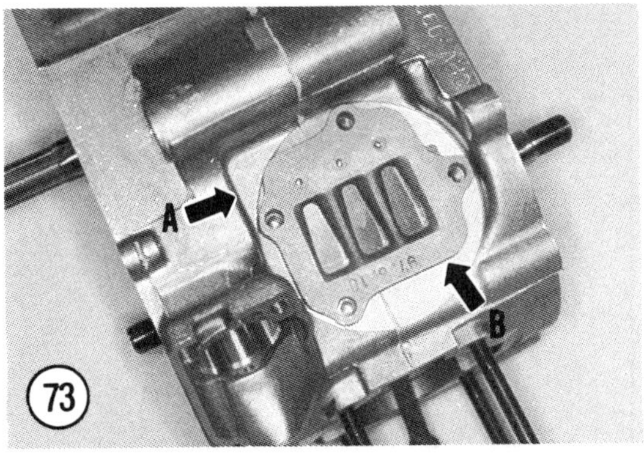

8. Install the intake manifold (**Figure 70**) and its mounting screws. Tighten the screws securely in a crisscross pattern.
9. If necessary, install the carburetor and air box (Chapter Seven).

Inspection

When measuring the reed valve components, compare the actual measurements to the specifications in **Table 2**. Replace all parts that are damaged or out of specification.

1. Carefully examine the reed block (A, **Figure 74**) for visible signs of wear, distortion or damage.
2. Check the reed valve (B, **Figure 74**) for cracks or other damage. A damaged reed valve will cause hard engine starting and reduce engine performance.
3. Check the reed stop (C, **Figure 74**) for cracks or other damage.
4. Use a flat feeler gauge and measure the clearance between the reed valve and the reed block sealing surface (**Figure 75**). Replace the reed valve if its bend clearance exceeds the service limit.

CAUTION
Many riders turn reed valves over if out of tolerance; however, bear in mind an out of tolerance condition is caused by metal fatigue. Metal fatigue may cause the reed valve to break and enter the engine, resulting in serious and expensive damage. Fiber reed valves are available and do not cause engine damage when they break.

5. Measure the reed stop height distance as shown in **Figure 76**. If the reed valve stop height measures

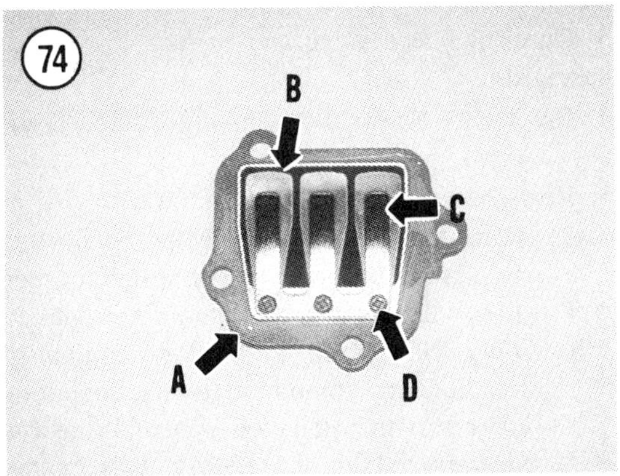

0.3 mm (0.012 in.) more or less than the specification in **Table 2**, either remove the reed stop and bend it back into specification, or replace it. Do *not* try to bend the reed stop while it is mounted on the reed block.

CAUTION
After bending the reed stop, check it carefully for cracks or other damage before reinstalling it back into the engine.

6. Inspect the intake manifold (**Figure 71**) and replace if cracked or damaged.
7. Measure the intake manifold flatness with a straightedge and feeler gauge. If the intake manifold warpage exceeds the service limit in **Table 2**, resurface the manifold as follows:
   a. Tape a piece of 400-600 grit wet emery sandpaper onto a piece of thick plate glass or surface plate.
   b. Slowly resurface the intake manifold by moving it in figure-eight patterns on the sandpaper.
   c. Rotate the manifold several times to avoid removing too much material from one side. Check progress often with the straightedge and feeler gauge.
   d. If the warpage cannot be corrected by this method, replace the intake manifold.

Reed Valve/Reed Stop Replacement

1. Remove the screws (D, **Figure 74**) securing the reed stop and reed valve to the reed block.
2. Clean and dry all parts. Remove all thread sealer residue from the mounting screws and the threaded holes in the reed stop.
3. Check the reed valve and replace if worn or damaged.
4. Replace the screws if the threads or screw heads are damaged.
5. Reassemble the reed cage as follows:
   a. The reed valve is not perfectly flat, but instead, one side will bow out slightly. Install the reed valve so that the bowed section faces out.
   b. Apply ThreeBond TB1342 or equivalent threadlocking compound to the mounting screws prior to installation. Assemble the reed valve and reed stop and secure with the mounting screws and lockwashers. Tighten the screws securely.

PRIMARY DRIVE GEAR AND OIL PUMP DRIVE GEAR

Refer to **Figure 77** when servicing the primary drive gear and oil pump drive gear assembly.

Removal

1. Remove the clutch cover (Chapter Six).
2. Lock the primary drive gear to the clutch gear by stuffing a thick folded rag (several layers thick) at the point shown in A, **Figure 78**. Then loosen the primary drive gear locknut (B, **Figure 78**).
3. Remove the clutch (Chapter Six).
4. Remove the locknut (B, **Figure 78**).
5. Remove the spring washer (A, **Figure 79**).
6. Remove the tapered washer (**Figure 80**).

75

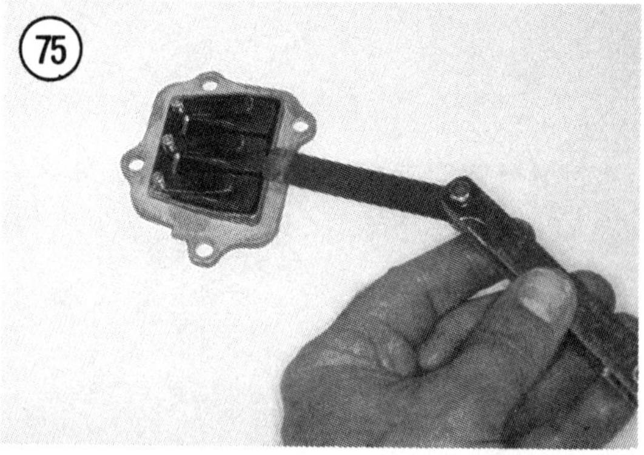

76

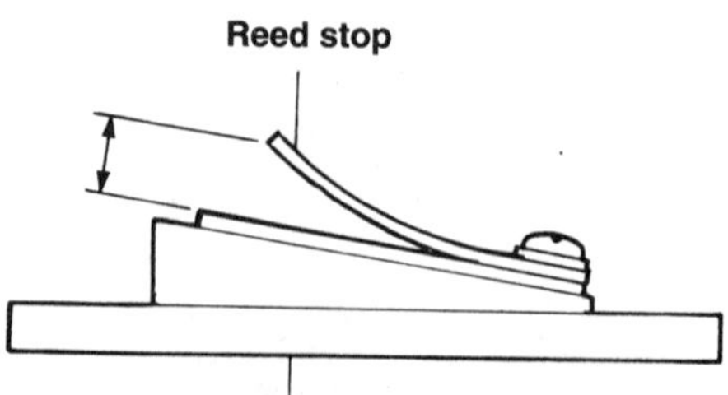

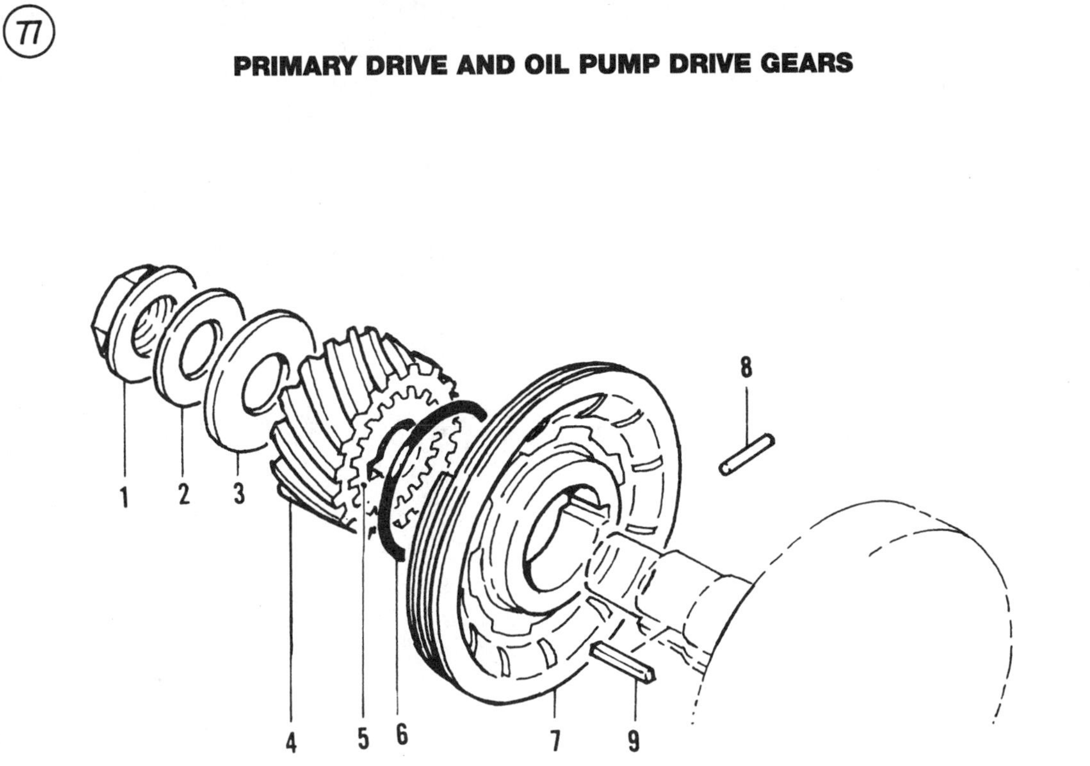

1, Locknut
2. Spring washer
3. Tapered washer
4. Outer primary drive gear
5. Inner primary drive gear
6. O-ring
7. Oil pump drive gear
8. Pin
9. Square key

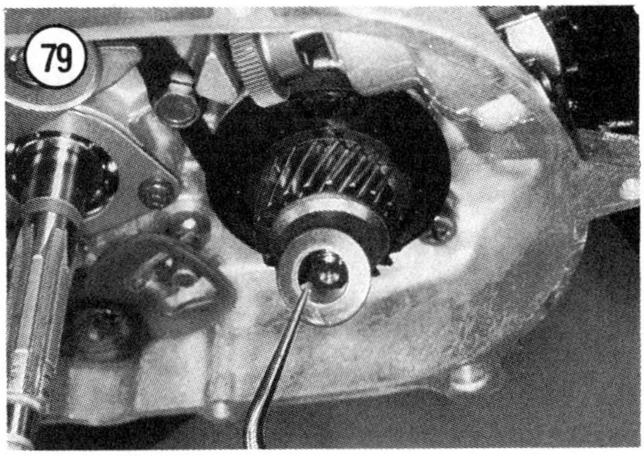

7. Remove the outer primary drive gear (**Figure 81**).
8. Remove the inner primary drive gear (A, **Figure 82**) and the square key (B, **Figure 82**).
9. Remove the O-ring (A, **Figure 83**) and the oil pump drive gear (B, **Figure 83**). On early models, remove the pin (**Figure 77**).

Inspection

Replace all worn or damaged parts as described in this section.

1. Clean and dry all parts (**Figure 84**).
2. Inspect the primary drive gear assembly (**Figure 85**) for:
   a. Missing, broken or chipped teeth.
   b. Cracked or scored gear bore.
   c. Damaged keyway.
   d. Damaged washers.
3. Inspect the oil pump drive gear (**Figure 86**) for:
   a. Missing, broken or chipped teeth.
   b. Damaged gear surface or bore.
   c. Worn or damaged O-ring.
   d. Damaged pin (early models).

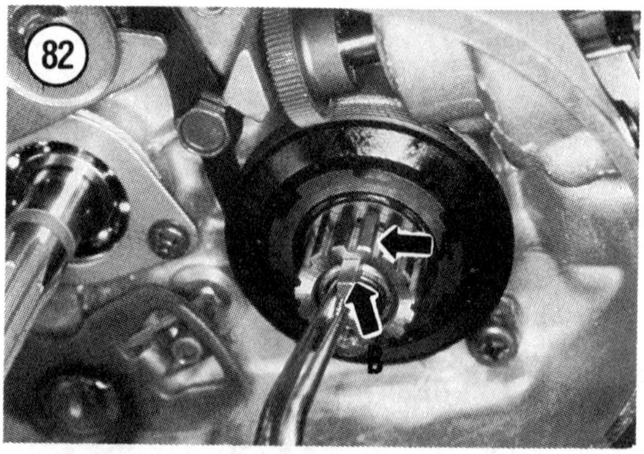

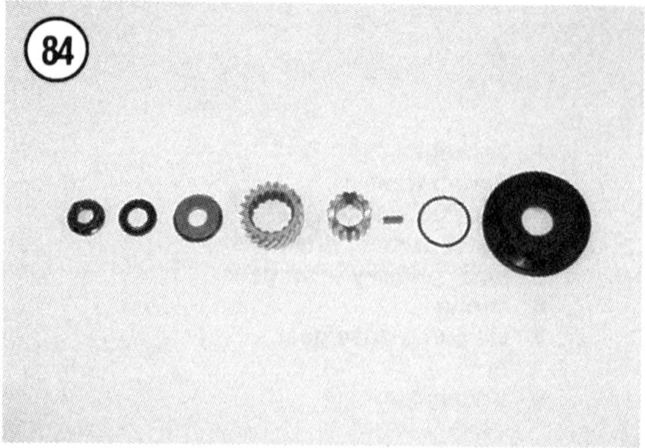

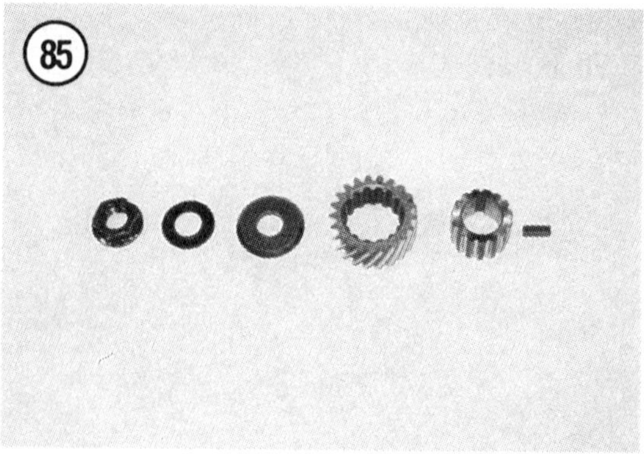

86

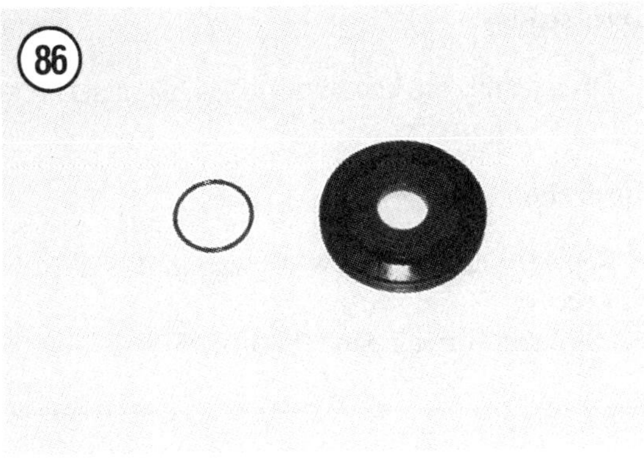

87

88

89

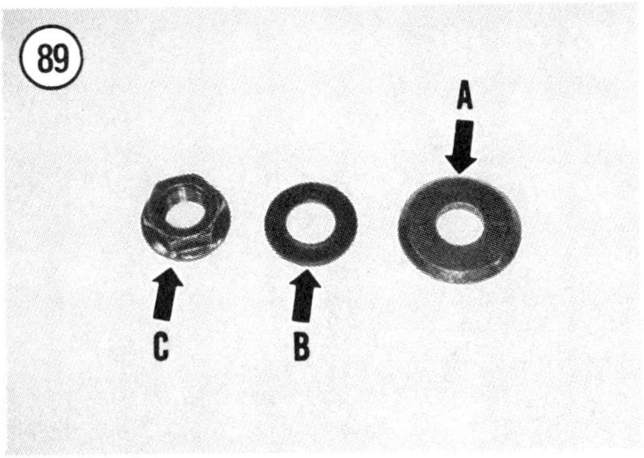

Installation

1. Install the oil pump drive gear over the crankshaft. Push the gear on slowly to mesh it with the oil pump driven gear (B, **Figure 83**). On early models, install the pin (**Figure 77**).
2. Install the O-ring (A, **Figure 83**) into the oil pump drive gear groove.
3. Install the inner primary drive gear with its shoulder (**Figure 87**) facing in. See A, **Figure 82**.
4. Align the gear and crankshaft keyways and install the square key (B, **Figure 82**). Push the key all the way in.
5. Install the outer primary drive gear with its shoulder (**Figure 88**) facing in. See **Figure 81**.
6. Install the washers and locknut (**Figure 89**) as follows:
   a. Install the tapered washer (A, **Figure 89**) with its tapered shoulder side facing out. See **Figure 80**.
   b. Install the spring washer (B, **Figure 89**) so its convex side faces out. See **Figure 79**.
   c. Install the locknut (C, **Figure 89**) and tighten finger-tight. See **Figure 90**.
7. Install the clutch (Chapter Six).
8. Lock the primary drive gear to the clutch gear by stuffing a thick folded rag (several layers thick) at the point shown in C, **Figure 78**. Then tighten the primary drive gear locknut (**Figure 90**) as specified in **Table 6**.
9. Install the right crankcase cover (Chapter Six).

KICKSTARTER

Refer to **Figure 91** for this procedure.

90

5

Removal

1. Remove the clutch as described in Chapter Six.
2. Remove the outer washer (**Figure 92**).
3. Unhook the spring (**Figure 93**) and allow it to unwind.
4. Pull the kickstarter assembly (**Figure 94**) out and remove from the engine.

Disassembly

Disassemble the kickstarter assembly in the order shown in **Figure 95**.

Inspection

Replace parts that show damage as described in this section.

1. Clean and dry all parts (**Figure 95**).

91

KICKSTARTER (BW80 AND PW80)

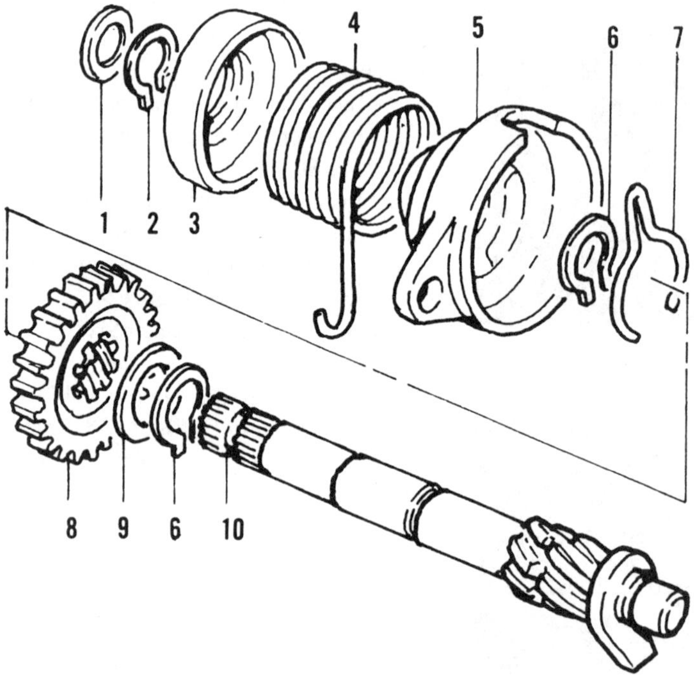

1. Outer washer
2. Circlip
3. Spring cover
4. Spring
5. Spring guide
6. Circlip
7. Clip
8. Kick gear
9. Washer
10. Kick shaft

92

93

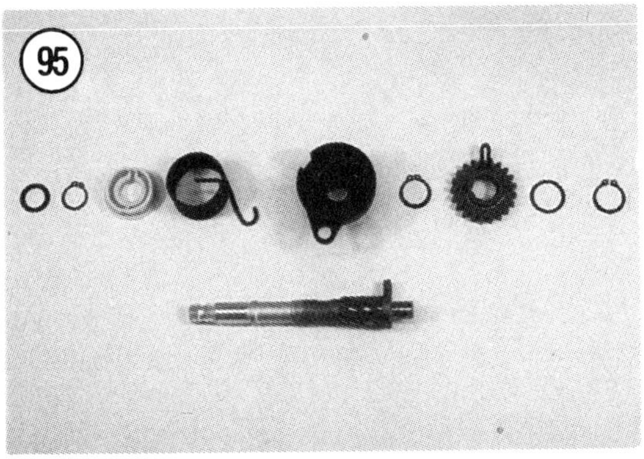

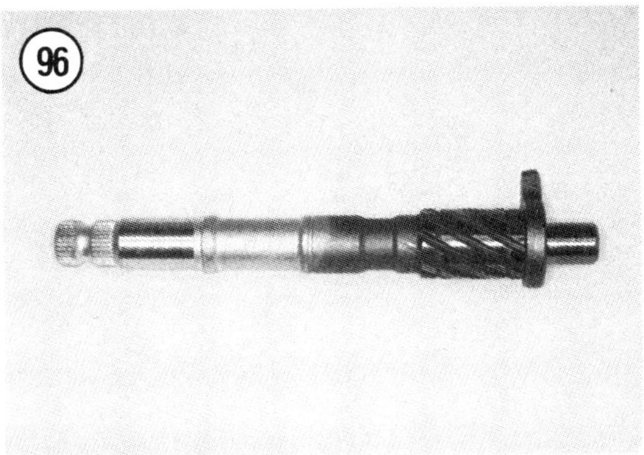

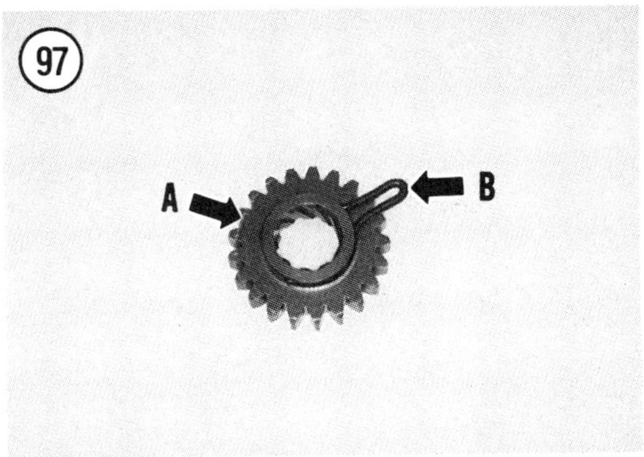

2. Inspect the kick shaft (**Figure 96**) for:
   a. Bent kick shaft.
   b. Stripped kick shaft splines.
   c. Damaged circlip grooves.
   d. Seized or severely worn bearing surfaces.
   e. Worn or elongated kick spring hole.
3. Inspect the kick gear (A, **Figure 97**) for:
   a. Missing, broken or chipped teeth.
   b. Worn or damaged splines.
   c. Damaged clip groove.
4. Check the clip (B, **Figure 97**) as follows:
   a. Check the clip for any visible wear or damage.
   b. Check the clip tension by hooking a spring scale onto the clip as shown in **Figure 98**. Hold the kick gear while pulling the spring scale. The clip should not slip or move on the kick gear until the spring scale reads 0.8-1.2 kg (1.8-2.6 lb.). Replace the clip if out of specification.
5. Inspect the spring (**Figure 95**) for:
   a. Spread or damaged coils.
   b. Damaged spring ends.
6. Inspect the spring cover and spring guide (**Figure 95**) for:
   a. Worn or damaged outer surface.
   b. Cracked or damaged bore inside diameter.
7. Replace the circlips (**Figure 95**) if they appear weak, bent or damaged.
8. Replace the washers (**Figure 95**) if bent or damaged.

Assembly

Refer to **Figure 91** for this procedure.

1. Lubricate all of the bearing and sliding surfaces with transmission oil.

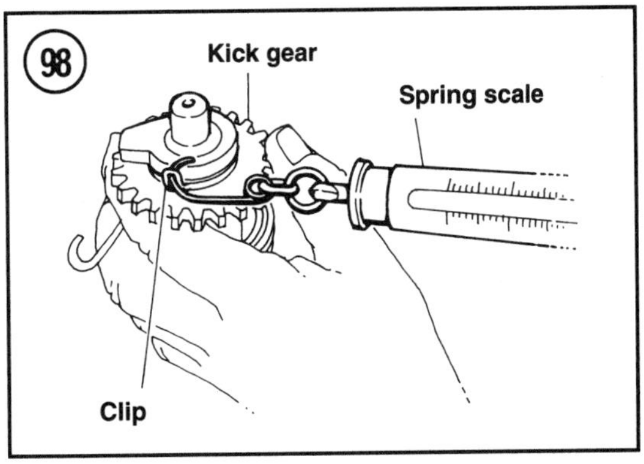

5

NOTE
*The kickstarter uses 3 circlips. The circlips shown in **Figure 99** (A and D) are identical (same part number). The third circlip (2, **Figure 91**) is smaller in size and is installed in the outer kick shaft groove.*

2. Install the first circlip (A, **Figure 99**) into the kick shaft groove (**Figure 100**).
3. Install the clip (B, **Figure 97**) onto the kick gear.
4. Install the kick gear with its clip (A, **Figure 101**) facing toward the outside of the shaft.
5. Install the second circlip into the kick shaft groove (B, **Figure 101**).
6. Install the spring guide (A, **Figure 102**), then center its notch over the clip as shown in B, **Figure 102**.
7. Install the spring with its hooked end (A, **Figure 103**) facing toward the spring guide. Then insert the opposite spring end into the hole in the kick shaft (B, **Figure 103**).
8. Install the spring cover (A, **Figure 104**); seat the notch (B, **Figure 104**) in the cover over the spring end.

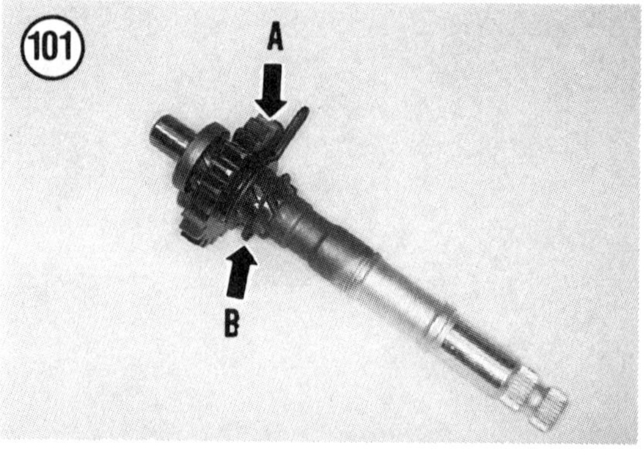

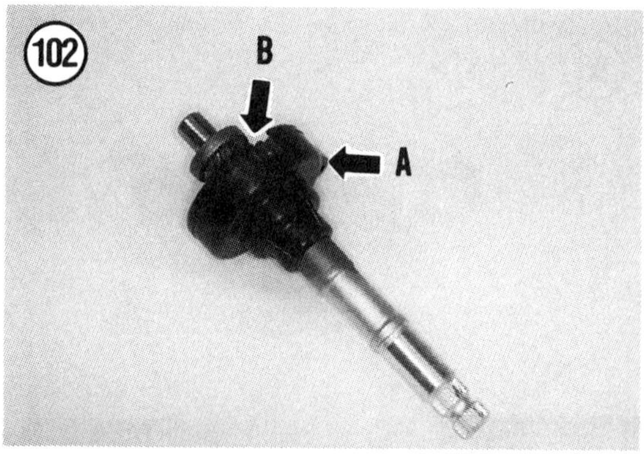

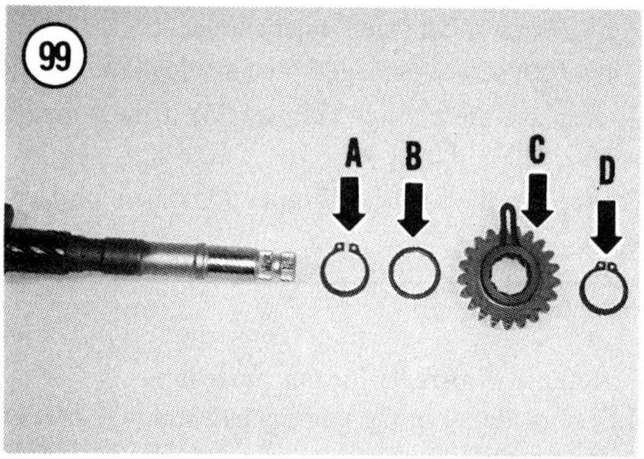

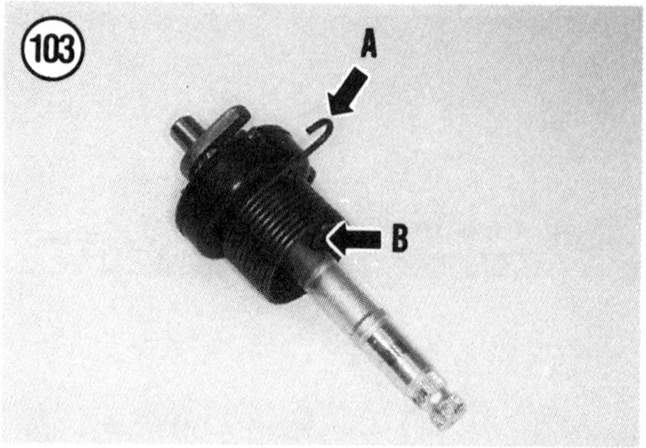

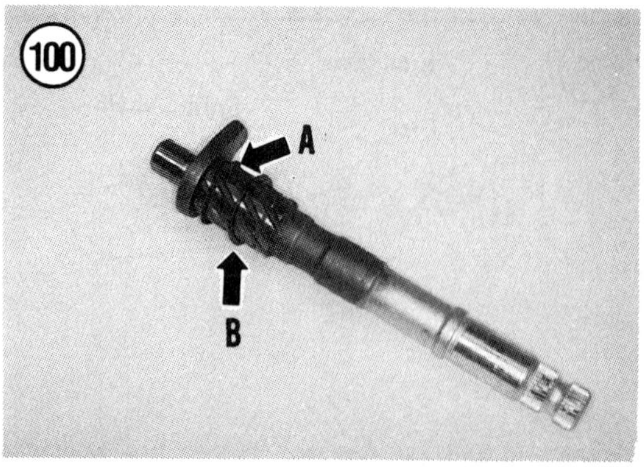

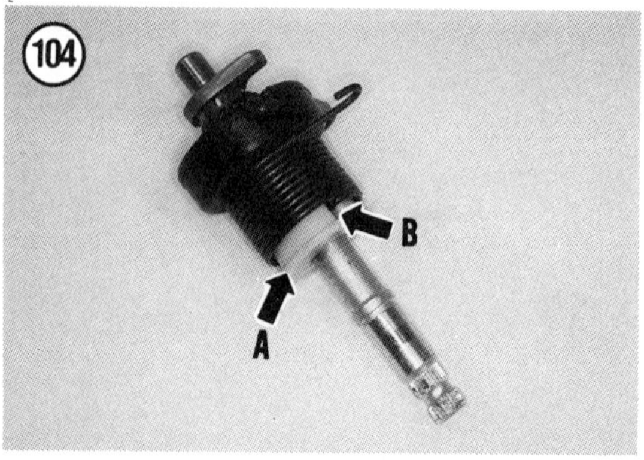

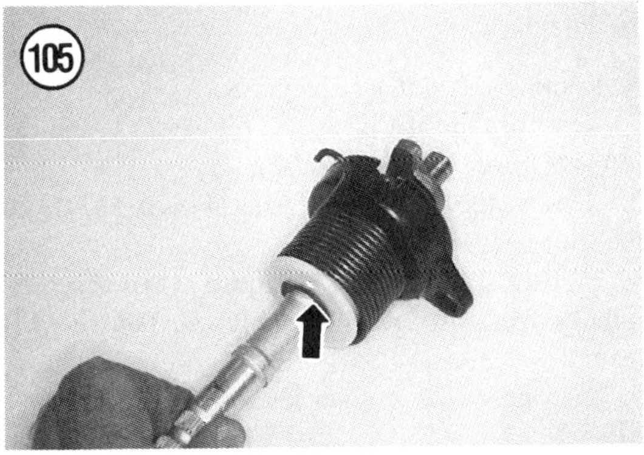

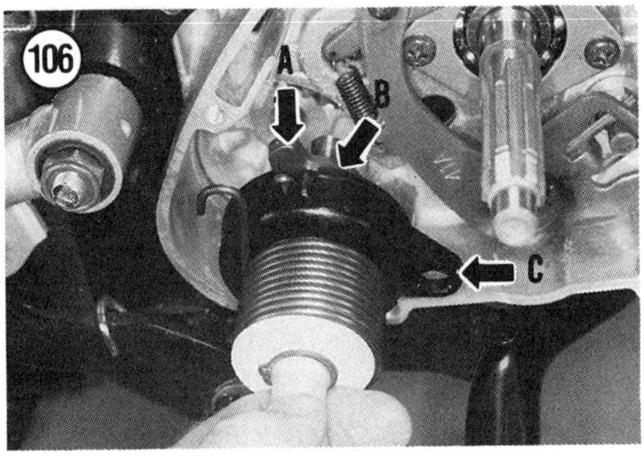

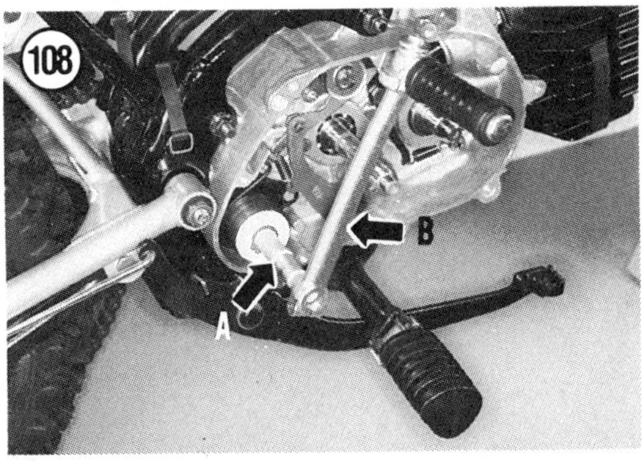

9. Install the circlip (**Figure 105**) into the outer kick shaft groove.

Installation

1. Before installing the kickstarter, note the following:
   a. The kick boss (A, **Figure 106**) fits against the crankcase projection's left side (A, **Figure 107**).
   b. The clip (B, **Figure 106**) fits into the crankcase notch (B, **Figure 107**).
   c. The hole in the spring guide (C, **Figure 106**) fits over the crankcase pin (C, **Figure 107**).
2. Install the kickstarter shaft (A, **Figure 108**) into the crankcase (do not align any of the parts described in Step 1).
3. Install the kickstarter pedal (B, **Figure 108**) onto the kick shaft.
4. Using the kickstarter pedal, rotate the kick shaft and align the parts as described in Step 1. See A (clip) and B (spring guide), **Figure 109**. The kick boss (A, **Figure 106**) is hidden during assembly.
5. Wind the kick spring (**Figure 93**) clockwise and hook it onto the crankcase post as shown in **Figure 110**.

5

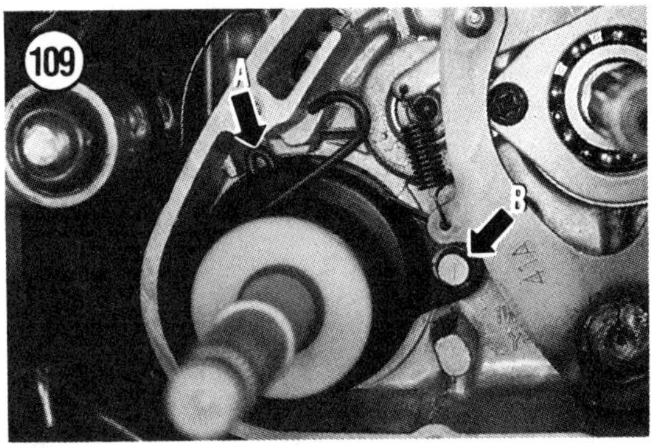

6. Install the washer (**Figure 92**) and seat it against the kick axle shoulder.

7. Operate the kickstarter pedal (**Figure 108**) by hand. Check that the kick shaft returns under spring pressure.

8. Install the clutch as described in this chapter.

EXTERNAL SHIFT MECHANISM

Refer to **Figure 111** for this procedure.

Removal

1. Remove the clutch (Chapter Six).
2. Remove the shift pedal (A, **Figure 112**) and the left side cover (B, **Figure 112**).
3. Remove the E-clip and washer (**Figure 113**) from the shift lever.
4. Push the selector arm (A, **Figure 114**) down, then remove the shift lever assembly (B, **Figure 114**) from the engine.
5. Disconnect the stopper lever spring (A, **Figure 115**).

(111)

INTERNAL SHIFT MECHANISM (BW80 AND PW80)

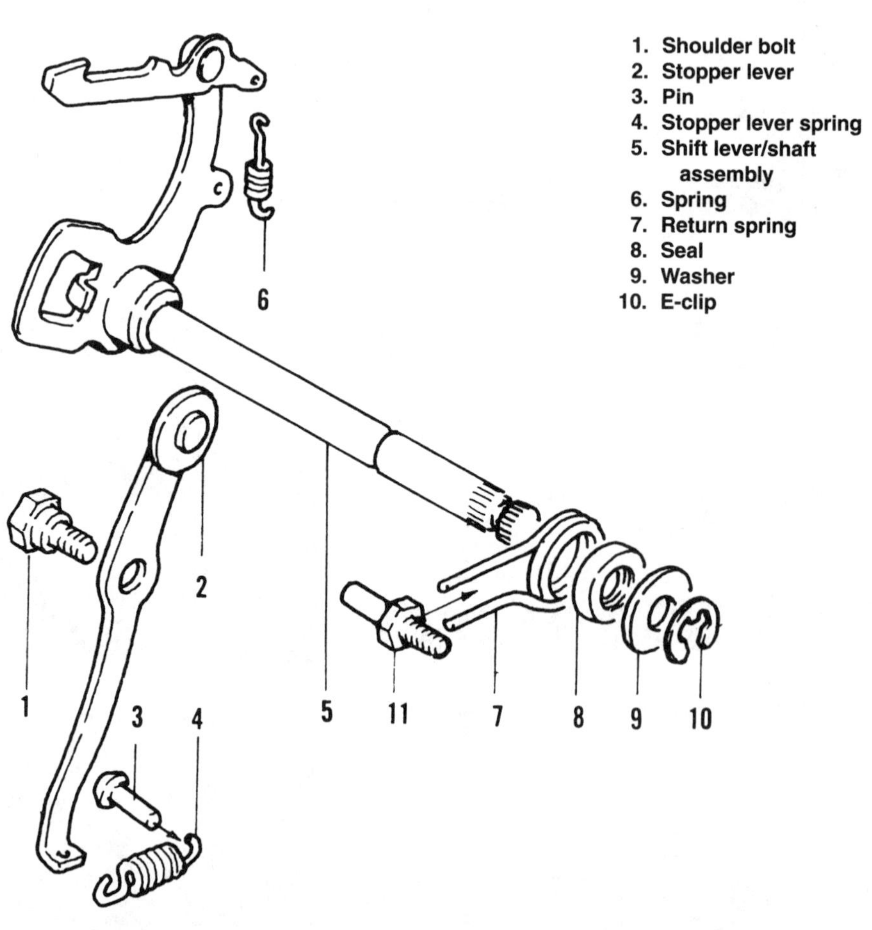

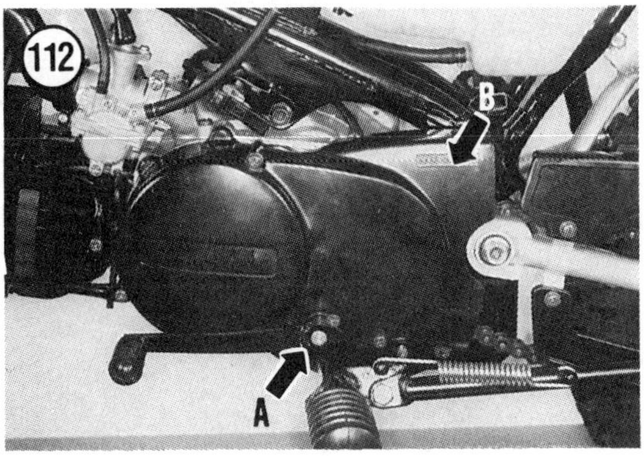

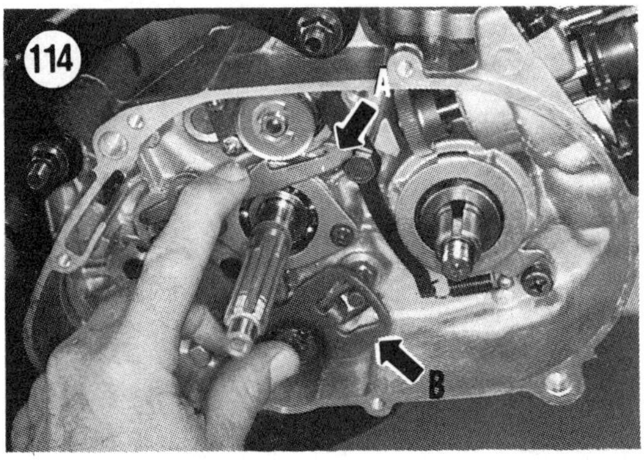

6. Remove the shoulder bolt (B, **Figure 115**) and stopper lever (C, **Figure 115**).

Inspection

Replace all parts that show damage as described in this section.

1. Clean and dry all parts (**Figure 116**).
2. Inspect the shift lever (**Figure 117**) for:
   a. Bent or twisted shaft.
   b. Worn or damaged splines.
   c. Damaged circlip groove.
   d. Worn or damaged selector arm (A, **Figure 118**).
   e. Weak or damaged tension spring (B, **Figure 118**).
   f. Weak or damaged return spring (C, **Figure 118**).
3. Inspect the stopper lever assembly (**Figure 119**) for:
   a. Worn or damaged stopper lever.
   b. Seized or damaged stopper lever roller.
   c. Weak or damaged spring.
   d. Damaged shoulder bolt.

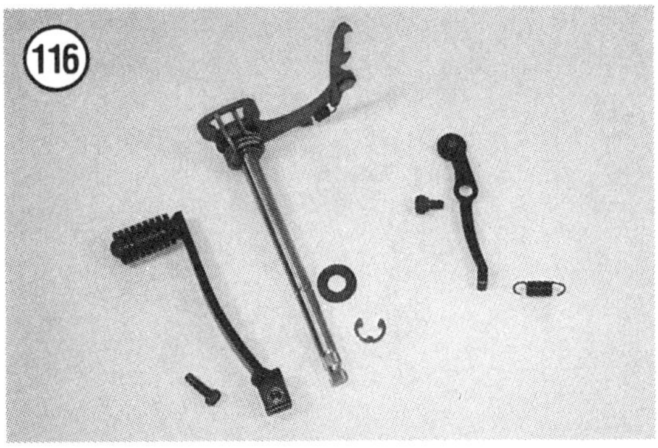

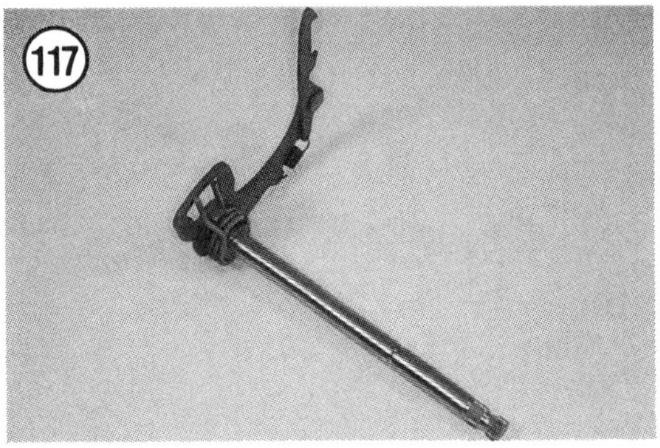

5

Installation

1. Install the shoulder bolt through the stopper lever as shown in A, **Figure 120**. Note that the stopper lever roller (B, **Figure 120**) is on the lever's rear side. Apply a medium strength threadlocking compound onto the shoulder bolt's threads.
2. Install the stopper lever so its roller engages with the shift cam (A, **Figure 121**), then install and tighten the shoulder bolt (B, **Figure 121**) as specified in **Table 6**. Make sure you can pivot the stopper lever back and forth by hand; if not, the bolt is installed incorrectly.
3. Install the stopper lever spring (**Figure 122**).
4. See **Figure 118**. Before installing the shift lever, make sure the tension (B) and return (C) springs are installed on the lever.
5. Apply some grease onto the shift lever splines (**Figure 117**). This may help to prevent the lever from damaging the oil seal as the splines and lever pass through the oil seal in Step 6.
6. Install the shift lever partway into the crankcase. Then push the selector arm (A, **Figure 114**) down and push the lever all the way in, making sure the return spring centers around the pin as shown in **Figure 123**. Release the selector arm so it engages with the shift drum pins.

118

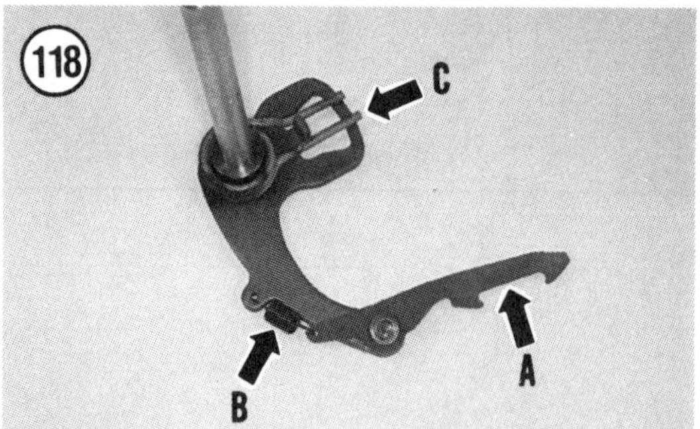

119

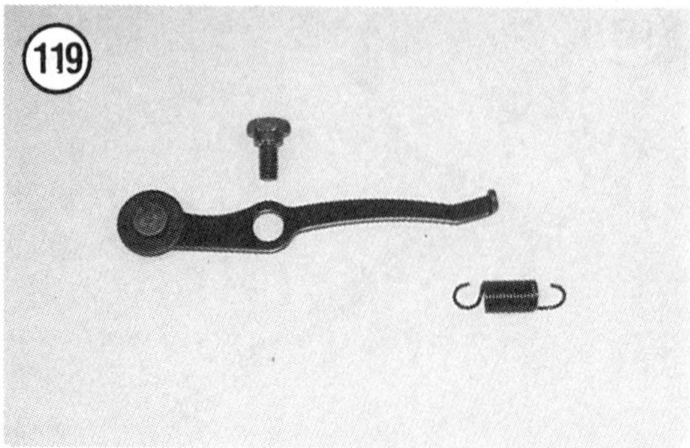

120

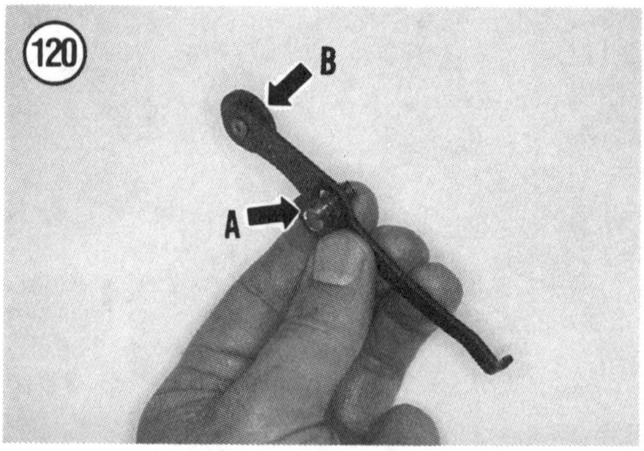

121

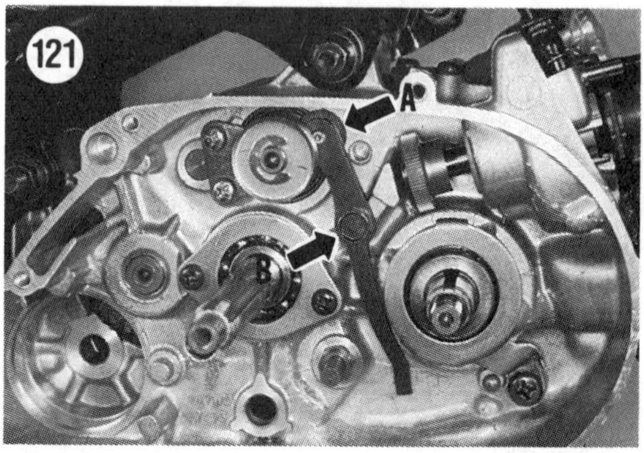

122

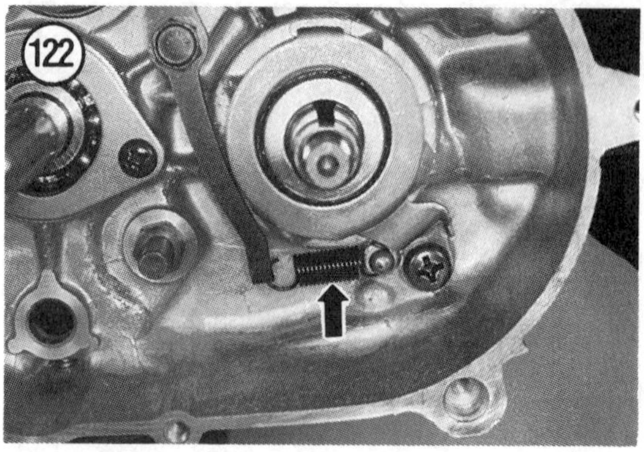

123

7. Remove the E-clip and plate (**Figure 124**) from the shift drum. Then make sure the clearance between the selector arm fingers and the shift drum pins are equal on both sides as shown in **Figure 125**. If not, check the selector arm and shift lever assembly for damage. Because there is no clearance adjustment, replace any damaged parts and recheck the clearance. Reinstall the plate (with its shoulder facing out) and the E-clip (**Figure 124**).

8. Install the washer over the shift lever and secure it with the E-clip (**Figure 113**).

9. Install the clutch (Chapter Six).

CRANKCASE AND CRANKSHAFT

The crankcase is made in 2 halves (**Figure 126**) of a precision diecast aluminum alloy.

The crankshaft assembly is made up of 2 full-circle flywheels pressed together on a hollow crankpin. The connecting rod big end bearing on the crankpin is a needle bearing assembly. The crankshaft assembly is supported by 2 ball bearings in the crankcase.

Special Tools

To disassemble and reassemble the crankcase assembly, the following special tools or their equiva-

5

124

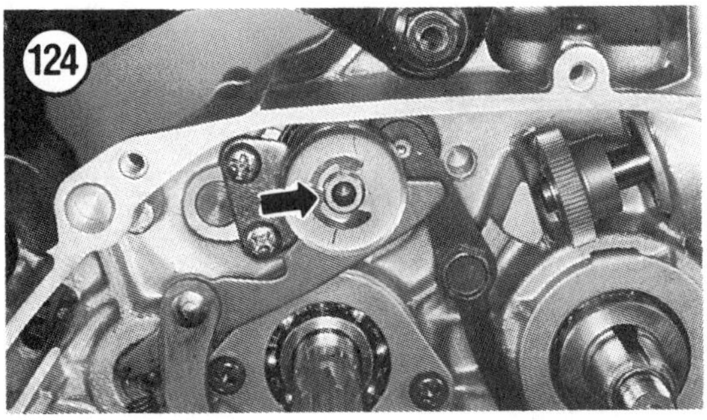

126

125

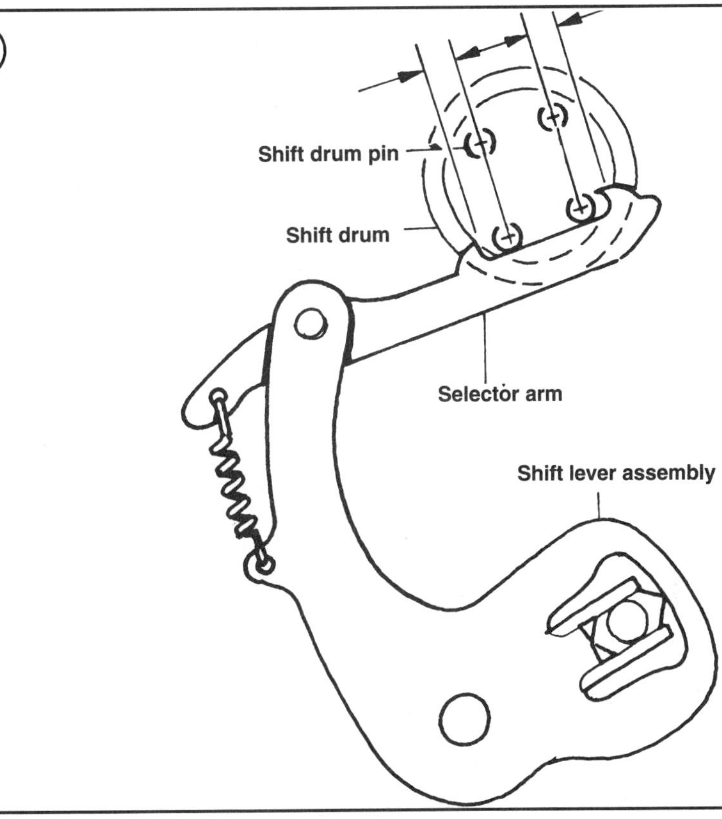

lents are required. These tools allow easy disassembly and reassembly of the engine without prying or hammer use.

a. Yamaha crankcase separating tool (part No. YU-01135) or equivalent. See **Figure 127**. This tool is used to separate the crankcase halves and to press the crankshaft out of the crankcase.
b. Yamaha crankshaft installing tool (part No. YU-90500) and adapter (part No. YU-90063); (**Figure 128**).
c. When handling the engine cases, 2 wooden blocks or a fixture made of wood (**Figure 129**) will assist in engine disassembly and reassembly.
d. A hand impact driver with a No. 3 Phillips bit is required to loosen and tighten the Phillips screws used to secure the crankcase halves and holder plates. See *Impact Driver* in Chapter One for a description of this tool.

Crankcase Disassembly

This procedure describes disassembly of the crankcase halves and removal of the crankshaft, transmission, and internal shift mechanism.

1. Remove all exterior engine assemblies as described in this chapter, unless otherwise noted:
   a. Cylinder head, cylinder and piston.
   b. Clutch (Chapter Six).
   c. Drive sprocket (Chapter Thirteen).
   d. Oil pump (Chapter Nine).
   e. Primary drive gear and oil pump drive gear.
   f. Kickstarter.
   g. External shift mechanism.
   h. Flywheel and stator plate (Chapter Eight).

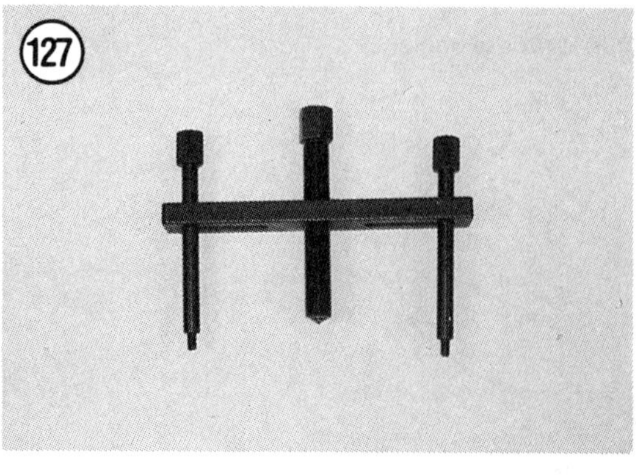

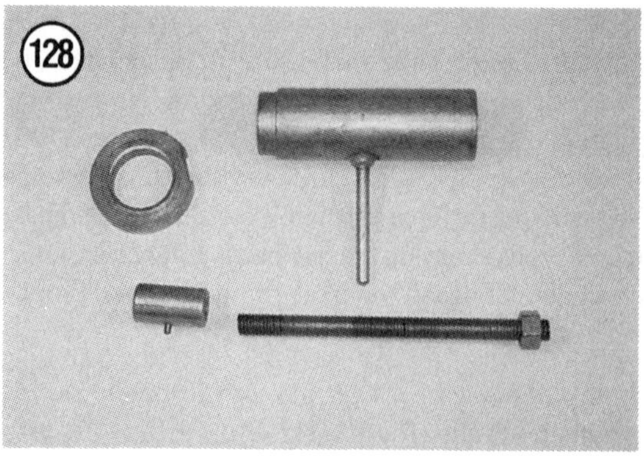

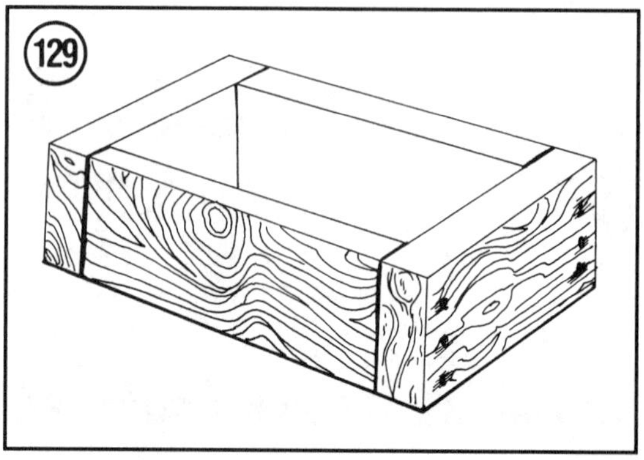

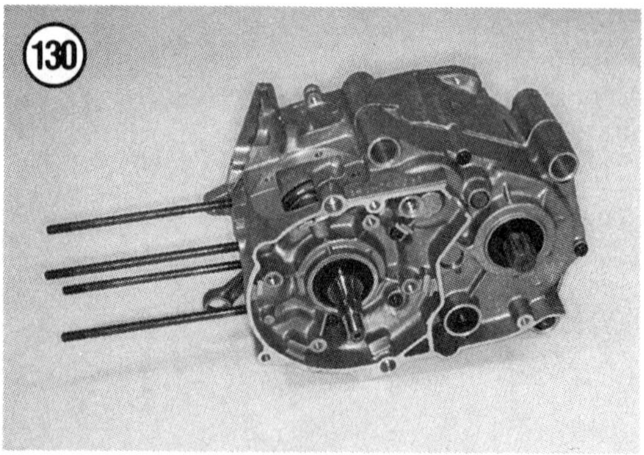

132

133

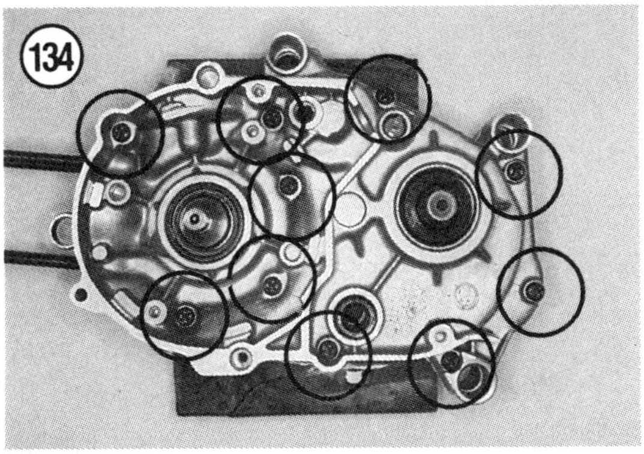
134

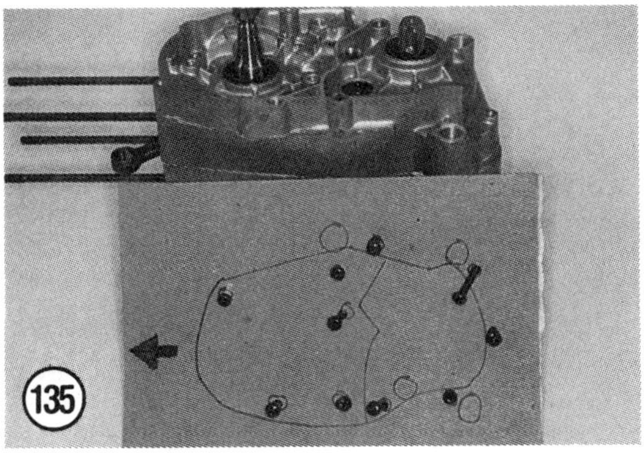
135

2. Make sure there are no other external engine assemblies mounted on the crankcase (**Figure 130**).

3. Place the engine assembly on wooden blocks with the right side facing up.

4. Remove the right crankshaft seal stopper plate and collar as follows:

   a. Remove the Phillips screw and holder plate (**Figure 131**).

   b. Remove the collar (**Figure 132**).

5. Remove the shift drum holder plate screws and holder plate (**Figure 133**).

6. Turn the engine over so the left side faces up.

7. Loosen the crankcase screws (**Figure 134**) one-quarter turn at a time following a crisscross pattern.

8. Before removing the crankcase mounting screws, draw an outline of the cover on a piece of cardboard. Then punch holes along the outline for the placement of each mounting screw. See **Figure 135**.

9. Remove the left crankcase mounting screws and place them in the corresponding holes in the cardboard (**Figure 135**).

NOTE

Steps 10-16 describe crankcase seperation and crankshaft removal with the Yamaha special tool. If the special tool is not available, have the crankcase seperated and the crankshaft removed at a dealership. Do not drive on the end of the crankshaft to remove it. This will severely damage the crankshaft threads.

10. Mount the crankcase separating tool onto the crankcase and over the crankshaft as shown in **Figure 136**. Apply grease onto the end of the crankshaft before running the tool's pressure bolt against it.

11. Run the tool's pressure bolt against the end of the crankshaft. Then check to make sure the tool's

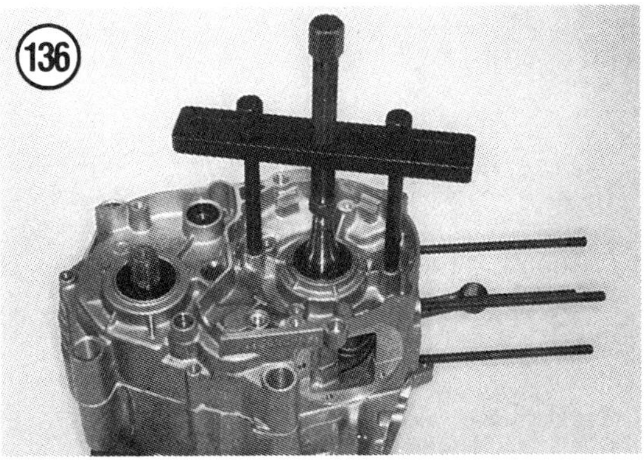
136

body is parallel with the crankcase (**Figure 136**). If not, readjust the tool's mounting bolts.

CAUTION
If the separating tool is not parallel with the crankcase surface, it will put an uneven stress on the case halves and may damage them.

12. Hold the engine with one hand and then turn the tool's pressure bolt *clockwise* until the left case half begins to separate. You may hear a loud pop when the case halves separate. This is normal, but stop and investigate all the way around the case halve mating surfaces. If everything is normal, continue with this step. If there is a problem, release tension from the pressure bolt and make sure all of the crankcase screws were removed.

NOTE
As the left case half is pulled up, the mainshaft and/or countershaft may ride up and cause the case halves to bind. After every 1/4 to 1/2 turn of the tool's pressure bolt, tap the ends of both shafts with a plastic or rubber mallet to release any binding. This will help the case halves separate more easily.

CAUTION
Crankcase separation requires only hand pressure on the pressure bolt. Applying excessive force will damage the case halves. If the pressure bolt becomes tight, **stop immediately**. *Check for crankcase bolts still in place, an external part that is still attached, or a binding transmission shaft(s).*

13. Continue turning the pressure bolt until the left case half is free, then lift it off the engine. The

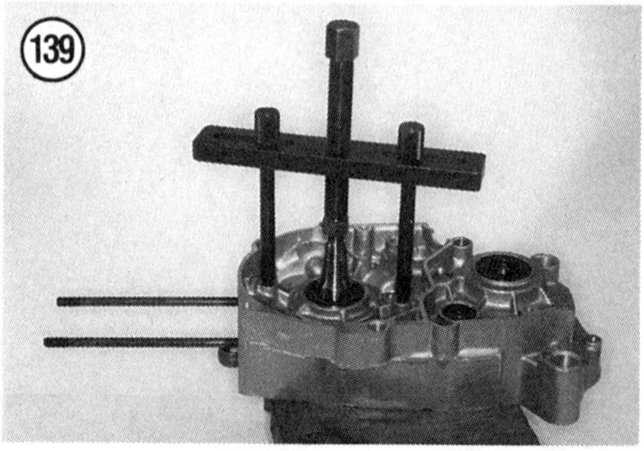

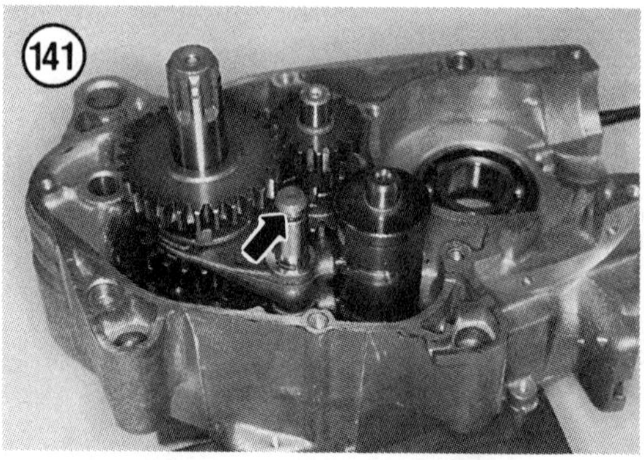

142

143

144

crankshaft will remain in the left case half. See **Figure 137**.

14. Remove the 2 dowel pins (**Figure 138**).

NOTE

If a dowel pin is stuck, leave it in the crankcase half.

15. Remove the crankshaft (**Figure 137**) as follows:
   a. Apply some thick grease onto the end of the crankshaft threads.
   b. Mount the crankcase separating tool onto the left crankcase half. Center the pressure bolt with the crankshaft as shown in **Figure 139**. Make sure the tool's body is parallel with the case half. If necessary, back one of the bolts out to level the tool body.
   c. Hold the connecting rod, then turn the pressure bolt clockwise and press the crankshaft out of the left crankcase half. See **Figure 140**.

16. Remove the transmission assembly from the right case half as follows:
   a. Remove the shift fork shaft (**Figure 141**) along with its E-clip and O-ring.
   b. Remove the left side shift fork (A, **Figure 142**) and the shift drum (B, **Figure 142**).
   c. Remove the right side shift fork (**Figure 143**).
   d. Remove the mainshaft and countershaft assemblies (**Figure 144**) from the right crankcase half at the same time (**Figure 145**).
   e. Remove the countershaft washer (**Figure 146**) if it stayed on the crankcase bearing.

17. Clean and inspect the crankcase halves, bearings, crankshaft and transmission as described in this chapter.

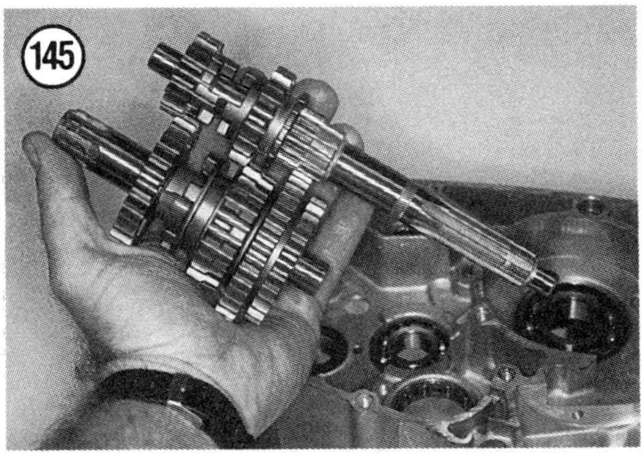
145

146

Crankcase Cleaning and Inspection

1. Remove the crankcase seals as described under *Crankcase Seal Replacement* in this chapter.
2. Remove all gasket and sealer residue from both crankcase mating surfaces.
3. Clean both crankcase halves (**Figure 126**).
4. Dry the case halves and bearings with compressed air. When doing so, hold the inner bearing races to prevent them from turning. When the bearings are dry, lubricate them with oil.
5. Check the crankcase halves (**Figure 126**) for cracks or fractures in the stiffening webs, around the bearing bosses, and at threaded holes.
6. Inspect machined surfaces for burrs, cracks or other damage. Repair minor damage with a fine-cut file or oilstone. A severely damaged mating surface may require welding and machining.

NOTE
If cracks or fractures are found, have them repaired at a reputable shop experienced in this type of welding and repair.

7. Check the cylinder studs (**Figure 147**) and threaded holes for stripping, cross-threading or deposit buildup. Clean threaded holes with compressed air. If necessary, repair threads with a tap or die. Replace damaged studs as described under *Stud Replacement* in Chapter One.
8. Check all of the crankcase bearings for pitting, galling and wear. See A, **Figure 148**, typical. Rotate the bearings by hand and feel for roughness and play. They should turn smoothly and evenly and there should be no apparent radial play. If any bearing is suspect, replace it as described in this section.
9. Check the needle bearings for visible wear or damage. See B, **Figure 148**, typical. These bearings are harder to check than ball bearings and unless there is obvious wear or visible damage, the amount of wear may not be detectable. However, because the transmission is bathed in a supply of oil, these bearings should be in good condition if the oil was changed regularly and kept at its correct operating level.

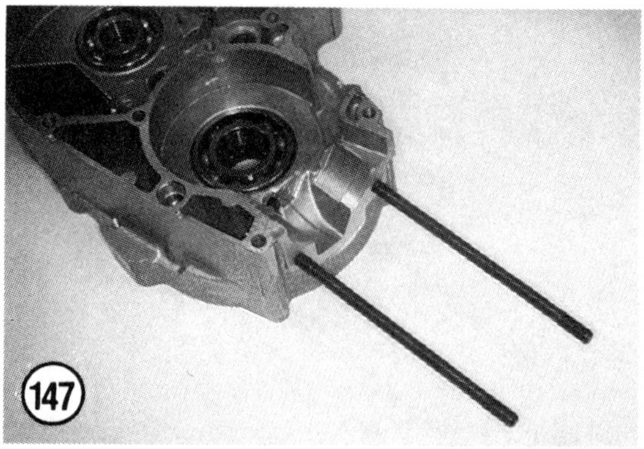

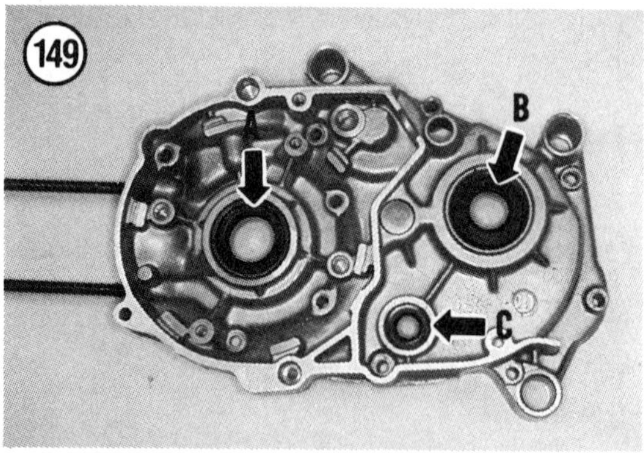

Crankcase Seal Replacement

Identify the crankcase seals as follows:

a. Left main bearing oil seal (A, **Figure 149**).

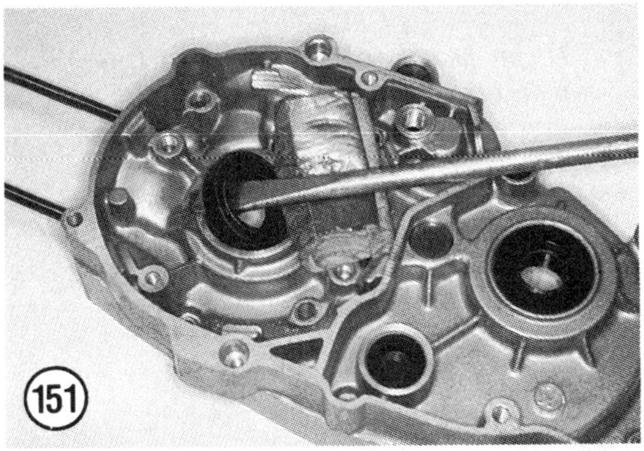
151

152

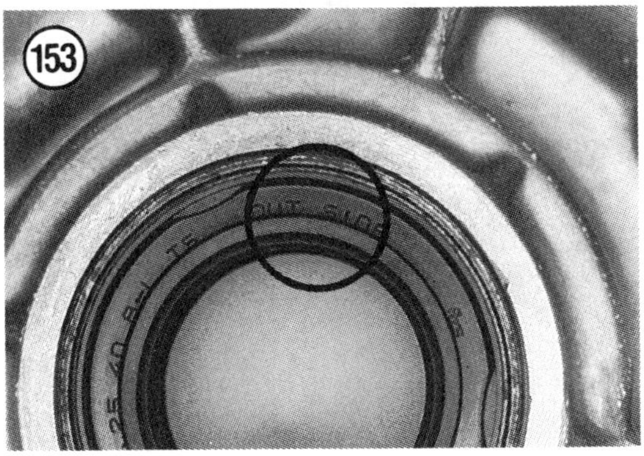
153

154

b. Countershaft seal (B, **Figure 149**).
c. Shift shaft seal (C, **Figure 149**).
d. Right main seal (**Figure 150**).

1. Before removing the oil seals, inspect them for damage or any type of unusual wear.
2. Remove the seals with a screwdriver, taking care not to damage the crankcase bore. Pad the pry area under the screwdriver to avoid damaging the crankcase. See **Figure 151**, typical.
3. Inspect and service the crankshaft bearings before installing the new oil seals. Refer to *Crankshaft Bearing Replacement* in this section.
4. Compare the new and old seals before installation.
5. Pack grease between the seal lips (**Figure 152**).
6. Install the left (A, **Figure 149**) and right (**Figure 150**) main seals as follows:
   a. These seals use a double lip design and can be incorrectly installed backwards.
   b. Install both main seals with their OUT SIDE mark facing out (away from main bearing). See **Figure 153**.
   c. The left main seal has a smaller inside diameter than the right seal. You can identify the main bearing oil seals by matching their inside diameter to the respective left and right side bearing bores.
   d. These seals have a hard outer diameter and require force during installation. Install both seals using a socket or bearing driver with the same outside diameter as that of the seal (**Figure 154**). Install both seals so their outer surface is flush with the top of its mounting bore.
7. Install the countershaft seal (B, **Figure 149**) and the shift shaft seal (C, **Figure 149**) with your hands or a suitable socket or bearing driver. Install both seals so that their outer surface is flush with the top of their mounting bore. Install both seals with their closed side facing out.

Crankcase Bearing Replacement

Identify the left side crankcase bearings as follows:

a. Left main bearing (A, **Figure 155**).
b. Left countershaft bearing (B, **Figure 155**).
c. Left mainshaft needle bearing (C, **Figure 155**).

Identify the right side crankcase bearings as follows:

a. Right main bearing (A, **Figure 156**).
b. Right countershaft bushing (B, **Figure 156**). This bushing is not available separately.
c. Right mainshaft bearing (C, **Figure 156**).
d. Right shift drum needle bearing (D, **Figure 156**).

1. All bearings are marked on one side with their respective size code and usually with some type of manufacturer code or name. Before removing the bearings, note and record the direction in which the manufacturer's marks face for proper assembly. Bearings are usually installed with these marks facing out (the marks are visible from the side the bearing is installed from).

2. If a bearing came off with the crankshaft, remove it with a bearing puller.

3. Before removing the right mainshaft bearing, remove the retainer plate screws and plate (**Figure 157**).

NOTE
Two methods of replacing the crankcase bearings are described below. Before you begin, read the ***Ball Bearing Replacement*** *section in Chapter One.*

4A. To replace the bearings using heat, perform the following steps:

a. Before heating the case half, select all of the appropriate bearing drivers for the bearings being removed.
b. Before heating the case half, place the new bearings in a freezer. Chilling them will slightly reduce their overall diameter while the hot crankcase is slightly larger due to heat expansion. This will make installation much easier.

CAUTION
Before heating the crankcases in this procedure to remove the bearings, wash the cases thoroughly with detergent and water. Rinse and rewash the cases as required to remove all traces of oil and other chemical deposits.

c. The bearings are installed with a slight interference fit. Heat the crankcase to a temperature of about 212° F (100° C) in a shop oven or on a hot plate. Heat only one case at a time.

CAUTION
Do not heat the cases with a torch (propane or acetylene)—never bring a flame into contact with the bearing or case. The direct heat will destroy the case hardening of the bearing and will likely warp the case half.

d. Remove the case from the shop oven or hot plate—*it is hot.*

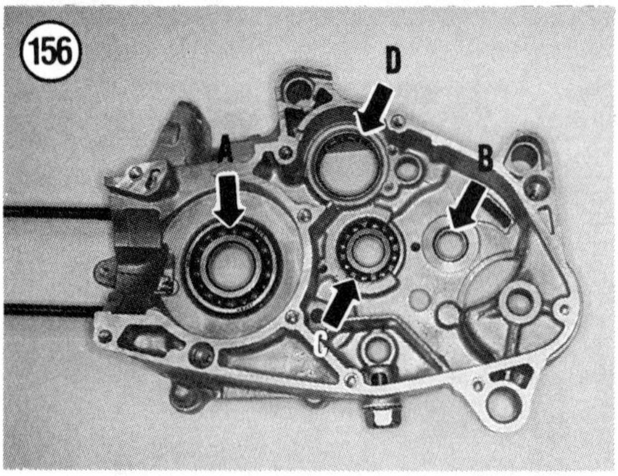

e. Support the crankcase on wooden blocks and drive the bearing out from its opposite side. Use a pilot bearing tool to remove bearings installed in a blind hole.

NOTE

Install new bearings with their manufacturer's name and size code facing in the same direction recorded before disassembly. If you did not record this information, install the bearings so that their marks are visible from the side the bearing is installed from.

f. While the crankcase is still hot, install the new bearing(s) into the crankcase. Install the bearing into its bore and drop it into place. If necessary, lightly tap the bearing(s) into the case with a driver placed on the outer bearing race. *Do not* install new bearings by driving on the inner bearing race. Install the bearing(s) until it seats completely.

4B. To replace bearings with a press:

a. Support the crankcase on 2 wooden blocks and center the bearing under the press ram.

b. Press the bearing out of the crankcase (**Figure 158**).

c. Support the crankcase on 2 wooden blocks and center the bearing and bearing bore under the press ram.

d. Place a bearing driver on the outer bearing race (**Figure 159**, typical) and press the bearing into the crankcase until it bottoms out. See **Figure 160**.

5. Install and tighten the mainshaft bearing retainer plate (**Figure 157**)as follows:

a. Remove all sealer residue from the retainer screw threads and the crankcase threaded holes.

b. Apply a medium strength threadlock onto the bearing retainer screw threads.

c. Install the mainshaft bearing retainer plate (**Figure 157**) and tighten the screws as specified in **Table 6**.

6. Install the oil seals as described under *Crankcase Seal Replacement* in this chapter.

158

159

160

Crankshaft Inspection

When measuring the crankshaft compare the actual measurements to the in **Table 4**. Replace the connecting rod assembly as described in this section if it is out of specification. To replace the connecting rod assembly, a 20-30 ton press and adapters, V-blocks or crankshaft truing stand and dial indicator are required. If necessary, refer crankshaft overhaul to a dealership or service shop. You can save considerable expense by disassembling the engine and taking the crankshaft in for repair at a dealership or machine shop familiar with this type of work.

(161)

CRANKSHAFT

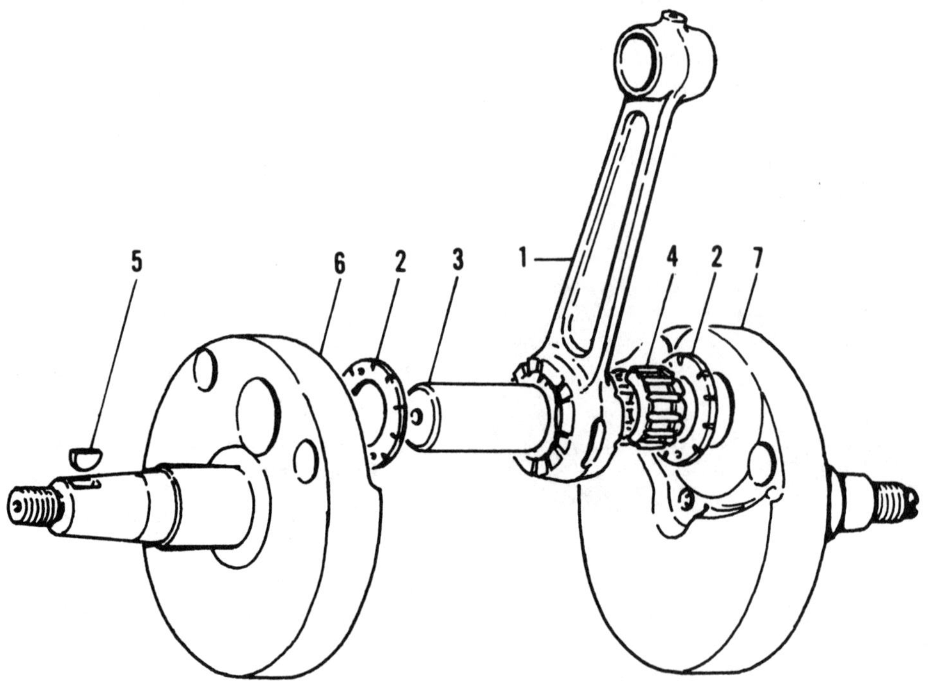

1. Connecting rod
2. Thrust washer
3. Crankpin
4. Needle bearing
5. Woodruff key
6. Left-hand crank half
7. Right-hand crank half

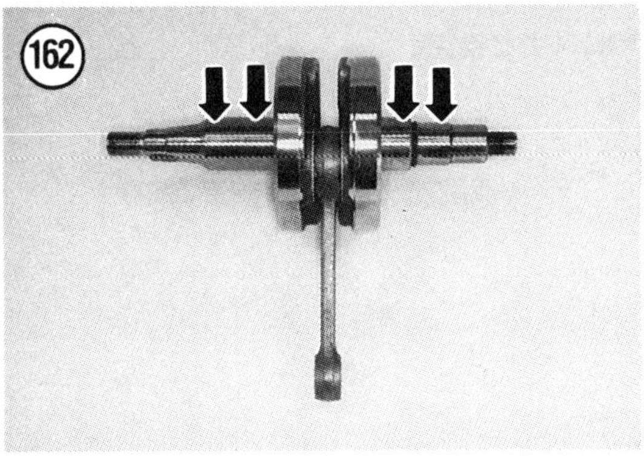

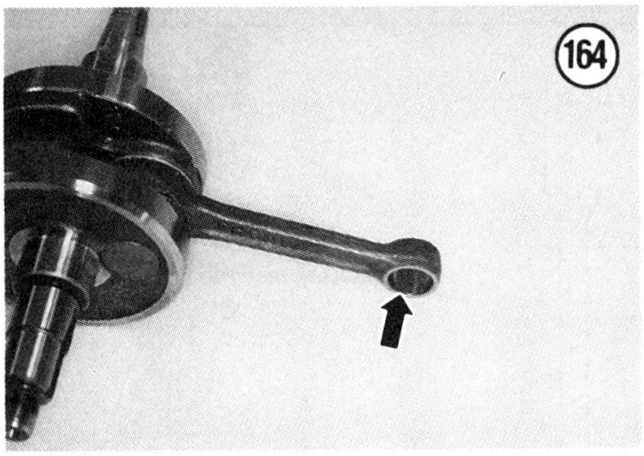

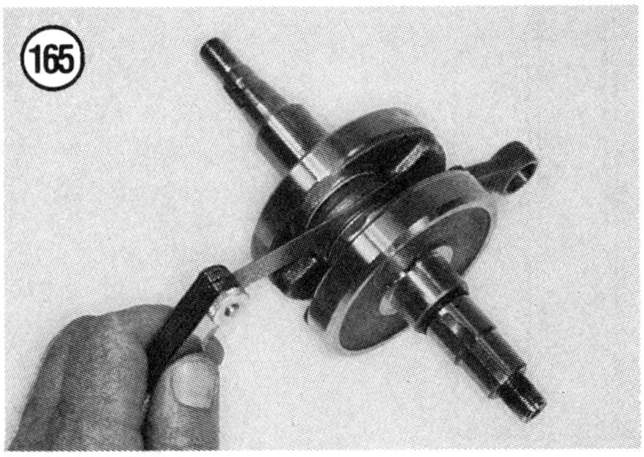

When rebuilding a crankshaft, always install a new connecting rod, crankpin, bearing and both thrust washers (**Figure 161**).

1. Clean and dry the crankshaft. Then lubricate the bottom end bearing and crankshaft journals with a 2-stroke engine oil.
2. Check the crankshaft journals (**Figure 162**) for scratches, heat discoloration or other defects.
3. Check the crankshaft oil seal surfaces (**Figure 162**) for grooving, pitting or scratches.
4. Check the crankshaft bearing surfaces (**Figure 162**) for chatter marks and excessive or uneven wear. Clean minor damage with 320 grit carborundum cloth.
5. Check the left crank half flywheel taper, threads and keyway (**Figure 162**) for damage.
6. Check the right crank half keyway and threads (**Figure 162**) for damage.
7. Check the connecting rod big end (**Figure 163**) for signs of heat or damage. Check the needles and cage for damage.
8. Check the connecting rod small end (**Figure 164**) for signs of heat or damage. To determine wear at the rod's small end, perform the *Piston Pin and Needle Bearing Inspection* procedure in this chapter.
9. Measure the connecting rod side clearance between the connecting rod and thrust washer with a feeler gauge (**Figure 165**). Replace the connecting rod assembly if the clearance is out of specification.
10. Measure connecting rod small end free play (**Figure 166**) as follows:
    a. Mount the crankshaft on a set of V-blocks.
    b. Turn the crankshaft so that the connecting rod is at top dead center (TDC).
    c. Mount a dial indicator so that its plunger contacts the connecting rod small end (**Figure 167**).
    d. Slide the connecting rod over so that it seats against the lower thrust washer that is on the same side the dial indicator is installed on. Hold the connecting rod in this position.
    e. While holding the lower part of the connecting rod, move the upper end by hand. Any movement is small end free play.
    f. Replace the connecting rod if the clearance is out of specification.
11. Measure connecting rod big end radial clearance (**Figure 166**) as follows:
    a. Turn the crankshaft so that the connecting rod is at TDC.

5

166

CONNECTING ROD INSPECTION

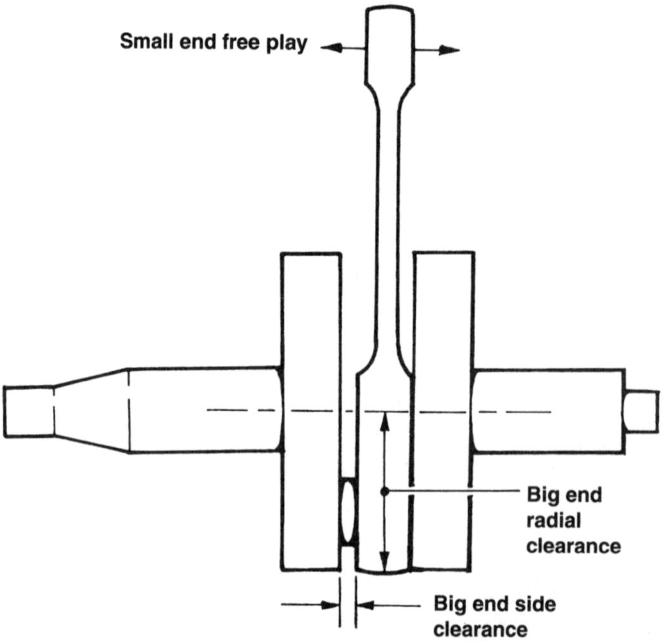

167

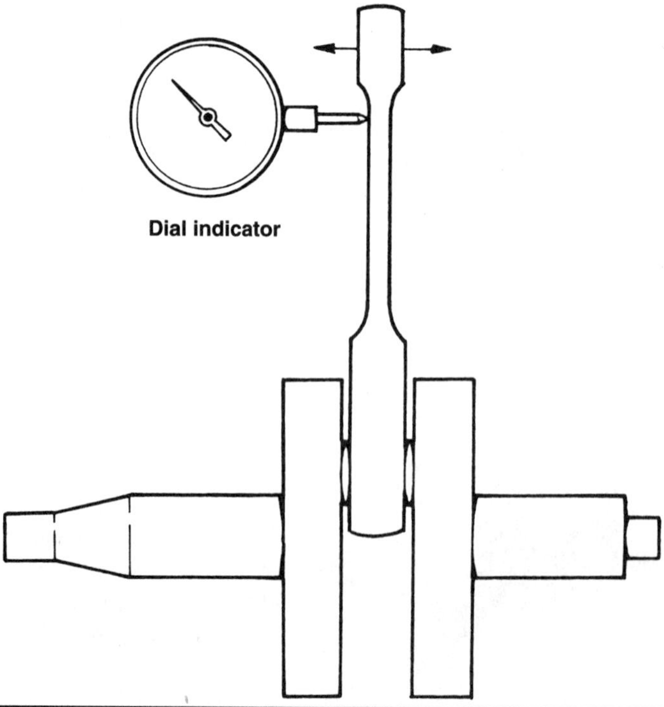

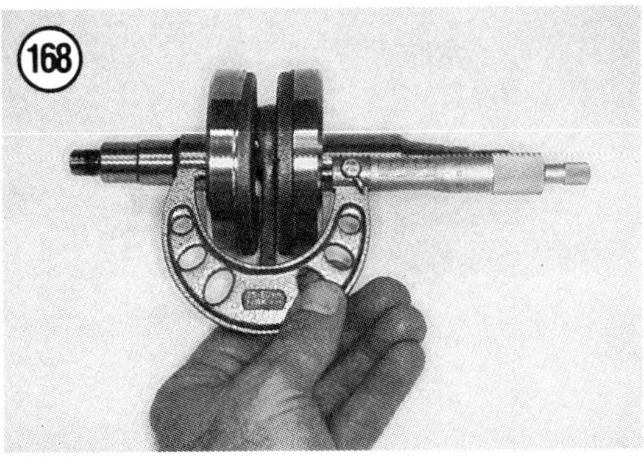

b. Move the connecting rod over so that it seats against one of the lower thrust washers.
c. Mount a dial indicator with its plunger contacting the connecting rod big end.
d. Hold the connecting rod in this position, then try to move it up and down as shown in **Figure 166**. Any movement is big end radial clearance.
e. Replace the connecting rod if any measurable play is present.

12. Measure the crank wheel width every 90° at its machined edge with a micrometer (**Figure 168**) or vernier caliper. Retrue the crankshaft if out of specification.

13. Measure crankshaft runout with a dial indicator and V-blocks as shown in **Figure 169**. Retrue the crankshaft if out of specification.

14. Replace the crankshaft O-ring (**Figure 170**) if worn or damaged.

Transmission Service

To service the transmission, refer to the *Transmission* section in this chapter.

Crankshaft Installation

The crankshaft is installed in the left case half (**Figure 171**) using the Yamaha crankcase tools described under *Special Tools* in this chapter. The tools are identified as follows:

a. Threaded adapter (A, **Figure 172**).
b. Installing pot (B, **Figure 172**).
c. Threaded rod and nut (C, **Figure 172**).
d. Spacer (D, **Figure 172**).

CAUTION

If you do not have access to these or similar special crankshaft tools, take

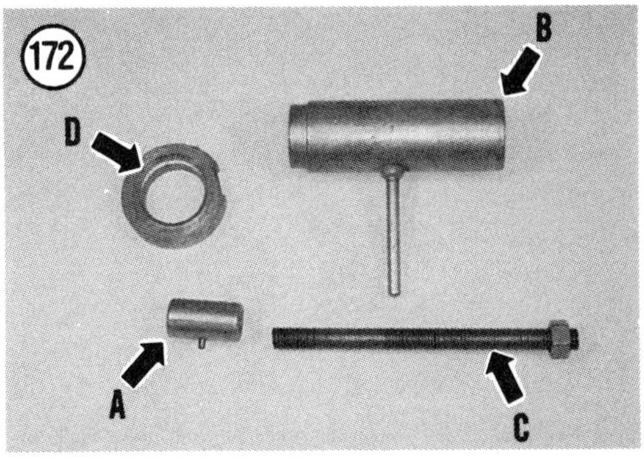

the crankshaft and crankcase half to a dealership and have it installed.

1. Clean the crankshaft before installation. Lubricate the big end bearing with 2-stroke injection oil.
2. Install the left main bearing oil seal as described under *Crankcase Seal Replacement* in this chapter.
3. Lubricate the left crankshaft main bearing with 2-stroke engine oil.
4. Carefully install the crankshaft's left end (side with taper) into the main bearing in the left crankcase half. Push it in until it stops (**Figure 173**).
5. Thread the Yamaha threaded adapter (part No. YU-90063) onto the crankshaft until it bottoms out, then back out 1/2 turn. See A, **Figure 174**.
6. Thread the threaded rod (B, **Figure 174**) all the way into the adapter.
7. Install the installing pot (A, **Figure 175**) over the threaded rod and engage its slot with the pin in the adapter to lock them together. Then install the nut (B, **Figure 175**) and thread it against the installing pot.

CAUTION

*Hold the connecting rod at TDC or BDC (**Figure 176**) when pressing the crankshaft into its main bearing; otherwise, the rod may contact the side on the crankcase, causing rod and crankcase damage.*

8. Hold the installing pot rod, then turn the nut (B, **Figure 175**) to pull the crankshaft into its main bearing. Continue until you feel the crankshaft shoulder bottom against the bearing. See **Figure 177**.
9. Spin the crankshaft by hand, making sure it turns smoothly with no roughness or binding.

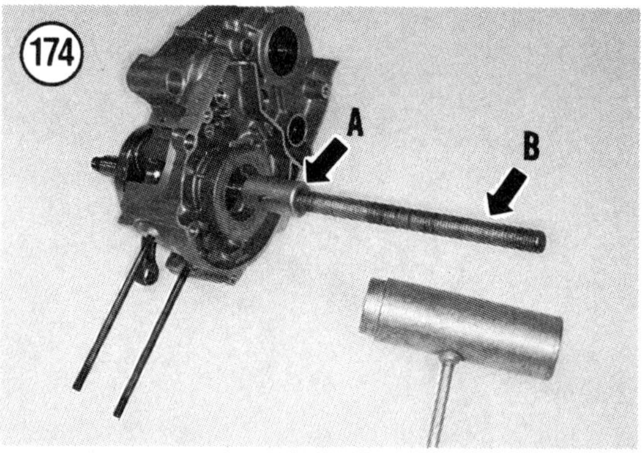

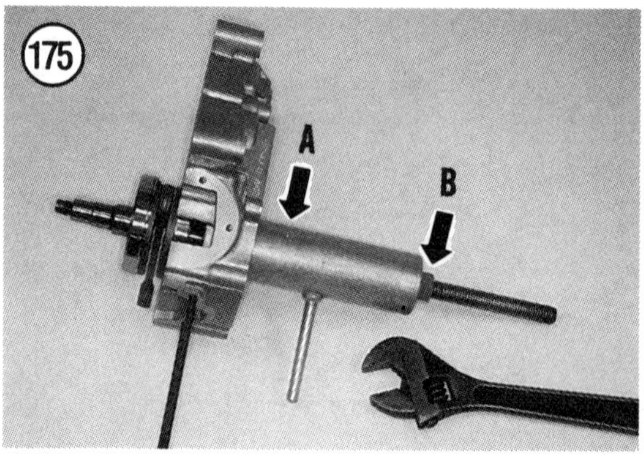

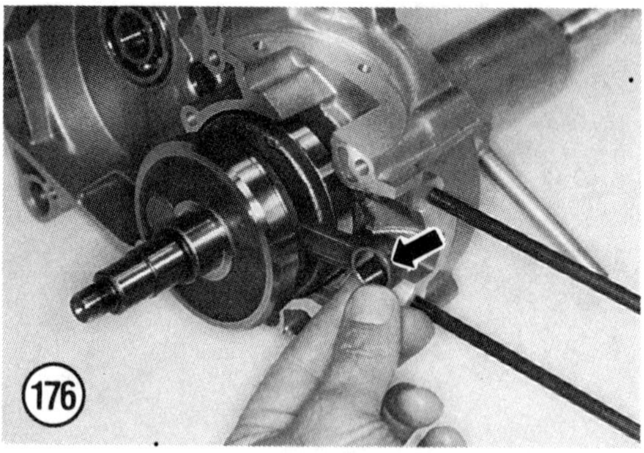

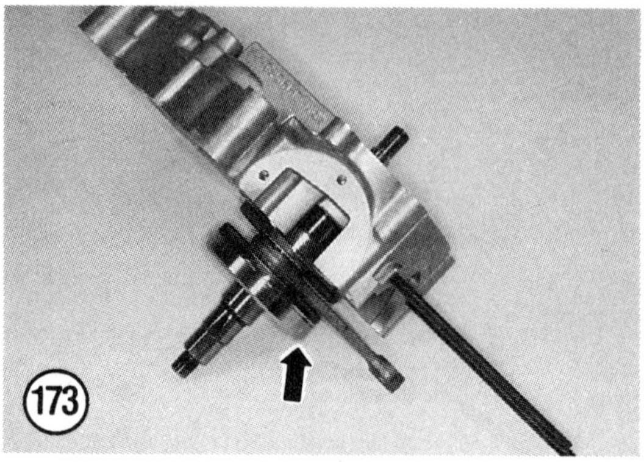

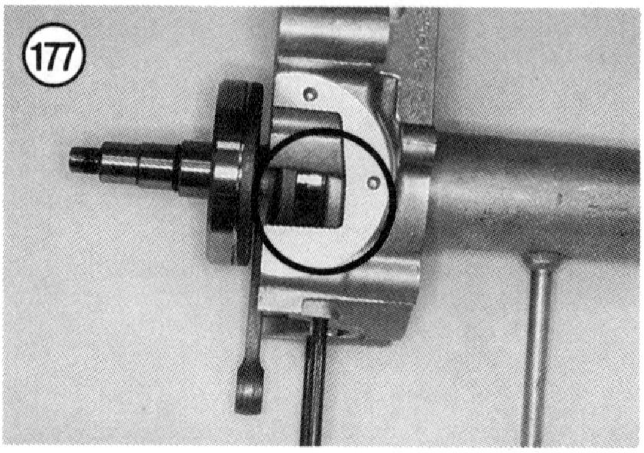

178

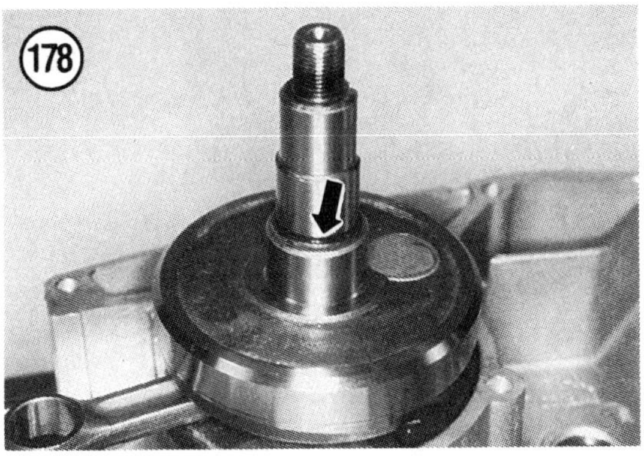

179

180

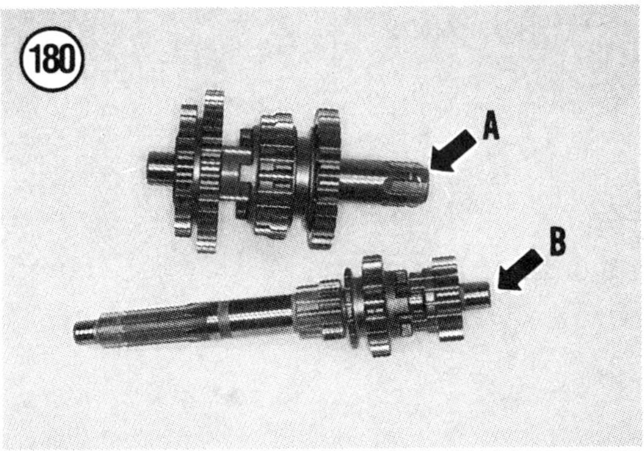

181

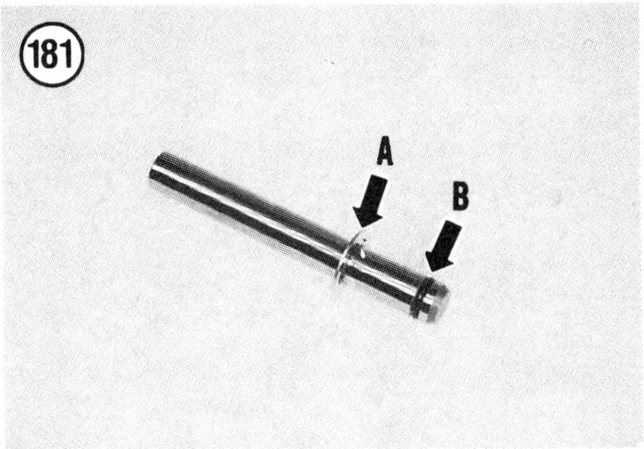

10. Lubricate a new O-ring with grease and install it over the crankshaft as shown in **Figure 178**.

Crankcase Assembly

This procedure describes installation of the transmission, internal shift mechanism and crankcase assembly.

1. Clean all engine parts before assembly.
2. Pack all of the crankcase oil seal lips with grease as described under *Crankcase Seal Replacement* in this chapter.
3. Install the crankshaft into the left crankcase half as described under *Crankshaft Installation* in this chapter. Lubricate a new O-ring with grease and install it over the crankshaft as shown in **Figure 178**. Then set this case aside as the transmission will be installed in the right crankcase half.
4. Lubricate all transmission bearings and transmission shaft bearing surfaces with gear oil.
5. Place the right crankcase half on wooden blocks (**Figure 179**).
6. Before installing the transmission shafts in the following steps, note the following:
   a. Check the countershaft (A, **Figure 180**) to make sure all of the gears, washers and circlips are properly installed. The mainshaft (B, **Figure 180**) is a pressed unit and should not be disassembled. See *Transmission* in this chapter.
   b. Apply some grease to the countershaft sprocket splines (C, **Figure 180**) to help protect the left crankcase seal as the shaft passes through it.
   c. See **Figure 181**. Make sure the E-clip (A) and O-ring (B) are installed on the shift fork shaft.
   d. Install a guide pin (**Figure 182**) into each shift fork. Both guide pins are identical (same part number).
   e. Refer to **Figure 183** to identify the shift forks: mainshaft shift fork (A) and countershaft shift fork (B). The mainshaft shift fork is to be installed first.
7. Lubricate the countershaft washer with transmission oil, then center it over the right countershaft bushing as shown in **Figure 184**.
8. Install the transmission shafts and the mainshaft shift fork as follows:
   a. Mesh the mainshaft and countershaft assemblies together (**Figure 185**), then install part-

5

way into the right crankcase at the same time (**Figure 186**).

b. Hold the transmission in this position and install the mainshaft shift fork into the mainshaft gear fork groove as shown in **Figure 187**, then install the transmission shafts all the way. See **Figure 188**.

9. Make sure the countershaft washer did not fall off the end of the countershaft.

10. Install the shift drum (**Figure 189**), then engage the mainshaft shift fork pin into the lower shift drum groove.

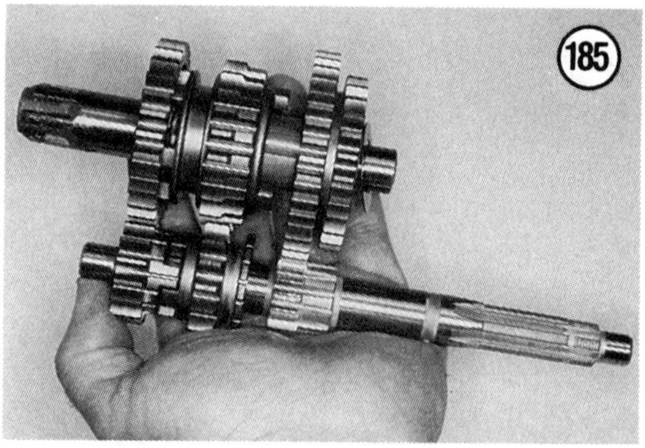

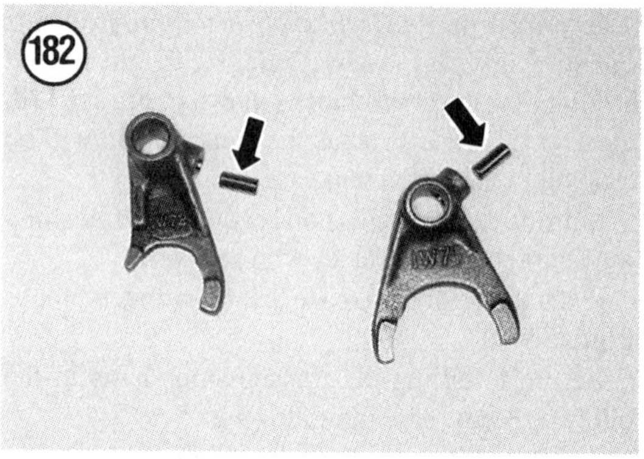

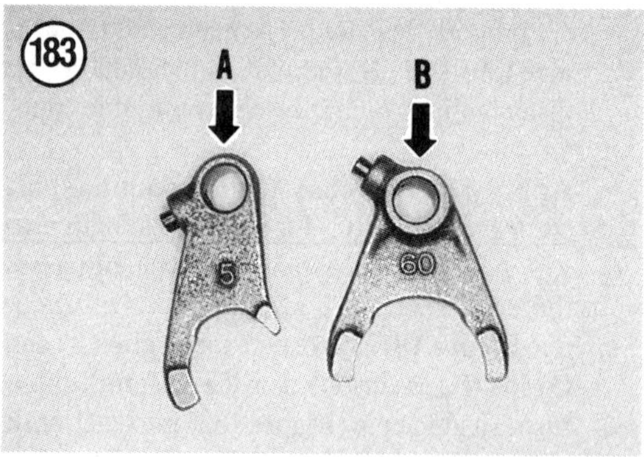

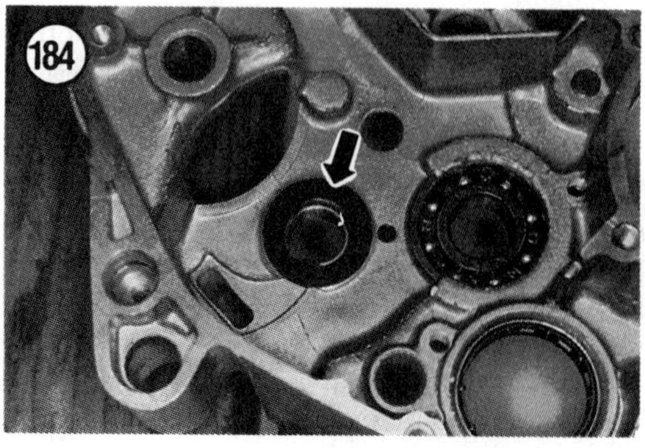

189

190

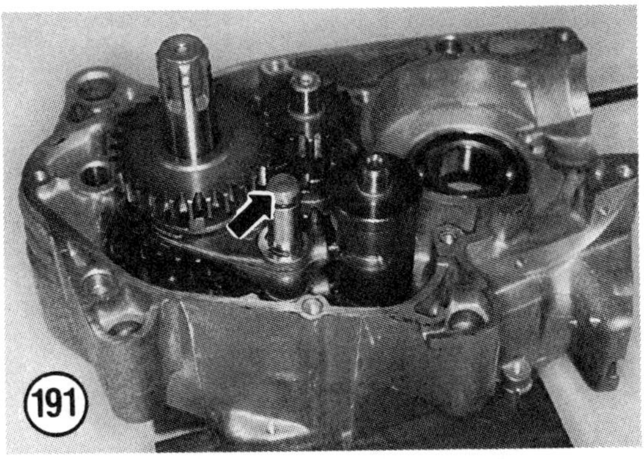

191

11. Install the countershaft shift fork into the countershaft gear fork groove (**Figure 190**), then engage the shift fork pin into the upper shift drum groove.
12. Install the shift fork shaft (**Figure 191**) through both shift forks and bottom it out in the right crankcase.
13. Spin the transmission shafts and shift through the gears using the shift drum. Make sure you can shift into all 3 gears.
14. Shift the transmission assembly into NEUTRAL.
15. Support the right crankcase assembly on wooden blocks.
16. Install the 2 dowel pins (**Figure 192**) into the crankcase holes.

NOTE
Make sure both crankcase mating surfaces are clean and free of all old sealer residue or oil.

17. Apply a light coat of a *nonhardening* liquid gasket sealer, such as Yamabond No. 4 or ThreeBond 1104, onto the right side crankcase gasket surface (**Figure 192**).
18. Align the left crankcase half and crankshaft with the right crankcase half, then install it over the transmission shafts and dowel pins and seat it against the right crankcase half (**Figure 193**). Then check that the gasket surfaces are flush all the way around the crankcase halves. Turn the crankshaft and both transmission shafts by hand. They should turn smoothly with no roughness or binding.

CAUTION
The crankcase halves should fit together without excessive force. If the crankcase halves do not fit together completely, do not pull them together with the crank-

192

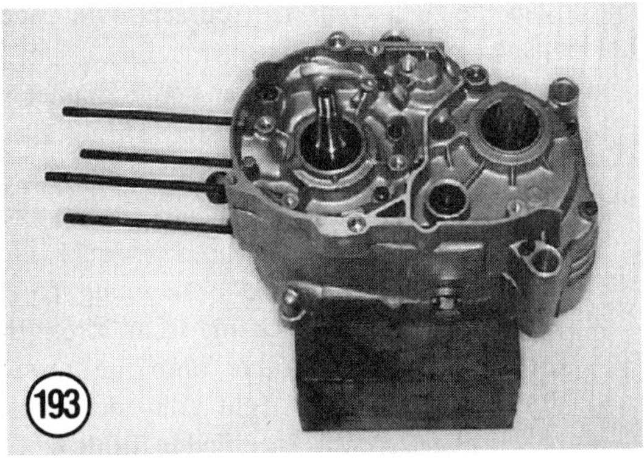

193

*case screws. If the crankshaft turns roughly or is binding, it may be off center in the cases; tap one end of the crank lightly with a mallet and check that it turns freely. If the crankshaft is properly centered in the right case main bearing, it may not have been installed properly in the left case main bearing (it did not bottom out against the bearing). If the crankshaft was rebuilt, measure the crankshaft wheel width with a micrometer (**Figure 168**) and compare the specification in **Table 4**. If the wheels are spaced too far apart, they can interfere with crankcase assembly. If necessary, separate the crankcase halves and investigate the cause of the interference. Do not risk damage by trying to force the cases together.*

19. Install all of the crankcase mounting screws (**Figure 194**) finger-tight.

NOTE

If the crankcase mounting screws were not identified, check that each one sticks up the same amount before you screw them all in. If not, there is a short screw in a long hole, and vice versa.

20. Tighten the crankcase mounting screws (**Figure 194**) in 2 stages as specified in **Table 6**.
21. Rotate the crankshaft and each transmission shaft and check for binding; each shaft must turn freely.
22. Install the shift drum holder plate and mounting screws (**Figure 195**); apply a medium strength threadlocking compound onto the mounting screws. Tighten the screws as specified in **Table 6**.
23. Check the shifting as described under *Transmission Shifting Check* in this chapter.
24. Install the right crankshaft oil seal collar and holder plate as follows:
   a. Apply grease onto the collar's outer diameter.
   b. Install the collar—shoulder side (**Figure 196**) facing down—over the crankshaft and seat it into the oil seal. Turn the collar as it enters and passes through the oil seal.
   c. Install the holder plate and its mounting screw (**Figure 197**); apply a medium strength threadlocking compound onto the screw threads. Tighten the right crankshaft seal holder plate screw as specified in **Table 6**.
25. Install the engine in the frame as described in this chapter.
26. Install all exterior engine assemblies as described in this chapter, unless otherwise noted:
   a. Flywheel and stator plate (Chapter Eight).
   b. External shift mechanism.
   c. Kickstarter.
   d. Primary drive gear and oil pump drive gear.
   e. Oil pump (Chapter Nine).
   f. Drive sprocket (Chapter Thirteen).
   g. Clutch (Chapter Six).

h. Cylinder head, cylinder and piston.

27. After filling the transmission with gear oil and bleeding the oil pump, start the engine and check for leaks.

TRANSMISSION

This section describes service to the 3-speed transmission and internal shift mechanism.

197

198

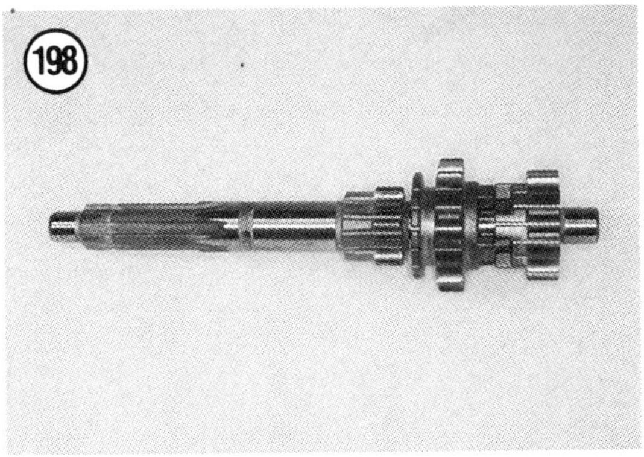

199

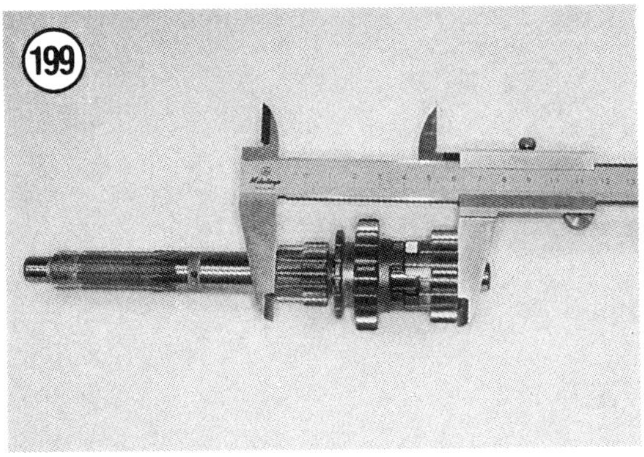

Removal/Installation

Remove and install the transmission assembly as described under *Crankcase and Crankshaft* in this chapter.

Mainshaft Inspection

The mainshaft (**Figure 198**) is a pressed unit and should not be disassembled. If the mainshaft shows damage as described in this section, it must be replaced as an assembly.

1. Clean and dry all parts.
2. Measure the mainshaft assembled length as shown in **Figure 199**. The correct length is 71.5-71.8 mm (2.815-2.827 in.).
3. Check the mainshaft (**Figure 198**) for:
   a. Worn or damaged splines.
   b. Worn or damaged bearing surfaces.
4. Check each mainshaft gear (**Figure 198**) for:
   a. Missing, broken or chipped teeth.
   b. Worn, damaged or rounded-off gear lugs.
5. Place the mainshaft on a set of V-blocks or truing stand and measure runout with a dial indicator. Replace the mainshaft if its runout exceeds the service limit in **Table 5**.

Countershaft Disassembly/Reassembly

Refer to **Figure 200** for this procedure.

1. To disassemble the countershaft, remove the circlip with circlip pliers. Carefully lay out all the clips, washers, and gears in the order you remove them. See **Figure 200** and **Figure 201**. When removing third gear, place it near the workbench for easy retrieval of the 9 bearing balls (**Figure 202**).
2. Inspect the countershaft as described under *Countershaft Inspection* in this chapter.

NOTE
Steps 3-8 describe countershaft reassembly.

3. To install third gear and the 9 bearing balls, perform the following:
   a. Third gear is equipped with 2 circlips (4 and 6, **Figure 200**). Remove the circlip (4, **Figure 200**) from the side of the gear opposite the shift drum groove. The opposite circlip (6, **Figure 200**) should be remain in the gear.

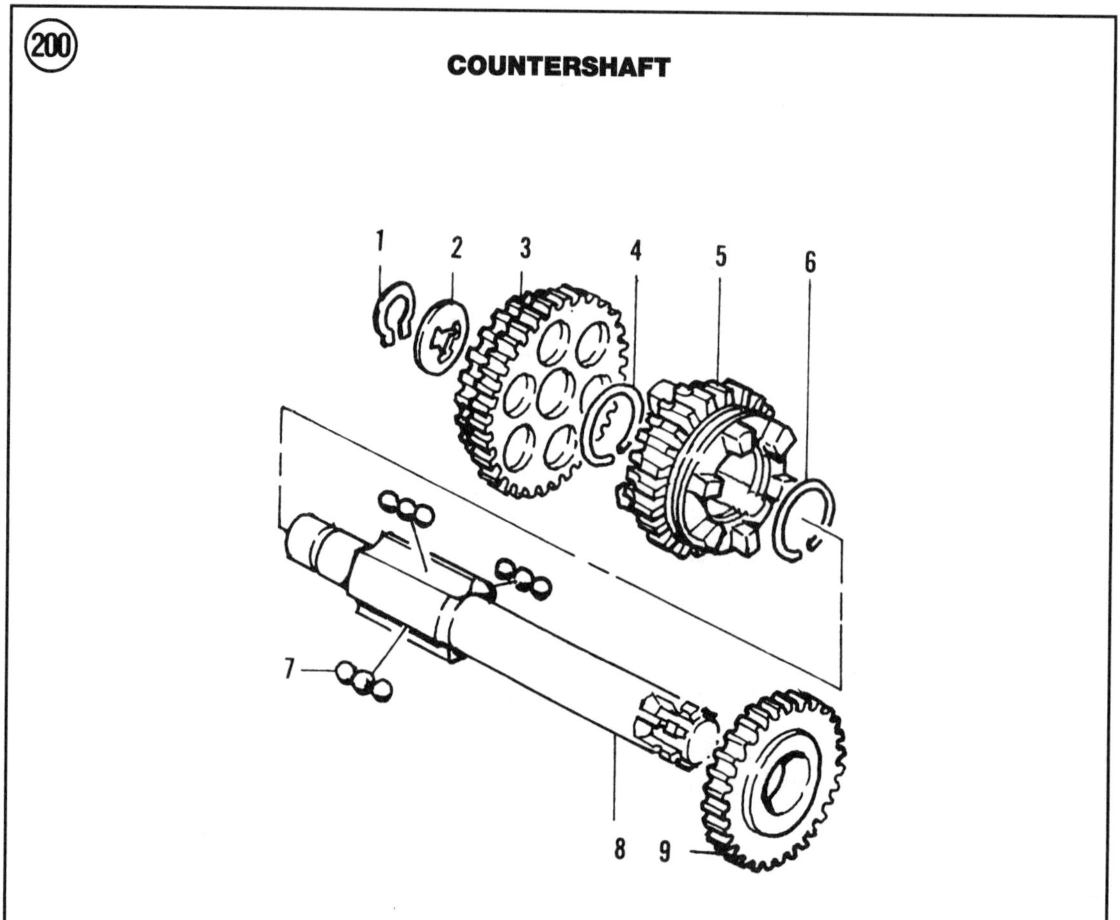

1. Circlip
2. Washer
3. First gear
4. Circlip
5. Third gear
6. Circlip
7. Balls (9 total)
8. Countershaft
9. Second gear

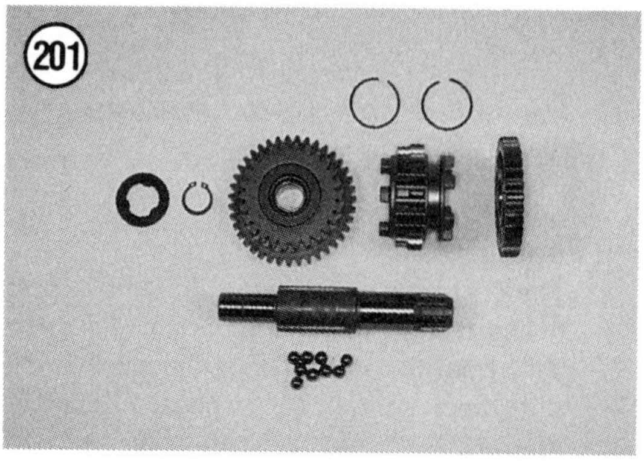

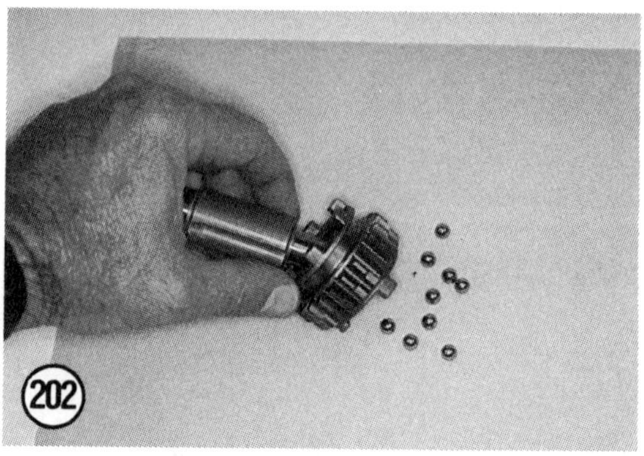

203
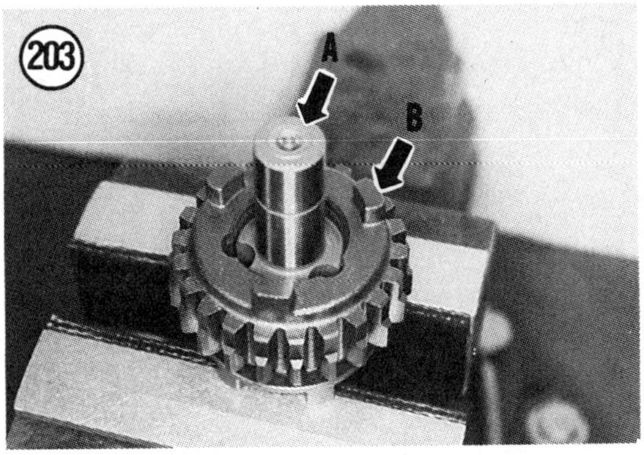

204
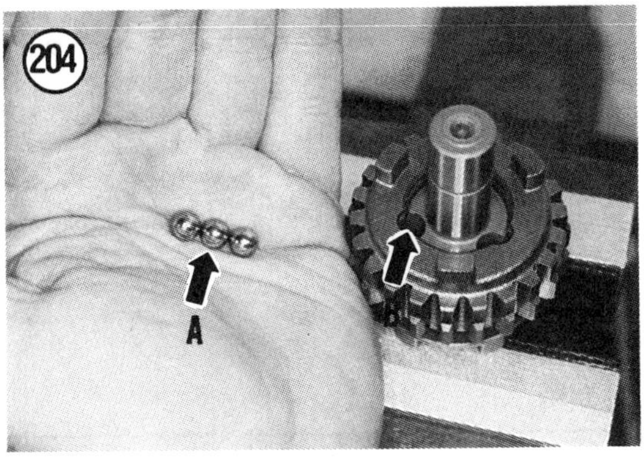

205

206

b. Position and secure the countershaft (A, **Figure 203**) in a vise with soft jaws as follows. Install third gear over the countershaft as shown in B, **Figure 203**. Then position the countershaft in the vise so that third gear rests on top of the vise with the circlip groove in the gear accessible just beyond the countershaft's shoulder (**Figure 203**). This position will allow you to install the balls and circlip easily.

c. Install 3 balls (A, **Figure 204**) into each of the 3 countershaft slots (B, **Figure 204**).

d. Install a new circlip (4, **Figure 200**) into the third gear groove.

e. **Figure 205** shows third gear properly installed on the countershaft.

4. Install the first gear assembly (**Figure 206**) with its larger gear facing toward third gear.
5. Install a new circlip (A, **Figure 207**) into the countershaft groove.
6. Install the washer (B, **Figure 207**) and seat it next to the circlip.
7. Turn the countershaft around and install second gear with its flat side (**Figure 208**) facing away from third gear. **Figure 209** shows the countershaft assembly.

Countershaft Inspection

Replace all parts that show damage as described in this section.

1. Clean and dry all parts (**Figure 201**).
2. Check the countershaft (**Figure 201**) for:
   a. Worn or damaged splines.
   b. Damaged circlip groove.
   c. Worn or damaged bearing surfaces.

207

d. Worn or damaged bearing ball operating surfaces.

3. Check each countershaft gear (**Figure 201**) for:
   a. Missing, broken or chipped teeth.
   b. Worn, damaged or rounded-off gear dogs and holes (**Figure 210**).
   c. Worn shift fork groove.
   d. Worn or damaged gear dogs.
   e. Worn or damaged third gear circlip groove(s).
4. Check the bearing balls (**Figure 201**) for flat spots, cracks or other damage. Replace all of the balls as a set.
5. Place the countershaft on a set of V-blocks or truing stand and measure runout with a dial indicator. Replace the countershaft if its runout exceeds the service limit in **Table 5**.

Internal Shift Mechanism Inspection

Replace all parts that show damage as described in this section.

1. Clean and dry all parts (**Figure 211**).
2. Inspect the shift drum (A, **Figure 211**) for:
   a. Worn or damaged bearing surfaces.
   b. Worn or damaged shift grooves.
   c. Worn or damaged shift drum pins. Replace the pins by removing the E-clip and washer (**Figure 212**). On reassembly, install the washer with is shoulder side facing out (away from shift drum) and install a new E-clip.
3. Inspect the shift forks (B, **Figure 211**) for:
   a. Damage at the slider gear contact fingers (A, **Figure 213**). Check for excessive wear, bending, cracks or heat discoloration (bluing).
   b. Excessively worn or seized bore surface (B, **Figure 213**).
   c. Damaged shift drum pins. Check the pin holes in the shift forks for cracks or other damage.
4. Check the shift drum shaft (C, **Figure 211**) for:
   a. Bending, galling or seizure. Remove the O-ring and E-clip from the shaft, then roll the shaft on a flat surface. Check for bending and visible damage. Then install the shift forks onto the shaft and slide back and forth. There must be no binding or tight spots.
   b. Damaged O-ring or E-clip groove. Install a new E-clip during reassembly.
   c. Worn or damaged O-ring.

208

209

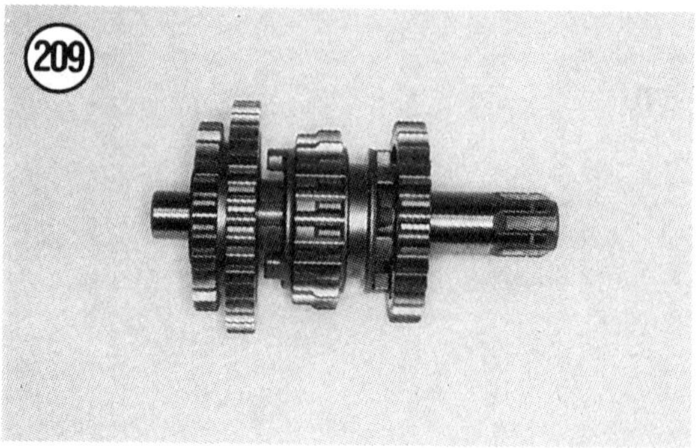

210

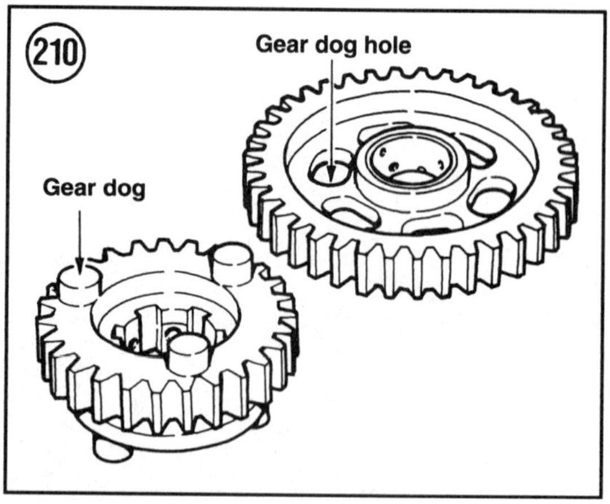

211

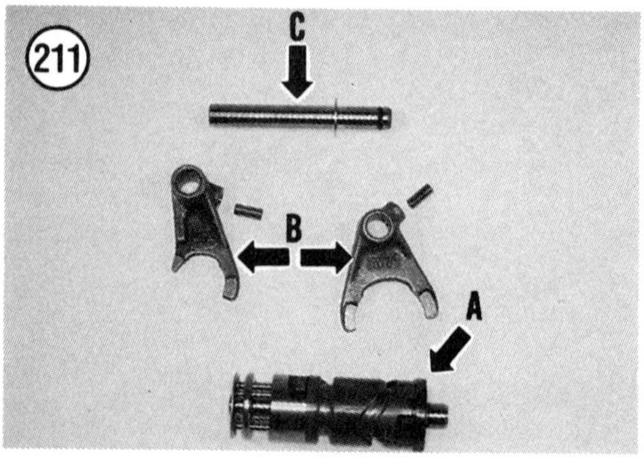

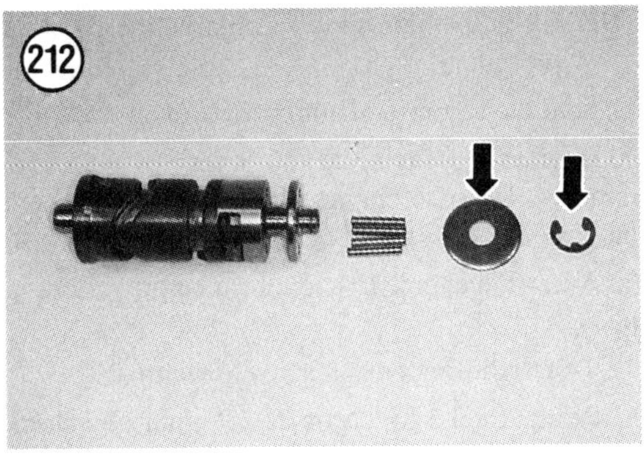

212

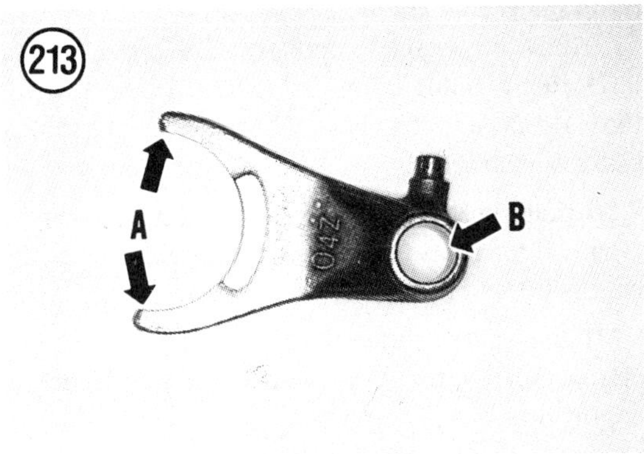

213

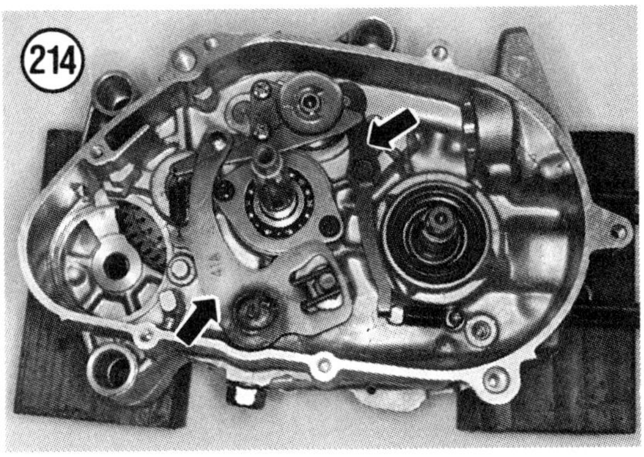

214

215

TRANSMISSION SHIFTING CHECK

The transmission can be checked with the engine mounted in the frame or with it mounted on the workbench. Always check the shifting after reassembling the engine cases.

1. Install the complete external shift mechanism assembly (**Figure 214**) as described in this chapter. The clutch or kickstarter assemblies do not have to be installed for this procedure. Make sure to install the washer and circlip onto the shift shaft groove (left side of engine) to prevent the shift shaft from backing out of the engine when checking the shifting in the following steps.

2. Install the shift pedal (A, **Figure 215**) onto the end of the shift lever. Secure the shift pedal with its pinch bolt so that you ddo not strip the mating splines.

3. Turn the mainshaft (B, **Figure 215**) rapidly and shift the transmission into each gear with the shift pedal (A, **Figure 215**). When the transmission is in NEUTRAL, the countershaft and mainshaft will turn freely from each other (that is, when you turn one shaft, the other shaft will not turn). The transmission is in gear when the stopper arm roller seats into between 2 shift drum pins. When the transmission is in gear, the countershaft and mainshaft are engaged and will turn together.

4. If the transmission does not shift properly into each gear, first check the external shift mechanism (**Figure 214**) for incorrectly assembled or damaged parts. If the mechanism is okay, the engine will have to be disassembled and the transmission and internal shift mechanism checked for damage or incorrectly installed parts.

ENGINE BREAK-IN

Engine performance and durability depends on a sensible and accurate engine break-in procedure. If the rings were replaced, a new piston installed, the cylinder rebored, the crankshaft rebuilt or replaced, or new engine bearings installed, the engine must be broken in just as if it were new. If a proper engine break-in procedure is not followed, accelerated engine wear and overheating will result, reducing engine life.

Before starting the break-in procedure, note the following:

a. Make sure the engine oil tank is full (Chapter Three) and the oil pump bled of all air (Chapter Nine).
b. Make sure the air filter is clean, oiled, and properly installed.
c. Make sure the correct heat range spark is installed in the engine.
d. Perform the break-in procedure on flat ground. To prevent engine overheating, avoid riding in sand, mud or up hills.
e. Do not run the engine with the throttle in the same position for more than a few seconds.
f. Short bursts of full throttle operation (no more than 2-3 seconds at a time) are acceptable. However, rest the engine after each full throttle operation by cruising at a low engine speed for a few minutes. This will allow the engine to rid itself of any excessive heat buildup.
g. Check the spark plug frequently during the break-in procedure. The electrode should be dry and clean and the color of the insulation should be light to medium tan. Refer to Chapter Three for further information on spark plug reading.
h. Keep accurate time records of the break-in procedure.

1. Start the engine and allow to warm up.
2. Operate the engine at lower speeds for 3 to 5 minutes. Turn the engine off and check the spark plug condition.
3. Allow the engine to cool down before restarting it.
4. Restart the engine and allow to warm up.
5. Repeat Step 2 for 5 minutes. Periodically check full throttle response. Turn the engine off and check the spark plug condition.
6. Allow the engine to cool down before restarting it. During this down time, check the motorcycle for loose or missing fasteners. Check the front and rear brake adjustments.
7. Restart the engine and allow to warm up. Run the engine through its full operating range, then turn the engine off and recheck the spark plug.
8. If the spark plug reading is okay, restart the engine and ride for 10-15 minutes. At this point, the engine break-in is complete.

Table 1 GENERAL ENGINE SERVICE SPECIFICATIONS (BW80 AND PW80)

Type	Air-cooled 2-stroke, reed valve induction
Cylinder arrangement	Single cylinder, forward inclined
Displacement	79 cc
Bore × stroke	47.0 × 45.6 mm (1.850-1.795 in.)
Compression ratio	6.6:1
Starting system	Kickstarter
Lubrication system	Autolube oil injection pump
Clutch	Wet, centrifugal automatic
Transmission	
Primary reduction system	Gear
Primary reduction ratio	66/21 (3.143)
Secondary reduction system	Chain drive
Secondary reduction ratio	32/15 (2.133)
Transmission type	3-speed constant mesh
Gear ratio	
First	39/12 (3.250)
Second	30/15 (2.000)
Third	26/18 (1.444)

Table 2 ENGINE TOP END SERVICE SPECIFICATIONS

	New mm (in.)	Service limit mm (in.)
Cylinder head warpage limit	—	0.03 (0.0012)
Cylinder		
Bore size	47.00-47.02 (1.8504-1.8511)	47.10 (1.854)
Taper limit	—	0.05 (0.0020)
Out-of-round limit	—	0.01 (0.0004)
Piston		
Diameter	46.964-46.983 (1.8490-1.8497)	—
Piston measuring point	5 (0.2)	—
Piston clearance		
BW80	0.045-0.050 (0.0018-0.0020)	—
PW80	0.033-0.038 (0.0013-0.0015)	—
Piston offset (exhaust side)	0.2 (0.008)	—
Piston rings (top and second rings)		
End gap		
BW80	0.15-0.30 (0.006-0.012)	—
PW80	0.15-0.35 (0.006-0.0024)	—
Side clearance		
BW80	0.03-0.05 (0.0012-0.0020)	— —
PW80	0.02-0.06 (0.0008-0.0024)	—
Intake manifold warp limit	—	0.1 (0.004)

(continued)

Table 2 ENGINE TOP END SERVICE SPECIFICATIONS (continued)

	New mm (in.)	Service limit mm (in.)
Reed valve		
Thickness	0.2 (0.008)	—
Reed valve stop height	6.3-6.7 (0.25-0.26)	—
Reed valve bend clearance limit	0.3 (0.012)	—

Table 3 PISTON RING SECTIONAL DIMENSIONS

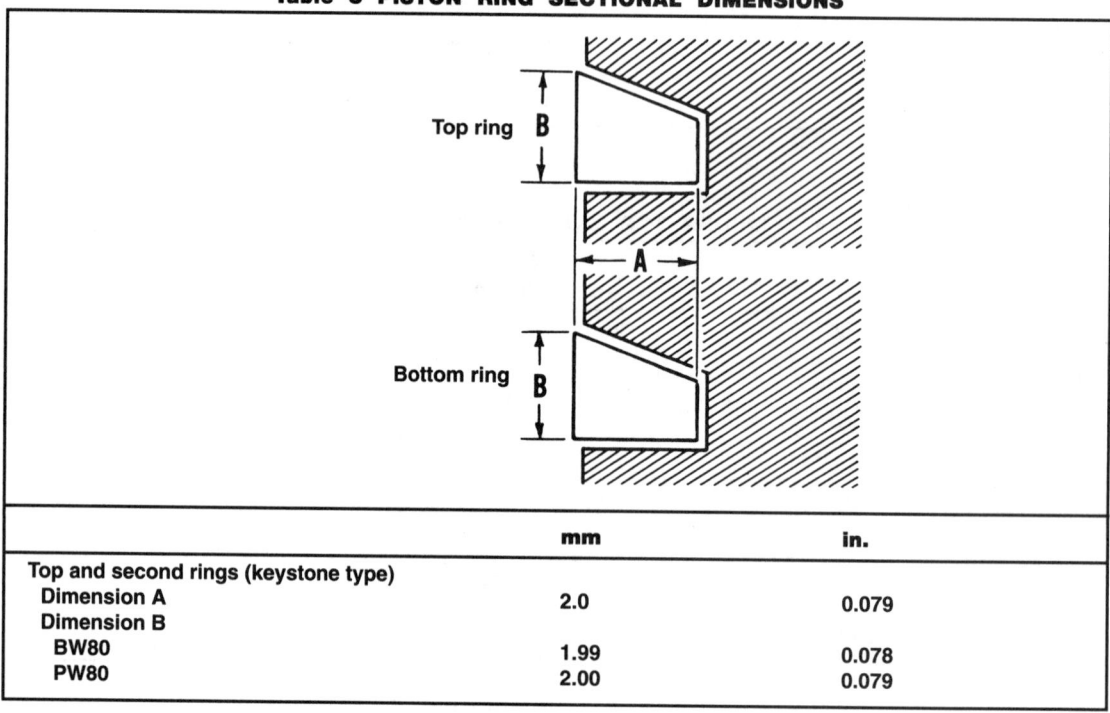

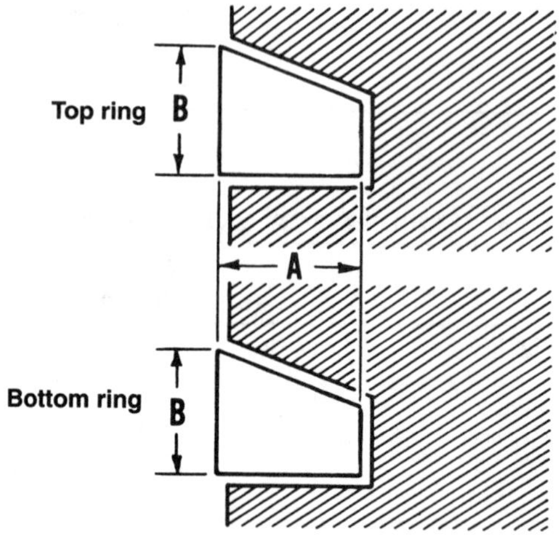

	mm	in.
Top and second rings (keystone type)		
Dimension A	2.0	0.079
Dimension B		
BW80	1.99	0.078
PW80	2.00	0.079

Table 4 CRANKSHAFT SERVICE SPECIFICATIONS

	New mm (in.)	Service limit mm (in.)
Crankshaft wheel width	47.90-47.95 (1.886-1.888)	—
Crankshaft runout limit		
BW80	—	0.03 (0.0012)
PW80	—	0.05 (0.0020)
Connecting big rod end side clearance	0.30-80 (0.012-0.031)	—
Connecting rod small end free play	1.0	—

Table 5 TRANSMISSION SERVICE SPECIFICATIONS

	New mm (in.)	Service limit mm (in.)
Countershaft runout limit	—	0.08 (0.003)
Mainshaft runout limit	—	0.08 (0.003)

Table 6 ENGINE TIGHTENING TORQUES

	N•m	in.-lb.	ft.-lb.
Bearing stopper plate mounting screw	8	70	—
Crankcase mounting screws	8	70	—
Cylinder head nuts			
BW80	10	88	—
PW80	14	—	10
Engine drain bolt	20	—	14
Engine mounting bolts			
BW80 (all)	23	—	17
PW80			
Front and center bolts	23	—	17
Under bolt	26	—	19
Exhaust pipe mounting bolts	18	—	13
Flywheel mounting nut	50	—	36
Left crankcase cover mounting screws	8	70	—
Kickstarter pinch bolt	12	106	—
Mainshaft bearing retainer plate screws	8	70	—
Oil pump cover mounting bolts	8	70	—
Oil seal stopper plate mounting screw	16	—	11
Primary drive gear locknut	50	—	36
Reed valve mounting screws	8	70.0	—
Right crankshaft oil seal holder plate mounting screw	16	—	11
Shift drum holder plate mounting screws	8	70	—
Shift pedal pinch bolt	10	88	—
Spark plug	20	—	14
Stopper lever shoulder bolt	14	—	10

CHAPTER SIX

CLUTCH (BW80 AND PW80)

This chapter contains service procedures for the right crankcase cover and clutch for the BW80 and PW80 models. The clutch can be serviced with the engine mounted in the frame.

Clutch specifications are listed in **Table 1** and **Table 2**. Tightening torques are listed in **Table 3**. **Tables 1-3** are found at the end of the chapter.

RIGHT CRANKCASE COVER

Removal/Installation

1. Drain the transmission oil (Chapter Three).
2. Remove the kickstarter pedal pinch bolt and remove the kickstarter pedal (A, **Figure 1**).
3. Remove the clutch cover mounting screws and cover (B, **Figure 1**). Note the washer (C, **Figure 1**) installed on the kickstarter shaft. Find the washer after removing the cover and reinstall it onto the kickstarter shaft. The washer will sometimes stick to the back of the cover.
4. Remove the dowel pins (A, **Figure 2**) and clutch cover gasket (B, **Figure 2**).
5. Remove all gasket residue from the crankcase cover and crankcase gasket surfaces.
6. Inspect the right crankcase cover seals as described in this section and replace if necessary.
7. Install the right crankcase cover by reversing these removal steps, noting the following:
   a. Tighten all of the right crankcase cover mounting screws in a crisscross pattern to the torque specification in **Table 3**.
   b. Refill the transmission with the correct type and quantity gear oil (Chapter Three). Check for leaks.
   c. Install the kickstarter pedal and its pinch bolt and tighten as specified in **Table 3**.

Right Crankcase Cover Oil Seals Inspection and Replacement

1. Inspect the kickstarter (**Figure 3**) and mainshaft (**Figure 4**)seals and replace if worn or damaged.
2. Pry the oil seal out of the cover with a wide-blade screwdriver. Pad the screwdriver to prevent it from damaging the cover.
3. Clean the oil seal bore.
4. Pack the lips of the new seal with grease.
5. Align the new seal with the cover so that its closed side is facing out. Then install the seal until it bottoms out in its mounting bore. See **Figure 3** or **Figure 4**.

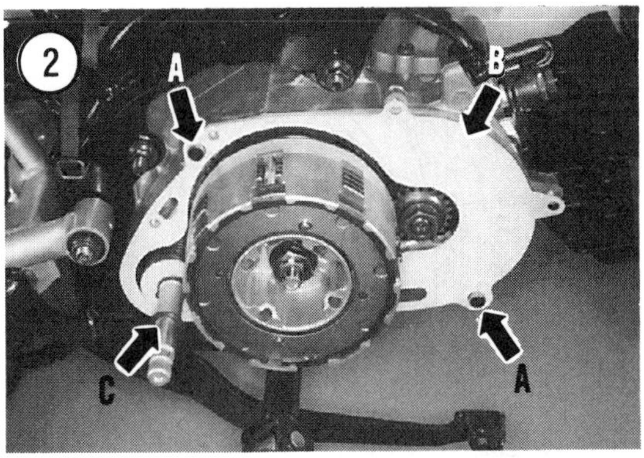

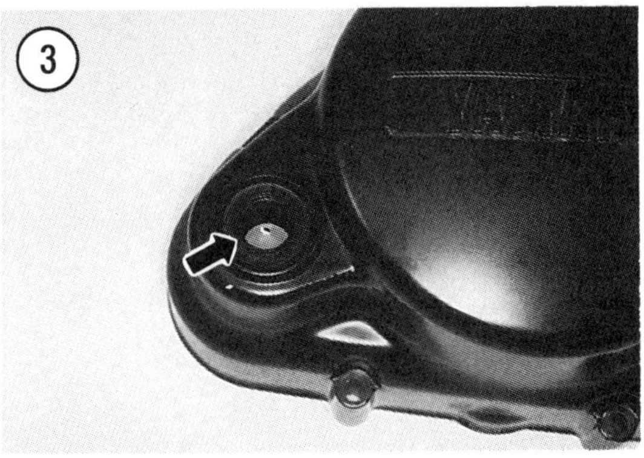

CLUTCH SERVICE

Refer to **Figure 5** when servicing the clutch in this section.

Special Tools

A flywheel (rotor) holder is required to hold the clutch boss when loosening and tightening the clutch locknut; see *Flywheel Holder* in Chapter One.

Removal/Installation

The clutch can be removed as a complete assembly without disassembling it.

1. Remove the right crankcase cover as described in this chapter.
2. Secure the clutch boss with the Yamaha rotor holding tool (part No. YU-01235 [A, **Figure 6**]) or similar tool, then loosen and remove the clutch locknut (B, **Figure 6**) and spring washer.
3. Slide the clutch assembly (**Figure 7**) off the mainshaft.
4. Remove the spacer (A, **Figure 8**) and thrust plate (B, **Figure 8**).
5. Service the clutch as described in this chapter.
6. Install the clutch by reversing these removal steps, noting the following.
7. Lubricate the spacer, thrust plate and clutch housing bore with transmission oil before reassembly.
8. Install the spring washer (A, **Figure 9**) so that its convex side faces out.
9. Install the clutch locknut with its shoulder (B, **Figure 9**) facing in (toward clutch).
10. Hold the clutch boss and tighten the clutch locknut (B, **Figure 6**) as specified in **Table 3**.

Clutch Disassembly

1. Remove the clutch as described in this chapter.

WARNING
To prevent eye injury, wear safety glasses when removing the snap ring in Step 2.

(5)

CLUTCH

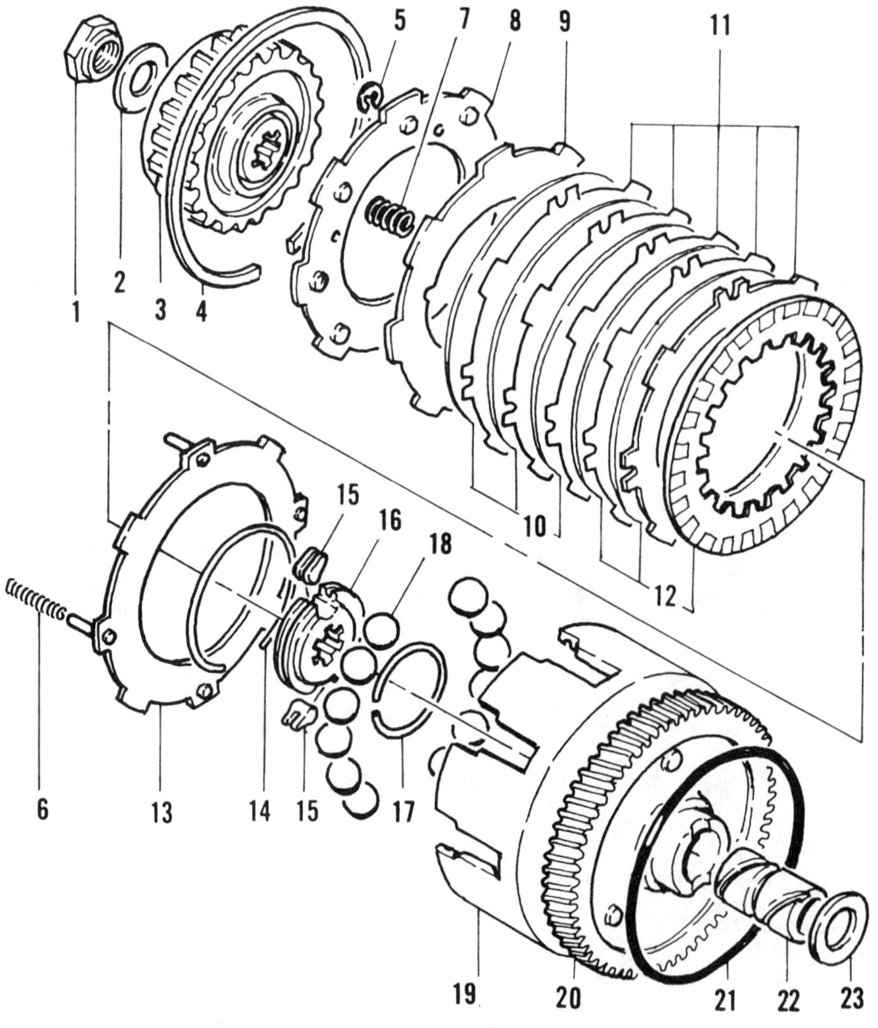

1. Clutch locknut
2. Spring washer
3. Clutch boss
4. Snap ring
5. E-clip
6. Clutch springs
7. Springs
8. Pressure plate (outer)
9. Pressure plate (inner)
10. Friction plates (silver)
11. Clutch plates
12. Friction plates (brown)
13. Thrust weight plate
14. Snap ring
15. One-way boss cam
16. One-way boss
17. Spring clip
18. Balls (12)
19. Clutch housing
20. Primary driven gear
21. O-ring
22. Spacer
23. Thrust plate

2. Using a screwdriver, pry the snap ring (4, **Figure 5**) out of the clutch housing groove. See A, **Figure 10**.

3. Remove the pressure plate assembly (B, **Figure 10**).

NOTE
*Unless you are going to service the pressure plate, do not remove the E-clips (5, **Figure 5**) that hold the pressure plate assembly together.*

4. Remove the compression springs (**Figure 11**).

5. Remove the clutch plates in the order shown in **Figure 5**.

6. Remove the clutch boss (**Figure 12**).

7. Remove the thrust weight plate (A, **Figure 13**).

8. Remove the 12 bearing balls (B, **Figure 13**).

9. Remove the one-way boss (16, **Figure 5**) as follows:

   a. Pry the snap ring (14, **Figure 5**) out of the clutch housing groove. See **Figure 14**.

   b. Remove the one-way boss assembly (**Figure 15**).

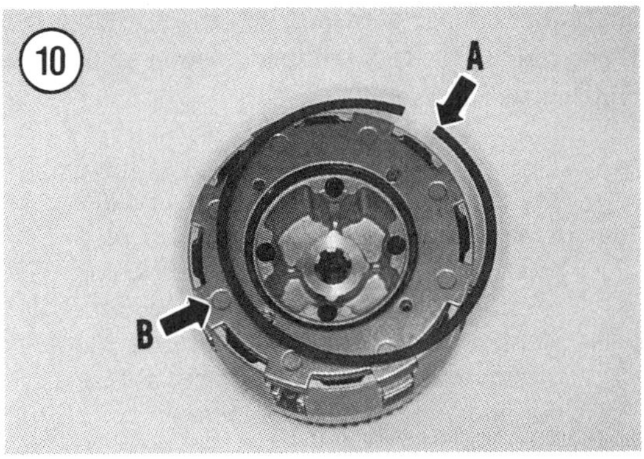

Clutch Inspection

When measuring the clutch components, compare the measurements to the specifications in **Table 2**. Replace parts that are out of specification or show damage as described in this section.

1. Clean and dry all parts (**Figure 16**).
2. Measure the free length of each clutch spring (**Figure 17**) with a vernier caliper. Replace the springs as a set if any one spring is too short.
3. Inspect the friction plates (A, **Figure 18**) for wear or damage. Then measure the thickness of each friction plate with a vernier caliper. If one friction plate is out of specification, replace all friction plates as a set.

NOTE
*There are two different types of friction plates used in the stock clutch—silver and brown identification colors (10 and 12, **Figure 5**). When you replace the friction plates as a set, make sure to purchase 3 silver and 3 brown plates.*

4. Inspect the clutch plates (B, **Figure 18**) for wear, bluing (indicating heat damage) or other damage. Then place each clutch plate on a flat surface and check for warpage with a feeler gauge (**Figure 19**). If one clutch plate is out of specification, replace the clutch plates as a set.

NOTE
*The clutch plates are available in 3 different thicknesses for adjustment purposes; see **Table 2** for thickness specifications. Before purchasing replacement clutch plates, perform the friction plate height adjustment during the clutch reassembly procedure.*

5. Check the pressure plate assembly (A, **Figure 16**) for warpage, cracks or other damage. If the pressure plate is warped, remove the E-clips (5, **Figure 5**) and disassemble the pressure plate. Check the springs (7, **Figure 5**) for weakness or other damage. Check the pressure plates (8 and 9, **Figure 5**) for warpage or other. Replace any damaged part(s) and reassemble with new E-clips.
6. Check the thrust weight plate (B, **Figure 16**) for:
   a. Warpage.
   b. Cracks.
   c. Loose or damaged spring pins.
7. Check the clutch boss (C, **Figure 16**) for:

12
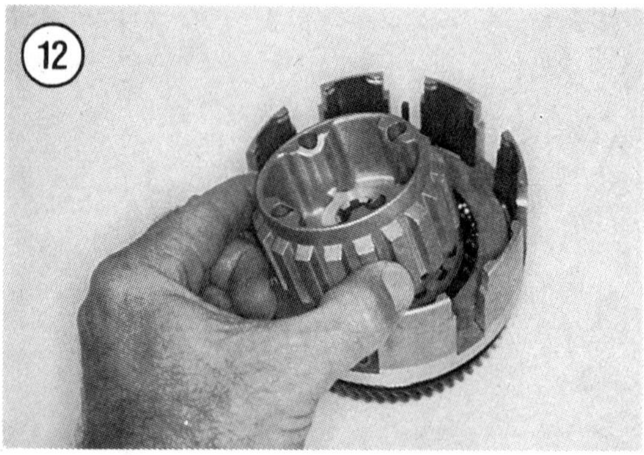

13

14
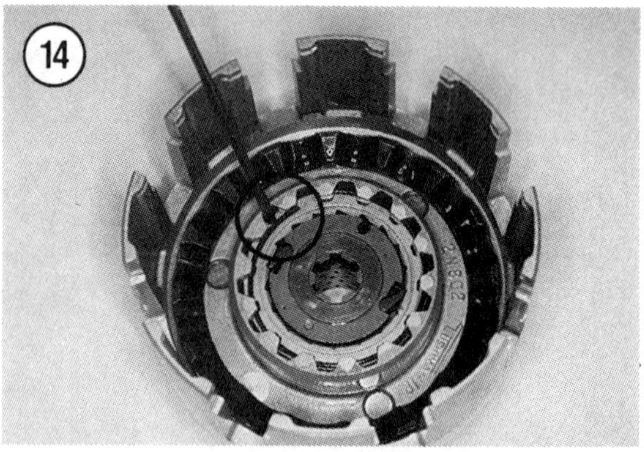

15
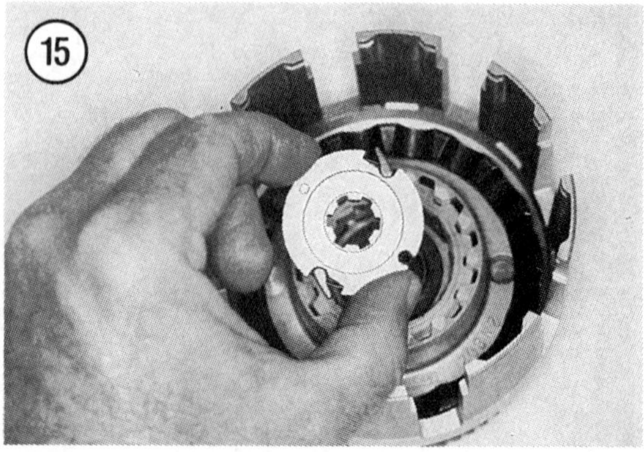

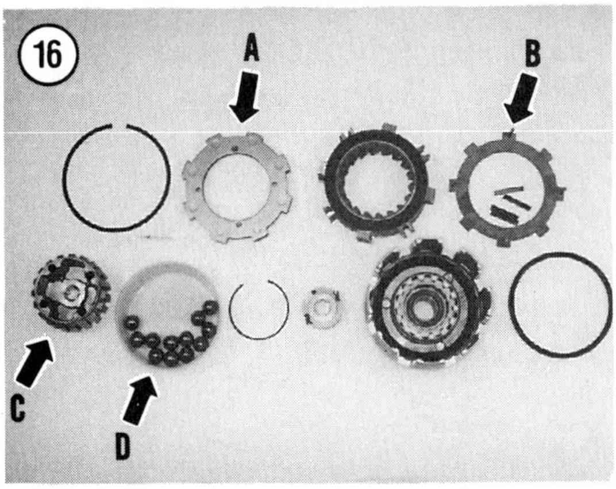

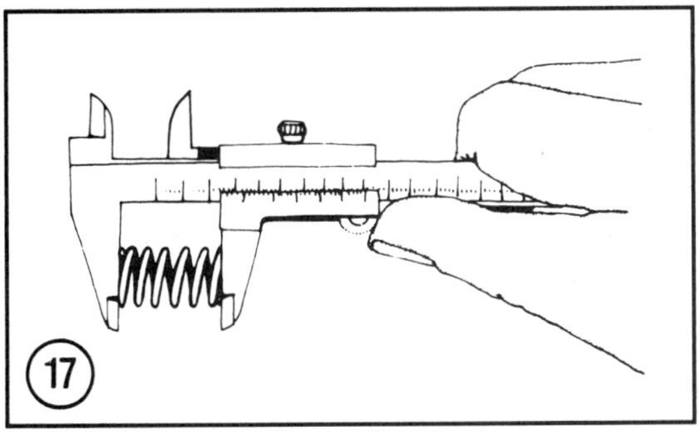

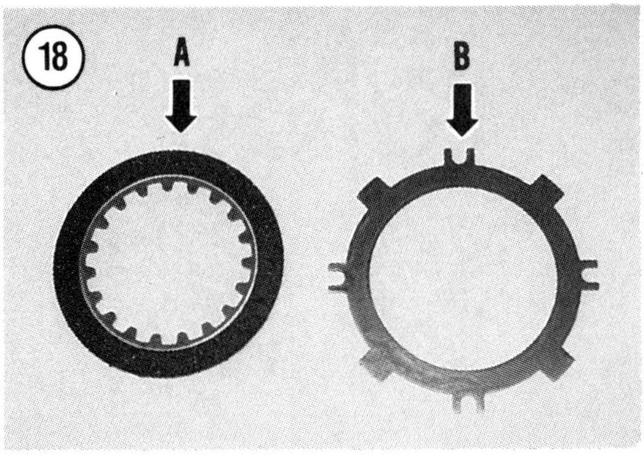

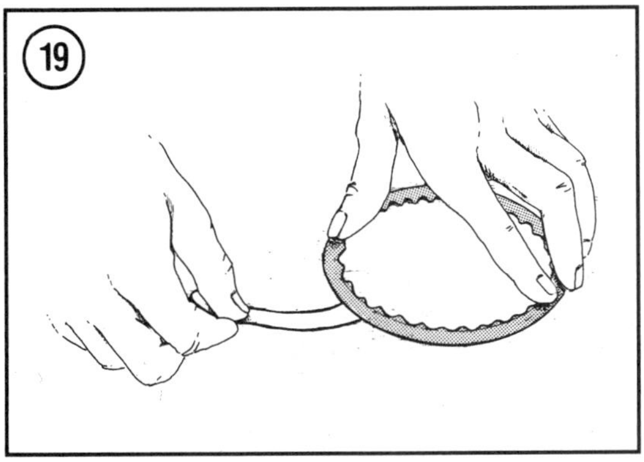

a. Worn or damaged outer splines. Damaged outer splines will cause erratic clutch operation.
b. Other wear or damage.

8. Check the clutch bearing balls (D, **Figure 16**) for pitting, excessive wear or damage. Replace all 12 bearing balls as a set.

9. Check for excessive wear or damage at the following clutch housing (**Figure 20**) positions:
   a. Clutch plate guide grooves (A). Repair light damage with a file. Replace the clutch housing if damage is severe.
   b. Bearing ball ramps (B).
   c. Clutch boss splines (C).
   d. Bushing (D).
   e. Snap ring grooves.

10. Inspect the primary driven gear (20, **Figure 5**) for missing, broken or chipped gear teeth. If this gear is damaged, check the primary drive gear (Chapter Five) for the same type of damage.

11. Refer to **Figure 5** and check the following parts for severe wear or damage:
   a. O-ring (21). Install the O-ring into the clutch housing groove.
   b. Spacer (22).
   c. Thrust plate (23).

12. Inspect the clutch locknut and spring washer (**Figure 9**) for damage.

13. Inspect the one-way boss cams (**Figure 21**) for severe wear or damage. To replace the cams, perform the following:
   a. Pry the spring clip (**Figure 22**) out of the one-way boss and remove the 2 cams. See **Figure 23**.
   b. Install the new cams into the one-way boss so that they face in the direction shown in **Figure 21**, then secure the cams with the spring clip.

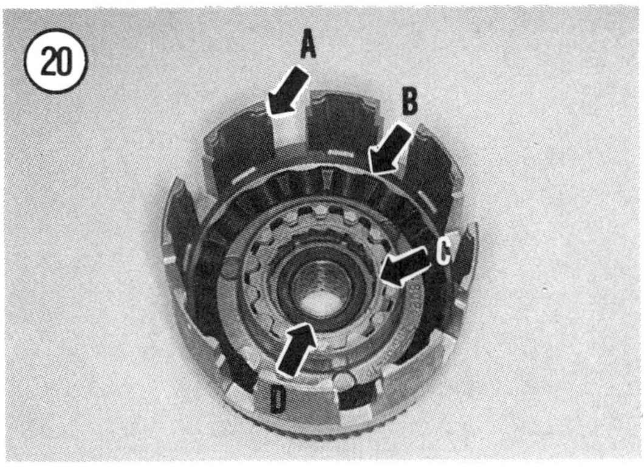

6

Position the spring clip so that its end gap fits around the split pin as shown in **Figure 22**.

Installation

1. Make sure all clutch parts are clean.
2. Lubricate all of the components with transmission oil during reassembly.
3. Install the one-way boss (**Figure 15**) into the clutch housing as shown in A, **Figure 24**.
4. Install the circlip (B, **Figure 24**) into the clutch housing groove. Make sure the circlip seats in the groove completely.
5. Install the 12 bearing balls into the clutch housing ball ramps as shown in **Figure 25**. Position the balls so that there is an empty space between each 3 ball set.
6. Install the thrust weight plate (A, **Figure 13**) and seat it into the clutch housing as shown in **Figure 26**. Make sure none of the bearing balls were repositioned.
7. Install the clutch boss (**Figure 12**) and seat it into the clutch housing as shown in **Figure 27**.

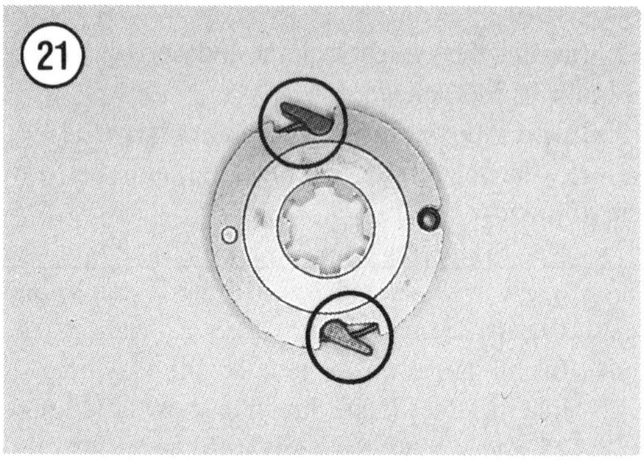
21

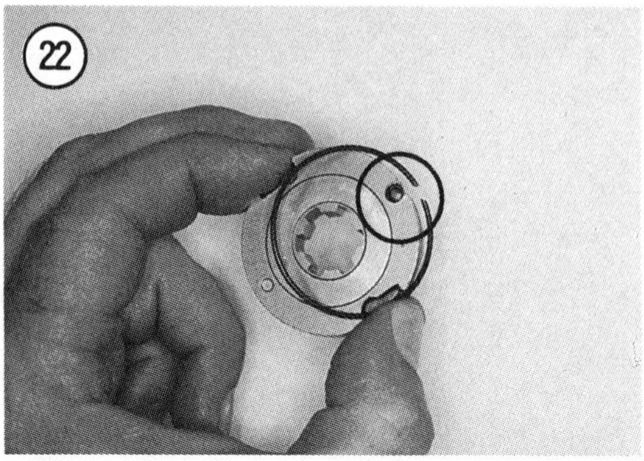
22

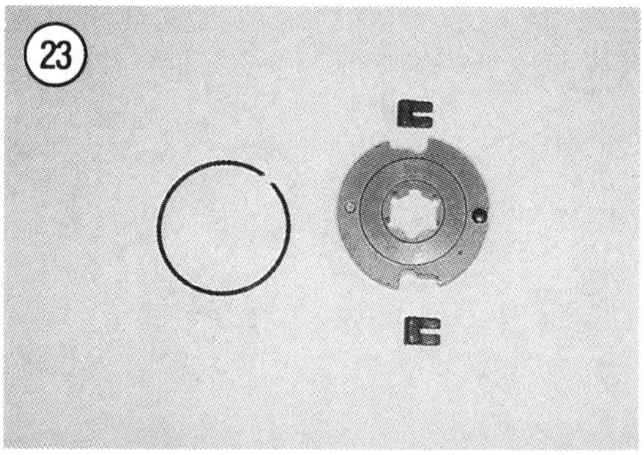
23

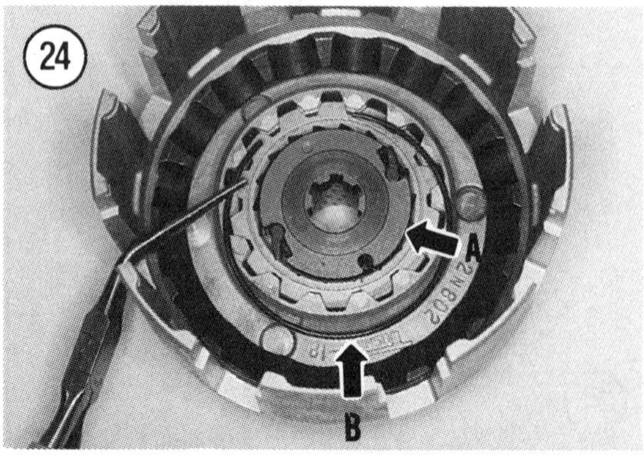

24

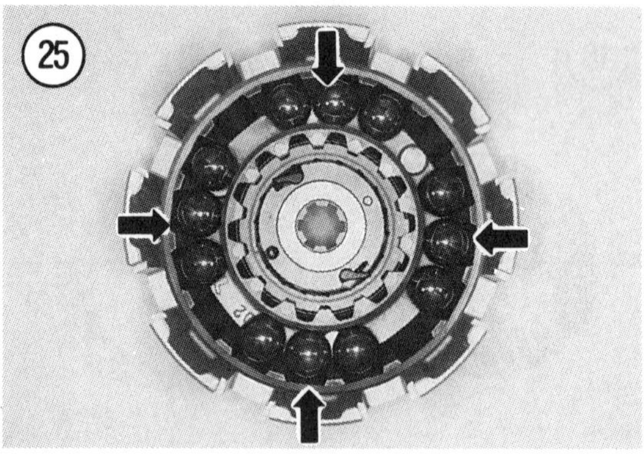
25

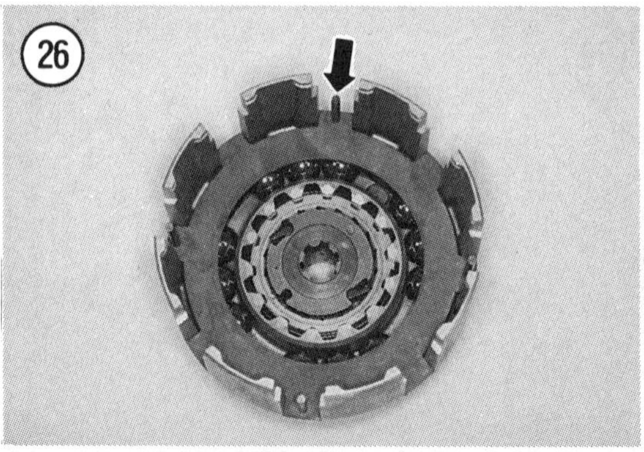
26

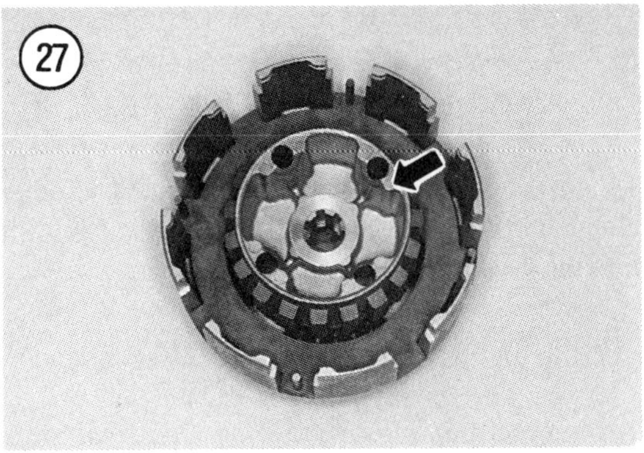

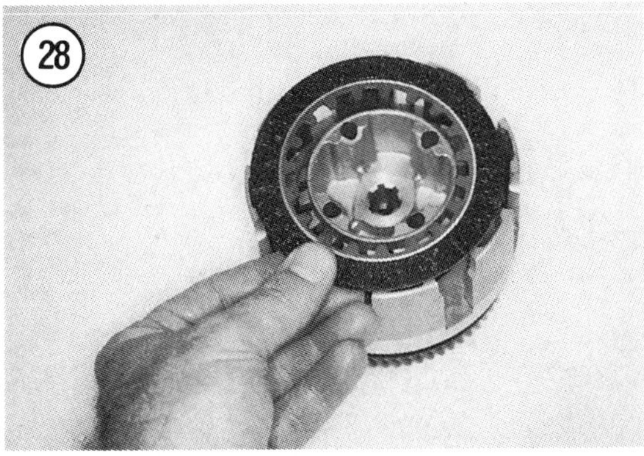

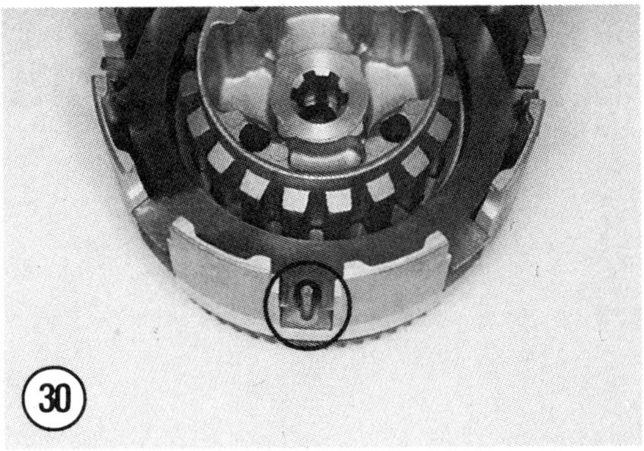

8. Identify the brown (12, **Figure 5**) and silver (10, **Figure 5**) friction plate sets. There should be 3 plates in each color set.

9. Install the clutch plates in the following order:
   a. Brown friction plate (**Figure 28**).
   b. Clutch plate (**Figure 29**). Align the 4 cutouts in each clutch plate with the spring posts on the thrust weight plate (**Figure 30**).
   c. Brown friction plate.
   d. Clutch plate.
   e. Brown friction plate.
   f. Clutch plate.
   g. Silver friction plate.
   h. Clutch plate.
   i. Silver friction plate.
   j. Clutch plate.
   k. Silver friction plate.

10. Check the friction plate height adjustment as follows:
   a. With the clutch housing resting on the workbench, push the clutch plate assembly down by hand.
   b. Measure the distance between the top of the outer friction plate down to the step on the clutch housing (**Figure 31**). This distance is the friction plate height. Compare with the friction plate height specification in **Table 2**.
   c. If the friction plate height is out of specification, perform Step 11. If the height is correct, go to Step 12.

11. To adjust the friction plate height, perform these steps:
   a. Remove all of the friction and clutch plates.
   b. The clutch plates (**Figure 29**) are available in 3 different thicknesses: 1.2, 1.4 and 1.6 mm (0.047, 0.055 and 0.063 in.). Replace the stock clutch plates with clutch plates of a thinner or

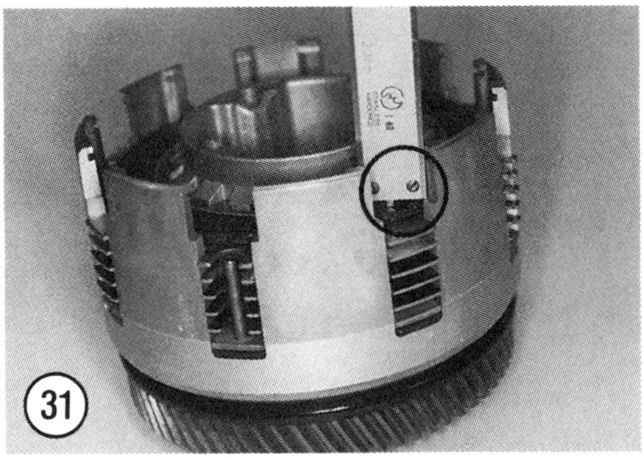

6

thicker thickness to correct the friction plate height adjustment.

c. Repeat Step 9 to install the friction and clutch plate assembly. Then remeasure the friction plate height.

d. Repeat these steps until the friction height adjustment is correct.

12. Install the clutch springs (**Figure 32**).

13. Turn the clutch boss (A, **Figure 33**) and align its splines (B, **Figure 33**) with the clutch housing splines.

14. Install the pressure plate (**Figure 34**) into the clutch housing. Install the pressure plate so that the side with the E-clips (5, **Figure 5**) face up (away from clutch housing).

WARNING
To protect your eyes, wear safety glasses when installing the snap ring in Step 15.

15. Install the circlip (4, **Figure 5**) into the outer clutch housing groove. Start at one end and push it into the groove by hand. See **Figure 35**.

NOTE
After installing the snap ring, check that the clutch boss and clutch housing splines are aligned.

16. Install the clutch as described in this chapter.

32

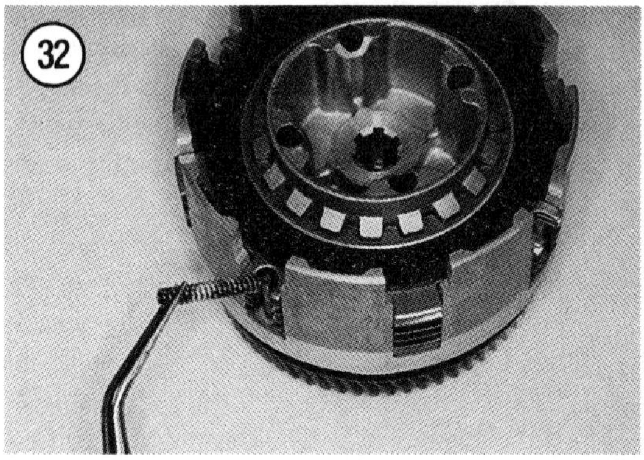

34

33

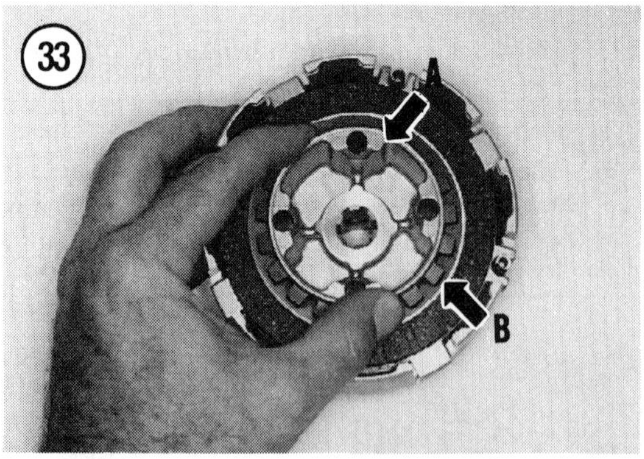

35

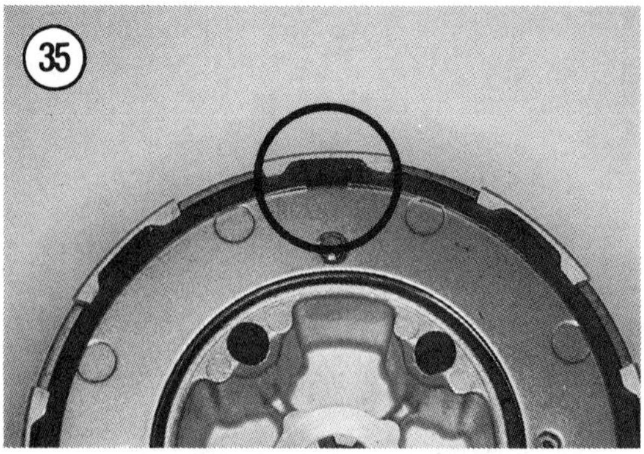

Table 1 CLUTCH SPECIFICATIONS

Type	Wet, centrifugal automatic
Friction plate quantity	
Brown plates	3
Silver	3
Clutch plate quantity	5
Clutch ball quantity	12
Clutch spring quantity	6

Table 2 CLUTCH SERVICE SPECIFICATIONS

	New mm (in.)	Service limit mm (in.)
Friction plate thickness	3.0 (0.118)	2.9 (0.114)
Friction plate height (adjustment gap)	1.40-1.75 (0.055-0.069)	—
Clutch plates thickness	1.2 (0.0470)	1.4 (0.055)
Warp limit	—	0.05 (0.002)
Clutch spring free	12.9 (0.51)	12.0 (0.47)
Clutch pushrod bend limit	—	0.15 (0.006)

Table 3 CLUTCH TIGHTENING TORQUES

	N•m	in.lb.	ft.-lb.
Clutch locknut	50	—	36
Engine drain bolt	20	—	14
Kickstarterpedal pinch bolt	12	106	—
Primary drive gear	50	—	36
Right crankcase cover	12	106	—
Stopper lever mounting bolt	14	—	10
Stopper plate	8	70	—
Stopper screw	25	—	18

6

CHAPTER SEVEN

FUEL SYSTEM

The fuel system consists of the fuel tank, fuel shutoff valve, carburetor and air filter.

This chapter includes service procedures for all parts of the fuel system, throttle cable and choke cable. Air filter service is covered in Chapter Three. Reed valve service is covered in Chapter Four (PW50) or Chapter Five (BW80 and PW80).

Tables 1-3 list stock carburetor specifications. **Tables 1-4** are at the end of the chapter.

CARBURETOR (PW50)

Table 1 lists carburetor specifications for the PW50.

Carburetor Removal

1. Support the bike on its centerstand.
2. Turn the fuel valve off and disconnect the fuel hose at the fuel valve or carburetor.
3. Remove the air box screw (A, **Figure 1**). Then spread the hose clamp (B, **Figure 1**) and remove the air box (C, **Figure 1**).
4. Disconnect the oil delivery hose (A, **Figure 2**) from the carburetor as follows:

CAUTION

The metal band used to secure the oil delivery hose to the carburetor fitting is a tight fit and can be difficult to remove. When removing the metal band in the next step, work carefully so you do not damage the band or tear the oil hose. A loose hose connection or torn hose will allow the oil pump to draw in air. This will prevent oil from reaching the engine and cause engine seizure. Replace any weak or damaged part during reassembly.

a. Loosen the metal band and slide it up the hose and off the carburetor fitting. Then disconnect the oil delivery hose from the carburetor.

1

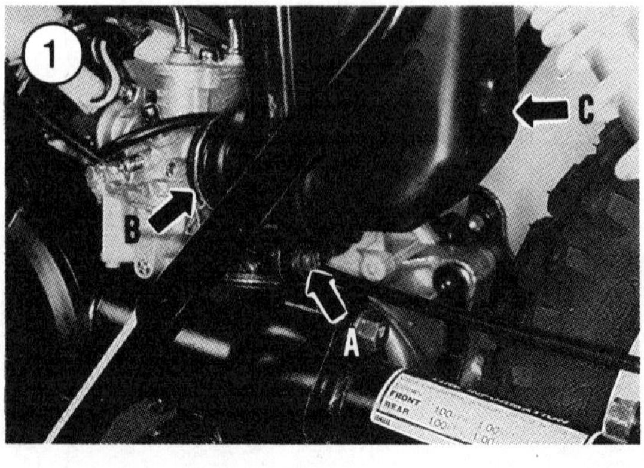

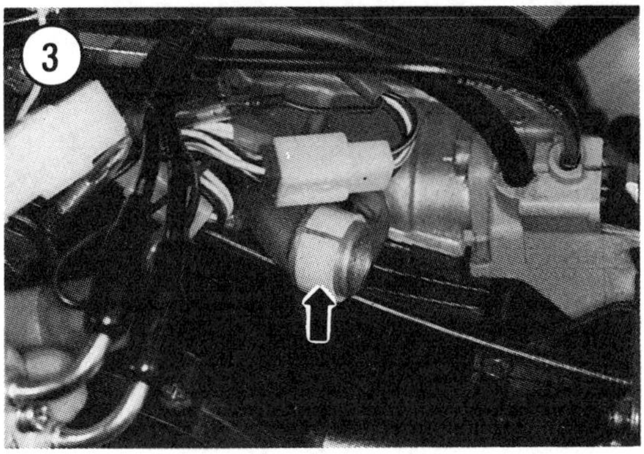

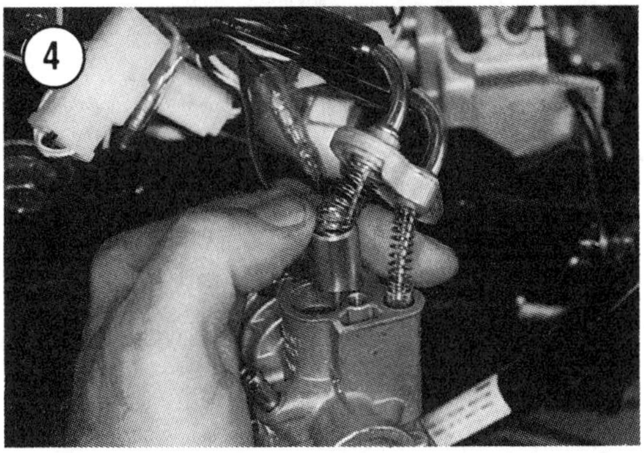

b. Plug the hose to prevent oil leakage and contamination.

5. Loosen the carburetor pinch bolt (B, **Figure 2**), then slide the carburetor off the intake manifold.

6. Remove the seal band (**Figure 3**) from the intake manifold. The seal band may come off with the carburetor.

7. Remove the carburetor cap screw, then remove the cap and pull the throttle and choke valve assemblies (**Figure 4**) from the carburetor.

NOTE
If you are not going to service the throttle or choke valve assemblies, position the cap assembly over the upper frame tube to prevent jet needle damage. Place the assemblies in a reclosable plastic bag to prevent contamination.

8. Plug the intake manifold opening to prevent dust and other debris from entering the engine.

NOTE
If there is any accumulation of dirt or other abrasive dust on the intake side of the carburetor, inspect and service the air filter (Chapter Three) and its connecting hose before restarting the engine.

Carburetor Installation

1. Install the throttle valve into the carburetor housing by aligning the groove in the throttle valve (A, **Figure 5**) with the pin (B, **Figure 5**) in the carburetor housing.

2. Install the choke valve (**Figure 4**) into its carburetor bore.

3. Push the carburetor cap down and center it on its gasket on top of the carburetor, then install and tighten its mounting screw and lockwasher securely.

4. Operate the throttle lever and then choke lever a few times. Both the throttle valve and choke valve assemblies must move through their carburetor bores with no binding or roughness. If there is any binding or roughness, note the following:

   a. If the throttle valve does not move or moves roughly, check the groove and pin alignment as described in Step 1. If the alignment is good, check the throttle valve assembly (at the handlebar) and the throttle cable for incorrect assembly, routing or adjustment.

6

THROTTLE AND CHOKE VALVES (PW50)

1. Cable boot
2. Choke cable adjuster
3. Throttle cable adjuster
4. Screw
5. Lockwasher
6. Cover
7. Gasket
8. Choke valve spring
9. Choke valve
10. Throttle spring
11. Throttle cable hook
12. E-clip
13. Jet needle
14. Throttle valve

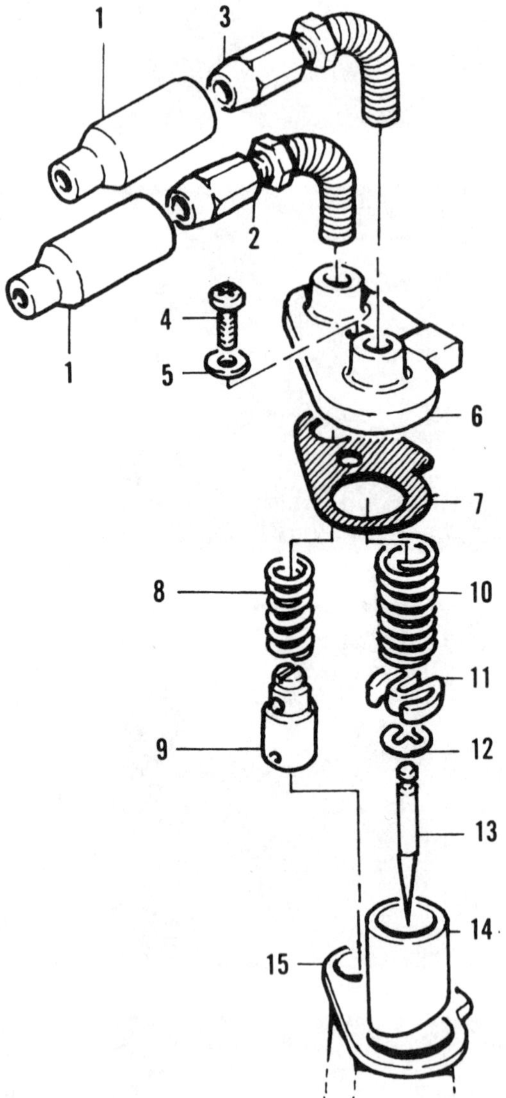

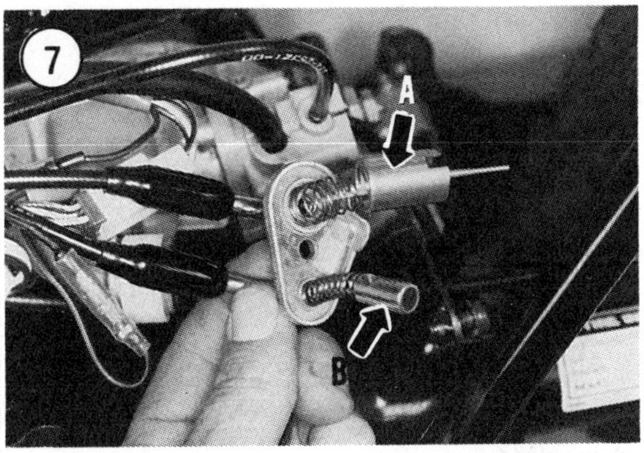

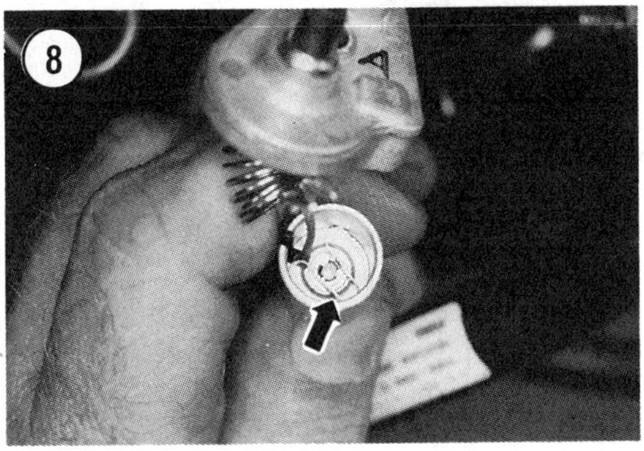

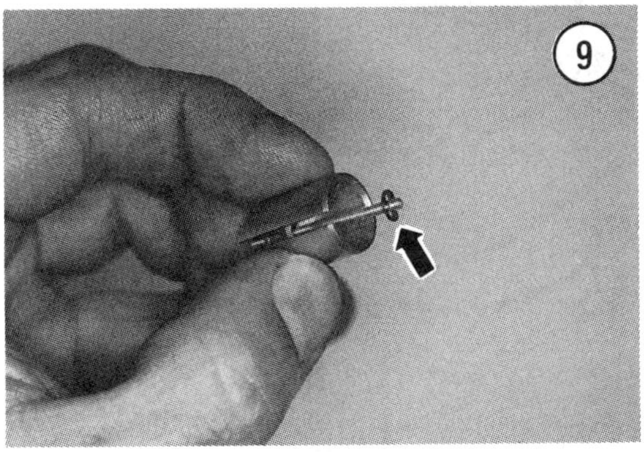

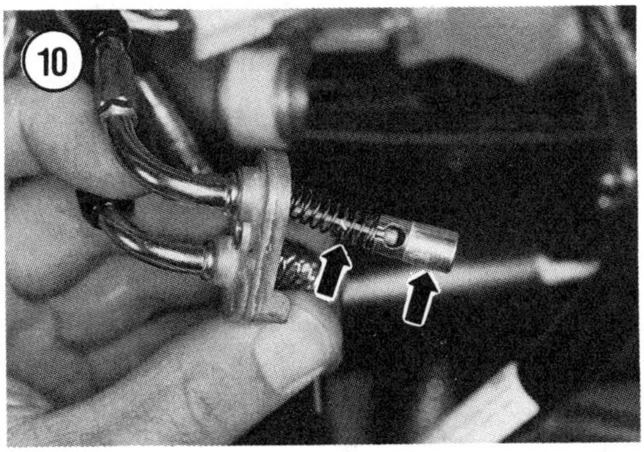

b. If the choke valve does not move or moves roughly, check the choke valve and spring assembly. Then check the choke lever and cable for incorrect assembly, routing or adjustment.

c. If necessary, service the throttle and choke valve assemblies as described in the following procedure.

5. If the seal band is not installed inside the carburetor, install it onto the intake manifold (**Figure 3**).

6. Slide the carburetor over the seal band and intake manifold. Level the carburetor with the engine and tighten its pinch bolt (B, **Figure 2**) securely.

7. Reconnect the oil delivery hose (A, **Figure 2**) onto the carburetor hose nozzle, then push the metal band over the hose nozzle to secure the hose. Replace the metal band if damaged or if it does not tighten the hose connection.

8. Spread the air box clamp (B, **Figure 1**) and slide the air box over the carburetor. Then install and tighten the air box mounting screw (A, **Figure 1**).

9. Reconnect the fuel hose onto the fuel tank. Secure the hose with its hose clamp.

10. Check the throttle valve and choke valve operation once again (see Step 4).

11. Bleed the oil pump as described in Chapter Nine.

12. After turning the fuel valve on, check the hose and carburetor for leaks.

Throttle Valve/Choke Valve Removal/Installation

Refer to **Figure 6**.

1. Remove the throttle and choke valve assemblies (**Figure 4**) from the carburetor as described under *Carburetor Removal* in this section.

2. Remove the throttle valve (A, **Figure 7**) as follows:

a. Compress the throttle valve spring into the cap and remove the throttle cable lock (**Figure 8**).

b. Push down and then lift out the throttle cable.

c. Remove the throttle valve spring.

d. Remove the jet needle (**Figure 9**).

3. Remove the choke valve (B, **Figure 7**) by compressing the choke spring and then sliding it off the cable (**Figure 10**).

4. Replace the carburetor cover gasket (7, **Figure 6**) if damaged.

(11)

CARBURETOR (PW50)

1. Carburetor body
2. Screw
3. Nut
4. Spring
5. Pilot air screw
6. Spring
7. Throttle stop screw
8. Pilot jet
9. Needle jet
10. Main jet
11. Needle valve
12. Float
13. Float pin
14. Float bowl gasket
15. Float bowl
16. Screw
17. Spring
18. Drain screw
19. Hose

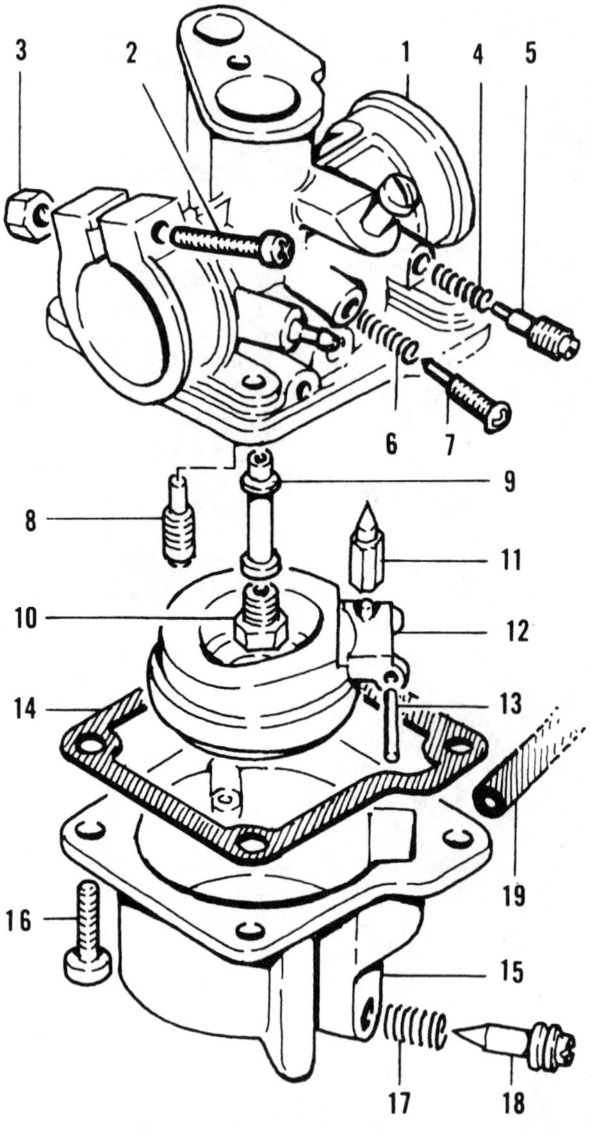

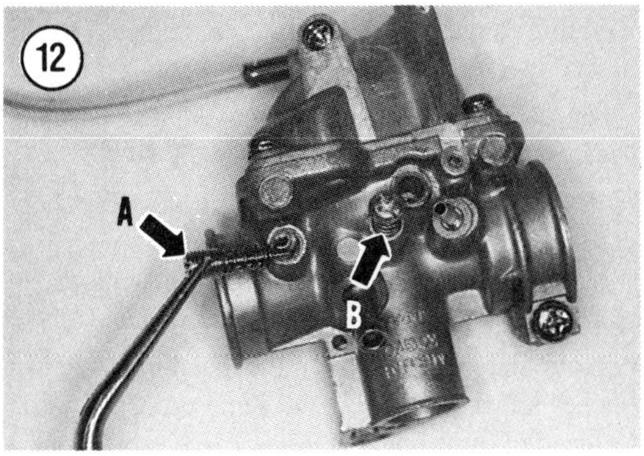

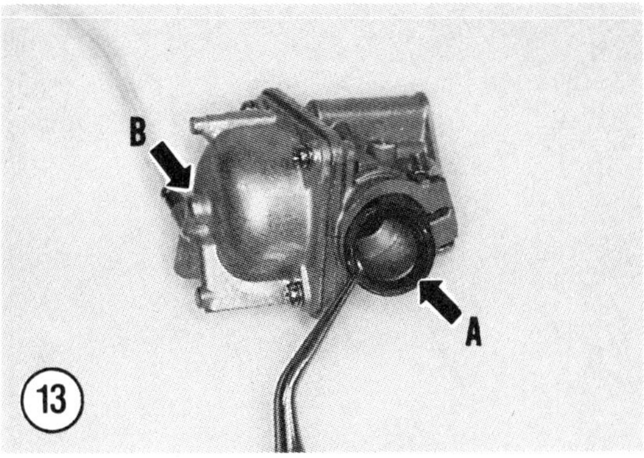

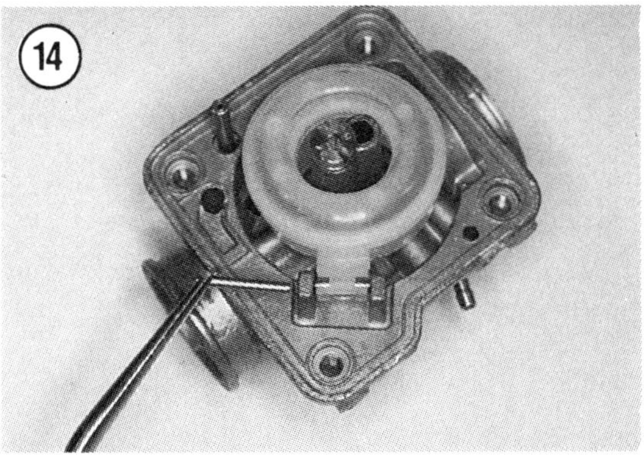

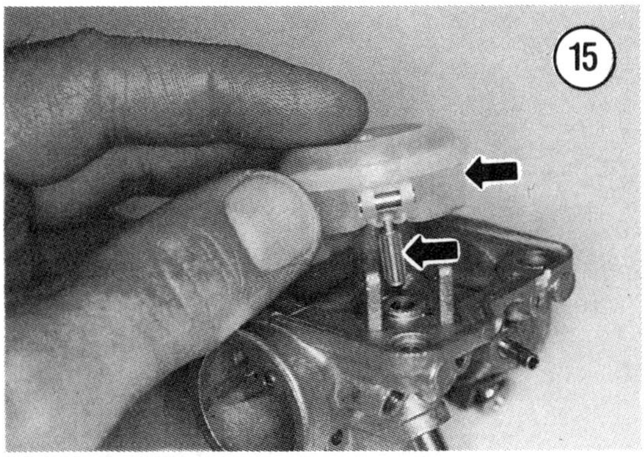

5. Inspect the throttle valve, spring and jet needle for damage. If the throttle valve has deep score marks or is severely worn, dirt may be passing through the air filter.

6. Inspect the choke valve and spring for damage.

7. Install the throttle and choke valve assemblies by reversing these removal steps, noting the following:

 a. Make sure the E-clip is installed in the correct jet needle clip groove. See **Table 1** for the stock groove position.
 b. If a cable was removed or replaced, adjust the cable as described in Chapter Three.

8. Install the throttle and choke valve assembles and carburetor cap (**Figure 7**) as described under *Carburetor Installation* in this section.

Carburetor Disassembly

Refer to **Figure 11**.

1. Remove the carburetor as described in this chapter.

2. Lightly seat the pilot air screw, counting the number of turns for reassembly reference, then back the screw out and remove it and its spring (A, **Figure 12**) from the carburetor.

3. Remove the throttle stop screw and spring (B, **Figure 12**).

4. Remove the rubber seal (A, **Figure 13**) from the carburetor bore.

5. Remove the float bowl screws and float bowl (B, **Figure 13**). Be careful of any gas that may spill out of the float bowl.

6. Carefully remove the float bowl gasket.

7. Remove the float pin with a pair of needlenose pliers (**Figure 14**), then remove the float and needle valve (**Figure 15**). Unhook the needle valve from the float.

8. Unscrew and remove the main jet (**Figure 16**).

9. Unscrew and remove the pilot jet (**Figure 17**).

10. Unscrew and remove the drain screw (18, **Figure 11**) and spring.

11. Push the needle jet (9, **Figure 11**) through the carburetor and remove it.

12. Clean and inspect all parts as described under *Carburetor Cleaning and Inspection (All Models)* in this chapter.

Carburetor Assembly

Refer to **Figure 11** when assembling the carburetor body.

1. Install the needle jet (9, **Figure 11**) through the carburetor and seat it into position.
2. Install the drain screw (18, **Figure 11**) and spring into the float bowl. Tighten the drain screw securely.
3. Install and tighten the pilot jet (**Figure 17**).
4. Install and tighten the main jet (**Figure 16**).
5. Hook the needle valve onto the float, then install the needle valve into its seat (**Figure 15**). Install the float pin through the carburetor pedestal arms and float (**Figure 14**).
6. Check the float height as described in this chapter.
7. Install the float bowl gasket, making sure all holes align. If the holes do not align, turn the gasket over.
8. Install the float bowl (B, **Figure 13**) and its mounting screws. Tighten each screw securely.
9. Install the rubber seal (A, **Figure 13**) into the carburetor bore.
10. Install the throttle stop screw and spring (B, **Figure 12**).

NOTE

Because the throttle stop screw sets the engine's idle speed, do not turn it too far into the carburetor or it will position the throttle valve too high in the carburetor. This condition will lean the air/fuel mixture and make the engine hard to start, especially when it is cold. Position the throttle stop screw so that it just raises the throttle valve in the carburetor bore. Make any final adjustments after installing the carburetor on the bike and starting the engine.

11. Install the pilot air screw (A, **Figure 12**) and lightly seat it. Then back the screw out the number of turns recorded during removal, or set it to the number of turns listed in **Table 1**.
12. Install the carburetor as described in this chapter.

Float Height Adjustment

The needle valve and float maintain a constant fuel level in the carburetor float bowl. Because the float level affects the fuel mixture throughout the engine's operating range, this level must be adjusted to the factory specifications.

The carburetor must be removed and partially disassembled for this adjustment.

1. Remove the carburetor as described in this chapter.
2. Remove the float bowl screws, float bowl (B, **Figure 13**) and gasket.
3. Hold the carburetor so the needle valve just touches the float arm. At the same time, fully seat the needle valve into its needle valve seat. Then

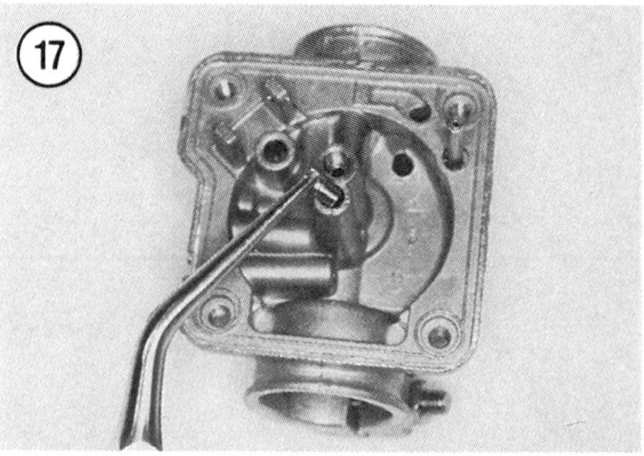

measure the float height distance from the carburetor body gasket surface to the top of the float using a ruler (**Figure 19**) or vernier caliper. See **Table 1** for the correct float height specification. If the float height is incorrect, note the following:

a. Inspect the needle valve and seat for severe wear or damage. Because the PW50 float is not adjustable, replace the float if the float height is incorrect and the needle valve and seat do not show any excessive wear or damage.

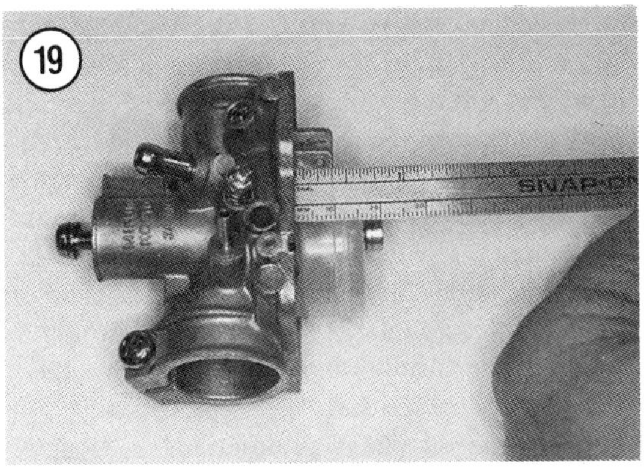

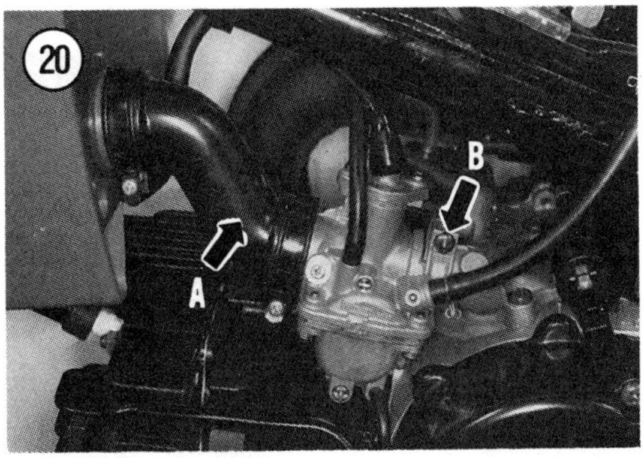

b. After installing a new float, remeasure the float height.

4. If removed, hook the needle valve onto the float, then install the needle valve into its seat (**Figure 15**). Install the float pin through the carburetor pedestal arms and float (**Figure 14**). Pivot the float up and down, making sure it moves smoothly.

5. Install the float bowl gasket, making sure all holes align. If the holes do not align, turn the gasket over.

6. Install the float bowl (B, **Figure 13**) and its mounting screws. Tighten each screw securely.

7. Install the carburetor as described in this chapter.

CARBURETOR (BW80 AND PW80)

7

See **Table 2** (BW80) or **Table 3** (PW80) for carburetor specifications.

Carburetor Removal

1. Support the bike on its sidestand.
2. Turn the fuel valve off and disconnect the fuel hose at the fuel valve or carburetor.
3. Loosen both air box hose clamps and remove the hose (A, **Figure 20**).
4. Loosen the carburetor pinch bolt (B, **Figure 20**), then slide the carburetor off the intake manifold.
5. Disconnect the oil delivery hose (A, **Figure 21**) from the carburetor as follows:

CAUTION
The metal band used to secure the oil delivery hose to the carburetor fitting is a tight fit and can be difficult to remove. When removing the metal band in the next step, work carefully so that you don't damage the band or tear the oil hose. A loose hose connection or torn hose will allow the oil pump to draw in air. This will prevent oil from reaching the engine and cause engine seizure. Replace any weak or damaged part during reassembly.

a. Loosen the metal band and slide it up the hose and off the carburetor fitting. Then disconnect the oil delivery hose from the carburetor.
b. Plug the hose to prevent oil leakage and contamination.

6. Remove the carburetor cap screws, then remove the cap (B, **Figure 21**) and pull the throttle and choke valve assemblies (**Figure 22**) from the carburetor.

NOTE
If you are not going to service the throttle or choke valve assemblies, position the cap assembly over the upper frame tube to prevent jet needle damage. Place the assemblies in a reclosable plastic bag to prevent contamination.

7. Plug the intake manifold opening to prevent dust and other debris from entering the engine.

NOTE
If there is any accumulation of dirt or other abrasive dust trapped around the intake side of the carburetor, inspect and service the air filter (Chapter Three) and its connecting hose before restarting the engine.

Carburetor Installation

1. Install the throttle valve into the carburetor housing by aligning the groove in the throttle valve (A, **Figure 23**) with the pin (B, **Figure 23**) in the carburetor housing.
2. Install the choke valve (**Figure 22**) into its carburetor bore.
3. Push the carburetor cap down and center it on its gaskets on top of the carburetor, then install and tighten its mounting screws (B, **Figure 21**) and lockwasher and tighten securely.
4. Operate the throttle lever and the choke lever a few times. Both the throttle valve and choke valve assemblies must move through their carburetor bores with no binding or roughness. If there is any binding or roughness, note the following:
   a. If the throttle valve does not move or moves roughly, check the groove and pin alignment as described in Step 1. If the alignment is good, check the throttle valve assembly (at the handlebar) and the throttle cable for incorrect assembly, routing or adjustment.
   b. If the choke valve does not move or moves roughly, check the choke valve and spring assembly. Then check the choke lever and cable for incorrect assembly, routing or adjustment.
   c. If necessary, service the throttle and choke valve assemblies as described in the following procedure.
5. If removed, install the seal band (**Figure 24**) into the carburetor or over the intake manifold.
6. Reconnect the oil delivery hose (A, **Figure 21**) onto the carburetor hose nozzle, then push the metal band over the hose nozzle to secure the hose. Replace the metal band if it is damaged or if it does not tighten the hose onto the carburetor hose nozzle.
7. Slide the carburetor over the intake manifold and turn it to align its slot with the raised boss mark on the intake manifold (A, **Figure 25**). Hold the carburetor in this position and tighten its pinch bolt (B, **Figure 20**) securely.
8. Install the air box hose onto the air box and carburetor so that the side of the hose with the raised "CARB" mark (B, **Figure 25**) is up and faces toward the carburetor. Tighten both hose clamps securely.
9. Reconnect the fuel hose onto the fuel valve or carburetor. Secure the hose with its hose clamp.
10. Check the throttle valve and choke valve operation once again (see Step 4).
11. Bleed the oil pump as described in Chapter Nine.

22

23

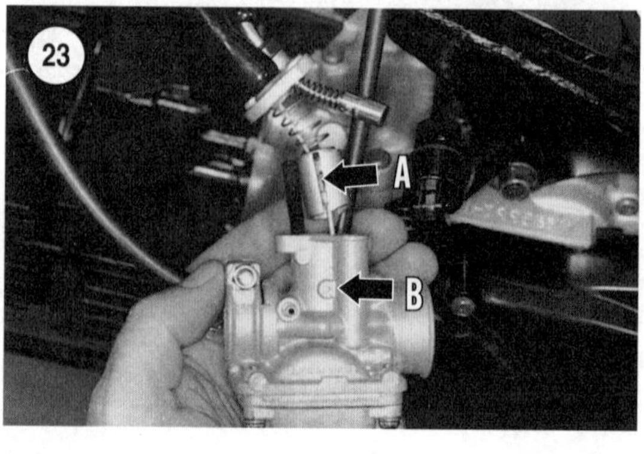

12. Turn the fuel valve on and check the hose and carburetor for leaks.

Throttle Valve/Choke Valve Removal/Installation

Refer to **Figure 26**.

1. Remove the throttle and choke valve assemblies (**Figure 22**) as described under *Carburetor Removal* in this section.
2. Remove the throttle valve (A, **Figure 27**) as follows:
   a. Compress the throttle valve spring into the cap and remove the throttle cable lock (**Figure 28**).
   b. Push down and then lift out the throttle cable.
   c. Remove the throttle valve spring.
   d. Remove the jet needle (**Figure 9**).
3. Remove the choke valve (B, **Figure 27**) by compressing the choke spring and then removing the choke valve (**Figure 29**) from the end.
4. Replace the gasket (7, **Figure 26**) if damaged.
5. Inspect the throttle valve, spring and jet needle for damage. If the throttle valve has deep score marks or is excessivley worn, dirt may be passing through the air filter.
6. Inspect the choke valve and spring for damage.
7. Install the throttle and choke valve assemblies by reversing these removal steps, noting the following:
   a. Make sure the E-clip is installed in the correct jet needle clip groove. See **Table 2** or **Table 3** for the stock clip groove positions.
   b. If a cable was removed or replaced, readjust it as described in Chapter Three.
8. Install the throttle and choke valve assembles and carburetor cap (**Figure 27**) as described under *Carburetor Installation* in this section.

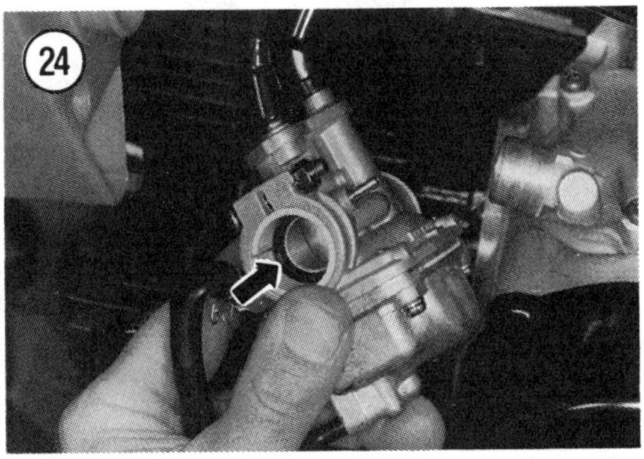

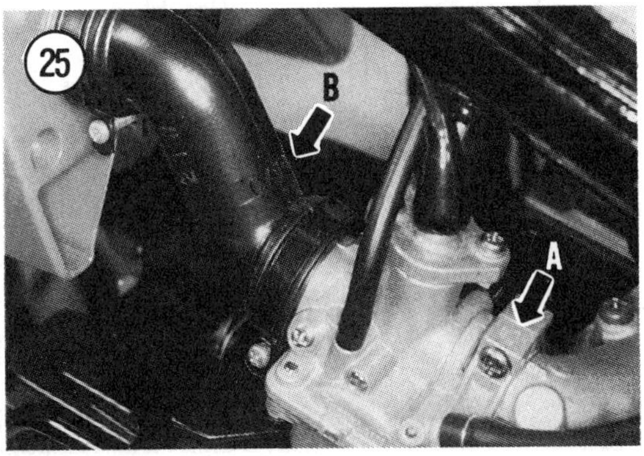

Carburetor Disassembly

Refer to **Figure 30**.

1. Remove the carburetor as described in this chapter.
2. Remove the hoses (A, **Figure 31**) connected to the carburetor and float bowl nozzles.
3. Remove the seal band and rubber seal (**Figure 32**) from the carburetor bore.
4. Lightly seat the pilot air screw (A, **Figure 33**), counting the number of turns for reassembly reference, then back the screw out and remove it and its spring from the carburetor. Remove the O-ring (4, **Figure 30**) and flat washer (5, **Figure 30**), if used.
5. Remove the throttle stop screw and spring (B, **Figure 33**). Remove the washer (8, **Figure 30**), if used.
6. Remove the float bowl screws and float bowl (B, **Figure 31**). Be careful of any gas that spills out of the float bowl.
7. Carefully remove the float bowl gasket.
8. Remove the float pin (**Figure 34**) with a pair of needlenose pliers, then remove the float and needle valve (**Figure 35**). Unhook the needle valve from the float.
9. Unscrew and remove the needle valve seat (A, **Figure 36**) and its gasket (B, **Figure 36**).
10. Unscrew and remove the main jet (**Figure 37**).
11. Unscrew and remove the needle jet (**Figure 38**).
12. Unscrew and remove the pilot jet (**Figure 39**).
13. Remove the drain screw (22, **Figure 30**) from the float bowl.

(26)

THROTTLE AND CHOKE VALVES (BW80 AND PW80)

1. Rubber boot
2. Choke cable adjuster
3. Throttle cable adjuster
4. Screw
5. Lockwasher
6. Carburetor cap
7. Gasket
8. Spring
9. Choke valve
10. Spring
11. Throttle cable lock
12. E-clip
13. Jet needle
14. Throttle valve
15. Carburetor body

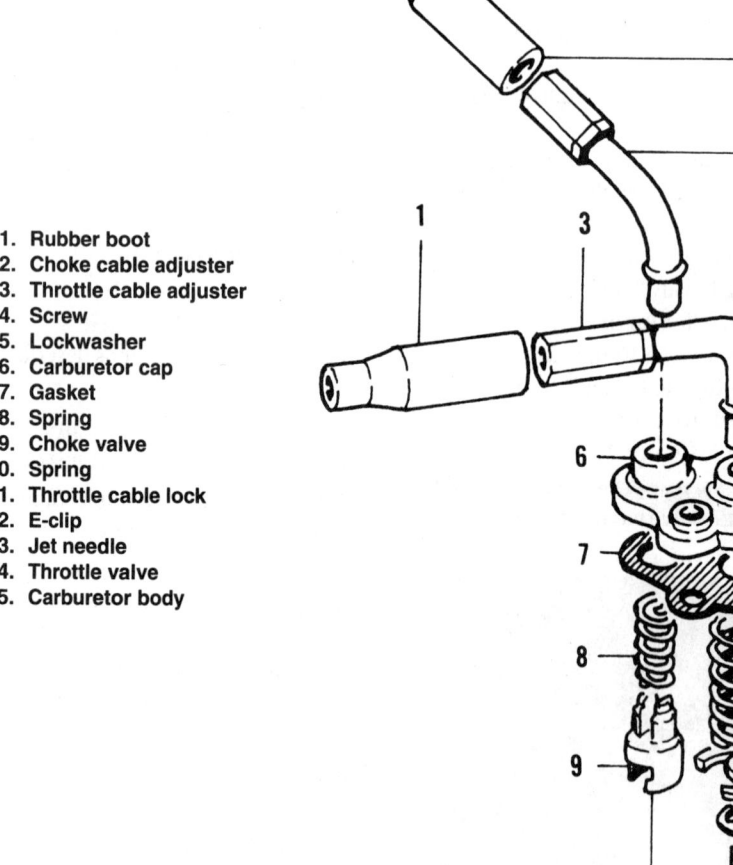

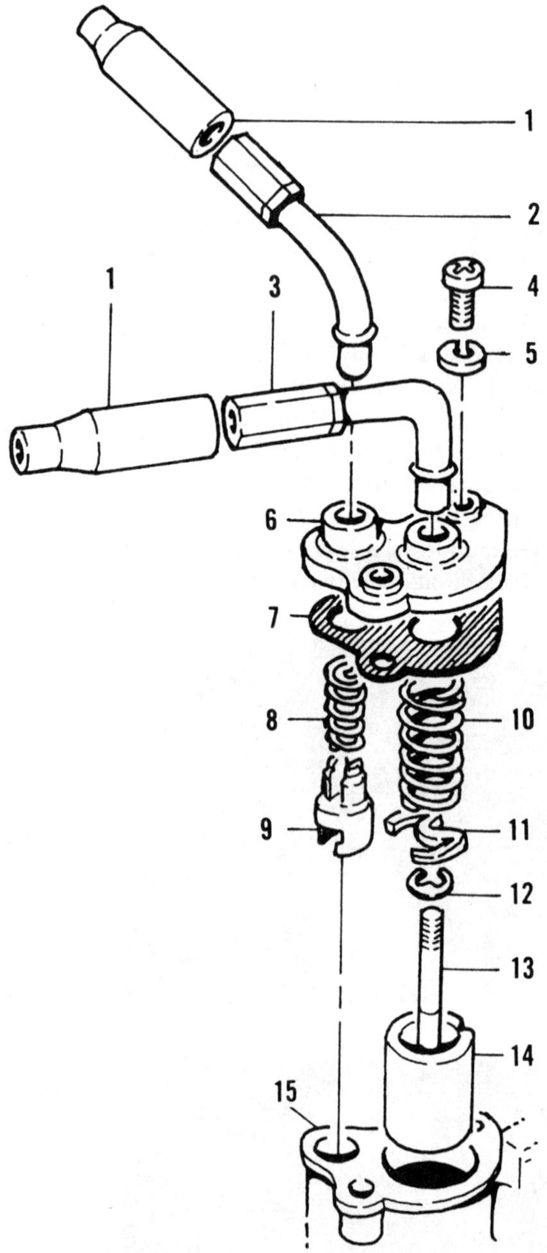

14. Clean and inspect all parts as described under *Carburetor Cleaning and Inspection (All Models)* in this chapter.

Carburetor Assembly

Refer to **Figure 30** when assembling the carburetor body.

1. Install the drain screw (22, **Figure 30**) into the float bowl and tighten securely.
2. Install and tighten the pilot jet (**Figure 39**).

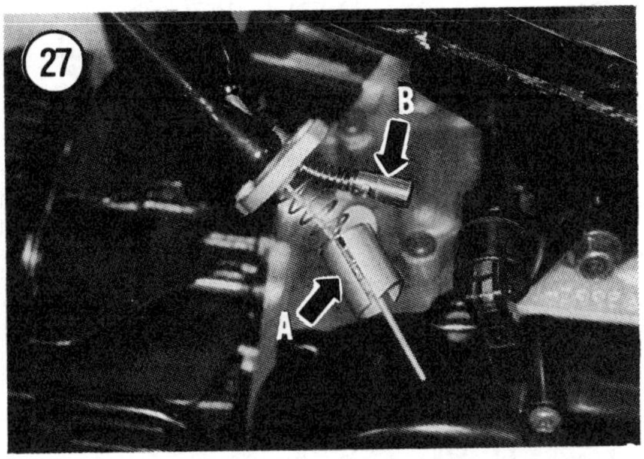

27

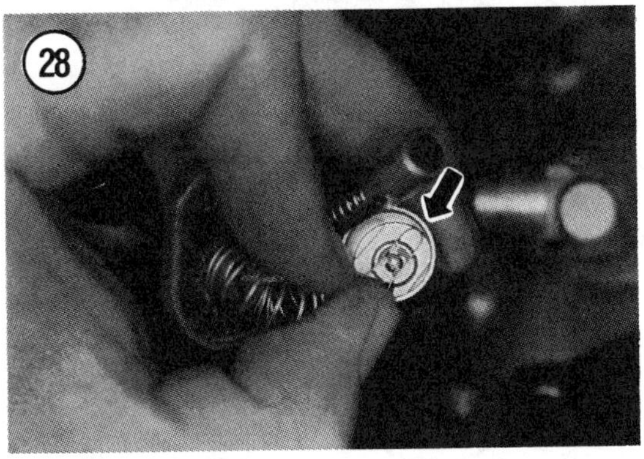
28

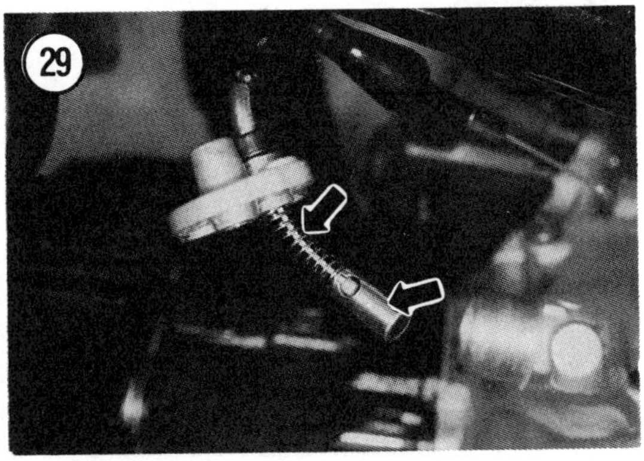
29

3. Install and tighten the needle jet (**Figure 38**)
4. Install and tighten the main jet (**Figure 37**).
5. Install the needle valve seat (A, **Figure 36**) and its gasket (B, **Figure 36**) and tighten securely.
6. Hook the needle valve onto the float (**Figure 40**), then install the needle valve into its seat (**Figure 35**). Install the float pin through the carburetor pedestal arms and float (**Figure 34**).
7. Measure the float height as described in this chapter.
8. Install the float bowl gasket, making sure all holes align. If the holes do not align, turn the gasket over.
9. Install the float bowl (B, **Figure 31**) and its mounting screws. Tighten each screw securely.
10. Install the throttle stop screw and spring (B, **Figure 33**) and washer (8, **Figure 30**) if used.

NOTE

Because the throttle stop screw sets the engine's idle speed, do not turn it too far into the carburetor or it will position the throttle valve too high in the carburetor. This condition will make the engine hard to start, especially when it is closed. Position the throttle stop screw so that it just raises the throttle valve in the carburetor bore. Final adjustment will take place after the carburetor is installed on the bike and when starting the engine.

11. Install the pilot air screw (A, **Figure 33**) assembly and lightly seat it. Then back the screw out the number of turns recorded during removal, or set it to the number of turns listed in **Table 2** and **3**.
12. Install the rubber seal and seal band (**Figure 32**) into the carburetor bore.
13. Reconnect all hoses (A, **Figure 31**) onto the carburetor body and float bowl nozzles.
14. Install the carburetor as described in this chapter.

Float Height Adjustment

The needle valve assembly and float maintain a constant fuel level in the carburetor float bowl. Because the float level affects the fuel mixture throughout the engine's operating range, this level must be adjsuted to the factory specification.

The carburetor must be removed and partially disassembled for this adjustment.

30

CARBURETOR (BW80 AND PW0)

1. Carburetor body
2. Screw
3. Nut
4. O-ring (BW80)
5. Washer (BW80)
6. Spring
7. Pilot air screw
8. Washer (BW80)
9. Spring
10. Throttle stop screw
11. Needle jet
12. Main jet
13. Needle valve seat washer
14. Needle valve and seat
15. Pilot jet
16. Floats
17. Float pin
18. Float bowl gasket
19. Float bowl
20. Lockwasher
21. Screw
22. Drain screw

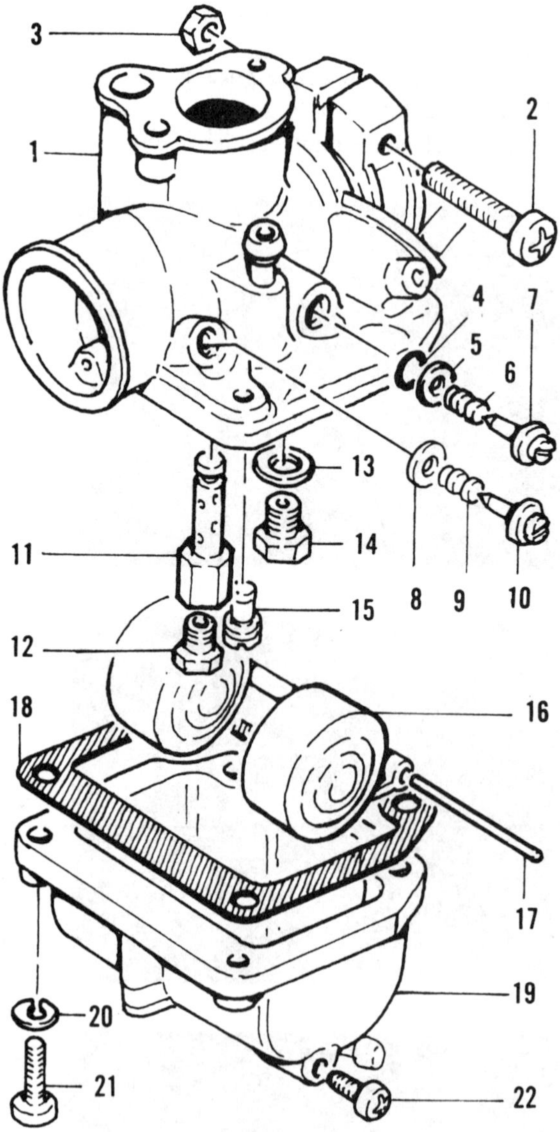

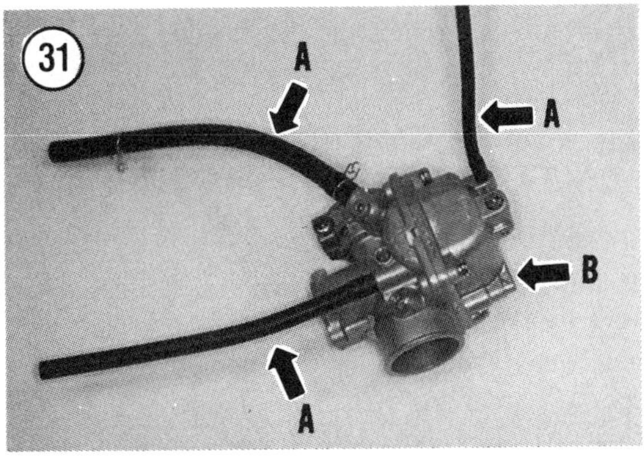

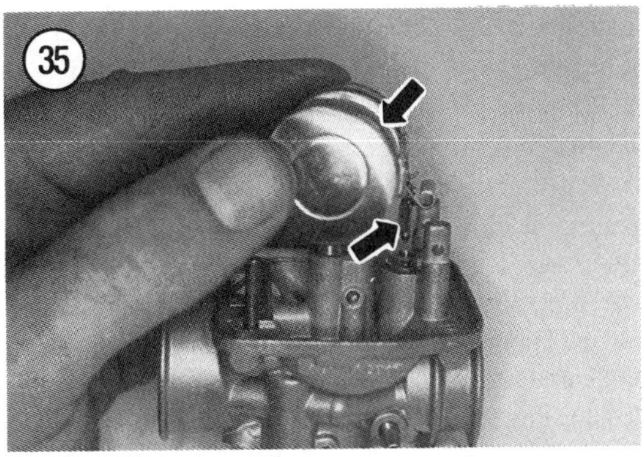

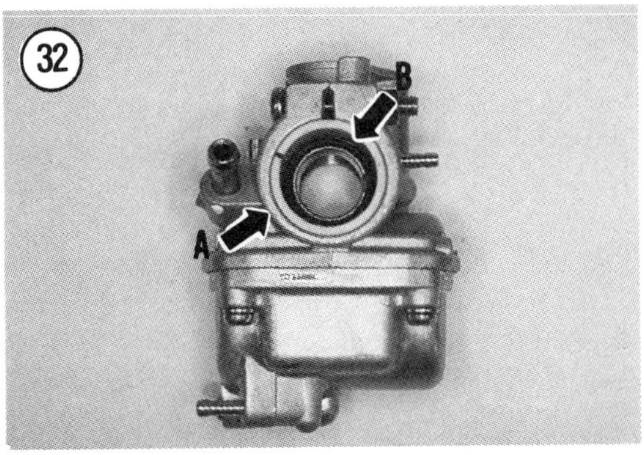

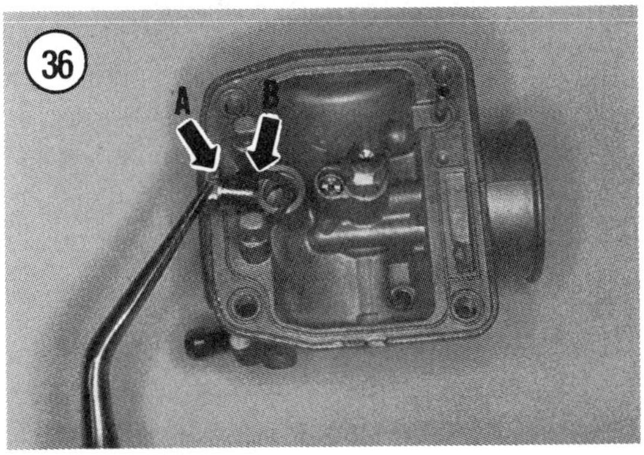

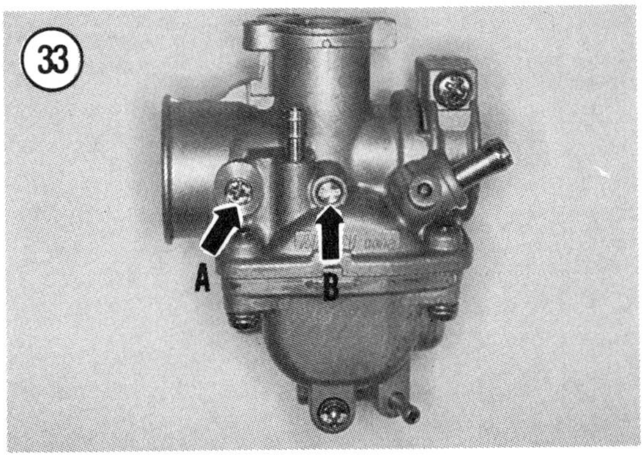

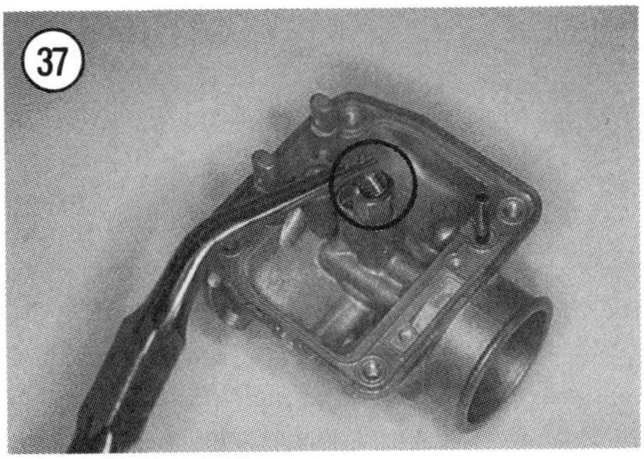

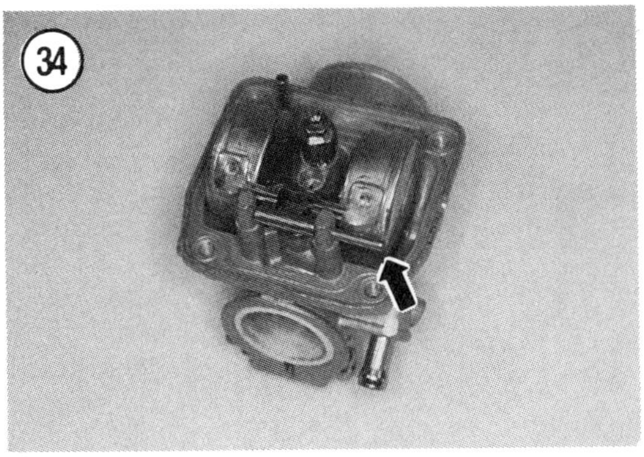

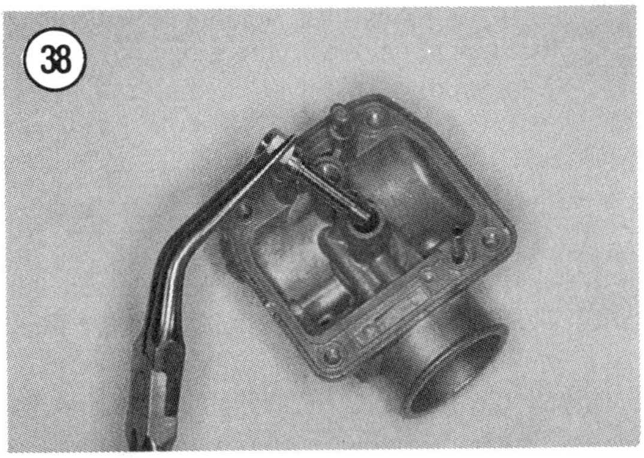

7

1. Remove the carburetor as described in this chapter.
2. Remove the float bowl screws, float bowl (B, **Figure 31**) and gasket.
3. Position the carburetor so that the needle valve is resting in its seat. At the same time make sure the float arm is resting on the needle valve without compressing the small pin in the top of the needle valve. Then measure the float height distance from the carburetor body gasket surface to the top of the float using a ruler (**Figure 41**) or vernier caliper. See **Table 2** (BW80) or **Table 3** (PW80) for the correct float height specifications. Note the following:
   a. If the float height is correct, go to Step 5.
   b. If the float height is incorrect, inspect the needle valve and seat and replace both parts as a set if there is any excessive wear or damage.
   c. If the needle valve and seat are good and the float height is incorrect, adjust the float height as described in Step 4.
4. To adjust the float height, note the following:
   a. The brass twin floats used on the BW80 and PW80 carburetors do not work independently. Raising or lowering the center float tang (**Figure 42**) adjusts the float's level in the carburetor. Do not bend the arms that extend from each float, or the floats themselves, in an attempt to adjust the float level. Doing so will make it difficult to measure and adjust the float height accurately.
   b. If the float height is incorrect, remove the float pin (**Figure 34**) with a pair of needlenose pliers, then remove the float and needle valve (**Figure 35**).
   c. Bend the center float tang with a screwdriver (**Figure 42**) to move the float up or down. Make each adjustment in small increments to avoid breaking off the center float tang.
   d. Hook the needle valve onto the float (**Figure 40**), then install the needle valve into its seat (**Figure 35**). Install the float pin through the carburetor pedestal arms and float (**Figure 34**).
   e. Remeasure the float height. Repeat these steps until the float height is correct.
5. Install the float bowl gasket, making sure all holes align. If the holes do not align, turn the gasket over.
6. Install the float bowl (B, **Figure 31**) and its mounting screws. Tighten each screw securely.
7. Install the carburetor as described in this chapter.

CARBURETOR CLEANING AND INSPECTION (ALL MODELS)

1. Initially clean all parts in a petroleum-based solvent, then clean in hot soapy water. Rinse parts with cold water and blow dry with compressed air. If a special carburetor cleaning solution is used, the float, needle valve and all gaskets and O-rings

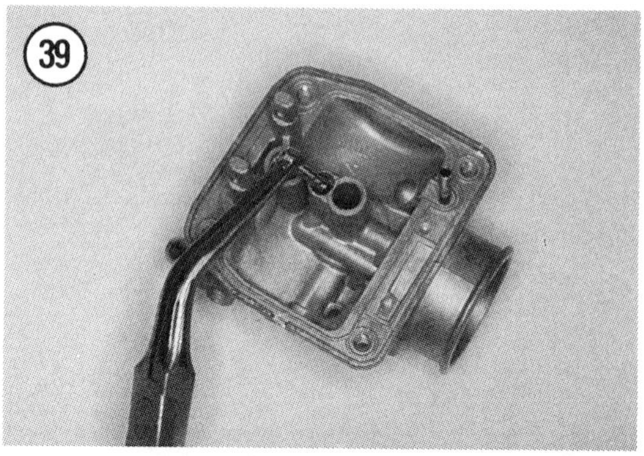

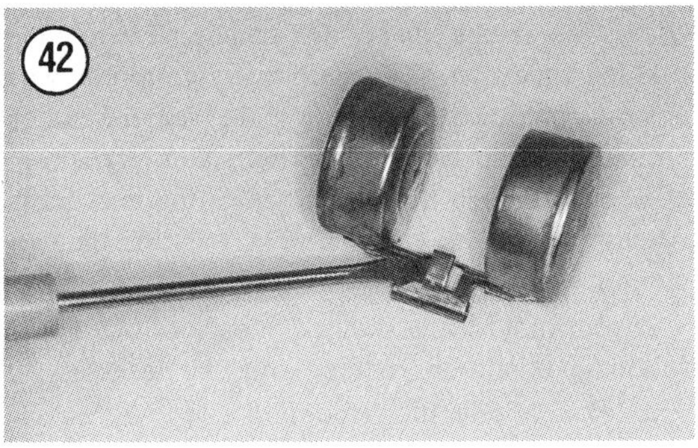
42

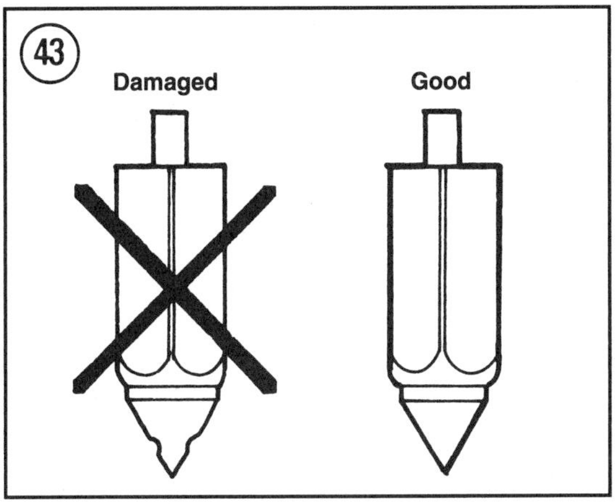

43

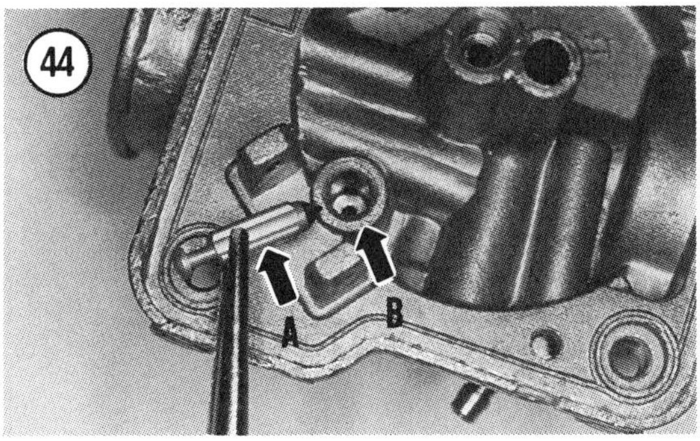

44

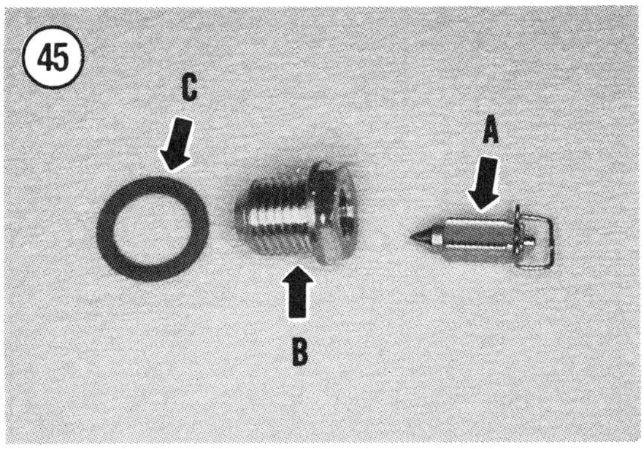

45

should be omitted from the bath and cleaned separately.

CAUTION
*Do **not** use wire or drill bits to clean jets as minor gouges in the jet can alter flow rate and change the air/fuel mixture.*

2. Clean all of the vent and overflow tubes with compressed air.
3. Replace the pilot jet if the screwdriver slot at the top of the jet is cracked or damaged. If the top of the jet breaks off while the jet is installed inside the carburetor, it may not come out.
4. Replace the float bowl gasket if leaking or damaged.
5. Inspect the needle valve assembly as follows:

NOTE
The needle valve and seat controls the flow of fuel from the fuel tank to the float bowl. The needle valve is closed by the float when there is a sufficient amount of fuel in the float bowl. A worn or damaged needle valve and/or seat, or dirt in the needle valve seat, can prevent the needle valve from closing. If this happens, the engine will operate with an excessively rich fuel mixture at all throttle openings. If the condition is severe, fuel will leak from the float bowl overflow tube when the engine is turned off with the fuel valve left on. When the engine is experiencing these types of conditions, and the float height measurement is correct, inspect the needle valve and seat for damage.

a. Check the end of the needle valve (**Figure 43**) and replace it if scored, worn or damaged. See A, **Figure 44** (PW50) or A, **Figure 45** (BW80 and PW80).
b. Inspect the needle valve seat (B, **Figure 44** or B, **Figure 45**) for steps, uneven wear or other damage. Because the needle valve seat is an integral part of the carburetor body on PW50 models, the carburetor body must be replaced if the seat is excessively worn or damaged. However, before replacing the carburetor body, install a new needle valve (A, **Figure 44**) and determine whether the condition improves or remains the same. On BW80 and PW80 models, replace the needle valve and

7

seat (**Figure 45**) as a set. On these same models, replace the washer (C, **Figure 45**) if leaking or damaged.

5. Inspect the float for deterioration or other visual damage. Check the float by submersing it in a container of water. If the float emits bubbles and takes on water, replace it.
6. Inspect the pilot air screw assembly for severe wear or damaged parts. A damaged screw tip will prevent smooth low-speed engine operation. Replace the O-ring (if used) if severely worn or damaged.
7. Inspect the choke valve assembly for wear or damage. Check the valve for deep scratches or other wear patterns. Replace the choke valve if necessary.
8. Make sure all passages and openings in the carburetor body and float bowl are clear. Clean with compressed air.

CARBURETOR REJETTING

Changes in altitude, temperature, humidity and track conditions can noticeably affect engine performance. This also includes changes that affects the engine's ability to breathe, such as jetting changes, or a different exhaust pipe and air filter. To obtain maximum performance from your Yamaha, jetting changes may be necessary. However, before you change the jetting, make sure the engine is in good running condition. For example, if your motorcycle is now running poorly during the same weather, altitude and track conditions where it once ran properly, it is unlikely the carburetor jetting is at fault. Attempting to tune the engine by rejetting the carburetor would only complicate matters.

If your motorcycle shows evidence of one of the following conditions, rejetting may be necessary:

a. Poor acceleration (too rich).
b. Excessive exhaust smoke (too rich).
c. Fouling spark plugs (too rich).
d. Engine misfires at low speeds (too rich).
e. Erratic acceleration (too lean).
f. Ping (spark knock) or rattle (too lean).

NOTE
Old gasoline or gasoline with an insufficient octane rating can also cause engine pinging or detonation.

g. Running hot (too lean).
h. The engine accelerates cleanly, but then cuts out.

Before checking the carburetor for one of the previously listed operating conditions, consider the following tuning and adjustment variables:

a. Carburetor float level—an incorrect float level will cause the engine to run rich or lean.

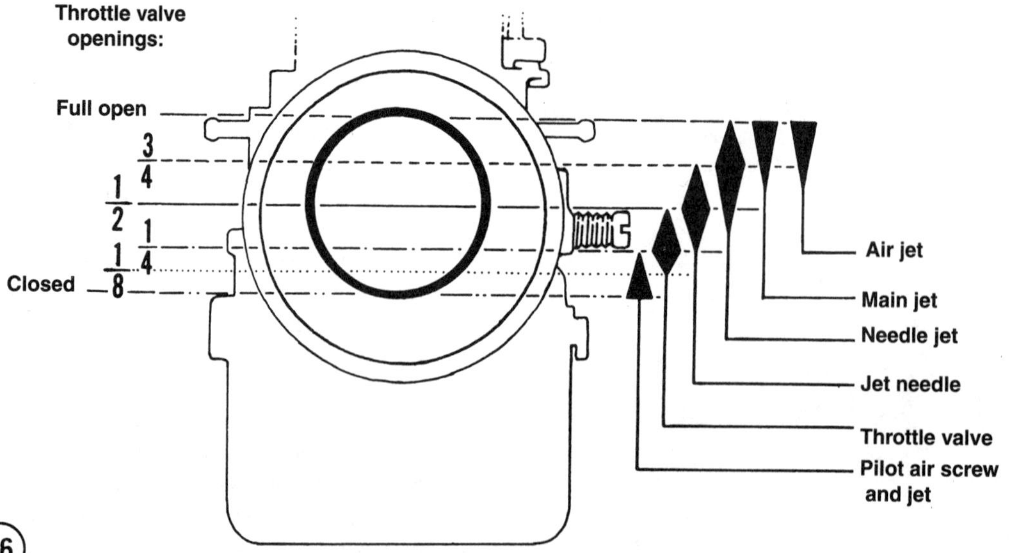

46

b. Air filter element—a dirty air filter element will cause the engine to run rich. Attempting to jet the engine with a dirty air filter element will only complicate engine tuning.
c. Ignition timing—incorrect ignition timing will decrease the engine's performance.
d. Exhaust flow—a plugged exhaust pipe silencer, or a heavily carbonized engine top end will reduce engine performance.

If the previously mentioned service items are good, the carburetor may require rejetting if any of the following conditions hold true:

a. A nonstandard air filter element is being used.
b. A nonstandard exhaust system is being used.
c. The engine was modified (piston, porting, compression ratio, etc.).
d. The motorcycle is operating in a much higher or lower altitude, or in a hotter or colder, or wetter or drier climate than in the past.
e. An aftermarket reed valve is being used.
f. A previous owner changed the jetting or the needle position in your motorcycle. See **Tables 1-3** for the stock carburetor jetting and jet needle clip specifications.

Carburetor Variables

The following carburetor parts may be changed when rejetting the carburetor. **Figure 46** shows the jetting circuits and how they relate to the different throttle valve opening positions.

47

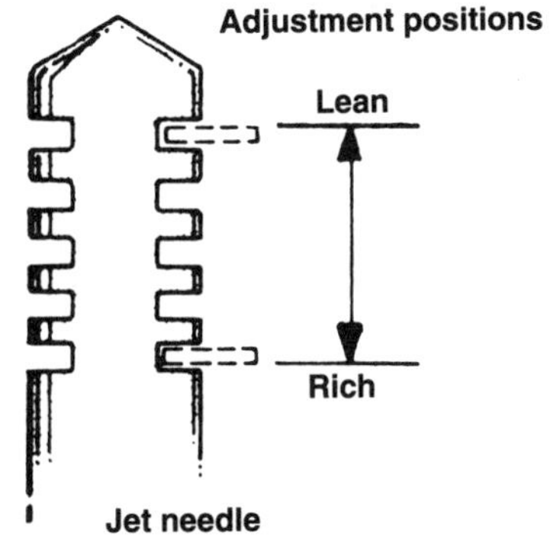

Pilot jet

The pilot jet and pilot air screw setting controls the fuel mixture from 0 to about 1/8 throttle. Note the following:

a. As the pilot jet numbers increase, the fuel mixture gets richer.
b. Turning the pilot air screw clockwise richens the mixture.
c. Turning the pilot air screw counterclockwise leans the mixture.

Throttle valve

The throttle valve cutaway affects airflow at small throttle openings. The smaller the cutaway, the richer the fuel mixture. The larger the cutaway, the leaner the fuel mixture. Mikuni throttle valves are identified by their cutaway sizes, where a larger number results in a leaner mixture. The cutaway numbers are in millimeters and are listed from 0.5 to 3.5 mm where 0.5 is rich and 3.5 is lean.

Jet needle

The jet needle controls the mixture at medium speeds, from approximately 1/8 to 3/4 throttle. The top of the needle has 5 evenly spaced clip grooves (**Figure 47**). The bottom half of the needle is tapered; this portion extends into the needle jet. While the jet needle is fixed into position by the clip, fuel cannot flow through the space between the needle jet and jet needle until the throttle valve is raised approximately 1/8 open. As the throttle valve is raised, the jet needles tapered portion moves out of the needle jet. The grooves permit adjustment of the mixture ratio. If the clip is raised (thus dropping the needle deeper into the jet), the mixture will be leaner; lowering the clip (raising the needle) will result in a rich mixture.

Needle jet

The needle jet works in conjunction with the jet needle.

On Mikuni carburetors, the letter and number stamped on the side of the needle jet indicates its inside diameter. The mixture gets richer in large steps as the letter size increases (front N through R), and in small steps within the letter range as the number increases (from 0 through 9). Some needle jets have a tab extending 2 to 8 mm into the throttle bore, indicated by /2 through /8 following the letter and number mark. This is called the primary choke, and it causes the mixture to be leaner at low speeds and richer at high speeds.

Main jet

The main jet controls the mixture from 3/4 to full throttle, and has some effect at lesser throttle openings. Each main jet is stamped with a number. Larger numbers provide a richer mixture, smaller numbers a leaner mixture.

Rejetting

CAUTION

An excessively lean mixture caused by running main jet that is too small can cause serious engine damage in a matter of seconds. When determining proper jetting, always start rich and progress toward the corrrect mixture, one step at a time. The engine must be at normal operating temperature when checking jetting. Attempting to jet an engine that is not yet at normal operating temperature, will result in an excessively lean mixture when the engine does reach operating temperature.

When jetting the carburetor, perform the procedures in Steps 1-3 to ensure accurate results. Note the following before carburetor jetting:

a. Referring to **Figure 46**, note the different jetting circuits and how they overlap each other in relation to the different throttle positions. Then determine the throttle position at which the adjustment should be made. Too often, the main jet is changed when actually the jet needle should be adjusted.
b. When checking the jetting, run the motorcycle on a track or private road where you can safely run at top speed. Keep accurate records as to weather, altitude and track conditions.
c. Check the jetting in the following order: pilot air screw, main jet and jet needle.

1. Adjust the pilot air screw and engine idle speed as described in Chapter Three.

WARNING

If you are taking spark plug readings, the engine will be HOT! Use caution and have a fire extinguisher and an assistant standing by when performing this procedure.

2. Because the main jet controls the mixture from 3/4 to full throttle, run the motorcycle at full throttle for a short distance. Stop the engine with the engine stop switch while the motorcycle is running at full throttle and coast to a stop. Remove and examine the spark plug after each test. The insulator must be a light tan color. If the insulator is soot black, the mixture is too rich; install a smaller main jet as described in this chapter. If the insulator is white, or blistered, the mixture is too lean; install a larger main jet.
3. Repeat the jetting check in Step 2 at different throttle positions. You may find that the full open throttle position is correct but that the 1/4 to 3/4 operating range is too rich or too lean. Refer to *Carburetor Variables*. If changing the jet needle clip position is necessary, refer to *Jet Needle Adjustment* in this chapter.

Main Jet Replacement

The following steps list instructions for changing the carburetor's main jet without disassembling the carburetor. When removing the carburetor in this procedure, do not remove the carburetor cap or disconnect the oil pump feed hose unless necessary. You can then remove the float bowl and service the main jet without having to perform other removal and service steps while at the same time reducing the chances of getting dirt into the carburetor. If this is the first time you have rejetted a carburetor, you may want to practice removing the carburetor while the engine is cold.

WARNING

If you are taking spark plug readings, the engine will be HOT! Use caution and have a fire extinguisher and an assistant standing by when performing this procedure.

WARNING

Some fuel will spill from the carburetor when performing this procedure. Because gasoline is extremely flammable, perform this procedure away from all open flames and sparks. Do not smoke or allow someone to smoke in the work area. Always work in a well-ventilated area. Wipe up any spills immediately.

1. Turn the engine off.
2. Turn the fuel shutoff valve to the OFF position.
3. Loosen the drain screw on the float bowl and drain the float bowl of all fuel.
4. Remove the float bowl screws and float bowl. Because the float bowl gaskets usually seat against the bottom of the carburetor body, do not remove the gasket unless its loose and starts to fall off the carburetor. If the gasket tears while removing the float bowl, install a new gasket.
5. Remove the carburetor as described under *Carburetor Removal* for your model in this chapter. Note the following:
   a. Do not disconnect the oil pump feed hose unless necessary.
   b. Do not remove the carburetor cap unless necessary.
6. Remove the main jet and replace it with a different one. Remember, change only one jet size at a time. Reinstall the float bowl and tighten its mounting screws securely.
7. Install the carburetor as described under *Carburetor Installation* for your model in this chapter. If the oil pump feed hose was disconnected, reconnect the hose and secure it with its clamp. Then after installing the carburetor, bleed the oil pump as described in Chapter Nine.

Jet Needle Adjustment

1. Remove the throttle valve and jet needle as described under *Carburetor* in this chapter.
2. Note the position of the clip. Raising the needle (lowering the clip) will enrich the mixture during mid-throttle opening, while lowering it (raising the clip) will lean the mixture. Refer to **Figure 47**.
3. See **Tables 1-3** for your model for the standard jet needle clip position.
4. Reverse these steps to install the jet needle.

FUEL TANK AND FUEL VALVE (PW50)

Refer to **Figure 48** when servicing the fuel tank and fuel valve in this section. **Table 4** lists the fuel tank capacity for the PW50 model.

Fuel Tank Removal/Installation

WARNING
Some fuel may spill from the fuel tank and carburetor when performing this procedure. Because gasoline is extremely flammable, perform this procedure away from all open flames (including pilot lights) and sparks. Do not smoke or allow anyone to smoke in the work area. Always work in a well-ventilated area. Wipe up any spills immediately.

1. Support the motorcycle on its centerstand.
2. Remove the seat (Chapter Fifteen).
3. Turn the fuel valve off and disconnect the fuel hose from the carburetor side of the fuel valve (A, **Figure 49**). Plug the end of the fuel hose. Remove the screw (B, **Figure 49**) securing the fuel valve to the frame.
4. Disconnect the rubber strap securing the rear of the tank (A, **Figure 50**) to the frame.
5. Remove the nut, bolt (B, **Figure 50**) collars and washers securing the fuel tank to the frame and remove the fuel tank.
6. Check for damaged or missing fuel tank collars and bushings. Replace parts as required.
7. Install the fuel tank by reversing these removal steps, noting the following.
8. Service the fuel valve as described later in this section.
9. Replace any damaged or leaking fuel hoses.
10. Replace any weak or damaged fuel hose clamps.
11. Secure the fuel hose to the fuel tank with its hose clamp. Check that all hose clamps (**Figure 48**) are in place.
12. After tightening the fuel valve and reconnecting the hose, turn the fuel valve on and check the hose and valve for leaks. Repair any leaks before riding the motorcycle.

(48)

FUEL TANK AND FUEL VALVE (PW50)

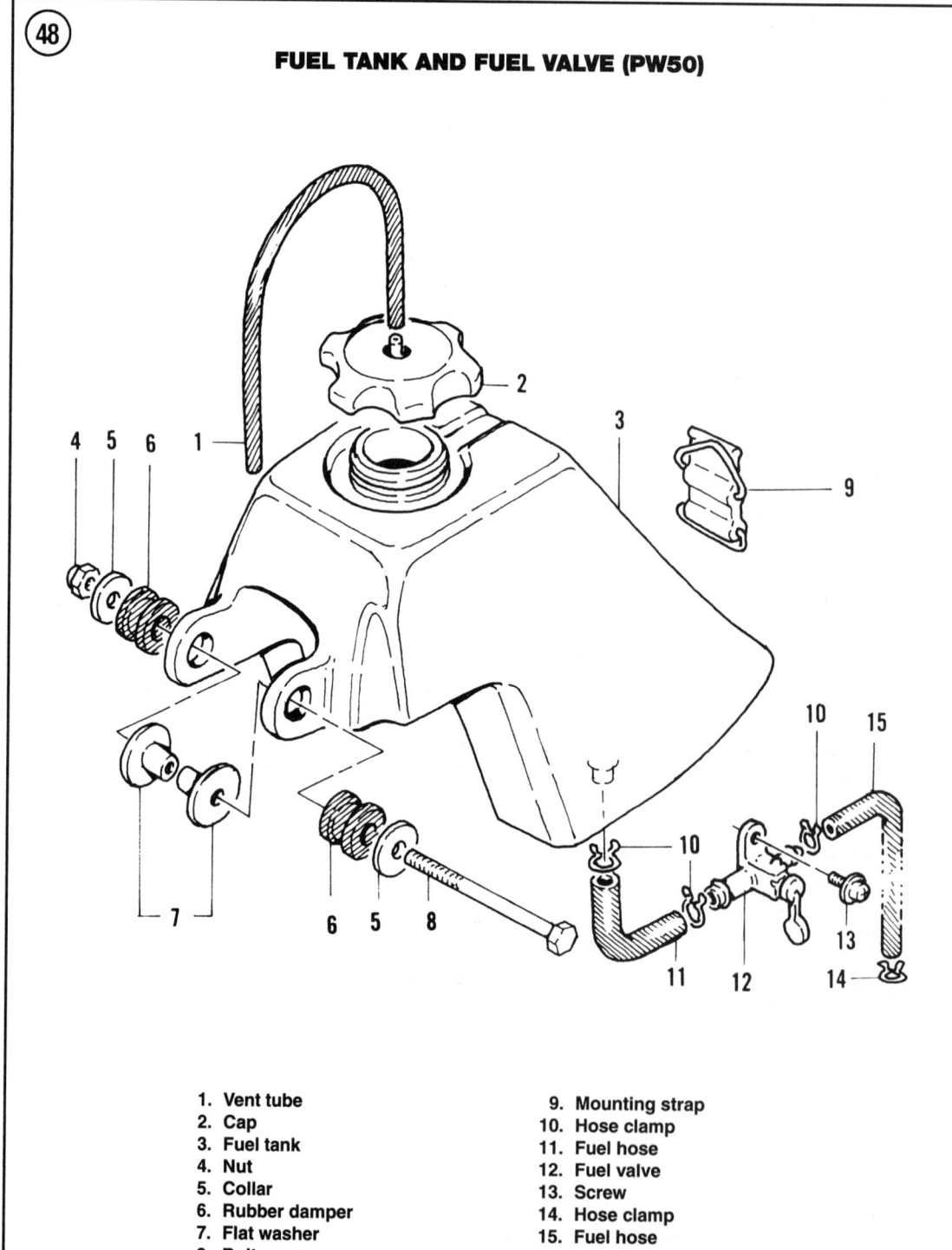

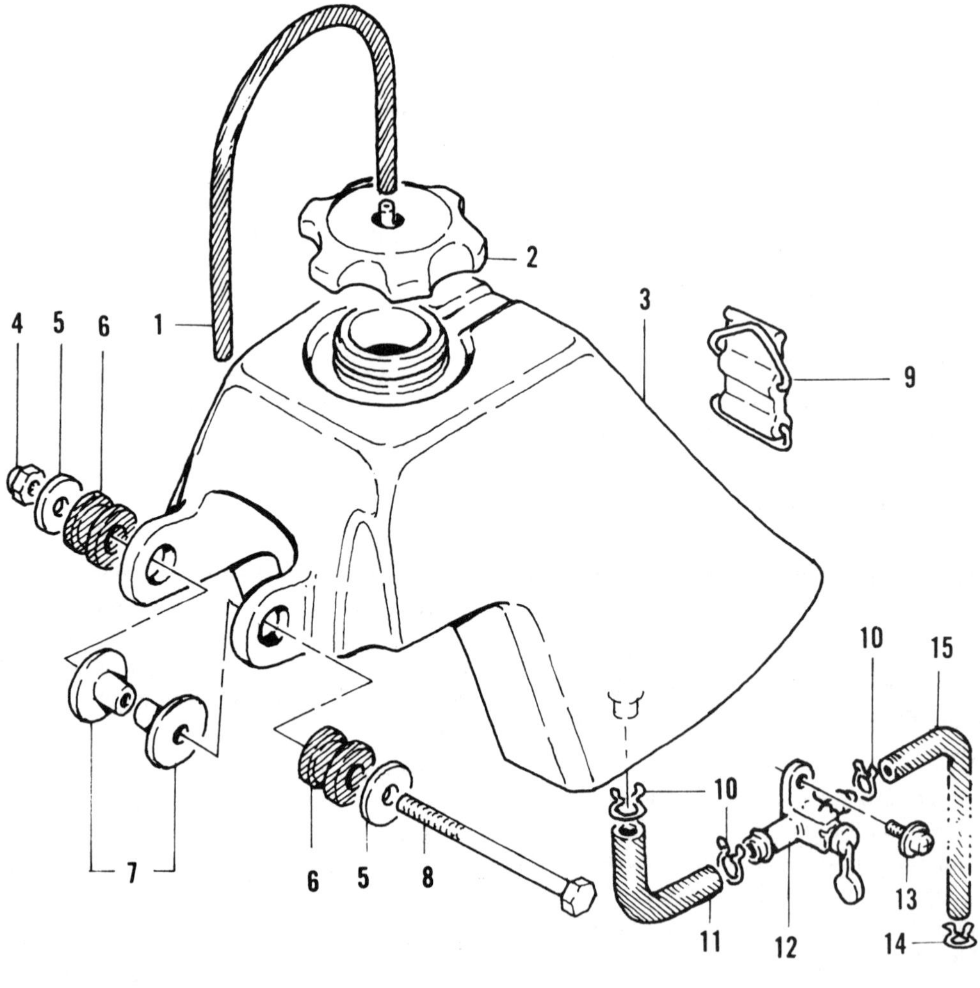

1. Vent tube
2. Cap
3. Fuel tank
4. Nut
5. Collar
6. Rubber damper
7. Flat washer
8. Bolt
9. Mounting strap
10. Hose clamp
11. Fuel hose
12. Fuel valve
13. Screw
14. Hose clamp
15. Fuel hose

Fuel Valve Removal/Installation

The PW50 model is equipped with a non-serviceable fuel valve (**Figure 51**); replacement parts are not available from Yamaha. Replace the fuel valve if it is leaking or if its passages are contaminated or plugged up.

WARNING
Some fuel may spill from the fuel tank and carburetor when performing this procedure. Because gasoline is an extremely flammable and explosive petroleum, perform this procedure away from all open flames (including pilot lights) and sparks. Do not smoke or allow someone to smoke in the work area. Always work in a well-ventilated area. Wipe up any spills immediately.

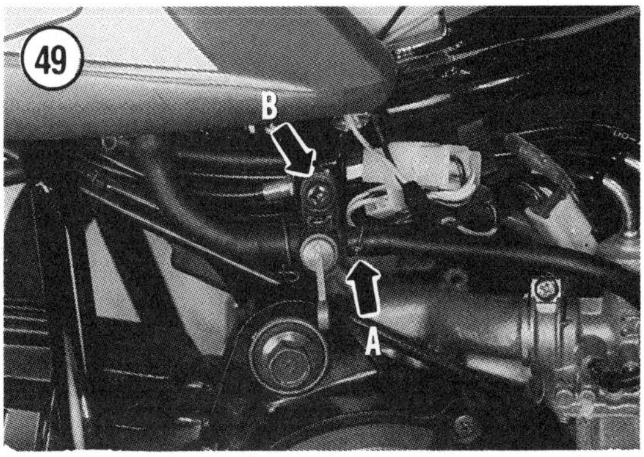

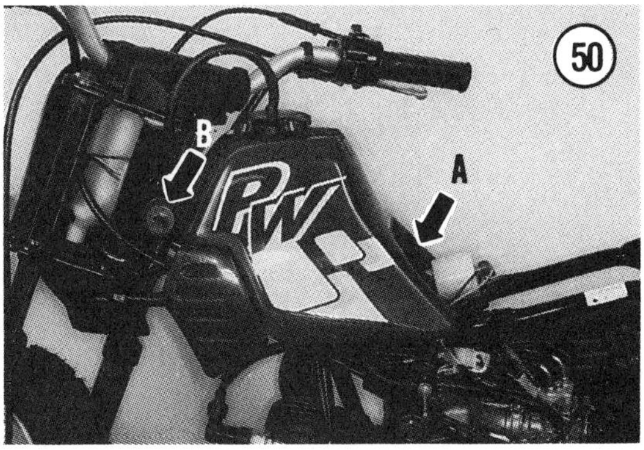

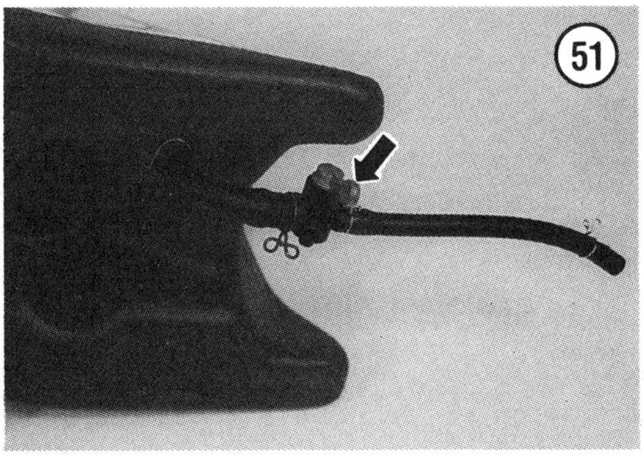

1. Turn the fuel valve off and disconnect the fuel line from the carburetor side of the fuel valve (A, **Figure 49**). Disconnect the fuel hose at the fuel valve assembly and not at the carburetor.
2. Connect a suitable piece of hose onto the fuel valve that is long enough to reach from the fuel valve to an empty gasoline storage can. Put the end of the hose into the gasoline storage can and turn the fuel valve to its ON position to drain the fuel into the can.
3. Disconnect both fuel hoses at the fuel valve and remove the valve.
4. Install a new fuel valve so that the lever side of the valve faces out as shown in **Figure 51**. Secure each hose end onto the valve fittings with a hose clamp.
5. Refill the fuel tank and check the fuel valve and hoses for leaks. Repair any leaks before riding the motorcycle.

FUEL TANK AND FUEL VALVE (BW80 AND PW80)

Refer to **Figure 52** (BW80) or **Figure 53** (PW80) when servicing the fuel tank and fuel valve in this section. **Table 4** lists fuel tank capacity for the BW80 and PW80 models.

Fuel Tank Removal/Installation

WARNING
Some fuel may spill from the fuel tank and carburetor when performing this procedure. Because gasoline is extremely flammable, perform this procedure away from all open flames (including pilot lights) and sparks. Do not smoke or allow anyone who is smoking in the work area. Always work in a well-ventilated area. Wipe up any spills immediately.

1. Support the motorcycle on its sidestand.

2. Remove the seat (Chapter Fifteen).

3. Turn the fuel valve off and disconnect the fuel hose (**Figure 54**) from the fuel valve. Plug the end of the fuel hose.

4A. On BW80 models, remove the bolt and washer securing the rear of the tank to the frame.

4B. On PW80 models, disconnect the rubber strap securing the rear of the tank to the frame.

5. Remove the front fuel tank mounting bolts and washers (**Figure 55**) and remove the fuel tank.

6. Check for damaged or missing fuel tank collars and bushings. Replace parts as required.

7. Install the fuel tank by reversing these removal steps, noting the following.

8. Service the fuel valve as described later in this section.

9. Replace any damaged or leaking fuel hoses.

10. Replace any weak or damaged fuel hose clamps.

11. Secure the fuel hose to the fuel tank with its hose clamp. Check that all hose clamps are in place.

(52)

FUEL TANK (BW80)

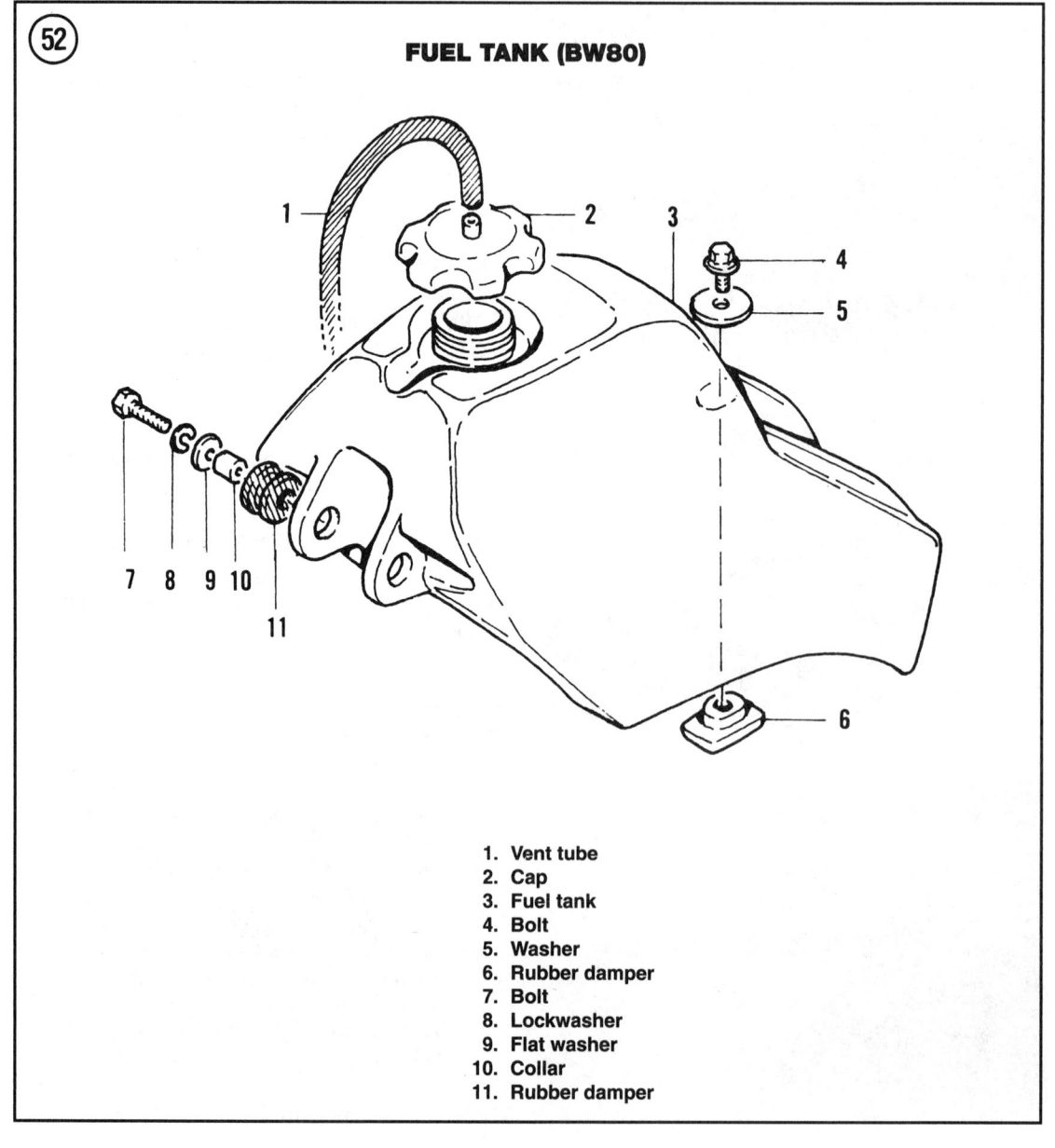

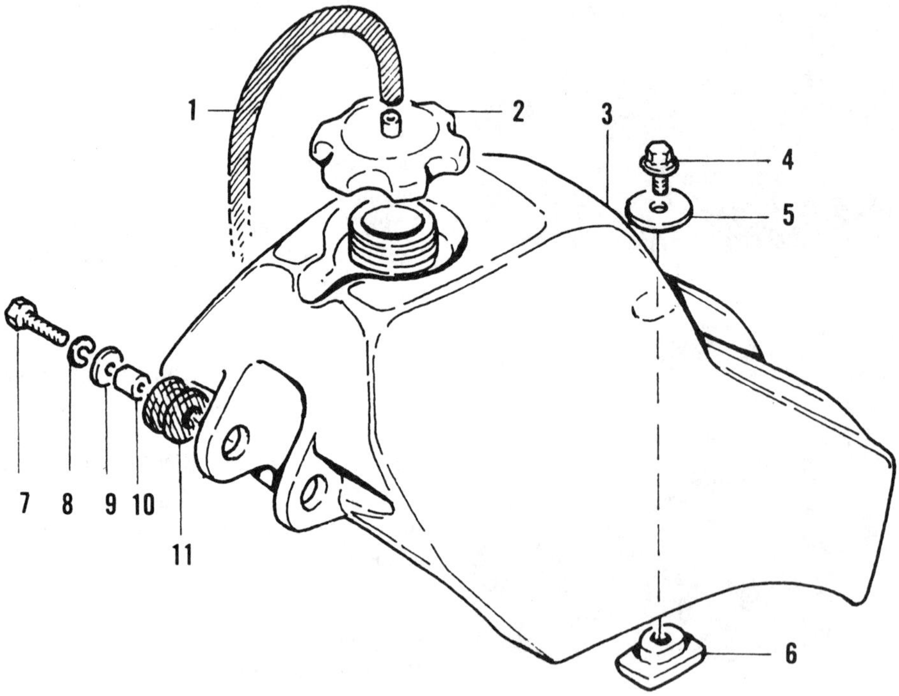

1. Vent tube
2. Cap
3. Fuel tank
4. Bolt
5. Washer
6. Rubber damper
7. Bolt
8. Lockwasher
9. Flat washer
10. Collar
11. Rubber damper

53

FUEL TANK (PW80)

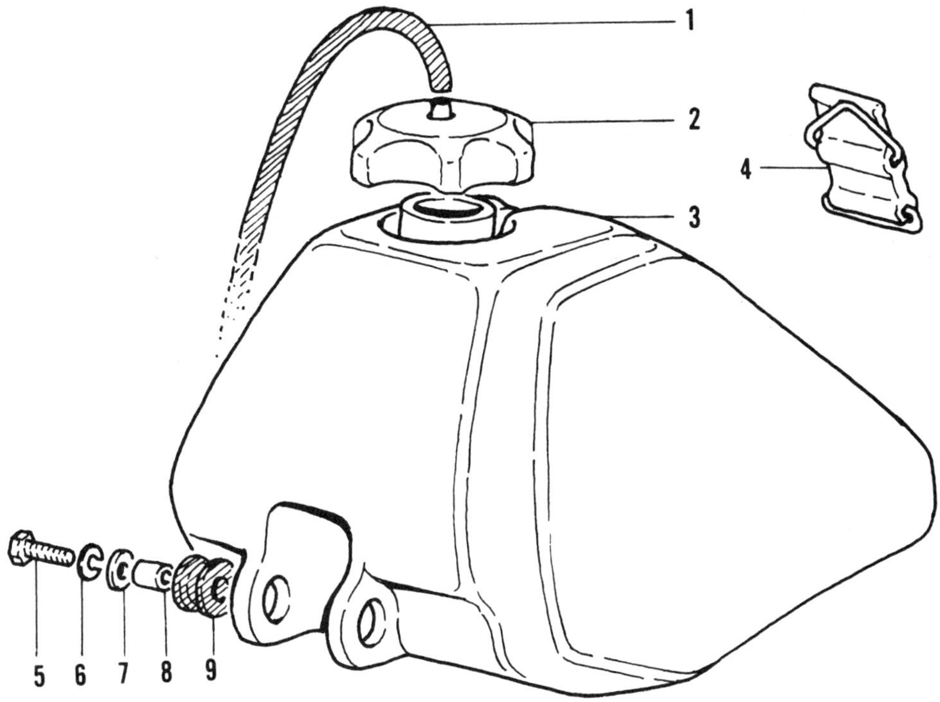

1. Vent tube
2. Cap
3. Fuel tank
4. Mounting strap
5. Bolt
6. Lockwasher
7. Flat washer
8. Collar
9. Rubber damper

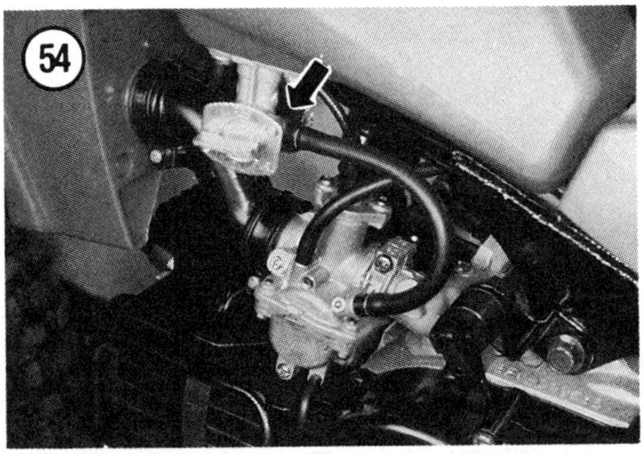

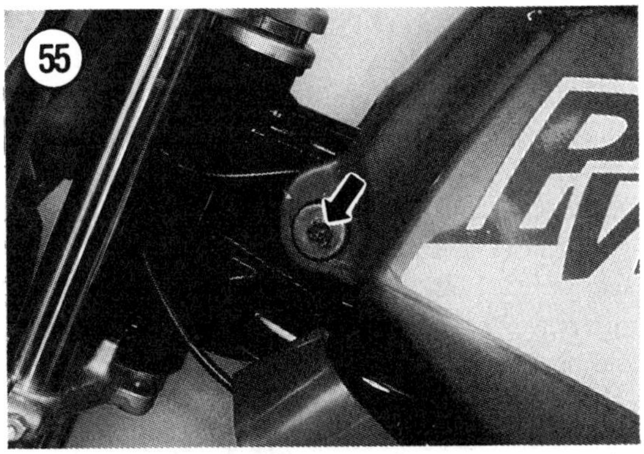

12. After reconnecting the hose, turn the fuel valve on and check the hose and valve for leaks. Repair any leaks before riding the motorcycle.

Fuel Valve Removal/Installation

Refer to **Figure 56** (BW80) or **Figure 57** (PW80) when servicing the fuel valve in this section.

WARNING

Some fuel may spill from the fuel tank and carburetor when performing this procedure. Because gasoline is extremely flammable, perform this procedure away from all open flames (including pilot lights) and sparks. Do not smoke or allow anyone to smoke in the work area. Always work in a well-ventilated area. Wipe up any spills immediately.

1. Remove the fuel tank as described in this chapter.
2. Drain the fuel into a gasoline storage can.
3. Remove the screws and washers that hold the fuel valve (**Figure 58**) to the fuel tank and remove the fuel valve. See **Figure 59**.
4. Remove the handle screws and disassemble the valve as shown in **Figure 56** or **Figure 57**. Clean all parts in solvent with a medium soft toothbrush, then dry. Check the small O-ring within the valve and the O-ring gasket; replace if they are starting to deteriorate or get hard.
5. Reassemble the valve and install it on the tank. Do not forget to install the gasket between the fuel valve and tank.

THROTTLE CABLES

On all models, the throttle cable is a subassembly consisting of 3 separate cables and a connector housing. The upper cable is connected between the throttle housing and connector housing. The 2 lower cables are connected between the connector housing and the carburetor and oil pump. Each cable is different. When you replace a cable, compare the old and new cables to make sure you have the correct cable. If you want to replace all 3 cables at the same time, you must purchase each cable separately, then

(56)

FUEL VALVE (BW80)

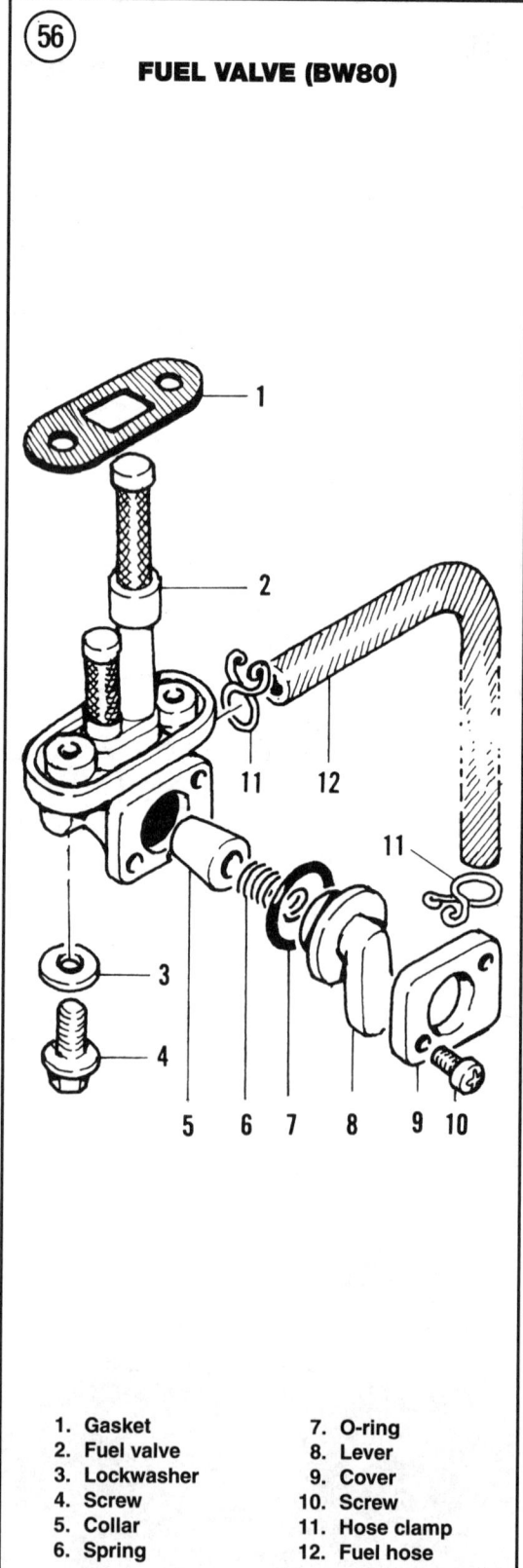

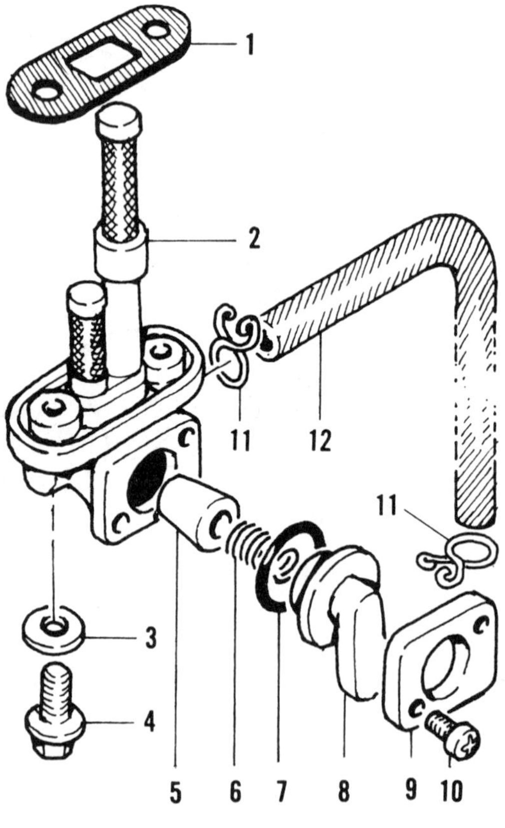

1. Gasket
2. Fuel valve
3. Lockwasher
4. Screw
5. Collar
6. Spring
7. O-ring
8. Lever
9. Cover
10. Screw
11. Hose clamp
12. Fuel hose

assemble them into the connector housing. Replace one cable at a time to avoid incorrect installation.

Cable wear and stretch will affect the operation of the throttle, oil pump and carburetor. Normal amounts of cable wear and stretch can be controlled by the adjustments described in Chapter Three. If you cannot adjust a cable within its adjustment limits as specified in Chapter Three, the cable is severely worn and requires replacement. Also, replace cables that show outer cable damage.

Replacement

1. Support the bike on its centerstand or sidestand.
2. Remove the fuel tank as described in this chapter.
3. Disconnect the throttle cable from the throttle lever as follows:
   a. Remove the screws holding the throttle housing together, then separate the housing halves. See **Figure 60** (PW50) or **Figure 61** (BW80 and PW80).

(57)

FUEL VALVE (PW80)

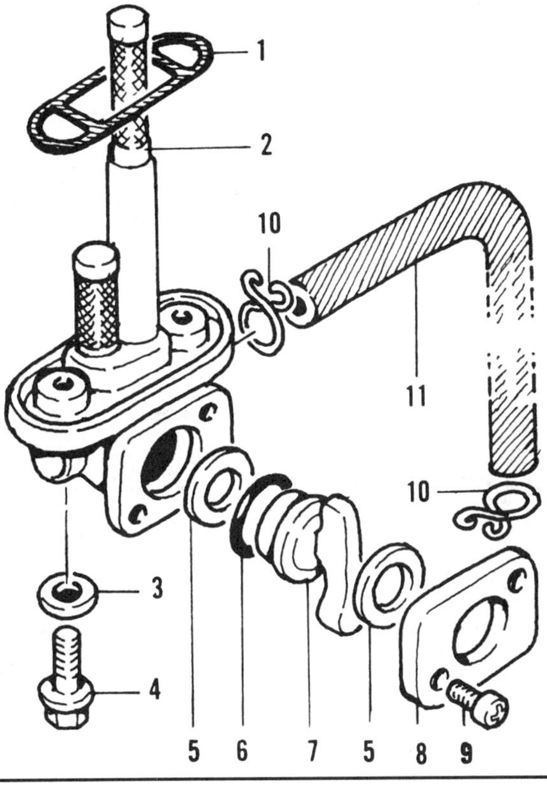

1. Gasket
2. Fuel valve
3. Lockwasher
4. Screw
5. Wave washer
6. O-ring
7. Lever
8. Cover
9. Screw
10. Hose clamp
11. Fuel hose

(58)

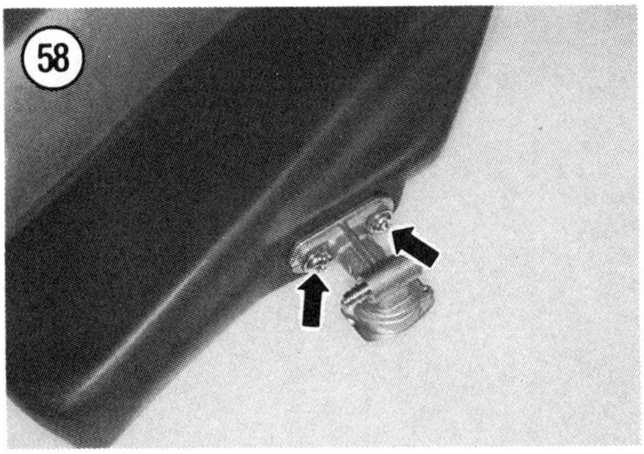

(59)

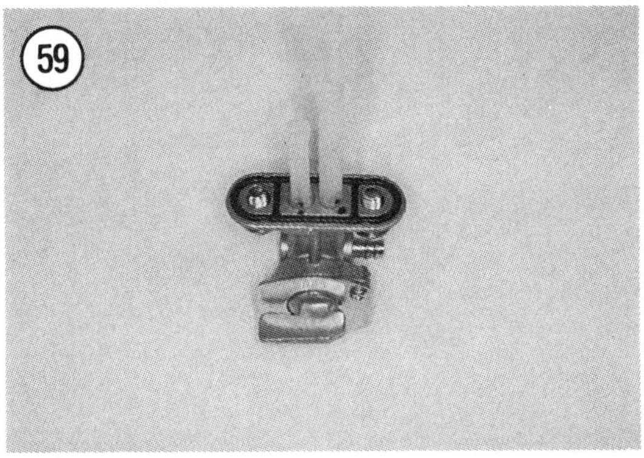

b. Disconnect the upper throttle cable from the throttle tube and remove it from the upper throttle housing half. See **Figure 62** (PW50) or **Figure 63** (BW80 and PW80).

4. Disconnect the lower throttle cable from the carburetor as described under *Carburetor* in this chapter. See **Figure 64** (PW50) or **Figure 65** (BW80 and PW80).

5. Disconnect the second lower throttle cable from the oil pump as described in Chapter Nine. See **Figure 66** (PW50) or **Figure 67** (BW80 and PW80).

6A. On PW50 models, disconnect the cable(s) from the connector housing (**Figure 68**).

6B. On BW80 and PW80 models, perform the following:

a. Remove the connecting housing cover screws and cover.
b. Disconnect the cable(s) from the connector housing (**Figure 69**).

7. Disconnect the cable(s) from any clips holding the cable(s) to the frame.

8. Make a drawing of the cable(s) routing path through the frame, then remove the cable(s).

60

61
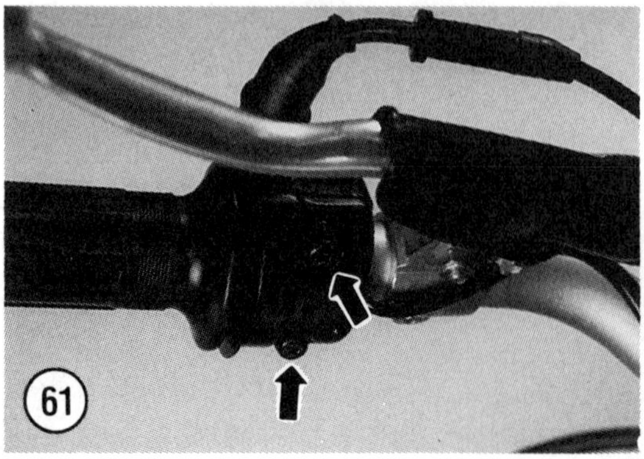

62
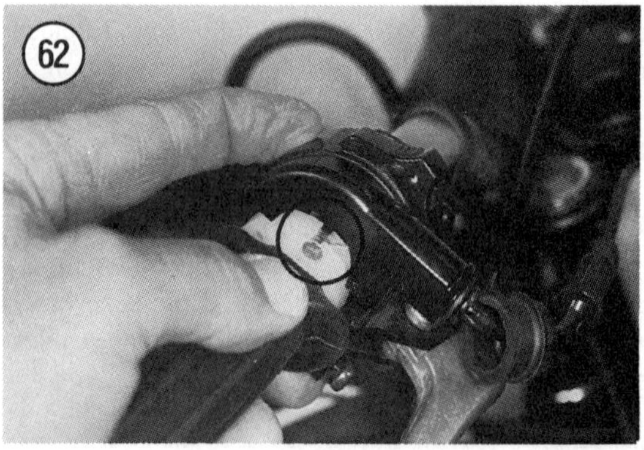

63
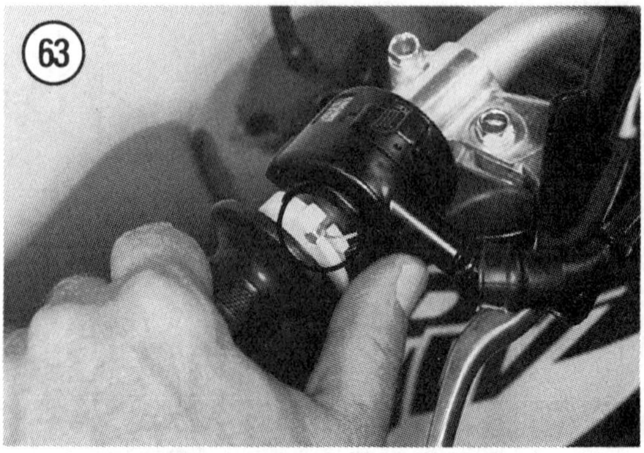

64
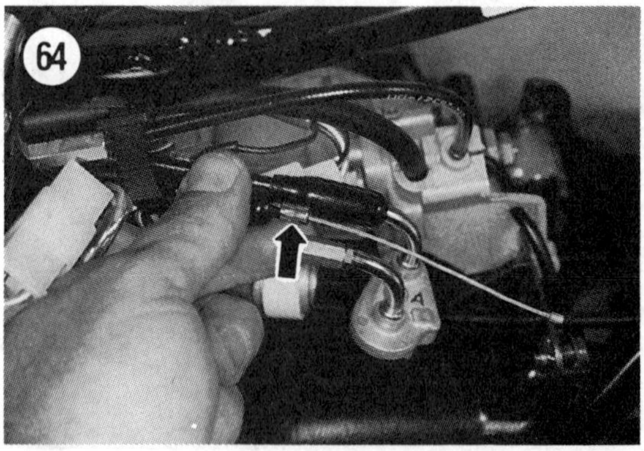

65
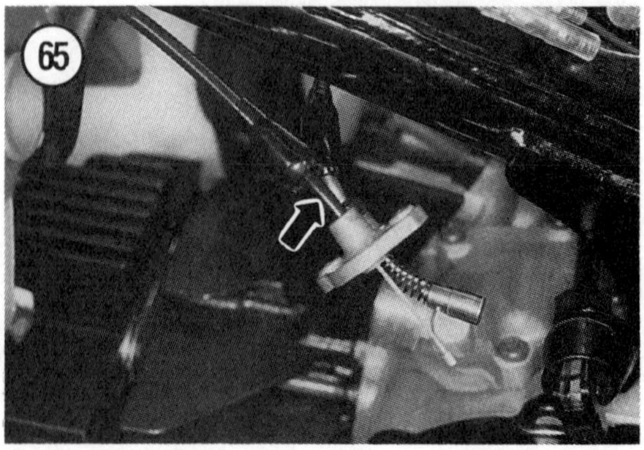

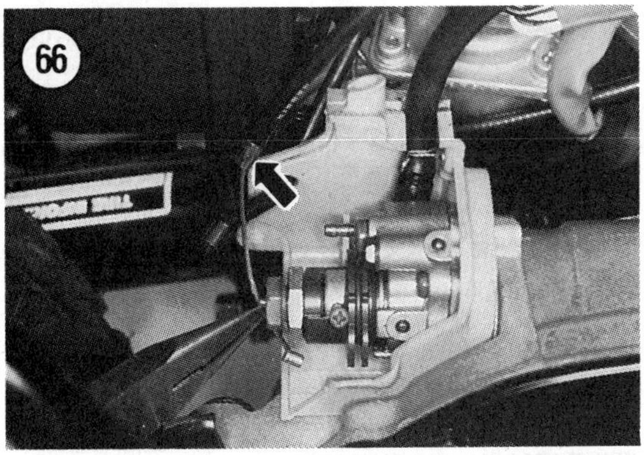
66

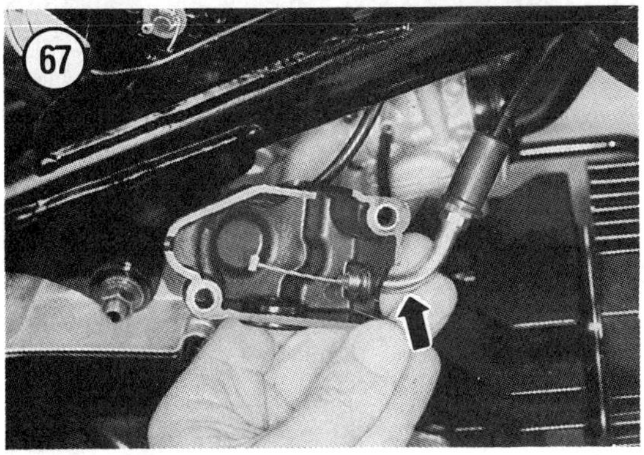
67

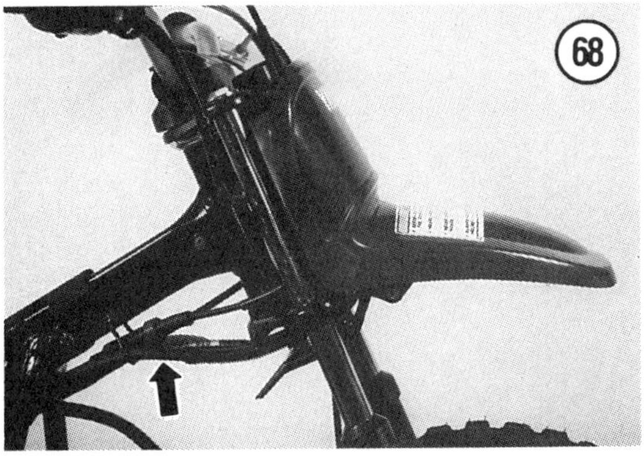
68

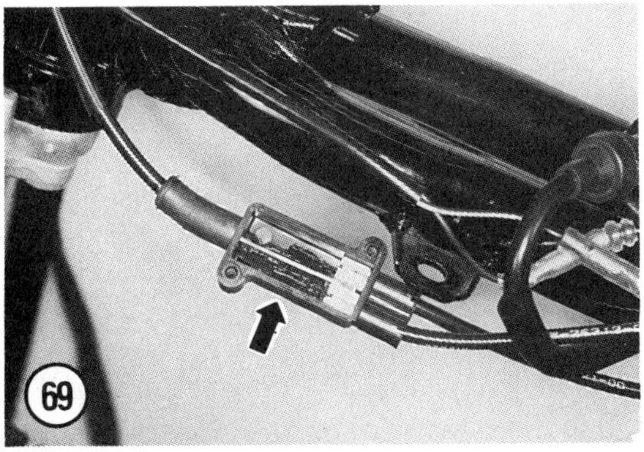
69

9. Lubricate the new throttle cable(s) as described in Chapter Three.
10. Install the new cable(s) by reversing these removal steps, noting the following:
11. Adjust the throttle cable as described in Chapter Three.

NOTE
The throttle cable adjustment described in Chapter Three adjusts the upper throttle cable and the lower cable that attaches to the carburetor. The oil pump cable is then adjusted separately.

12. Adjust the oil pump cable as described in Chapter Three.
13. Operate the throttle lever to make sure the cable is installed and routed properly. If operation is rough or if there is any binding, recheck the throttle cable installation and routing path.

CHOKE CABLE

The choke cable connects the choke lever to the choke valve installed inside the carburetor.

Removal/Installation

1. Support the bike on its centerstand or sidestand.
2. Remove the fuel tank as described in this chapter.
3A. On PW50 models, perform the following:
   a. Remove the front fender (Chapter Fifteen).
   b. Loosen the choke cable hex nut (**Figure 70**) and disconnect the cable from its mounting position on the upper steering stem.
   c. Disconnect the choke cable from the carburetor as described under *Carburetor* in this chapter. See **Figure 71**.

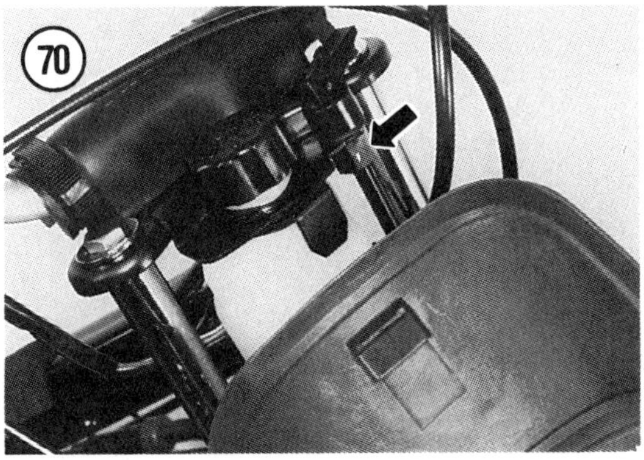
70

3B. On BW80 and PW80 models, perform the following:

a. Loosen the choke cable hex nut (A, **Figure 72**) and disconnect the cable from its mounting position on the frame.
b. Disconnect the choke cable from the carburetor as described under *Carburetor* in this chapter. See B, **Figure 72**.

4. Disconnect the cable from any clips holding the cable to the frame.

5. Make a drawing of the cable routing path through the frame, then remove the cable.

6. Lubricate the new choke cable as described in Chapter Three.

7. Install the new choke cable by reversing these removal steps, noting the following:

8. Adjust the choke cable as described in Chapter Three.

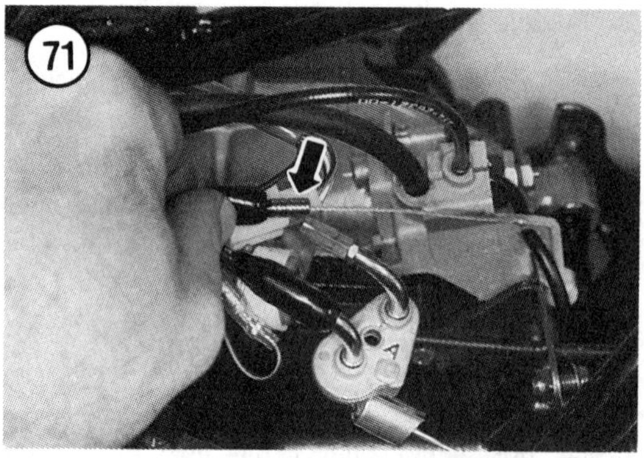

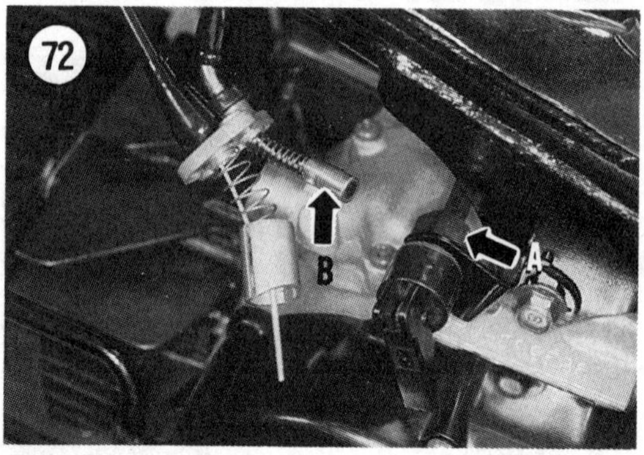

Table 1 CARBURETOR SPECIFICATIONS (PW50)

Type	Mikuni VM12Sc
Identification mark	4X400
Main jet	70
Pilot jet	40
Needle jet	E-2
Jet needle	3X1
Clip position	2
Throttle valve cutaway	4.0
Air screw setting (turns out)	1 3/8
Air jet	2.5
Pilot outlet size	0.9
Valve seat size	1.2
Starter jet	30
Float height	15.5-17.5 mm (0.61-0.69 in.)

Table 2 CARBURETOR SPECIFICATIONS (BW80)

Type	Mikuni VM15
Identification mark	1RY00
Main jet	82.5
Pilot jet	20
Needle jet	D-8
Jet needle	3X8
Clip position	4
Throttle valve cutaway	3.0
Air screw setting (turns out)	1 1/4
Air jet	2.5
Valve seat size	1.2
Starter jet	30
Float height	22.5-23.5 mm (0.89-0.93 in.)

Table 3 CARBURETOR SPECIFICATIONS (PW80)

Type	Mikuni VM15Sc
Identification mark	21W00
Main jet	125
Pilot jet	15
Needle jet	E-4
Jet needle	3E3
Clip position	3
Throttle valve cutaway	2.5
Air screw setting (turns out)	1 1/2
Air jet	2.5
Pilot outlet size	0.9
Valve seat size	1.2
Starter jet	30
Float height	20.8-22.8 mm (0.82-0.90 in.)

Table 4 FUEL TANK CAPACITY

	U.S. gal.	Liters	Imp. gal.
Full			
PW50	0.53	2.0	0.44
BW80	1.06	4.0	0.88
PW80	1.29	4.9	1.08
Reserve			
PW50	Not specified		
BW80	0.11	0.4	0.09
PW80	0.26	1.0	0.22

7

CHAPTER EIGHT

ELECTRICAL SYSTEM

This chapter describes service procedures for the ignition system.

Electrical system service specifications are found in **Table 1**. Tightening torques are listed in **Table 2**. Both tables are listed at the end of the chapter.

COMPONENT TESTING

An ohmmeter (described in Chapter One) must be used for accurate testing of the ignition coil, stator plate coils, switches and wiring.

Resistance Testing

1. Make sure the test leads are connected properly. **Table 1** lists the wire connections for each test.
2. Make all ohmmeter readings when the engine is cold (68° F[20° C]). Readings taken on a hot engine will show increased resistance and may lead you to replace parts that are not faulty without solving the basic problem.

NOTE

With the exception of certain semiconductors, the resistance of a conductor increases as its temperature increases. In general, the resistance of a conductor increases 10 ohms per each degree of temperature increase. The opposite is true if the temperature drops. To ensure accurate testing, Yamaha performs their tests at a controlled temperature of 68° F(20° C) and base their specifications on tests performed at this temperature.

3. When using an analog ohmmeter and switching between ohmmeter scales, always cross the test leads and zero the needle to ensure a correct reading.

CAPACITOR DISCHARGE IGNITION

All models are equipped with a capacitor discharge ignition (CDI) system. This system consists of the magneto assembly, CDI unit, ignition coil and engine stop switch; see the wiring diagram for your model at the end of this manual. The magneto assembly consists of the flywheel and stator plate. The flywheel is equipped with magnets and is mounted on the crankshaft. The stator plate is mounted onto the engine. The flywheel and magnets revolve around the stator assembly.

Alternating current from the magneto is rectified and used to charge the capacitor. As the piston approaches the firing position, a pulse from the pulser coil is rectified, shaped, and then used to trigger the silicone controlled rectifier. This in turn allows the capacitor to discharge quickly into the primary side of the high-voltage ignition coil where it is increased, or stepped up, to a high enough voltage to jump the gap between the spark plug electrodes.

CDI Cautions

Certain measures must be taken to protect the CDI unit when serving and troubleshooting the ignition system.

1. Keep all connections between the various units clean and tight. Be sure that the wiring connectors are pushed together firmly (**Figure 1**). Check the connectors for loose, corroded or damaged pins (**Figure 2**).
2. Never disconnect any of the electrical connections while the engine is running.
3. When kicking the engine over with the spark plug removed, make sure the spark plug is installed in its plug cap and grounded against the cylinder head (**Figure 3**). If not, excessive resistance may damage the CDI unit.
4. The CDI unit is mounted on a rubber vibration isolator or on rubber dampers. Make sure that the CDI unit is mounted correctly.

FLYWHEEL

The flywheel is mounted on the end of the crankshaft. See **Figure 4** (PW50) or **Figure 5** (BW80 and PW80).

Use one of the following pullers to remove the flywheel:

a. Yamaha flywheel puller part No. YU-01235.

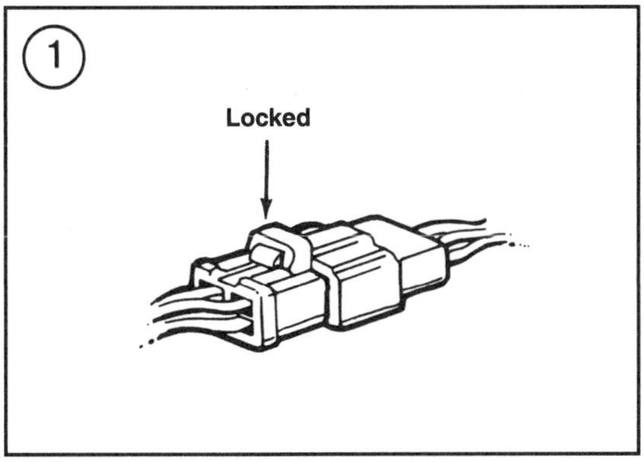

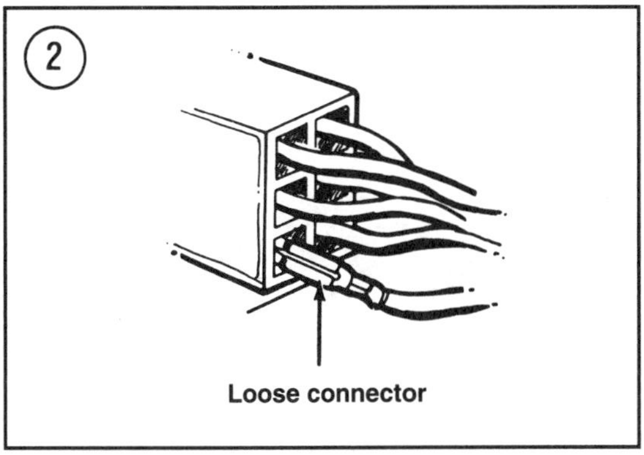

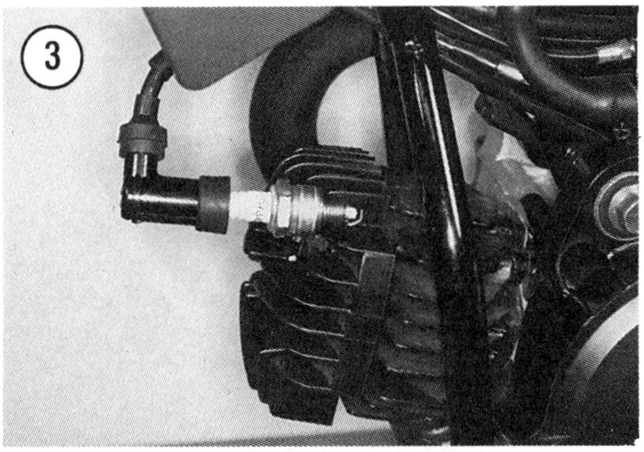

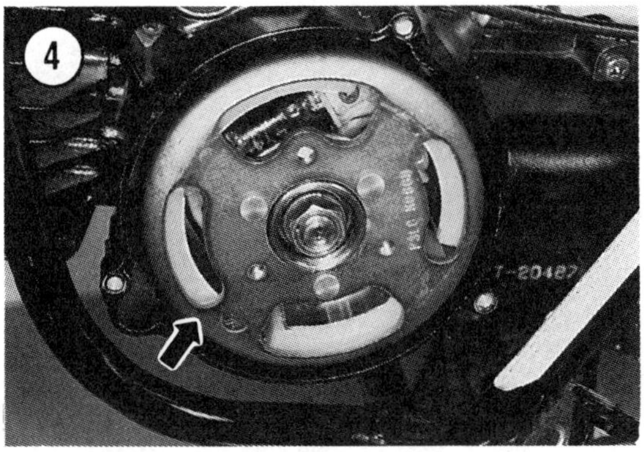

b. Motion Pro flywheel puller part No. 08-026 (**Figure 6**).
c. K&N flywheel puller part No. 82-0150.

Removal/Installation

Handle the flywheel carefully when removing and installing it in this procedure. A flywheel can lose magnetism from a sharp blow when dropped on a hard surface.

1. Support the bike on its side or centerstand.
2A. On PW50 models, remove the left side cover (**Figure 7**).
2B. On BW80 and PW80 models, remove the shift pedal and the left side cover (**Figure 8**).
3. Secure the flywheel with a holding tool (A, **Figure 9**) and loosen the flywheel nut (B, **Figure 9**). On PW50 models, remove the nut, lockwasher and flat washer. On BW80 and PW80 models, remove the nut, flat washer (if equipped) and lockwasher.

CAUTION
Flywheel removal requires a puller that threads into the face of the flywheel. Do not pry or hammer on the flywheel or try to remove it with a different type of puller. Damage will result, and you may destroy the flywheel's magnetism or damage the coils mounted on the stator plate. Use the proper type of puller described.

4. Apply a dab of grease onto the flywheel puller's pressure bolt where it will contact the crankshaft. Then thread the flywheel puller (**Figure 10**) into the flywheel. Screw the flywheel puller into the flywheel threads until it stops, then back out 1/2 turn.

CAUTION
Do not apply excessive force to the puller when removing the flywheel. Doing so can cause the puller to strip the threads in the flywheel or damage the end of the crankshaft. If necessary, take the engine to a dealership and have them remove the flywheel.

5. Hold the flywheel puller and turn its pressure bolt (**Figure 11**) clockwise. When tightening the pressure bolt against the crankshaft, check the puller body to make sure that it has not started to pull out of the flywheel threads. Continue until the flywheel pops free.
6. Remove the flywheel and puller. Do not loosen the Woodruff key (A, **Figure 12**) on the crankshaft.

CAUTION
*Inspect the inside of the flywheel (**Figure 12**) for small bolts, washers or other metal particles that may be picked up by the magnets. These small metal bits can damage the stator plate coils.*

7. Install the flywheel by reversing these removal steps, while noting the following.

6

7

8
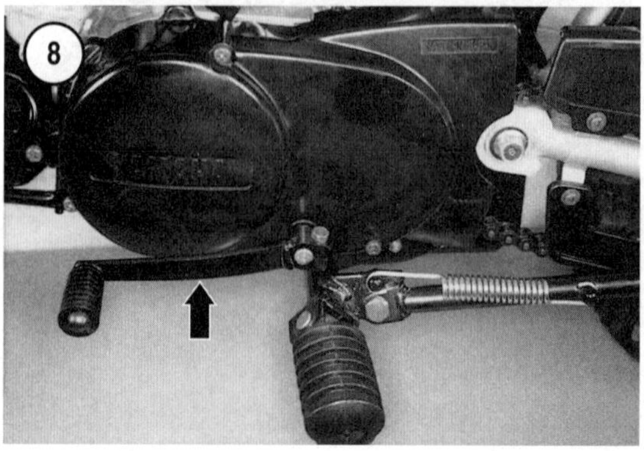

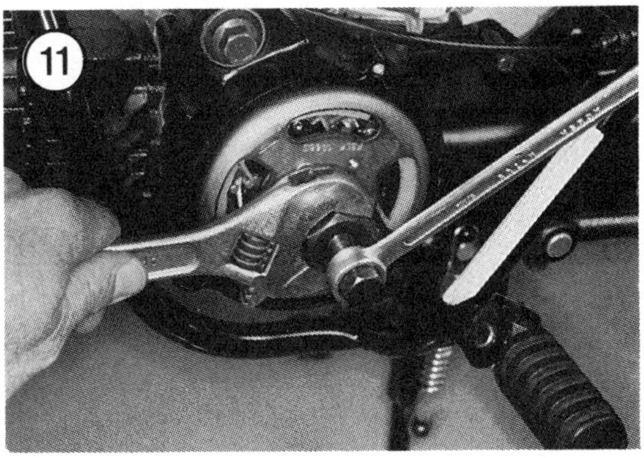

8. Make sure the Woodruff key (A, **Figure 12**) is in place on the crankshaft, then align the keyway in the flywheel (B, **Figure 12**) with the Woodruff key and install the flywheel.

9. Hold the flywheel with the holding tool (A, **Figure 9**), then tighten the flywheel nut (B, **Figure 9**) as specified in **Table 2**.

10. Tighten the left side cover mounting screws securely. See **Figure 7** (PW50) or **Figure 8** (BW80 or PW80). On BW80 and PW80 models, tighten the shift pedal pinch bolt as specified in **Table 2**.

CAUTION

Do not overtighten the side cover screws or you can crack or warp the cover. A damaged cover allows dirt and water to enter the cover, contaminating the flywheel and stator plate surfaces. Dirt is also forced against the crankcase seal where it wears the seal surface at the crankshaft, causing an air leak.

Flywheel Inspection

The flywheel is permanently magnetized and cannot be tested. To isolate the flywheel as a problem area, you would have to install a flywheel known to be good and then try to restart the engine. If the engine starts with the new flywheel, but did not run with the original flywheel and all other conditions remain the same, the original flywheel is defective. If defective, the flywheel must be replaced; it cannot be remagnetized.

1. Check the flywheel (**Figure 12**) carefully for cracks or breaks.
2. Check the flywheel for loose or missing rivets.
3. Check the tapered bore of the flywheel and the crankshaft taper (**Figure 12**) for cracks or other damage.
4. Check the Woodruff key and the crankshaft keyway for cracks or other damage.

Stator Assembly Removal/Installation

1. Remove the flywheel as described in this chapter.
2. Remove the fuel tank as described in Chapter Seven.
3. Disconnect the electrical wire connectors from the magneto to the CDI unit. See the wiring diagram

for your model at the end of this manual to identify the connectors and wire colors.

4. Remove the screws securing the stator plate to the engine and remove the stator plate. See **Figure 13** (PW50) or **Figure 14** (BW80 or PW80).

5. Install by reversing these removal steps, while noting the following.

6. Clean the wiring harness connectors with contact cleaner.

7. Route the wiring harness along its original path.

8. Insert the stator plate wiring harness grommet into the crankcase.

9. Tighten the stator plate screws as specified in **Table 2**.

Stator Coil Testing and Replacement

The stator coils (**Figure 13** or **Figure 14**) can be tested while mounted on the engine. With the engine off, disconnect the stator plate electrical connectors and measure the resistance between the pairs of wire leads listed in **Table 1**. If the resistance is zero (short circuit) or infinite (open circuit), check the wiring to the coils and the connector pins. If the wiring and its connectors are good, the coil is damaged and must be replaced.

On PW50 models, the stator plate coils can be replaced separately. Identify the stator coils as follows:

a. Charge coil: A, **Figure 15**.
b. Pulser coil: B, **Figure 15**.
c. Lighting coil: C, **Figure 15**.

On BW80 and PW80 models, the source coil (**Figure 16**) can be replaced separately.

When replacing a damaged coil, note the following:

a. Note any screws and clamps securing the wiring harness to the stator plate. Make a drawing of the wiring harness as it routed through the stator plate to the coil(s). Reinstall the wiring harness so that it follows its original path.
b. Using a soldering gun, unsolder the wiring harness connector at the damaged coil.
c. Resolder the new coil to the wiring harness using rosin core solder—never use acid core solder.

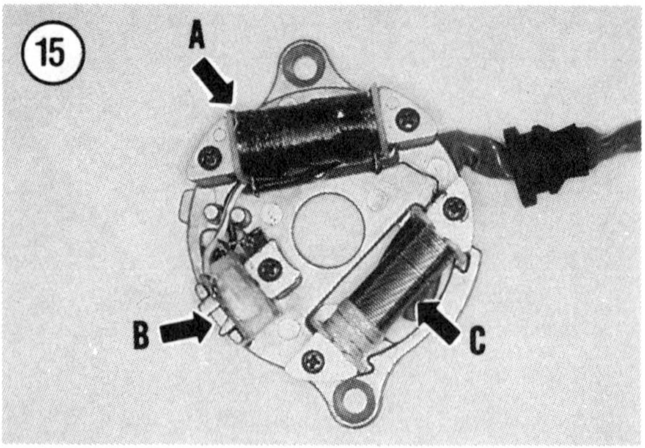

CDI UNIT

On PW50 models, the CDI unit is mounted partway inside the main frame tube (**Figure 17**). On BW80 and PW80 models, the CDI unit is mounted between the 2 main frame tubes (A, **Figure 18**).

Removal/Installation

1. Remove the fuel tank (Chapter Seven).
2. Disconnect the CDI electrical connectors.

3A. On PW50 models, pull the CDI unit out of its frame mounting position and remove it.
3B. On BW80 and PW80 models, remove the screw securing the CDI unit to the frame and remove the CDI unit.
4. Install by reversing these steps.
5. Clean the connectors with electrical contact cleaner.

Testing

The CDI unit can not be tested using conventional equipment. Accepted practice is to troubleshoot the ignition system, testing all components, switches, coils and wiring. If a problem in the ignition system is not found, then consider that the CDI unit is faulty and requires replacement. To troubleshoot the ignition system, refer to Chapter Two.

IGNITION COIL

On PW50 models, the ignition coil is mounted at the base of the upper frame tube (**Figure 19**). On BW80 and PW80 models, the ignition coil is mounted between the 2 main frame tubes (B, **Figure 18**).

Removal/Installation

1. Remove the fuel tank (Chapter Seven).
2. Disconnect the spark plug lead.
3. Disconnect the primary wires at the ignition coil.
4. Remove the screws securing the ignition coil to the frame and remove it. See B, **Figure 18** or **Figure 19**.
5. Install by reversing these removal steps. Make sure all electrical connectors are tight and free of corrosion. Make sure the ground wire connection point on the frame is free of rust and corrosion.

Testing

When testing the ignition coil in this section, compare the resistance readings to the specified resistance in **Table 1**. Replace the ignition coil if out of specification or if it shows damage as described in this section.

The ignition coil can be checked while mounted on the bike.

1. Remove the fuel tank (Chapter Seven).
2. Disconnect the spark plug lead.
3. Disconnect the primary wires at the ignition coil.
4. Inspect the ignition coil body for cracks, carbon tracks or other visible signs of damage. Check the primary and secondary wires for cracks or other damage.
5. Read the information listed under *Component Testing* in this chapter before testing the ignition coil.
6. Measure the coil primary resistance using an ohmmeter set at R × 1. Measure the resistance between the ignition coil orange lead and the ground terminal on the ignition coil (**Figure 20**).
7. Measure the secondary resistance as follows:
   a. Remove the spark plug cap (**Figure 21**) from the secondary wire.
   b. Switch the ohmmeter to its R × 1000 scale.
   c. Measure the resistance between the secondary lead (without spark plug cap) and the ignition coil orange lead.
8. Measure the spark plug cap resistance as follows:
   a. Switch the ohmmeter to its R × 1000 scale.
   b. Measure the spark plug cap resistance as shown in **Figure 22**.
   c. Replace the spark plug if the resistance reading is out of specification.

NOTE
Continuity in both the primary and secondary windings is not a guarantee that the ignition coil is working properly; only an operational spark test can tell if the coil is producing an adequate spark. To confirm the coil's condition, take it to your dealership and have a spark test performed.

9. Thread the spark plug cap onto the secondary coil wire. Then pull the spark plug cap to make sure it is secured to the coil wire.

SWITCH TESTING

Use and ohmmeter or test light and check the ignition control switch (PW50) or the engine stop switch (BW80 and PW80) as follows:

1. Remove the fuel tank (Chapter Seven).
2. Disconnect the ignition control switch (PW50) or the engine stop switch (BW80 and PW80) electrical connectors. See **Figure 23**, typical.
3. Switch an ohmmeter to the R × 1 scale.

20 IGNITION COIL TESTING

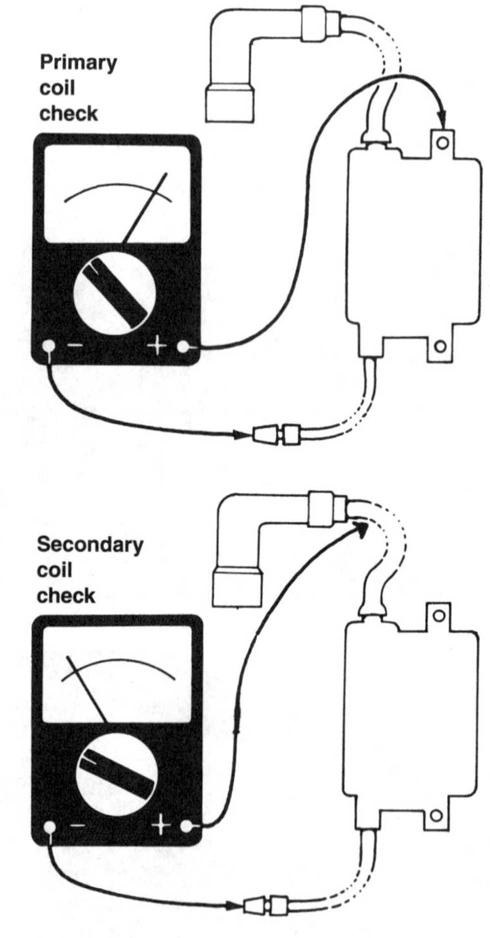

21

4A. On PW50 models, connect the ohmmeter leads between the black/red and black connector leads. Note the following:

a. The ohmmeter should read continuity with the switch in the OFF position and no continuity in the START/RUN position.

b. Replace the switch if it failed either test.

4B. On BW80 and PW80 models, connect the ohmmeter leads between the black/white and black connector leads. Note the following:

a. The ohmmeter should read continuity with the switch in the OFF position and no continuity in the RUN position.

b. Replace the switch if it failed either test.

5. Reconnect the ignition switch electrical connectors.

6. Install the fuel tank (Chapter Seven).

WIRING DIAGRAMS

Wiring diagrams for all models are located at the back of this manual.

22

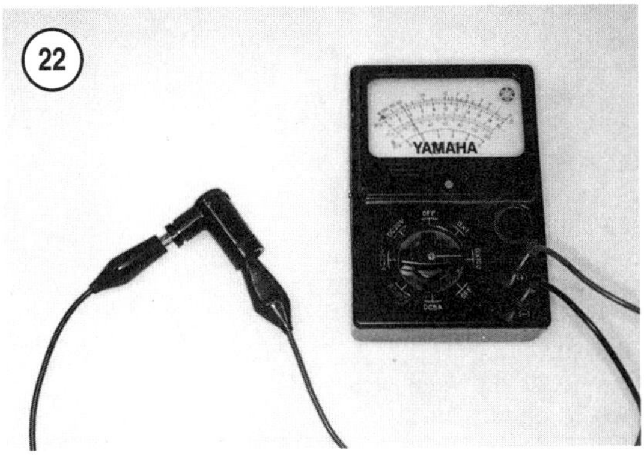

23

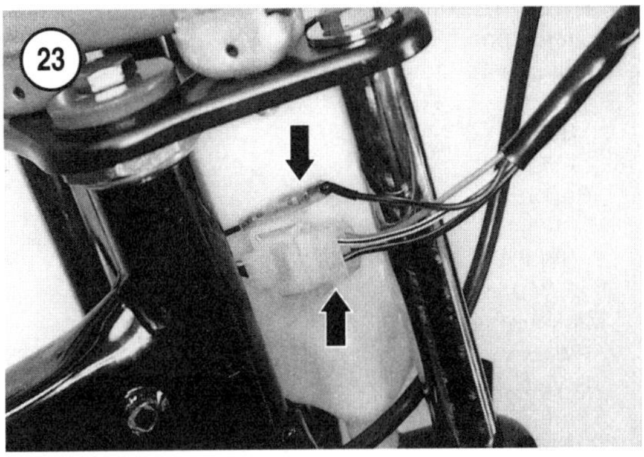

Table 1 and Table 2 are on the following page.

Table 1 ELECTRICAL SPECIFICATIONS

Ignition system	Capacitor discharge ignition (CDI)
Charging system	Flywheel magneto
Stator coil	
Model/Manufacturer	
PW50	4X4/Yamaha
BW80	F3T80771/Mitsubishi
PW80	F4T80571/Mitsubishi
Source coil resistance	
BW80 (black to black/red)	360-440 ohms*
PW80 (black to black/red)	189-231 ohms*
Charge coil resistance	
PW50 (black to black/red)	297-363 ohms*
Pickup coil resistance	
PW50 (black to white/red)	18-22 ohms*
Lighting coil resistance	
PW50 (black to white)	0.57-0.69 ohm*
Ignition coil	
Primary coil resistance	
PW50	0.32-0.48 ohm*
BW80	0.85-1.15 ohms*
PW80	0.26-0.36 ohms*
Secondary coil resistance	
PW50	5.68-8.52K ohms*
BW80	5.0-6.8K ohms*
PW80	3.5-4.7K ohms*
Minimum tester spark gap	
PW50 and PW80	6 mm (0.24 in.)
BW80	5 mm (0.20 in.)
Spark plug cap resistance	4.0-6.0K ohms*

*All measurements taken at 68° F (20° C).

Table 2 TIGHTENING TORQUES

	N•m	in.-lb.	ft.-lb.
Flywheel nut			
PW50	43	—	31
BW80 and PW80	50	—	36
Shift pedal pinch bolt	10	88	—
Stator plate screws	7	62	—

CHAPTER NINE

OIL INJECTION SYSTEM

All of the models covered in this manual are equipped with an oil injection system.

Oil pump specifications are listed in **Tables 1-3** (end of chapter).

OIL PUMP CABLE ADJUSTMENT

Refer to *Throttle And Oil Pump Cable Adjustment* in Chapter Three for your model.

OIL PUMP BLEEDING

The oil pump must be bled if air enters one of the oil lines or oil pump. When air enters the oil injection system, it blocks the flow of oil to the engine. The oil pump must be bled when one of the following conditions have occurred:

a. The oil tank ran empty.
b. When any one of the oil injection hoses were disconnected.

The oil pump is equipped with a bleed screw installed in the pump body. Removing the screw allows oil from the oil tank to flow through the oil delivery and pump passage, forcing air out of the system.

PW50

1. Support the bike on its centerstand.
2. Check that the oil tank is full of oil. See *Engine Oil* in Chapter Three.
3. Remove the exhaust system as described in Chapter Four.
4. Remove the upper cover screw and cover (**Figure 1**) from the oil pump.
5. Place a drain pan underneath the engine.
6. Remove the bleed screw and gasket (A, **Figure 2**) from the oil pump.

WARNING
The engine must be running when bleeding the oil pump. When doing so,

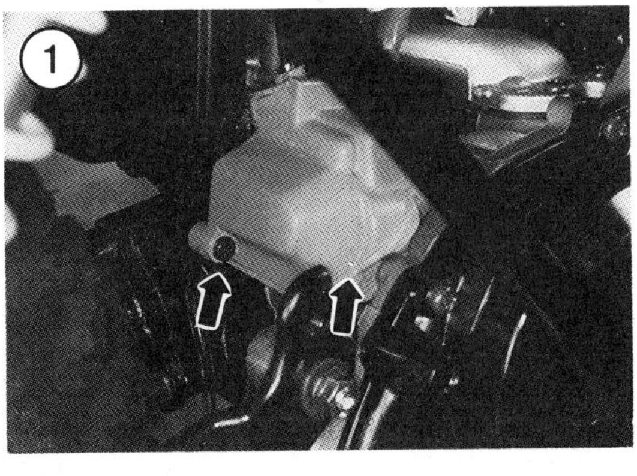

do not run the engine in an enclosed area. The exhaust gases contain carbon monoxide, a colorless, tasteless, poisonous gas. Carbon monoxide levels build quickly in a small enclosed area and can cause unconsciousness and death in a short time. Start and run the engine in an area with plenty of ventilation.

7. Start the engine and allow it to run at idle speed. Then pull the oil pump cable (B, **Figure 2**) away from the oil pump to open the pump pulley as far as possible. Hold the cable in this position with the engine running at idle speed until the oil draining from the bleed hole is free of air bubbles. When the oil flowing from the oil pump is free of air bubbles, release the oil pump cable and reinstall the bleed screw and washer and tighten securely. Then turn the engine off.

NOTE

If oil does not flow from the oil pump and there is oil in the oil tank, remove the oil fill cap from the top of the oil tank. If oil now starts to flow, the vent hole in the cap is clogged with dirt or other debris. Clean the vent hole and reinstall the cap. A clogged vent hole will cause a vacuum to build in the tank and prevent oil from flowing out of the tank. If oil still does not flow, check for a clogged oil supply hose (from the tank to the oil pump).

CAUTION

If the engine is hot, allow it to cool down before continuing with Step 8.

8. Wipe up as much oil from around the oil pump and engine as possible.

9. Remove the drain pan.

10. Check that the oil pump cable is seated correctly in the lower oil pump cover and that the control wire is routed correctly through the pulley with its end piece mounted into the pulley hole.

11. Install the upper cover (**Figure 1**) and its mounting screw (**Figure 1**).

12. Install the exhaust system (Chapter Four).

13. Top off the oil tank. See *Engine Oil* in Chapter Three.

BW80 and PW80

1. Remove the exhaust system as described in Chapter Five.

2. Remove the oil pump cover bolts (A, **Figure 3**). Then remove the oil pump cover (B, **Figure 3**) while at the same time disconnecting the oil pump cable from the oil pump. See **Figure 4**.

3. Check that the oil tank is full of oil. See *Engine Oil* in Chapter Three.

4. Place a drain pan or rag underneath the oil pump.

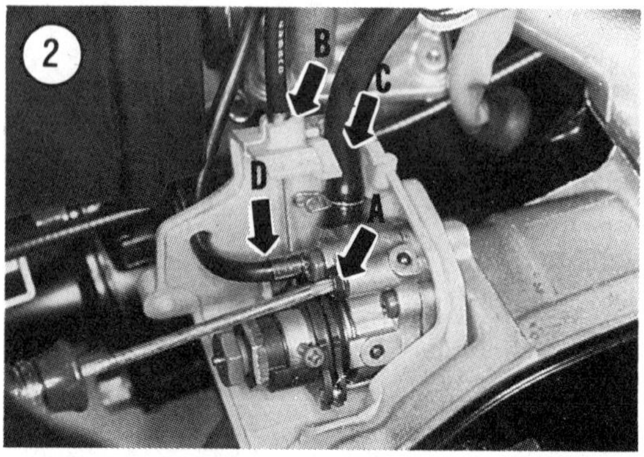

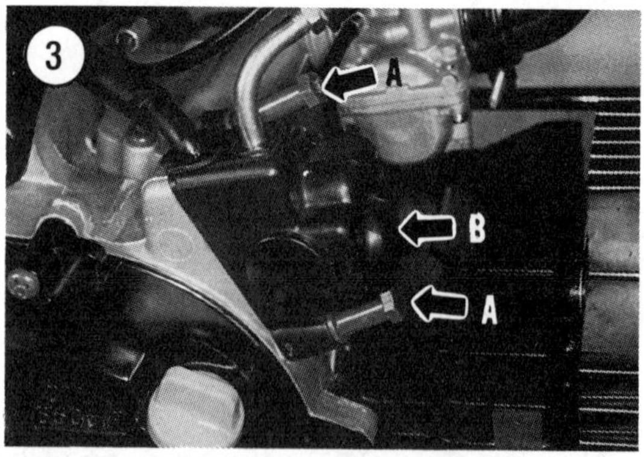

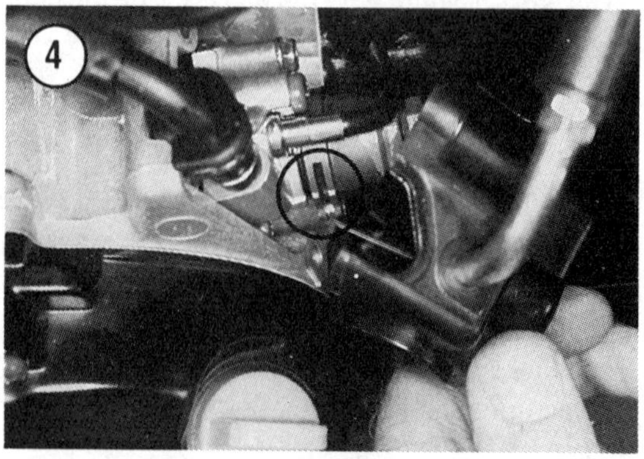

5. Remove the bleed screw and gasket (A, **Figure 5**) from the oil pump. Oil should begin to flow fromthe oil pump.

NOTE

If oil does not flow out of the oil pump and there is oil in the oil tank, remove the oil fill cap from the top of the oil tank. If oil starts to flow from the oil tank, the vent hole in the cap is clogged with dirt or other debris. Clean the vent hole and reinstall the cap. A clogged vent hole will cause a vacuum to build in the tank and prevent oil from flowing out of the tank. If oil still does not flow, check for a clogged oil supply hose (from the tank to the oil pump).

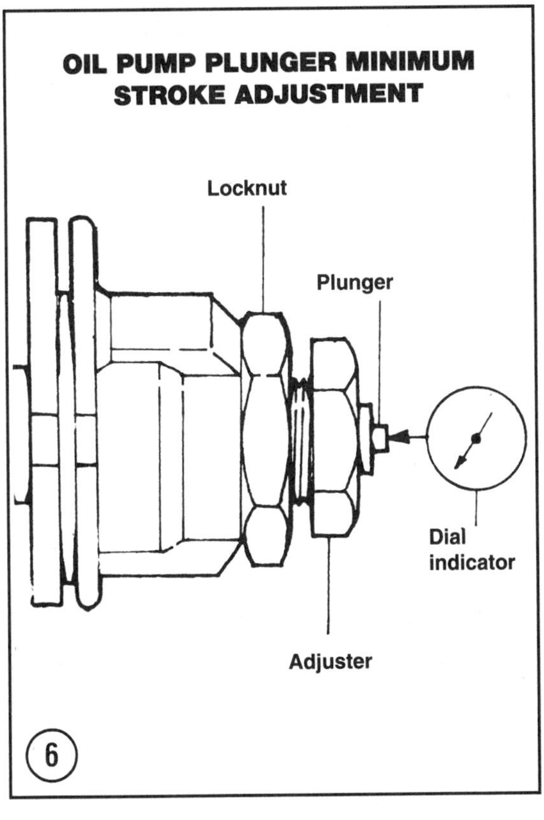

6. If there is air in the system, air bubbles will be mixed with the oil. Allow the oil to run fromthe oil pump until there are no air bubbles in the oil. Then install the bleed screw (A, **Figure 5**) and its gasket and tighten securely.
7. Wipe up as much oil from the oil pump and engine as possible.
8. Remove the drain pan or rag from underneath the oil pump.
9. Reconnect the oil pump cable onto the pulley (**Figure 4**) and reinstall the cover (B, **Figure 3**). Install and tighten the cover mounting bolts (A, **Figure 3**) as specified in **Table 3**.
10. Install the exhaust system (Chapter Five).
11. Top off the oil tank. See *Engine Oil* in Chapter Three.

9

OIL PUMP PLUNGER STROKE ADJUSTMENT

When it seems that the engine is getting too much or too little oil, measure the oil pump plunger stroke and then adjust if necessary. A dial indicator and magnetic stand is required for this procedure.

1A. On PW50 models, perform the following:
   a. Support the bike on its centerstand.
   b. Remove the exhaust system as described in Chapter Four.
   c. Remove the upper cover screw and cover (**Figure 1**) from the oil pump.

1B. On BW80 and PW80 models, perform the following:
   a. Remove the exhaust system as described in Chapter Five.
   b. Remove the oil pump cover bolts (A, **Figure 3**). Then remove the oil pump cover (B, **Figure 3**) while at the same time disconnecting the oil pump cable from the oil pump. See **Figure 4**.

2. Mount a dial indicator so that its tip seats against the end of the oil pump plunger as shown in **Figure 6**.

WARNING

The engine must be running when measuring the plunger stroke. Do not run the engine in an enclosed area. The exhaust gases contain carbon monoxide, a colorless, tasteless, poisonous gas. Carbon monoxide levels build quickly in a small enclosed area and can cause unconsciousness and death in a short time. Start and run the engine in an area with plenty of ventilation.

3. Start the engine and allow to run at idle speed.

4. Read the minimum stroke on the dial indicator and compare to the specification in **Table 1** or **Table 2**. Note the following:

   a. If the minimum stroke is correct, go to Step 5.
   b. If the minimum stroke is incorrect, loosen the oil pump locknut (**Figure 6**) and turn the adjuster (**Figure 6**) clockwise or counterclockwise until the minimum stroke measurement is correct. Then tighten the locknut and recheck the minimum stroke.

5. Turn the engine off.

6. Remove the dial indicator and magnetic stand from the bike.

7A. On PW50 models, perform the following:

   a. Install the upper cover (**Figure 1**) and its mounting screw (**Figure 1**).
   b. Install the exhaust system (Chapter Four).

7B. On BW80 and PW80 models, perform the following:

   a. Reconnect the oil pump cable onto the pulley (**Figure 4**) and reinstall the cover (B, **Figure 3**). Install and tighten the cover mounting bolts (A, **Figure 3**) as specified in **Table 3**.
   b. Install the exhaust system (Chapter Five).

(7)

OIL PUMP (PW50)

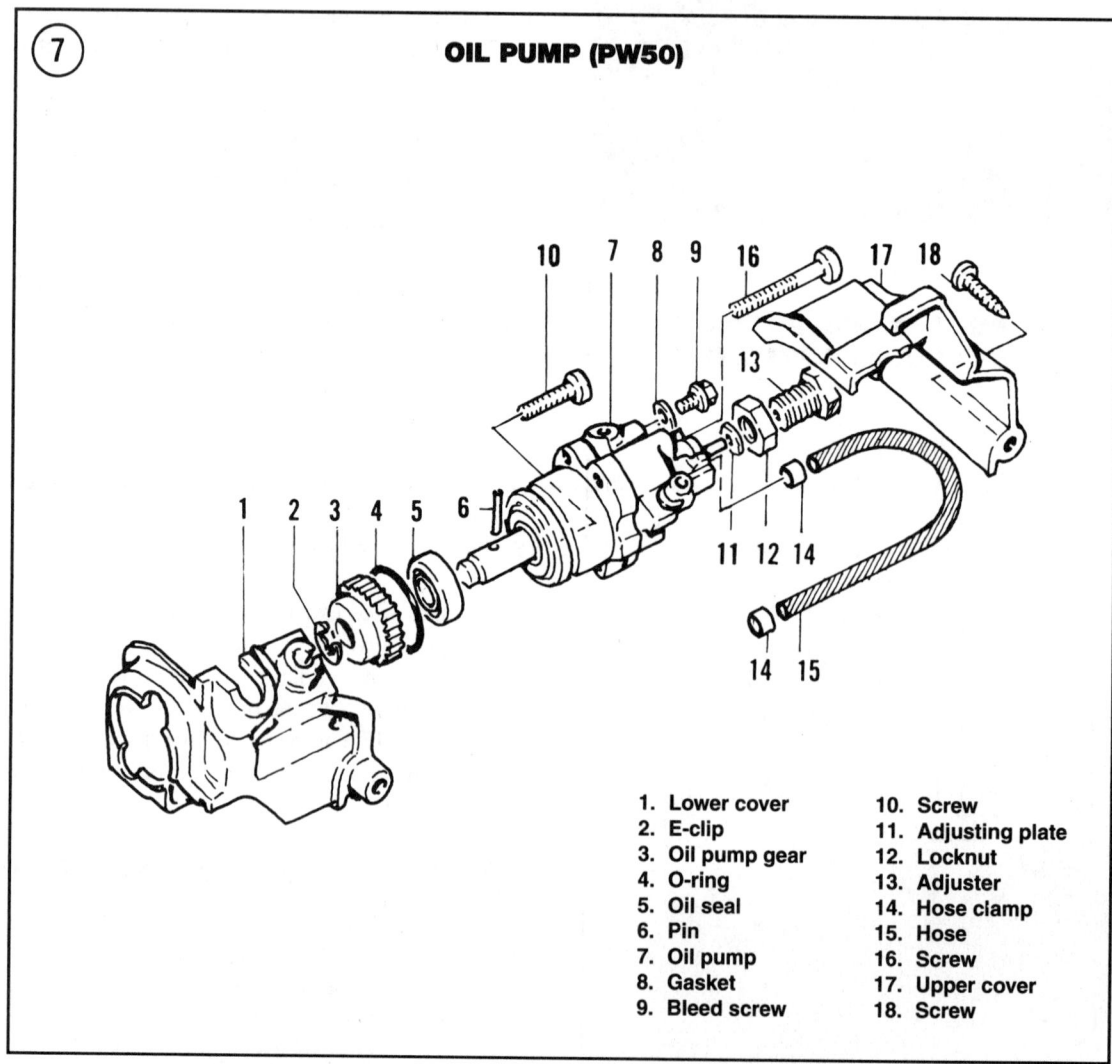

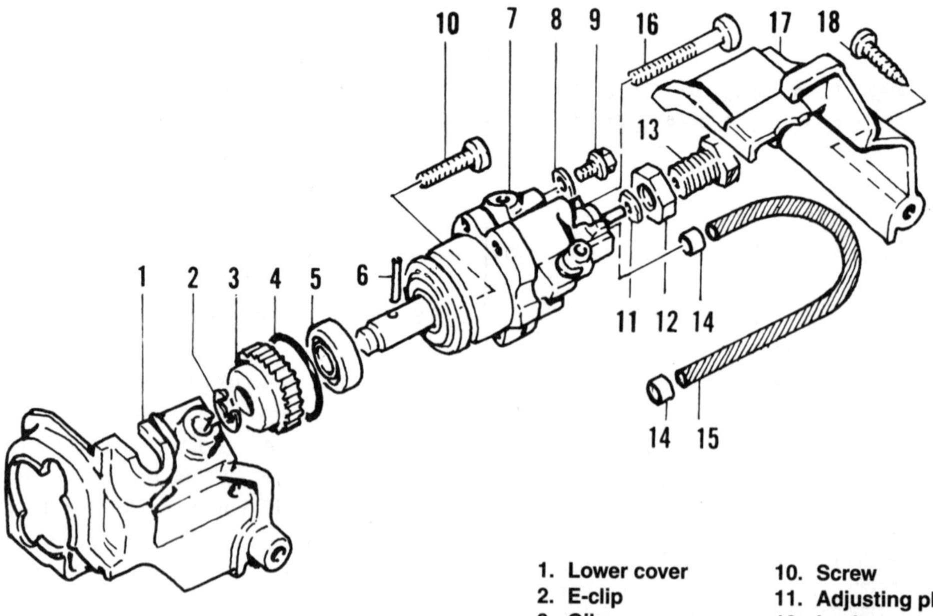

1. Lower cover
2. E-clip
3. Oil pump gear
4. O-ring
5. Oil seal
6. Pin
7. Oil pump
8. Gasket
9. Bleed screw
10. Screw
11. Adjusting plate
12. Locknut
13. Adjuster
14. Hose clamp
15. Hose
16. Screw
17. Upper cover
18. Screw

OIL PUMP

This section describes removal, inspection and installation procedures for the oil pump assembly. The oil pump is a sealed unit and should not be disassembled.

Removal/Installation (PW50)

Refer to **Figure 7** for this procedure.

1. Support the bike on its centerstand.
2. Remove the exhaust system as described in Chapter Four.
3. Remove the upper cover screw and cover (**Figure 1**) from the oil pump.
4. Disconnect the oil supply hose (C, **Figure 2**) and the oil delivery hose (D, **Figure 2**) from the oil pump. Plug both hoses to prevent oil leakage and hose contamination.
5. Disconnect the oil pump cable (B, **Figure 2**) from the pulley.
6. Remove the screws that secure the oil pump and the lower cover to the crankcase. Then remove the oil pump and lower cover assembly (**Figure 8**).
7. Store the oil pump in a sealed plastic bag until inspection and installation.
8. Inspect the oil pump as described under *Inspection* in this section.
9. Install the oil pump and lower cover by reversing these removal steps, noting the following.
10. Lubricate the oil pump O-ring with transmission oil.
11. When installing the oil pump (**Figure 8**) into the crankcase, align the drive and driven gears.
12. Tighten the oil pump mounting screws as specified in **Table 3**.

8

13. Secure each hose with its clamp (C and D, **Figure 2**).
14. Bleed the oil pump as described in this chapter.

Removal/Installation (BW80 and PW80)

Refer to **Figure 9** for this procedure.

1. Support the bike on its sidestand.
2. Remove the exhaust system as described in Chapter Five.
3. Remove the oil pump cover bolts (A, **Figure 3**). Then remove the oil pump cover (B, **Figure 3**) while at the same time disconnecting the oil pump cable from the oil pump. See **Figure 4**.
4. Disconnect the oil supply hose (A, **Figure 5**) and the oil discharge hose (B, **Figure 5**) from the oil pump. Plug both hoses to prevent oil leakage and hose contamination.
5. Remove the screws that secure the oil pump to the crankcase, then remove the oil pump (**Figure 10**).
6. Store the oil pump in a sealed plastic bag until inspection and reassembly.
7. Inspect the oil pump as described under *Inspection* in this section.
8. Install the oil pump and lower cover by reversing these removal steps, noting the following.
9. Lubricate the oil pump O-ring with transmission oil.
10. When installing the oil pump (**Figure 10**) into the crankcase, align the drive and driven gears.
11. Tighten the oil pump mounting screws as specified in **Table 3**.
12. Secure each hose with its clamp.
13. Bleed the oil pump as described in this chapter.
14. Tighten the oil pump cover mounting bolts as specified in **Table 3**.

9

Inspection

Refer to **Figure 7** (PW50) or **Figure 9** (BW80 and PW80) for this procedure. Replace parts that show damage as described in this section.

1. **Figure 7** and **Figure 9** show the assembled oil pump with their mating parts that can be replaced separately. Do not disassemble the oil pump assembly.
2. Visually inspect the oil pump for a cracked housing or other damage. Replace the oil pump if any leakage or damage is noted. The oil pump is a sealed

unit and must not be disassembled. If the oil pump is okay, store it in a sealed plastic bag until reassembly. See **Figure 11** (PW50) or **Figure 10** (BW80 and PW80).

3. Inspect the oil pump driven gear for severe wear, cracks or other damage.

4. Replace the external oil pump O-ring if leaking or damaged.

OIL HOSES

Fresh oil hoses should be installed whenever the old hoses become hard and brittle or damaged. When replacing damaged or worn oil hoses, use Yamaha replacement hoses and make sure to install hoses with the correct inside diameter. When reconnecting hoses, secure each hose end with a clamp. Bleed the oil pump after reconnecting one or both oil hoses.

OIL TANK

Replace the engine oil tank (**Figure 12** [PW50] or **Figure 13** [PW80 and BW80]) if it leaks or is damaged. If the inside of the tank becomes contaminated, remove the oil tank and discard the oil according to local EPA regulations. Flush the tank thoroughly and allow to air dry before refilling with oil. Refill the oil tank with the correct type of 2-stroke engine oil (Chapter Three).

Then bleed the oil pump as described in this chapter.

OIL PUMP OUTPUT TEST (PW50)

Yamaha does not list output test specifications for the PW50 models.

9 **OIL PUMP (BW80 AND PW80)**

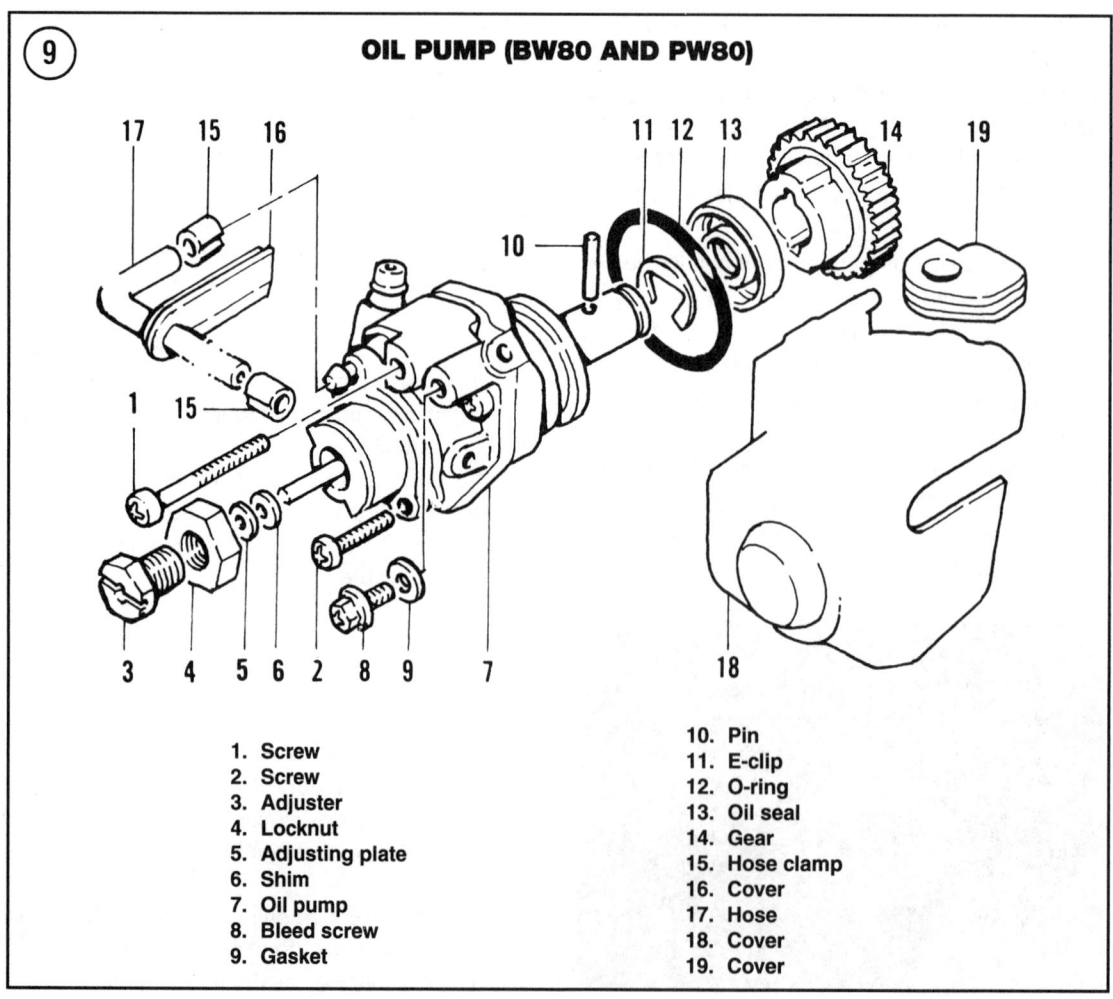

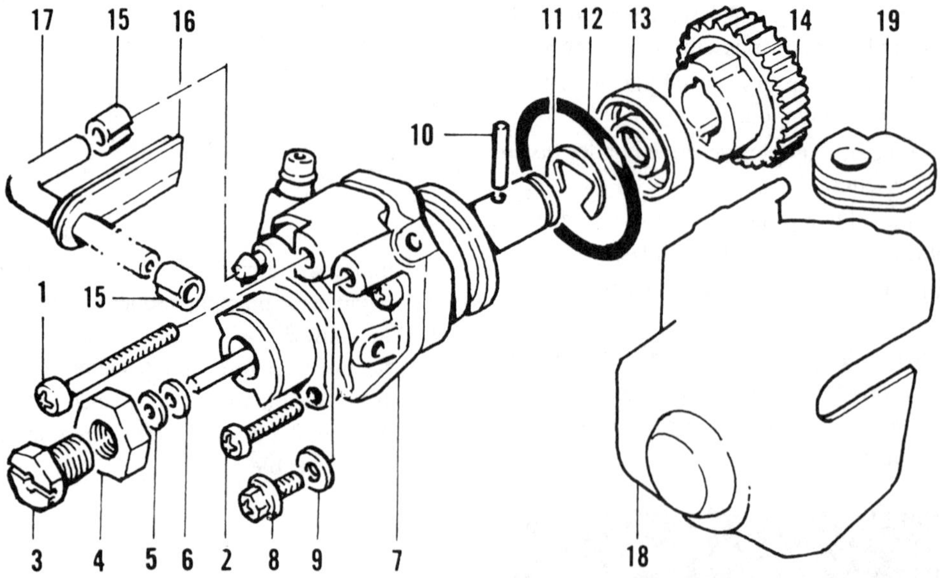

1. Screw
2. Screw
3. Adjuster
4. Locknut
5. Adjusting plate
6. Shim
7. Oil pump
8. Bleed screw
9. Gasket
10. Pin
11. E-clip
12. O-ring
13. Oil seal
14. Gear
15. Hose clamp
16. Cover
17. Hose
18. Cover
19. Cover

10

11

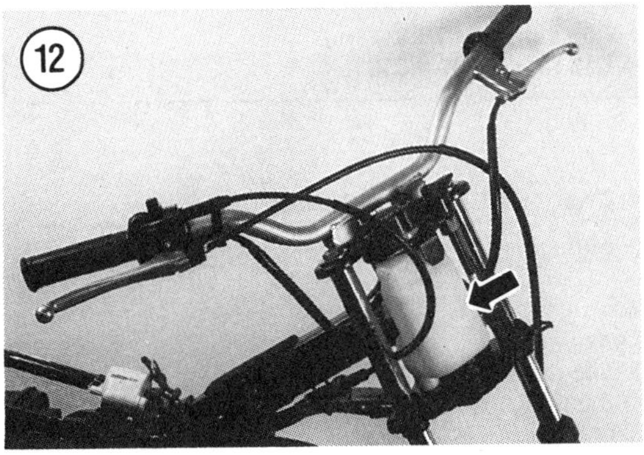
12

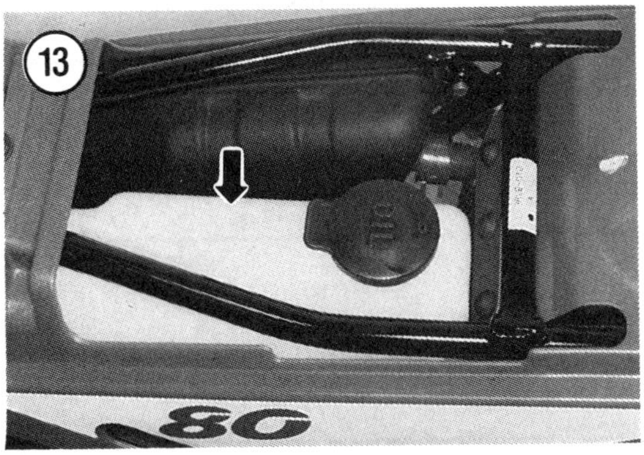
13

OIL PUMP OUTPUT TEST (BW80 AND PW80)

Table 2 lists specifications for checking the output of the oil pump. While the oil pump is dependable and seldom fails, perform this test when troubleshooting an oil supply problem. The test consists of disconnecting the oil delivery line from the carburetor and running the engine at idle while counting a specified number of pump strokes. The oil that is pumped from the delivery line is measured to determine the oil pump output. Because the oil delivery line is disconnected from the carburetor during this test, engine lubrication is provided by premixing a small mount of gasoline and oil and adding it the fuel tank.

1. Connect one end of a long piece of fuel hose to the fuel valve on the fuel tank. Insert the other end into an empty fuel can. Turn the fuel valve to RES and drain the fuel tank of all fuel. When the fuel tank is empty, remove the fuel hose and reconnect the carburetor fuel hose to the fuel valve.
2. Remove the drain screw from the bottom of the carburetor and drain it also, then reinstall the drain screw.
3. Prepare a 24:1 premix as follows:
   a. To make a 24:1 premix, add 2.7 ounces of Yamalube 2-R (or equivalent 2-stroke engine oil) to 1/2 gallon of gasoline.
   b. Shake the can thoroughly to mix the oil with the gasoline, then pour the premix into the fuel tank.
4. Remove the exhaust system as described in Chapter Five.
5. Remove the oil pump cover bolts (A, **Figure 3**). Then remove the oil pump cover (B, **Figure 3**) while at the same time disconnecting the oil pump cable from the oil pump. See **Figure 4**.
6. Slide the band clamp down the oil delivery hose, then disconnect the hose from the carburetor nozzle. Insert the open end of the delivery hose into a graduated beaker that can measure a small amount of liquid (0-10 cc). Install a longer hose, if necessary.
7. Plug the nozzle on the carburetor to prevent air from being drawn into the engine during this procedure.

WARNING

The engine must be running when checking the pump oil output. When doing so, do not run the engine in an enclosed area. The exhaust gases contain carbon monoxide, a colorless, tasteless, poisonous gas. Carbon monoxide levels build quickly in a small enclosed area and can cause unconsciousness and death in a short time. Start and run the engine in an area with plenty of ventilation.

NOTE

Start counting the oil pump strokes as soon as the engine is started.

8. Have an assistant start the engine and allow to idle. Count the number of piston strokes up to 200, then turn the engine off and measure the amount of oil discharged into the beaker. The correct oil output capacity for 200 strokes is listed in **Table 2**. Note the following:
   a. The accuracy of this test depends on your accuracy in counting the pump strokes and measuring the oil output.
   b. If the output measurement is correct for 200 strokes, the oil pump is working correctly.
   c. If the output quantity differs from the output specification listed in **Table 2**, the oil pump is faulty and should be replaced. Replace the oil pump as described in this chapter.

9. Drain the premix from the fuel tank and refill the tank with unmixed gasoline.

10. Reconnect the oil delivery hose onto the carburetor. Secure the hose with its hose clamp.

11. Bleed the oil pump as described in this chapter.

12. Reconnect the oil pump cable onto the pulley (**Figure 4**) and reinstall the cover (B, **Figure 3**). Install and tighten the cover mounting bolts (A, **Figure 3**) as specified in **Table 3**.

13. Install the exhaust system (Chapter Five).

Table 1 OIL PUMP SPECIFICATIONS (PW50)

Minimum stroke	0.25-0.30 mm (0.010-0.012 in.)
Maximum stroke	1.00-1.15 mm (0.039-0.045 in.)

Table 2 OIL PUMP SPECIFICATIONS (BW80 AND PW80)

Adjusting mark at idle	Auto adjuster
Color code	
BW80	Brown
PW80	Not specified
Minimum stroke	0.40-0.45 mm (0.016-0.018 in.)
Maximum stroke	1.0-1.1 mm (0.039-0.043 in.)
Output specifications	
Minimum output @ 200 strokes	0.077-0.087 mL (0.0026-0.0029 U.S. oz./0.0027-0.0032 Imp. oz.)
Maximum output @ 200 strokes	0.192 mL (0.0065 U.S. oz./0.0068 Imp. oz.)

Table 3 LUBRICATION SYSTEM TIGHTENING TORQUES

	N•m	in.-lb.
Oil pump		
PW50	4	35
BW80 and PW80	5	44
Oil pump cover		
PW50	—	
BW80 and PW80	8	71

CHAPTER TEN

FRONT SUSPENSION AND STEERING (PW50)

This chapter describes repair and maintenance on the front wheel, wheel bearings, steering components and front forks.

Steering and front suspension specifications are listed in **Table 1**. Tire and wheel specifications are listed in **Table 2**. **Tables 1-3** are at the end of the chapter.

FRONT WHEEL

Refer to **Figure 1** when servicing the front wheel in this section.

Removal/Installation

1. Support the motorcycle with the front wheel off the ground.
2. Loosen the front brake adjuster (A, **Figure 2**) at the front wheel.
3. Remove the axle nut cotter pin (B, **Figure 2**) and discard it.
4. Remove the axle nut and flat washer (**Figure 3**).
5. Remove the front axle (**Figure 4**) and pull out the wheel and brake assembly. Remove the brake assembly (**Figure 5**) from the front wheel.
6. Remove the collar (**Figure 6**) from the right side of the wheel.
7. Perform the *Inspection* procedure in this section to clean and inspect the parts.
8. Install the front wheel by reversing these removal steps. Note the following:
   a. Apply a light coat of grease to the axle and dust seal lips (**Figure 7**).
   b. Install the axle from the right side (**Figure 4**).
   c. When installing the wheel in the forks, make sure the anchor boss on the left fork tube fits between the lugs cast into the brake panel (**Figure 8**).
   d. To center the brake shoes in the drum, tighten the axle nut lightly, spin the wheel and apply the front brake forcefully, then tighten the axle nut as specified in **Table 3**.
   e. Install a *new* cotter pin and bend its ends over (**Figure 9**) to lock it in place.

WARNING
Never reuse the cotter pin.

   f. Adjust the front brake as described in Chapter Three.

1

FRONT WHEEL (PW50)

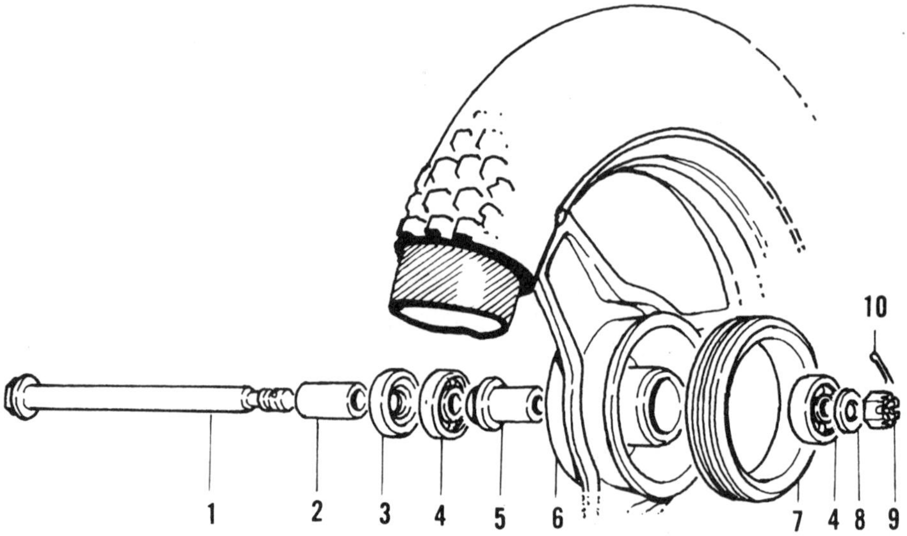

1. Front axle
2. Collar
3. Axle seal
4. Wheel bearings
5. Collar
6. Wheel assembly
7. Cover
8. Washer
9. Axle nut
10. Cotter pin

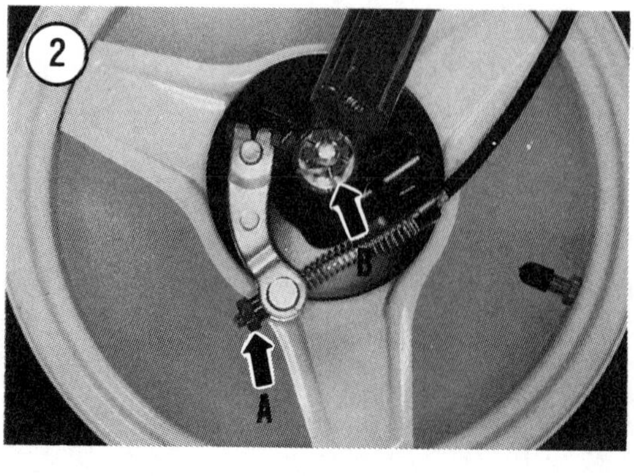

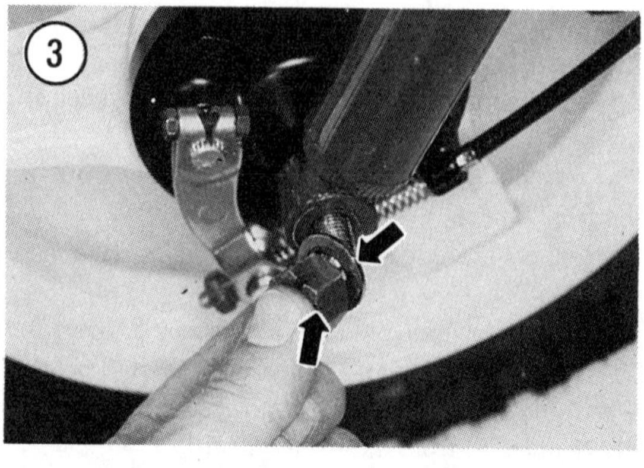

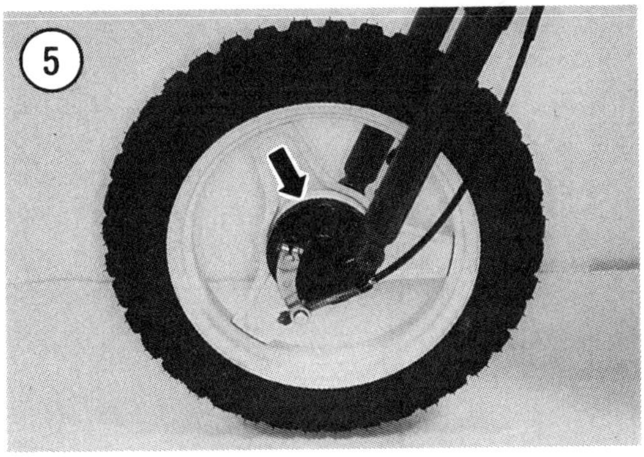

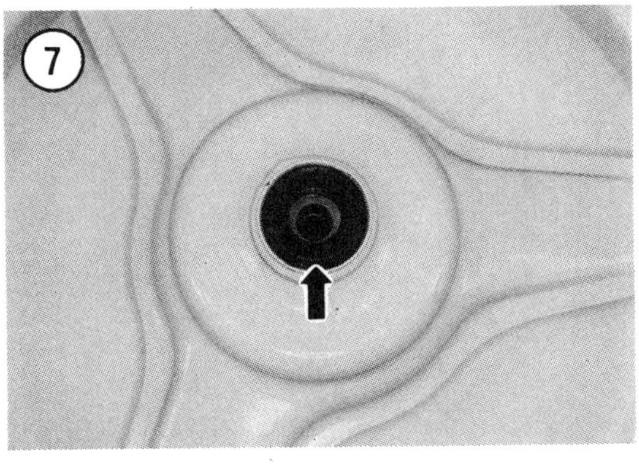

g. After the wheel is completely installed, rotate it and then apply the brake a couple of times to make sure the wheel rotates freely and that the brake is operating correctly.

Inspection

Replace all parts that show damage as described in this section.

1. Inspect the dust seal (**Figure 7**) for wear, hardness, cracks or other damage. If necessary, replace the dust seal as described under *Front Hub* in this chapter.
2. Turn each bearing inner race (**Figure 10**) by hand. The bearing must turn smoothly with no roughness, catching, binding or excessive noise. Some axial play is normal, but radial play must be negligible; see **Figure 11**. If one bearing is damaged, replace both bearings as a set. Refer to *Front Hub* in this chapter.
3. Clean and dry the axle, collar, washer and axle nut.
4. Replace the axle if it is bent or damaged. Do not try to straighten a bent axle.

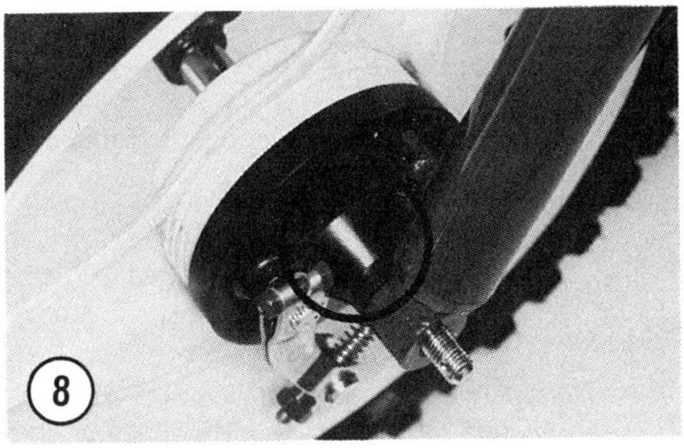

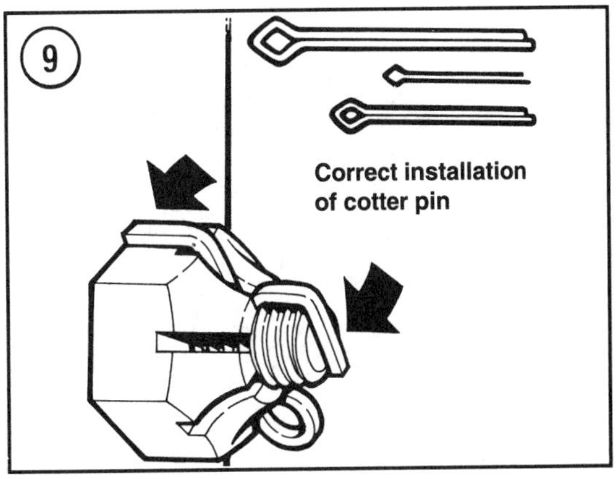

5. Check the wheel (**Figure 12**) for:
   a. Cracks or other damage.
   b. Breaks or other damage where the spokes are welded to the rim.
6. Service the brake drum and brakes as described in Chapter Fourteen.
7. Check wheel runout in the following procedure.

Wheel Runout

Wheel rim runout is the amount of wobble a wheel shows as it rotates. You can check runout with the wheels on the bike by simply supporting the wheel off the ground and turning the wheel slowly while you hold a pointer solidly against a fork leg or the drive shaft. Just be sure any wobble you observe isn't caused by your own hand.

Off the motorcycle, runout can be checked with a dial indicator as shown in **Figure 13**.

Table 2 lists the maximum allowable side-to-side and up-and-down runout limits.

If the runout exceeds the service limit in **Table 2**, check the wheel bearings for severe wear or damage. If the wheel bearings are in good condition, the wheel must be replaced.

FRONT HUB

Refer to **Figure 1** when servicing the front hub.

Inspection

Inspect each wheel bearing as follows:

CAUTION
Do not remove the wheel bearings for inspection purposes as they may be damaged during removal. Remove the

11

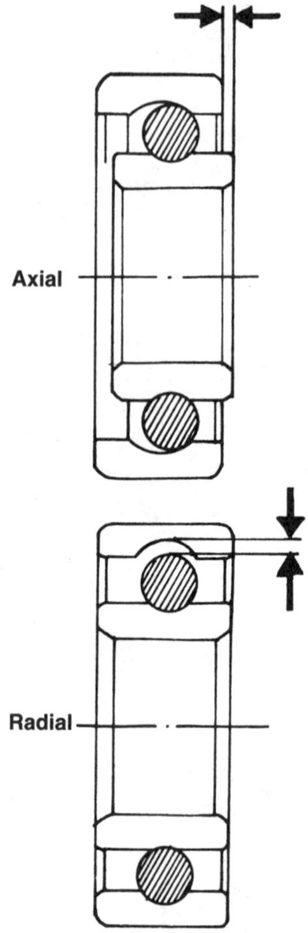

10

12

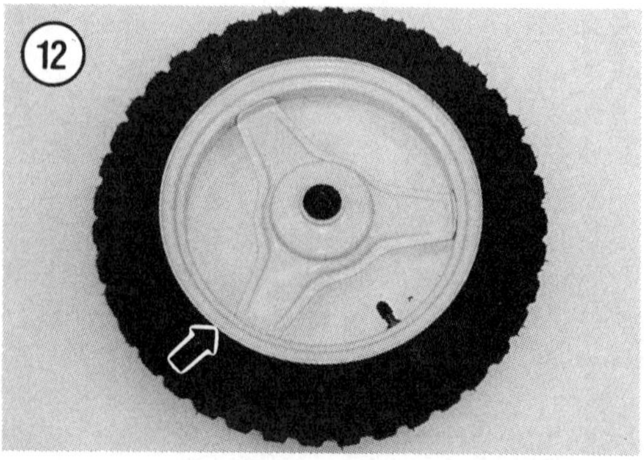

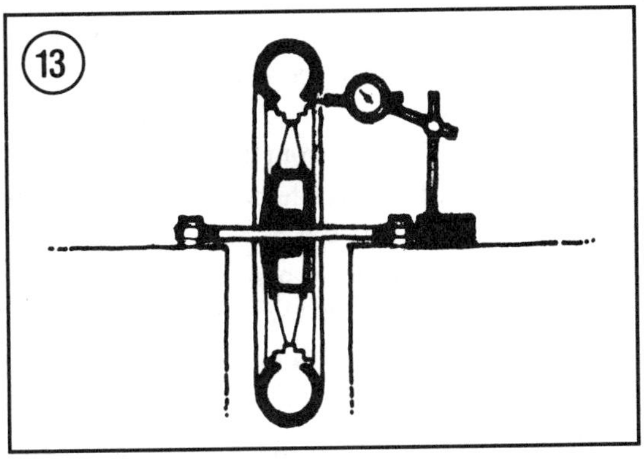

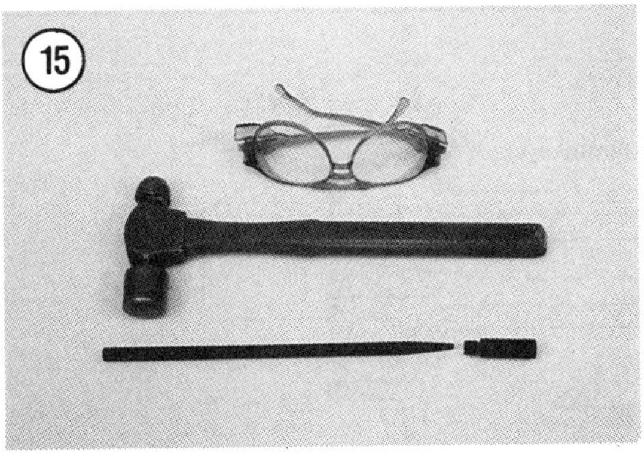

wheel bearings only if they are to be replaced.

1. Pry the dust seal out of the hub with a wide-blade screwdriver (**Figure 14**). Support the screwdriver with a rag to avoid damaging the hub.
2. Turn each bearing inner race (**Figure 10**) by hand. The bearings must turn smoothly without excessive noise or play. Some axial play (end play) is normal, but radial play (side play) must be negligible; see **Figure 11**.
3. If one bearing is damaged, replace both bearings as a set.

Disassembly

NOTE
Step 1 describes 2 methods of removing the front wheel bearings. Step 1A requires the use of the Kowa Seiki Wheel Bearing Remover set. Step 1B describes how to remove the bearing using a drift and hammer.

1A. To remove the hub bearings (**Figure 10**) with the Kowa Seiki Wheel Bearing Remover set:

NOTE
*The Kowa Seiki Wheel Bearing Remover set shown in **Figure 15** is available from K & L Supply Co., in Santa Clara, CA. You can order this tool set through your Yamaha dealer.*

a. Select the correct size remover head tool and insert it into one of the hub bearings (**Figure 16**).
b. From the opposite side of the hub, insert the remover shaft into the slot in the backside of the remover head (**Figure 17**). Then position

10

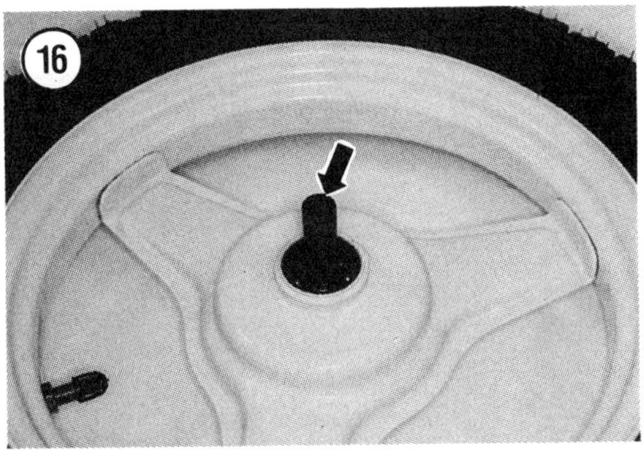

the hub with the remover head tool resting against a solid surface and strike the remover shaft to force it into the slit in the remover head. This will wedge the remover head tool against the inner bearing race. See **Figure 18**.

c. Position the hub and strike the end of the remover shaft with a hammer to drive the bearing (**Figure 19**) out of the hub. Remove the bearing and tool. Release the remover head from the bearing.

d. Remove the coolar (**Figure 20**) from the hub.

e. Repeat to remove the opposite bearing.

1B. To remove the hub bearings without special tools:

a. Using a long drift, tilt the center hub spacer away from one side of the bearing (**Figure 21**).

NOTE
Try not to damage the hub spacer's machined surface when positioning and driving against the long drift. You may have to grind a clearance groove in the drift to enable it to contact the bearing while clearing the spacer.

b. Tap the bearing out of the hub with a hammer, working around the perimeter of the bearing's inner race.

c. Remove the collar from the hub (**Figure 20**).

d. Drive out the opposite bearing using a large socket or bearing driver.

e. Inspect the collar for burrs created during removal. Remove burrs with a file.

2. Clean and dry the hub (**Figure 22**) and center hub spacer.

3. Inspect the hub bore (**Figure 22**) for cracks or excessive wear. If a bearing was a loose fit in the hub, the hub is excessive worn or damaged; replace the wheel assembly.

Assembly

Before installing the new bearings and dust seals, note the following:

a. The left and right side bearings are identical (same part number); see **Figure 23**.

b. Install both bearings with their numbered side (**Figure 24**) facing out.

18

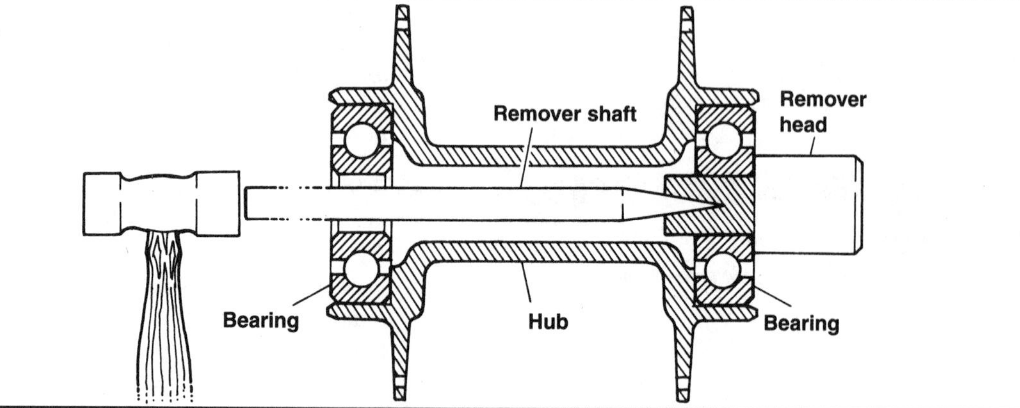

19

20

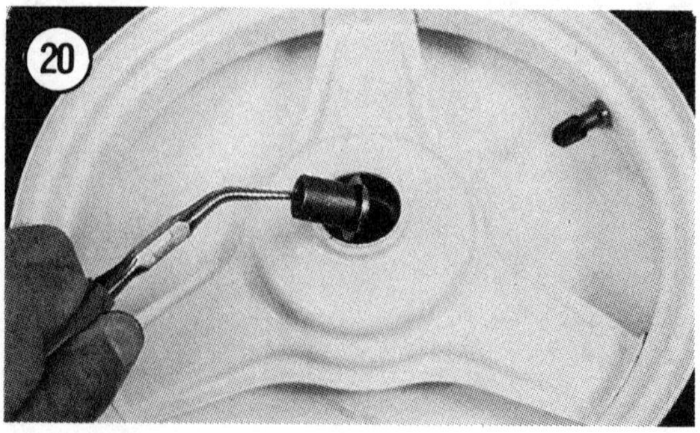

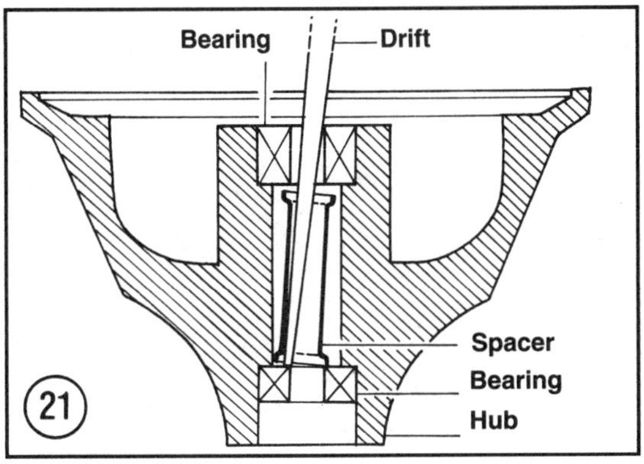

21

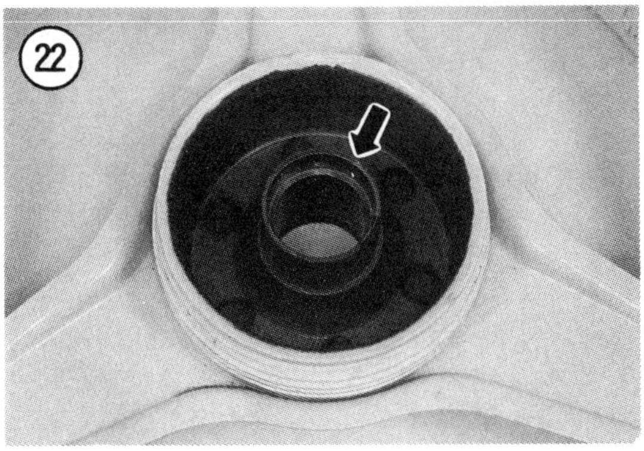
22

c. When grease is called for in the following steps, use a Lithium based multipurpose grease (NLGI # 2) or equivalent.

1. Blow any dirt or foreign matter out of the hub (**Figure 22**).

2. Pack the open side of each bearing (**Figure 24**) with grease.

3. Place the first bearing squarely against the bore opening. Select a driver (**Figure 25**) with an outside diameter just a little smaller than the bearing's outside diameter. Then drive the bearing into the bore until it bottoms out (**Figure 26**).

4. Install the center hub spacer (**Figure 20**) and center it against the first bearing's center race.

5. Place the second bearing squarely against the bore opening. Using the same driver as before, drive the bearing partway into the bearing bore. Then stop and make sure the collar is centered in the hub. If not, install the front axle through the hub to center the spacer with the bearing. Then remove the axle and continue installing the bearing until it bottoms out.

6. Pack the dust seal lip with grease.

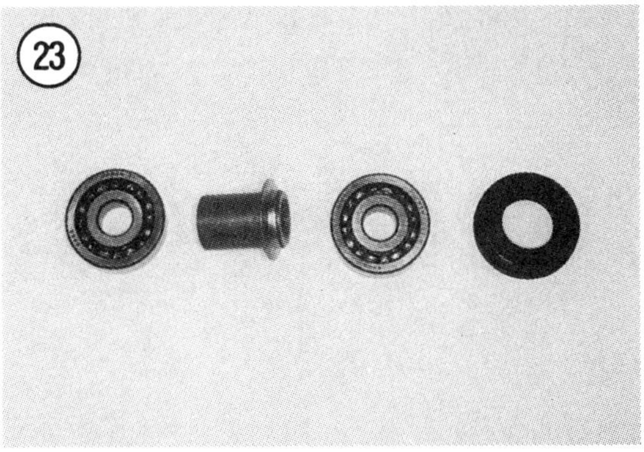
23

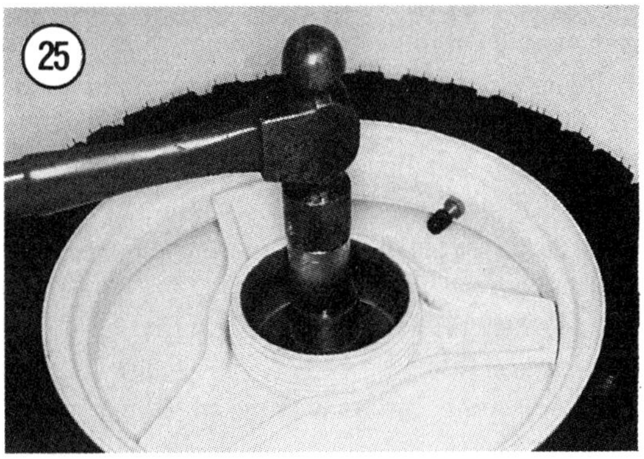
25

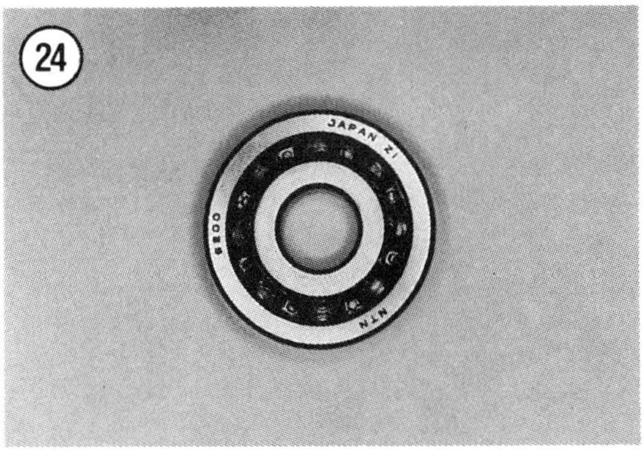
24

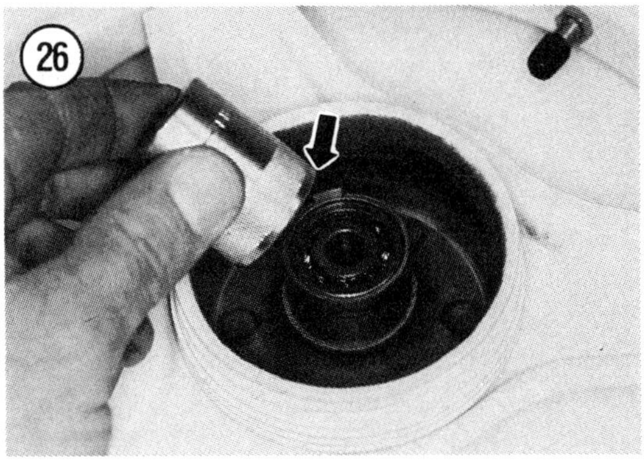
26

7. Place the dust seal squarely against the bore opening with its closed side facing out. Then drive the dust seal in the bore until it bottoms out (**Figure 27**).

8. Check that inner race on each bearing turns without any binding or damage.

TIRE CHANGING

Refer to *Tire Changing* in Chapter Eleven.

HANDLEBAR

Removal/Installation

1. Remove the handlebar pad (**Figure 28**).
2. Loosen the rear brake cable adjuster (**Figure 29**) at the rear wheel.
3. Disconnect the rear brake cable at the handlebar (**Figure 30**).
4. Disconnect the engine stop switch electrical connectors (**Figure 31**).
5. Loosen the throttle housing screws and slide the housing (**Figure 32**) off the handlebar. Do not bend or damage the throttle or front brake cables.
6. Remove the handlebar mounting nuts and washers (**Figure 33**), then remove the handlebar.
7. Inspect the handlebar as described under *Inspection* in this section.
8. To install the handlebar, reverse the removal steps while noting the following:
   a. Tighten the handlebar mounting nuts as specified in **Table 3**.
   b. Adjust the rear brake as described in Chapter Three.

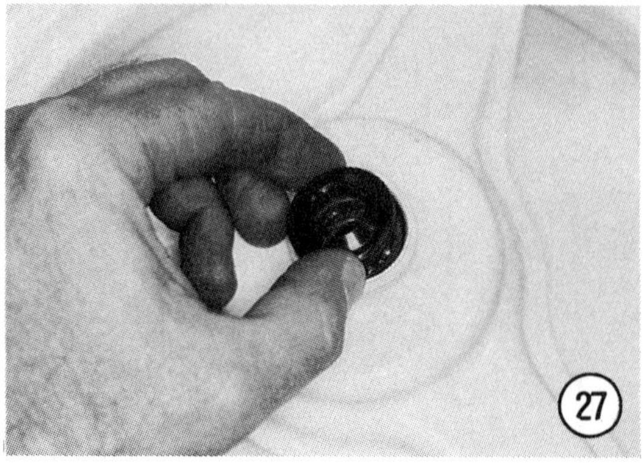
27

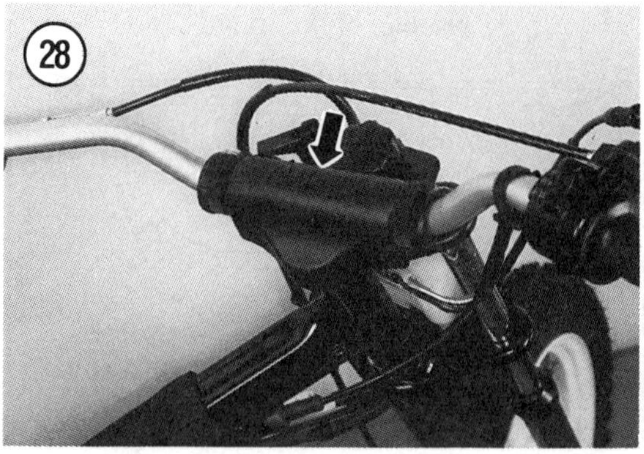
28

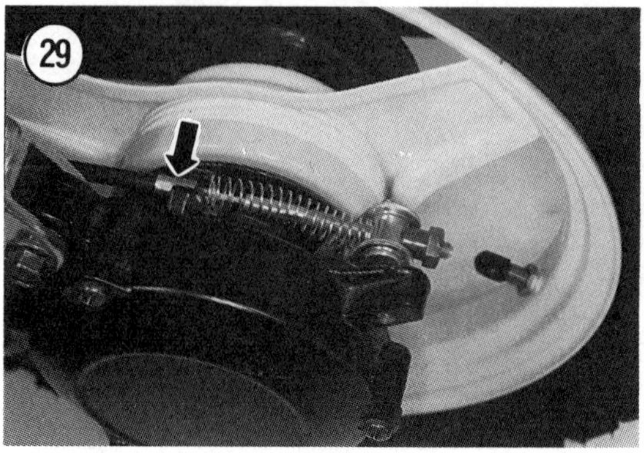
29

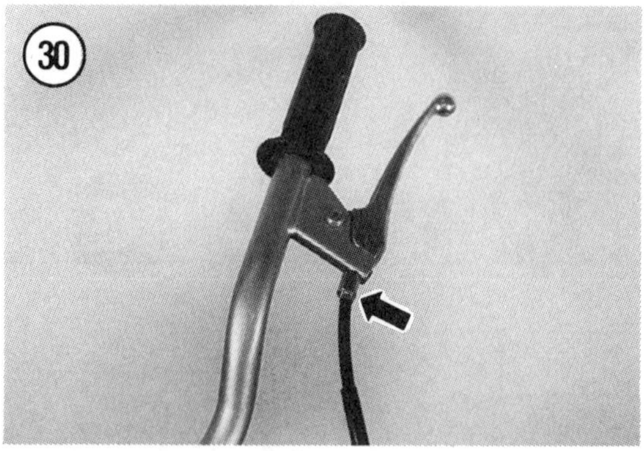
30

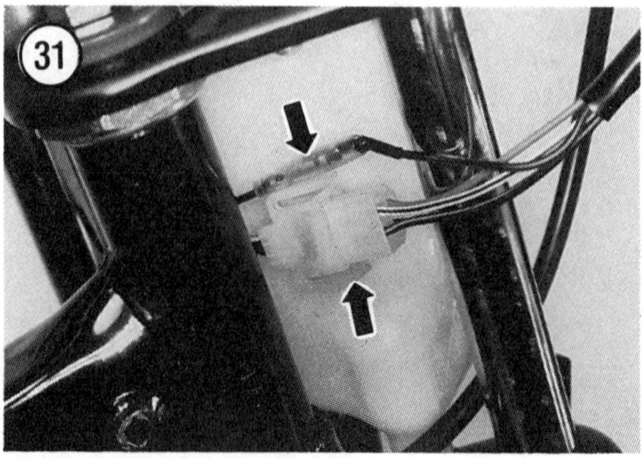
31

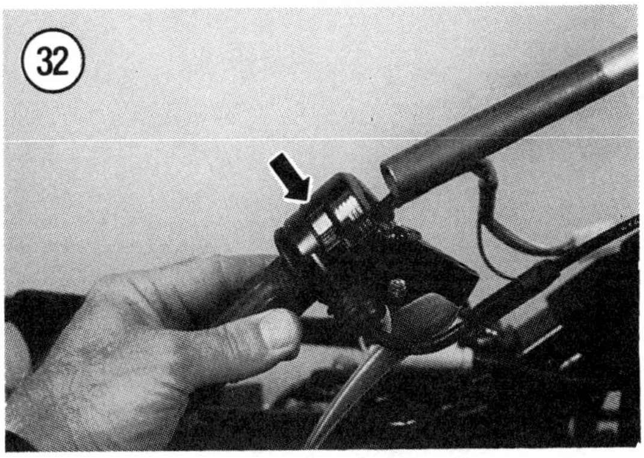

c. Check the throttle cable routing after reinstalling the throttle housing onto the handlebar.
d. Check the throttle cable adjustment as described in Chapter Three.
e. Reconnect the engine stop switch electrical connectors before starting the engine.

WARNING
Make sure the front brake, rear brake, throttle and engine stop switch are operating correctly before riding the bike.

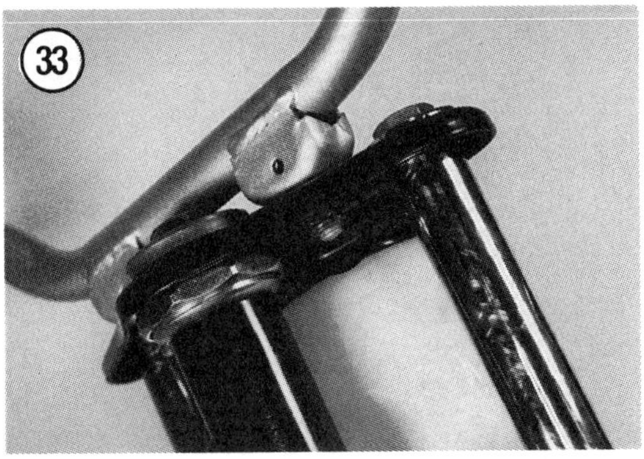

Inspection

1. Check the handlebar for loose or damaged handlebar mounting threads or mounting bracket (**Figure 34**). Replace if necessary.
2. Check the handlebar for a damaged or broken rear brake lever perch (A, **Figure 35**). Replace if necessary.
3. Replace the grips (B, **Figure 35**) if excessively worn or damaged.

NOTE
Replace the grips while the handlebar is mounted on the motorcycle.

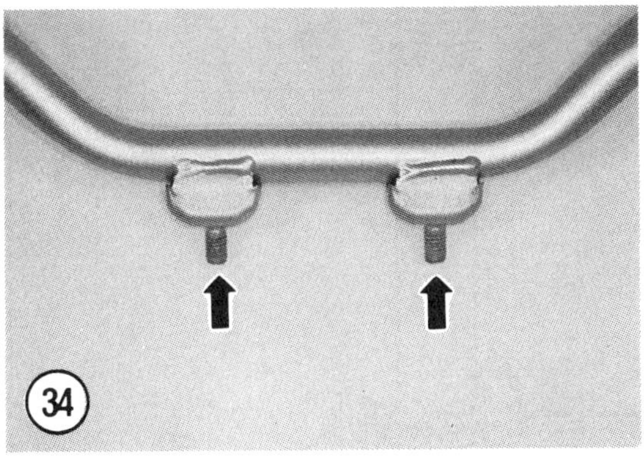

4. Replace a lever that is severely worn, cracked, or if the end ball is broken off (**Figure 36**).

WARNING
The balls on the end of control levers help to prevent the lever from puncturing a rider's body in the event of a crash and forceful contact with the lever. Do not allow the motorcycle to be ridden with a damaged control lever.

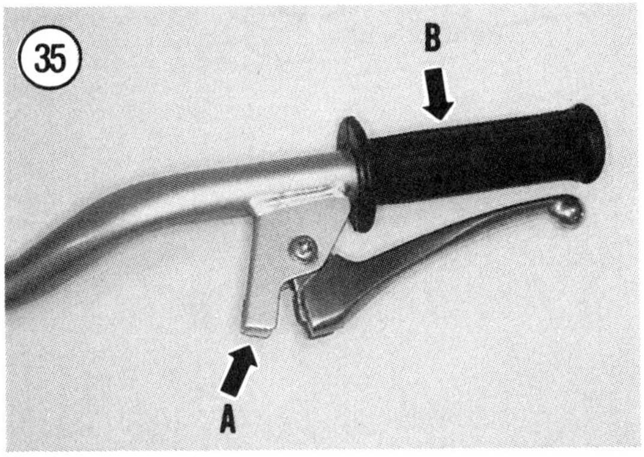

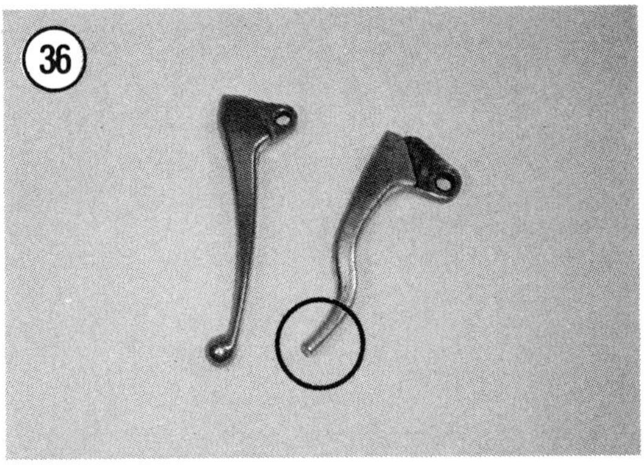

10

(37)

STEERING ASSEMBLY

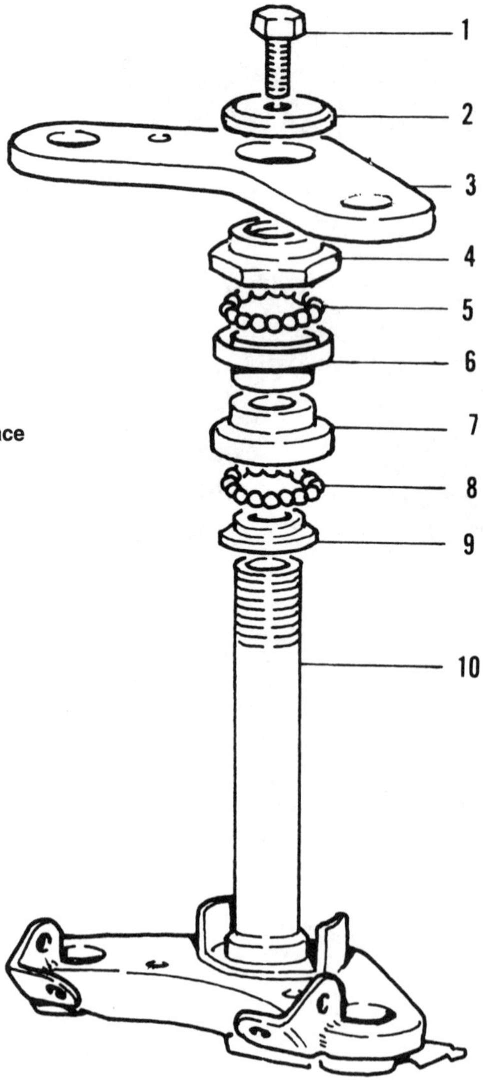

1. Steering stem bolt
2. Washer
3. Upper fork bridge
4. Steering stem nut and bearing race
5. Bearing balls
6. Steering head bearing race (upper)
7. Steering head bearing race (lower)
8. Bearing balls
9. Steering head bearing race
10. Steering stem

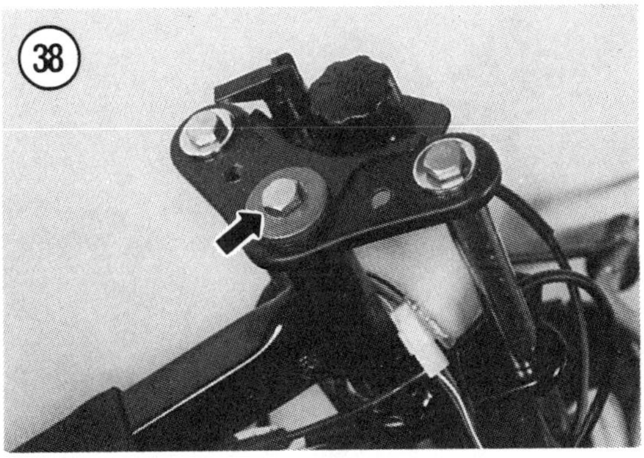

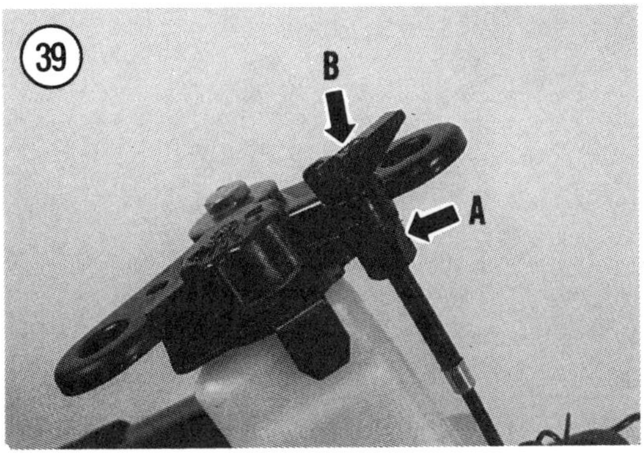

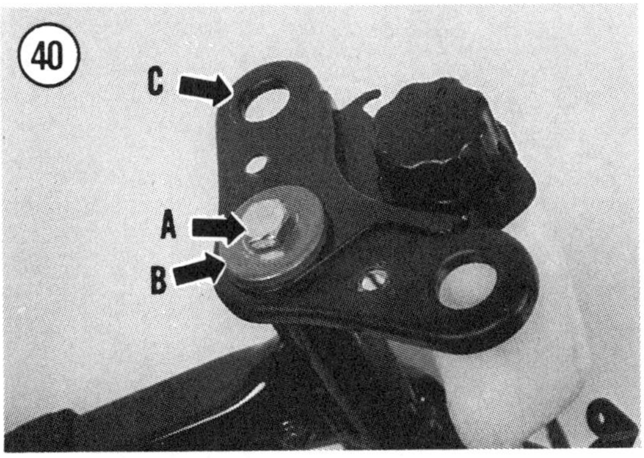

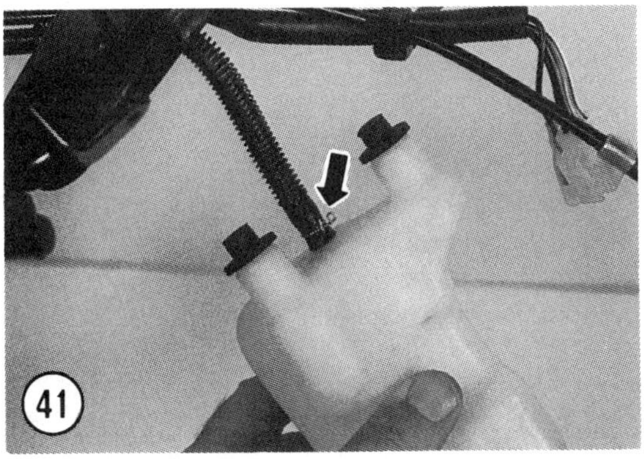

STEERING HEAD

The steering head (**Figure 37**) on the PW50 uses individual bearing balls at the top and bottom pivot positions. The steering head bearing races and the steering stem bearing race need to be removed only if they require replacement.

Table 1 lists steering specifications.

Disassembly

1. Remove the front wheel as described in this chapter.
2. Remove the front fender (Chapter Fifteen).
3. Remove the handlebar as described in this chapter.
4. Loosen, but do not remove, the steering stem bolt (**Figure 38**).
5. Remove the front forks as described in this chapter.
6. Loosen the choke cable mounting nut (A, **Figure 39**) and remove the choke lever (B, **Figure 39**) from the notch in the upper fork bridge.
7. See **Figure 40**. Remove the steering stem bolt (A), washer (B) and upper fork bridge (C).
8. Remove the oil tank from the lower steering stem. Disconnect the oil tank hose (**Figure 41**) from the bottom of the oil tank. Plug the hose and oil tank to prevent oil leakage and contamination. Do not loose the 2 rubber dampers installed on the bottom of the oil tank (**Figure 41**).
9. Remove the oil hose, choke cable and wiring harness from the bracket on the bottom of the steering stem (**Figure 42**).

NOTE

Have an assistant hold the steering stem to keep it from dropping out while hold-

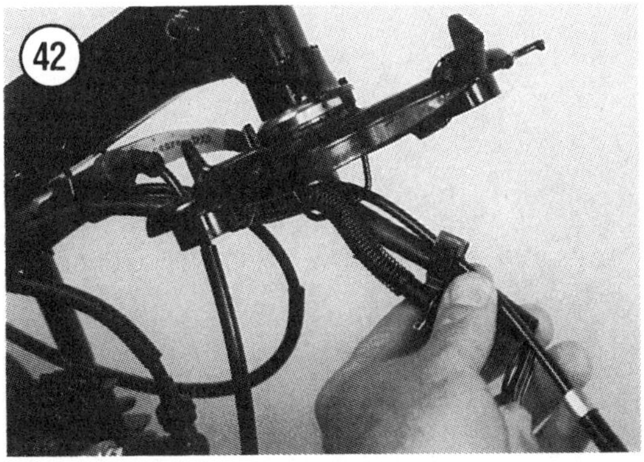

10

ing a large pan directly under the steering stem to catch loose bearing balls.

10. Loosen and remove the steering stem nut (**Figure 43**) and the steering stem (**Figure 44**). See **Figure 45**.

NOTE

In Step 11, remove the bearing balls only. Do not remove the steering head or steering stem bearing races.

11. Remove the upper and lower bearing balls sets (**Figure 46**). Remove any balls stuck in the lower bearing race (**Figure 47**).

NOTE

There are 52 bearing balls 5/32 in. [4.0 mm] diameter)—26 on the top and 26 on the bottom.

Inspection

1. Clean and dry all parts (**Figure 48**).

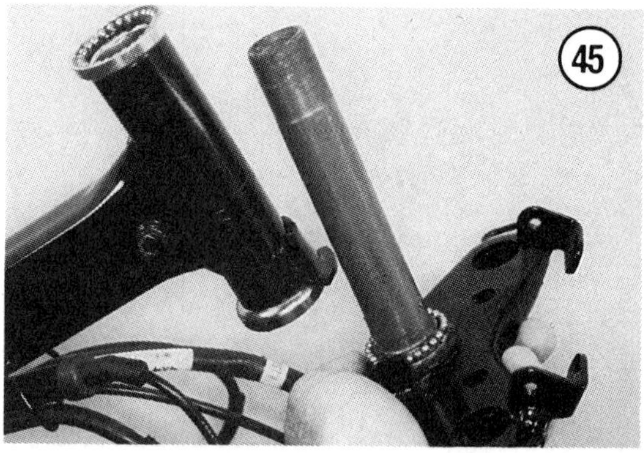

45

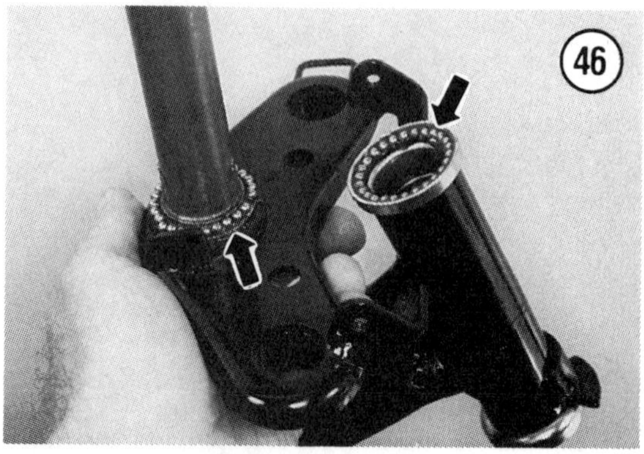

46

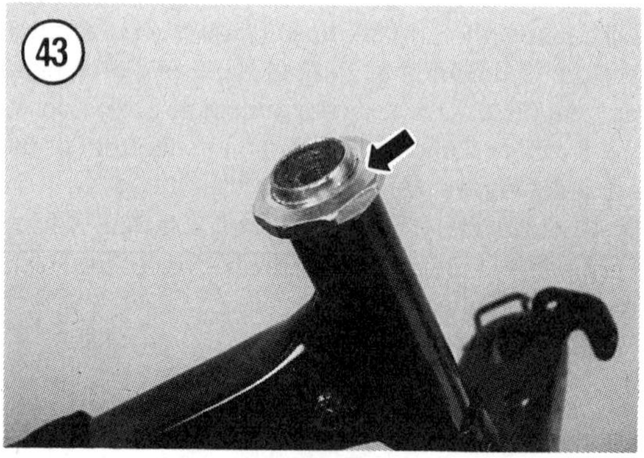

43

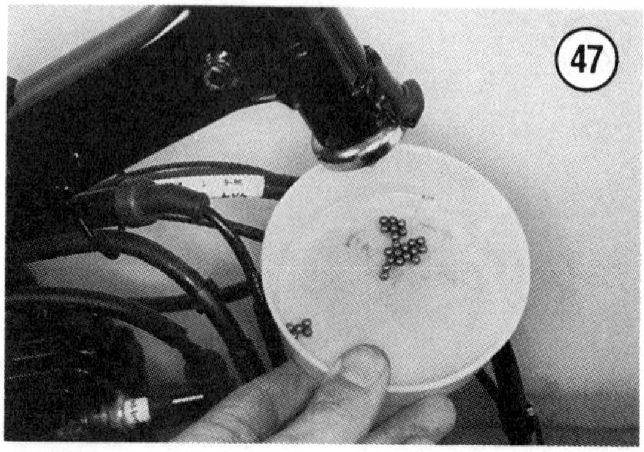

47

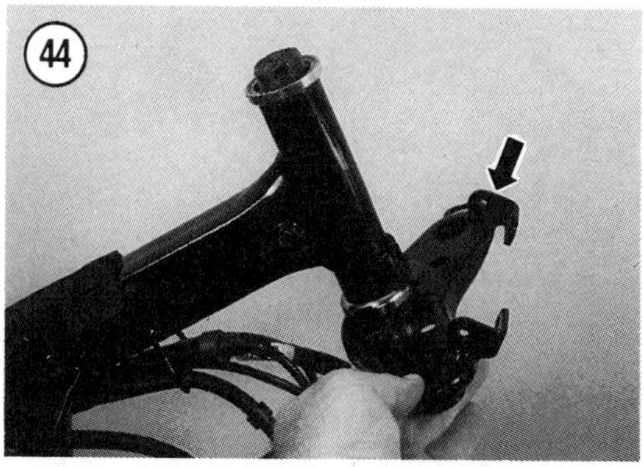

44

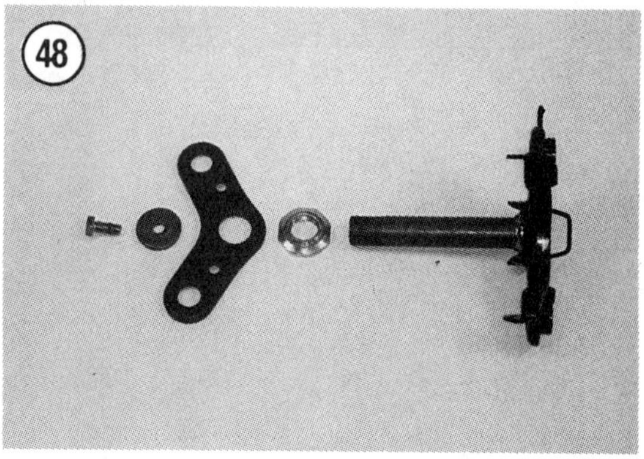

48

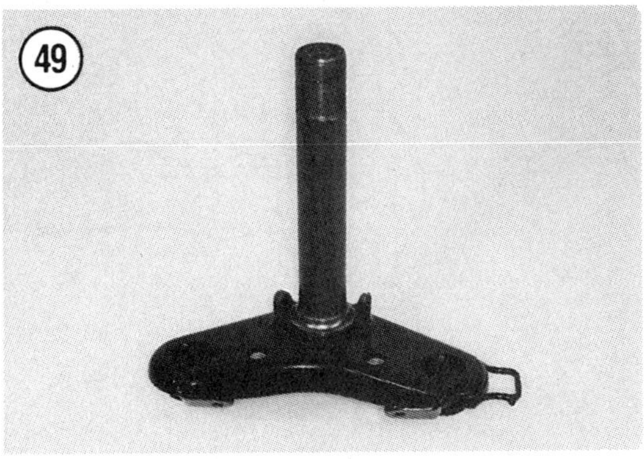

49

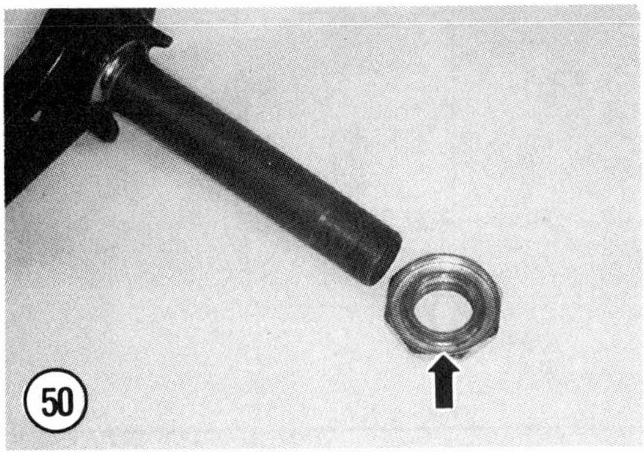

50

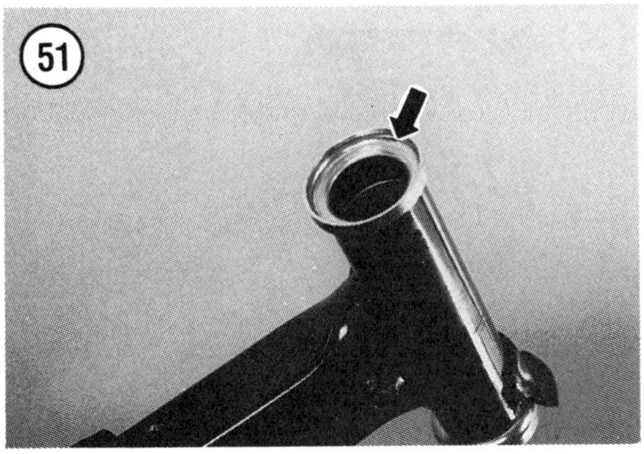

51

52

2. Check the steering head frame welds for cracks and fractures. Refer repair to a qualified frame shop or welding service.
3. Check the steering stem bolt, washer and steering nut (**Figure 48**) and replace if damaged. Check the mating threads in the steering stem for damage.
4. Check the upper fork bridge (**Figure 48**) and steering stem (**Figure 49**) assembly for cracks and damage.
5. Check the bearing races for pitting, galling and corrosion. If a race is worn or damaged, replace both race sets and all bearing balls. Replace bearing races as described in this section. The bearing races are identified as follows:
   a. Upper bearing races—**Figure 50** and **Figure 51**.
   b. Lower bearing races—**Figure 52** and **Figure 53**.
6. Check all of the bearing balls (**Figure 47**) for flat spots, cracks, excessive wear or other damage. If the bearing balls are worn or damaged, replace all bearing races and bearing balls as a set.

Steering Head Bearing Race Replacement

The steering head bearing races (**Figure 51** and **Figure 53**) are pressed into place. Do not remove them unless they are worn and require replacement; ball races are easily bent.

To remove the steering head races (**Figure 51** and **Figure 53**), insert an aluminum or brass drift into the head tube and carefully tap the race out from the inside (**Figure 54**). Tap all the way around the race so that neither the race nor the head tube is bent. To install a race, grease it and fit it into the end of the head tube. Tap it slowly and squarely with a socket

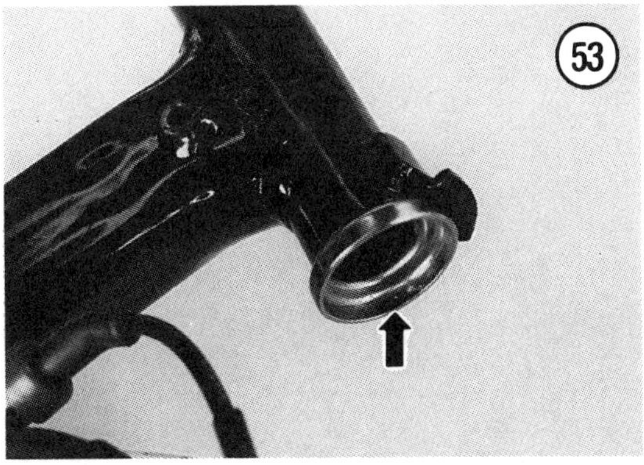

53

or a block of wood (**Figure 55**). Make sure it is fully seated. You will notice a distinct change in the hammering sound as the race bottoms-out.

NOTE

*The upper (**Figure 51**) and lower (**Figure 53**) steering head races are different. Be sure that you install them in the proper ends of the head tube.*

Steering Stem Bearing Race Replacement

The steering stem bearing race (**Figure 52**) is pressed into place. Do not remove this race unless it is worn and requires replacement.

1. Thread the steering nut onto the steering stem (**Figure 56**).
2. Remove the steering stem bearing race with a chisel as shown in **Figure 57**. Work around the race in a circle, prying a little at a time.
3. Clean the steering stem with solvent and dry thoroughly.
4. Inspect the steering stem and replace if it bent or otherwise damaged.
5. Slide the new race onto the steering stem until it stops.
6. Tap the race down with a piece of hardwood or a piece of pipe of the proper size (**Figure 58**). Make sure it is seated squarely and all the way down (**Figure 52**).

Assembly

Refer to **Figure 37** when assembling the steering assembly.

55

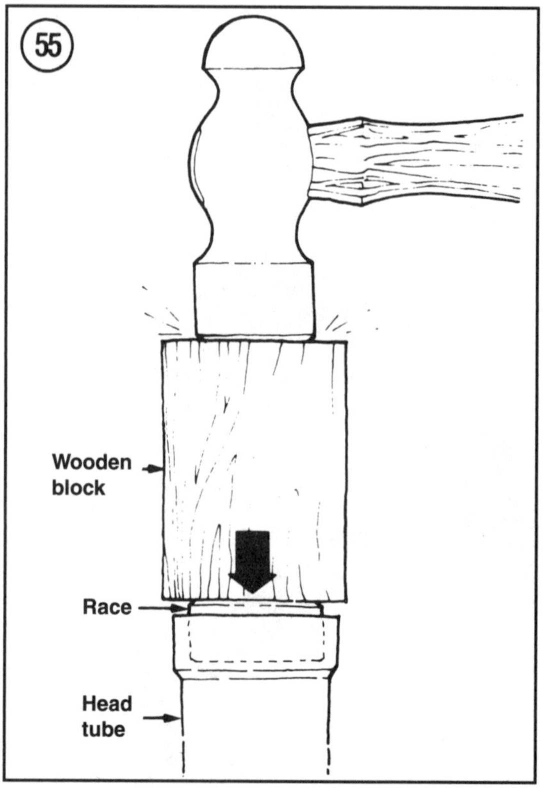

56

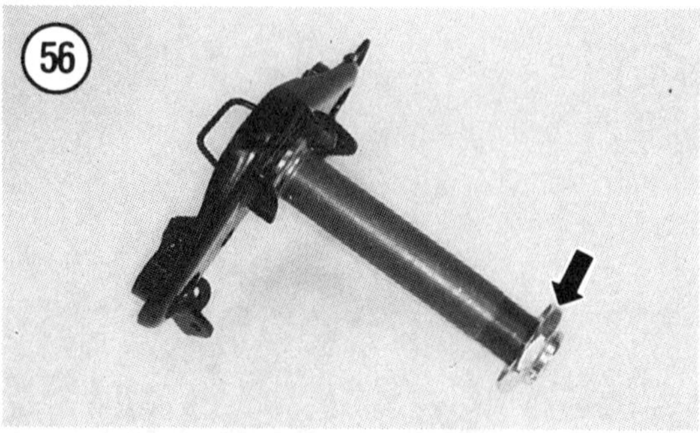

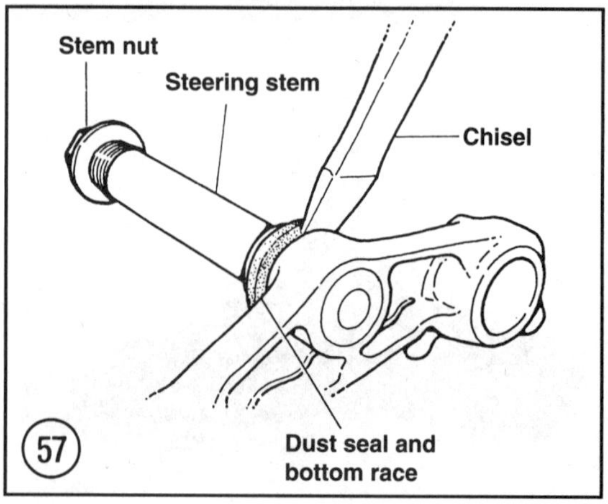

57

54

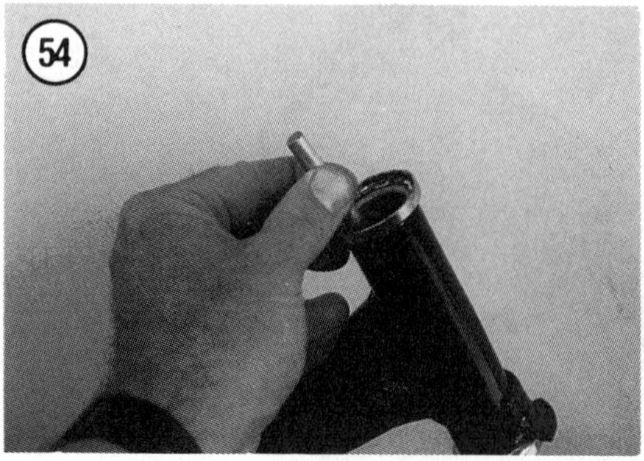

58

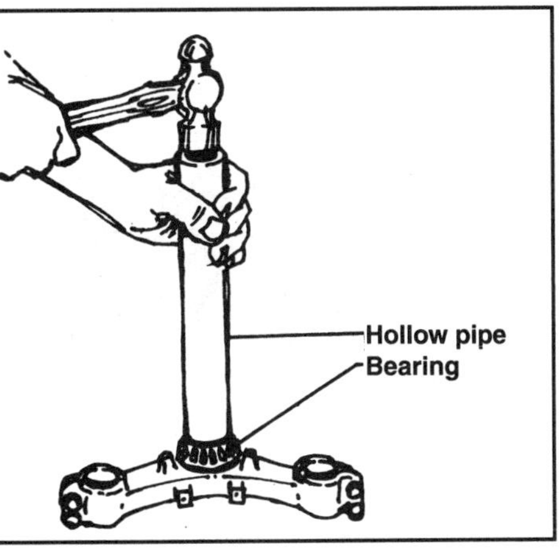

59

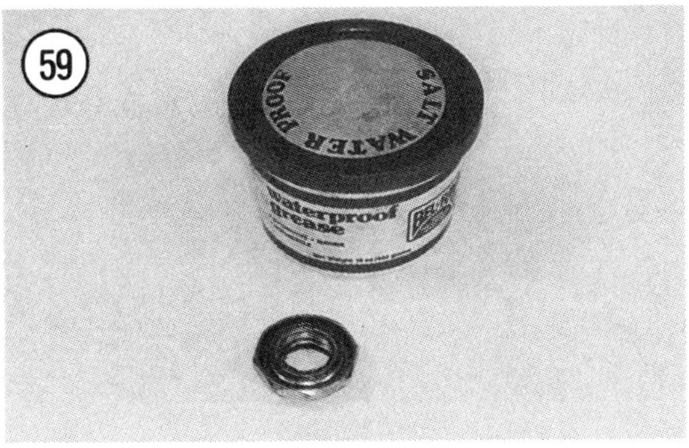

60

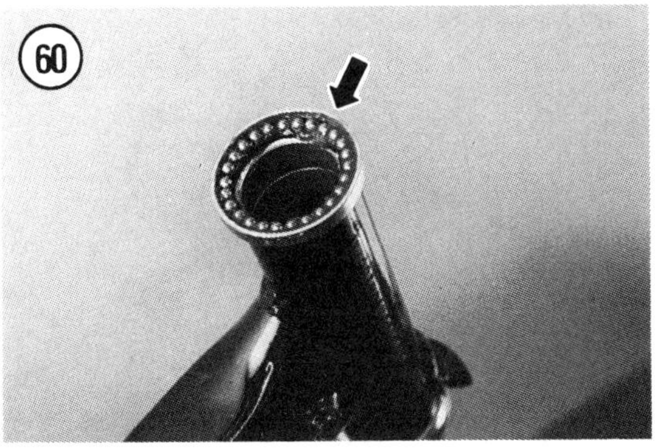

61

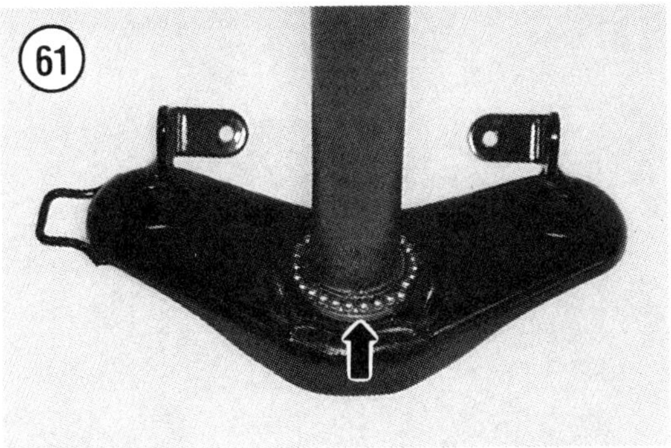

1. Make sure the upper (**Figure 51**) and lower (**Figure 53**) steering head bearing races are properly seated in the frame.
2. Lubricate all of the bearing races with a waterproof bearing grease (**Figure 59**).
3. Fit 26 bearing balls around the upper steering head bearing race (**Figure 60**). The grease will hold them in place.
4. Fit 26 bearing balls around the steering stem bearing race (**Figure 61**). Grease will hold them in place.
5. Insert the steering stem (**Figure 44**) into the steering head. Hold it firmly in place.
6. Check that none of the upper bearing balls (**Figure 62**) were dislodged.
7. Screw the steering nut (**Figure 63**) onto the steering stem.

NOTE:

Yamaha lists the steering nut torque at 6 N•m (53 in.-lb.). While you can torque the nut to this specification, you will obtain a more accurate steering adjustment by performing the procedure in Steps 8-10. Also, the steering nut may

62

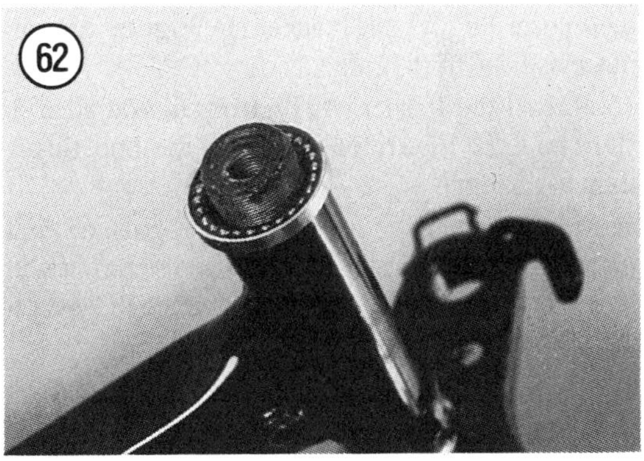

63

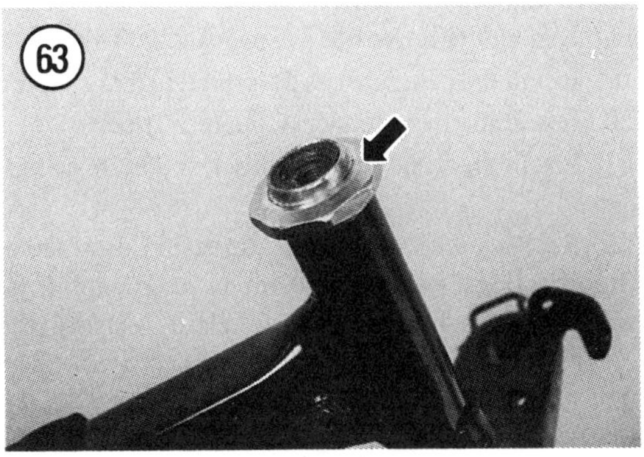

have to be readjusted after tightening the steering stem bolt later in this procedre.

8. Tighten the steering nut (**Figure 63**) firmly to seat the bearings.
9. Loosen the steering nut (**Figure 63**) until there is noticeable play in the steering stem.
10. Tighten the steering nut (**Figure 63**) just enough to remove all play, both horizontal and vertical, yet loose enough that the assembly will turn under its own weight after an initial assist.
11. Feed the oil hose, choke cable and wiring harness back through the bracket on the bottom of the steering stem (**Figure 42**).
12. Remove the plug, then reconnect the oil hose onto the bottom of the oil tank (**Figure 41**). Secure the hose with its clamp.
13. Fit the 2 rubber dampers onto the bottom of the oil tank (**Figure 41**), then install the tank into the 2 holes in the steering stem (**Figure 64**).

CAUTION
If the rubber dampers are not used, the oil tank may crack and leak.

14. Install the upper fork bridge (A, **Figure 65**), then push the oil tank bracket (B, **Figure 65**) into place over the fork bridge.
15. Install the washer (A, **Figure 66**) and steering stem bolt (B, **Figure 66**). Tighten the bolt finger-tight at this time.
16. Fit the choke lever bracket (A, **Figure 67**) into the notch in the upper fork bridge and secure it with its mounting nut (B, **Figure 67**). Operate the lever to make sure it works correctly.
17. Slide the fork tubes into the steering head assembly and secure them in place with their lower pinch bolts as described in this chapter.
18. With both fork tubes in place, tighten the steering stem bolt (**Figure 68**) as specified in **Table 3**.
19. Install the handlebar as described in this chapter.
20. Install the front fender (Chapter Fifteen).
21. Install the front wheel as described in this chapter.
22. Recheck the steering adjustment as described in Step 10. If the steering adjustment is now too tight (after tightening the steering stem bolt), perform the *Steering Adjustment* procedure in this chapter.
23. Bleed the oil pump as described in Chapter Nine.

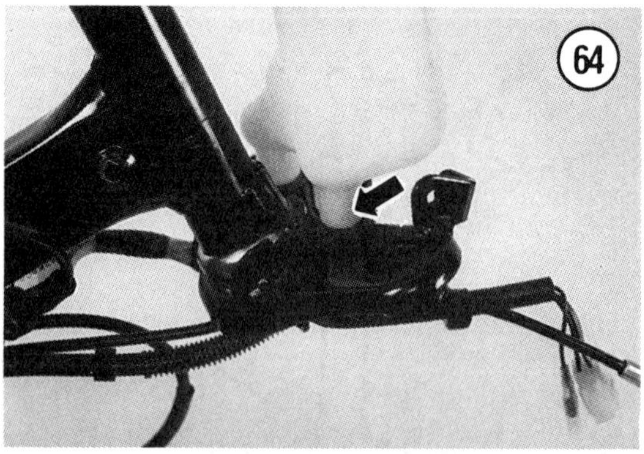

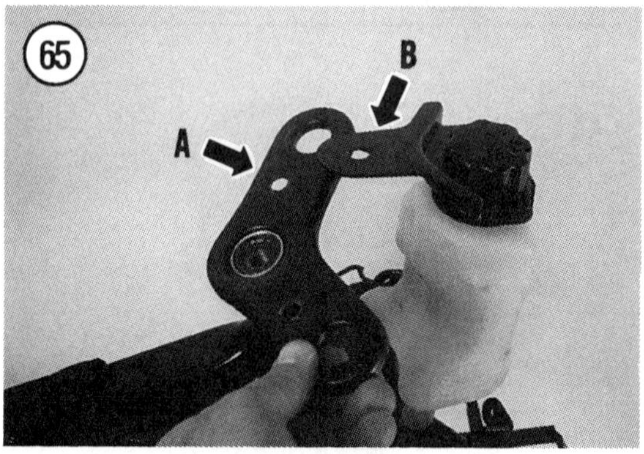

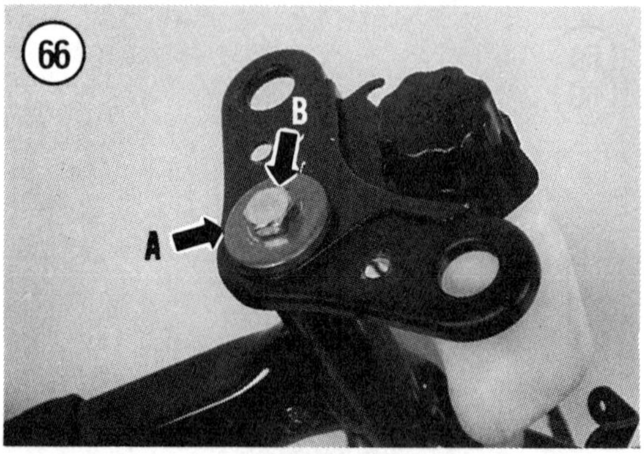

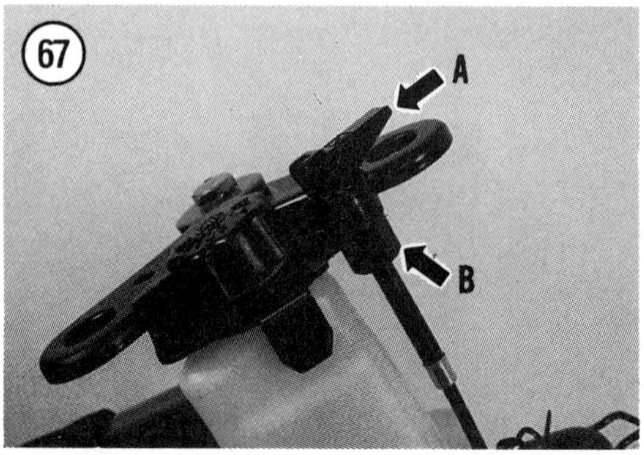

24. After 30 minutes to 1 hour of riding time, recheck the steering adjustment.

Steering Adjustment

If your periodic checks detect excessive steering play, adjust the steering as described in this section. The steering head should also be disassembled, cleaned and inspected for wear on the bearing balls and races, then lubricated with a waterproof grease according to the maintenance schedule in Chapter Three.

The steering adjustment can be checked and adjusted with the front wheel and front forks mounted on the bike.

1. Support the bike with the front wheel off the ground.
2. Check bearing play by turning the steering stem from lock-to-lock. The steering stem must pivot smoothly with no binding or roughness. There should be no horizontal or vertical play, yet the steering should be loose enough so that the front end will turn under its own weight after an initial assist. If there is any noticeable binding or roughness, first check that the control cables are not causing the condition. If they are routed properly, continue with Step 3.

NOTE

Steps 3-10 describe steering play adjustment.

3. Remove the handlebar as described in this chapter.
4. Remove the steering stem bolt and washer (**Figure 68**), then pivot the oil tank and its mounting bracket forward (A, **Figure 69**).
5. Remove the 2 upper fork tube mounting bolts and washers (B, **Figure 69**), then remove the upper fork bridge (C, **Figure 69**).
6. Loosen or tighten the steering nut (**Figure 70**) to adjust the steering play.
7. Recheck steering play by turning the steering stem from side to side. If the steering play is okay, turn the handlebar so that the front forks are facing straight ahead. Then grasp the fork tubes and try to move them back and forth (front to back). Do this several times while trying to detect any play in the bearings. If there is play, but the steering adjustment feels okay, the bearings and races are probably worn and require replacement. It helps to have someone steady the bike when checking steering head play.
8. Reposition the oil tank and then install the upper fork bridge (C, **Figure 69**)
9. Install the steering stem bolt and washer and tighten as specified in **Table 3**.
10. Recheck the steering play. If necessary, repeat these steps until the steering play adjustment is correct. Then continue with Step 11.
11. Install the upper fork tube mounting bolts and washers (B, **Figure 69**); tighten both bolts securely.

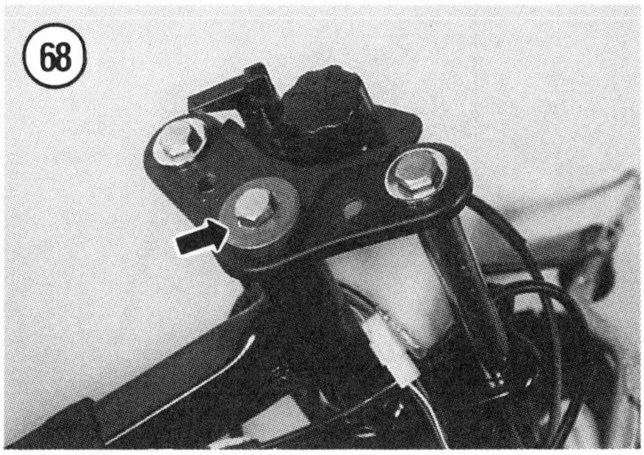

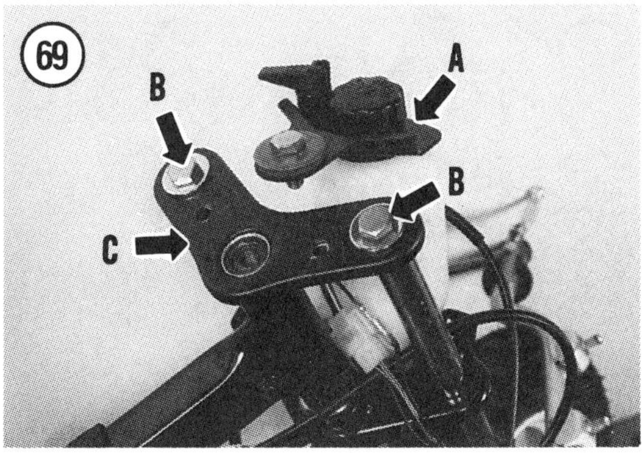

10

12. Install the handlebar as described in this chapter.

FRONT FORKS

Each fork consists of the fork tube (inner tube), slider (outer tube), fork spring and the damper rod with its components. To simplify fork service and to prevent the mixing of parts, the forks should be removed, serviced and reinstalled individually.

Table 1 lists fork tube specifications.

Removal/Installation

1. Support the bike with the front wheel off the ground.
2. Remove the front wheel as described in this chapter.
3. Remove the handlebar as described in this chapter.
4. Remove the upper fork tube mounting bolt and washer (B, **Figure 69**).
5. Remove the fork tube pinch bolt (**Figure 71**). Then work the fork tube down and out with a twisting motion.
6. Install the fork tube by reversing these removal steps, plus the following:
   a. Route the throttle cable between the right fork tube and oil tank as shown in **Figure 72**.
   b. Install the fork tube with the front brake anchor boss (**Figure 73**) on the left side.
   a. Tighten the fork tube pinch bolt (**Figure 71**) as specified in **Table 3**.
   b. Tighten the upper fork tube mounting bolt (B, **Figure 69**) securely.

Disassembly

Refer to **Figure 74**.

1. Remove the fork tube as described in this chapter.
2. Slide the dust cover (**Figure 75**) off the fork tube.
3. Clamp the slider in a vise with soft jaws.
4. Remove the circlip (**Figure 76**) from the groove in the top of the slider.
5. Grasp the slider and then twist and pull the fork tube and damper assembly out (**Figure 77**).

NOTE

Because these fork tubes do not operate in oil (grease only), they can be difficult to separate under the best of conditions. If any water has leaked inside the fork tube, rust on the parts will make fork separation difficult.

6. Slide the dust seal, collar and rebound spring (**Figure 78**) off the top of the fork tube.
7. Remove the rubber cap (**Figure 79**) from the end of the lower spring seat.
8. Remove the pin (A, **Figure 80**) and the lower spring seat (B, **Figure 80**).
9. Remove the fork spring (**Figure 81**) and the bumper stop (**Figure 82**).

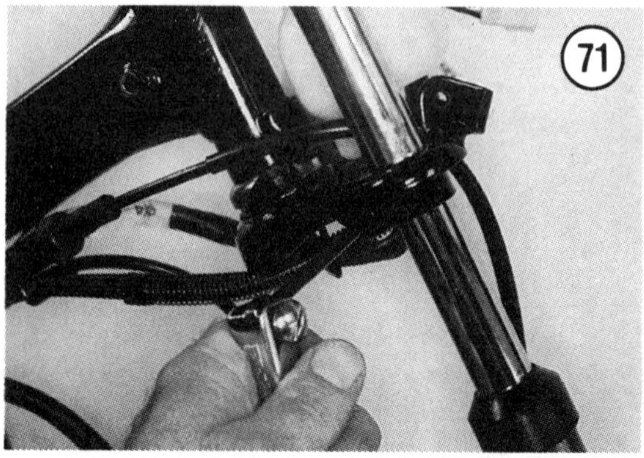

71

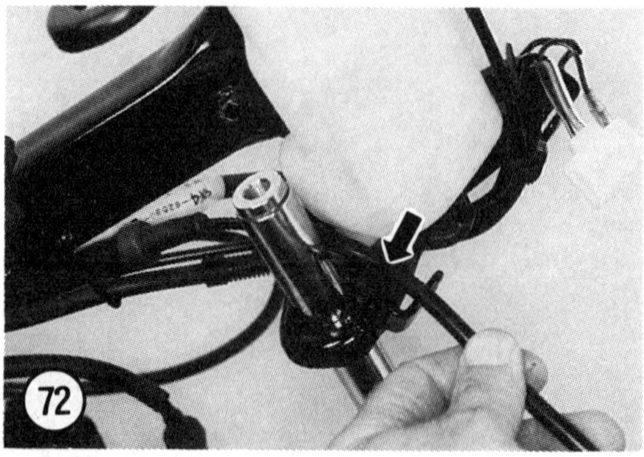

72

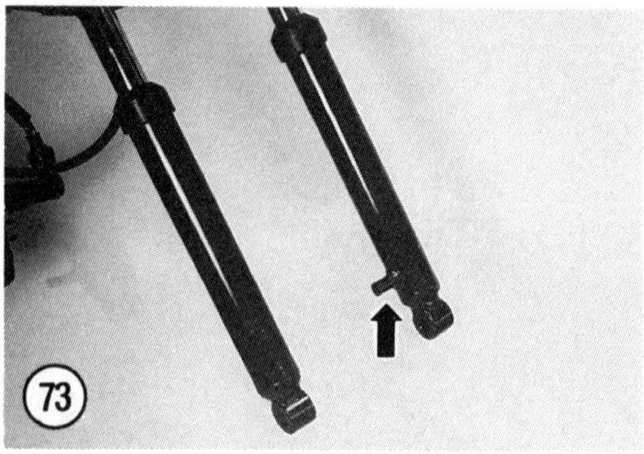

73

(74)

FRONT FORK

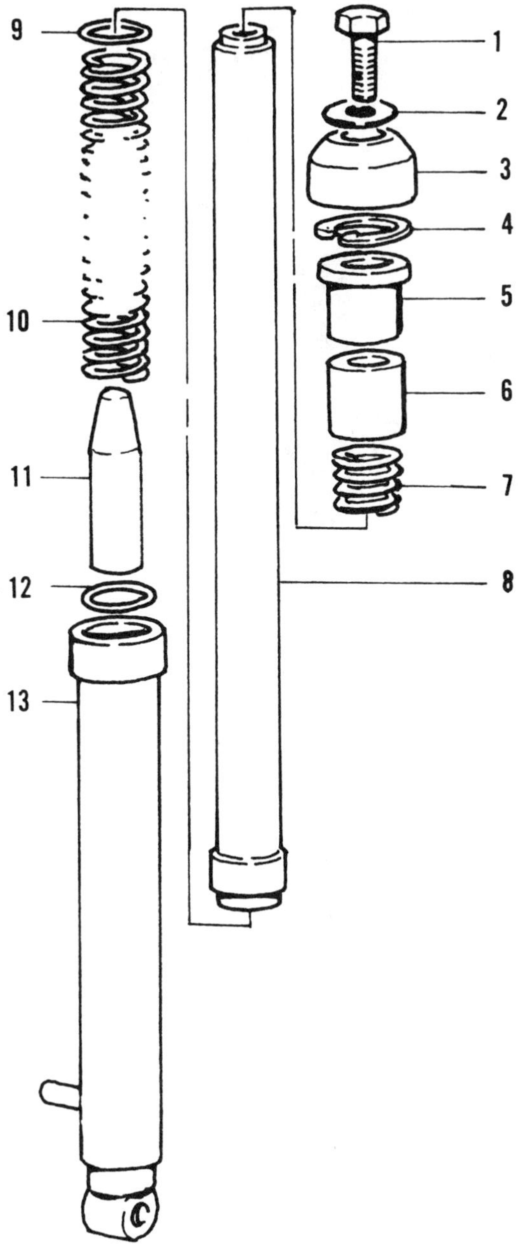

1. Front fork upper mounting bolt
2. Washer
3. Dust cover
4. Circlip
5. Dust seal
6. Collar
7. Rebound spring
8. Fork tube
9. Spring seat
10. Fork spring
11. Bumper stop
12. Lower spring seat
13. Slider

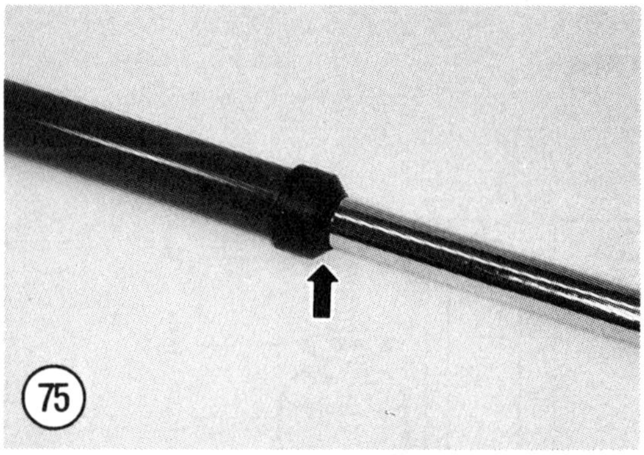

75

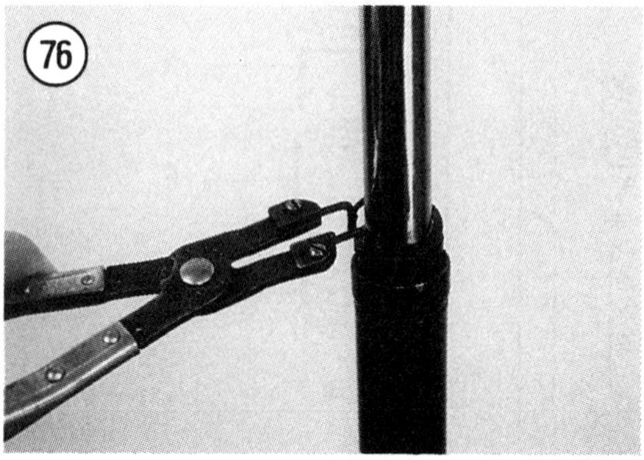

76

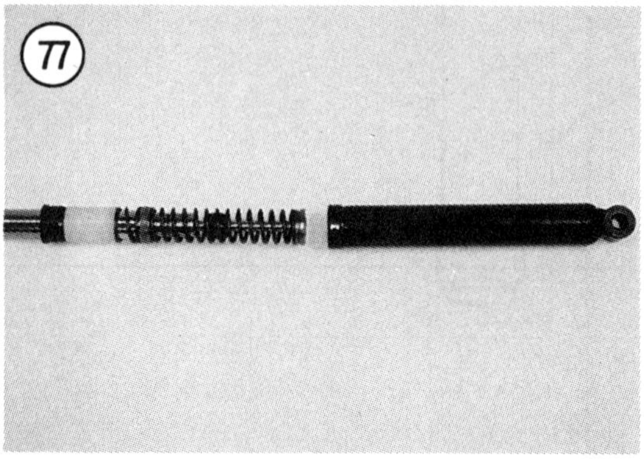

77

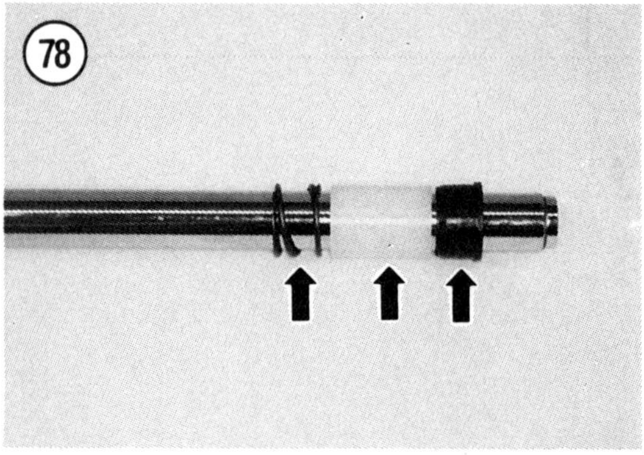

78

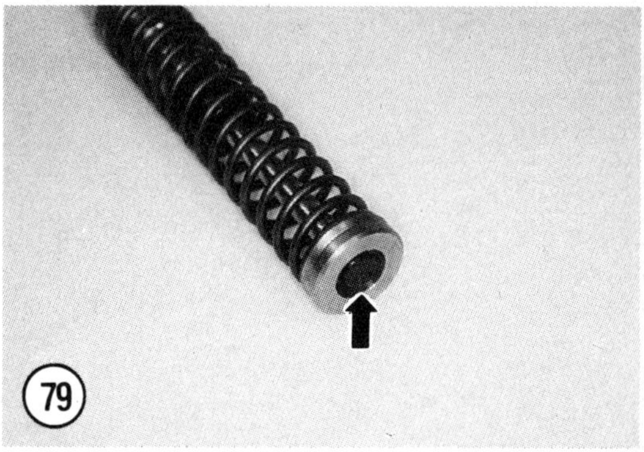

79

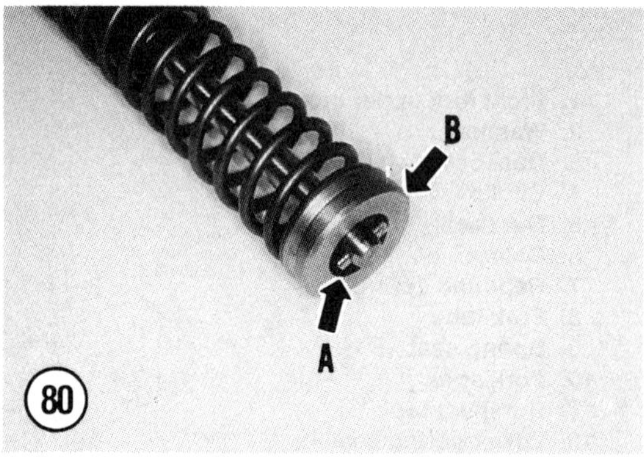

80

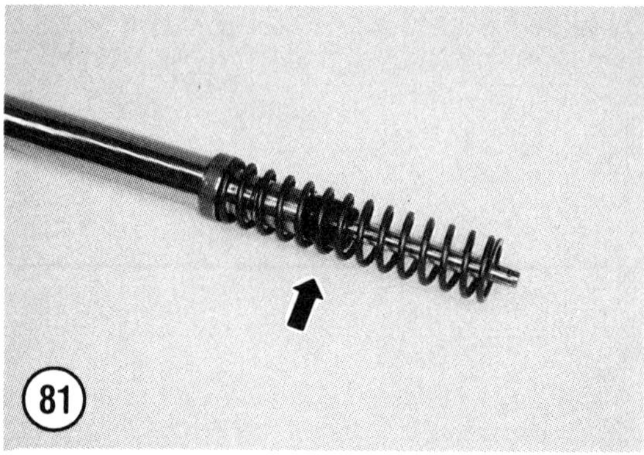

81

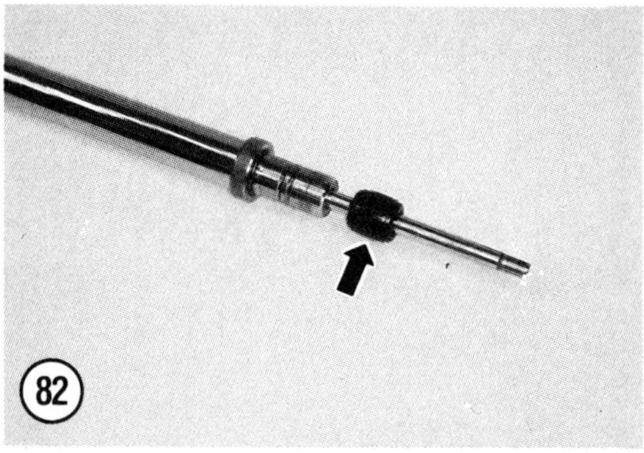

82

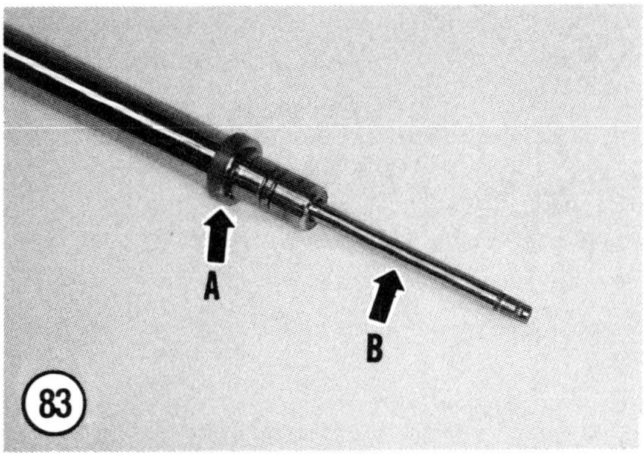

83

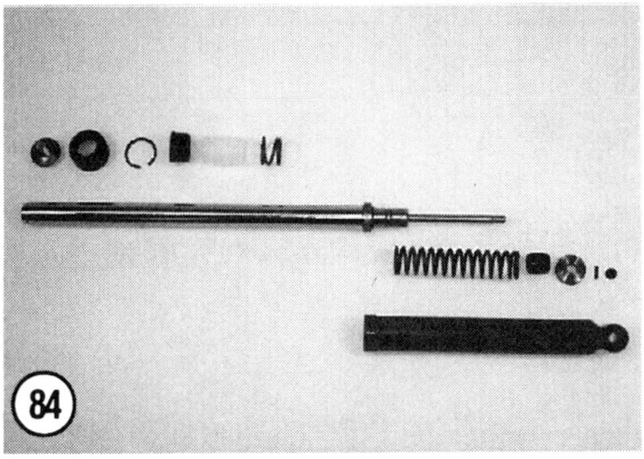
84

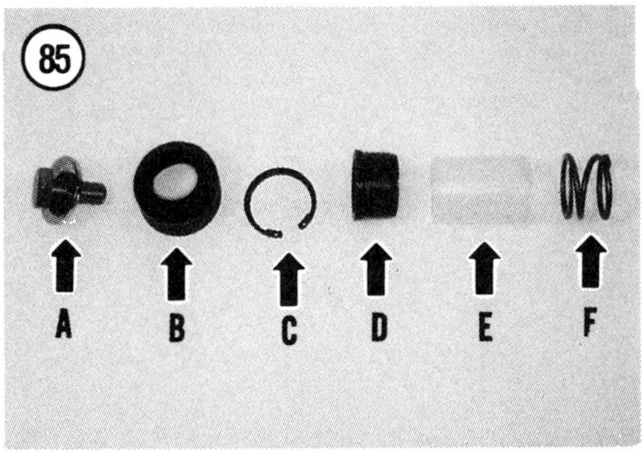

85

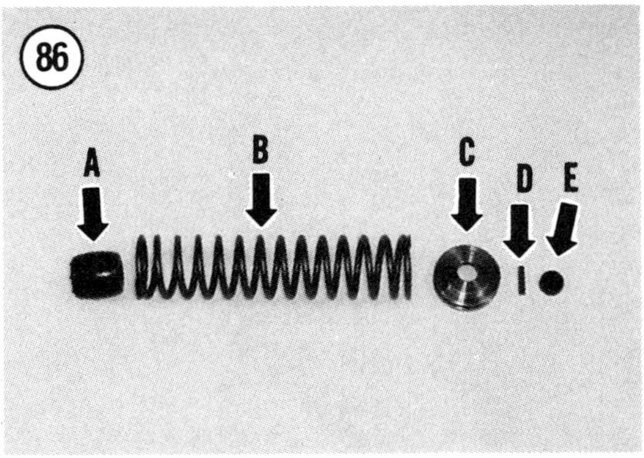

86

NOTE

The upper spring seat (A, ***Figure 83****) and the damper assembly (B,* ***Figure 83****) are fixed units and must not be removed from the fork tube.*

Inspection

Replace parts that show damage as described in this section.

1. Clean and dry all parts (**Figure 84**).
2. Check the upper assembly (**Figure 85**) for:
   a. Damaged fork tube mounting bolt (A) and washer.
   b. Worn or damaged dust cover (B). A damaged dust cover will allow water to enter the lower slider assembly.
   c. Weakened or bent circlip (C).
   d. Worn or damaged dust seal (D) or collar (E).
   e. Weak or damaged rebound spring (F).
3. Check the lower assembly (**Figure 86**) for:
   a. Damaged bumper stop (A).
   b. Fatigued or damaged fork spring (B). Measure the free length of the fork spring and compare to the specification listed in **Table 1**. Because the specification lists the length of the new spring, replace the spring if it is appreciably shorter than the new spring length.
4. Check the fork tube (**Figure 87**) for:
   a. Bent or scratched tube.
   b. Loose or damaged upper spring seat (A, **Figure 83**).
   c. Bent or damaged damper rod (B, **Figure 83**).
5. Check the slider (**Figure 88**) for:
   a. Dents or exterior damage that may cause the upper fork tube to hang up during riding conditions.

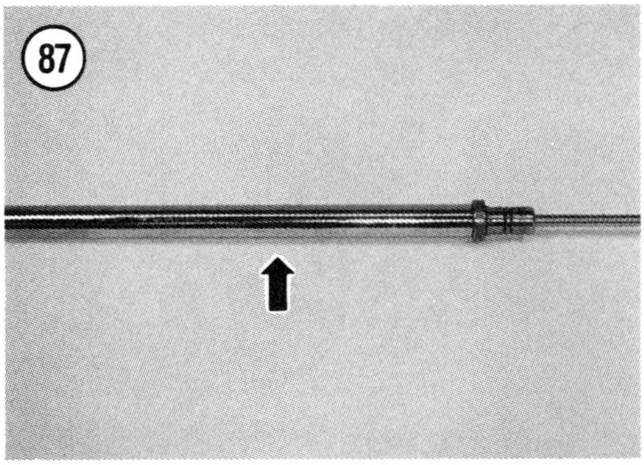
87

b. A worn or damaged circlip groove (**Figure 89**).

Assembly

1. Make sure all parts are clean before starting assembly.
2. Lubricate both springs with grease.
3. Install the bumper stop (**Figure 82**) onto the damper rod.
4. Install the fork spring (**Figure 81**) over the damper rod and seat it against the upper spring seat.
5. Install the lower spring seat with its shoulder side (**Figure 90**) facing toward the damper rod. See **Figure B, Figure 80**.
6. Compress the spring seat and spring by hand, then install the pin (A, **Figure 80**) through the hole in the end of the damper rod. Release the spring seat and spring.
7. Install the rubber cap (**Figure 79**) into the end of the spring seat.

NOTE
***Figure 91** shows the lower part fully assembled.*

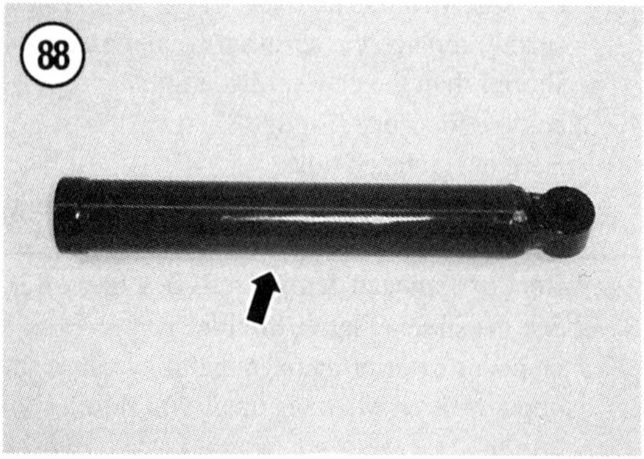
88

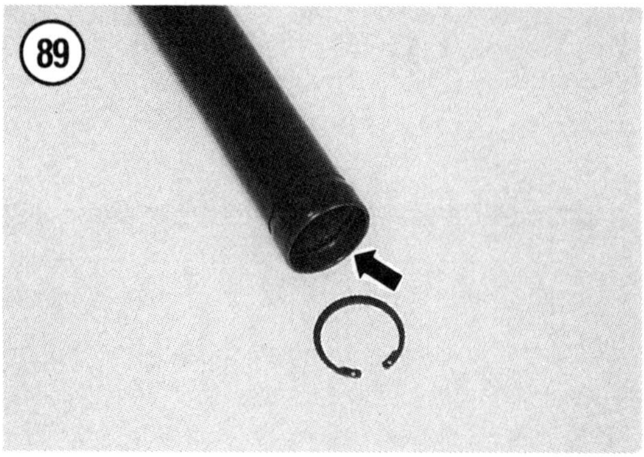
89

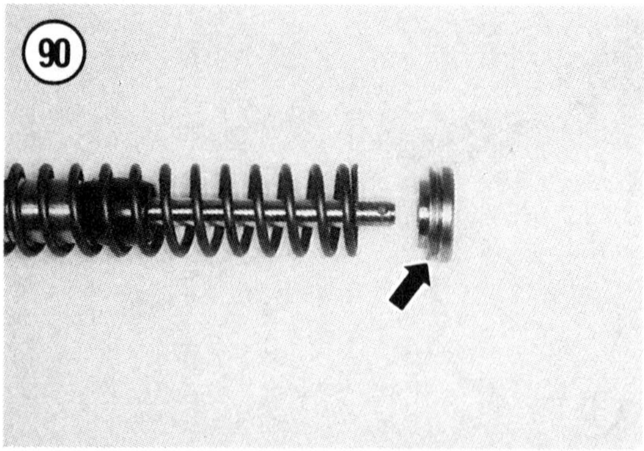
90

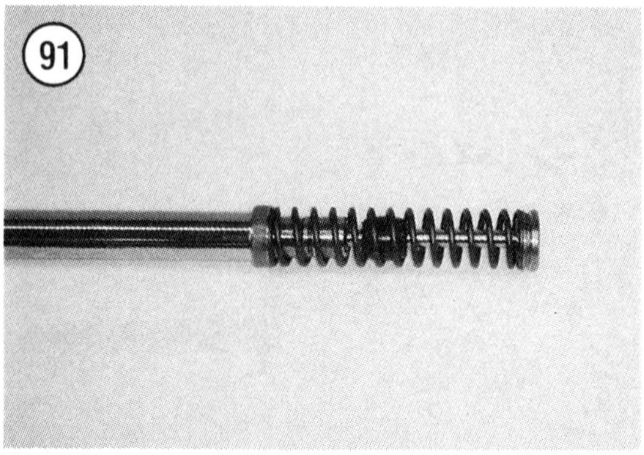
91

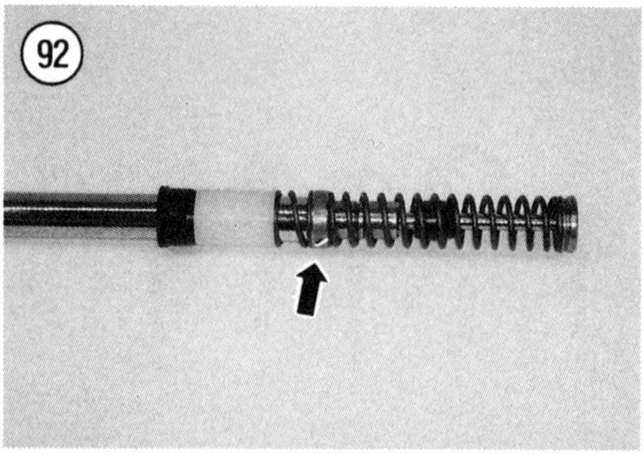
92

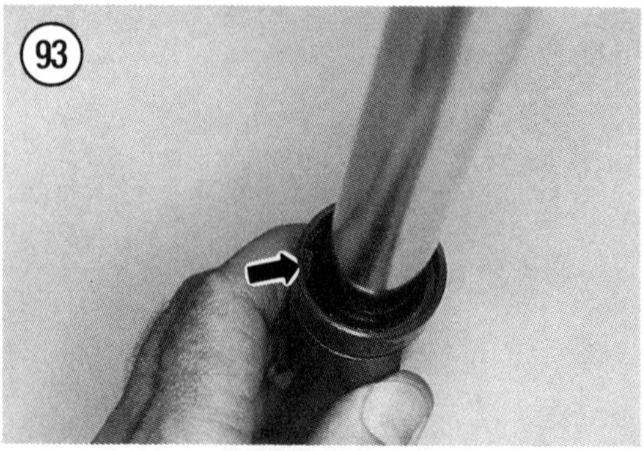
93

8. Install the rebound spring, collar and dust seal (**Figure 78**) over the fork tube and seat against the upper spring seat as shown in **Figure 92**. Install the dust seal with its shoulder facing away from the collar.
9. Lubricate all of the internal fork components with grease.
10. Insert the fork tube assembly into the slider (**Figure 77**).
11. Install the circlip over the fork tube with its square side facing away from the slider.
12. Compress the dust seal, then install the circlip into the groove in the top of the slider (**Figure 76**). Make sure it seats in the groove completely (**Figure 93**).
13. Install the dust cover (**Figure 75**) and seat it into the groove in the slider.
14. Install the fork tubes as described in this chapter.

Table 1 FRONT SUSPENSION AND STEERING SPECIFICATIONS (PW50)

Frame type	Steel tube backbone
Caster angle	25.5°
Trail	50 mm (1.97 in.)
Steering	
Type	Individual steel balls
Ball diameter	5/32 in.
Number of balls in steering head	
Upper race	26 pieces
Lower race	26 pieces
Front fork travel	60 mm (2.4 in.)
Fork spring	
Free length	115 mm (4.53 in.)
Spring rate	0.4 kg/mm (22.4 in.-lb.)

Table 2 TIRE AND WHEEL SPECIFICATIONS (PW50)

Rim size	
Front	10 × 1.50/steel
Rear	10 × 1.50/steel
Tire size	
Front	2.50 × 10-4PR (tube type)
Rear	2.50 × 10-4PR (tube type)
Tire pressure	
Front	100 kPa (15 psi)
Rear	100 kPa (15 psi)
Rim runout limit	
Side-to-side	1 mm (0.04 in.)
Up and down	1 mm (0.04 in.)

Table 3 FRONT SUSPENSION TIGHTENING TORQUES (PW50)

	N•m	in.-lb.	ft.-lb.
Front axle nut	40	—	29
Handlebar mounting nuts	19	—	13
Steering nut	See text		
Fork tube pinch bolt	32	—	23
Steering stem bolt	32	—	23

CHAPTER ELEVEN

FRONT SUSPENSION AND STEERING (BW80 AND PW80)

This chapter describes repair and maintenance on the front wheel, wheel bearings, steering components, front forks and tire changing.

Steering and front suspension specifications are listed in **Table 1**. Tire and rim specifications are listed in **Table 2**. **Tables 1-3** are at the end of the chapter.

FRONT WHEEL

Refer to **Figure 1** (BW80) or **Figure 2** (PW80) when servicing the front wheel in this section.

Removal/Installation

1. Support the motorcycle with the front wheel off the ground.
2. Loosen the front brake adjuster (A, **Figure 3**) at the front wheel.
3. Remove the axle nut cotter pin and discard it. See **Figure 4** (BW80) or B, **Figure 3** (PW80).
4. Remove the axle nut and flat washer (BW80). See **Figure 4** (BW80) or B, **Figure 3** (PW80).
5. Remove the front axle (A, **Figure 5** or A, **Figure 6**) and pull out the wheel and brake assembly. Remove the brake assembly from the front wheel.
6. Remove the collar and dust cover from the right side of the wheel. See B, **Figure 5** (BW80) or B, **Figure 6** (PW80). The dust cover will come off with the collar (**Figure 7**).
7. Perform the *Inspection* procedure in this section to clean and inspect the parts.
8. Install the front wheel by reversing these removal steps. Note the following:
   a. On PW80 models, a special washer is attached onto the outside of each fork tube (**Figure 8**). If a washer falls off after removing the front axle, secure it in place with silicone sealant.
   b. If removed, install the dust cover onto the collar (**Figure 7**).
   c. Apply a light coat of grease onto the axle and dust seal lips (**Figure 9**).
   d. Install the axle from the right side.
   e. When installing the wheel in the forks, make sure the anchor boss on the left fork tube fits between the lugs cast into the brake panel. See **Figure 4** (BW80) or C, **Figure 3** (PW80).

① **FRONT WHEEL (BW80)**

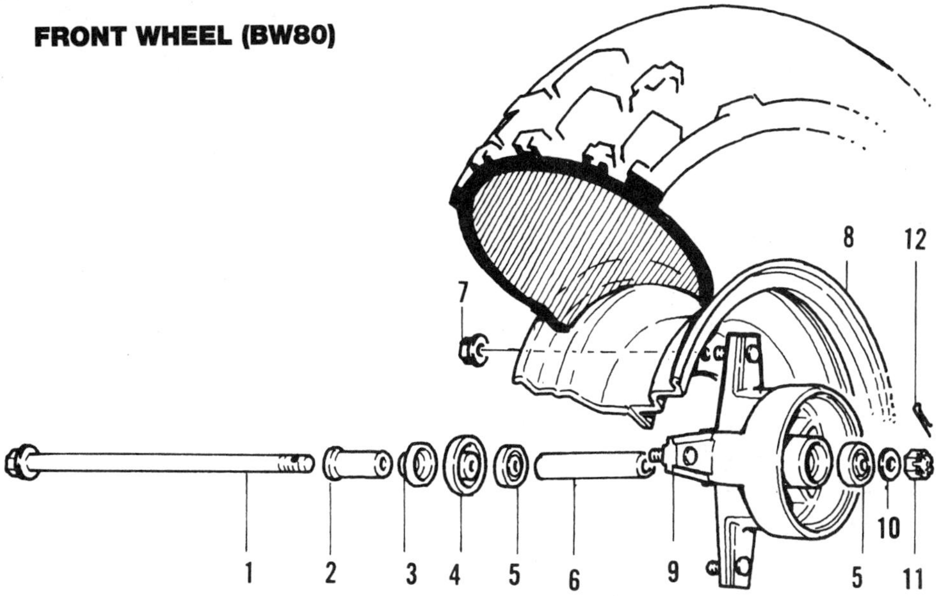

1. Front axle
2. Collar
3. Dust cover
4. Dust seal
5. Bearing
6. Collar
7. Nut
8. Wheel
9. Front hub
10. Washer
11. Axle nut
12. Cotter pin

② **FRONT WHEEL (PW80)**

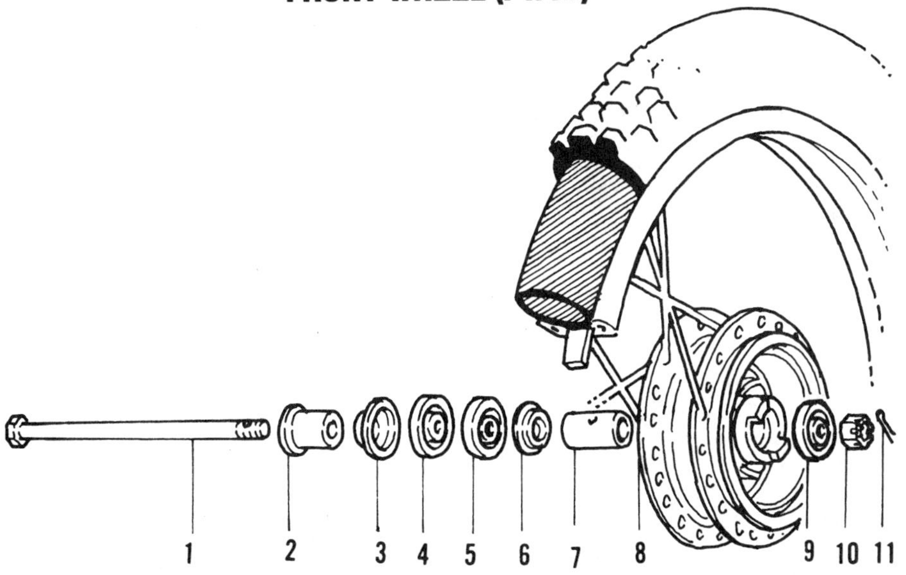

1. Front axle
2. Collar
3. Dust cover
4. Dust seal
5. Bearing
6. Shield
7. Collar
8. Front hub
9. Bearing
10. Axle nut
11. Cotter pin

f. To center the brake shoes in the drum, tighten the axle nut lightly, spin the wheel and apply the front brake forcefully, then tighten the axle nut as specified in **Table 3**.

g. Install a *new* cotter pin and bend its ends over (**Figure 10**) to lock it in place.

WARNING
Never reuse a cotter pin.

h. Adjust the front brake as described in Chapter Three.

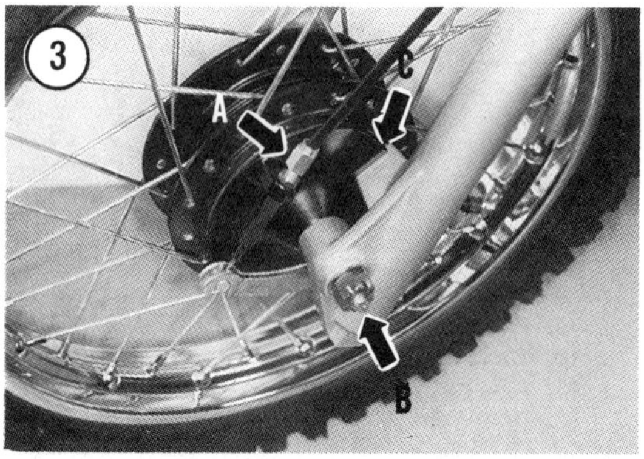

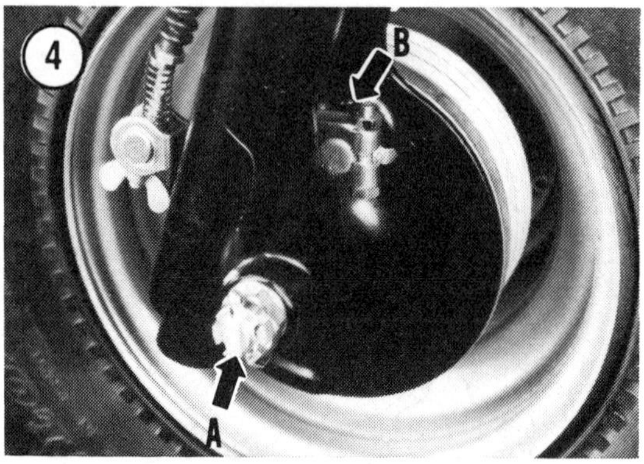

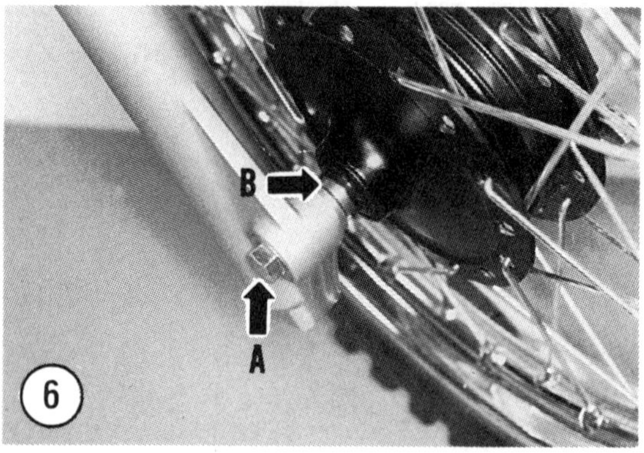

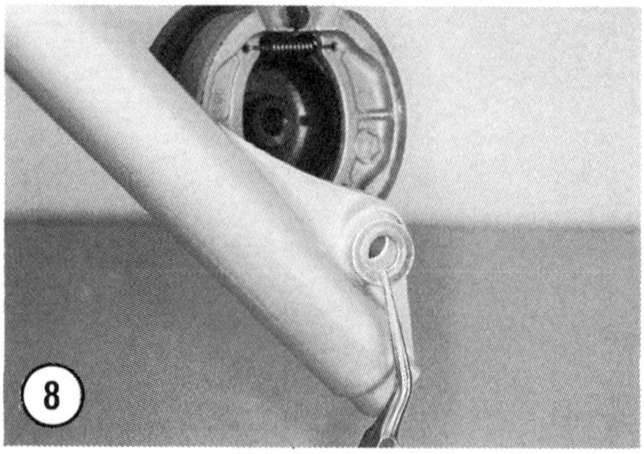

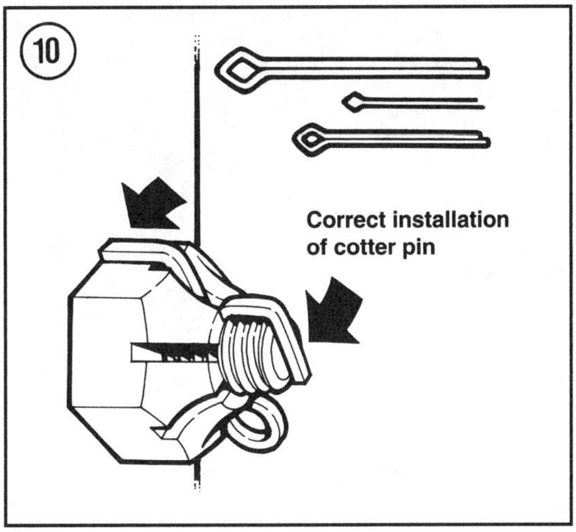

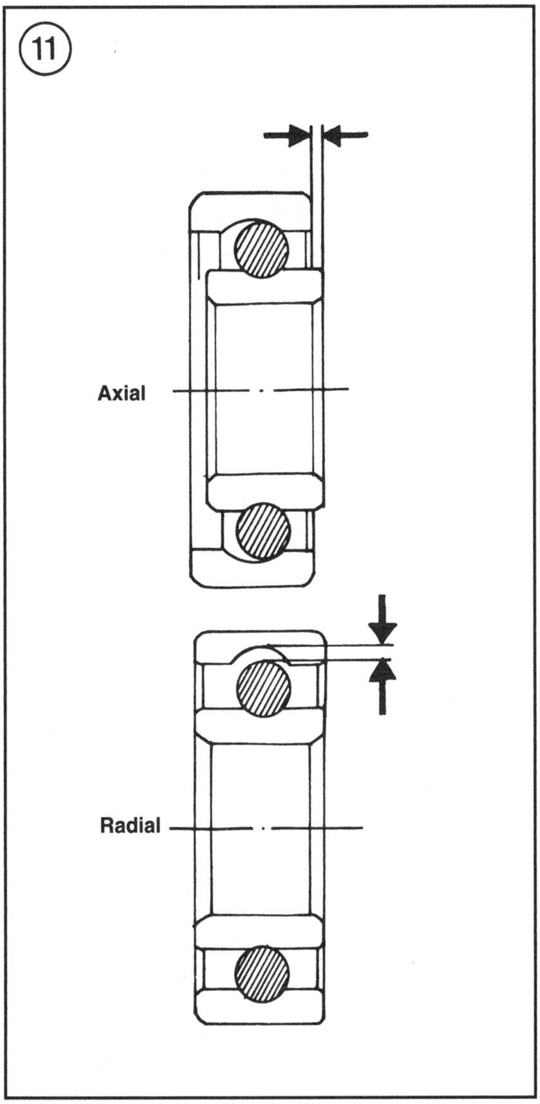

i. After the wheel is completely installed, rotate it and then apply the brake a couple of times to make sure the wheel rotates freely and that the brake is operating correctly.

Inspection

Replace parts that show damage as described in this section.

1. Inspect the dust cover (**Figure 7**) for excessive wear or cracks.
2. Inspect the dust seal (**Figure 9**) for excessive wear, hardness, cracks or other damage. If necessary, replace the dust seal as described under *Front Hub* in this chapter.
3. Turn each bearing inner race by hand. The bearing must turn smoothly with no roughness, catching, binding or excessive noise. Some axial play is normal, but radial play must be negligible; see **Figure 11**. If one bearing is damaged, replace both bearings as a set. Refer to *Front Hub* in this chapter.
3. Clean and dry the axle, collar, washer and axle nut.
4. Roll the front axle on a flat surface to see if it is bent. Then check the axle for cracks, severe wear or thread damage. Replace the axle if it is bent or damaged.

WARNING

Do not try to straighten a bent axle as axle failure could occur under riding conditions.

5. Check the wheel assembly for:
   a. Dents or broken welds.
   b. Loose or damaged spokes on PW80 models.
   c. Cracked or damaged hub.
   d. Breaks or other damage where the center spoke assembly is mounted to the rim (BW80).
6. Service the brake drum and brakes as described in Chapter Fourteen.
7. Check wheel runout as described in this chapter.

Wheel Runout (BW80)

1. Raise the bike so that the front wheel is off the ground.
2. Clean the rim of all dirt and debris.

3. Mount a dial indicator against the rim as shown in **Figure 12**.
4. Turn the tire slowly by hand and read the movement indicated on the dial indicator. See **Table 2** for runout limits. Note the following:
   a. If the runout limit is excessive, first check the condition of the wheel assembly. If the wheel is damaged, it may require replacement.
   b. If the wheel is in good condition, but the runout is excessive, remove the wheel and check the wheel bearings as described under *Inspection* in this section. The bearings should turn smoothly with no sign of roughness, excessive play or other abnormal conditions. Replace the wheel bearings as described under *Front Hub* in this chapter.
5. Remove the dial indicator and lower the vehicle to the ground.

Wheel Runout (PW80)

Wheel runout is the amount of wobble a wheel shows as it rotates. You can check runout with the wheels on the bike by simply supporting the wheel off the ground and turning the wheel slowly while you hold a pointer solidly against a fork leg or swing arm (**Figure 13**).

Table 2 lists the rim side-to-side and up and down runout limits.

NOTE
*Make sure you use the correct size spoke wrench (**Figure 14**) when checking and tightening the spokes in the following steps.*

12

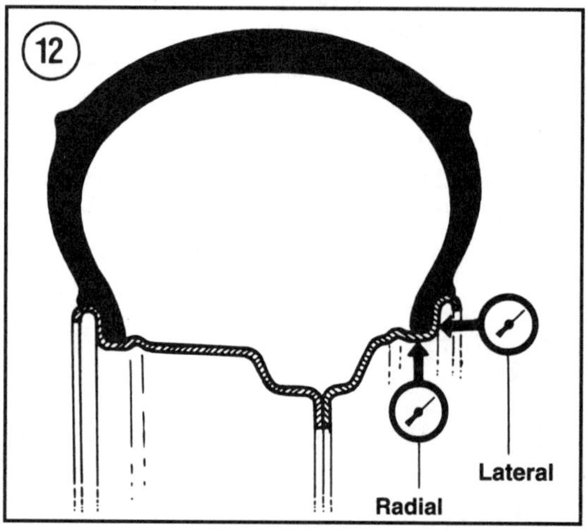

13

14

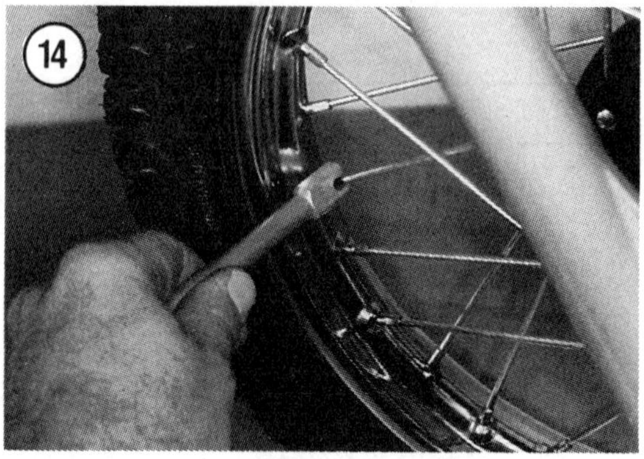

15

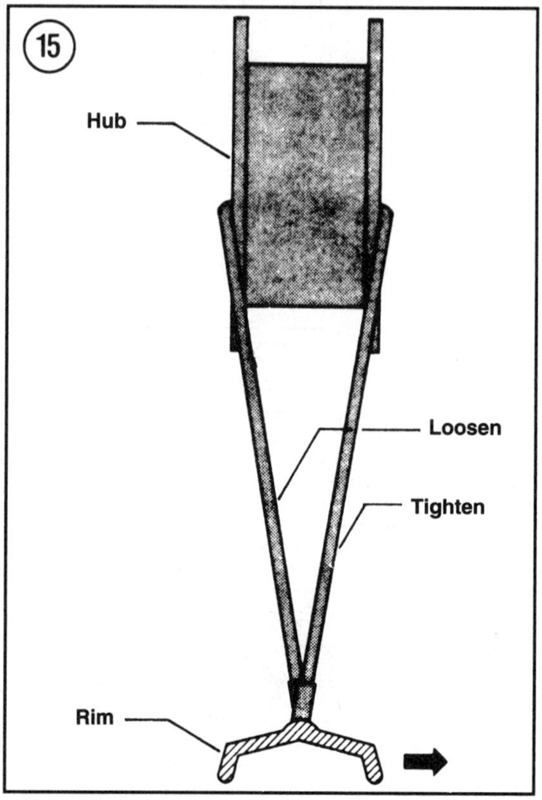

1. Draw the high point of the rim toward the centerline of the wheel by loosening the spokes in the area of the high point and on the same side as the high point, and tightening the spokes on the side opposite the high point (**Figure 15**).
2. Rotate the wheel and check runout. Continue adjusting until the runout is within specifications. Be patient and thorough, adjusting the position of the rim a little at a time. If you loosen 2 spokes at the high point 1/2 turn, loosen the adjacent spokes 1/4 turn. Tighten the spokes on the opposite side equivalent amounts.

CAUTION
During break-in of a new wheel, check the spoke tension after the first 10, 30 and 60 minutes of riding. Most spoke seating takes place during initial use.

NOTE
If a spoke(s) is loose but its nipple is hard to turn, do not force the nipple or you will round it off, making further adjustment almost impossible. Rust is usually the cause of tight or frozen spoke nipples. When you find one or more spokes in this condition, spray the nipple with a penetrating liquid and wait for it to soak in. Hopefully this will loosen the nipple(s) so that it can be turned. If not, the spoke will have to cut and a new spoke and nipple installed in its place.

16

17

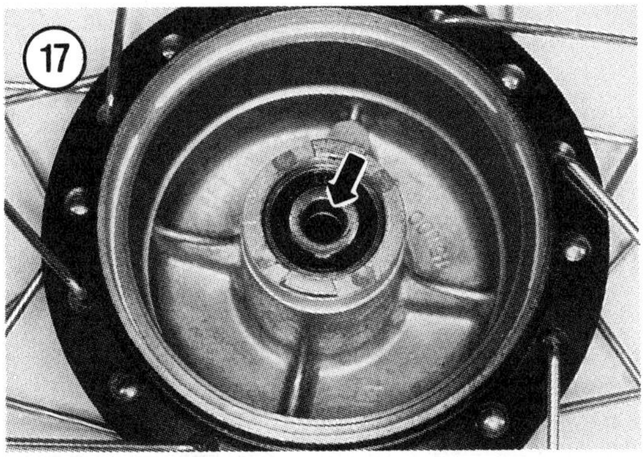

FRONT HUB

Refer to **Figure 1** or **Figure 2** when servicing the front hub. The following procedures are performed on a PW80 model. The BW80 and PW80 models use the same bearing arrangement.

Inspection

Inspect each wheel bearing as follows:

CAUTION
Do not remove the wheel bearings for inspection purposes as they may be damaged during their removal. Remove the wheel bearings only if they are to be replaced.

1. Pry the dust seal out of the hub with a wide-blade screwdriver (**Figure 16**). Support the screwdriver with a rag to avoid damaging the hub.
2. Turn each bearing inner race (**Figure 15**) by hand. The bearings must turn smoothly with no roughness, catching, binding or excessive noise. Some axial play is normal, but radial play must be negligible; see **Figure 11**.
3. If one bearing is damaged, replace both bearings as a set.

Disassembly

NOTE
Step 1 describes 2 methods of removing the front wheel bearings. Step 1A requires the use of the Kowa Seiki Wheel Bearing Remover set. Step 1B describes how to remove the bearing with a drift and hammer.

1A. To remove the hub bearings (**Figure 17**) with the Kowa Seiki Wheel Bearing Remover set:

NOTE
*The Kowa Seiki Wheel Bearing Remover set shown in **Figure 18** is available from K & L Supply Co., in Santa*

Clara, CA. You can order this tool set through your Yamaha dealer.

a. Select the correct size remover head tool and insert it into one of the hub bearings (**Figure 19**).
b. From the opposite side of the hub, insert the remover shaft into the slot in the backside of the remover head (**Figure 20**). Then position the hub with the remover head tool resting against a solid surface and strike the remover shaft to force it into the slit in the remover head. This will wedge the remover head tool against the inner bearing race. See **Figure 21**.
c. Position the hub and strike the end of the remover shaft with a hammer to drive the bearing (A, **Figure 22**) out of the hub. Remove the bearing and tool. Release the remover head from the bearing.
d. Remove the collar (B, **Figure 22**) from the hub.
e. Repeat to remove the opposite bearing.

1B. To remove the hub bearings without special tools:

a. Using a long drift, tilt the center hub spacer away from one side of the bearing (**Figure 23**).

NOTE

Do not damage the hub spacer's machined surface when positioning and driving against the long drift. You may have to grind a clearance groove in the

19

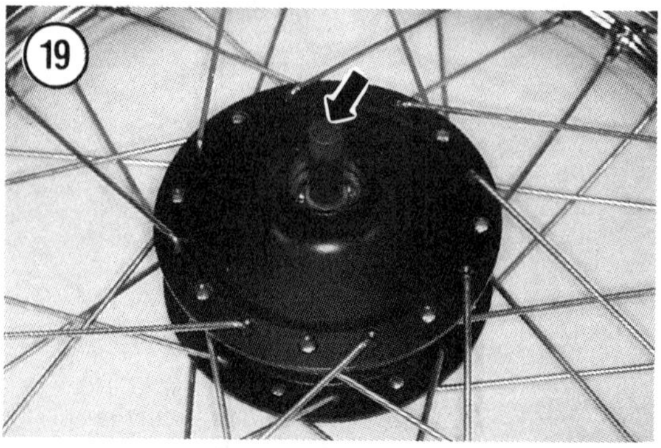

18

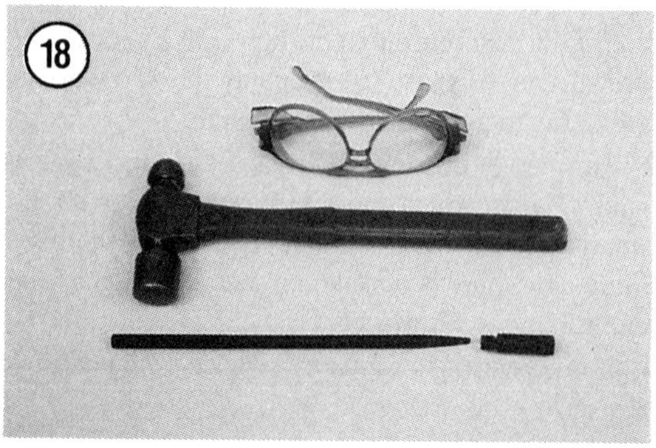

20

21

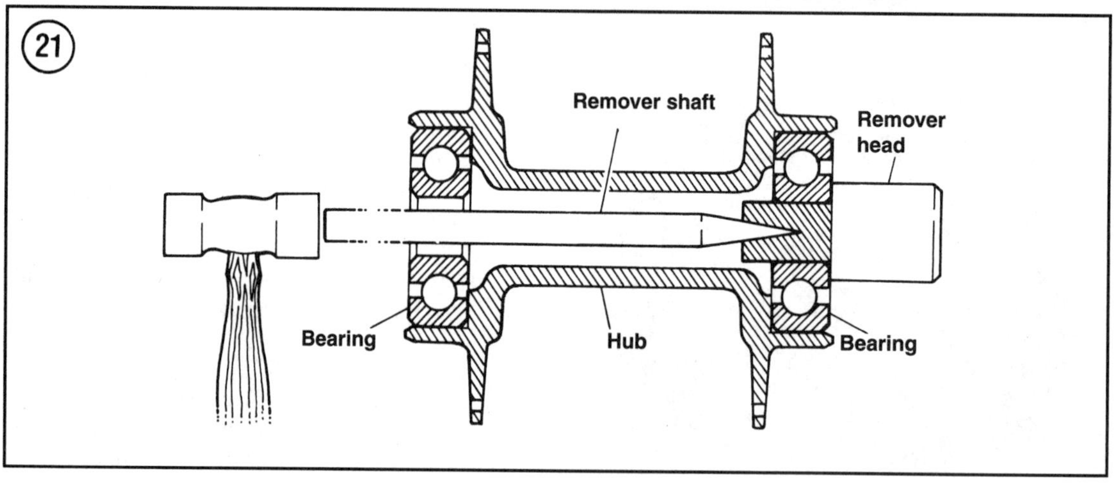

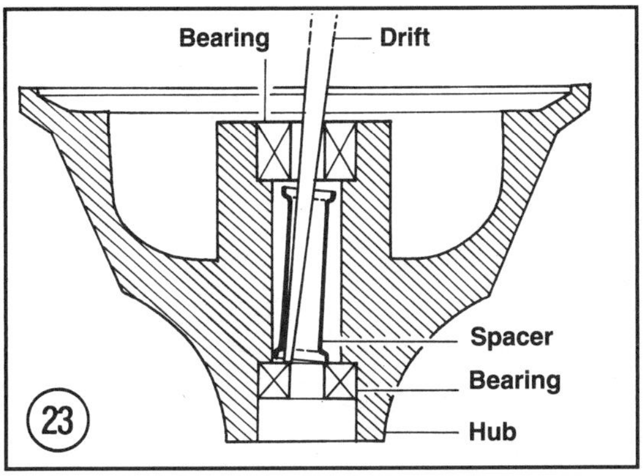

drift to enable it to contact the bearing while clearing the spacer.

b. Tap the bearing out of the hub with a hammer, working around the perimeter of the bearing's inner race.
c. Remove the collar from the hub (B, **Figure 22**).
d. Drive out the opposite bearing using a large socket or bearing driver.
e. Inspect the center hub spacer for burrs created during removal. Remove burrs with a file.

2. Clean and dry the hub and center hub spacer.

3. Inspect the hub bore (**Figure 24**) for cracks or excessive wear. If a bearing was a loose fit in the hub, the hub is excessively worn or damaged; replace the hub.

Assembly

Before installing the new bearings and dust seals, note the following:

a. The left and right side bearings (**Figure 25**) are different. If you did not identify the bearings before removing them, have your dealership parts manager identify them for you.
b. When grease is called for in the following steps, use a Lithium based multipurpose grease (NLGI # 2) or equivalent.

1. Blow any dirt or foreign matter out of the hub (**Figure 24**).

2. Pack the open side of each bearing (**Figure 25**) with grease.

3. Place the brake hub side bearing into its mounting bore with its closed side facing out (**Figure 17**). Select a driver (**Figure 26**) with an outside diameter just a little smaller than the bearing's outside diame-

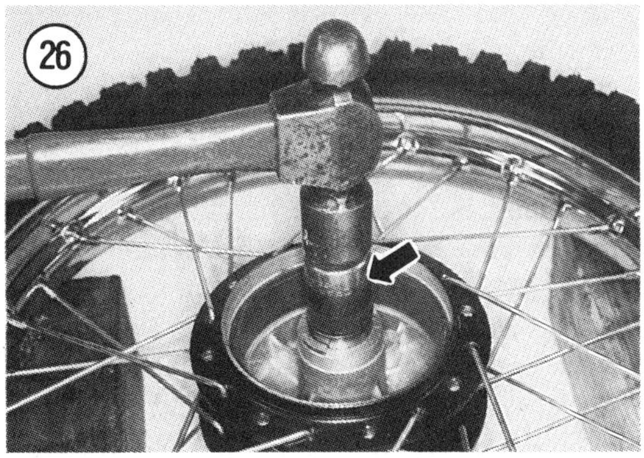

ter. Then drive the bearing into the bore until it bottoms (**Figure 17**).

4. Install the collar (**Figure 27**) and center it against the first bearing's center race.
5. Place the second bearing squarely against the bore opening. Using the same driver as before, drive the bearing partway into the bearing bore. Then stop and check that the collar is centered in the hub. If not, install the front axle through the hub to center the spacer with the bearing. Then remove the axle and continue installing the bearing until it bottoms.
6. Pack the dust seal lip with grease.
7. Place the dust seal squarely against the bore opening with its closed side facing out. Then drive the dust seal in the bore until it bottoms out (**Figure 9**).
8. Check that inner race on each bearing turns without any binding or damage.

HANDLEBAR

Removal/Installation

1. Remove the front fender (Chapter Fifteen).
2. Remove the fuel tank (Chapter Seven).
3. Disconnect the front brake cable (A, **Figure 28**) at the handlebar.
4. Disconnect the engine stop switch electrical connectors from the left side of the engine. Disconnect the wiring harness band (A, **Figure 29**)at the handlebar.
5. Loosen the throttle housing screws (B, **Figure 28**).
6. Remove the handlebar mounting bolts and washers and the upper holders (B, **Figure 29**), then slide the throttle housing off the handlebar and remove the handlebar. Do not bend or damage the throttle or front brake cables.
7. Inspect the handlebar as described under *Inspection* in this section.
8. To install the handlebar, reverse the removal steps while noting the following:
   a. Each handlebar holder is machined with a slot (**Figure 30**) on one side. Install both handlebar holders so the slot in each holder faces toward the inside of the bike (**Figure 31**).
   b. Tighten the front and then the rear handlebar mounting bolts as specified in **Table 3**.
   c. Adjust the front brake as described in Chapter Three.

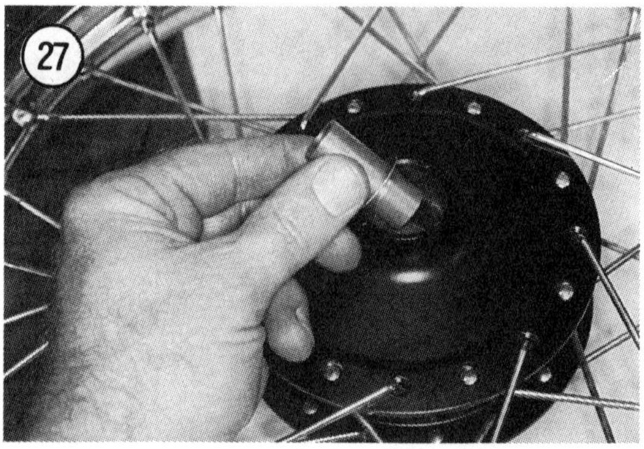

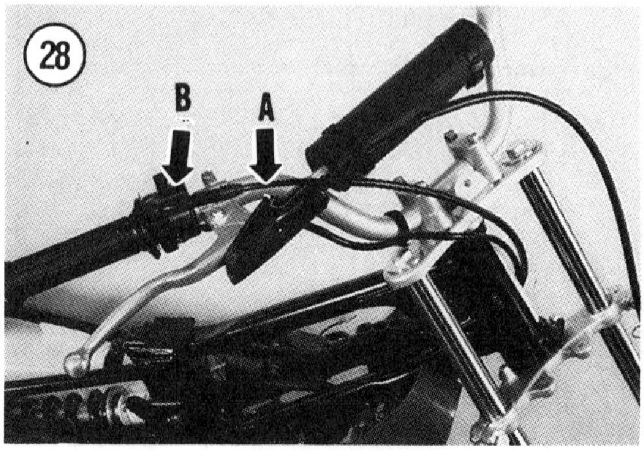

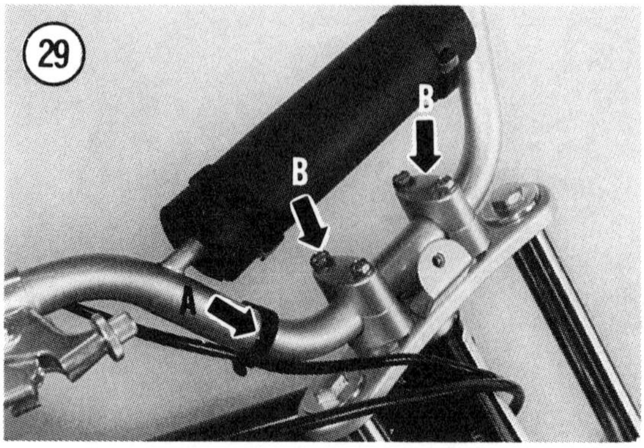

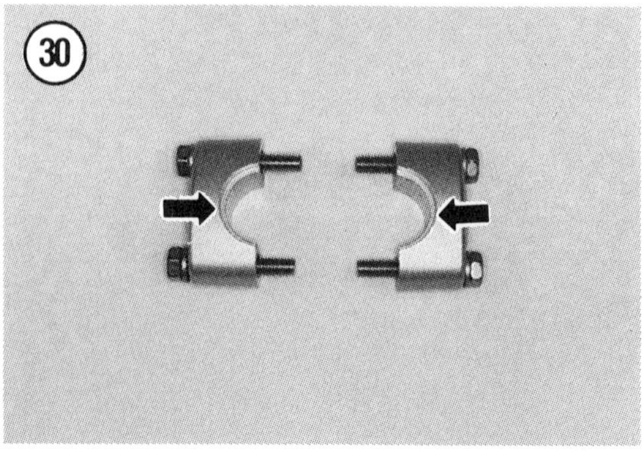

d. Check the throttle cable routing after reinstalling the throttle housing onto the handlebar.

e. Check the throttle cable adjustment as described in Chapter Three.

f. Reconnect the engine stop switch electrical connectors before starting the engine.

WARNING
Make sure the front brake, throttle and engine stop switch are operating correctly before riding the bike.

31

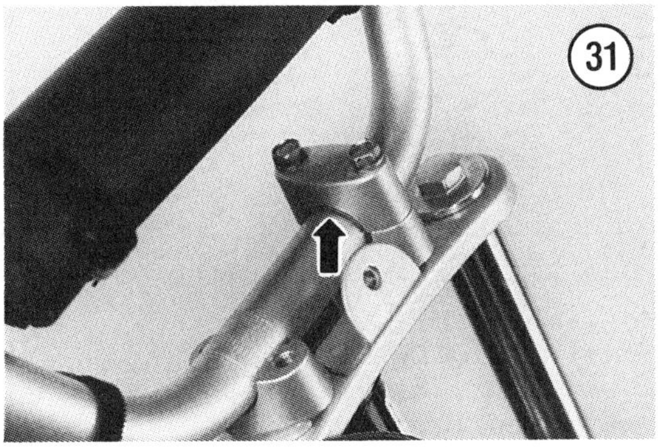

32

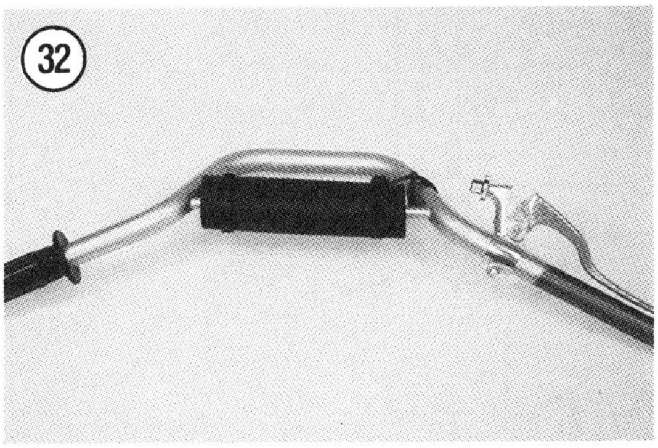

33

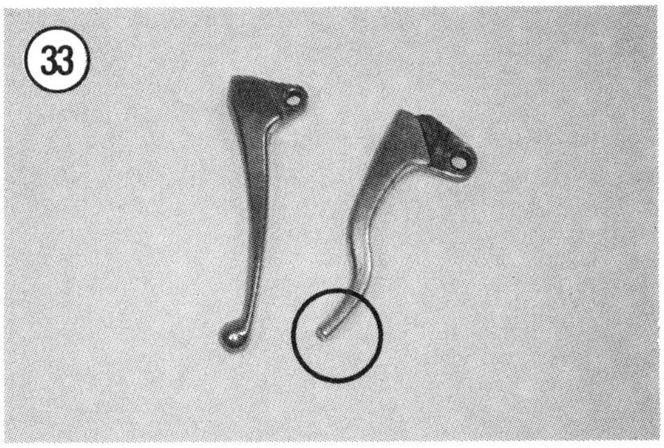

Inspection

1. Check the handlebar (**Figure 32**) and replace if cracked, bents or shows other damage. Do not attempt to straighten or repair a damaged handlebar.
2. Replace the grips (**Figure 32**) if worn or damaged. Follow the grip manufacturer's directions when installing and gluing grips onto the handlebar.

NOTE
It is easier to replace the grips while the handlebar is mounted on the motorcycle.

3. Replace a lever that is worn, cracked, or if the end ball is broken off (**Figure 33**).

WARNING
The balls on the end of control levers help to prevent the lever from puncturing a rider's body in the event of a crash and forceful contact with the lever. Do not allow the motorcycle to be ridden with a damaged control lever.

STEERING HEAD

The steering head (**Figure 34**) uses individual bearing balls at the top and bottom pivot positions. The steering head bearing races and the steering stem bearing race need to be removed only if they require replacement.

Table 1 lists steering specifications.

Disassembly

1. Remove the front wheel as described in this chapter.
2. Remove the front fender (Chapter Fifteen).
3. Remove the handlebar as described in this chapter.
4. Loosen, but do not remove, the steering stem bolt (A, **Figure 35**).
5. Remove the front forks as described in this chapter.
6. Remove the steering stem bolt and washer (A, **Figure 35**) and the upper fork bridge (B, **Figure 35**).

NOTE
Have an assistant hold the steering stem to keep it from dropping out. At the same time have them hold a large pan directly

11

(34)

STEERING (BW80 AND PW80)

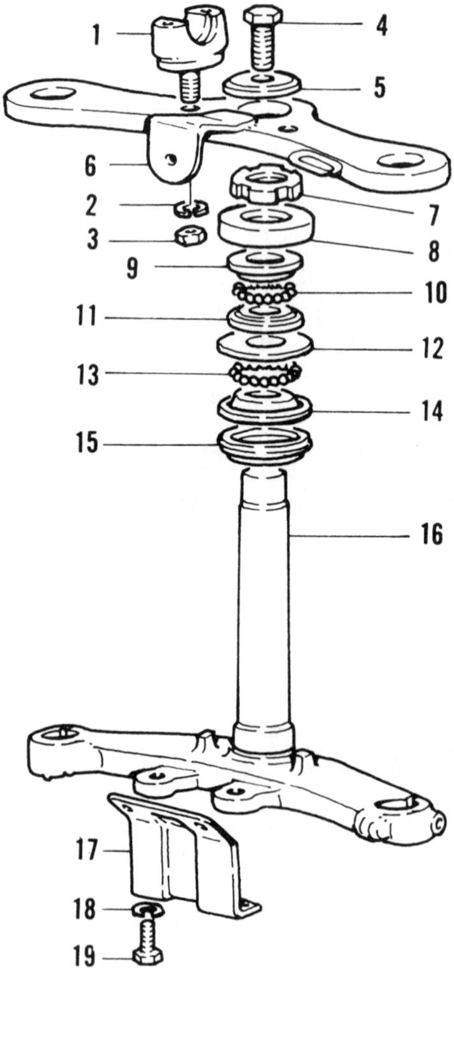

1. Lower handlebar holder
2. Lockwasher
3. Nut
4. Steering stem bolt
5. Washer
6. Upper fork bridge
7. Steering stem nut
8. Cover
9. Upper bearing race
10. Bearing balls (22 pieces)
11. Steering head bearing race
12. Lower bearing race
13. Bearing balls (19 pieces)
14. Steering stem bearing race
15. Seal
16. Steering stem
17. Fender bracket
18. Lockwasher
19. Bolt

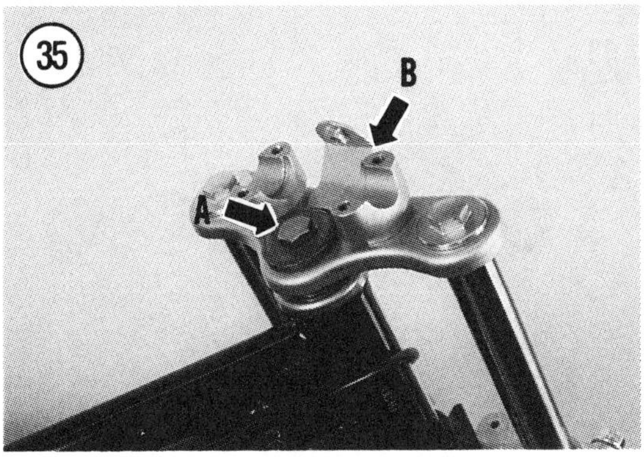

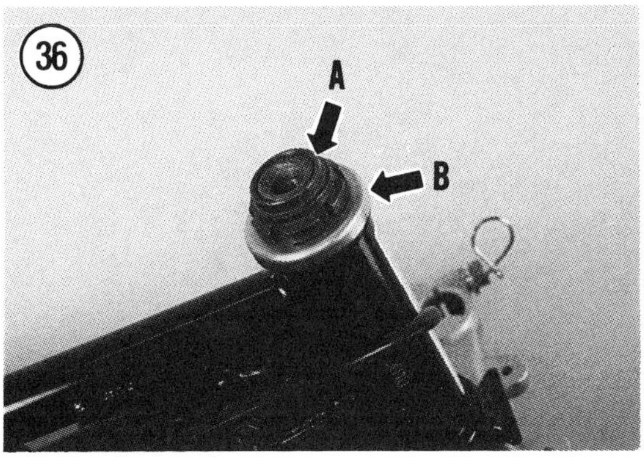

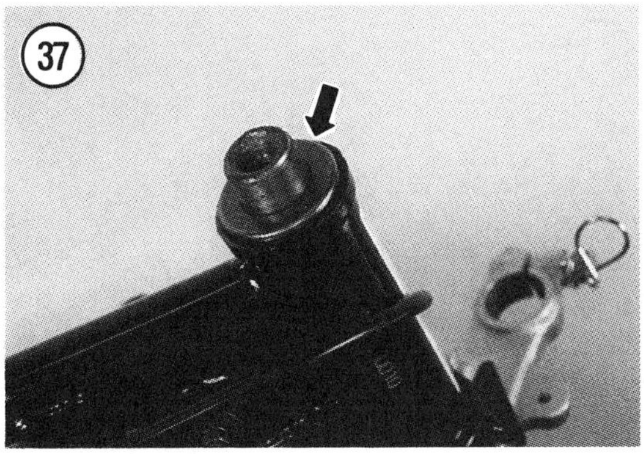

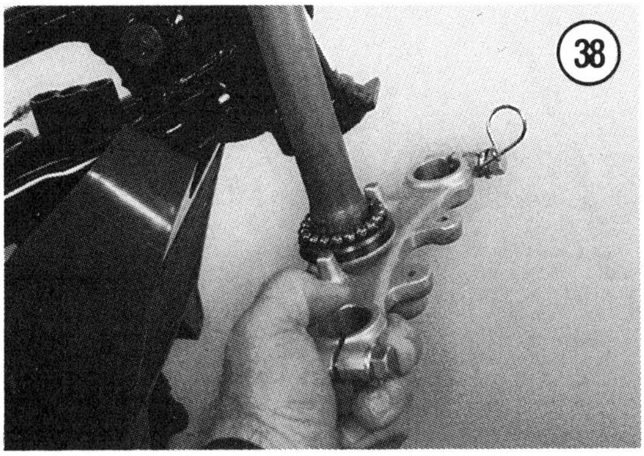

under the steering stem to catch loose bearing balls.

7. Loosen and remove the steering stem nut (A, **Figure 36**), cover (B, **Figure 36**), upper bearing race (**Figure 37**) and steering stem (**Figure 38**).

NOTE
In Step 8, remove the bearing balls only. Do not remove the steering head or steering stem bearing races.

8. Remove the upper (**Figure 39**) and lower (**Figure 40**) bearing balls sets. Remove any bearing balls stuck in the steering stem bearing race (13, **Figure 34**).

NOTE
*The upper and lower bearing balls are different sizes. See **Table 1** for bearing sizes and quantities.*

Inspection

Replace all parts that show damage as described in this section.

11

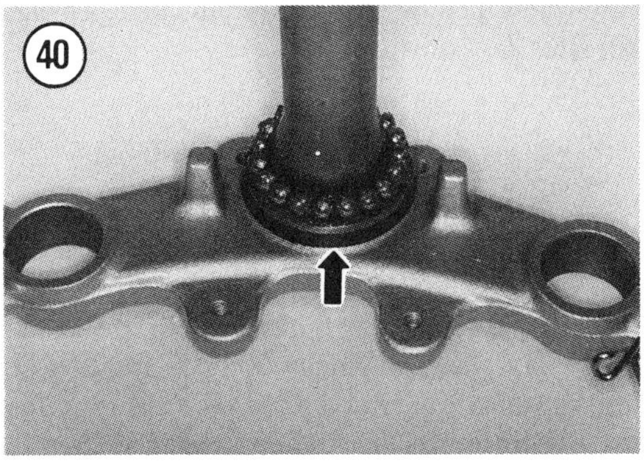

1. Clean and dry all parts.
2. Check the steering head frame welds for cracks and fractures. Refer repair to a qualified frame shop or welding service.
3. Check the steering stem bolt, washer, cover and steering stem nut (**Figure 41**) and replace if damaged. Check the mating threads in the steering stem for damage.
4. Check the upper fork bridge (**Figure 41**) for damage.
5. Check the lower handlebar holders (**Figure 42**) for looseness or damage. Note the following:
   a. Install the lower handlebar holders so that the groove in each holder faces toward the inside as shown in **Figure 42**.
   b. Tighten the lower handlebar holder mounting nuts (3, **Figure 34**) as specified in **Table 3**.
6. Check the steering stem (**Figure 38**) assembly for cracks and damage.
7. Check the bearing races for pitting, galling and corrosion. If a race is worn or damaged, replace both race sets and all bearing balls. Replace bearing races as described in this section. The bearing races are identified as follows:
   a. Upper bearing races—9, **Figure 34** and **Figure 43**.
   b. Lower bearing races—**Figure 44** and A, **Figure 45**.
8. Check all of the bearing balls for pitting, flat spots, cracks, severe wear or other damage. If the bearing balls are severely worn or damaged, replace all bearing races and bearing balls as a set.

Steering Head Bearing Race Replacement

The steering head bearing races (**Figure 43** and **Figure 44**) are pressed into place. Do not remove them unless they are worn and require replacement; ball races are easily bent.

NOTE

*The upper (**Figure 43**) and lower (**Figure 44**) steering head races are different. Be sure that you install them in the proper ends of the head tube.*

To remove the steering head races (**Figure 43** and **Figure 44**), insert an aluminum or brass drift into the head tube and carefully tap the race out from the inside (**Figure 46**). Tap all the way around the race

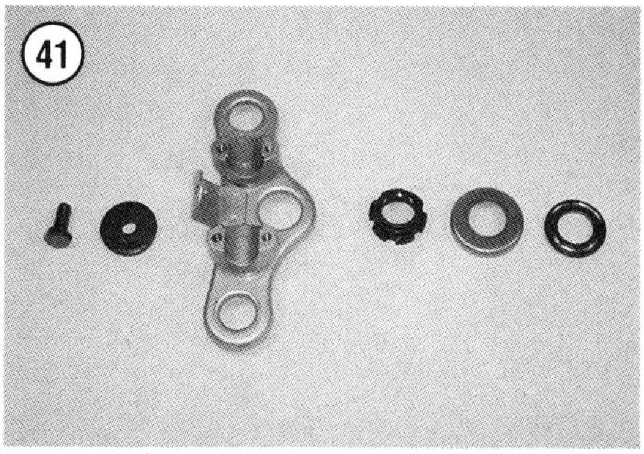

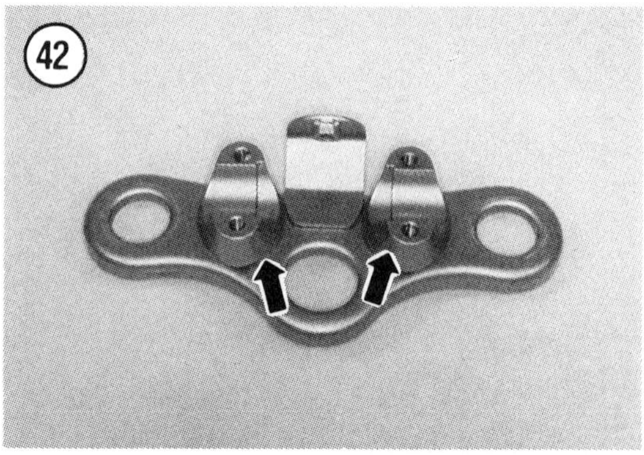

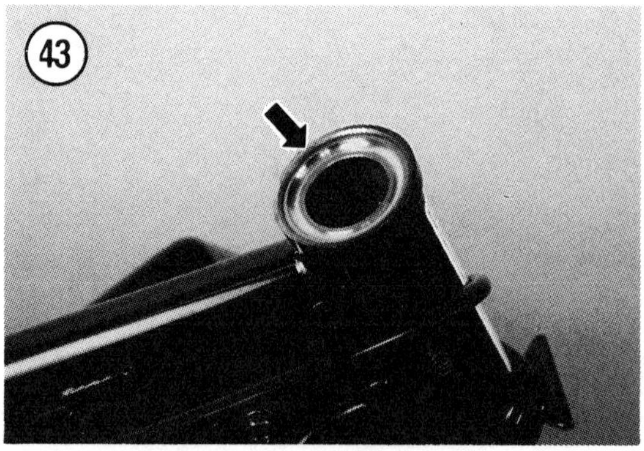

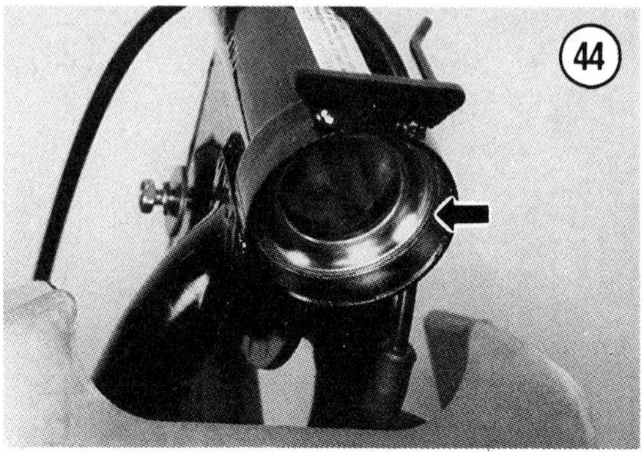

so that neither the race nor the head tube is bent. To install a race, grease it and fit it into the end of the head tube. Tap it slowly and squarely with a socket or a block of wood (**Figure 47**). Make sure it is fully seated. You will notice a distinct change in the hammering sound as the race bottoms-out.

Steering Stem Bearing Race Replacement

The steering stem bearing race (A, **Figure 45**) is pressed into place. Do not remove this race unless it requires replacement.

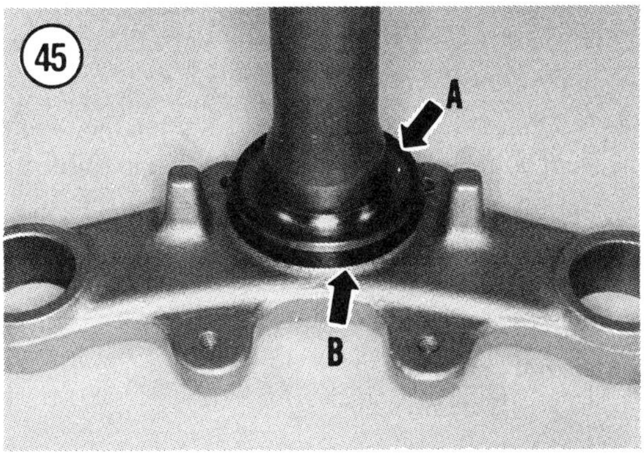

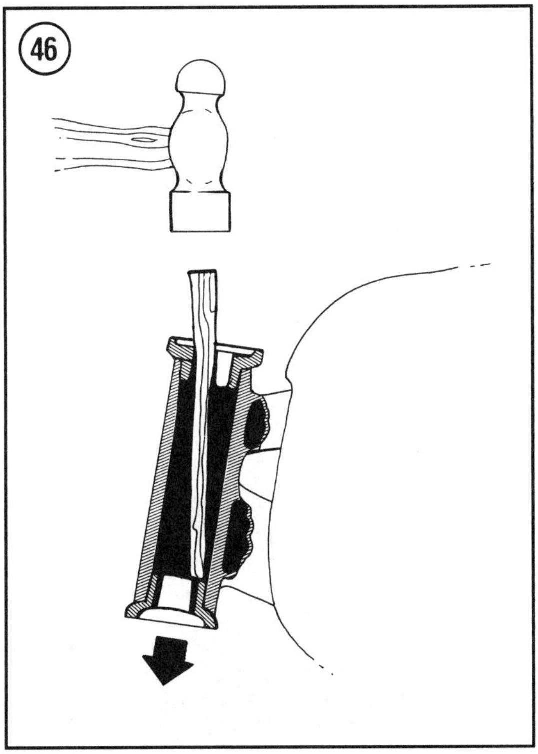

1. Thread the steering stem nut onto the steering stem (**Figure 48**).
2. Remove the steering stem bearing race with a chisel as shown in **Figure 48**. Work around the race in a circle, prying a little at a time. Remove and discard the seal (B, **Figure 45**).
3. Clean and dry the steering stem.
4. Inspect the steering stem and replace if it is bent or otherwise damaged.
5. Slide a new seal down the steering stem (B, **Figure 45**).
6. Slide the new race onto the steering stem until it stops.
7. Tap the race down with a piece of hardwood or a piece of pipe of the proper size (**Figure 49**). Make sure it is seated squarely and all the way down (A, **Figure 45**).

Assembly

Refer to **Figure 34** when assembling the steering assembly.

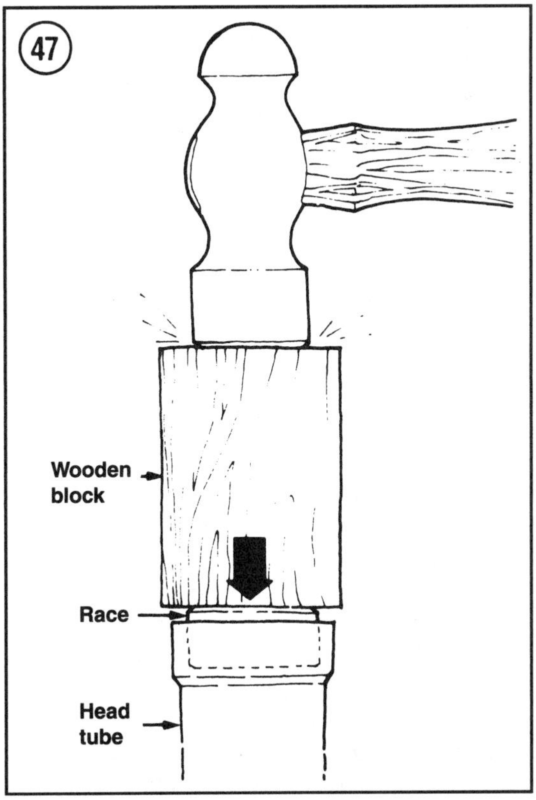

11

1. Make sure the upper (**Figure 43**) and lower (**Figure 44**) steering head bearing races are properly seated in the frame.
2. Lubricate all of the bearing races with a waterproof bearing grease.

NOTE
*See **Table 1** to identify the bearing ball sizes.*

3. Fit 22 bearing balls around the upper steering head bearing race (**Figure 39**). The grease will hold them in place.
4. Fit 19 bearing balls around the steering stem bearing race (**Figure 40**). Grease will hold them in place.
5. Insert the steering stem (**Figure 38**) into the steering head. Hold it firmly in place.
6. Check that none of the upper bearing balls were dislodged.
7. Install the upper bearing race (**Figure 37**).
8. Install the cover (B, **Figure 36**).
9. Screw the steering stem nut (A, **Figure 36**) onto the steering stem.

NOTE
Step 10 describes two methods on how to tighten the steering stem nut. Step 10A requires the use of a ring nut torque adapter wrench and a torque wrench. Step 10B does not require special tools.

10A. To tighten the steering stem nut (A, **Figure 36**) using the Yamaha ring nut wrench (part No. YU-33975):

a. Mount the ring nut wrench onto the torque wrench so that it forms a right angle as shown in **Figure 50**.
b. Tighten the ring nut (**Figure 50**) to 38 N•m (27 ft.-lb.) to seat the bearings.
c. Remove the tool and loosen the steering stem nut 1/4 turn.
d. Turn the steering stem from side-to-side to check bearing play. The steering stem must be tight enough to remove all play, both horizontal and vertical, yet loose enough so that the assembly will turn under its own weight after an initial assist.
c. If the steering play is too loose or tight, readjust the steering stem nut.

10B. To tighten the steering stem nut (A, **Figure 36**) without special tools, perform the following:

a. Tighten the steering stem nut (A, **Figure 36**) firmly to seat the bearings.
b. Loosen the steering stem nut (A, **Figure 36**) until there is noticeable play in the steering stem.
c. Tighten the steering stem nut (A, **Figure 36**) just enough to remove all play, both horizontal and vertical, yet loose enough so that the assembly will turn under its own weight after an initial assist.

11. Install the upper fork bridge (B, **Figure 35**).
12. Install the washer and steering stem bolt (A, **Figure 35**). Tighten the bolt finger-tight at this time.
13. Slide the fork tubes into the steering head assembly and secure them in place with their lower pinch bolts as described in this chapter.
14. With both fork tubes in place, tighten the steering stem bolt (A, **Figure 35**) as specified in **Table 3**.
15. Install the handlebar as described in this chapter.
16. Install the front fender (Chapter Fifteen).

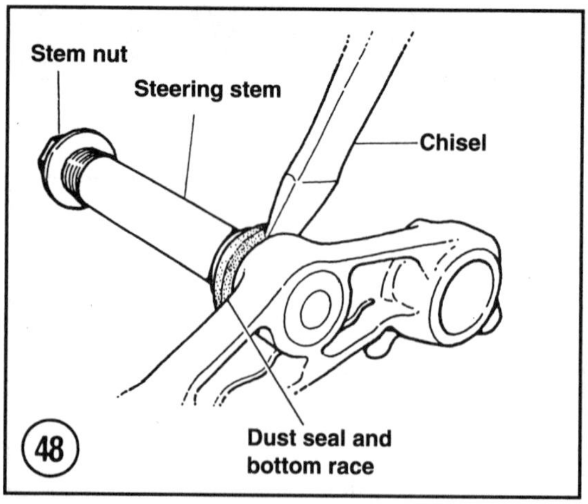

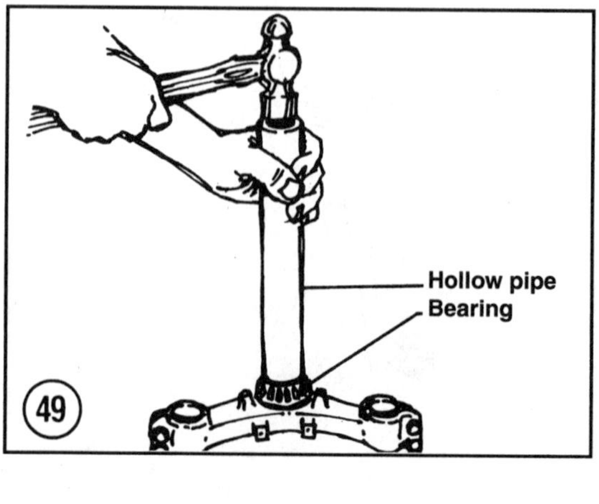

17. Install the front wheel as described in this chapter.

18. Recheck the steering adjustment as described in Step 10. If the steering adjustment is now too tight (after tightening the steering stem bolt), perform the *Steering Adjustment* procedure in this chapter.

19. After 30 minutes to 1 hour of riding time, recheck the steering adjustment.

Steering Adjustment

If your periodic checks detect excessive steering play, adjust the steering as described in this section. The steering head should also be disassembled, cleaned and inspected for wear on the bearing balls and races, then lubricated with a waterproof grease according to the maintenance schedule in Chapter Three.

The steering adjustment can be checked and adjusted with the front wheel and front forks mounted on the bike.

1. Support the bike with the front wheel off the ground.

50

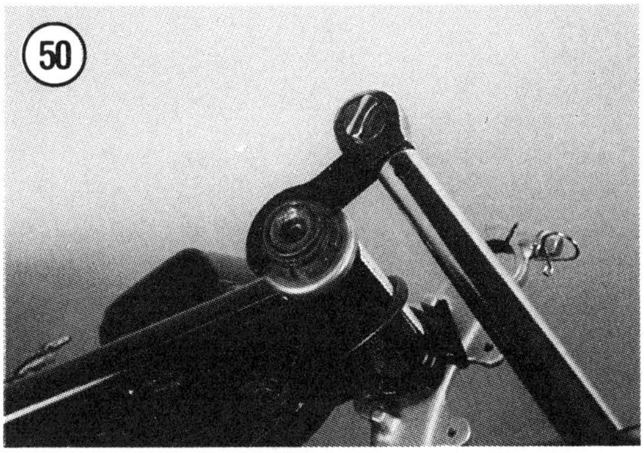

51

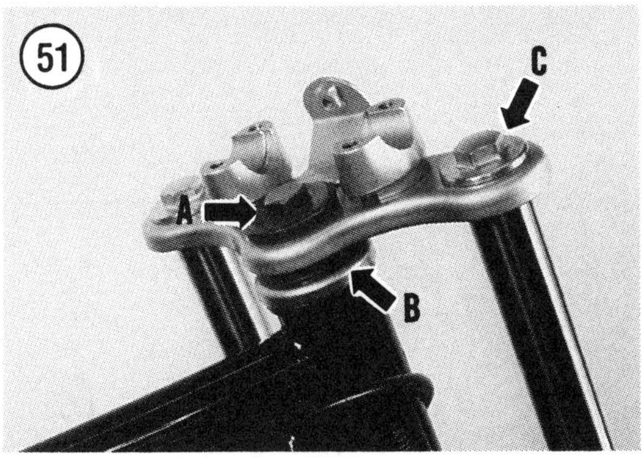

2. Check bearing play by turning the steering stem from lock to lock. The steering stem must pivot smoothly with no binding or roughness. There should be no horizontal or vertical play, yet the steering should be loose enough so that the front end will turn under its own weight after an initial assist. If there is any noticeable binding or roughness, first make sure the control cables are not causing the condition. If they are routed properly, continue with Step 3.

NOTE

Steps 3-7 describe steering play adjustment.

3. Remove the handlebar as described in this chapter.

4. Loosen the steering stem bolt and washer (A, **Figure 51**).

5. Loosen or tighten the steering stem nut (B, **Figure 51**) to adjust the steering play.

6. Recheck steering play by turning the steering stem from side to side. If the steering play is okay, turn the handlebar so that the front forks are facing straight ahead. Then grasp the fork tubes and try to move them back and forth (front to back). Do this several times while trying to detect any play in the bearings. If there is play, but the steering adjustment feels okay, the bearings and races are probably worn and require replacement. It helps to have someone steady the bike when checking steering head play.

7. Install the steering stem bolt and washer (A, **Figure 51**) and tighten as specified in **Table 3**.

8. Recheck the steering play. If necessary, repeat these steps until the steering play adjustment is correct.

9. Install the handlebar as described in this chapter.

FRONT FORKS

Each fork consists of the fork tube (inner tube), slider (outer tube), fork spring and the damper rod with its components. To simplify fork service and to prevent the mixing of parts, the forks should be removed, serviced and reinstalled individually.

Table 3 lists fork tube specifications.

Fork Oil Change

The forks are not equipped with drain screws. It is necessary to remove the fork assembly and partially disassemble the fork to drain and replace the fork oil. If you are only going to change the fork oil, proceed to the *Disassembly* procedure and follow the instructions listed for changing the foil oil.

Removal/Installation

1. Support the bike with the front wheel off the ground.
2. Remove the front wheel as described in this chapter.
3. Loosen and remove the fork cap (**Figure 52**) from the fork tube. If the handlebars are mounted on the bike, you may not be able to remove the fork cap from the upper fork bridge.
4. Loosen the fork tube pinch bolt (A, **Figure 53**). Then work the fork tube (B, **Figure 53**) down and out with a twisting motion.
5. If you are not going to disassemble the fork tube, install the fork cap and tighten hand tight. The cap will prevent oil from draining or leaking out if the fork tube is turned on its side.
6. Install the fork tube by reversing these removal steps, plus the following:
   a. Install the fork tube with the brake plate anchor boss (A, **Figure 54**) onto the left side of the motorcycle.
   b. Tighten the fork tube pinch bolt (A, **Figure 53**) as specified in **Table 3**.
   c. Tighten the fork cap (**Figure 52**) as specified in **Table 3**.

Special Tools

A 6 mm and 8 mm hex socket (A, **Figure 55**) is required during fork service. Also, a damper rod holder (Yamaha part No. YM-01300-1 or equivalent [B, **Figure 55**]) may be required when loosening and tightening the front fork Allen bolt. This tool is mounted onto a long T-handle where it is inserted through the fork tube and pushed into the top of the damper rod. The sharp corners on the tool help it to bite into the damper rod (**Figure 56**), thus preventing the damper rod from turning when loosening and tightening the fork tube Allen bolt. Steps on how to work around using this tool are described in the following service procedures. However, if they fail to hold the damper rod in place, the damper rod holder will be required.

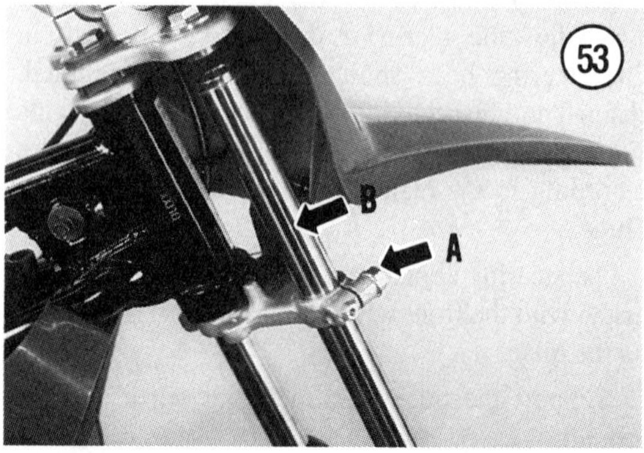

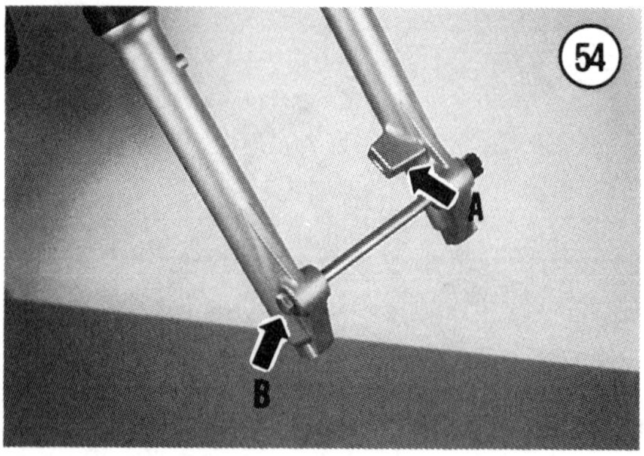

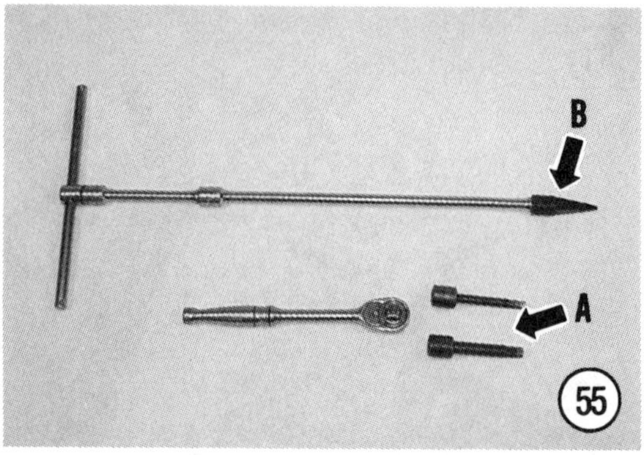

(56)

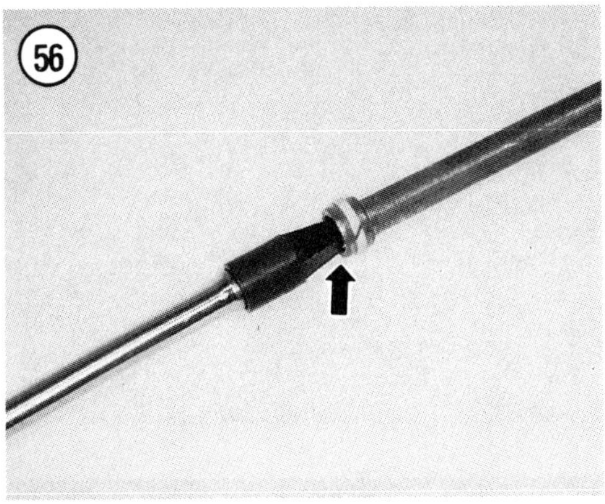

Disassembly

Refer to **Figure 57**.

NOTE
*If you are only changing the fork oil, perform Steps 1, 2, 4, 5, 6, 8, 9 and 10 in this procedure. Then continue by performing Steps 7, 8, 9, 10 and 11 under the **Reassembly** procedure.*

NOTE
To help with disassembly, Steps 1-4 are performed with the forks mounted on the bike.

(57)

FRONT FORK (BW80 AND PW80)

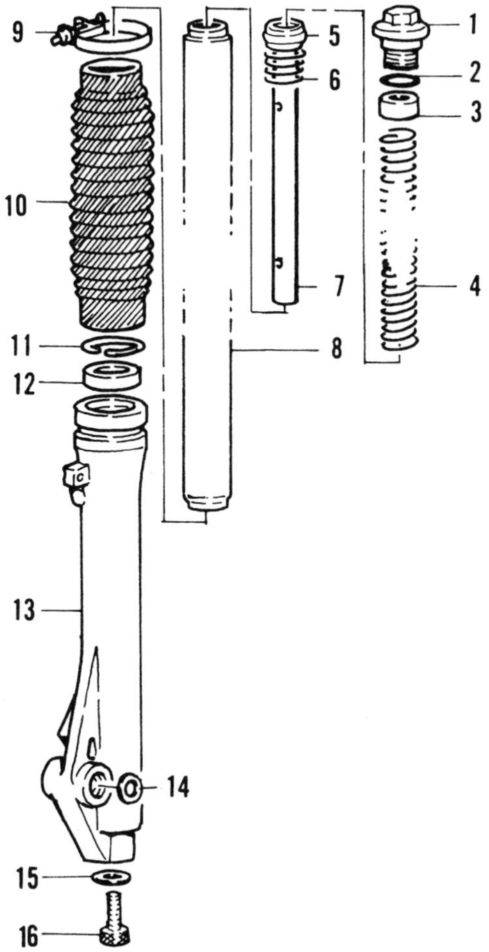

1. Fork cap
2. O-ring
3. Spring seat
4. Fork spring
5. Piston ring
6. Return spring
7. Damper rod
8. Fork tube
9. Hose clamps
10. Fork boot (BW80)
11. Circlip
12. Oil seal
13. Slider
14. Washers (PW80)
15. Washer
16. Allen bolt

1. Remove the handlebar as described in this chapter.
2. Remove the front wheel as described in this chapter. Then reinstall the front axle (B, **Figure 54**) through both fork tubes to hold the sliders in place.
3. With the fork spring applying pressure against the damper rod, loosen, but do not remove, the fork tube Allen bolt (**Figure 58**).

NOTE
If the damper rod turns with the Allen bolt, the damper rod holder tool, described under Special Tools, will be required to complete disassembly. Steps on how to use this tool are described later in this procedure.

4. Remove the fork cap (C, **Figure 51**).

WARNING
The fork spring is under pre-load. Keep your face away from the fork tube when loosening the spring seat in Step 5. The spring seat may fly out unexpectedly.

5. Loosen, but do not remove, the spring seat (**Figure 59**) installed inside the fork tube.
6. Loosen the fork tube pinch bolt and remove the fork tube from the bike.
7. Remove the fork boot (10, **Figure 57**) from the fork tube.
8. Mount the fork tube in a vise with soft jaws.
9. Remove the spring seat (A, **Figure 60**) and fork spring (A, **Figure 60**).
10. Remove the fork from the vise and pour the oil out and discard it. Pump the fork several times to expel the remaining oil.

NOTE
Step 11 describes removal of the Allen bolt and gasket. If you were able to loosen the Allen bolt during Step 3, perform Step 11A. If not, perform Step 11B.

11A. If the Allen bolt is loose, remove it and its gasket (**Figure 61**) from the bottom of the slider.
11B. If the Allen bolt is tight, remove it as follows:
  a. See *Special Tools* for a description of the damper rod holder tool (B, **Figure 55**). Mount the tool onto a long T-handle.
  b. Mount the slider in a vise with soft jaws.

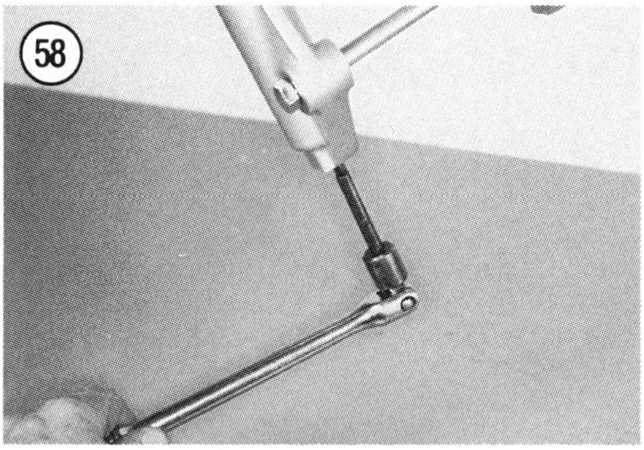

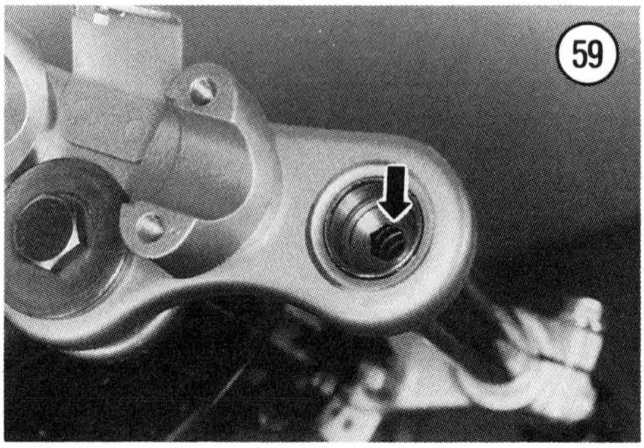

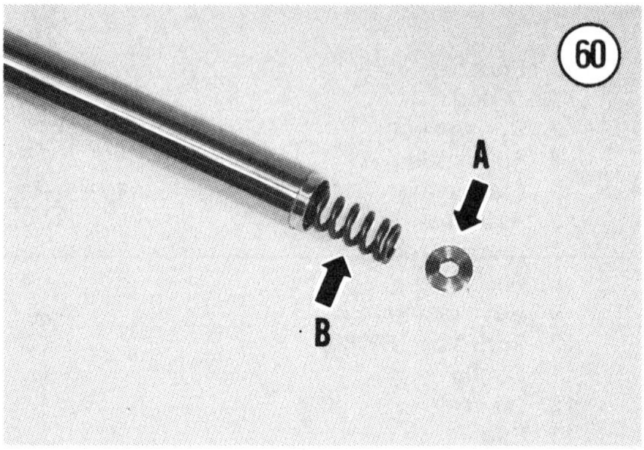

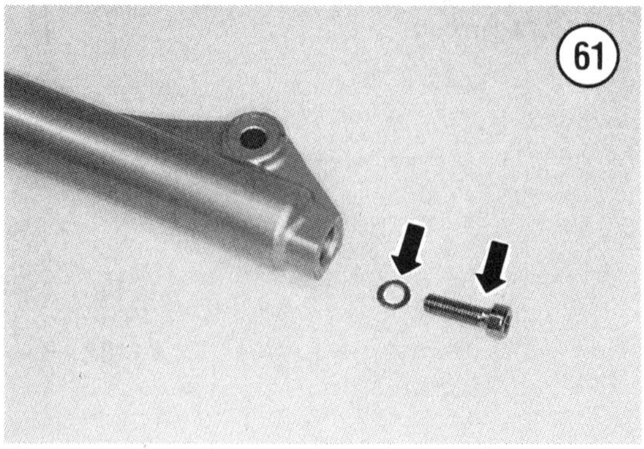

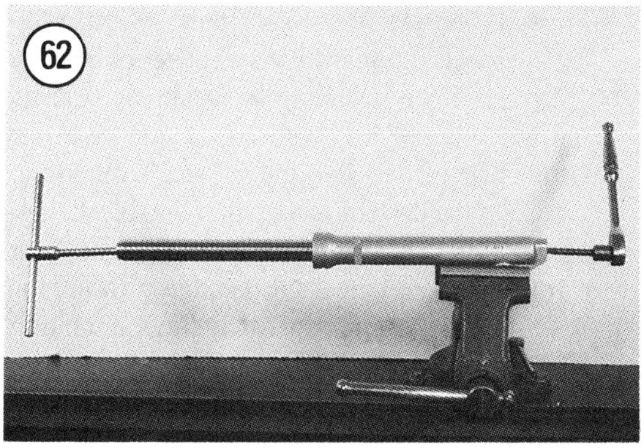
62

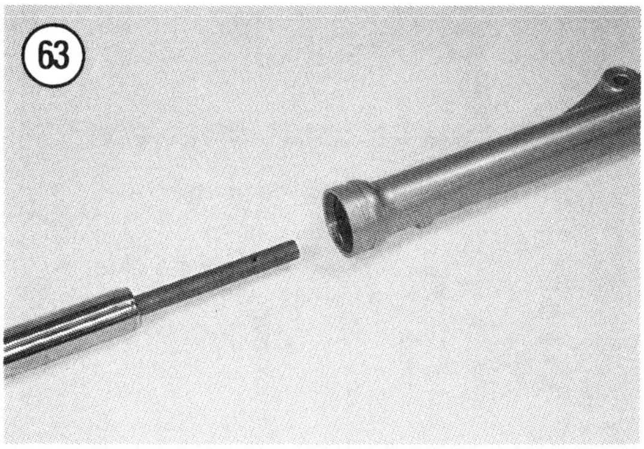
63

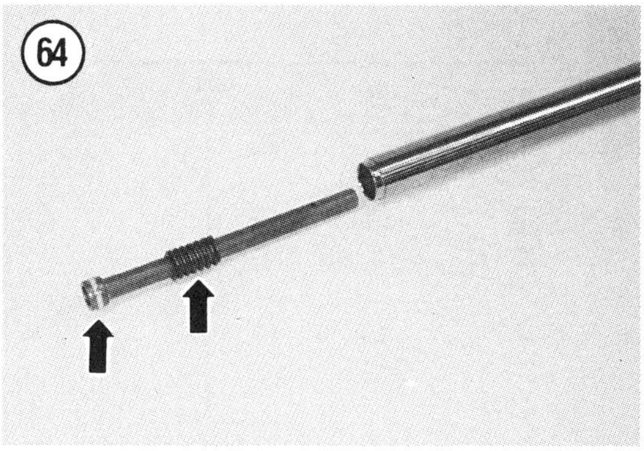
64

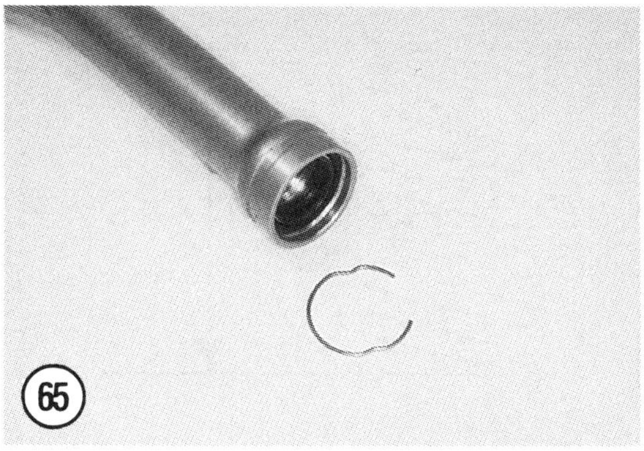
65

c. Insert the tool through the fork tube and into the top of the damper rod (**Figure 62**). **Figure 56** shows the tool and damper rod with the damper rod removed for clarity.

d. Twist the T-handle to "bite" the tool into the damper rod, then hold the T-handle and loosen the Allen bolt with the hex socket (figure 62). If necessary, have an assistant hold the T-handle while you turn the hex socket.

e. Remove the Allen bolt and socket (**Figure 61**).

f. Remove the slider from the vise.

12. Pull the fork tube out of the slider (**Figure 63**).

13. Remove the damper rod and rebound spring (**Figure 64**) from the fork tube.

14. To remove the oil seal, perform the following:

a. Remove the circlip (**Figure 65**) from the top of the slider.

b. Mount the slider in a vise with soft jaws.

CAUTION

While the oil seal is normally a tight fit in the slider, it can sometime be very difficult to remove. The following step describes how to remove the oil seal by prying it out of the slider. If this method fails to move the oil seal, don't apply excessive force as you can easily damage the slider or cause injury to yourself. If the oil seal does not move outward, take the slider to a dealership and have the oil seal removed for you.

WARNING

To protect your eyes, wear safety glasses when removing the oil seal in the following step.

c. Using a wide-blade screwdriver and rag as shown in **Figure 66**, pry the oil seal out of the

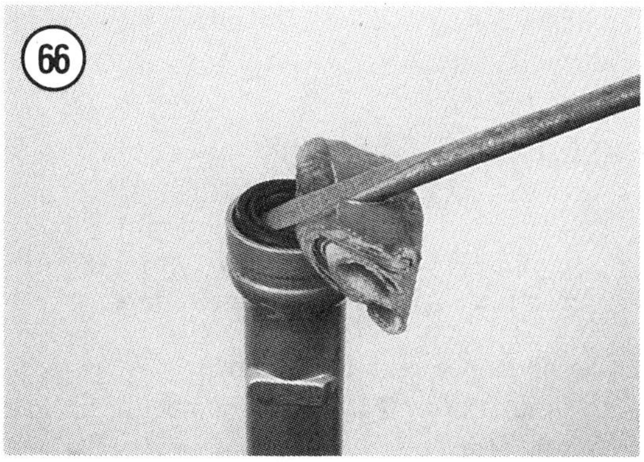
66

11

slider. To help break the seal loose, pry at different points around the seal.

Inspection

Replace parts that are out of specification or show damage as described in this section.

1. Clean and dry all parts (**Figure 67**). Remove all sealer residue from the damper rod and Allen bolt threads.
2. Check the fork tube (A, **Figure 67**) for wear or scratches that would damage the oil seal.
3. Check the fork tube (A, **Figure 67**) for straightness and replace if bent.

WARNING

Do not straighten a bent fork tube. Doing so may weaken the tube and cause it to fail during riding conditions.

4. Check the slider (B, **Figure 67**) for:
   a. Dents or exterior damage that may cause the fork tube to hang up during riding conditions.
   b. Damaged circlip groove.
   c. Damaged oil seal mounting bore.
5. Check the damper rod (C, **Figure 67**) for:
   a. Bending or other damage.
   b. Stripped threads.
   c. Worn or damaged piston ring (5, **Figure 57**). The piston ring can be replaced separately.
   d. Damaged return spring.
6. Measure the free length of the fork spring (**Figure 68**). Replace the spring if it is shorter than specified in **Table 1**. Compare the length of the left and right fork springs. Replace them both if one is much shorter than the other.
7. Replace the fork cap O-ring if damaged.
8. Replace the Allen bolt (16, **Figure 57**) if the hex part of the bolt has started to round off. Replace the washer if damaged.

Assembly

NOTE

If you are only changing the fork oil, perform Steps 7-11 in this procedure.

1. Install the new oil seal as follows:
   a. Install the oil seal with its number or marked side facing up.
   b. Install the new seal with a press (**Figure 69**) or drive it into place with a socket or bearing driver. When selecting a socket or bearing driver, choose one with an outside diameter that will just fit into the oil seal's mounting bore. If the driver has a smaller outside diameter, it will apply more pressure to the inside or softer part of the seal and damage it. Install the seal until it bottoms out in the slider mounting bore. See **Figure 70**.
   c. Lubricate the oil seal lip with fork oil.

67

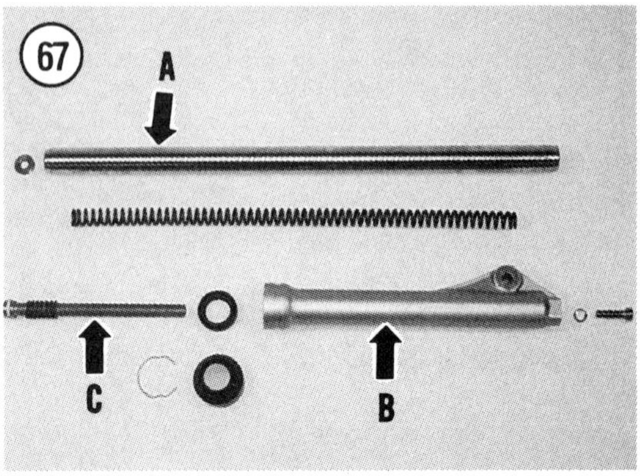

68

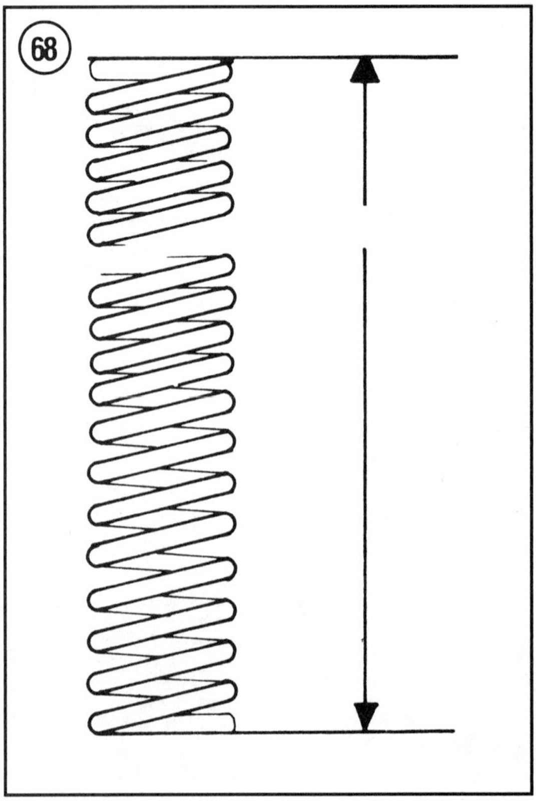

d. Install the circlip (**Figure 65**) into the slider groove.

2. Lubricate the damper rod piston ring (5, **Figure 57**) with fork oil.

3. Slide the return spring onto the damper rod, then install the damper rod into the fork tube (**Figure 64**).

4. Slide the fork tube and damper rod into the slider (**Figure 63**).

5. Apply a medium strength thread lock to the threads of the Allen bolt, then install the bolt and its washer and tighten hand tight. See **Figure 61**.

NOTE

Step 6 describes 2 methods of tightening the Allen bolt.

6A. To tighten the Allen bolt without special tools, perform the following:

a. Temporarily install the fork spring and spring seat (**Figure 60**) into the fork tube.

b. Install the fork tube into the steering stem and secure it with the lower steering stem pinch bolt.

c. Install the front axle (B, **Figure 54**) through both fork tubes to secure the slider in place.

d. Tighten the Allen bolt (**Figure 58**) as specified in **Table 3**.

e. If the damper rod turns with the Allen bolt, the fork spring is not providing enough pressure against the damper rod. Tighten the Allen bolt as described in Step 6B.

f. Remove the front fork from the bike, then remove the spring seat and fork spring (**Figure 60**).

6B. To tighten the Allen bolt with the use of the damper rod holder tool (B, **Figure 55**), perform the following:

a. See *Special Tools* for a description of the damper rod holder tool (B, **Figure 55**). Mount the tool onto a long T-handle.

b. Mount the slider in a vise with soft jaws.

c. Insert the tool through the fork tube and into the top of the damper rod (**Figure 62**). **Figure 56** shows the tool and damper rod with the damper rod removed for clarity.

d. Twist the T-handle to bite the tool into the damper rod, then hold the T-handle and tighten the Allen bolt as specified in **Table 3**. If necessary, have an assistant hold the T-handle while you tighten the Allen bolt.

e. Remove the slider from the vise.

7. Add fork oil to the fork and then set the oil level as follows:

a. Bottom out the fork tube in the slider.

b. Add the correct weight and amount of fork oil as specified in **Table 1**. If you are going to set the oil level, add more to the fork than that specified in **Table 1**.

c. Set the oil level with a commercial type oil level gauge. Follow the manufacturer's instructions when using the tool.

8. Support the slider in a vise with soft jaws.

9. Pull the fork tube all the way up. Install the fork spring and spring seat (**Figure 60**).

10. Install the boot (10, **Figure 57**). On BW80 models, secure the boot with the 2 hose clamps. On PW80 models, seat the boot lip into the groove in the top of the slider.

11. Complete assembly by installing the front fork onto the bike as described in this chapter. After installing the front fork, tighten the fork cap as specified in **Table 3**.

69

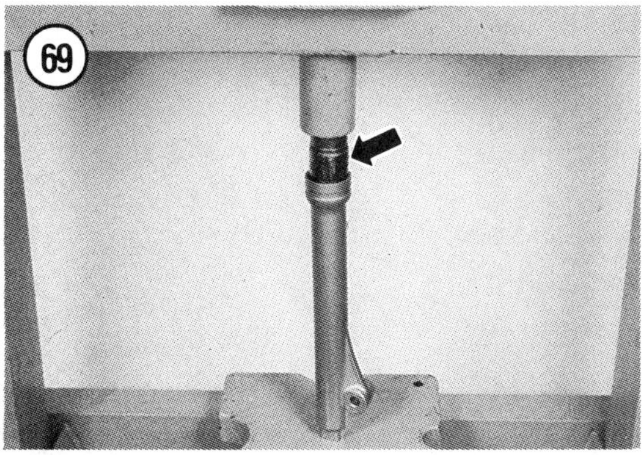

70

11

TIRE CHANGE (BW80)

The BW80 is equipped with tubeless, low pressure tires designed specifically for off-road use only. Rapid tire wear will occur if the vehicle is ridden on paved surfaces.

Tire Changing

The front and rear tire rims are of the 2-piece type and have a very deep built-in ridge (**Figure 71**) to keep the tire bead seated on the rim under severe riding conditions. Unfortunately it also tends to keep the tire on the rim during tire removal as well.

A bead breaker (**Figure 72**) is required for breaking the tire away from the rim.

1. Remove the wheel from the bike as described in this chapter (front) or Chapter Thirteen (rear).
2. Remove the brake hub from the wheel as described in Chapter Fourteen.
3. Remove the valve stem cap and core and deflate the tire. Do not reinstall the core at this time.
4. Lubricate the tire bead and rim flanges with a liquid dish detergent or any rubber lubricant. Press the tire sidewall/bead down to allow the liquid to run into and around the bead area. Also apply lubricant to the area where the bead breaker arm will come in contact with the tire sidewall.
5. Position the wheel into the tire removal tool (**Figure 72**).
6. Slowly work the tire tool, making sure the tool is up against the inside of the rim, and break the tire bead away from the rim.
7. Using your hands, press down on the tire on either side of the tool and try to break the rest of the bead free from the rim.
8. If the rest of the tire bead cannot be broken loose, raise the tool, rotate the tire/rim assembly and repeat Steps 4 and 5 until the entire bead is broken loose from the rim.
9. Turn the wheel over and repeat to break the opposite loose.
10. Remove the tire rims from the tire.
11. Inspect the rim sealing surface of the rim. If the rim has been severely hit it will probably cause an air leak. Repair or replace the rim as required.
12. Inspect the tire for cuts, tears, abrasions or any other defects.
13. Clean the rims and tire sealing surfaces.
14. Set the tire into position on the outer rim.
15. Install the inner rim into the tire and onto the outer rim. Align the bolt holes.
16. Install the brake hub as described in Chapter Fourteen.
17. Install the valve stem core.
18. Apply tire mounting lubricate to the tire bead and inflate the tire to the seating pressure specifications listed in **Table 2**.
19. Check the rim line molded into the tire around the edge of the rim (**Figure 73**). It must be equally

71 TIRE SEATING

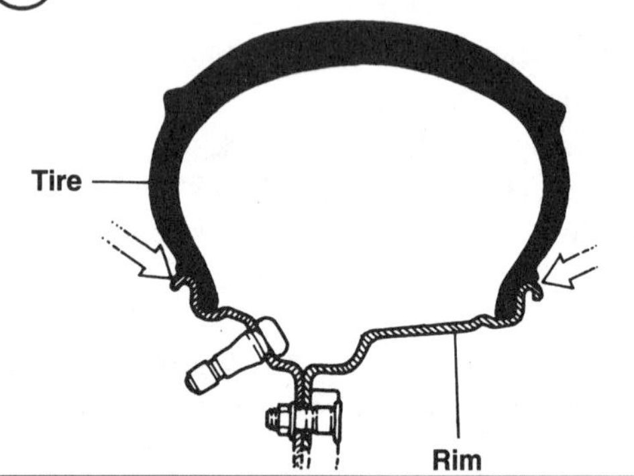

72

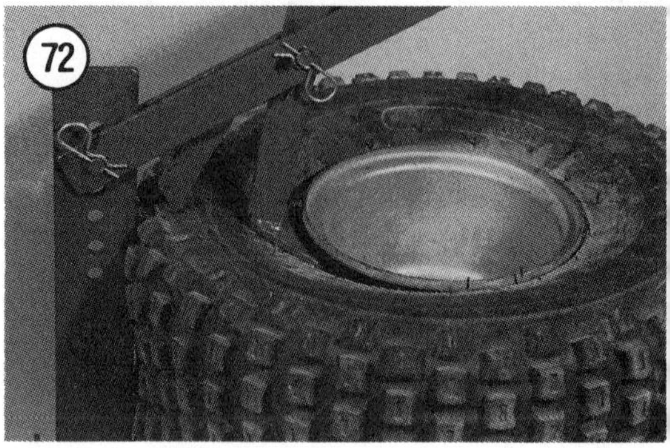

73

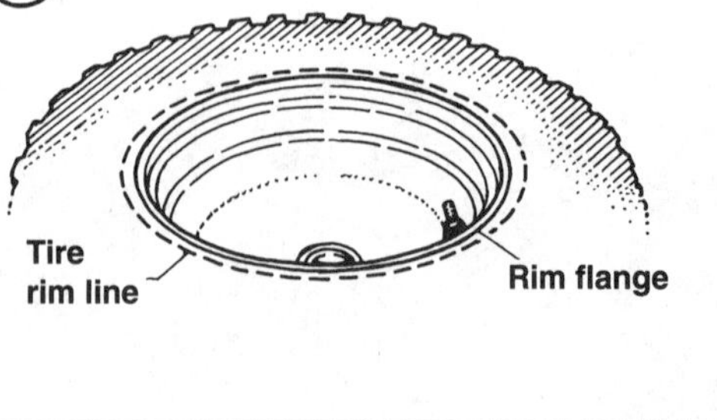

spaced all the way around. If the rim line spacing is not equal the tire bead is not properly seated. Deflate the tire and unseat the bead completely. Lubricate the bead and reinflate the tire.

20. Check for air leaks and install the valve cap.

21. Install the wheel assembly onto the bike as described in this chapter (front) or Chapter Thirteen (rear).

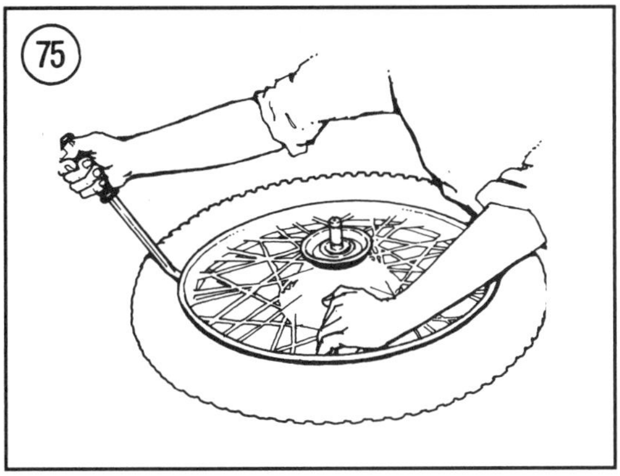

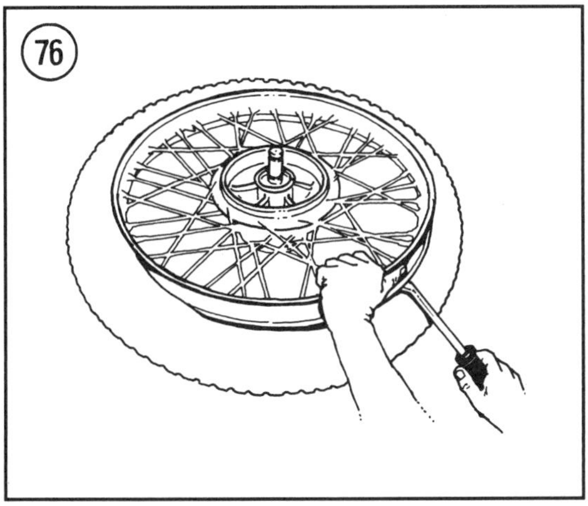

TIRE CHANGE (PW50 AND PW80)

Removal

1. Remove the valve core (**Figure 74**) and deflate the tire.

2. Press the entire bead on both sides of the tire into the center of the rim.

3. Lubricate the beads with soapy water.

4. Insert the tire iron under the bead next to the valve (**Figure 75**). Force the bead on the opposite side of the tire into the center of the rim and pry the bead over the rim with the tire iron.

5. Insert a second tire iron next to the first to hold the bead over the rim. Then work around the tire with the first tire iron, prying the bead over the rim. Be careful not to pinch the inner tube with the tire irons.

6. Remove the valve from the hole in the rim and remove the tube from the tire.

7. Stand the tire upright. Insert the tire iron between the second bead and the side of the rim that the first bead was pried over (**Figure 76**). Force the bead on the opposite side from the tire iron into the center of the rim. Pry the second bead off of the rim, working around as with the first.

11

Installation

1. Carefully check the inside and outside of the tire for any damage.

2. On PW80 models, check that the spoke ends do not protrude through the nipples into the center of the rim to puncture the tube. Grind or file off any protruding spoke ends.

3. Install the rubber rim band with its rough side toward the rim. Align the holes in the band with the holes in the rim.

4. Liberally sprinkle the inside tire casing with talcum powder. Talcum powder reduces chafing between the tire and tube and helps to minimize tube damage.

5. Lubricate one bead with soapy water. Then align the tire with the rim and push the tire onto the rim (**Figure 77**). Work around the tire in both directions (**Figure 78**).

6. Install the core into the inner tube valve. Put the tube in the tire and insert the valve stem through the hole in the rim. Inflate just enough to round it out. Too much air will make installing it in the tire

difficult, and too little will increase the chances of pinching the tube with the tire irons.

7. Lubricate the upper tire bead and rim with soapy water.

8. Press the upper bead into the rim opposite the valve. Pry the bead into the rim on both sides of the initial point with your hands and work around the rim to the valve. If the tire wants to pull up on one side, either use a tire iron or one of your knees to hold the tire in place. The last few inches are usually the toughest to install and it is also where most pinched tubes occur. If you can, continue to push the tire into the rim with your hands. Relubricate the bead if necessary. If the tire bead wants to pull out from under the rim use both of your knees to hold the tire in place. If necessary, use a tire iron for the last few inches.

9. Wiggle the valve to be sure the tube is not trapped under the bead. Set the valve squarely in its hole before screwing on the valve nut.

10. Check the bead on both sides of the tire for even fit around the rim, then relubricate both sides of the tire. Inflate the tire to approximately 172 kPa (25 psi) psi to insure the tire bead is seated properly on the rim. If the tire is hard to seat, release the air from the tube and then reinflate.

11. Bleed the tire pressure back down to 100 kPa (15 psi). Screw on the valve stem nut but do not tighten it against the rim. Instead, tighten it against the air cap. Doing this will prevent the valve stem from pulling away from the tube if the tire slips on the rim.

77

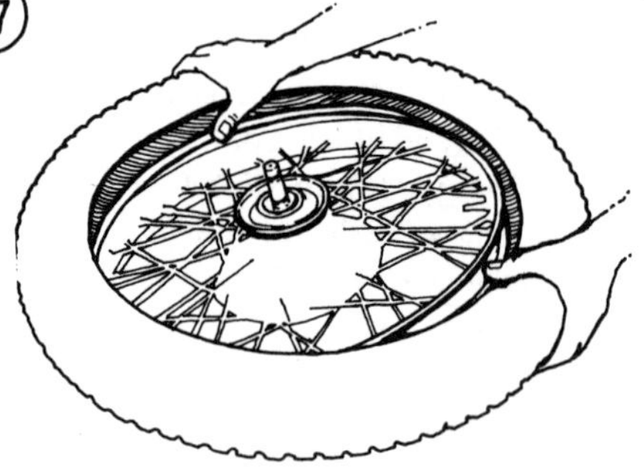

78

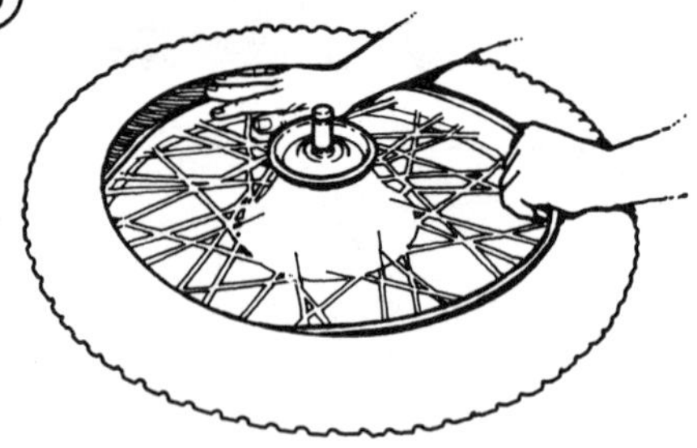

Table 1 FRONT SUSPENSION AND STEERING SPECIFICATIONS (BW80 AND PW80)

Frame type	Steel tube backbone
Caster angle	
BW80	26° 10 minutes
PW80	26°
Trail	
BW80	54 mm (2.13 in.)
PW80	62 mm (2.44 in.)
Steering	
Type	Individual steel balls
Number of balls in steering head	
Upper race	22
Lower race	19
Front fork travel	110 mm (4.3 in.)
Fork spring	
Spring free length	
New	425.1 mm (16.74 in.)
Service limit	420.8 mm (16.57 in.)
Spring rate	0.35 kg/mm (19.6 lbs./in.)
Fork oil	
Type	15 wt. fork oil
Oil capacity	
BW80	69 mL (2.33 U.S. oz. [2.43 Imp. oz.])
PW80	60 mL (2.0 U.S. oz. [2.1 Imp. oz.])
Oil level	
BW80	172 mm (5.5 in.)
PW80	188.5 mm (7.42 in.)

11

Table 2 TIRE AND WHEEL SPECIFICATIONS (BW80 AND PW80)

Rim size/material	
Front	
BW80	5.00 × 10/steel
PW80	1.40 × 14/steel
Rear	
BW80	6.50 × 7/steel
PW80	1.60 × 12/steel
Tire size	
Front	
BW80	19 × 7.00-10 (tubeless)
PW80	2.50 × 14-4PR (tube type)
Rear	
BW80	19 × 9.00-7 (tubeless)
PW80	3.00 × 12-4PR (tube type)
Tire pressure	
Front and rear tires	
BW80	29.4 kPa (0.3 kg/cm^2; 4.3 psi)
PW80	100 kPa (1.0 kg/cm^2; 15 psi)
Rim runout limit	
Side-to-side	2 mm (0.08 in.)
Up and down	2 mm (0.08 in.)

Table 3 FRONT SUSPENSION TIGHTENING TORQUES (BW80 AND PW80)

	N•m	in.-lb.	ft.-lb.
Fork cap	40	—	29
Fork tube pinch bolts (lower)	33	—	24
Front axle nut			
BW80	50	—	36
PW80	35	—	25
Front fork Allen bolt	20	—	14
Handlebar holder			
Upper holder bolts	13	115	—
Lower holder mounting nuts	40	—	29
Steering stem nut	see text		
Steering stem bolt	40	—	29

CHAPTER TWELVE

REAR SUSPENSION AND FINAL DRIVE (PW50)

This chapter describes repair and maintenance on the rear wheel, rear arm, final drive assembly and rear shocks.

Rear suspension specifications are listed in **Table 1**. Tightening specifications are listed in **Table 2**. **Tables 1** and **2** are at the end of the chapter.

REAR WHEEL

Removal/Installation

Refer to **Figure 1**.

1. Support the motorcycle on its centerstand.
2. Remove the spark arrestor and exhaust pipe (Chapter Four).
3. Apply the rear brake, then loosen and remove the rear axle nut and washer (A, **Figure 2**).
4. Remove the right side shock absorber's lower mounting bolt (B, **Figure 2**). Then swing the shock absorber up and tie it to the frame tube (**Figure 3**).
5. Remove the 2 front rear arm mounting nuts and washers (**Figure 4**), then remove the rear arm assembly (**Figure 5**) and the inner washer (**Figure 6**).

NOTE
*The washers removed in Steps 3 and 5 are identical (same part number); see 2 and 6, **Figure 1**.*

6. Slide the rear wheel to the right side and remove it from the ring gear shaft (**Figure 7**). Do not loose the washer installed between the rear wheel and the ring gear assembly (**Figure 8**).
7. Perform the *Inspection* procedure in this section to clean and inspect the parts.
8. Install the rear wheel by reversing these removal steps. Note the following:
   a. Apply a light coat of grease onto the axle and ring gear shaft splines.
   b. Tighten the rear axle nut (A, **Figure 1**) as specified in **Table 2**.
   c. Tighten the rear arm mounting nuts (**Figure 4**) as specified in **Table 2**.
   d. Tighten the shock absorber's lower mounting bolt (B, **Figure 2**) as specified in **Table 2**.
   e. Check the rear brake adjustment (Chapter Three).

1

REAR WHEEL (PW50)

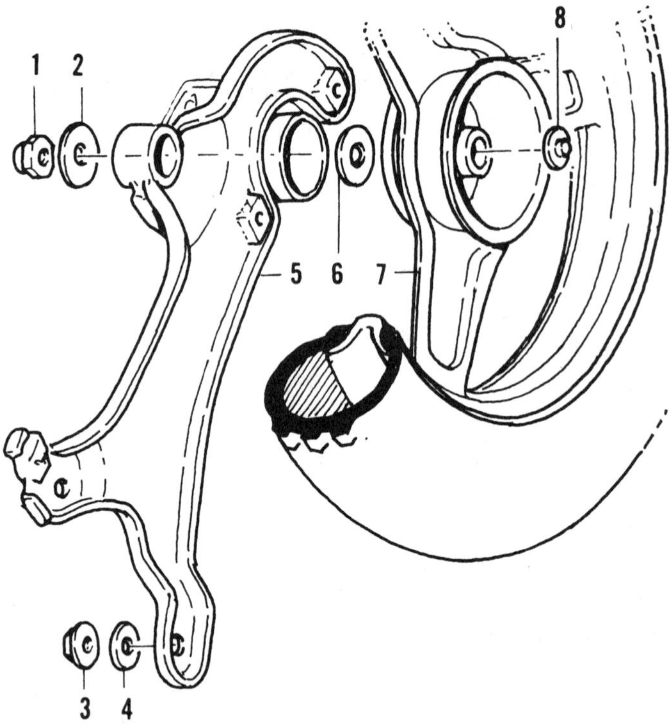

1. Axle nut
2. Washer
3. Nut
4. Washer
5. Rear arm
6. Washer
7. Rear wheel assembly
8. Washer

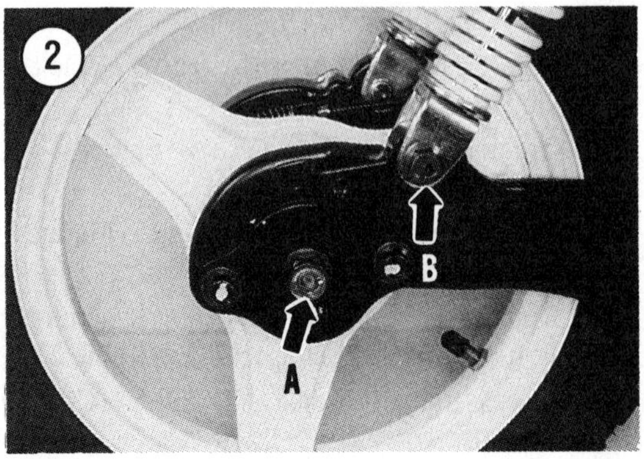

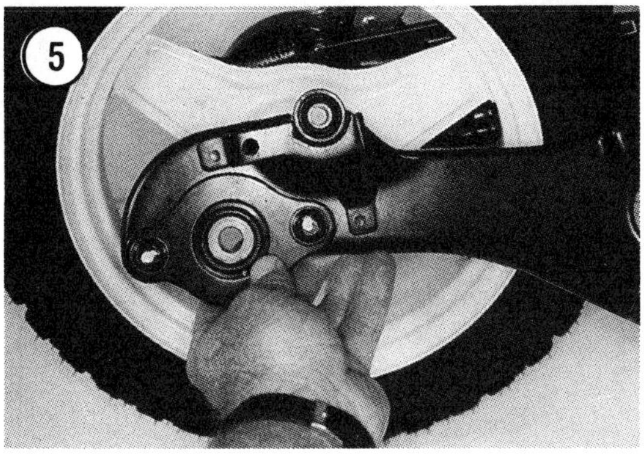

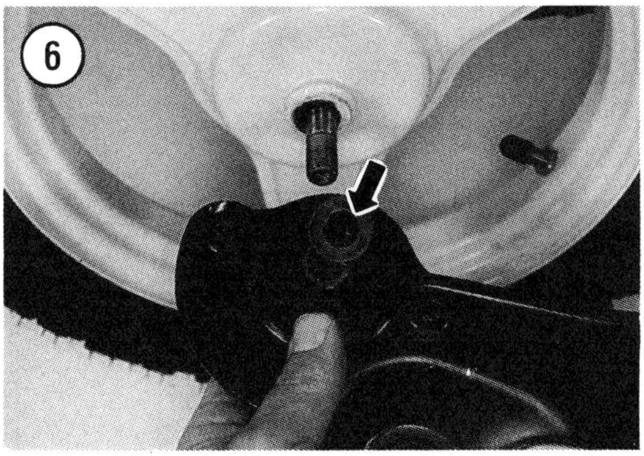

f. After the wheel is completely installed, rotate it and then apply the rear brake a couple of times to make sure the wheel rotates freely and that the brake is operating correctly.

Inspection

Replace parts that show damage as described in this section.

1. Check the wheel (**Figure 9**) for:
   a. Cracks or other damage.
   b. Breaks or other damage where the spokes are welded to the rim.
   c. Excessively worn or damaged splines (**Figure 10**).

2. Check the rear arm bearing as described under *Rear Arm* in this chapter.

3. Service the brake drum and brakes as described in Chapter Fourteen.

4. Check wheel runout as described under *Wheel Runout* in Chapter Ten.

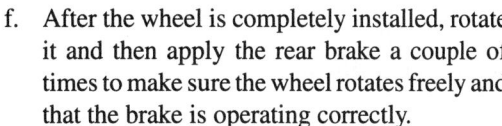

12

REAR ARM

Removal/Installation

1. Support the motorcycle on its centerstand.
2. Remove the spark arrestor and exhaust pipe (Chapter Four).
3. Apply the rear brake, then loosen and remove the rear axle nut and washer (A, **Figure 2**).
4. Remove the right side shock absorber's lower mounting bolt (B, **Figure 2**). Then swing the shock absorber up and tie it to the frame tube (**Figure 3**).
5. Remove the 2 front rear arm mounting nuts and washers (**Figure 4**), then remove the rear arm assembly (**Figure 5**) and the inner washer (**Figure 6**).

NOTE

The washers removed in Steps 3 and 5 are identical (same part number); see 2 and 6, ***Figure 1****.*

6. Perform the *Inspection* procedure in this section to clean and inspect the parts.
7. Install the rear arm by reversing these removal steps. Note the following:
   a. Tighten the rear axle nut (A, **Figure 1**) as specified in **Table 2**.
   c. Tighten the rear arm mounting nuts (**Figure 4**) as specified in **Table 2**.
   d. Tighten the shock absorber's lower mounting bolt (B, **Figure 2**) as specified in **Table 2**.

Inspection

1. Clean and dry the rear arm assembly (**Figure 11**).
2. Inspect the rear arm (**Figure 11**) for bending or other damage.
3. Check the shock bushing (**Figure 12**) for wear or damage. Replace the bushing with a press.
4. Turn the rear arm bearing's inner race (**Figure 13**) by hand. The bearing must turn with no roughness, catching, binding or excessive noise. Some axial play is normal, but radial play must be negligible; see **Figure 14**. If necessary, replace the bearing as described in this section.

Rear Arm Bearing Replacement

Refer to **Figure 15**.

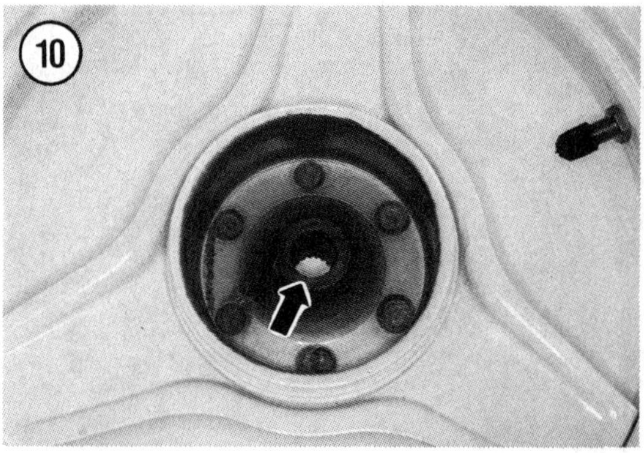
10

11

12

13

14

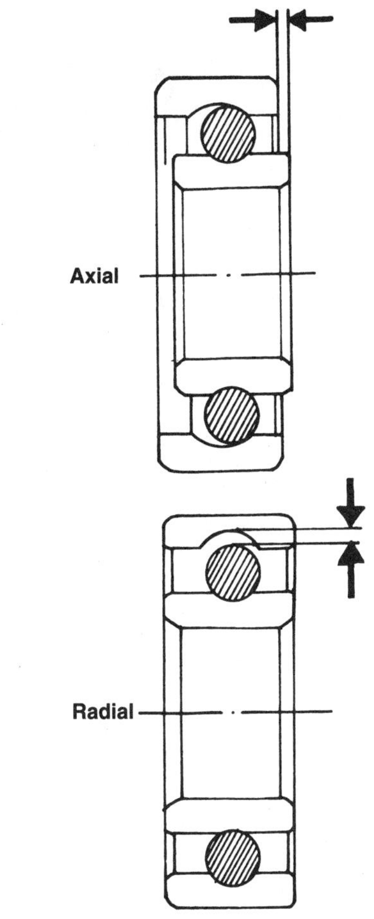

CAUTION
Do not remove the rear arm bearing for inspection purpose as it can be damaged during removal. Remove the bearing for replacement only.

1. Remove the 2 rear arm bearing housing mounting bolts and washers, then remove the bearing housing (**Figure 16**).
2. Remove the collar (**Figure 17**) from each seal.
3. Pry the dust seal out of the hub with a wide-blade screwdriver (**Figure 18**). Support the screwdriver with a rag to avoid damaging the housing.
4. Measure the bearing's installed depth (**Figure 19**) before removing it in Step 5.
5. Support the bearing housing in a press and press out the bearing (**Figure 20**).
6. Inspect the bearing housing for cracks (**Figure 21**), scoring or other damage. If the bearing is a loose fit in its mounting bore, replace the bearing housing.
7. Support the bearing housing in a press with its left side facing up (**Figure 22**).
8. Install the bearing in its mounting bore and press it into place with a suitable size bearing driver placed on the bearing's outer race (**Figure 22**). Press in the

16

15

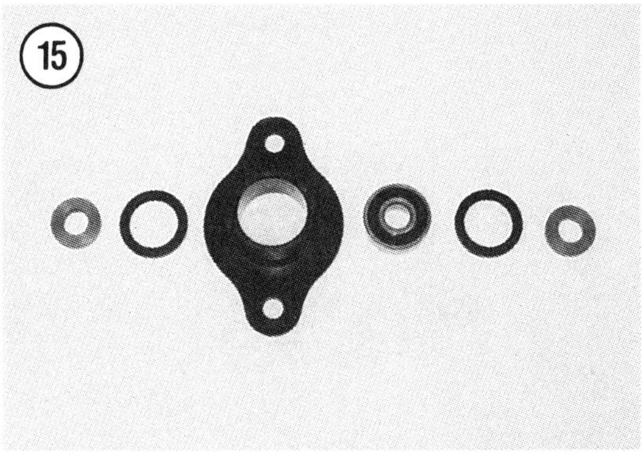

17

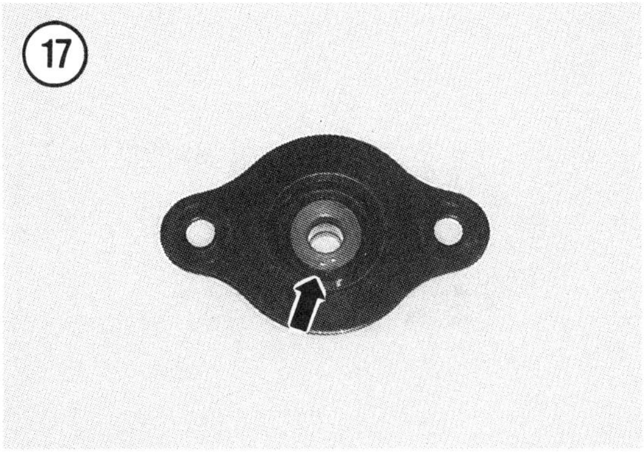

bearing to the dimension recorded in Step 4. See **Figure 23**.

9. Make sure the bearing's inner race turns without any binding or damage.
10. Pack each dust seal lip with grease (**Figure 24**).
11. Place the dust seal squarely against the bore opening with its closed side facing out. Then press or drive the dust seal in the bore until it bottoms against the bearing. Repeat for the other dust seal.
12. Install a collar (**Figure 17**) in each seal.

TIRE CHANGING

Refer to *Tire Changing* in Chapter Eleven.

FINAL DRIVE

The final drive assembly consists of the drive shaft and housing, final drive housing and ring gear (**Figure 25**).

Removal

1. Support the motorcycle on its centerstand.
2. Remove the rear wheel as described in this chapter.
3. Remove the rear brake assembly as described in Chapter Fourteen.
4. Remove the left shock absorber lower mounting bolt (**Figure 26**), then pivot the shock up and tie it to the frame tube (**Figure 27**).
5. Remove the bolts and lockwashers (A, **Figure 28**) that hold the final drive housing (B, **Figure 28**) to the drive shaft housing. Then withdraw the final drive housing (B, **Figure 28**) and remove it.
6. Remove the drive shaft assembly (**Figure 29**).

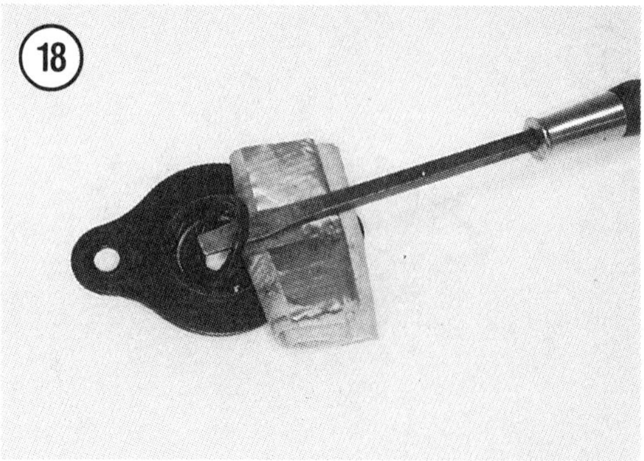
18

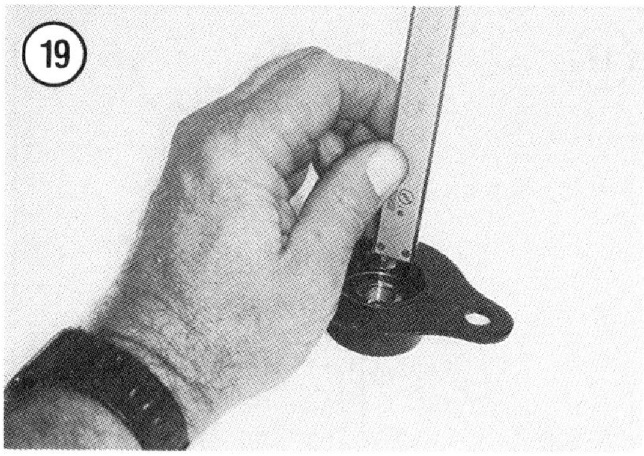
19

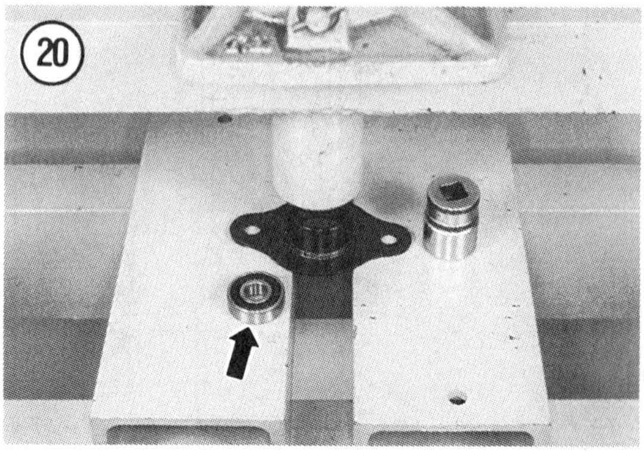
20

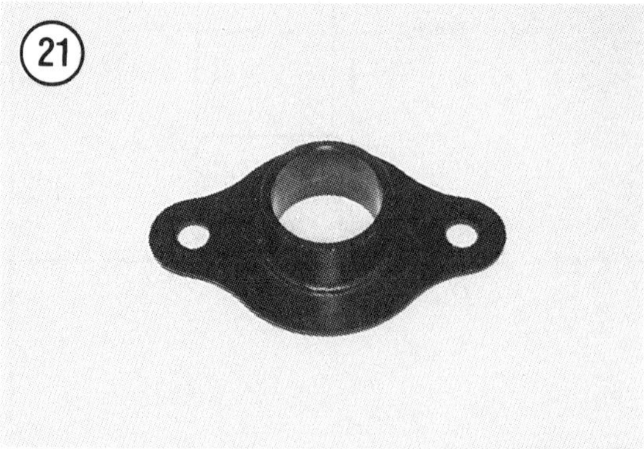
21

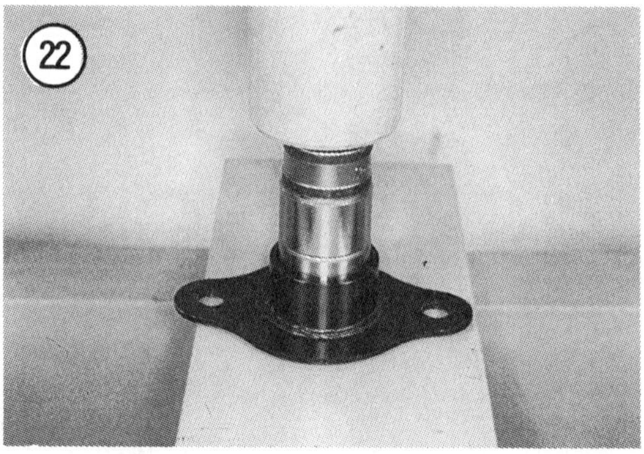
22

23

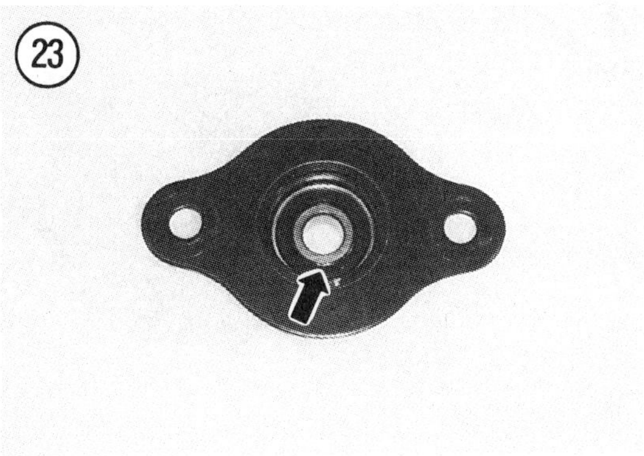

24

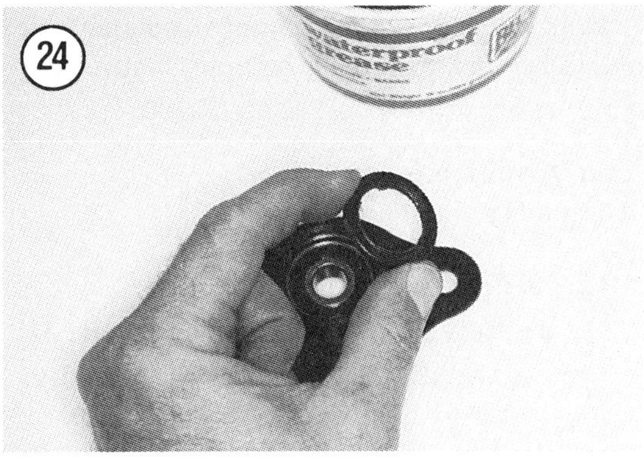

25

FINAL DRIVE

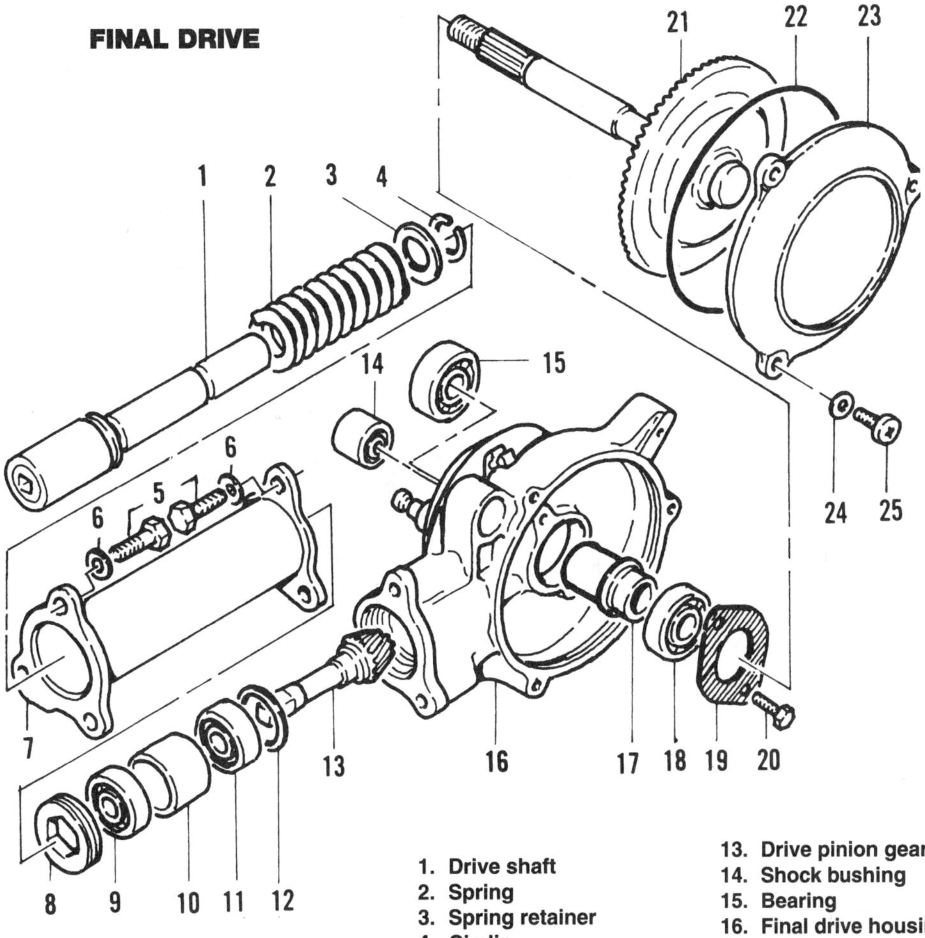

1. Drive shaft
2. Spring
3. Spring retainer
4. Circlip
5. Bolt
6. Lockwasher
7. Drive shaft housing
8. Drive pinion hex nut
9. Bearing
10. Spacer
11. Bearing
12. Drive pinion shim
13. Drive pinion gear
14. Shock bushing
15. Bearing
16. Final drive housing
17. Spacer
18. Bearing
19. Ring gear bearing plate
20. Bolt
21. Ring gear
22. O-ring
23. Housing cover
24. Washer
25. Screw

7. Remove the drive shaft housing mounting bolts and washers and remove the housing (**Figure 30**).

Final Drive Housing Disassembly

Refer to **Figure 25** for this procedure.

1. Clean and dry the final drive housing (**Figure 31**).
2. Remove the screws and washers that hold the housing cover to the final drive housing. Then remove the cover and its O-ring (A, **Figure 32**).
3. Pull the ring gear (B, **Figure 32**) out of the housing. See **Figure 33**.
4. Mount the final drive housing in a vise with soft jaws as shown in **Figure 34**.
5. Remove the drive pinion hex nut (**Figure 34**) as follows:
   a. The hex nut has right-hand threads. Turn the hex screw counterclockwise to remove it.
   b. A 22 mm hex wrench (Yamaha part No. YM-01307) or equivalent will be required to remove the hex screw. We made a tool using a 13/16 in. spark plug socket with a 7/8 in. (22

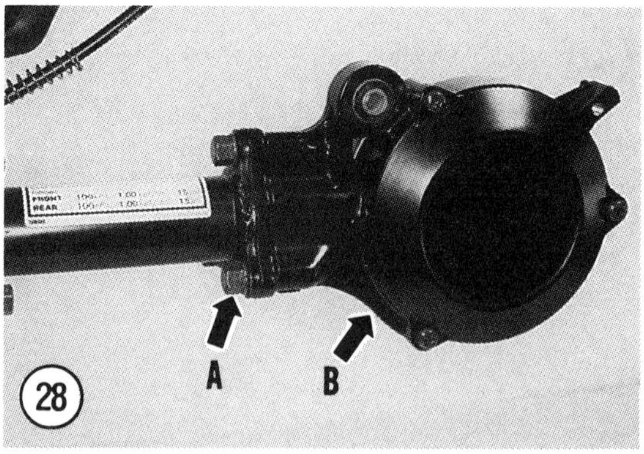

28

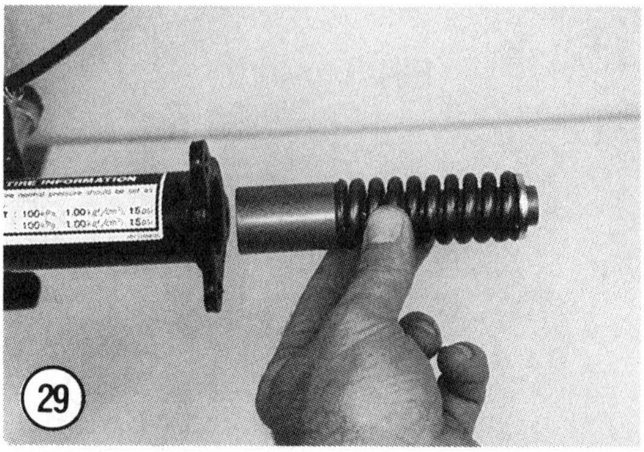
29

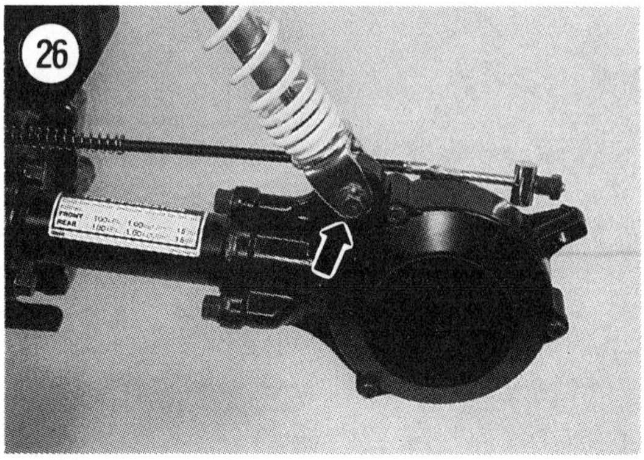
26

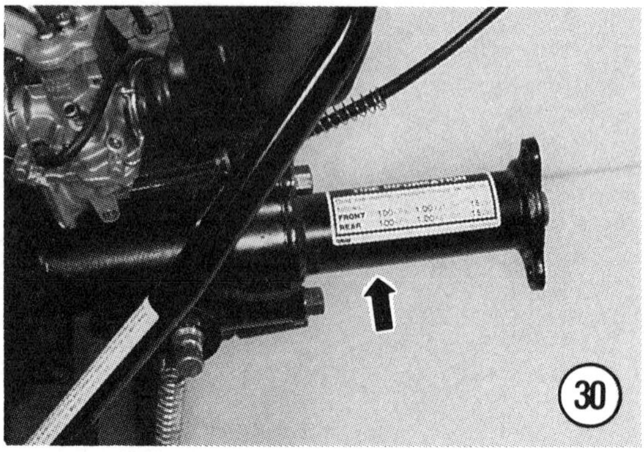
30

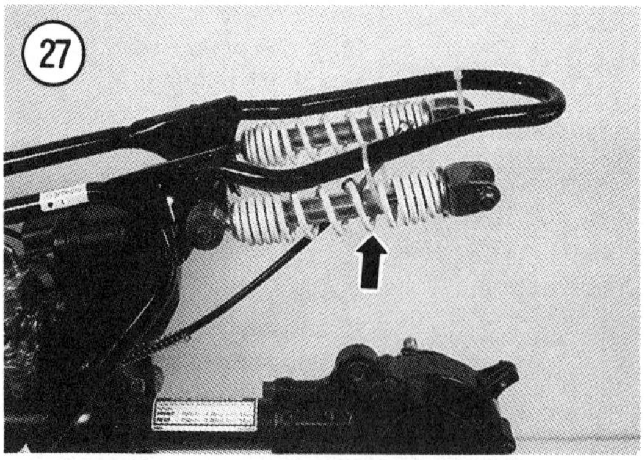
27

31

mm) male hex end and a suitable bolt with 2 jam nuts (**Figure 35**).

c. Using your hex wrench (**Figure 36**), loosen and remove the drive pinion hex nut. See **Figure 37**.

6. Remove the drive pinion gear assembly (**Figure 38**). The assembly will come apart as shown in **Figure 39**.

7. Locate and remove the drive pinion shim (**Figure 40**).

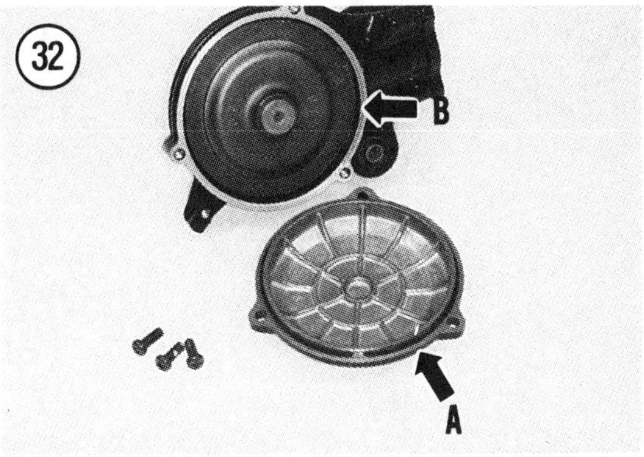

32

33

34

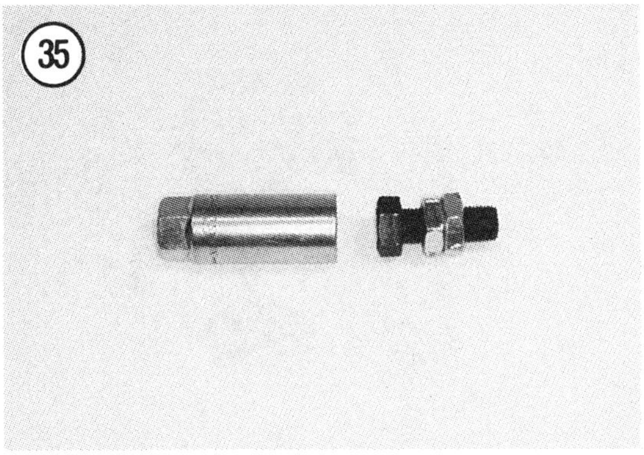

35

36

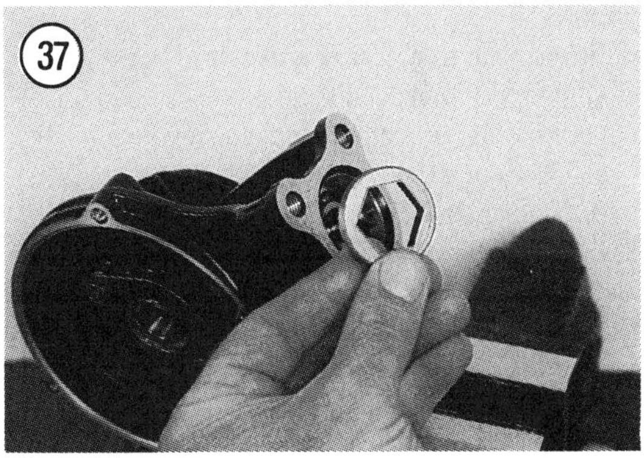

37

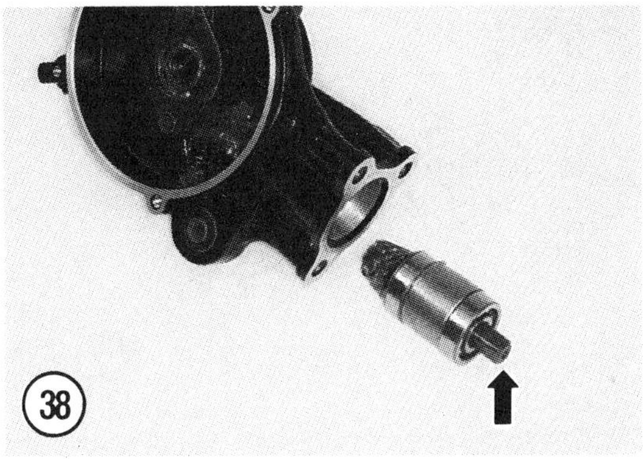

38

8. Remove the bolts and ring gear bearing plate (**Figure 41**), then remove the ring gear bearings and spacer. See **Figure 42**.

Inspection

Replace all parts that show damage as described in this section.

1. Clean and dry all parts (**Figure 43**) while noting the following:
   a. Clean the unshielded bearings with a bearing cleaner.
   b. Do not clean the rubber sealed bearing with a solvent as it may damage the rubber seal and contaminate the bearing's grease.
2. Inspect the final drive housing cover (A, **Figure 44**) for cracks or other damage.
3. Replace the cover O-ring (A, **Figure 44**) if severely worn or damaged.
4. Inspect the final drive housing (B, **Figure 44**) for:
   a. Cracks or other damage.
   b. Cracked or scored bearing bores.
   c. Damaged threads.
5. Inspect the shock bushing (**Figure 45**) for excessive wear or damage. Replace the bushing with a press.
6. Inspect the ring gear (**Figure 46**) for:
   a. Worn or damaged splines.
   b. Missing, broken or chipped ring gear teeth.
   c. Worn or damaged bearing surfaces.
   d. Damaged axle threads.
7. Support the ring gear between centers, then install a dial indicator and position its stem against the ring gear as shown in **Figure 47**. Slowly turn the ring gear to measure its deflection. Replace the ring gear if its deflection reading exceeds 0.08 mm (0.0031 in.).

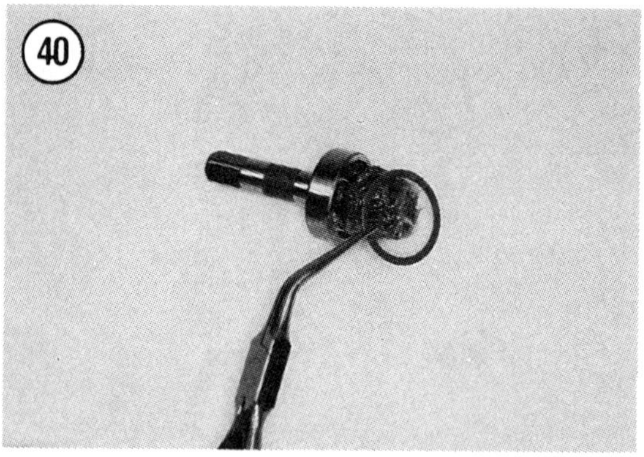
40

41

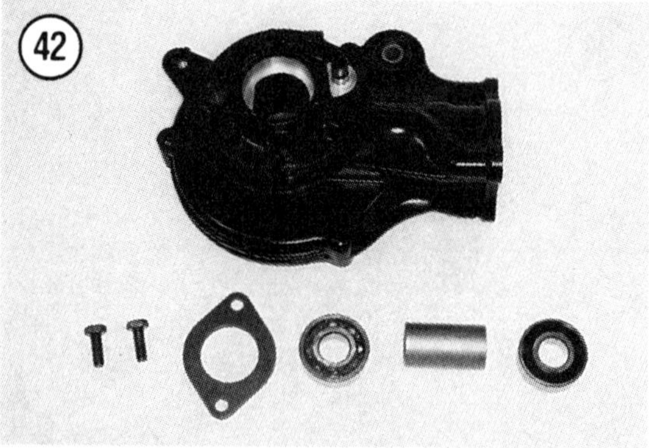
42

39

43

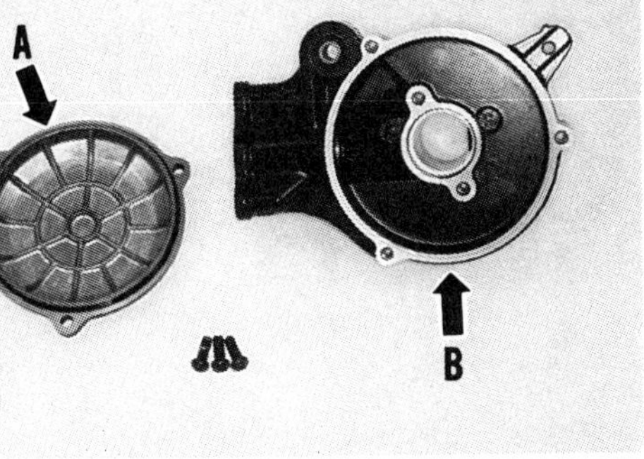

44

8. Inspect the drive pinion gear and shaft (**Figure 48**) for:

   a. Worn or damaged shaft end.
   b. Missing, broken or chipped pinion gear teeth.
   c. Worn or damaged bearing surfaces.

9. Inspect the drive pinion gear bearings (A and B, **Figure 49**) as follows:

   a. Make sure that both bearings are clean.
   b. Turn each bearing by hand. Make sure that the bearings turn smoothly. Check rollers for of wear, pitting or excessive heat (bluish tint).

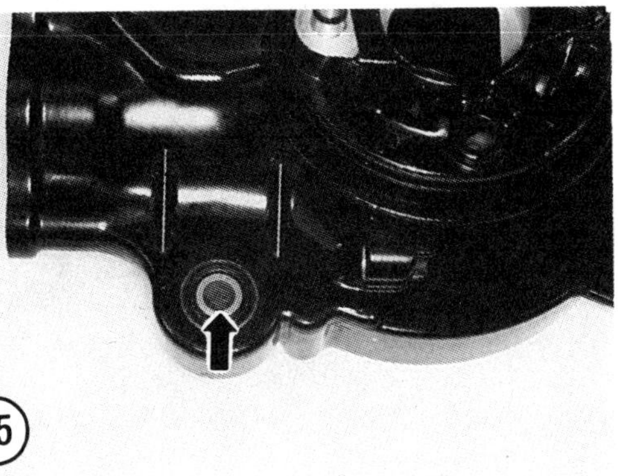

45

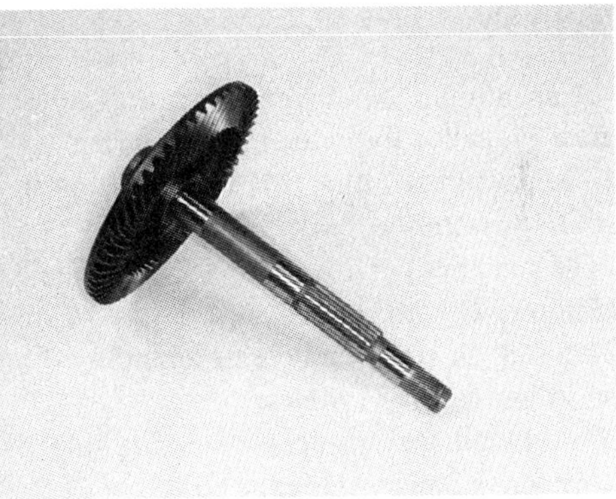

46

47

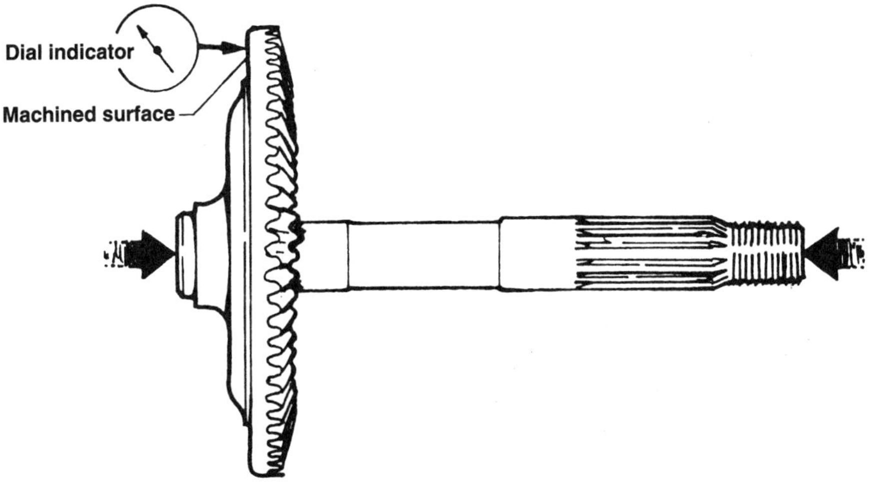

Replace bearings if there is any evidence of roughness or visible damage.

c. Replace the press fit bearing (B, **Figure 49**) with a press and suitable drivers.

10. See **Figure 49**. Inspect the hex nut (C), spacer (D) and drive pinion shim (E) for damage.
11. Inspect the ring gear bearings (A and B, **Figure 50**) as described in Step 9. Replace the outer bearing if its rubber seal (**Figure 51**) is cracked or damaged.
12. Pack all of the bearings (**Figure 52**) with lithium base wheel bearing grease.

Assembly

Use lithium base wheel bearing grease when grease is called for in the following steps.

1. Make sure all final drive parts are clean before starting assembly.
2. If you have not done so, pack all of the bearings (**Figure 52**) with grease.
3. Install the ring gear bearing assembly (**Figure 42** and **Figure 50**) as follows:
   a. Install the unshielded bearing into the final drive housing (**Figure 53**).
   b. Install the ring gear bearing plate and the 2 mounting bolts (**Figure 41**). Tighten the ring gear bearing plate bolts as specified in **Table 3**.
   c. Install the spacer (**Figure 54**) and center it against the bearing.
   d. Install the other bearing with its rubber seal facing out as shown in **Figure 55**.
   e. Place a strip of tape across the bearing to prevent it from falling out when completing final drive reassembly (**Figure 56**).
4. Pack the final drive housing with grease at the points shown in **Figure 57**.

49

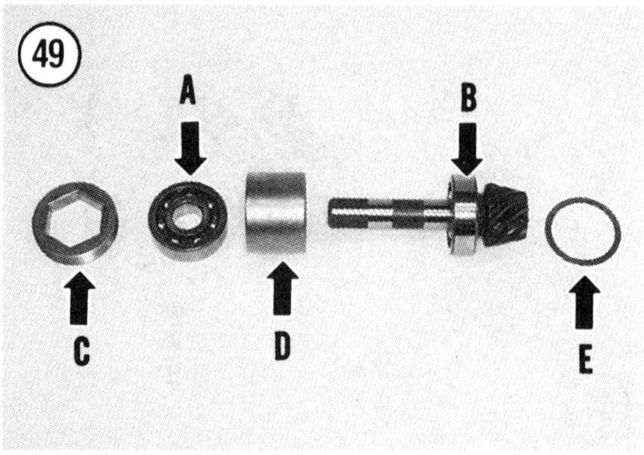

50

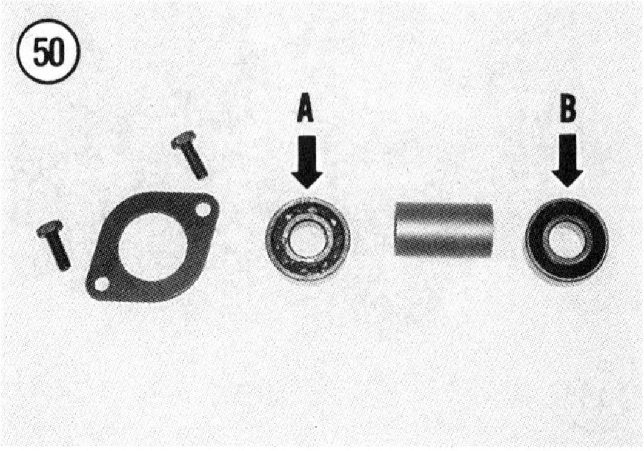

51

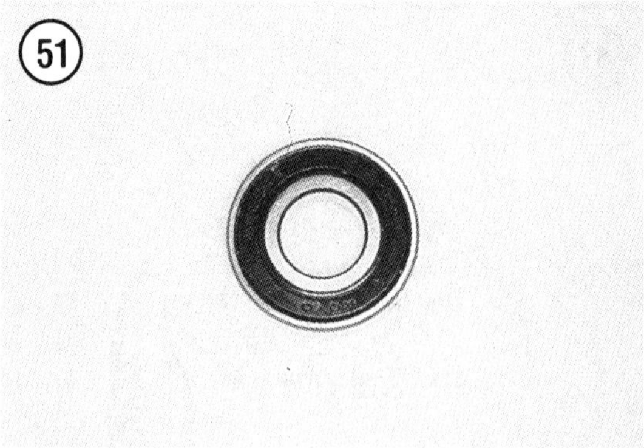

48

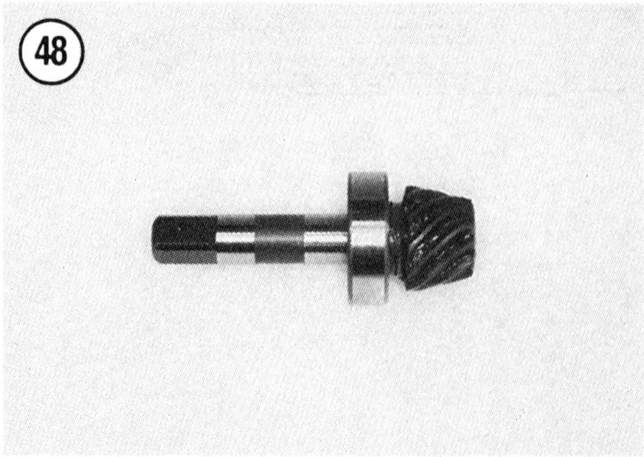

52

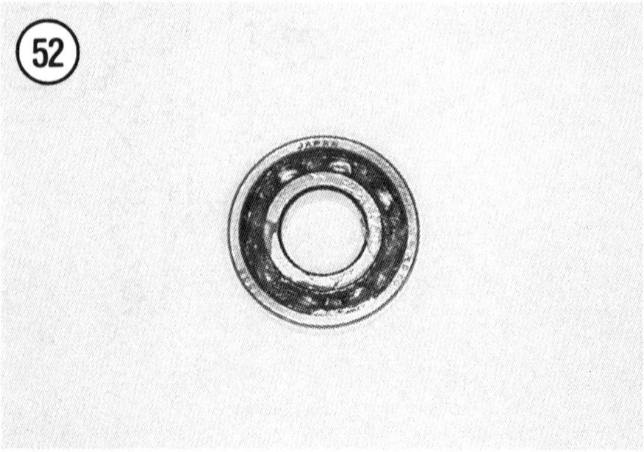

53

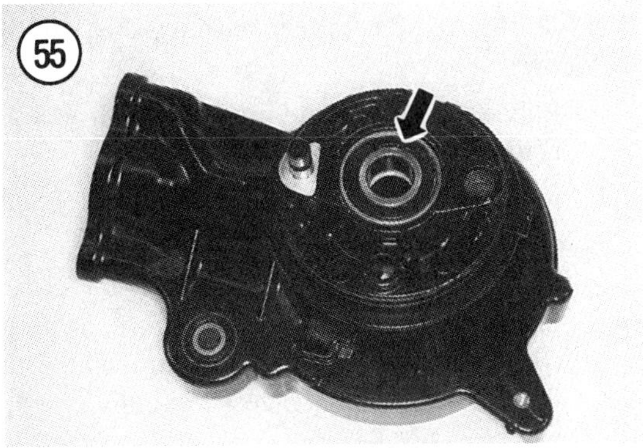
55

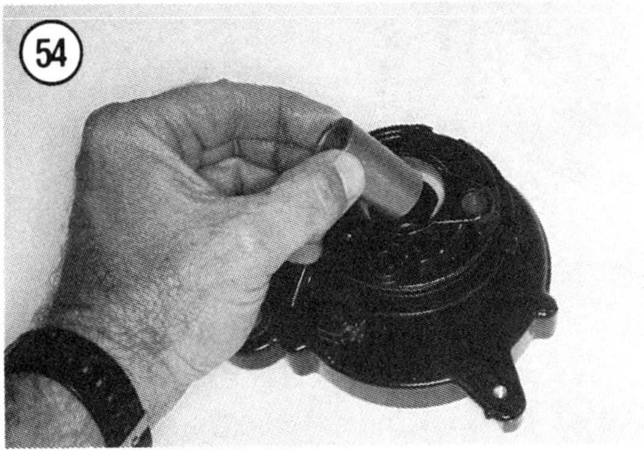
54

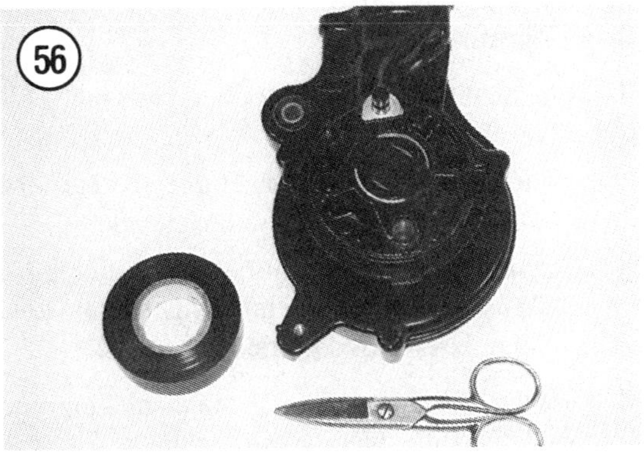
56

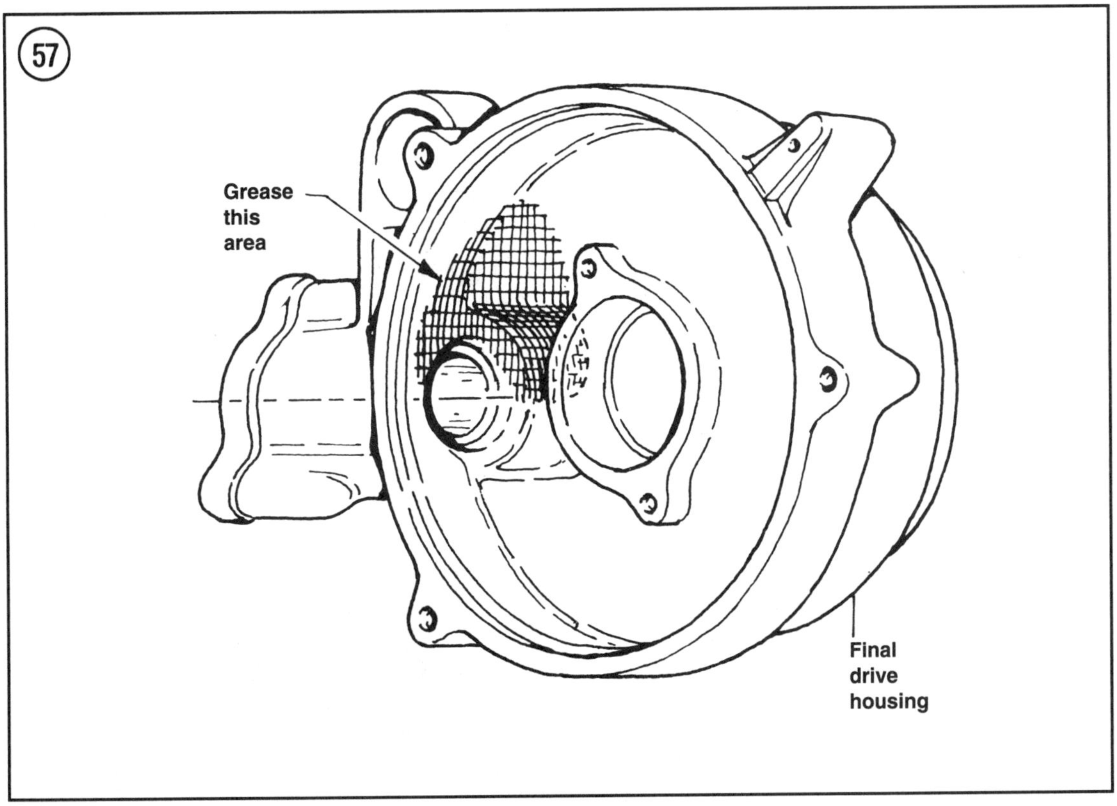
57
Grease this area
Final drive housing

5. Install the drive pinion gear assembly (**Figure 58**) as follows:

   a. Lubricate the drive pinion gear with grease (**Figure 59**).
   b. Install the drive pinion shim over the gear and center it against the bearing (**Figure 60**). Use grease to hold the shim in place.
   c. Install the spacer (A, **Figure 61**) and bearing (B, **Figure 61**) onto the drive pinion shaft, then install the drive pinion gear assembly into its mounting bore.

6. Mount the final drive housing in a vise with soft jaws (**Figure 62**).

7. Install and tighten the drive pinion hex nut (**Figure 62**) as follows:

   a. The hex nut has right-hand threads. Turn the hex screw clockwise to tighten it.
   b. Using the same 22 mm hex wrench (**Figure 63**) used during disassembly, tighten the drive pinion hex nut as specified in **Table 2**.

8. Turn the drive pinion shaft by hand, making sure it turns without any binding or roughness.

60

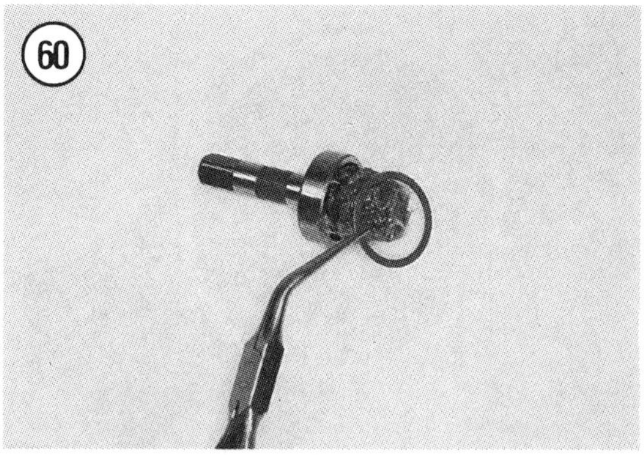

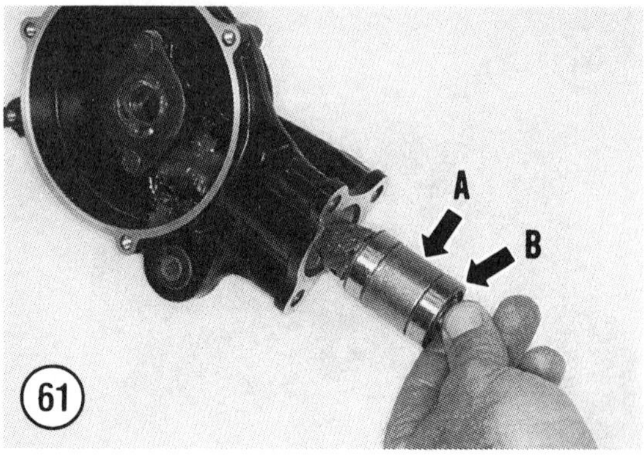

61

58

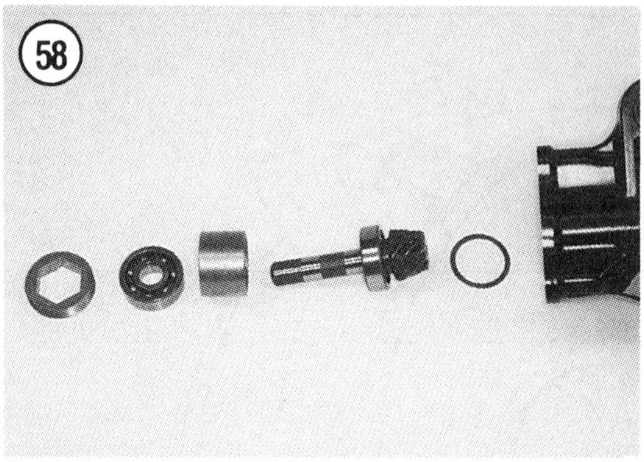

62

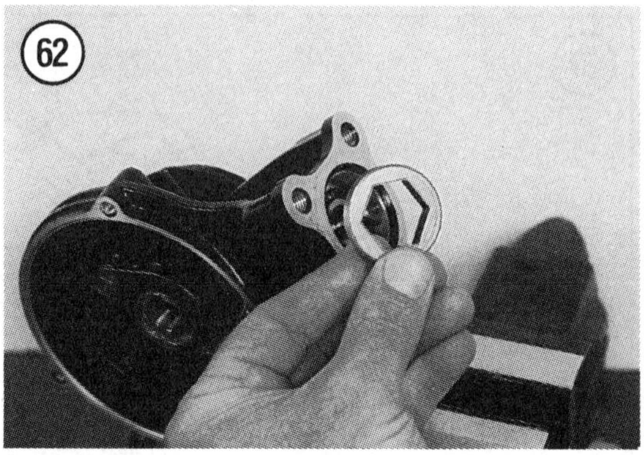

59

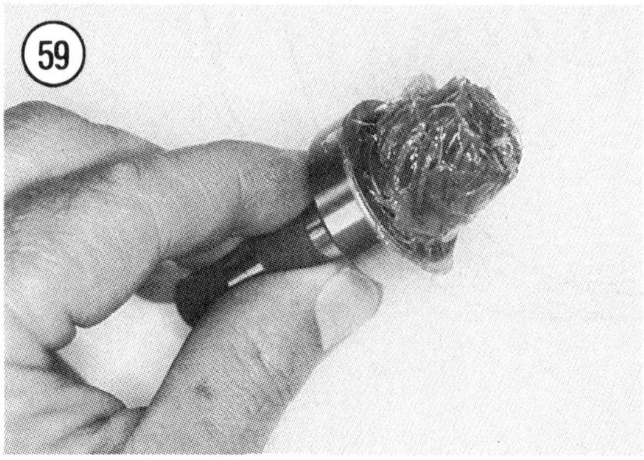

63

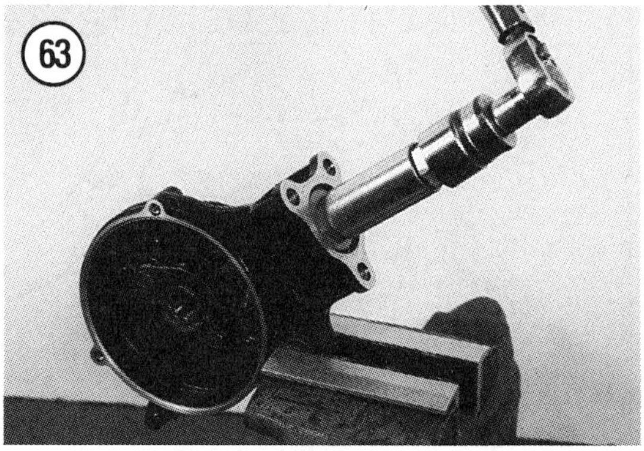

64

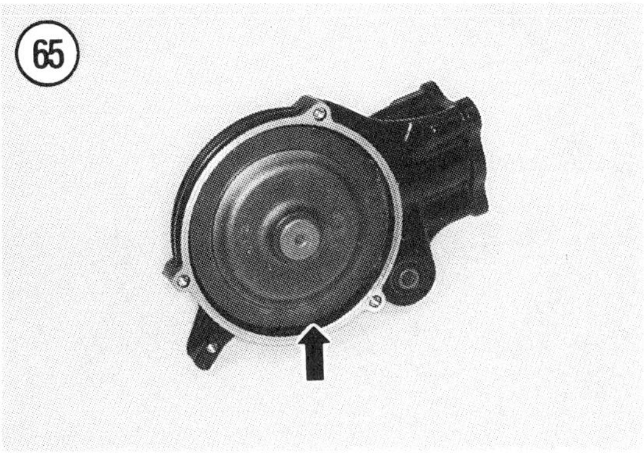
65

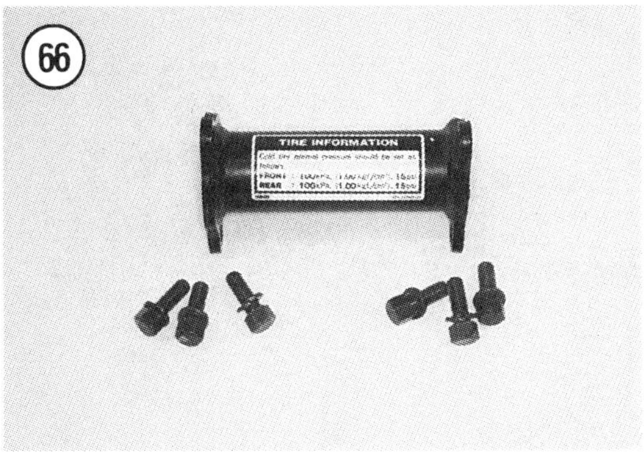
66

9. Lubricate the ring gear (**Figure 64**) with grease and install it into the final drive housing, meshing it with the pinion gear. See **Figure 65**.

10. Install the housing cover and O-ring and secure with its mounting screws and washers; tighten the screws as specified in **Table 2**.

Drive Shaft and Housing Inspection

1. Remove all sealer residue from the drive shaft housing mating surfaces.
2. Clean and dry the drive shaft and housing.
3. Inspect the housing (**Figure 66**) for cracks, warpage or other damage. Replace damaged mounting bolts.
4. Inspect the drive shaft (**Figure 67**) for a damaged spring or worn or damaged square hole ends (**Figure 68**). Refer drive shaft overhaul to a dealership.

WARNING
Without the proper tools and experience, disassembling the drive shaft can be dangerous. The spring seat and spring can fly off, causing injury.

Installation

1. Remove all sealer residue from the drive shaft housing, final drive housing and engine (A, **Figure 69**) mating surfaces.
2. Apply a thin coat of Yamabond No. 4 or an RTV sealant onto the engine (A, **Figure 69**), drive shaft housing (A, **Figure 70**) and final drive housing (B, **Figure 70**) mating surfaces.
3. Install the drive shaft housing (**Figure 71**) on the engine and secure it with its 3 mounting bolts and

67

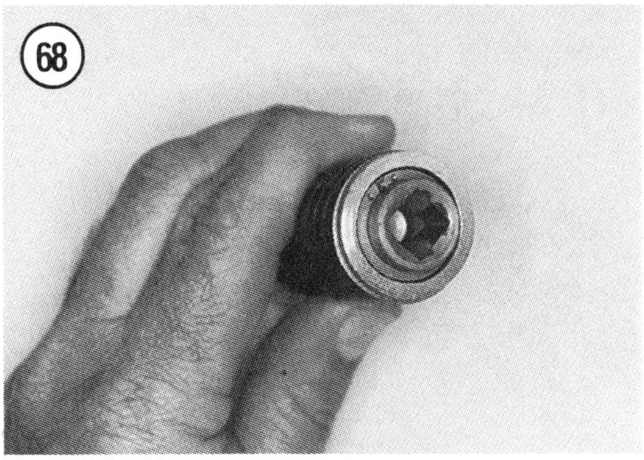
68

lockwashers. Install the housing with the tire decal facing out. Tighten the drive shaft housing mounting bolts as specified in **Table 2**.

4. Align the square hole in the drive shaft (**Figure 72**) with the middle driven pinion shaft (B, **Figure 69**), then install the drive shaft as shown in **Figure 73**.

5. Align the drive pinion gear shaft (**Figure 74**) with the drive shaft hole and install the final drive housing and its mounting bolts (**Figure 75**). Tighten the drive

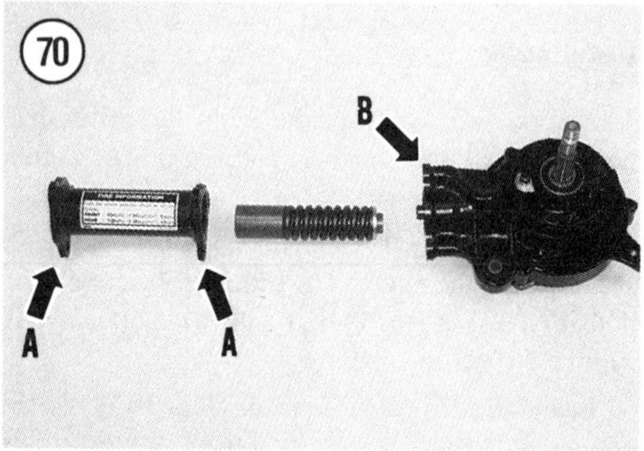

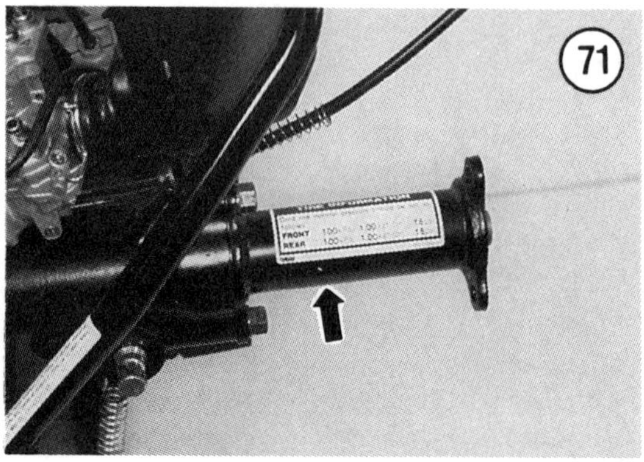

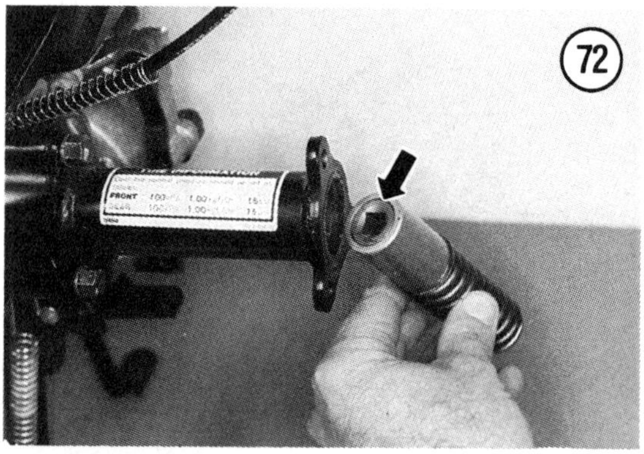

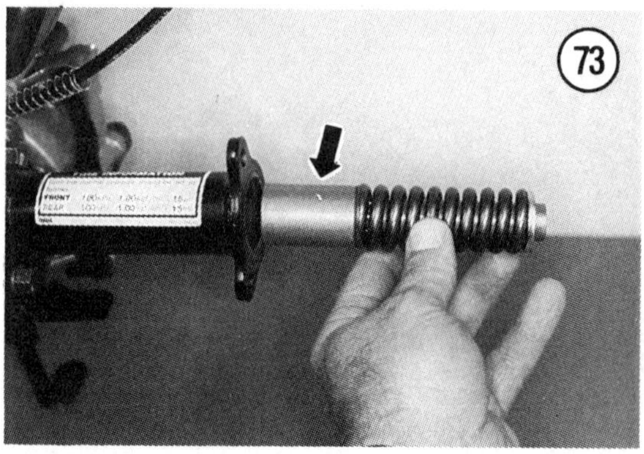

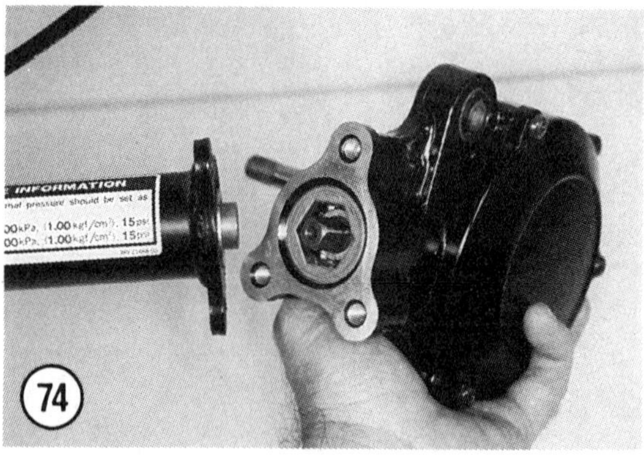

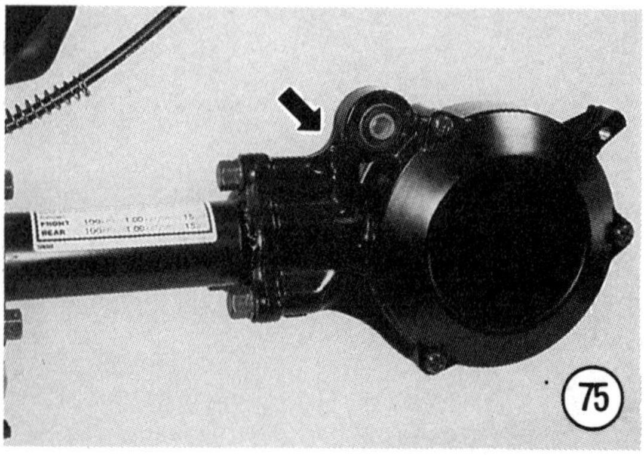

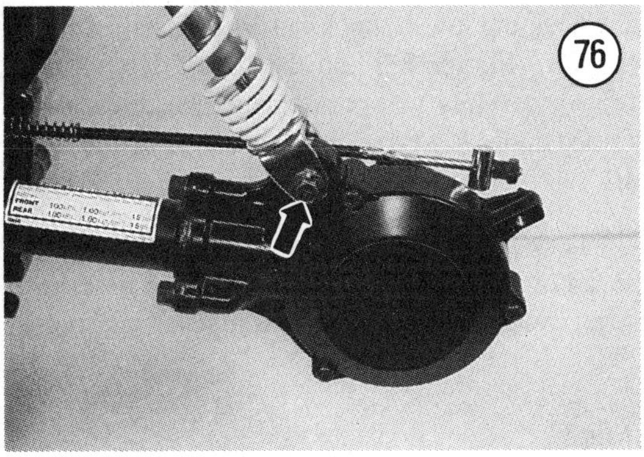

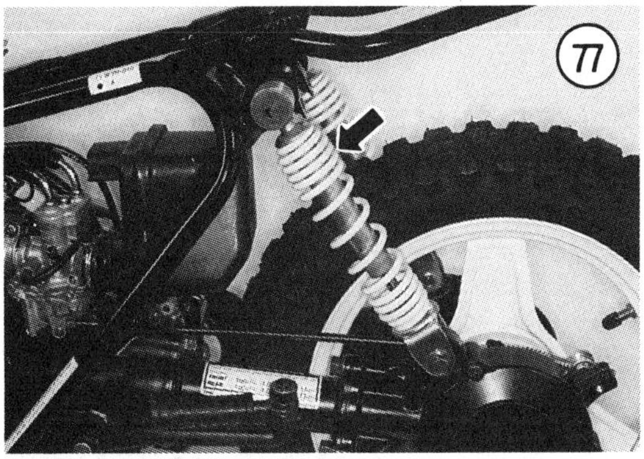

shaft housing mounting bolts as specified in **Table 2**.

6. Mount the left shock absorber (**Figure 76**) onto the final drive housing and install its mounting bolt, then tighten as specified in **Table 2**.

7. Install the rear brake assembly (Chapter Fourteen).

8. Install the rear wheel as described in this chapter.

REAR SHOCKS ABSORBERS

Removal/Installation

Refer to **Figure 77** and **Figure 78** for this procedure.

1. Support the bike on its centerstand.
2. Remove the lower mounting bolt (**Figure 79**).
3. Remove the upper mounting bolt and washer (**Figure 80**).
4. Remove the shock absorber.
5. Remove the washer (**Figure 81**) from the upper frame boss.

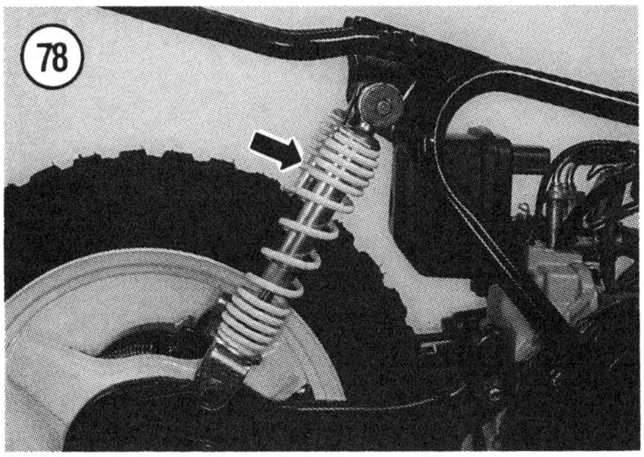

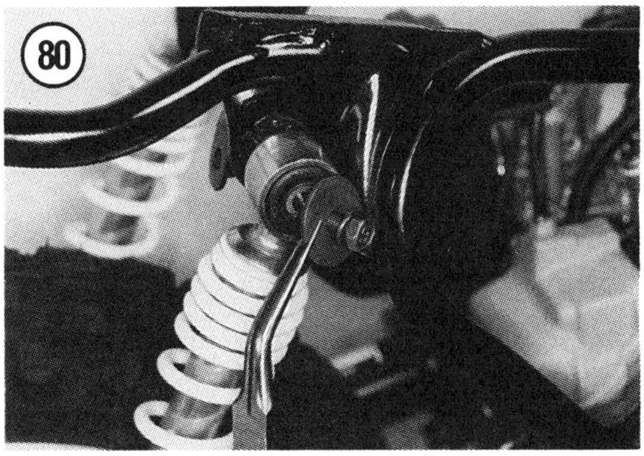

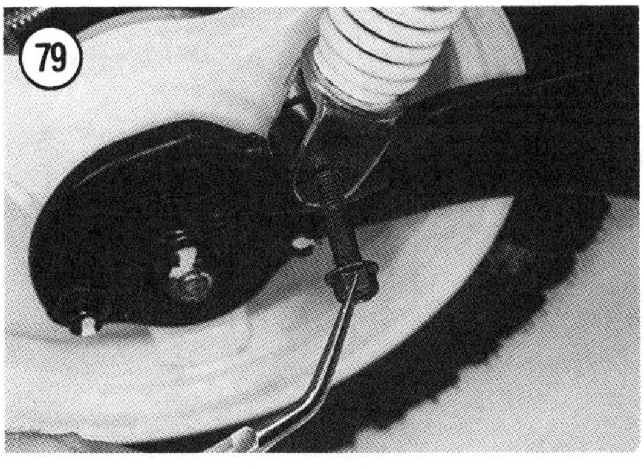

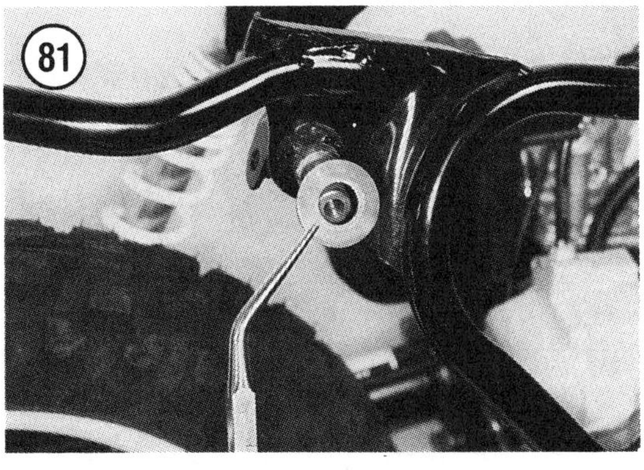

6. Inspect the shock absorbers as described in this section.
7. Install the shock absorbers by reversing these removal steps, plus the following:
   a. The left and right side shock absorbers are identical.
   b. The threaded part of the lower shock mounting bracket (**Figure 82**) must be facing in (toward wheel) when installing the shock absorber.
   c. Tighten the upper and lower shock absorber mounting bolts as specified in **Table 2**.

Inspection

The shock absorbers are not serviceable. Replace parts that show damage as described in this section.

1. Clean and dry all parts (**Figure 83**).
2. Check each shock absorber for:
   a. Leaking damper housing.
   b. Bent damper rod.
   c. Bent upper or lower clevis mounting bracket.
   d. Damaged shock spring.
   e. Worn or damaged shock bushing (**Figure 84**). This bushing is not replaceable.
3. Check the lower shock bushings installed in the rear arm (**Figure 85**) and the final drive housing. Replace severely worn or damaged bushings as described under *Rear Arm* or *Final Drive* in this chapter.

4. Check the shock mounting boss (**Figure 86**) for cracks or other damage. Refer repair to an experienced welder familiar with motorcycle frame repair.

82
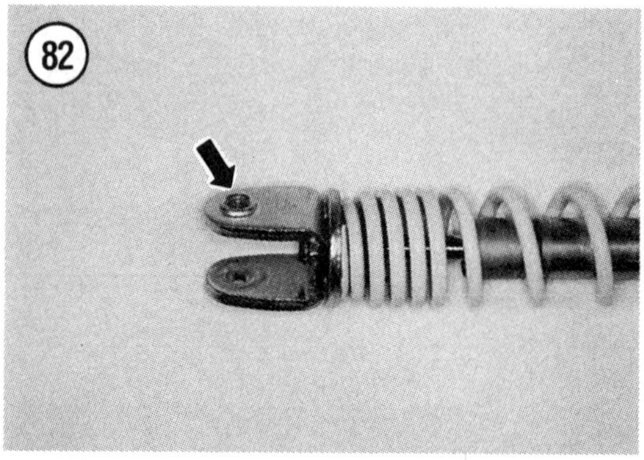

83
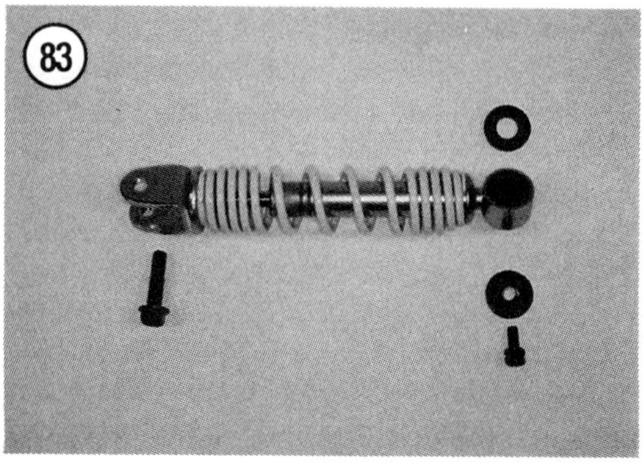

84
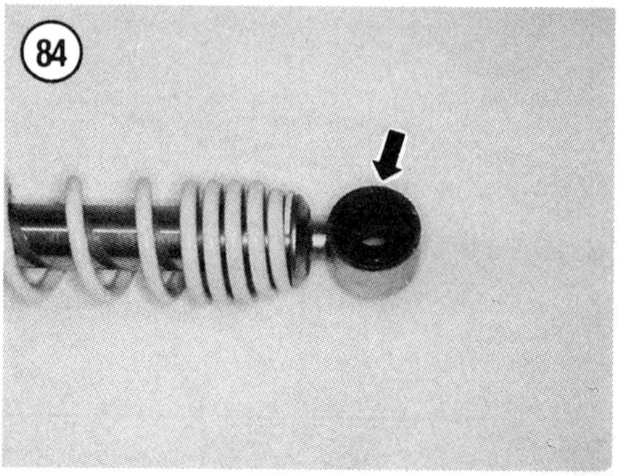

85

86
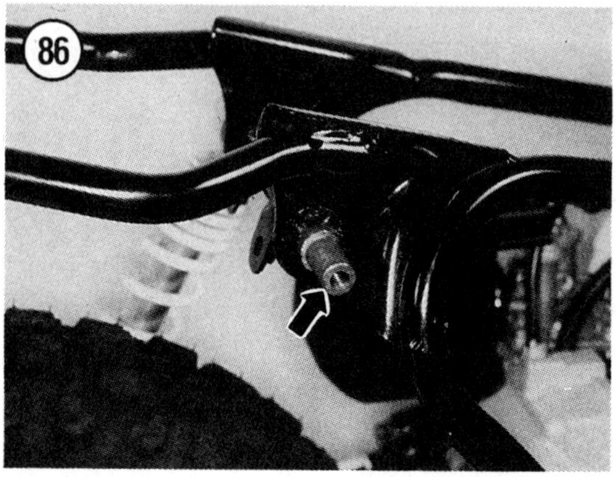

Table 1 REAR SUSPENSION SPECIFICATIONS (PW50)

Rear wheel travel	50 mm (2.0 in.)
Shock absorber travel	30 mm (1.2 in.)
Rear shock spring free length	
Spring rate	
K1	1.30 kg/mm (72.8 lbs./in.)
K2	3.17 kg/mm (177.5 lbs./in.)
Swing arm free play	0 mm (0 in.)

Table 2 REAR SUSPENSION TIGHTENING TORQUES (PW50)

	N•m	in.-lb.	ft.-lb.
Rear axle nut	60	—	44
Engine mount/pivot shaft nut	48	—	35
Rear shock absorber nuts			
Upper	11	97	—
Lower	23	—	17
Drive pinion hex screw	50	—	36
Ring gear bearing plate bolts	12	106	—
Housing cover	9	79	—
Drive shaft housing mounting bolts	26	—	19
Rear arm			
Bearing housing mounting bolts	33	—	24
Mounting nuts at engine	29	—	21

12

CHAPTER THIRTEEN

REAR SUSPENSION (BW80 AND PW80)

This chapter describes repair and maintenance on the rear wheel, wheel bearings, drive chain, rear shock absorber and rear swing arm.

Rear suspension specifications are listed in **Table 1**. Drive chain specifications are listed in **Table 2**. **Tables 1-4** are at the end of the chapter.

REAR WHEEL

Removal/Installation

Refer to **Figure 1** (BW80) or **Figure 2** (PW80).

1. Support the motorcycle with its rear wheel off the ground.
2. Remove the cotter pin, axle nut and washer (A, **Figure 3**).
3. Loosen the axle adjusters (B, **Figure 3**)
4. Disconnect the brake adjusting rod (A, **Figure 4**) from the rear wheel. Store the spring, collar and wing nut on the brake rod to prevent their loss.
5. On PW80 models, disconnect the brake stay arm (B, **Figure 4**) at the rear wheel. See **Figure 2** for the brake arm parts.
6. Push the rear wheel forward and slip the drive chain off of the driven sprocket.
7. Remove the rear axle.
8. Remove the rear wheel along with the right side collar (**Figure 5**) and chain adjusters.
9. If necessary, pull the final driven flange assembly (A, **Figure 6**) out of the rear hub.
10. Perform the *Inspection* procedure in this section to clean and inspect the parts.
11. Install the rear wheel by reversing these removal steps. Note the following:
    a. If necessary, assemble the final driven flange assembly (A, **Figure 6**) as described in this chapter.
    b. Lubricate the axle with a light coat of grease.
    c. On BW80 models, install the rear wheel so that the anchor boss on the right swing arm fits between the lugs cast into the brake backing plate (**Figure 7**, typical).
    d. Install the rear axle from the right side (**Figure 1** or **Figure 2**).
    e. On PW80 models, tighten the brake stay arm nut (B, **Figure 4**) as specified in **Table 4**.
    f. Adjust the drive chain and rear brake free play as described in Chapter Three.
    g. Tighten the rear axle nut (A, **Figure 3**) as specified in **Table 3** or **Table 4**. Then install a

new cotter pin through the axle nut and axle; bend its ends over to lock it in place.

h. After the wheel is completely installed, rotate it and then apply the rear brake a couple of times to make sure the wheel rotates freely and that the brake is operating correctly.

Inspection

Replace parts that show damage as described in this section.

1A. On BW80 models, check the wheel (**Figure 1**) for:

a. Cracks or other damage.
b. Loose or damaged brake drum and rear hub assembly.

1B. On PW80 models, check the wheel (**Figure 2**) for:

a. Loose, missing or damaged spokes.
b. Damaged rim.
c. Damaged hub.

1

REAR WHEEL (BW80)

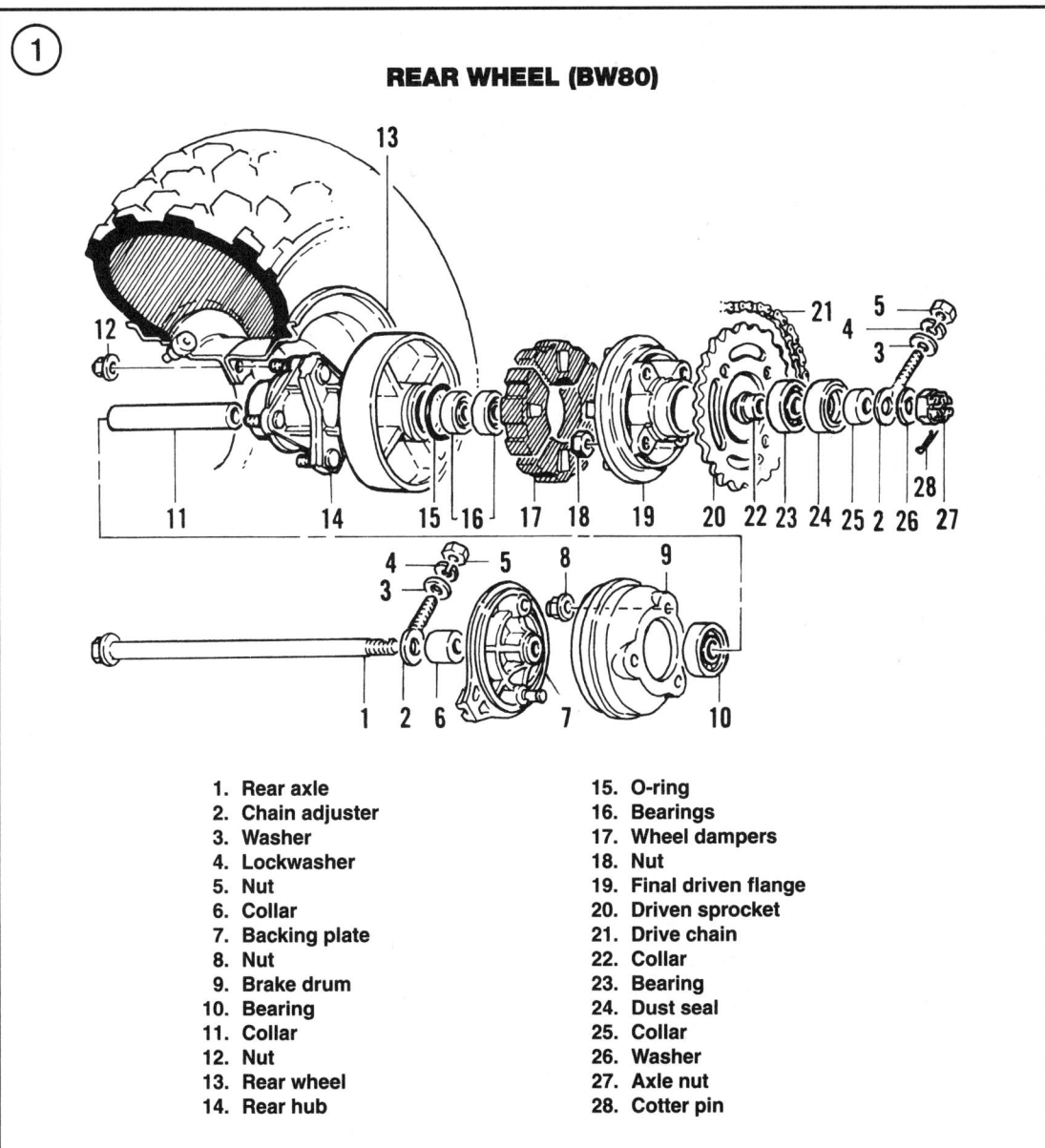

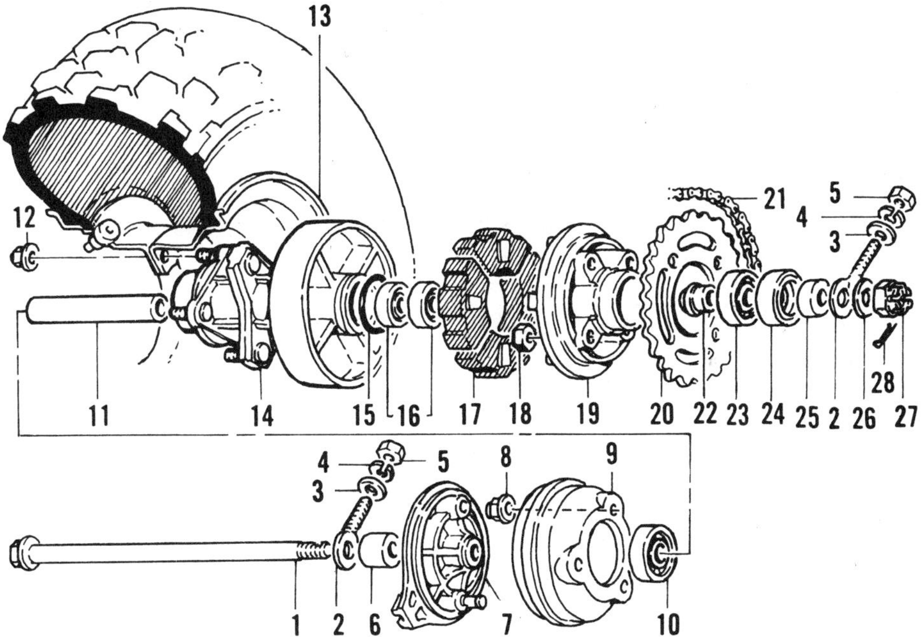

1. Rear axle
2. Chain adjuster
3. Washer
4. Lockwasher
5. Nut
6. Collar
7. Backing plate
8. Nut
9. Brake drum
10. Bearing
11. Collar
12. Nut
13. Rear wheel
14. Rear hub
15. O-ring
16. Bearings
17. Wheel dampers
18. Nut
19. Final driven flange
20. Driven sprocket
21. Drive chain
22. Collar
23. Bearing
24. Dust seal
25. Collar
26. Washer
27. Axle nut
28. Cotter pin

13

(2)

REAR WHEEL (PW80)

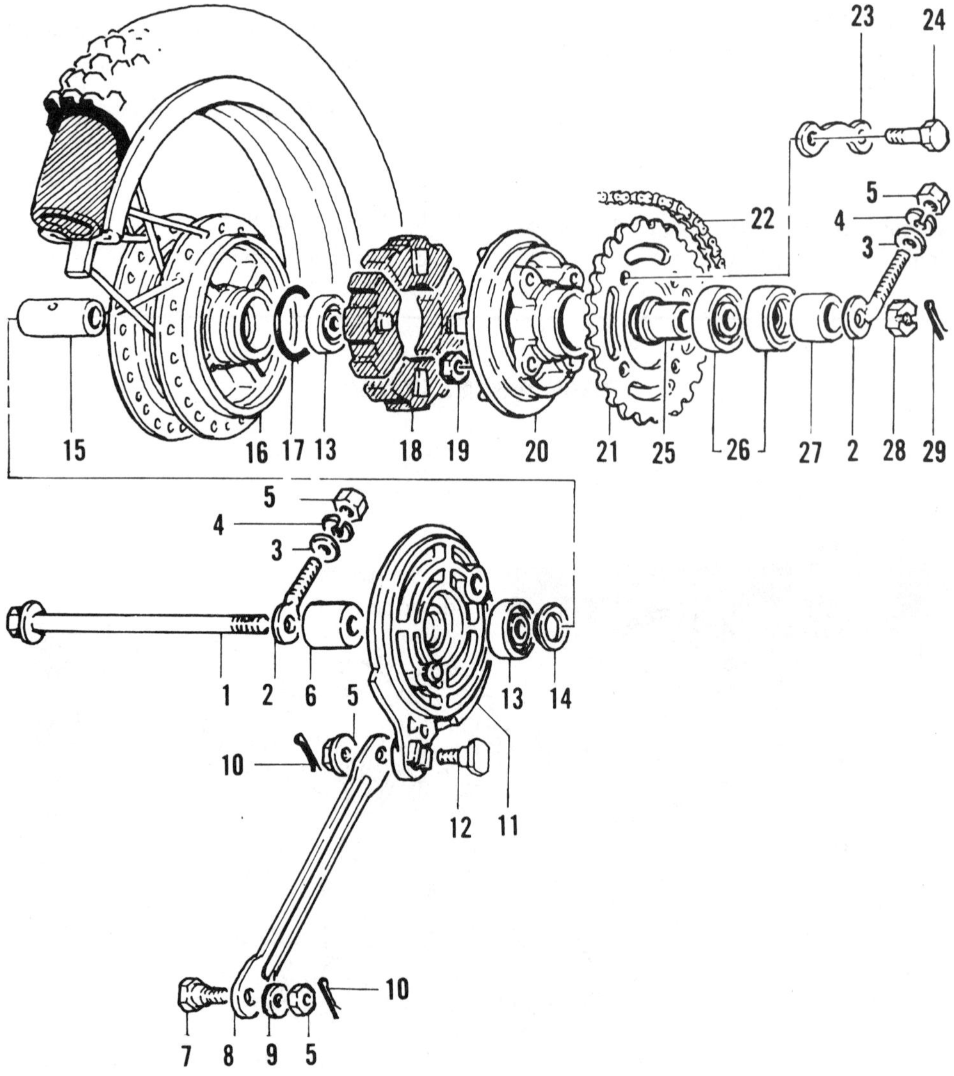

1. Rear axle
2. Chain adjuster
3. Washer
4. Lockwasher
5. Nut
6. Collar
7. Bolt
8. Brake stay arm
9. Washer
10. Cotter pin
11. Backing plate
12. Bolt
13. Bearing
14. Plate
15. Collar
16. Rear hub
17. O-ring
18. Wheel dampers
19. Nut
20. Final driven flange
21. Driven sprocket
22. Drive chain
23. Lockwasher
24. Bolt
25. Collar
26. Bearings
27. Collar
28. Axle nut
29. Cotter pin

3

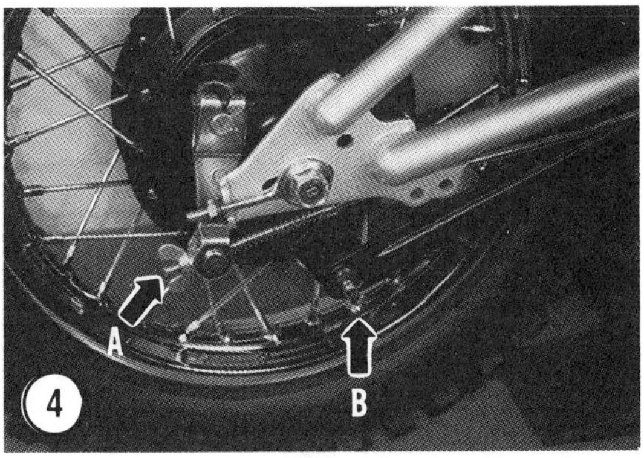

4

2. Turn each bearing inner race (**Figure 8**) hand. The bearing must turn smoothly with no roughness, catching, binding or excessive noise. Some axial play is normal, but radial play must be negligible; see **Figure 9**. If one bearing is damaged, replace both bearings as a set. Refer to *Front Hub* in this chapter.

3. Clean and dry the axle, axle adjusters, collar, washer and axle nut.

4. Roll the front axle on a flat surface to see it if it is bent. Then check the axle for cracks, excessive wear or thread damage. Replace the axle if it is bent or damaged.

WARNING

Do not straighten a bent axle as axle failure could occur under riding conditions.

5. Service the brake drum and brakes as described in Chapter Fourteen.

6. Service the rear damper assembly (**Figure 6**) as described under *Rear Hub* in this chapter.

7. Check wheel runout as described under *Wheel Runout* in Chapter Eleven.

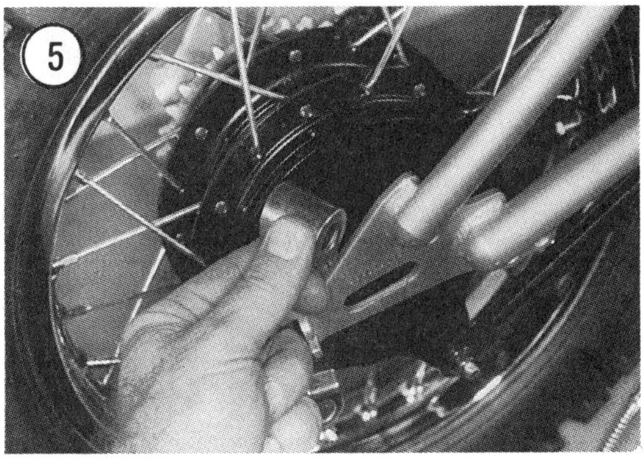
5

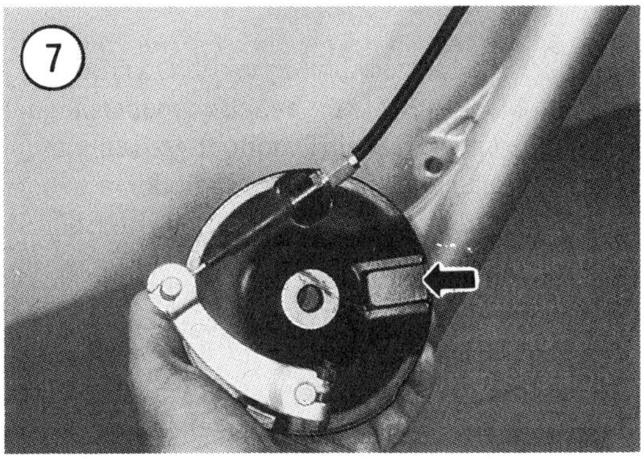
7

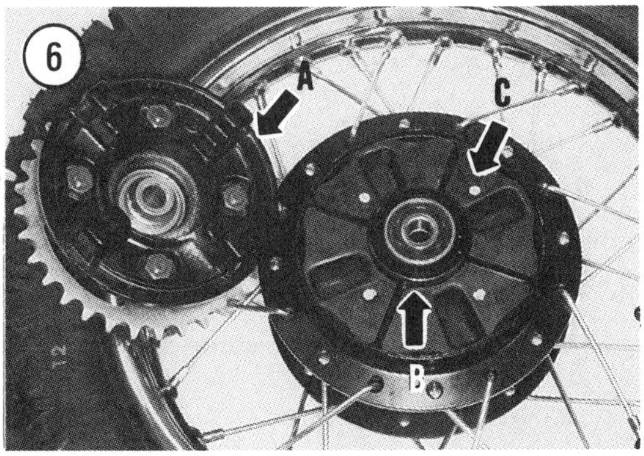

6

8

REAR HUB (PW80)

Refer to **Figure 2** when servicing the rear hub.

Inspection

Inspect each wheel bearing as follows:

CAUTION
Do not remove the wheel bearings for inspection purposes as they may be damaged during their removal. Remove the wheel bearings only if they are to be replaced.

1. Turn each bearing inner race (**Figure 8**) by hand. The bearings must turn with no roughness, catching, binding or excessive noise. Some axial play is normal, but radial play must be negligible; see **Figure 9**.
2. If one bearing is damaged, replace both bearings as a set.

Disassembly

NOTE
Step 1 describes 2 methods of removing the rear wheel bearings. Step 1A will require the use of the Kowa Seiki Wheel Bearing Remover set. Step 1B describes how to remove the bearings without special tools.

1A. To remove the hub bearings (**Figure 8**) with the Kowa Seiki Wheel Bearing Remover set:

NOTE
*The Kowa Seiki Wheel Bearing Remover set shown in **Figure 10** is available from K & L Supply Co., in Santa Clara, CA. You can order this tool set through your Yamaha dealer.*

a. Select the correct size remover head tool and insert it into one of the hub bearings (**Figure 11**).
b. From the opposite side of the hub, insert the remover shaft into the slot in the backside of the remover head (**Figure 12**). Then position the hub with the remover head tool resting against a solid surface and strike the remover shaft to force it into the slit in the remover

9

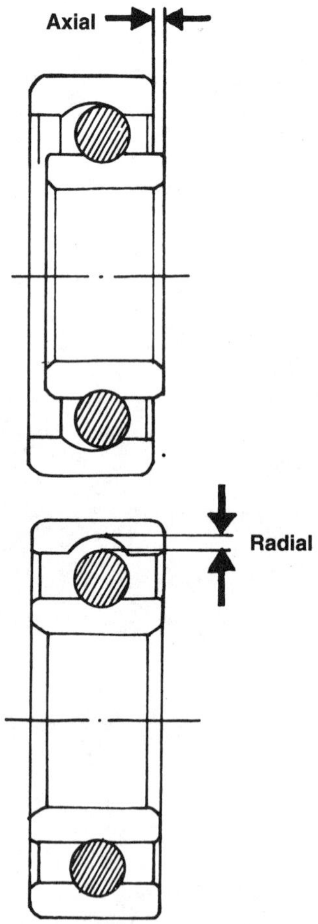

10

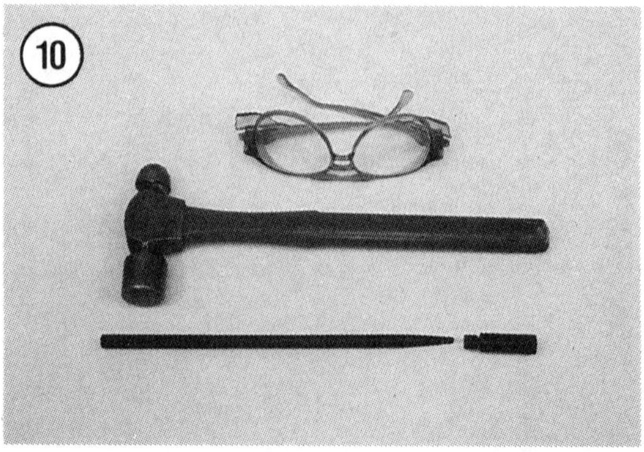

head. This will wedge the remover head tool against the inner bearing race. See **Figure 13**.

c. Position the hub and strike the end of the remover shaft with a hammer to drive the bearing (A, **Figure 14**) out of the hub. Remove the bearing and tool. Release the remover head from the bearing.

d. Remove the collar (B, **Figure 14**) from the hub.

e. Repeat to remove the opposite bearing.

1B. To remove the hub bearings without special tools:

a. Using a long drift, tilt the center hub spacer away from one side of the bearing (**Figure 15**).

NOTE

Do not damage the hub spacer's machined surface when positioning and driving against the long drift. You may have to grind a clearance groove in the drift to enable it to contact of the bearing while clearing the spacer.

b. Tap the bearing out of the hub with a hammer, working around the perimeter of the bearing's inner race.

c. Remove the collar from the hub (B, **Figure 14**).

d. Drive out the opposite bearing using a large socket or bearing driver.

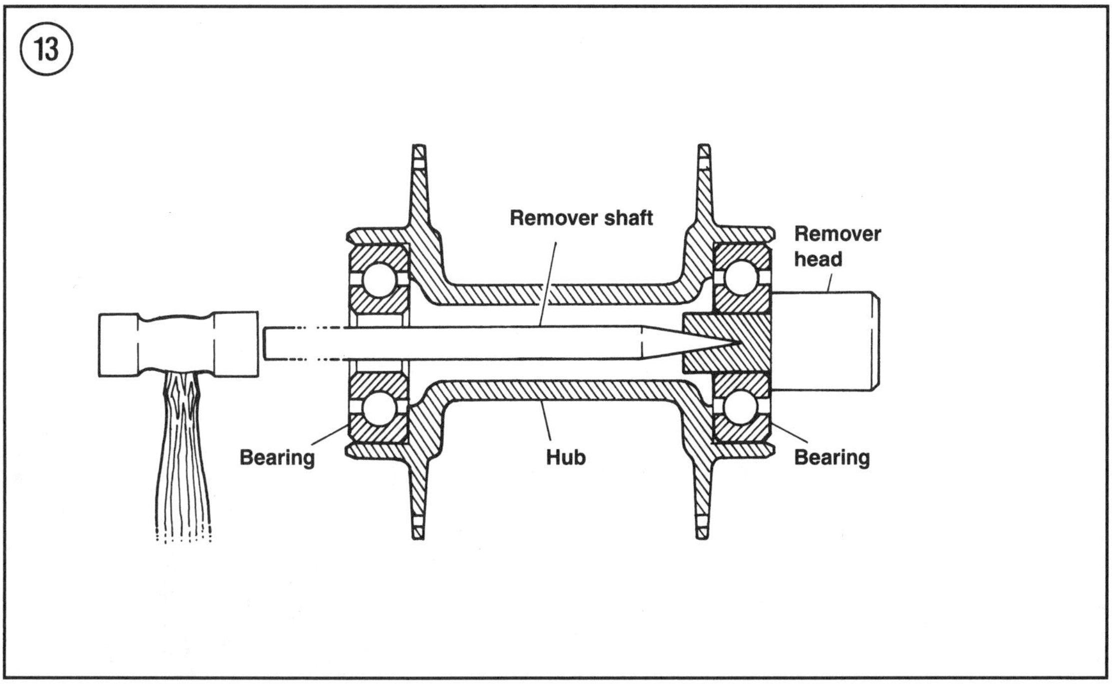

e. Inspect the collar for burrs created during removal. Remove burrs with a file.

2. Clean and dry the hub and collar.

3. Inspect the hub bore (**Figure 16**) for cracks or severe wear. If a bearing was a loose fit in the hub, the hub is severely worn or damaged; replace the wheel assembly.

Assembly

Before installing the new bearings note that the left and right side bearings (**Figure 17**) are different. If you did not identify the bearings before removing them, have your dealership parts manager identify them for you.

1. Blow any dirt or foreign matter out of the hub (**Figure 16**).

2. Pack the open side of each bearing with grease.

3. Place the brake hub side bearing into its mounting bore with its closed side facing out (**Figure 8**). Select a driver (**Figure 18**) with an outside diameter just a little smaller than the bearing's outside diameter. Then drive the bearing into the bore until it bottoms out (**Figure 8**).

4. Install the collar (**Figure 19**) and center it against the first bearing's center race.

5. Place the second bearing squarely against the bore opening with its marked side facing out (**Figure 20**). Using the same driver as before, drive the bearing partway into the bearing bore. Then stop and check that the collar is centered in the hub. If not, install the front axle through the hub to center the spacer with the bearing. Then remove the axle and continue installing the bearing until it bottoms out.

6. Check that inner race on each bearing turns without any binding or damage.

14

15
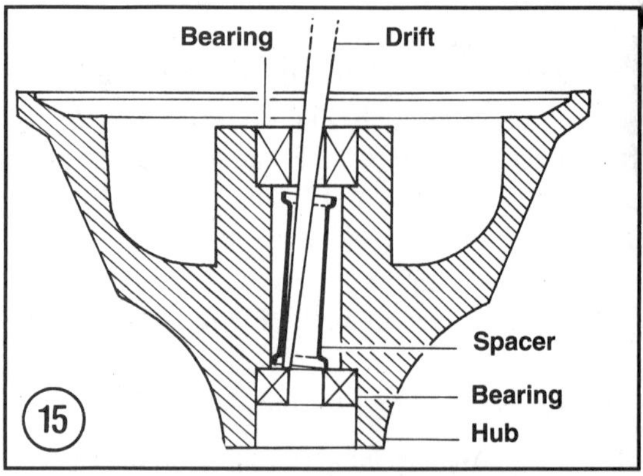

16

17

18
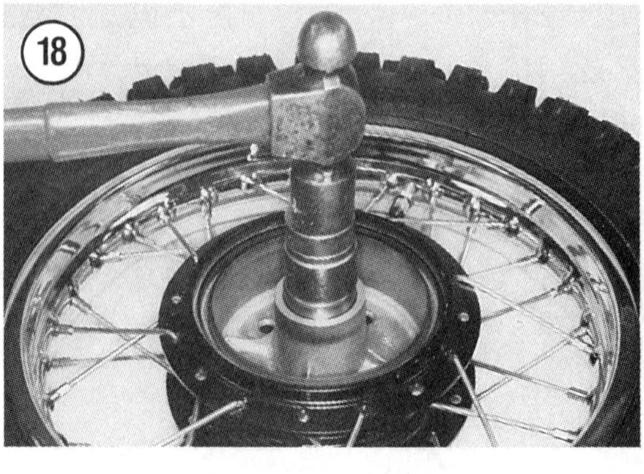

19

20

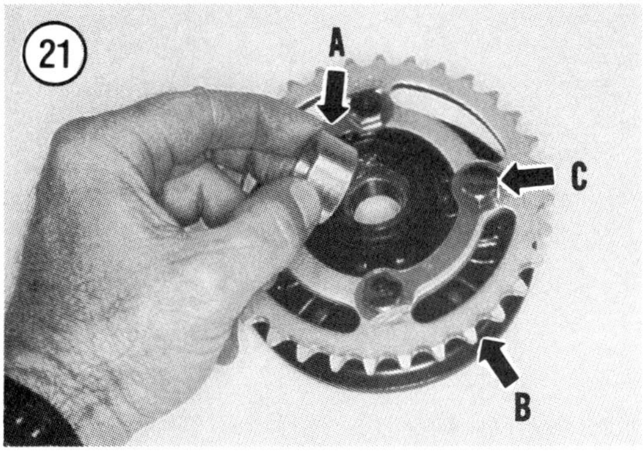

21

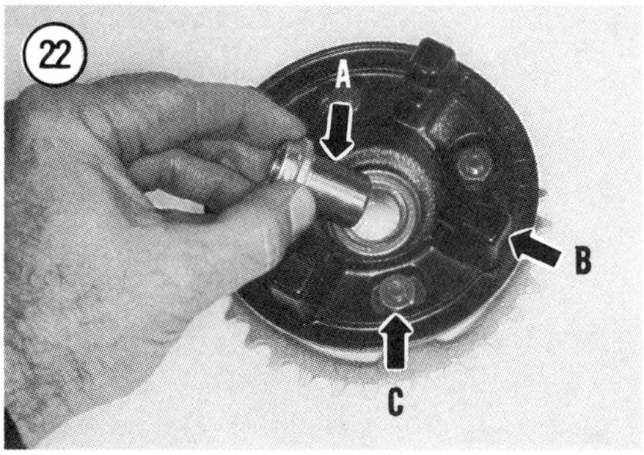

22

REAR HUB
(BW80)

Procedures and tools used to service the rear hub on the BW80 is the same as for the PW80 except that the BW80 rear hub is equipped with 2 left side bearings (**Figure 1**). When removing the left side bearings from the hub, remove the outer and inner bearings separately. Do not try to remove both bearings at the same time.

FINAL DRIVEN FLANGE

The rear hub is equipped with a final driven flange assembly that buffers clutch engagement and other conditions that exert excessive stress on the drive train components. The final driven flange consists of the flange housing, wheel dampers, collars and bearing assembly. The wheel dampers fit into grooves cast into the rear hub and separate the rear hub from the final driven flange housing.

Refer to **Figure 1** (BW80) or **Figure 2** (PW80) when servicing the final driven flange assembly.

Removal/Installation

1. Remove the rear wheel as described in this chapter.
2. Remove the final driven flange (A, **Figure 6**) from the rear hub.
3. Remove the O-ring (B, **Figure 6**) from the groove in the rear hub.
4. Remove the wheel dampers (C, **Figure 6**) from the rear hub.
5. Remove the outer (A, **Figure 21**) and inner (A, **Figure 22**) collars.
6. Perform the final driven flange inspection procedure.
7. Reverse these steps to install the final driven flange assembly, plus the following:
   a. Lubricate the collar outside diameters (A, **Figure 21** and A, **Figure 22**) and the dust seal lip (A, **Figure 23**) with wheel bearing grease.
   b. Align the boss arms on the flange housing (A, **Figure 6**) with the rectangular holes in the wheel dampers (C, **Figure 6**). Then push the driven flange housing into the rear wheel (**Figure 24**).

Inspection

Replace parts that show damage as described in this section

1. Inspect the final driven flange (**Figure 22**) assembly for:
   a. Worn or damaged boss arms (B, **Figure 22**).
   b. Damaged housing assembly.
2. Inspect the wheel dampers (C, **Figure 6**) for:
   a. Cracks, splitting or age deterioration.
   b. Excessive wear or damage.
3. Inspect the outer (A, **Figure 21**) and inner (A, **Figure 22**) collars for:
   a. Cracks.
   b. Severe wear.
4. Inspect the O-ring (B, **Figure 6**) and replace if cracked or damaged.
5. Service the driven sprocket (B, **Figure 21**) as described later in this chapter.
6. Inspect the dust seal (A, **Figure 23**) for wear or damage. Replace the dust seal as described in the following procedure.

CAUTION
In Step 7, do not remove the flange bearing for inspection purposes as you can damage it. Remove the bearing for replacement only.

7. Turn the flange bearing inner race (B, **Figure 23**) by hand. The bearing must turn smoothly with no roughness, catching, binding or excessive noise. Some axial play is normal, but radial play must be negligible; see **Figure 9**. If necessary, replace the bearing as described in the following procedure.

Dust Seal and Bearing Replacement

The final driven flange housing is equipped with a dust seal and bearing.

1. Pry the dust seal out of the hub with a wide-blade screwdriver (**Figure 25**). Support the screwdriver with a rag to avoid damaging the flange or mounting bore.
2. Clean and dry the mounting bore.
3. Check the mounting bore for cracks or other damage. If the bearing is a loose fit or slides out of its mounting bore, the flange housing is damaged and must be replaced.
4. Install the new bearing as follows:

a. Press in the new bearing with a bearing driver or socket placed on the outer bearing race.

b. Install the bearing with is open side (**Figure 26**) facing out.

c. Press in the bearing (**Figure 27**) until it bottoms out in its mounting bore.

5. Install the new dust seal as follows:

a. Pack the seal lips with grease. OEM replacement dust seals may be pre-packed with grease (**Figure 28**).

27

28

29

b. Install the dust seal with its closed side facing out (A, **Figure 23**).

c. Press in the dust seal until its outer surface is flush with or slightly below the mounting bore surface (A, **Figure 23**).

CHAIN AND SPROCKETS

This section describes replacement of the drive and driven sprocket and drive chain. Chapter Three lists information on how to determine drive chain and sprocket wear.

Table 2 lists drive chain specifications.

Removal/Installation

1. Support the bike with its rear wheel off the ground.
2. Remove the drive chain as follows:
   a. Turn the rear wheel until the master link is accessible.
   b. Remove the master link spring clip with a pair of pliers (**Figure 29**). Then remove the side plate and connecting link (**Figure 30**) and separate the drive chain.
   c. Remove the drive chain.
3. Remove the drive (front) sprocket as follows:
   a. Remove the shift pedal (A, **Figure 31**) and the left side cover (B, **Figure 31**).
   b. Remove the circlip (A, **Figure 32**) and drive sprocket (B, **Figure 32**).
4. Remove the driven (rear) sprocket as follows:
   a. Remove the rear wheel as described in this chapter.
   b. Pry the lockwasher tabs away from the sprocket bolts (C, **Figure 21**).
   c. Remove the final driven flange housing from the rear wheel.
   d. Hold the bolts and remove the sprocket nuts (C, **Figure 22**) from inside the final driven flange housing.
   e. Remove the sprocket bolts, lockwashers and sprocket.
5. Reverse these steps to install the sprockets and drive chain, noting the following:
   a. Install a new drive sprocket circlip (A, **Figure 32**). Install the circlip so that its flat side faces out (away from sprocket).
   b. Replace any damaged driven sprocket lockwashers, nuts or bolts.

c. One side of each sprocket is stamped with its number of sprocket teeth. Install the sprocket with the number side facing out (away from motorcycle).
d. Tighten the driven sprocket nuts (C, **Figure 22**) as specified in **Table 3** or **Table 4**.
e. Install a new master link. Install the spring clip so that its closed side (**Figure 30**) faces in the direction of chain travel.
f. Adjust the drive chain and tighten the rear axle nut as described in Chapter Three.

TIRE CHANGING

Refer to *Tire Changing* in Chapter Eleven.

REAR SHOCK ABSORBER

WARNING
The rear shock absorber contains highly compressed nitrogen gas. Observe the WARNING label mounted on the shock absorber. Do not tamper with

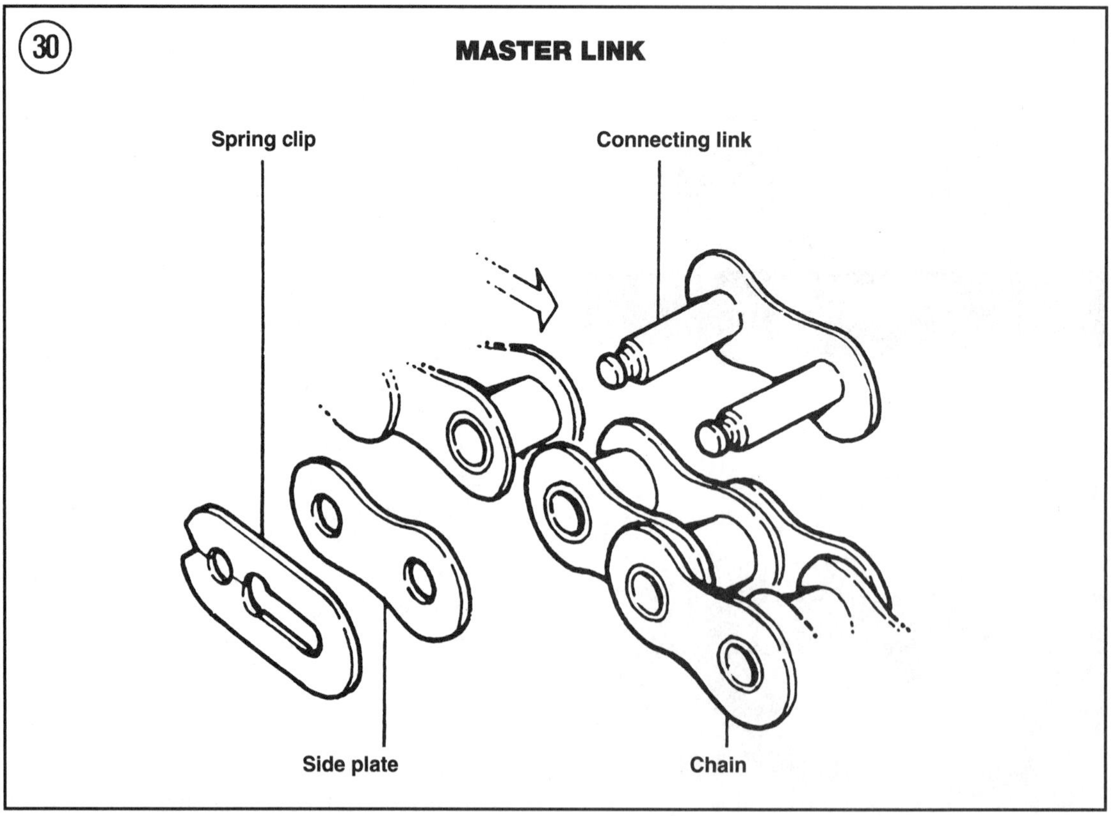

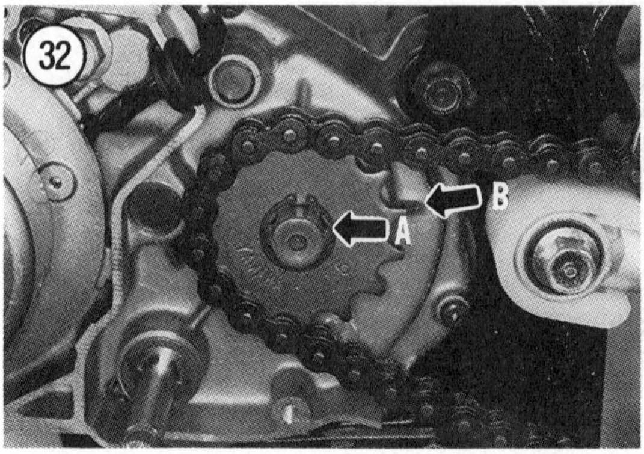

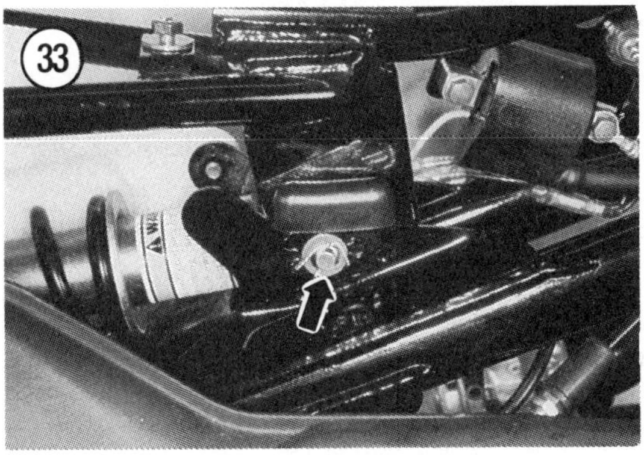

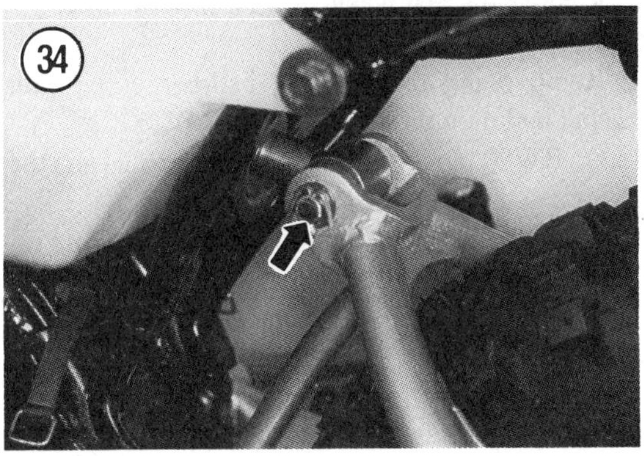

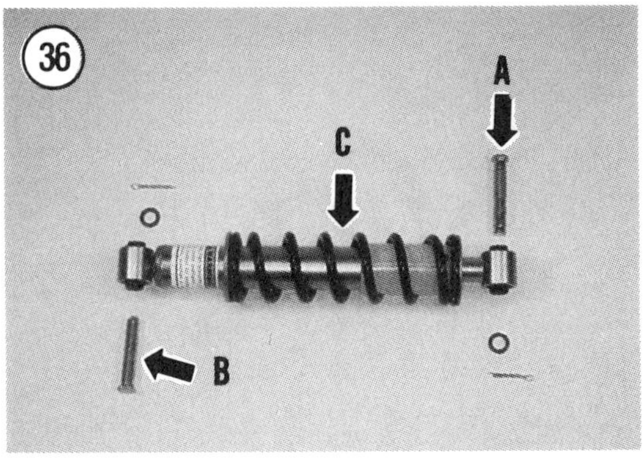

or attempt to open the damper assembly. Do not place it near an open flame or other extreme heat. Do not weld on the frame near it. Do not dispose of the damper unit yourself. Take it to a Yamaha dealership where it can be de-activated and disposed of properly.

Removal/Installation

1. Support the bike with the rear wheel off the ground.
2. Remove the fuel tank (Chapter Seven).
3. Remove the front cotter pin, washer and mounting pin (**Figure 33**).
4. Remove the rear cotter pin, washer and mounting pin (**Figure 34**).
5. Remove the shock absorber through the rear part of the frame (**Figure 35**).
6. Inspect the shock absorber as described under *Inspection* in this section.
7. Install the rear shock absorber by reversing these removal steps, noting the following:
   a. Install the shock absorber in the direction shown in **Figure 35**.
   b. The rear mounting pin (A, **Figure 36**) is longer than the front pin (B, **Figure 36**).
   c. Lubricate each mounting pin with lithium soap base grease before installing them.
   d. Install the front mounting pin (**Figure 33**) from the left side.
   e. Install the rear mounting pin (**Figure 34**) from the right side.
   f. Secure the mounting pins with *new* cotter pins. Bend the cotter pin ends over to lock them in place.

13

Inspection

The shock absorber are not serviceable. Replace parts that show damage as described in this section.

1. Clean and dry all parts (**Figure 36**).
2. Check the shock absorber for:
   a. Leaking damper housing.
   b. Bent damper rod.
   c. Bent upper or lower clevis mounting bracket.
   d. Damaged shock spring.
   e. Damaged spring seats.

3. Replace the mounting pins and/or washers if damaged. Install *new* cotter pins during shock installation.
4. Check the shock bushings for severe wear or damage (**Figure 37**). Check the rubber part of each bushing for cracks, age deterioration, separation or other damage. Replace both bushings as follows:
   a. The upper and lower bushings are identical (same part number).
   b. Support the shock and press out the old bushings.
   c. Check the mounting bore in each end of the shock for cracks or other damage; replace the shock absorber if necessary.
   d. Support the shock and press in the new bushings. Center each bushing in its mounting bore (**Figure 37**).

REAR SWING ARM

Refer to**Figure 38** when servicing the rear swing arm.

Swing Arm Free Play Inspection

The swing arm is equipped with bushings. In time they will wear to the point that they must be replaced. Before removing the swing arm, inspect the bushings as follows:

1. Support the bike on a stand with the rear wheel off the ground.
2. Remove the rear wheel as described in this chapter.
3. Remove the rear shock absorber cotter pin, washer and mounting pin (**Figure 34**).
4. Pivot the swing arm up and down. It should move smoothly with no binding or roughness.
5. Grasp the swing arm (A, **Figure 39**) and try to rock it back and forth by pulling one side back in a horizontal arc, then reversing. If you feel any more than a very slight movement of the swing arm (1.0 mm [0.04 in.]), and the pivot shaft is correctly tightened, the bushings are probably worn and should be replaced. If necessary, replace the bushings as described in this section.

NOTE
Make sure any motion you feel is not caused by the frame moving around on its stand.

6. Reverse these steps to reassemble the rear suspension, plus the following:
   a. Lubricate and install the rear shock absorber mounting pin as described under *Rear Shock Absorber*.
   b. Install the rear wheel as described in this chapter.

Removal/Installation

1. Support the bike on a stand with the rear wheel off the ground.
2. Remove the rear wheel as described in this chapter.
3. Remove the rear shock absorber cotter pin, washer and mounting pin (**Figure 34**).
4. On BW80 models, remove the shift pedal and the left crankcase cover.
5. Remove the upper and lower chain guides (**Figure 38**).
6. Disconnect the drive chain master link. Do not remove the drive chain unless necessary.
7. Remove the swing arm pivot shaft nut (**Figure 40**) and pivot shaft (B, **Figure 39**), then remove the swing arm assembly.

NOTE
If the pivot shaft is stuck or frozen in place, you may have to knock it out with an appropriate size rod. When doing so, use an aluminum or brass rod and take care not to damage the bushings.

8. Perform the *Inspection* procedure in this section.
9. To install the swing arm, reverse these removal steps, noting the following:
   a. Clean the pivot shaft hole in the frame of all old grease and dirt.

37

b. Install the drive chain guard (A, **Figure 41**) onto the swing arm.
c. Lubricate the pivot shaft (B, **Figure 41**) and both bushings (**Figure 42**) with a lithium base waterproof wheel bearing grease.
d. Install the pivot shaft from the left side (B, **Figure 39**).

NOTE
*If the pivot shaft is difficult to install, the swing arm mounting bores may be bent. Refer to **Swing Arm Bushing Replacement** in this section for steps on how to check the mounting bore alignment.*

e. Tighten the pivot shaft nut (**Figure 40**) as specified in **Table 3** or **Table 4**.
f. Perform the *Swing Arm Free Play Inspection* procedure to check the pivot shaft and swing arm bushings.
g. Reconnect the drive chain as described under *Chain and Sprockets* in this chapter.

38

REAR SWING ARM

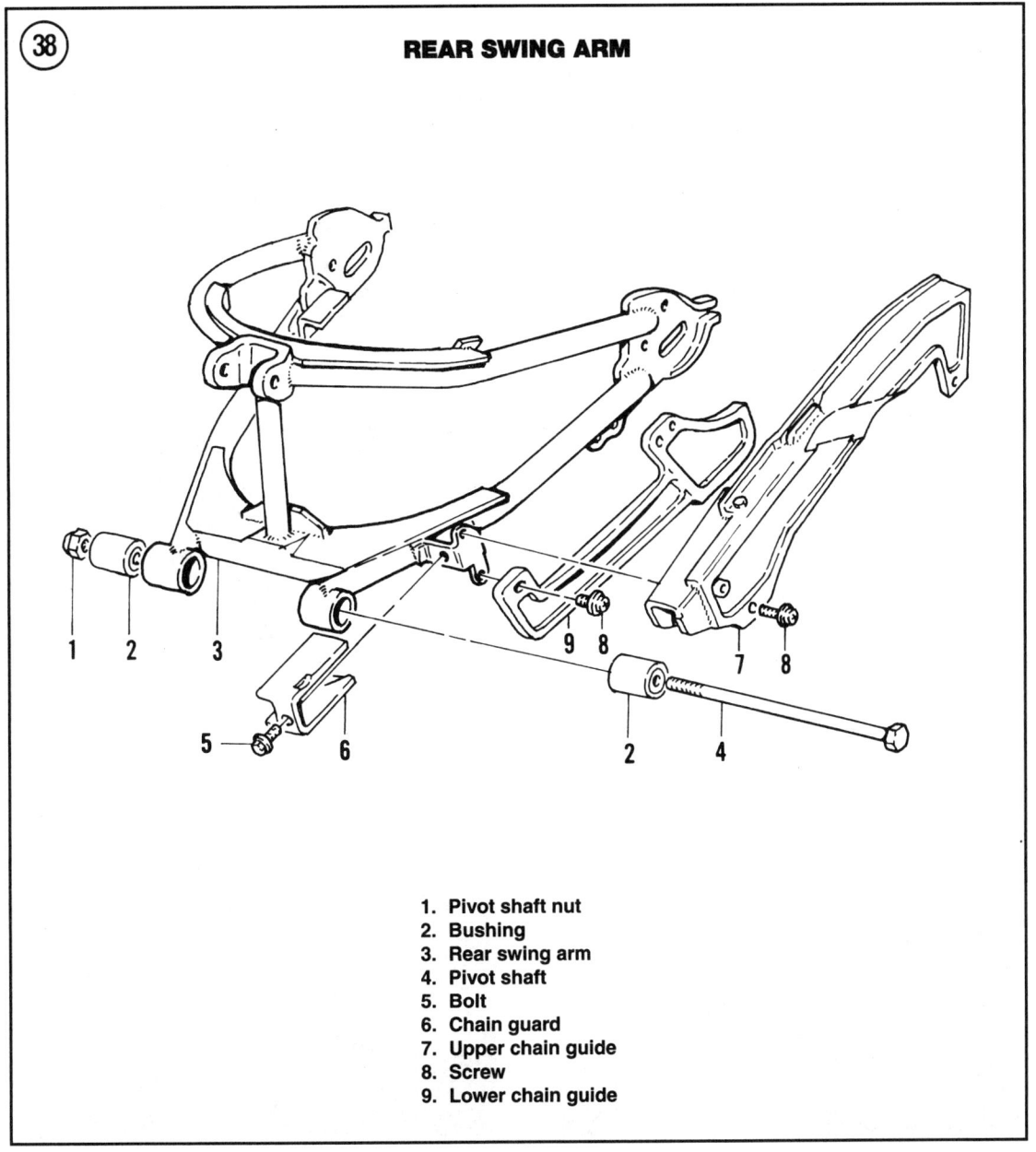

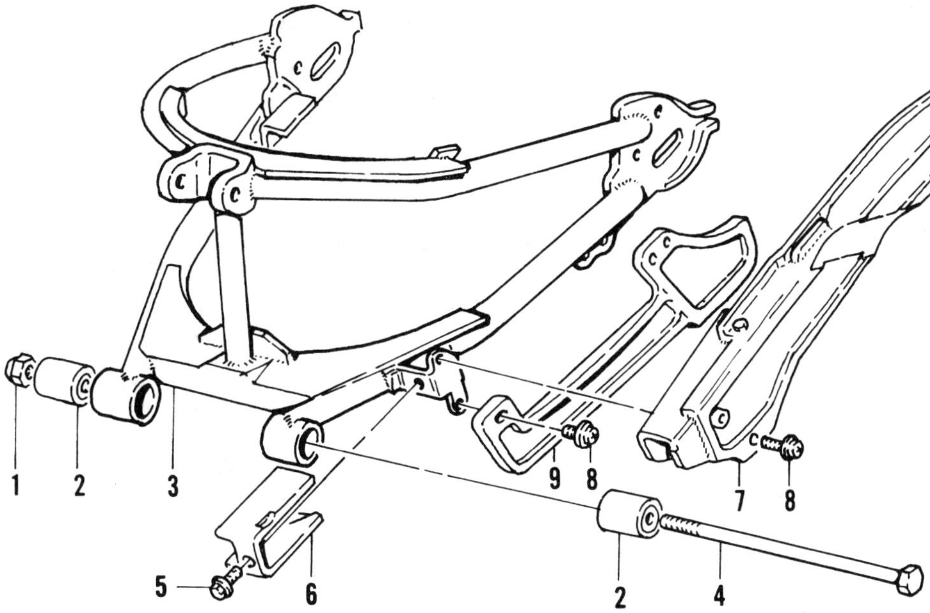

1. Pivot shaft nut
2. Bushing
3. Rear swing arm
4. Pivot shaft
5. Bolt
6. Chain guard
7. Upper chain guide
8. Screw
9. Lower chain guide

Inspection

Replace parts that show damage as described in this section.

1. Clean and dry all parts (**Figure 41**).
2. Inspect the swing arm (C, **Figure 41**) for:
   a. Cracks or other damage.
   b. Weak or damaged welds.
   c. Damaged brake stay arm (C, **Figure 41**) on PW80 models.
3. Replace the drive chain guard if worn or damaged.
4. Check the swing arm bushings (**Figure 42**) for severe wear or damage. Check the rubber part of each bushing for cracks, age deterioration, separation or other damage. Replace both bushings as a set as described in this section.
5. Check the pivot shaft (B, **Figure 41**) for:
   a. Bending. Roll it on a flat surface.
   b. Thread damage.
6. Replace the pivot shaft nut if damaged.

Swing Arm Bushing Replacement

To avoid bending the swing arm when removing the bushings, the mounting bore from which the bushing is being removed or installed must be supported as shown in the following photographs. A press, press adapters, supports and bearing drivers are required to safely replace the bushings. If you do not have access to the necessary equipment, take the swing arm to a dealership or machine shop and have them replace the bushings for you.

The left and right swing arm bushings (**Figure 38**) are identical. Always replace both bushings at the same time.

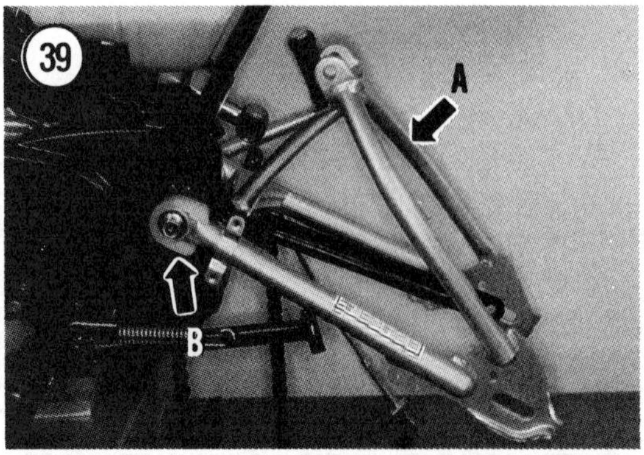

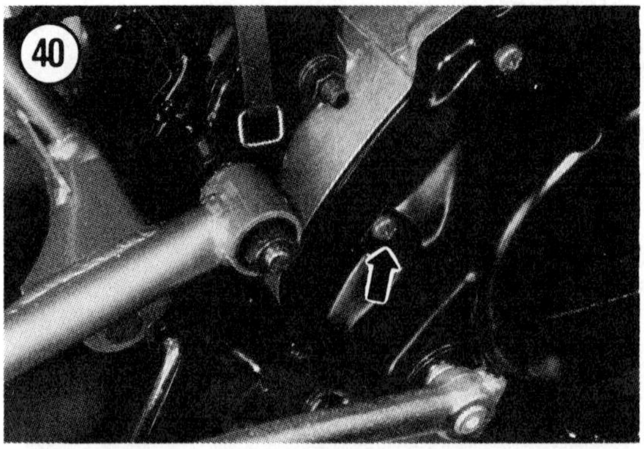

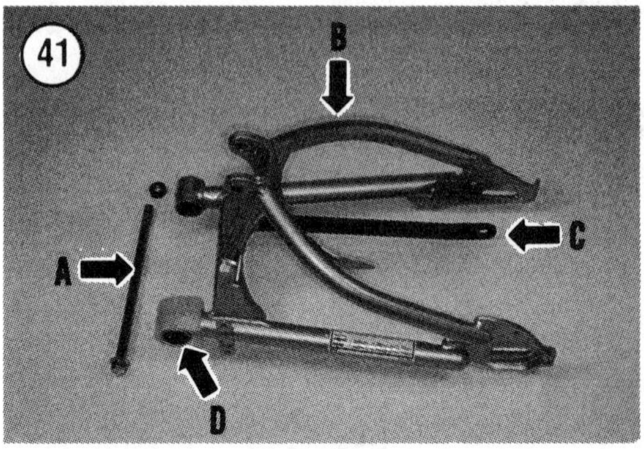

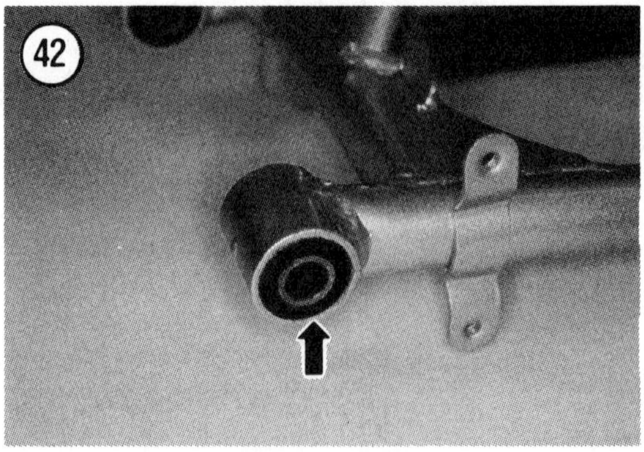

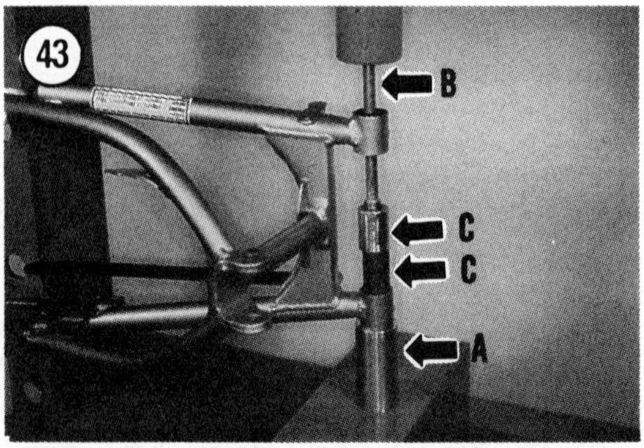

NOTE

The bushings used in the swing arm are not rebuildable and should not be removed unless you intend to replace them. They can be damaged during removal.

1. Support the swing arm in a press and on a hollow support (A, **Figure 43**) that has an inside diameter large enough to accept the bushing as it is being removed.
2. Run the driver (B, **Figure 43**) through the upper bushing and mount it onto a bushing driver with an outside diameter just a bit smaller than the bushings diameter. The driver must be able to pass through the mounting bore as the bushing is being removed.
3. Press the bushing out of the swing arm. As the bushing is pressed out, all of the tension placed against the swing arm is removed, allowing the swing arm and press adapters to fall. Be ready to catch the swing arm as the bushing is pressed out.
4. Turn the swing arm over and press out the opposite bushing.
5. Inspect the bushing mounting bores for cracks, bending or other damage. Replace the swing arm if any damage is found.
6. Support the swing arm mounting bore with 2 raised blocks and a horizontal steel bar as shown in A, **Figure 44**. Place the new bushing on top of its mounting bore and press it into place with a suitable driver (B, **Figure 44**). Press in the bushing until it is centered in its mounting bore.
7. Turn the swing arm over and install the second bushing.
8. Install the pivot shaft through both bushings (**Figure 45**). The pivot shaft should slide through both bushings without any force.

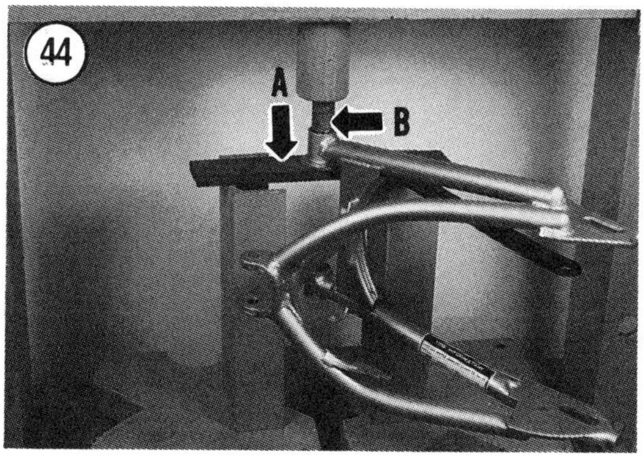

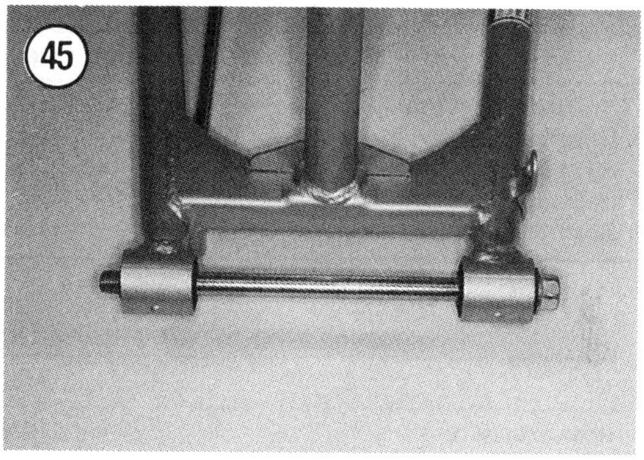

Table 1 REAR SUSPENSION SPECIFICATIONS (BW80 AND PW80)

Shock absorber travel	48 mm (1.89 in.)
Rear wheel travel	
BW80	110 mm (4.3 in.)
PW80	95 mm (3.7 in.)
Shock spring free length	
New	169 mm (6.65 in.)
Service limit	167 mm (6.57 in.)
Spring rate	
BW80	6.75 kg/mm (378 lbs./in.)
PW80	4.23 kg/mm (237 lbs./in.)
Rear swing arm free play limit	1.0 mm (0.04 in.)

Table 2 DRIVE CHAIN SPECIFICATIONS

Type/manufacturer	420M/DAIDO
No. of links	
BW80	89 (plus master link)
PW80	83 (plus master link)
Chain free play	15-20 mm (0.6-0.8 in.)

Table 3 REAR SUSPENSION TIGHTENING TORQUES (BW80)

	N•m	in.-lb.	ft.-lb.
Brake drum @ rear hub nuts	30	—	22
Driven sprocket nuts	25	—	17
Pivot shaft nut	50	—	36
Rear axle nut	85	—	62
Rear hub @ wheel nuts	30	—	22

Table 4 REAR SUSPENSION TIGHTENING TORQUES (PW80)

	N•m	in.-lb.	ft.-lb.
Rear axle nut	60	—	44
Pivot shaft nut	31	—	22
Brake stay arm	16	—	11
Driven sprocket nuts	26	—	19

CHAPTER FOURTEEN

BRAKES

Drum brakes are used at the front and rear wheels. **Figure 1** illustrates the major components of the brake assembly. Activating the brake hand lever or brake pedal (BW80 and PW80 only) pulls the cable or rod which in turn rotates the camshaft. This forces the brake shoes out into contact with the brake drum.

Brake lever and pedal free play must be maintained on both brakes to minimize brake drag and premature wear and maximize braking effectiveness. Refer to Chapter Three for complete adjustment procedures.

Glaze buildup on the brake shoes reduces brake effectiveness. The brake shoes should be removed and cleaned regularly to ensure maximum brake shoe contact.

The brake cables must be inspected and replaced periodically, as they stretch with use until they can no longer be properly adjusted.

Brake specifications are listed in **Tables 1-4** (end of chapter).

WARNING

*When working on the brake system, do **not** inhale brake dust. It may contain asbestos, which can cause lung injury and cancer. Wear a disposable face mask and wash your hands thoroughly after completing the work. Wet down the brake dust on brake components before working on them. Secure and dispose of all brake dust and cleaning materials properly. Do **not** use compressed air to blow off brake parts.*

DRUM BRAKES (EXCEPT PW50 REAR BRAKE)

The front and rear brake assemblies (except for the PW50 rear brake) are almost identical and both are covered in the same procedure. Where differences occur, they are identified in the procedure. To service the PW50 rear brake, refer to *Rear Drum Brake (PW50)* in this chapter.

Refer to the following parts diagram for your model when servicing the front or rear drum brake:

a. **Figure 2**: PW50 front brake.
b. **Figure 3**: BW80 front brake.
c. **Figure 4**: BW80 rear brake.
d. **Figure 5**: PW80 front brake.
e. **Figure 6**: PW80 rear brake.

Disassembly/Reassembly

1. Disconnect the front brake cable (**Figure 7** or **Figure 8**) or the rear brake rod (A, **Figure 9**) adjuster at the wheel.

2. On PW80 models, remove the cotter pin and nut and disconnect the brake stay arm at the rear backing plate (B, **Figure 9**). Discard the cotter pin.
3. Remove the front or rear wheel as described in Chapter Ten, Chapter Eleven or Chapter Thirteen for your model.

4. Pull the brake assembly straight up and out of the brake drum.

5. Spread some old newspapers over the ground and then place the backing plate on top of them with the brake shoes facing up. Spray the brake shoes and backing plate with an aerosol type brake cleaner to remove brake dust and dirt from the brake assembly. Wait until the brake cleaner evaporates from the brake assembly, then take it to your workbench for further service. Fold the newspapers over and store them in a sealed plastic bag. Dispose of the bag.

NOTE
Place a clean shop rag on the linings to protect them from oil and grease during removal.

NOTE
*Before removing the brake shoes from the backing plate, measure them as described under **Brake Inspection (All Models)** in this chapter.*

1

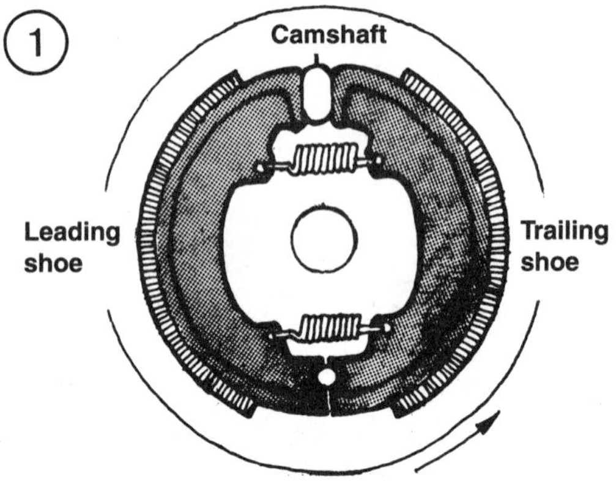

2

FRONT BRAKE (PW50)

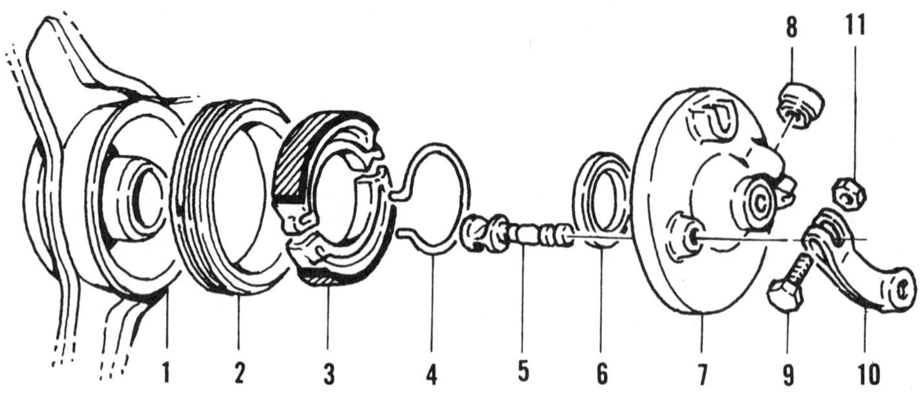

1. Wheel
2. Seal
3. Brake shoes
4. Spring
5. Brake cam
6. Oil seal
7. Backing plate
8. Plug
9. Bolt
10. Brake arm
11. Nut

③

FRONT BRAKE (BW80)

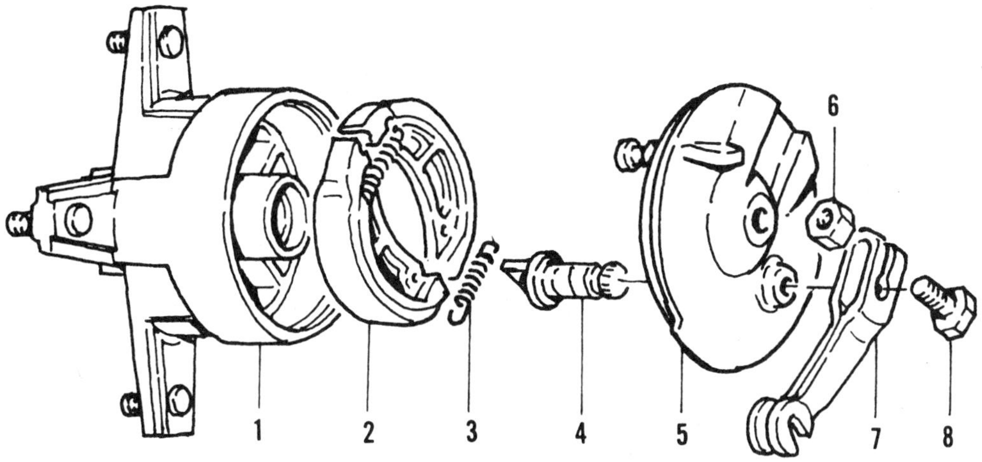

1. Front hub
2. Brake shoes
3. Spring
4. Brake cam
5. Backing plate
6. Nut
7. Brake arm
8. Bolt

6. Spread the brake shoes apart (**Figure 10**) and pull them off of the backing plate.

7A. On PW50 models, remove the brake return spring (**Figure 11**).

7B. On all other models, remove both brake return springs (**Figure 12**).

8. Remove the brake cam assembly as follows:

   a. Look for alignment marks on the brake lever and brake cam like those shown in **Figure 13**. If there are no marks, make your own as shown in **Figure 13**.
   b. Remove the pinch bolt and nut and then the brake arm (**Figure 13**).
   c. Remove the camshaft (**Figure 14**) from the backing plate.

9. Clean and dry all parts with an aerosol type brake cleaner.

10. Perform the inspection procedures listed under *Brake Inspection (All Models)* in this chapter.

NOTE
Use a high temperature waterproof wheel bearing grease when grease is

4

REAR BRAKE (BW80)

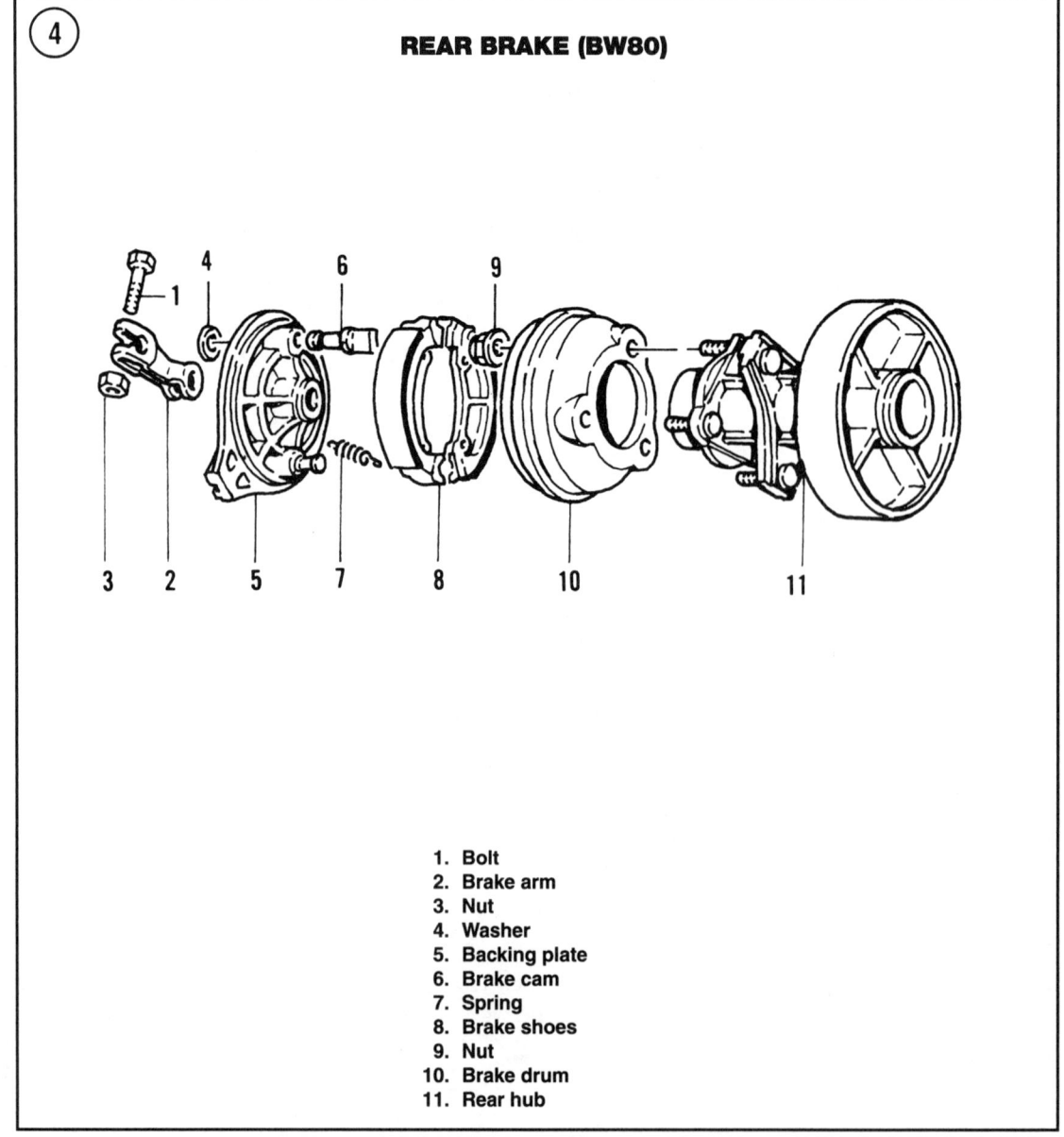

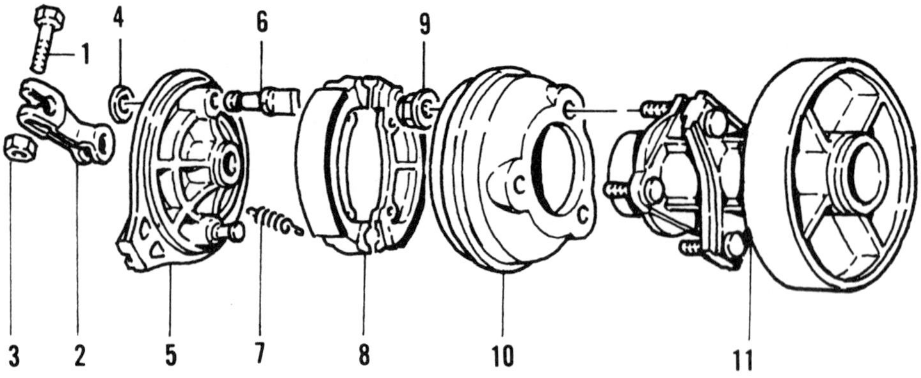

1. Bolt
2. Brake arm
3. Nut
4. Washer
5. Backing plate
6. Brake cam
7. Spring
8. Brake shoes
9. Nut
10. Brake drum
11. Rear hub

called for in the following steps. In all cases, apply the grease sparingly to keep it from getting on the brake linings or drums.

CAUTION
Do not use a low-temperature grease as it can thin under braking temperatures and run onto the brake linings and drum, contaminating both surfaces and reduce braking effectiveness.

11. On PW50 models, lubricate the backing plate seal lip (**Figure 15**) with grease.

12. Install the brake cam, brake arm, pinch bolt and nut (**Figure 13**). Align the index marks on the brake cam and brake arm (**Figure 13**). Hold the pinch bolt and tighten the nut as specified in **Table 4**.

13. Lubricate the brake cam face and groove and the fixed shaft groove with a small amount of grease.

14A. On PW50 models, connect the spring onto the brake shoes as shown in **Figure 11**.

(5)

FRONT BRAKE (PW80)

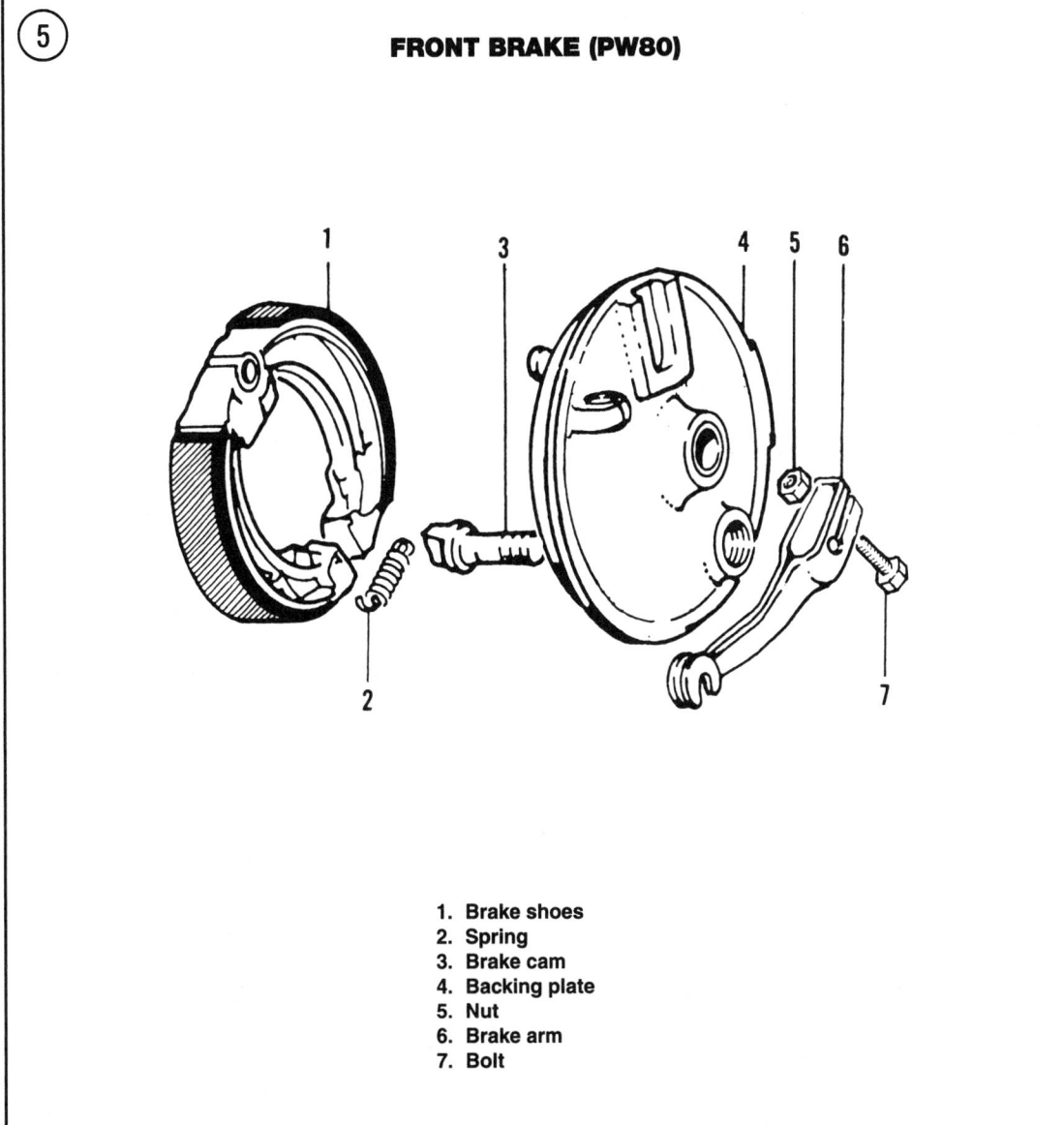

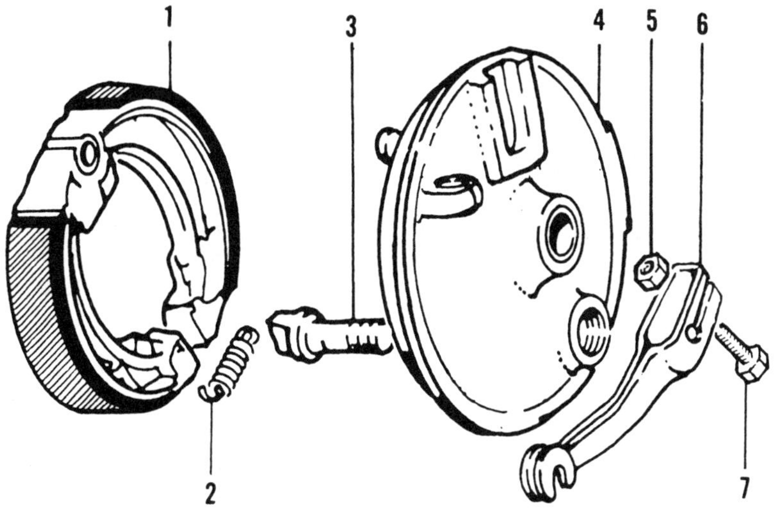

1. Brake shoes
2. Spring
3. Brake cam
4. Backing plate
5. Nut
6. Brake arm
7. Bolt

6

REAR BRAKE (PW80)

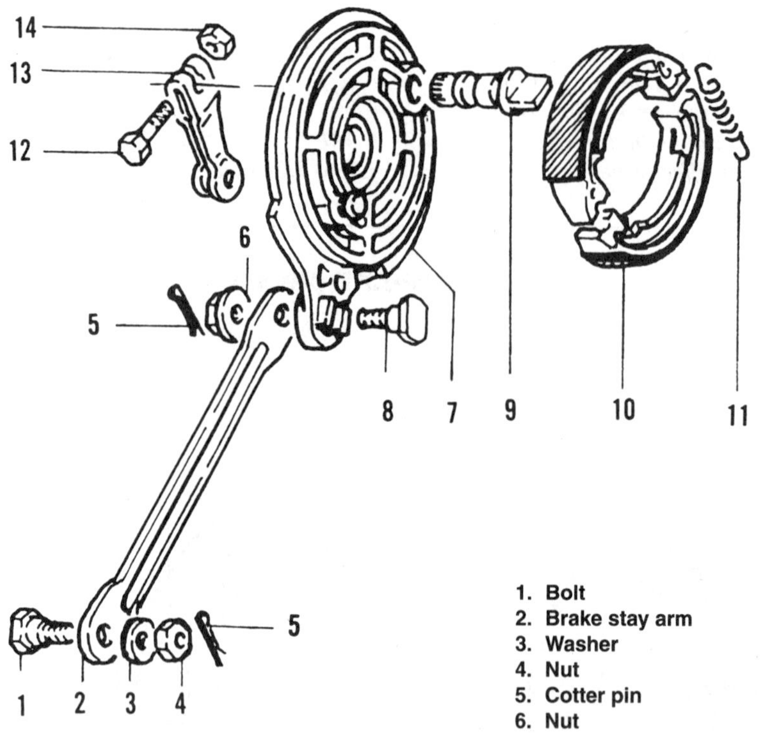

1. Bolt
2. Brake stay arm
3. Washer
4. Nut
5. Cotter pin
6. Nut
7. Backing plate
8. Bolt
9. Brake cam
10. Brake shoes
11. Spring
12. Bolt
13. Brake arm
14. Nut

7

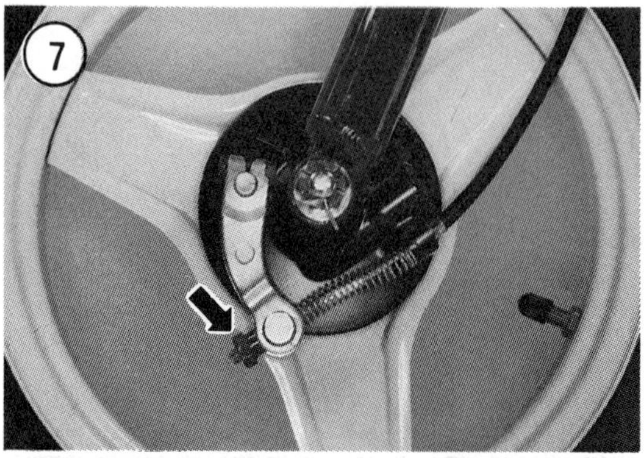

8

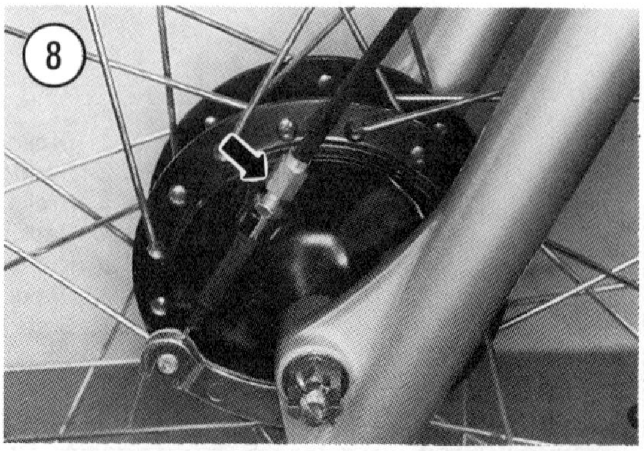

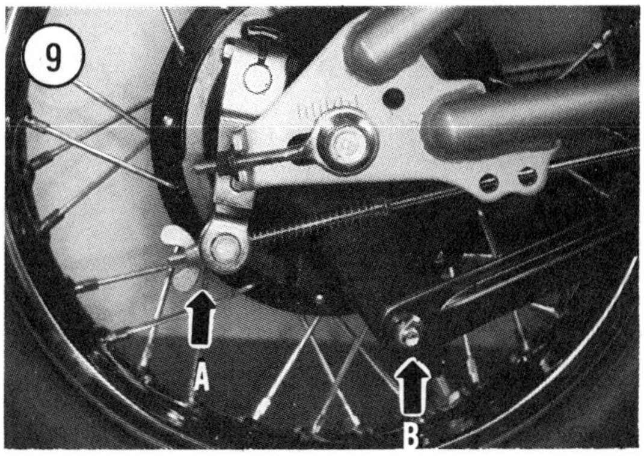

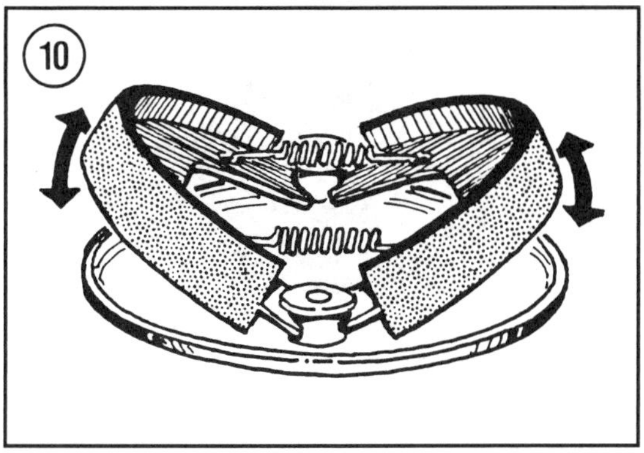

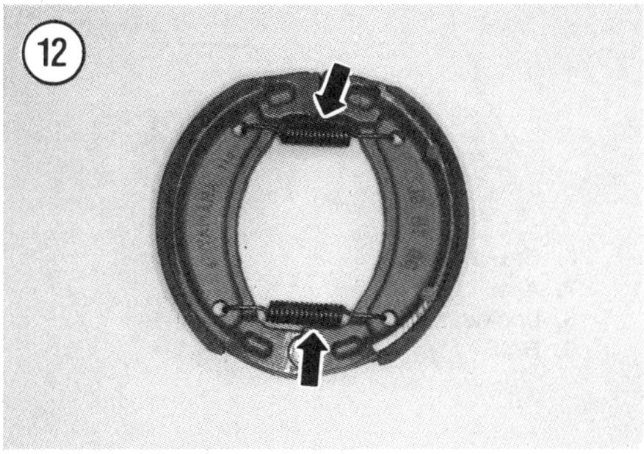

14B. On all other models, connect the return springs onto the brake shoes as shown in **Figure 12**.

15. Spread the brake shoes and install them against the brake cam and backing plate shaft. See **Figure 16** (PW50) or **Figure 17** (all other models). On PW50 models, install the brake shoes so that the brake shoe spring faces toward the backing plate. Wipe off any grease that was picked up on the brake linings.

16. Install the brake assembly into the wheel and then install the wheel as described in Chapter Ten, Chapter Eleven or Chapter Thirteen for your model.

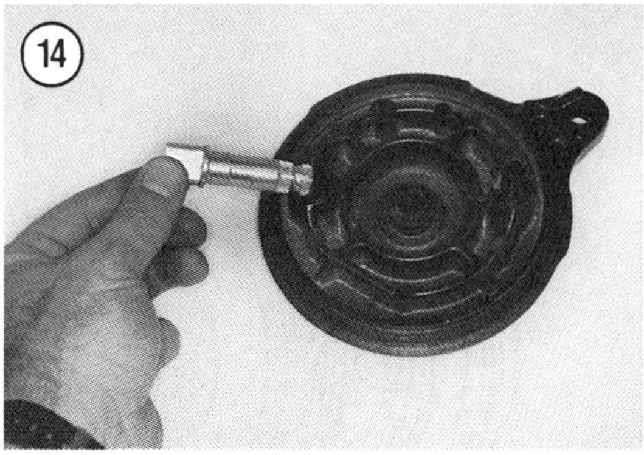

17. On PW80 models, reconnect the brake stay arm to the rear backing plate (B, **Figure 9**). Tighten the rear brake stay arm nut as specified in **Table 4**. Secure the brake stay arm bolt and nut with a new cotter pin. Bend the cotter pin arms over to lock it in place.

18. Reconnect the front brake cable (**Figure 7** or **Figure 8**) or the rear brake rod (A, **Figure 9**) adjuster at the wheel.

19. Adjust the brake as described in Chapter Three.

BRAKE DRUMS (BW80)

Refer to **Figure 3** (front) or **Figure 4** (rear) for this procedure.

Removal/Installation

1. Remove the wheel as described in Chapter Eleven or Chapter Thirteen.

16

17

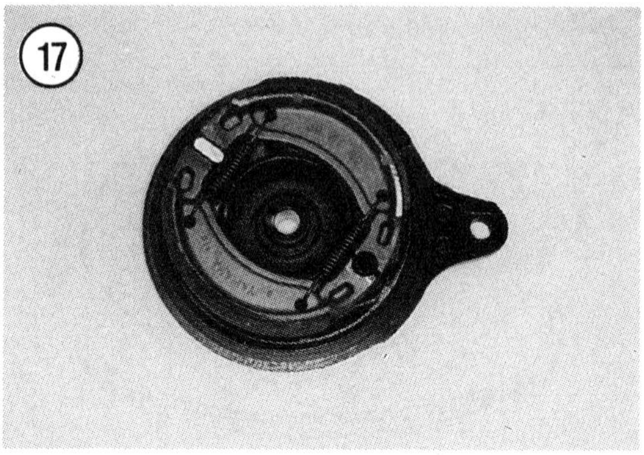

18

REAR BRAKE (PW50)

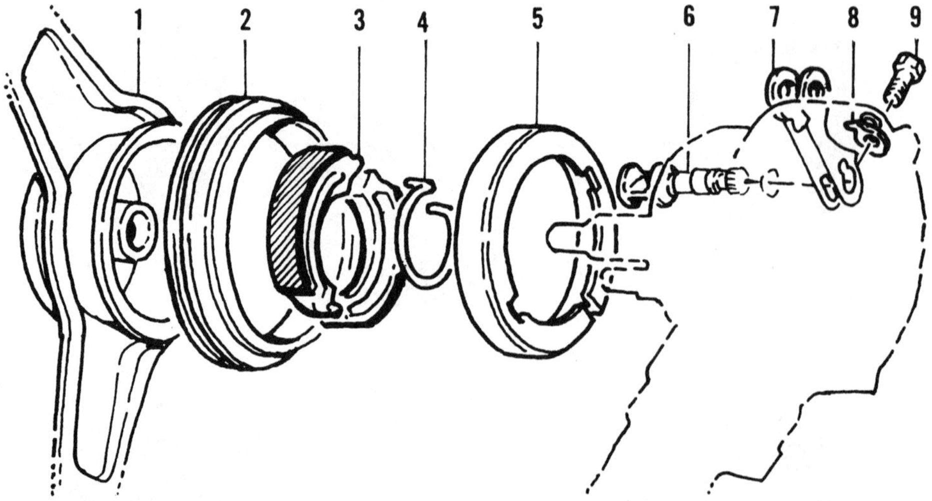

1. Wheel
2. Seal
3. Brake shoes
4. Spring
5. Cover
6. Brake cam
7. Arm
8. Lockwasher
9. Bolt

2A. Remove the nuts that secure the front hub to the front wheel assembly, then remove the front hub.
2B. Remove the nuts securing the rear brake drum and rear hub to the rear wheel assembly. Then remove the rear brake drum and rear hub.
3. Inspect the brake drum as described under *Brake Inspection (All Models)* in this chapter.
4. Install by reversing these removal steps, noting the following.
5. Tighten the rear hub nuts as specified in **Table 4**.

REAR DRUM BRAKE (PW50)

Refer to **Figure 18**.

Disassembly/Reassembly

1. Remove the rear wheel as described in Chapter Twelve.
2. Spread some old newspapers under the final drive housing and then spray the brake shoes and final drive housing with an aerosol type brake cleaner to remove brake dust and dirt from the brake assembly.

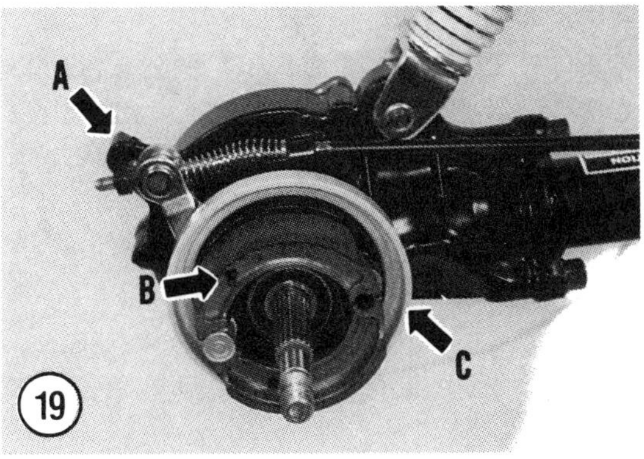

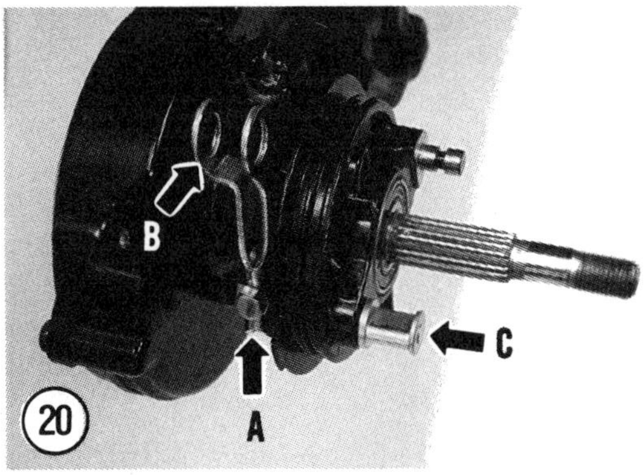

Wait until the brake cleaner evaporates before continuing with Step 3. Fold the newspapers over and store them in a sealed plastic bag. Dispose of the bag.
3. Disconnect the rear brake cable (A, **Figure 19**) from the brake arm.
4. Spread the brake shoes (B, **Figure 19**) and remove them from the final drive housing.
5. Remove the cover (C, **Figure 20**) from the final drive housing.
6. Remove the brake cam assembly as follows:
   a. Pry the lockwasher tab away from the pinch bolt (A, **Figure 20**).
   b. See **Figure 20**. Remove the pinch bolt and lockwasher (A), brake arm (B) and brake cam (C).
7. Remove the brake return spring (**Figure 11**) to separate the brake shoes.
8. Clean and dry all parts with an aerosol type brake cleaner.
9. Perform the inspection procedures listed under *Brake Inspection (All Models)* in this chapter.
10. Connect the spring onto the brake shoes as shown in **Figure 11**.

NOTE
Use a high-temperature waterproof wheel bearing grease when grease is called for in the following steps. In all cases, apply the grease sparingly to keep it from getting on the brake linings or drum.

CAUTION
Do not use a low-temperature grease as it can thin under braking temperatures and run onto the brake linings and drum, contaminating both surfaces and reduce braking effectiveness.

11. Lubricate the brake cam groove with grease and install it through the final drive housing as shown in A, **Figure 21**.
12. Align the index mark on the brake cam and brake arm (B, **Figure 21**), then install the brake arm onto the brake cam.

NOTE
***Figure 22** shows the brake cam and brake arm index marks with the parts removed for clarity.*

13. Install the pinch bolt and its lockwasher (A, **Figure 20**) and tighten as specified in **Table 4**. Bend

14

the lockwasher tab over the bolt's head to lock the bolt in place.

14. Spread the cover and install it into the final drive housing groove as shown in C, **Figure 19**. Position the cover so that its end gap seats into the notch in the bottom of the final drive housing as shown in **Figure 23**.

15. Lubricate the brake cam face and groove and the fixed shaft groove with a small amount of grease.

16. Spread the brake shoes and install them against the brake cam and backing plate shaft (**Figure 24**). Install the brake shoes so that the spring faces toward the final drive housing. Wipe off any grease picked up on the brake linings.

17. Reconnect the rear brake cable (A, **Figure 19**) at the brake arm.

18. Install the rear wheel as described in Chapter Twelve.

19. Adjust the brake as described in Chapter Three.

BRAKE INSPECTION (ALL MODELS)

When measuring the brake components in this section, compare the actual measurements to the new and service limit specifications in **Tables 1-3**. Replace parts that are out of specification or show damage as described in this section. When replacing brake shoes, replace them in sets.

1. Read the *Warning* in the introduction of this chapter.

2. Remove the wheel as described in Chapter Ten, Eleven, Twelve or Thirteen.

3. Spread some old newspapers over the ground and then place the backing plate on top of them with the brake shoes facing up. If you are servicing the PW50 rear brake, spread the newspapers under the final

21

22

23

24

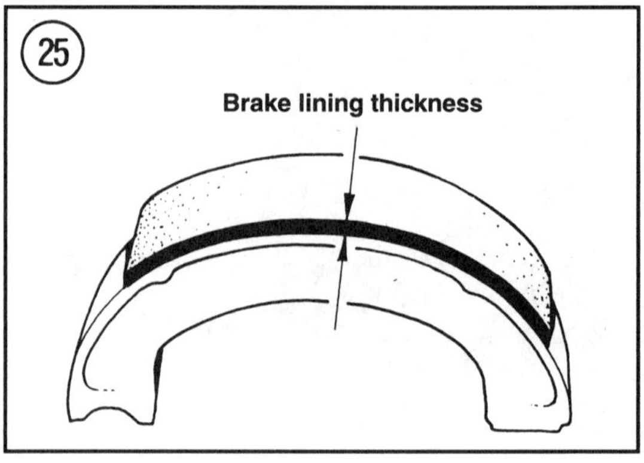

25

drive housing. Then spray the brake shoes and backing plate with an aerosol type brake cleaner to remove brake dust and dirt from the brake assembly. Wait until the brake cleaner evaporates from the brake assembly, then take it to your workbench for further service. Fold the newspapers over and store them in a sealed plastic bag. Dispose of the bag.

NOTE
*When measuring the brake shoes in Step 4A, measure the lining material (**Figure** 25) only. Do not include the thickness of the aluminum plate.*

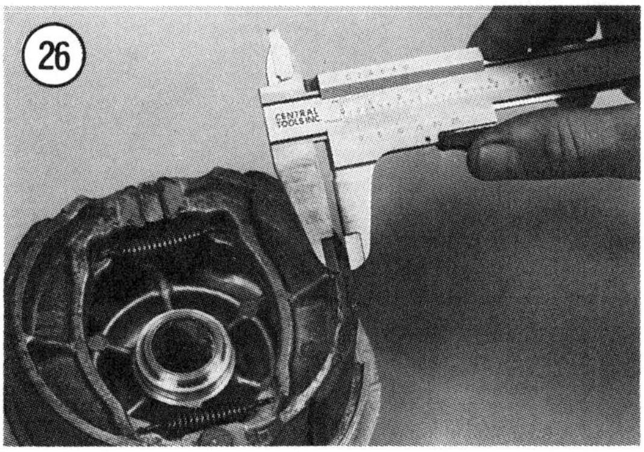
26

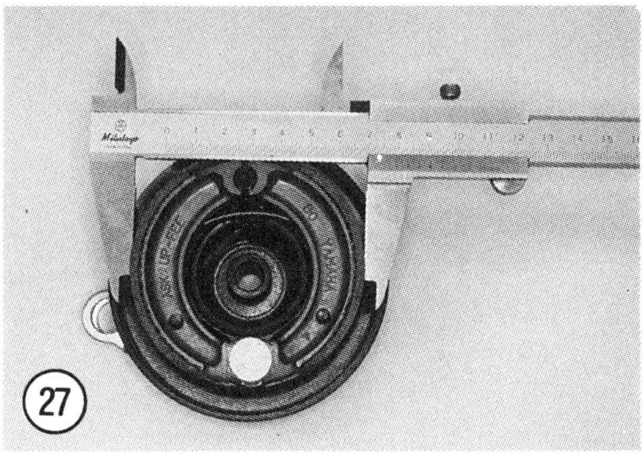
27

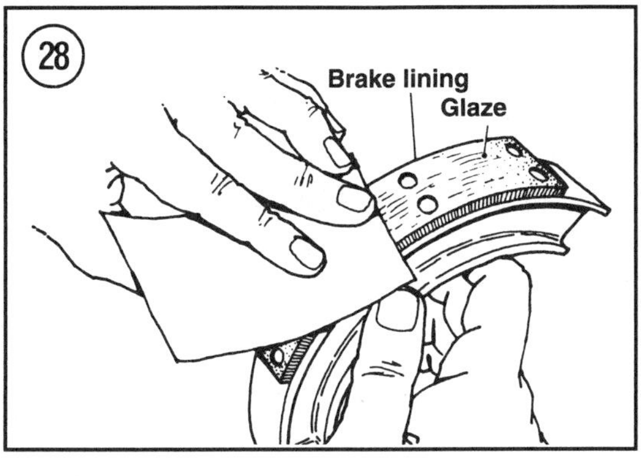

28

4A. On BW80 models, measure the brake shoe lining thickness at both ends and in the center with a vernier caliper (**Figure 26**). Replace the brake shoes if out of specification.

4B. On PW50 and PW80 models, measure the installed brake shoe set with a vernier caliper as shown in **Figure 27**. Replace the brake shoes if out of specification.

5. Remove the brake shoes from their mounting points as described in this chapter.

6. If the brake shoes can be reused, check for a hard glaze formation on the surface of each lining. Some glaze will be normal, but if the glaze is hard or heavy, the brake linings may have been dragging on the drum. To remove glaze from the linings perform the following:

WARNING
Perform this procedure outside, not in your garage or any other enclosed work area.

a. Remove glaze from the lining surface with a coarse grade sandpaper (**Figure 28**). Do not over-sand one spot as this will create a depression in the lining and reduce the lining-to-drum contact area. Sand just enough to remove the glaze.
b. Spray the brake linings and shoes with an aerosol type brake cleaner and allow to air dry.
c. Discard the sandpaper and wash your hands thoroughly.

7. Inspect the brake linings for imbedded foreign material. Remove dirt with a stiff wire brush. If the linings are severely worn or grooved, the brake drum may be damaged or out-of-round. Replace brake shoes that are contaminated with oil or grease.

8. To clean the brake drum, perform the following:
a. Turn the wheel over and pour any accumulated brake dust into a garbage bag. Tie the bag closed and discard it.
b. On BW80 and PW80 models, cover the wheel bearing with a piece of tape. Then on all models spray the brake drum with an aerosol type brake cleaner and allow to air dry.
c. Remove any rust on the brake drum surface with a fine-to-medium grade sandpaper and then reclean with brake cleaner.

9. Inspect the brake drum (**Figure 29**) for roughness, scoring, excessive glaze, cracks or distortion. Service the brake drum as follows:

a. Remove light roughness, rust, and glaze with a fine-to-medium grade sandpaper.
b. Drums that are cracked or damaged require replacement. On PW50 models, the wheel must be replaced as an assembly. On BW80 models, the brake drum can be replaced separately. On PW80 models, the hub/drum assembly must be removed from the wheel and a new one installed. This service requires wheel disassembly, relacing and truing.

10. Measure the brake drum inside diameter (lining surface) with a vernier caliper (**Figure 30**). Because the brake drum can wear unevenly, take a minimum of 3 measurements. Replace the brake drum if the inside diameter is out of specification. On original brake drums, the maximum brake drum diameter dimension is cast into each brake drum.

11A. On PW50 models, inspect the brake spring (**Figure 11**) for cracks or other damage.

11B. On BW80 and PW80 models, inspect the spring for stretched areas, hook damage or severe rust contamination. On BW80 models, measure the springs free length and compare with the new service dimension in **Table 2**. Yamaha does not list a service limit for spring free length. Replace both springs at the same time. Stretched or severely worn brake springs will not fully retract the brake shoes from the drum, resulting in a power-robbing drag on the drum and cause premature brake lining wear.

12. On PW50 models, inspect the front brake backing plate oil seal (**Figure 15**) for excessive wear or damage. If necessary, replace the oil seal as follows:

a. Pry the seal out of the backing plate with a screwdriver and support block as shown in **Figure 31**.
b. Place the new oil seal in its mounting bore so that its closed side faces out. Then drive it into place with a suitable bearing driver or socket. Install the oil seal until its outer surface is flush with the top of its mounting bore.

13. Inspect the brake cam and brake lever splines for damage.

14. On PW50 models, inspect the rubber seal (**Figure 32**) mounted on the wheel for excessive wear, cracks or other damage.

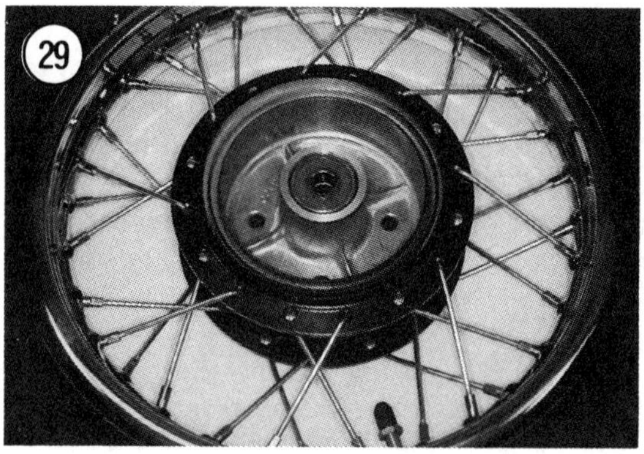

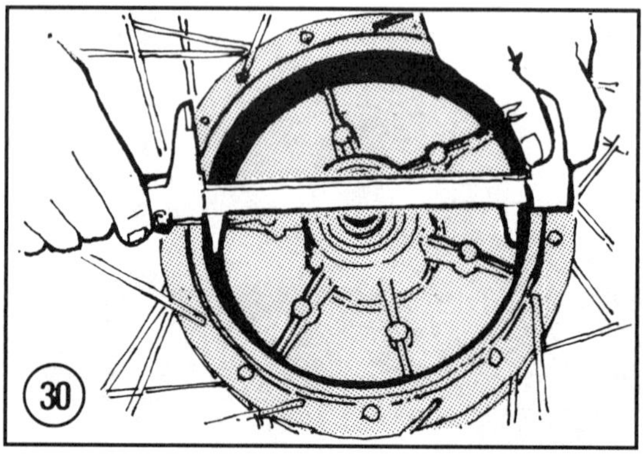

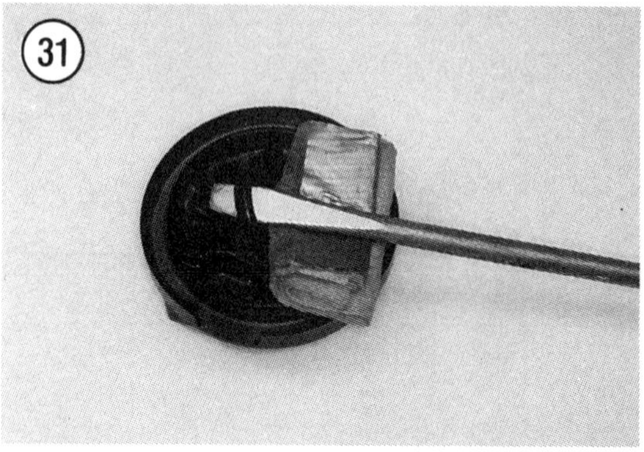

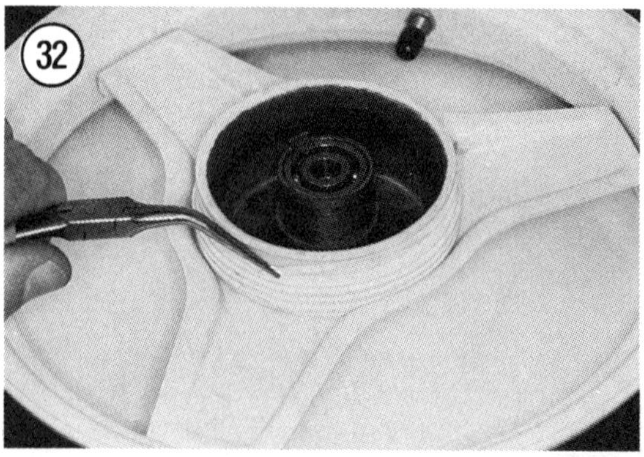

BRAKE LEVERS AND CABLES (PW50)

Brake Lever Replacement

The front brake lever (A, **Figure 33**) is mounted on the right handlebar. The rear brake lever (B, **Figure 33**) is mounted on the left handlebar. Replace the brake levers as described under *Handlebar* in Chapter Ten.

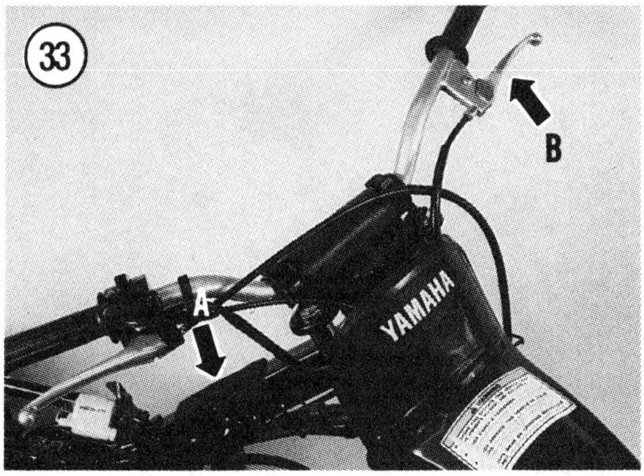

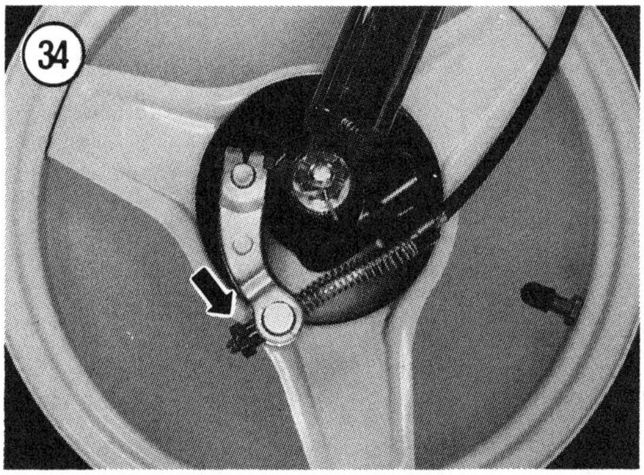

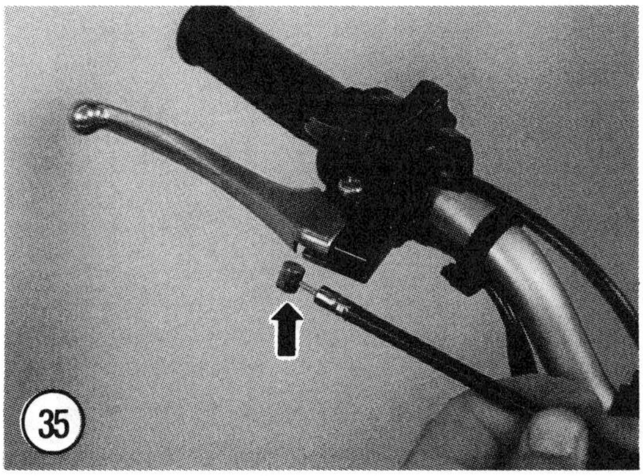

Front Brake Cable Replacement

1. After purchasing the new cable, lubricate it as described in Chapter Three.
2. Disconnect the front brake cable adjuster (**Figure 34**) at the front wheel.
3. Tie a piece of heavy string onto the end of the old cable. Cut the string so that it is longer than the new cable.
4. Disconnect the brake cable at the front brake lever (A, **Figure 33**).
5. Remove the old cable by pulling it from the top (upper cable end). Continue until the cable is removed from the frame, leaving the attached piece of string in its original mounting position.
6. Untie the string from the old cable and discard the cable.
7. Tie the string onto the bottom end of the new brake cable.
8. Pull the string to install the new cable along the original brake cable routing path. Continue until the brake cable is in position between the upper and lower brake levers, then untie the string and remove it from the bike.
9. Connect the upper cable end (**Figure 35**) onto the upper brake lever.
10. Reconnect the lower cable end into the boss in the front hub, then run the cable through the lower brake lever and install the spring, collar and adjust nut. See **Figure 34**).
11. Recheck the front brake cable alignment from the handlebar to the front wheel.
12. Adjust the front brake as described in Chapter Three.

Rear Brake Cable Replacement

1. Support the bike on its centerstand.
2. Remove the fuel tank (Chapter Seven).
3. After purchasing the new cable, lubricate it as described in Chapter Three.
4. Disconnect the rear brake cable adjuster (**Figure 36**) at the rear wheel.
5. Tie a piece of heavy string onto the end of the old cable. Cut the string so that it is longer than the new cable.
6. Disconnect the brake cable at the rear brake lever (B, **Figure 33**).
7. Remove the old cable by pulling it from the back. Continue until the cable is removed from the frame,

leaving the attached piece of string in its original mounting position.

8. Untie the string from the old cable and discard the cable.

9. Tie the string onto the bottom end of the new brake cable.

10. Pull the string to install the new cable along the original brake cable routing path. Continue until the brake cable is in position between the upper and lower brake levers, then untie the string and remove it from the bike.

11. Connect the upper cable end (**Figure 37**) onto the rear brake lever at the handlebar.

12. Reconnect the lower cable end into the boss in the final drive housing, then run the cable through the rear brake lever and install the spring, collar and adjust nut. See **Figure 36**.

13. Recheck the rear brake cable alignment from the handlebar to the rear wheel.

14. Adjust the rear brake as described in Chapter Three.

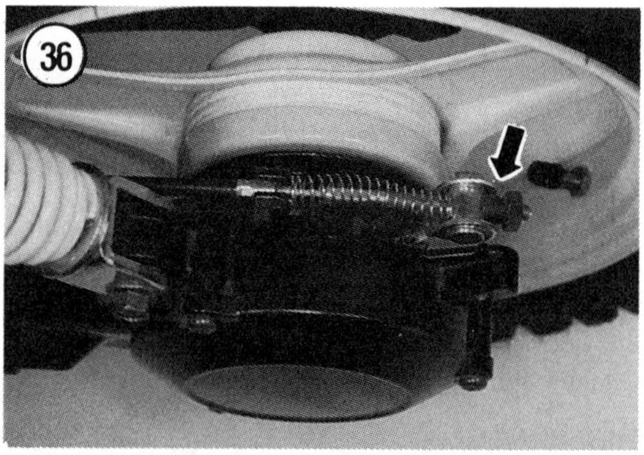

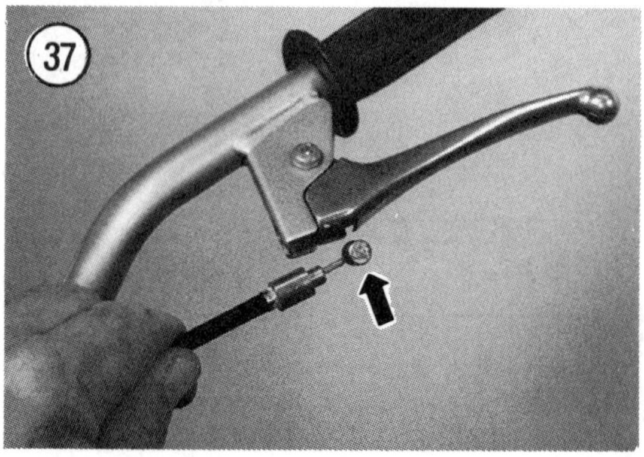

FRONT BRAKE CABLE REPLACEMENT (BW80 AND PW80)

1. After purchasing the new cable, lubricate it as described in Chapter Three.

1. Loosen the front brake cable adjuster locknut (**Figure 38**) at the handlebar.

2. Disconnect the front brake cable adjuster (**Figure 39**) from the front wheel.

3. Tie a piece of heavy string onto the end of the old cable. Cut the string so that it is longer than the new cable.

4. Disconnect the brake cable from the front brake lever (**Figure 38**).

5. Remove the old cable by pulling it from the top (upper cable end). Continue until the cable is removed from the frame, leaving the attached piece of string in its original mounting position.

6. Untie the string from the old cable and discard the cable.

7. Tie the string onto the bottom end of the new brake cable.

8. Pull the string to install the new cable along the original brake cable routing path. Continue until the brake cable is in position between the upper and lower brake levers, then untie the string and remove it from the bike.

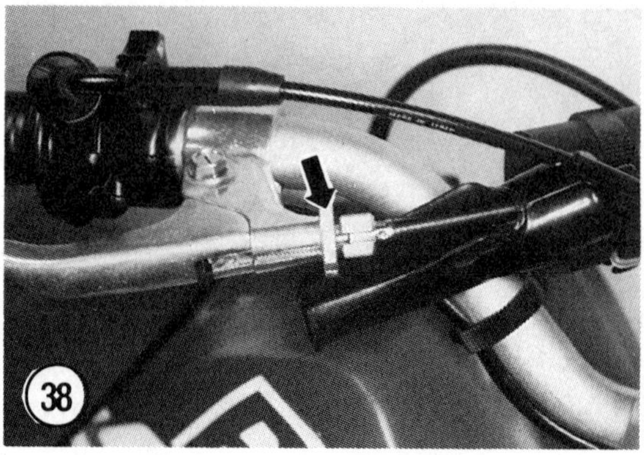

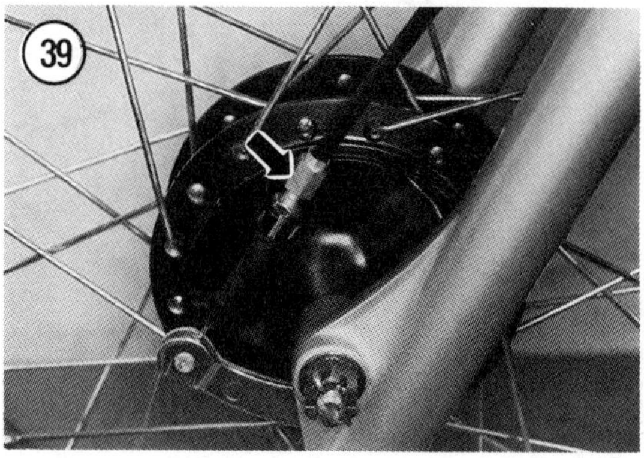

9. Connect the upper cable end (**Figure 38**) onto the upper brake lever.
10. Reconnect the lower cable end into the boss in the front hub, then run the cable through the lower brake lever and install the spring, collar and adjust nut. See **Figure 39**.
11. Recheck the front brake cable alignment from the handlebar to the front wheel.
12. Adjust the front brake as described in Chapter Three.

REAR BRAKE PEDAL AND ROD (BW80 AND PW80)

Removal/Installation

Refer to **Figure 40** for this procedure.

1. Unscrew the adjustment screw from the brake rod.
2. Depress the brake pedal and withdraw the brake rod from the brake lever. Remove the collar and spring.
3. Remove the E-clip and flat washer securing the rear brake pedal to its pivot shaft on the footpeg mounting bracket. Then remove the rear brake pedal and its return spring.
4. Remove the cotter pin and flat washer and disconnect the brake rod from the brake pedal.
5. Install by reversing these removal steps, noting the following:
   a. Clean all old grease from the rear brake pedal and its pivot shaft.
   b. Lubricate the pivot shaft with a waterproof grease.
   c. Secure the brake rod to the brake pedal with a new cotter pin and bend the ends over completely.
   d. Adjust the rear brake as described in Chapter Three.

(40)

REAR BRAKE PEDAL AND ROD (BW80 AND PW80)

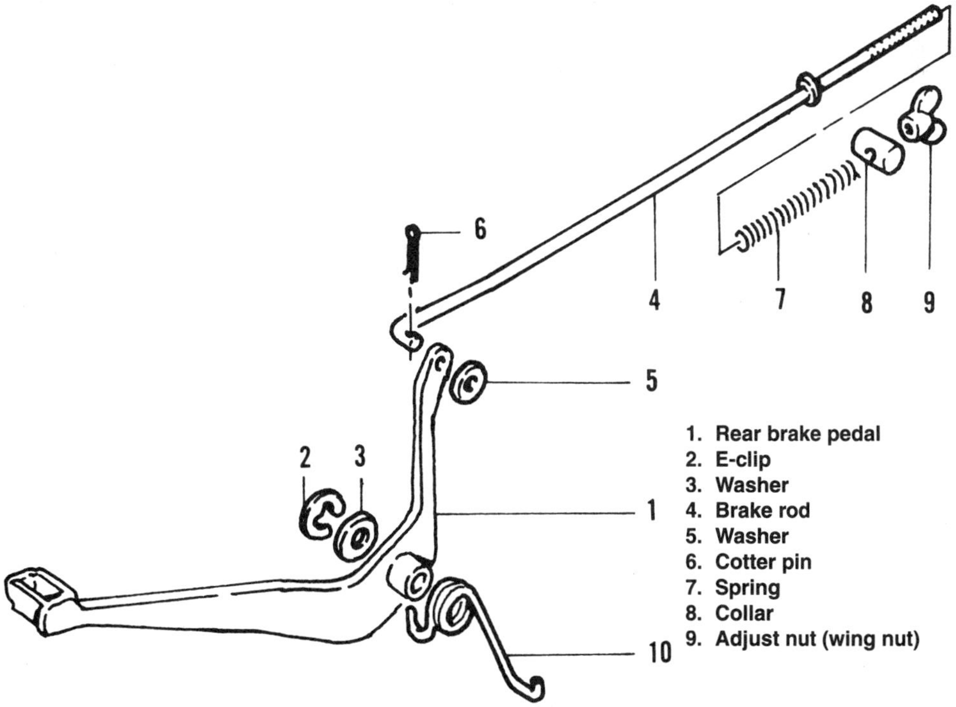

Table 1 FRONT AND REAR BRAKE SERVICE SPECIFICATIONS (PW50)

	New mm (in.)	Service limit mm (in.)
Brake drum inside diameter		
Front and rear	80 (3.15)	80.5 (3.17)
Brake shoe diameter		
Front and rear	80 (3.15)	77 (3.03)

Table 2 FRONT AND REAR BRAKE SERVICE SPECIFICATIONS (BW80)

	New mm (in.)	Service limit mm (in.)
Brake drum inside diameter		
Front and rear	95 (3.74)	96 (3.78)
Brake shoe lining thickness		
Front and rear	4 (0.16)	2 (0.08)
Brake shoe spring free length	32.7 (1.29)	—

Table 3 FRONT AND REAR BRAKE SERVICE SPECIFICATIONS (PW80)

	New mm (in.)	Service limit mm (in.)
Brake drum inside diameter		
Front	95 (3.74)	96 (3.78)
Rear	110 (4.33)	111 (4.37)
Brake shoe diameter		
Front	95 (3.74)	92 (3.62)
Rear	110 (4.33)	107 (4.21)

Table 4 BRAKE TIGHTENING TORQUES

	N•m	in.-lb.	ft.lb.
Brake camshaft pinch bolt nut			
PW50			
Front	4	35	—
Rear	6	53	—
BW80	10	88	—
PW80	7	62	—
Rear brake stay arm nuts at swing arm and brake backing plate			
PW80	16	—	11
Wheel hub nuts			
BW80	30	—	22

CHAPTER FIFTEEN

BODY

This chapter describes service procedures for the seat, side panels and fenders.

SEAT, SIDE COVERS AND REAR FENDER (PW50)

On the PW50, the side covers and rear fender are part of the same subassembly. The seat is secured separately to the rear fender with mounting bolts.

Removal/Installation

1. Remove the 2 fender bolts (A, **Figure 1**) and flap (B, **Figure 1**), then remove the seat and rear fender assembly.
2. To remove the seat from the rear fender, remove the mounting bolts and washers (if used).
3. Install by reversing these removal steps, noting the following.
4. When installing the rear fender assembly, insert the tab (A, **Figure 2**) on the front of the fender into the frame boss (B, **Figure 2**). Then install the flap and the 2 mounting bolts (A, **Figure 1**) and tighten securely.
5. Lift up on the front of the seat to make sure it is locked in place.

SEAT (BW80 AND PW80)

Removal/Installation

1. Remove the 2 nuts (**Figure 3**) securing the seat to the frame and remove the seat.

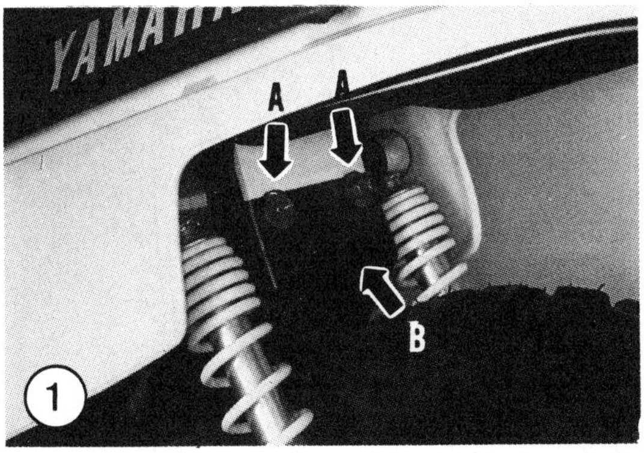

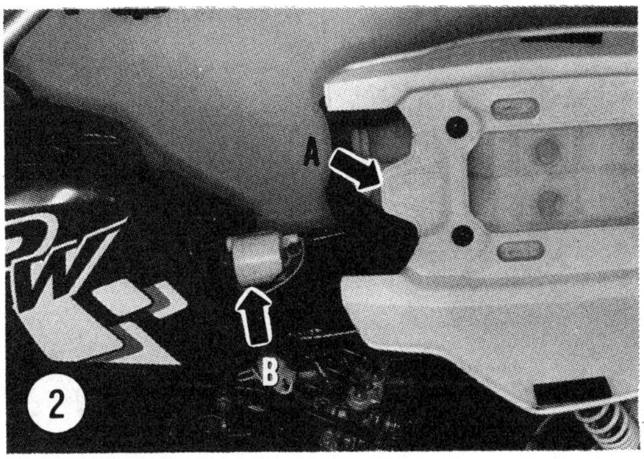

2. To remove the seat from the rear fender, remove the mounting bolts and washers (if used).
3. Install by reversing these removal steps, noting the following.
4. When installing the seat, insert the tab (A, **Figure 4**) on the bottom of the seat into the frame boss (B, **Figure 4**). Then install the 2 mounting nuts (**Figure 3**) and tighten securely.
5. Lift up on the front of the seat to make sure it is locked in place.

FRONT FENDER

Removal/Installation (PW50)

1. Remove the screws securing the front fender to its mounting brackets, then remove the fender (**Figure 5**).
2. Remove the screws securing the front fender mounting brackets (A, **Figure 6**) and fender flap to the steering stem. Then remove the brackets and fender flap.
3. Install by reversing these removal steps while noting the following.
4. When installing the fender flap, hook the tab on top of the fender flap onto the lower oil hose guide bracket (mounted on the bottom of the steering stem). Then install the front fender mounting brackets (A, **Figure 6**) and fender flap mounting screws and tighten securely.
5. When installing the front fender, hook the upper bracket slot the in the top of the fender into the tab on the oil tank mounting bracket.
6. Tighten all of the mounting screws securely.
7. Check the front brake cable and throttle cable routing.

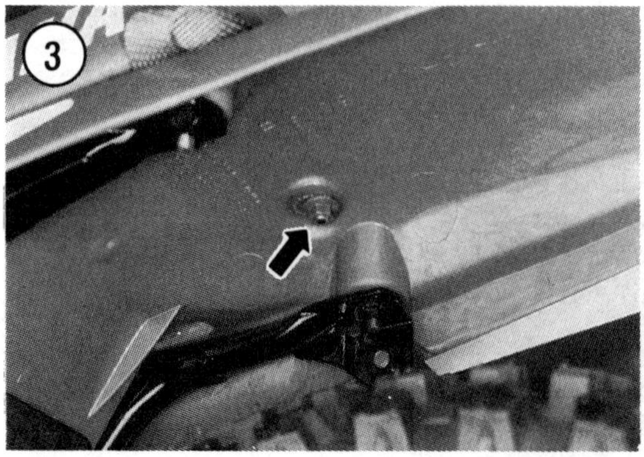

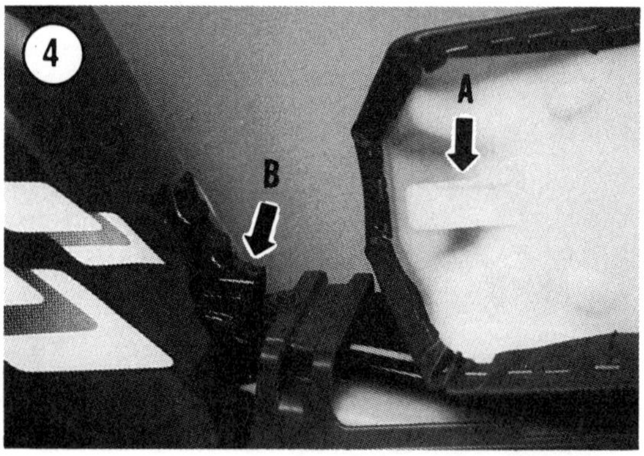

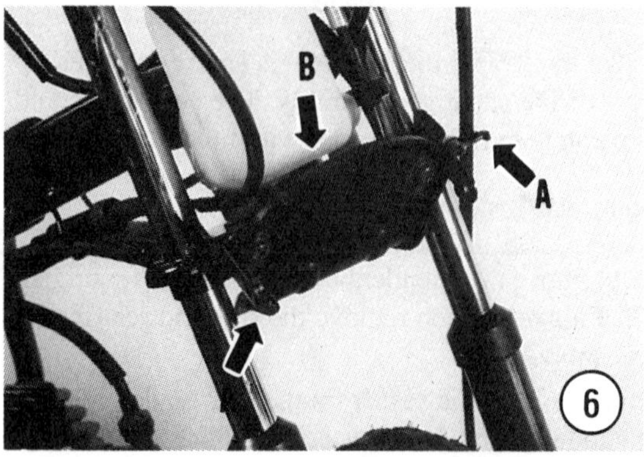

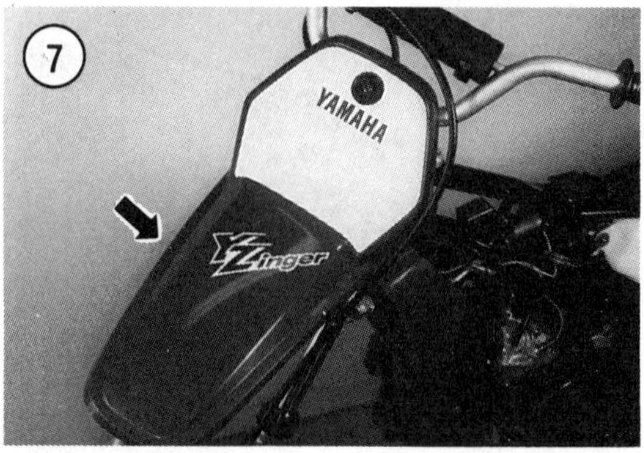

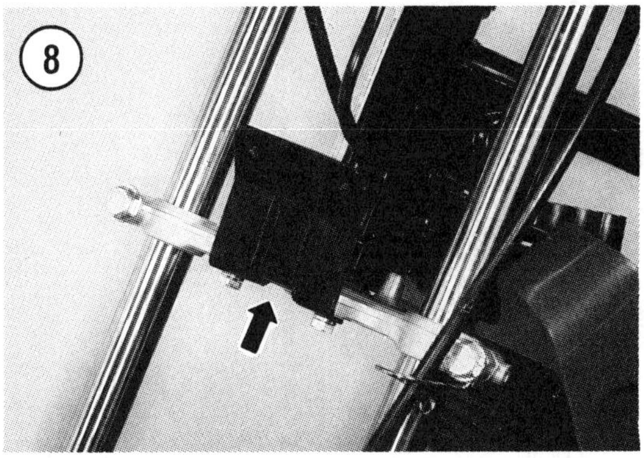

Removal/Installation (BW80 and PW80)

1. Remove the screws securing the front fender to its mounting brackets, then remove the fender (**Figure 7**).
2. Remove the screws securing the front fender mounting bracket to the steering stem and remove the bracket (**Figure 8**).
3. Install by reversing these removal steps while noting the following.
4. Tighten all of the mounting screws securely.
5. Check the front brake cable and throttle cable routing.

REAR FENDER (BW80 AND PW80)

Removal/Installation

1. Remove the seat as described in this chapter.
2. Remove the screws securing the rear fender to the frame, then remove the rear fender (**Figure 9**).
3. Install by reversing these removal steps while noting the following.
4. Tighten all of the mounting screws securely.

INDEX

A

B

C

D

E

W

Yamaha PW50 (1981-2002)

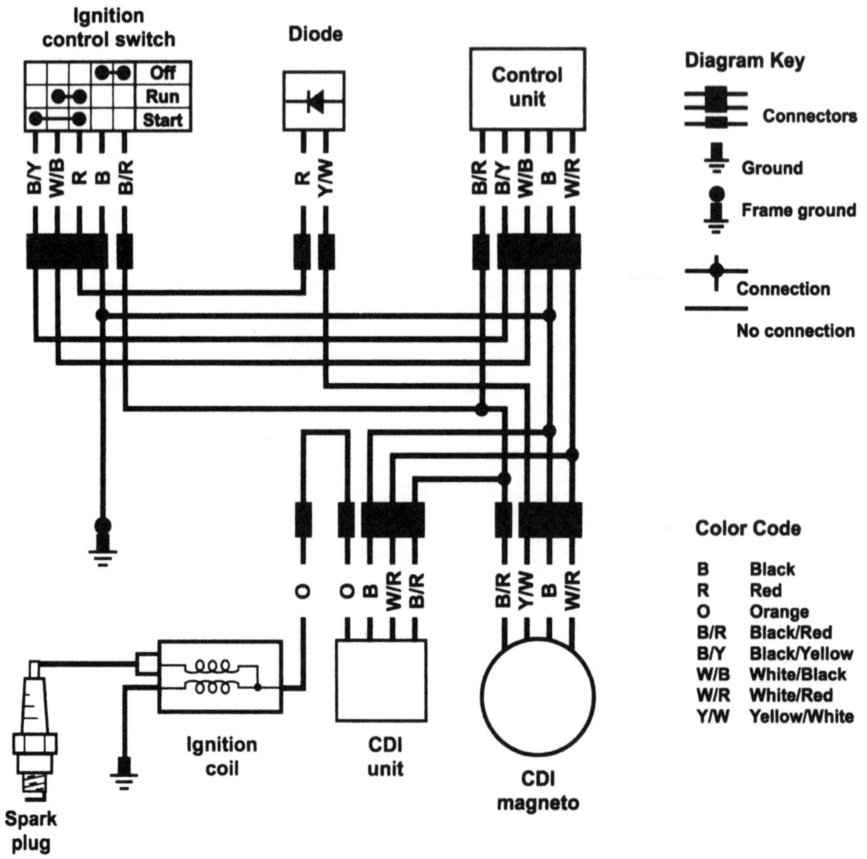

Yamaha BW80 (1986-1990)

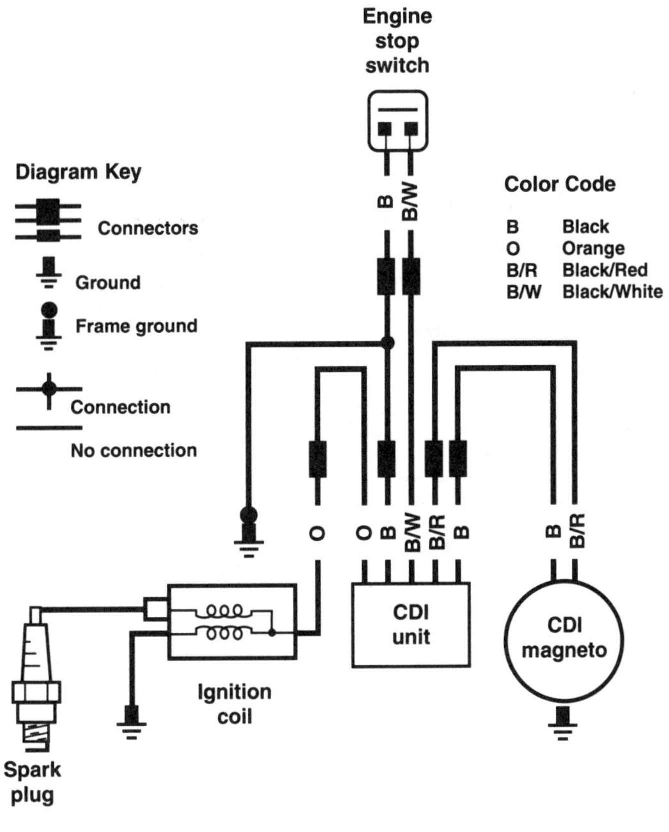

Yamaha PW80 (1981-2002)

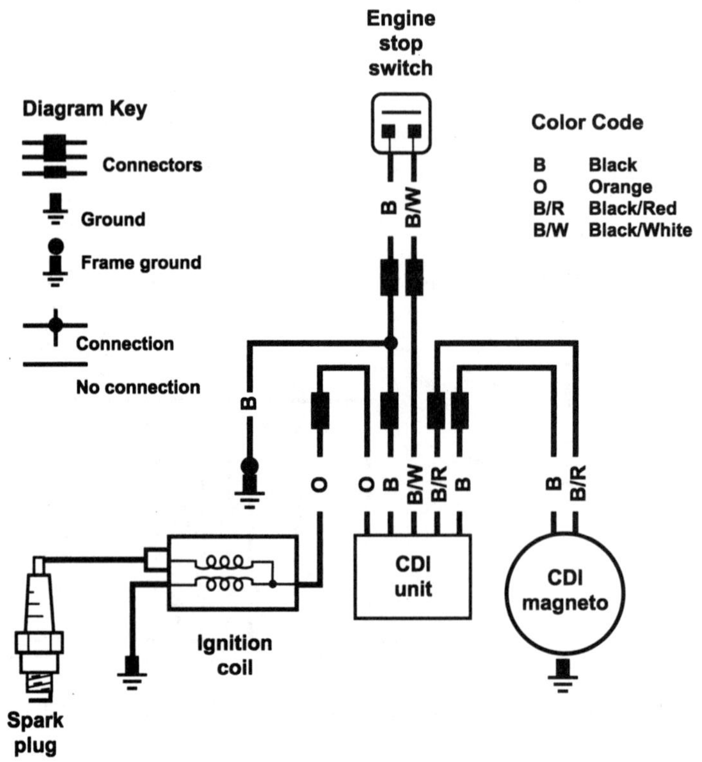

NOTES

NOTES

MAINTENANCE LOG

Date	Miles	Type of Service